CALLIMACHUS

CALLIMACHUS

THE HYMNS

Edited with Introduction, Translation, and Commentary by

Susan A. Stephens

OXFORD
UNIVERSITY PRESS

OXFORD
UNIVERSITY PRESS

Oxford University Press is a department of the
University of Oxford. It furthers the University's objective
of excellence in research, scholarship, and education
by publishing worldwide.

Oxford   New York

Auckland   Cape Town   Dar es Salaam   Hong Kong   Karachi
Kuala Lumpur   Madrid   Melbourne   Mexico City   Nairobi
New Delhi   Shanghai   Taipei   Toronto

With offices in

Argentina   Austria   Brazil   Chile   Czech Republic   France   Greece
Guatemala   Hungary   Italy   Japan   Poland   Portugal   Singapore
South Korea   Switzerland   Thailand   Turkey   Ukraine   Vietnam

Oxford is a registered trade mark of Oxford University Press
in the UK and certain other countries.

Published in the United States of America by
Oxford University Press
198 Madison Avenue, New York, NY 10016

© Oxford University Press 2015

A copy of this book's Cataloging-in-Publication Data is on file
with the Library of Congress.

ISBN 978–0–19–978304–5

1 3 5 7 9 8 6 4 2

Printed in the United States of America
on acid-free paper

Contents

Preface

My goal in writing this commentary is to provide readers with a convenient and accessible edition of all six of Callimachus' hymns in one volume, accompanied by notes sufficient for ease of reading. That such an edition does not already exist is my justification for undertaking the task, especially given the importance of this poet and the fact that the hymns and epigrams are his only complete works. In keeping with Callimachus' own stated poetic practice this is not a μέγα βιβλίον; thus constraints of space have required a certain amount of triage: the linguistic, metrical, historical, geographic, and cultic material I provide will necessarily lack the wealth of scholarly detail provided by those commentaries on individual hymns produced mainly in the 1970s and 1980s. Like all writers of commentaries I have depended heavily on my predecessors, though experience in teaching and in writing on the hymns has led me considerably to reduce the amount of linguistic detail (particularly about Homeric usage) and commensurately to increase parallels from tragedy and lyric. Also I situate Callimachus' divinities as much as possible within the context of cult practices relevant to early Ptolemaic Alexandria and Cyrene. I have tried to keep always before the reader the fact that Callimachus was a poet; thus literary parallels are selected in the main for their allusive potential and references kept, when possible, to easily accessed secondary materials. The translations do no more than aim for clarity and are intended to provide the reader with my understanding of the text.

It is my pleasure to acknowledge the colleagues who have offered encouragement, advice, and the generous donation of their time in reading various versions of this manuscript. Richard Martin has patiently enlightened me about many Homeric minutiae. Jim Clauss and Alex Sens have provided comments on individual hymns, but I am especially grateful for their perceptive advice about rethinking the shape of the whole. Keyne Cheshire, Ivana Petrovic, and Massimo Giuseppetti read and commented on individual hymns, and in addition provided me with their own work in advance of publication, from which I learned more than I can say. Flora Manakidou has very generously provided me with her forthcoming work on the *Hymn to Athena* and with a copy of her 2013 commentary. Dirk Obbink and Daniela Colomo very kindly facilitated my examination of hymns papyri. Israel McMullin has given me the student's perspective on what is useful (or more often, not); Jon Weiland has drawn the maps. Aaron Palmore and John Richards have helped with the proof reading. Andrew Dyck has done an exemplary job of editing and indexing (what errors remain are my own). Mark Edwards has read and commented on the whole and been particularly helpful with the metrical sections and in providing Homeric parallels. All of these individuals have facilitated the process of writing this commentary. However, I owe a special debt of gratitude to Marco Fantuzzi and Benjamin Acosta-Hughes, who have read through the whole manuscript more than once. Their learned advice has considerably improved what I now present, and I hope that in some measure it repays their efforts. Last but not least, I would like to thank the Press for their patience and support.

Illustrations

Abbreviations

Greek authors follow LSJ, and standard abbreviations for periodicals and editions of papyri are used, though they are sometimes expanded for clarity. Callimachus' fragments are cited by Pfeiffer's numbers, except for the *Hecale* (cited by Hollis' numbers) and those fragments of the *Aetia* not in Pfeiffer (cited by Harder's numbers). The following abbreviations are used throughout:

A-B	C. Austin and G. Bastianini, *Posidippi Pellaei quae supersunt omnia* (Milan, 2002).
Anacreontea	M. L. West, *Anacreontea* (Leipzig, 1993).
AP	*Anthologia Palatina.*
Buck	C. D. Buck, *The Greek Dialects: Grammar, Selected Inscriptions, Glossary* (Chicago, 1955).
Bühler	W. Bühler, *Die Europa des Moschos* (Wiesbaden, 1960).
Chantraine	P. Chantraine, *Grammaire homerique.* 2 vols. (Paris, 1958–62).
Chantraine *ED*	P. Chantraine, *Dictionnaire étymologique de la langue grecque: histoire des mots* (Paris, 1968, repr. 1999).
Denniston	J. D. Denniston, *Greek Particles.* 2nd edn. (Oxford, 1950).
D-K	H. Diels, *Die Fragmente der Vorsokratiker*, rev. W. Kranz. 6th edn. (Berlin, 1951–52).
FGrH	F. Jacoby, *Die Fragmente der griechischen Historiker* (Berlin and Leiden, 1923–58).
Goodwin *MT*	W. W. Goodwin, *Syntax of the Moods and Tenses of the Greek Verb* (New York, 1899, repr. 1965).
Gow	A. S. F. Gow, *Theocritus: Edited with a Translation and Commentary.* 2 vols. (Cambridge, 1950).
GLP	D.L. Page, *Greek Literary Papyri*, vol. 1 (Cambridge, MA, 1942).

G-P A. S. F. Gow and D. L. Page, *Hellenistic Epigrams*, 2 vols. (Oxford, 1965).

IEG² M. L. West, *Iambi et elegi Graeci*. 2nd edn. (Oxford, 1989–92).

IG *Inscriptiones Graecae* (Berlin 1873–).

Kidd D. Kidd, *Aratus*: Phaenomena (Cambridge, 1997, repr. 2004).

LIMC *Lexicon iconographicum mythologiae classicae*, 8 vols. (Zurich and Munich, 1981–99).

LSJ H. G. Liddell et al. *A Greek-English Lexicon, with a Revised Supplement*. 9th edn. (Oxford, 1996).

M-W R. Merkelbach and M. L. West, *Fragmenta Hesiodea*. 3rd edn. (Oxford, 1990).

OGIS W. Dittenberger, *Orientis Graeci inscriptiones selectae*, 2 vols. (Leipzig, 1903–5).

PCG R. Kassel and C. Austin, *Poetae comici Graeci*. 8 vols. (Berlin, 1983–2001).

Pf. R. Pfeiffer, *Callimachus*. 2 vols. (Oxford, 1949–53).

PGM K. Preisendanz, *Papyri Graecae magicae* (Leipzig, 1931).

PMG D. L. Page, *Poetae melici Graeci* (Oxford, 1962).

Powell J. U. Powell, *Collectanea Alexandrina* (Oxford, 1925).

RE G. Wissowa and W. Kroll, eds. *Paulys Realencyclopädie der classischen Altertumswissenschaft*. 34 vols. in 68 + index and 15 supplements. Stuttgart, 1893–1980.

Rose V. Rose, *Aristotelis fragmenta*. 2nd edn. (Leipzig, 1886).

Schmitt R. Schmitt, *Die Nominalbildung in den Dichtungen des Kallimachos von Kyrene* (Wiesbaden, 1970).

SEG *Supplementum epigraphicum Graecum* (Leiden, 1923–).

SH H. Lloyd-Jones and P. J. Parsons, *Supplementum Hellenisticum* (Berlin and New York, 1983).

SIG W. Dittenberger, *Sylloge Inscriptionum Graecarum*. 3rd edn. (Leipzig, 1915–24).

S-M B. Snell and H. Maehler, *Pindarus*. 2 vols. (Leipzig, 1974–75).

Smyth H. W. Smyth, *Greek Grammar*, rev. G. Messing (Cambridge, MA, 1956).

Spanoudakis K. Spanoudakis, *Philitas of Cos* (Leiden, 2002).

TrGF B. Snell, R. Kannicht, and S. Radt, *Tragicorum Graecorum fragmenta*. 5 vols. (Göttingen, 1971–2004).

V E.-M. Voigt, *Sappho et Alcaeus. Fragmenta* (Amsterdam, 1971).

Th. M. L. West, *Hesiod, Theogony* (Oxford, 1966).

Op. M. L. West, *Hesiod,* Works and Days (Oxford 1978, repr. 1998).

Wilamowitz, *HD* U. von Wilamowitz-Moellendorf, *Hellenistische Dichtung.* 2 vols. (Berlin, 1931–32).

Editors of Callimachus Cited by Name

Asper M. Asper, *Kallimachos Werke* (Darmstadt, 2004).

Blomfield C. J. Blomfield, *Callimachi quae supersunt* (London, 1815).

Bornmann F. Bornmann, *Callimachi Hymnus in Dianam.* Biblioteca di Studi Superiori 55 (Florence, 1968).

Bulloch A. W. Bulloch, *Callimachus: The Fifth Hymn* (Cambridge, 1985).

Cahen E. Cahen, *Callimaque* (Paris, 1939).

D'Alessio G.-B. D'Alessio, *Callimaco. Inni, Epigrammi, Ecale.* 2nd edn. (Milan, 2007).

Ernesti J. A. Ernesti, *Callimachi hymni epigrammata et fragmenta cum notis . . . quibus accedunt Ezechielis Spanhemii commentarii & notae Tiberii Hemsterhusii et Davidis Ruhnkenii.* 2 vols. (Leiden, 1761).

Gigante Lanzara V. Gigante Lanzara, *Callimaco.* Inno a Delo (Pisa, 1990).

Harder A. M. Harder, *Callimachus,* Aetia. *Introduction, Text and Translation; Commentary.* 2 vols. (Oxford, 2012).

Hollis H. A. Hollis, *Callimachus: Hecale. Introduction, Text, Translation, and Enlarged Commentary.* 2nd edn. (Oxford, 2009).

Hopkinson N. Hopkinson, *Callimachus:* The Hymn to Demeter (Cambridge, 1984).

Kuiper K. Kuiper, *Studia Callimachea. 1. De hymnorum I-IV dictione epica* (Leiden, 1896).

Mair G. R. Mair, *Callimachus. Hymns and Epigrams* (Cambridge, MA and London, 1921 [repr.]).

McLennan G. R. McLennan, *Callimachus,* Hymn to Zeus. *Introduction and Commentary* (Rome, 1977).

Meineke A. Meineke, *Callimachi hymni et epigrammata* (Berlin, 1861).

Mineur W. H. Mineur, *Callimachus.* Hymn to Delos. *Introduction and Commentary.* Mnemosyne Supplement 83 (Leiden, 1984).

Pfeiffer See above Pf.

Schneider O. Schneider, *Callimachea,* 2 vols. (Leipzig, 1870–73)

Wilamowitz U. von Wilamowitz-Moellendorf, *Callimachi hymni et epigrammata* (Berlin, 1881, repr. 1896).

Williams F. Williams, *Callimachus,* Hymn to Apollo (Oxford, 1978).

The following abbreviations are used for Callimachus' hymns: *hZeus (Hymn to Zeus)*, *hAp (Hymn to Apollo)*, *hArt (Hymn to Artemis)*, *hDelos (Hymn to Delos)*, *hAth (Hymn to Athena, On the Bath of Pallas)*, *hDem (Hymn to Demeter)*. Homeric hymns are abbreviated as follows: *HhDion (Homeric Hymn to Dionysus)*, *HhDem (Homeric Hymn to Demeter)*, *HhAp (Homeric Hymn to Apollo)*, *HhHerm (Homeric Hymn to Hermes)*, *HhAphr (Homeric Hymn to Aphrodite)*, *HhPan (Homeric Hymn to Pan)*; other Homeric hymns are cited by number.

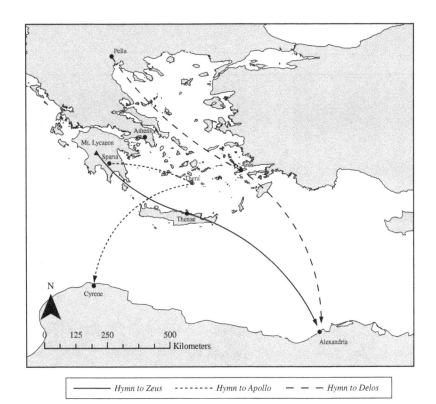

MAP 1 Movement from North to South

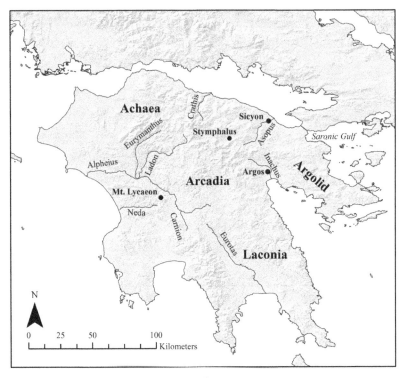

MAP 2 Peloponnese

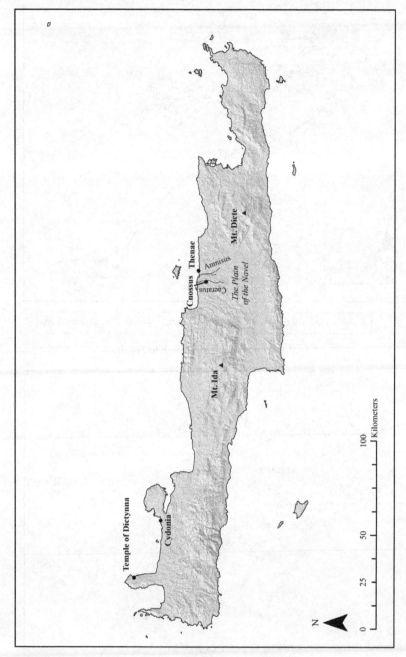

MAP 3 Crete

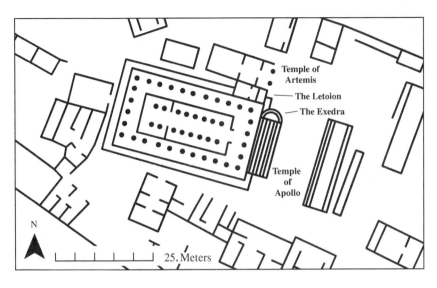

Inset of Apollo Sanctuary

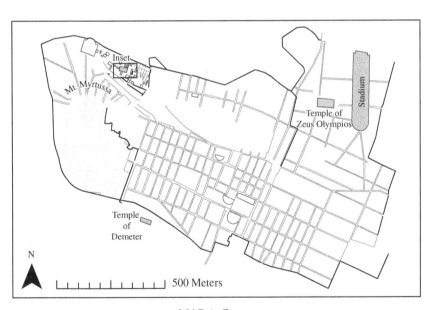

MAP 4 Cyrene

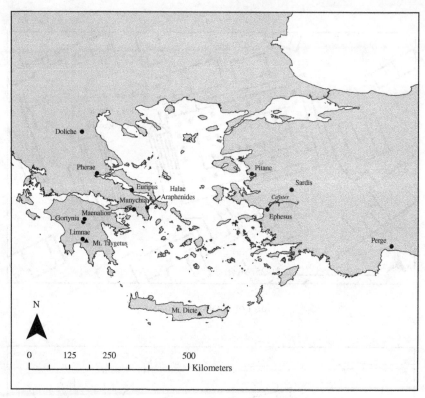

MAP 5 Locations in *Hymn to Artemis*

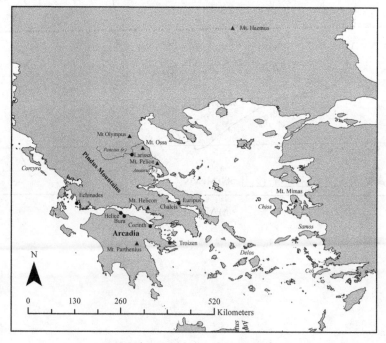

MAP 6 Locations in *Hymn to Delos*

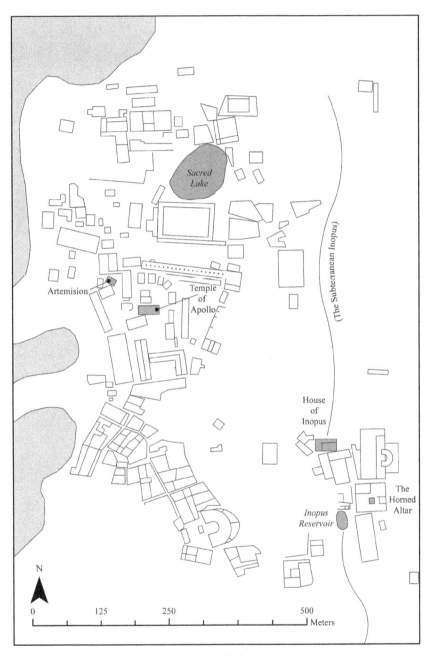

Sacred
Lake

(The Subterranean Inopus)

Artemision

Temple
of
Apollo

House
of
Inopus

The
Horned
Altar

Inopus
Reservoir

N

0   125   250   500
Meters

MAP 7 Delos

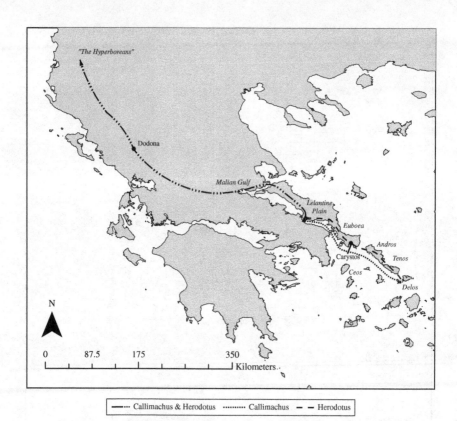

"The Hyperboreans"

Dodona

Malian Gulf

Lelantine
Plain

Euboea

Andros

Carystos

Tenos

Ceos

Delos

N

0   87.5   175   350
                                       Kilometers

······· Callimachus & Herodotus   ·········· Callimachus   — — Herodotus

MAP 8   Route of Delian offerings

CALLIMACHUS

Introduction

Life and Works

Callimachus of Cyrene was the most important poet of the Hellenistic age. He lived at the moment of transition from the classical world of old Greek city-states to the new foundation of Ptolemaic Alexandria in North Africa—a megacity that attracted people of diverse ethnicities from locations throughout the Mediterranean. Facilitated by this new environment, Callimachus appropriated the literary past and positioned himself between poetry as performance in traditional venues and the new possibilities afforded by the text. His poems contain explicit statements on poetic aesthetics, often constructed as responses to his "critics." Whether these statements were serious and systematic, or playful, and whether his enemies were real, or fictional foils to dramatize his own aesthetics, he was unique in his expression of what constituted excellence in contemporary poetics. His insistence on his own poetics as "new" in combination with his compositions in multiple genres provoked frequent and continuous imitation among later poets of both Greece and Rome.

His was a remarkable creative range. His poetry included hymns, epigrams, iambic poetry (*Iambi* and the *Ibis*), an elegiac poem of 4,000–6,000 lines on the origins of cultic practices throughout the Greek-speaking Mediterranean (*Aetia*), a hexameter poem of about 1,000 lines on an early exploit of Theseus and the bull of Marathon (*Hecale*), victory odes, and encomia of kings and queens. According to the *Suda* (T1Pf.), his prose writing embraced numerous topics, including foundations, nomenclature of various locations, paradoxography, and at least one essay that seems to have been about the critique of poetry (πρὸς Πραξιφάνην, fr. 460 Pf.). The most influential of his prose texts was the *Pinakes*, a comprehensive listing of earlier Greek literature by genre that included biographies of each author, citing their works with initial words or first lines.[1] His poetic works would have exceeded those of his contemporaries, Theocritus, Aratus, Posidippus, and Apollonius, combined, but unfortunately only his six hymns and around sixty of his epigrams have survived intact. The rest has been reduced to numerous citations in later Greek lexica and handbooks or, beginning in the late nineteenth century, has been discovered on papyrus.[2]

There are few verifiable facts about Callimachus' life, and much of what the ancient testimonia record is inference based on his writings. He claims to have been from the old Greek city of Cyrene in Libya, slightly over 500 miles to the west of Alexandria. The city was founded in the seventh century BCE. It was a Dorian colony settled by Arcadians, Spartans, Therans, and Cretans, and its foundation myth was narrated in Herodotus (4.151–67) as well as in Pindar's *Pythians* 4 and 5. Callimachus includes a brief version in his *Hymn to Apollo*. In the following epigram for his father, Callimachus claims to be related to the distinguished general of the same name, who is attested in other Cyrenean sources:

Ὅστις ἐμὸν παρὰ σῆμα φέρεις πόδα, Καλλιμάχου με
ἴσθι Κυρηναίου παῖδά τε καὶ γενέτην.
εἰδείης δ' ἄμφω κεν· ὁ μέν κοτε πατρίδος ὅπλων
ἦρξεν, ὁ δ' ἤεισεν κρέσσονα βασκανίης.

You, whoever walks by my tomb, know that I am the child and father of Callimachus the Cyrenean. You would know both. One once led the armies of his homeland; the other sang beyond the reach of envy. (*ep.* 21 Pf. = *AP* 7.525)

In the Cyrenean section of his *Hymn to Apollo*, Callimachus calls Cyrene "my city" and refers to "our kings" (lines 65 and 68); another poem (fr. 388 Pf.) mentions Magas of Cyrene and his daughter Berenice. A number of his poems showcase members of the ruling house of Alexandria (the Ptolemies). These include the *Hymn to Delos*, in which the birth of Ptolemy II on Cos is prophesied by Apollo,

---

1. On the nature and importance of the *Pinakes*, see Blum 1991.

2. For the discovery and assembly of his texts from book and papyrus fragments, see Lehnus 2011, Pontani 2011, and Massimilla 2011.

and the first line from a poem that seems to have been written for the marriage of Arsinoe II to her full brother, Ptolemy II (fr. 392 Pf.), an event that occurred between 279 and 274 BCE. Callimachus also wrote on Arsinoe II's death (fr. 228 Pf.), which fell in 270 BCE. Two other fragmentary poems now incorporated into the *Aetia* feature Berenice II, the daughter of Magas the king of Cyrene and wife of Ptolemy III: the *Victory of Berenice*, at the opening of *Aetia* book 3, commemorates the queen's chariot victory at the Nemean Games in either 245 or 241; the *Lock of Berenice*, which ends the *Aetia*, commemorates her marriage to Ptolemy III Euergetes in, probably, 246. According to the *Suda*, Callimachus also wrote poems (now lost) on the Gauls (the *Galatea*) and on Argos (the *Foundation of Argos*, the *Arrival of Io*), topics that seem calculated to support the self-fashioning of the ruling dynasty.[3] Callimachus' connection with Cyrene and Alexandria is not in doubt, but assertions that he traveled elsewhere are more problematic. An Athenian inscription that lists contributors to a special levy to aid the state includes the name Callimachus, without further qualification. It has recently been re-dated to a period well within the poet's lifetime (around 247 BCE), and therefore it may indicate his presence in Athens (Oliver 2002: 6); Callimachus was not, however, an uncommon name at Athens (cf. *RE* s.v. Kallimachos 1–3).

Further biographic details are less certain. The *Suda* claims that he was a schoolmaster (γραμματικός) in the Alexandrian suburb of Eleusis (T1 Pf.), although Tzetzes (T14c Pf.) asserts that he was a νεανίσκος τῆς αὐλῆς ("a youth of the court"), a rank incompatible with the position of an elementary school teacher. Cameron argues persuasively that other members of his family were highly placed, including a number who were known to be Cyrenaic philosophers (1995: 3–5). Why or when Callimachus moved from Cyrene to Alexandria is not known, and how long he resided in one or the other city is equally unclear. Between 275 and 246 the two cities were technically at war. Probably this did not require all traffic between them to cease; more probably exchanges continued, at least sporadically, especially in the long period of the betrothal of Magas' daughter Berenice to the son of Ptolemy II (c.253–246). Where Callimachus spent these years is not known, though his poem on the death of Arsinoe suggests that he was in Alexandria at least in 270. According to Athenaeus (6.252c), Callimachus recorded in his *Pinakes* that one Lysimachus wrote on the education of Attalus. The first Attalus of Pergamum took the throne only in 241, so if Athenaeus' statement is accurate, then Callimachus must still have been writing in 240, or even later.

A controversial piece of evidence for Callimachus' chronology is the elegiac epinician for Sosibius (frr. 384 and 384a Pf.). Athenaeus (4.144ε) claims that

---

3. For the successors of Alexander, the Gauls had come to occupy the ideological space that the Persians held in the Classical age; and the Ptolemaic house traced its Greek lineage from Argos, see *hAth* Introduction.

this elegy was written for a Sosibius who lived and wrote in the court of Cassander of Macedon. Cassander died in 297 BCE, so if the identification is correct, the elegy would be Callimachus' earliest known work, belonging some time in the 290s, and this presupposes a birthdate no later than 320–315. Most scholars now believe that Athenaeus was wrong and that the subject of the elegy was the notorious advisor of Ptolemy IV, the Sosibius later responsible for the death of Berenice II. In this case, the poem could not have been written much before 240 and may have been as late as 230. The epinician (fr. 384 Pf.) itself is ambiguous: in lines 39–41 Callimachus' speaker remarks: ἐκ δὲ διαύλου, | Λαγείδη, παρὰ σοὶ πρῶτον ἀεθλοφορεῖν | εἱλάμεθα, Πτολεμ[αῖ]ε ("we chose first to win a victory in the *diaulos* near by you, Ptolemy son of Lagus"). If the vocative refers to the living Soter, then the poetic subject must be the earlier Sosibius, but if the event recalled is the *Ptolemaia*, the festival established by Philadelphus *c.* 276 BCE to honor his deceased father, the epinician must be for the later Sosibius, and the apostrophized Ptolemy not the living sovereign but the deified Soter heralded as protector of the games.[4] As a corollary, Callimachus' birth would need to fall around 305 (to accommodate the dating of *hZeus* to around 284) and his death sometime after 240. In this commentary I follow the later dating.

Callimachus lived in Alexandria, a city that had been founded within a generation of his birth. His was not the city described by Strabo, who was writing at the end of the first century CE, but a city in the process of being built: high levels of immigration, dynamic physical changes, and rapid growth would have persisted during his lifetime. This earlier city had some sort of walls (the first mention of which is actually by Callimachus in *Iambus* 1), palace environs, and the *Museion* (which may or may not have included the Library). The lighthouse was built between 297 and 285; the stadium (*Lageion*) was probably completed by the time of the *Ptolemaia*. Polybius is the first to mention the theater (15.30.4) and a Thesmophorion (15.29.8) in connection with the events of 203/202, though these may well have been earlier constructions since documents refer to festivals of Demeter as early as 257 (Perpillou-Thomas 1993: 78–81).[5] Callimachus himself provides evidence for the Cape Zephyrium temple dedicated to Arsinoe-Aphrodite and for Arsinoe's mortuary temple. These were likely to have been constructed after Arsinoe II's death in 270, and the latter seems never to have been finished.

Within this rapidly expanding civic environment, the Greek community was a diverse mix. To judge from papyrus evidence drawn from the rest of Egypt,

4. See Fraser 1972: 2.1004–5 for a full discussion.

5. For details of Alexandrian monuments organized chronologically, see McKenzie 2007: 32–79.

Greek-speaking groups in descending order of concentration would have included Macedonians (mainly the soldiers), Cyreneans, Thracians, islanders, and Athenians.[6] The newness of the city dictated that everyone was an immigrant; therefore who came, where they came from, and the fact of migration itself constituted an essential dimension of poetic reception. Thus Callimachus reflects the variety of these ethnic groups in the hymns themselves: if *hZeus* was written for the *Basileia*, as many scholars believe, it was likely to have been the Macedonian holiday transplanted to Egypt; Cyrene figures in *hAp*; the southern Aegean islands, particularly Crete and Delos, are featured in *hArt* and *hDelos*. Argos (*hAth*) and Thessaly (*hDem*) were regions with strong Ptolemaic connections.

Callimachus and His Contemporaries

Callimachus did not write in a literary vacuum: Ptolemaic Alexandria was a fertile, thriving poetic environment, in part because monarchic patronage strove to make it so, in part because the new city provided opportunities in so many different venues, not the least of which was the newly established Library. Although Callimachus himself was never head of the Library, his composition of the *Pinakes* and the breadth of his poetic and prose intertexts testifies to his active engagement with this new (textual) mode of thinking. His prose works on paradoxography, on rivers, nymphs, birds, and winds, and on *Foundations of Islands and Cities and Their Name Changes* are all reflected in his hymns. So too were other contemporary prose writers. Demetrius of Phalerum, for example, collected the fables of Aesop; Callimachus uses Aesop in his own poetry. Euhemerus wrote the *Sacred Register*, notorious for its claims that Zeus and other gods had first been mortals who subsequently came to be worshipped for their benefits to mankind. Callimachus locates Euhemerus in Alexandria in his first *Iambus* (fr. 191.10–11 Pf.), making him an old man "scribbling his unrighteous books."

Callimachus' most important poetic contemporaries included Theocritus of Syracuse, the inventor of the bucolic genre. Associated with Sicily and Cos, he was among the earliest Hellenistic poets, and his residence in Alexandria most probably belongs between the 280s and the 260s. His *Encomium of Ptolemy* II (*Idyll* 17) and *Heracliscus* (*Idyll* 24) share numerous verbal and thematic parallels with Callimachus' *Hymn to Zeus* and *Hymn to Delos* (Stephens 2003: 123–70); the *Epithalamium*

---

6. See Mueller 2005. In addition to ethnic Greeks, about 50% of the early population would have been Egyptian, and there were non-Greek immigrants from other regions of the Mediterranean (e.g., Syria, Caria). The large concentration of Jews dates to the second century, and would not have been part of Callimachus' potential audience.

for Helen and Menelaus (*Idyll* 18) has close verbal parallels in the *Hymn to Athena* (F. Griffiths 1979: 89–90). Aratus of Soli (*c*.315–240 BCE) wrote the *Phaenomena*, a didactic treatment of Eudoxus' astronomy that was subsequently of great influence on Latin poetry. He probably wrote in the court of Antigonus Gonatas of Macedon, and he may never have been in Alexandria. Nonetheless, the proem to Zeus and other passages in the *Phaenomena* have clear parallels with Callimachus' hymns, even though priority cannot be established (Cuypers 2004: 102). Epigrammatists from a variety of locations also achieved prominence during this period. Their epigrams, often imitating earlier stone inscriptions, were beginning to be collected into poetry books. The most important of these writers were Asclepiades of Samos and Posidippus of Pella. A roll of more than a hundred epigrams of the latter, datable to the late third century BCE, was first published in 2001. The epigrams of this new collection share many features in common with Callimachus' poetry, including an emphasis on the athletic victories of Ptolemaic queens.

Apollonius of Rhodes, whose surviving poem is the epic *Argonautica*, is thought to have been a native Alexandrian and a slightly younger contemporary of Callimachus. He followed Zenodotus as head of the Alexandrian Library. The *Suda* makes him Callimachus' μαθητής (T 11a Pf.). Few scholars believe Apollonius was in fact Callimachus' pupil, but the term does imply a degree of artistic closeness that is borne out by the poems. A few examples will suffice to illustrate the relationship between the *Argonautica* and the hymns: Apollonius' poem has a hymnic opening and closing (1.1–2 and 4.1773–81); the beginning of the *Argonautica* includes references to Zeus, Apollo, and Artemis (1.508–9, 536–39, 569–72) that parallel moments in Callimachus' first three hymns respectively; the scene of Zeus's childhood on Crete appears twice, once in the context of Orpheus' cosmogony (1.508–9) and then at the opening of book 3. Aphrodite's description of the ball given to Zeus by his nurse Adrasteia includes several allusions to *hZeus* (e.g., 3.134: ἔτι νήπια κουρίζοντι = *hZeus* 54: μή σεο κουρίζοντος); finally, the narratives of Paraebius and of Phineus in book 2 are parallel to the paired narratives of *hAth* and *hDem*, see p. 22.[7]

The exact chronology of Callimachus' contemporaries will continue to be disputed, not least because they evidently wrote in response to each others' texts. But we know so little about strategies of poetic exchange—whether informal or public—that assertions about allusive priority must be made with extreme caution. The obviously shared subject matter of these poets indicates a rich and very interactive poetic environment, while also suggesting the growing importance of the text as a viable poetic and ideological medium.

---

7. See Stephens 2003: 200–10 (on *hZeus, hAp*); Köhnken 2003 (on *hAp, hDelos*); Eichgrün 1961: 111–18 (on *hArt*).

The Hymnic Tradition and Callimachus' Hymns

Hymns were among the oldest and most enduring elements in what comes to be the Greek poetic repertory. Hymns survive on stone and in manuscripts from the earliest recorded writing to the end of antiquity. They take many forms over time, and share many features with choral song; in essence, they were formal addresses to a god or group of gods on behalf of a community. That address could call upon the god in the second person (sometimes called *Du-Stil*) or speak about the god in the third person (sometimes called *Er-Stil*), or speak in the first person on behalf of the group. Hymns may have been sung by a communal group in unison, or performed by a chorus with musical accompaniment and dance, or performed by a solo singer. They might even be in prose like the so-called Isis aretalogies.

Traditionally, scholars have divided hymns into cultic, rhapsodic, and literary, depending on the assumed context of performance and audience. Cultic hymns were sung and/or danced performances for specific deities and in specific locations (e.g., the Palaikastro hymn to Zeus, paeans to Apollo at Delphi). To the extent that they survive, they were inscribed on stone (like the Palaikastro hymn) or cited in a later Greek author (see, for example, the hymn cited by Aelian, which is discussed in the introduction to *hAth*). Hymnlike lyric monody can be found in the archaic poets (e.g., Sappho, Alcaeus, Alcman, Pindar, Bacchylides), though scholars are divided about whether they were performed in cultic environments in real time (see, e.g., Athanassaki 2009: 242–43). Hymns were also a prominent feature within the choruses of Greek tragedy and comedy, and these examples, although removed from local performance, are helpful in understanding the structure and ubiquity of the genre (see, e.g., Swift 2010). Cult hymns vary in length: many are under thirty lines; others well over a hundred. But the formal elements of all types of hymns are more or less consistent, which prompts the following schematic:[8]

1. The invocation (*epiklesis*), or summoning of the divinity. The name will naturally occur at the beginning of a hymn, accompanied by relevant cult titles and epithets. In this formal opening there may be a genealogy that links the god to a particular place (see, e.g., *hZeus* 5–14), and companion deities may also be mentioned.
2. Praise of the divinity (*eulogia, euphemia*). This has various parts that may be more or less elaborated. They include a listing of the god's

---

8. See Furley and Bremer 2001: 1.1–64 for a full discussion of hymnic forms, and throughout for examples of Greek hymns.

unique powers, reminders of past benefits that the god has conferred
on worshippers, a narrative of the god's birth and relevant deeds of
prowess (e.g., killing the Pytho, defeating the Giants), descriptions of
the god's favorite locales and activities, interspersed throughout with
repeated addresses.

3. The prayer. Usually introduced by χαῖρε or other form of χαίρω, it expresses
the community's gratitude, for which it hopes for favor in return (see, e.g.,
hZeus 91–94). This section may include imperatives to summon the god
to appear.[9]

In addition to cultic, lyric, and dramatic hymns, thirty-three hexameter hymns
in an epic dialect were transmitted under the name of Homer, though compositional dates and provenances vary.[10] The majority of them are quite short (3–22
lines), but there are six major hymns ranging in size from forty-nine lines (to
Pan) to 580 lines (to Hermes). There is also a *Hymn to Dionysus*, from which
about sixty of the original 400+ lines survive (see West 2011: 29–43). This hymn
seems to have opened the collection in the manuscript tradition. Most of these
hymns begin by naming the god in the third person, or calling upon the Muses
to help the singer best hymn the god, though the hymns to Dionysus and Apollo
open with a *Du-Stil* address to the god himself. Homeric hymns continue with
the standard attention to the god's birth, nature, and deeds, the narratives of which
in the hymns to Dionysus, Demeter, Apollo, Hermes, and Aphrodite have been
expanded over several hundred lines. They close with a greeting to the god (at
this juncture the poet often uses the first person) and may call for another song
(see, e.g., *HhAphr* 292–93: χαῖρε, θεά, Κύπροιο ἐϋκτιμένης μεδέουσα· | σεῦ δ᾽ ἐγὼ
ἀρξάμενος μεταβήσομαι ἄλλον εἰς ὕμνον ["Hail, goddess, guardian of well-culti-
vated Cyprus. Having begun with you, I will turn to another hymn"]). They will
sometimes have internal references to performance (see, e.g., *HhAp* 171–78).
Homeric hymns are thought not to have been composed for a specific cultic
event, but are classified as "rhapsodic," from the practice in rhapsodic performance of beginning with a *prooimion* or prelude to the main event with a hymn
(see Pi. *Nem.* 2.1–5; [Plut.] *De musica* 6.1133C). The likely location for performance of these hymns would have been rhapsodic competitions at Panhellenic
centers and also, as J. S. Clay (1989: 3–16) has suggested, at banquets. These

9. Menander Rhetor (1.333–44 Russell-Wilson) divides hymns into eight types, the most significant of which are cletic (containing invocations of the god); scientific, i.e., those written by
philosophers expounding the nature of the deity; mythological; and genealogical. Elements
from all of these types may be found in Callimachus' hymns.

10. See Faulkner 2011b: 7–16 for a discussion of dating of the individual hymns. In his view
almost all would have been written by 300 BCE, and thus available to Callimachus.

hymns were transmitted as a group, along with Callimachus' six hymns, Orphic hymns, and hymns of Proclus; it is clear that Callimachus both knew the Homeric hymns individually, if not yet as a collection, and drew freely from the hymns to Dionysus, Demeter, Apollo, Hermes, Aphrodite, and Pan, and a few of the minor hymns.

Callimachus' hymns fall into two groups, usually described as non-mimetic and mimetic.[11] *HZeus*, *hArt*, and *hDelos* are "non-mimetic"; the speaker begins by invoking the god by name and proceeds to narrate his or her deeds in accordance with the schematic set out above. *HAp*, *hAth*, and *hDem* are "mimetic": the same parts are present but somewhat rearranged and presented as an immediate event taking place in the presence of the hearer or reader. The speaker creates the *mise en scène* of the ritual, invoking the participants and inserting a mythological narrative about the divinity into this frame. This mimetic effect is found also in choral lyric, particularly in forms like paean or prosodion, and Callimachus very likely modeled his own practice on these familiar antecedents. Like the Homeric, Callimachus' hymns are in stichic meters (hexameter, elegiacs), which means that they would not have been sung or danced, though they too may have been recited. (The majority of cult hymns in contrast is strophic.)

Scholars have long debated the exact relationship of Callimachus' hymns to real cultic events and to serious religious ideas. The consensus in the last forty years has been that the hymns were elegantly contrived poetic or metapoetic experiments that mimicked the hymnic form but lacked religious focus or content (e.g., Bing 2009: 33–48, Depew 1993). Thus they have been designated "literary," a category for which there were certainly contemporary examples: Philicus wrote a hymn to Demeter (*GLP* 90 = *SH* 676–80) that he specifically addressed to Alexandrian scholars (γραμματικοί) and Cleanthes' Stoic *Hymn to Zeus* was surely restricted to philosophical and literary circles. But it is important to note that even if these hymns were not attached to cultic events, they were not necessarily devoid of religious significance, and the Stoic hymn points in a direction that may be relevant for Callimachus. Philosophical debate over the nature of divinity is reflected in Cleanthes' hymn as Zeus is praised as the Stoic universal and first cause.[12] Cameron's tart criticisms (1995: 63–67) of those who would divorce ancient hymnody from context has led to some revisionism, and more recent trends have been to identify elements of the hymns as having analogues in known cult practice and in inscribed hymns but to reserve final judgment on whether, when,

---

11. See Harder 1992 for a detailed discussion of these terms; at 384 she makes the important observation that the distinction (mimetic, non-mimetic) obscures the "subtle play of *diegesis* and mimesis which pervades the whole collection of hymns and gives it a certain unity."

12. For a text and commentary on Cleanthes' hymn see Hopkinson 1989: 27–28, 131–36.

or where the hymns were or could have been performed.[13] What confuses the matter is that Callimachus seems, as a compositional strategy, deliberately to blur the distinction between a one-time real performance event and a carefully contrived fiction. He positions his poems to be both the mimesis of a specific event, as the cultic hymns seem to be, and the text that first creates, then enables the continual recreation of the event (see Acosta-Hughes and Stephens 2012: 145–47). Finally the extent to which mimicry was already incorporated in ancient ritual practices, particularly processions (see, e.g., Connelly 2007: 104–15), might be significant for Callimachus' compositional style, especially in the case of the mimetic hymns.

There can be no doubt that Callimachus consciously engages in a literary recollection of earlier poetic practice. In his treatment of cults in the hymns he adapts a lyric or hymnic persona, as the occasion demands. But the cultic information in each of these hymns, insofar as we can judge, accurately reflects contemporary religious practices. Certainly the locations Callimachus chooses to mention are often cult centers of the deity in question that are newly created or have been recently revived (e.g., Mt. Lycaeon in *hZeus*, Ephesus in *hArt*). It is also important to realize that archaeologists and scholars of ancient religion often rely upon Callimachus' hymns for local cultic information. While this by no means guarantees that Callimachus' information is accurate, it does guarantee that experts have not found it to be in error or to contradict what physical remains can tell them.[14] There continued to be a wide range of performance practices in the early Hellenistic period—established festivals like the Cyrenean *Carneia*, newly established festivals in Ptolemaic Alexandria (e.g., *Basileia, Ptolemaia, Arsinoeia*), continuing traditions of rhapsodic performance, and symposia of the Successors—at which Callimachus' hymns could have been performed, although this is not to say that they were.

The Hymns as a Collection

Whether it is Callimachus himself who is responsible or a later editor, the hymns give every indication of being a carefully arranged collection at both formal and thematic levels.

The six hymns fall into three pairs. *HZeus* and *hAp* locate their divinities respectively in Alexandria and Cyrene and insist on the closeness of the two divinities—Apollo (*hAp* 29) sits at the right hand of Zeus. These two, more than

13. For a summary of the debate with relevant bibliography see Petrovic 2011: 264–65. Hunter and Fuhrer 2002 and Vamvouri Ruffy 2004 discuss the theology of Callimachus' hymns in the context of early Ptolemaic Alexandria; Petrovic 2007, 2011 in terms of contemporary cultic practices.

14. See, e.g., Billot 1997–98 on Argive legends or Laronde 1987: 362–65 on the *Carneia*.

the others, focus on one specific area of concern for the divinity: kings for Zeus and song for Apollo. Both feature movement from north to south. The twin children of Leto—Artemis and Apollo—are the subjects of the next two hymns, which are also the longest. Both divinities move from the central to the eastern Mediterranean and both hymns end with vignettes of cult-sites important to the Ptolemies—Ephesus and Delos respectively. Both portray these cult-sites as under attack and successfully defended. Both are alive with cultic song and dance. The final pair feature Athena and Demeter in closely parallel narratives (see Hopkinson's very full analysis, pp. 13–17). Both are mimetic with inserted tales of young men from whom the goddess exacts retribution: Athena takes away the sight of Tiresias for accidentally seeing her as she bathed in the wild; Demeter punishes Erysichthon for deliberately trying to cut down her sacred tree. In contrast to the first four hymns written in epic Ionic, these two are in the Doric dialect.

Callimachus' hymns reflect the Homeric hymns in the following ways: the opening of the first hymn, *hZeus*, echoes the opening of the now fragmentary *HhDion*, which may have been the first hymn in the earlier collection, while the precocity of Zeus owes something to *HhHerm*. *HArt* depends on *HhAp* for its overall structure: like the earlier hymn, it falls into two parts, the first of which seems to provide closure, after which the hymn begins again. *HhPan* has influenced the Arcadian section of this hymn. *HDelos* reflects the Delian portion of *HhAp*. *HDem* exists in counterpoint with *HhDem*, and *hAth* with *HhAphr*. Finally, *hAp* reprises moments in *HhAp*, but its Cyrenean focus and paeanlike refrain makes it the least "Homeric" of the hymns. (See further Acosta-Hughes and Cusset 2012.)

The order of the individual hymns describes an arc, with the two longest in the center; their respective lengths are: 96 lines, 113 lines, 268 lines, 326 lines, 142 lines, and 138 lines. Hymns for two male divinities open, hymns for two female divinities close the group, and hymns devoted to Artemis and Apollo and their mother Leto occupy the center. Two-thirds of the way through the collection we find Apollo prophesying the birth of Ptolemy II on Cos and his subsequent rule over Egypt (*hDelos* 162–70). The mimetic and non-mimetic hymns are loosely interwoven: non-mimetic (*hZeus*), mimetic (*hAp*), non-mimetic (*hArt*), non-mimetic (*hDelos*), mimetic (*hAth*), and mimetic (*hDem*).

The middle four all have large narrative sections on specific cults—Cyrene, Ephesus, Delos, Argos; the flanking two do not, though *hZeus* is surely for Alexandria, and *hDem* is, according to the scholiast, also for Alexandria, though a number of scholars have argued for other locations (see p. 266). If the first and last are centered on Alexandria, however, that might account for their flanking positions and perhaps for their lack of local specificity.

The first four insist on the divine family of Zeus, Leto, and their twins. Hera, when she does appear, is hostile to both mother and children. Zeus pointedly remarks, "When goddesses would bear me such children as this, I would have little concern for the jealousy of an angry Hera" (*hArt* 29–31). Her wrathful pursuit of the pregnant Leto throughout the Mediterranean prevents Apollo's birth. The narratives include birth stories (*hZeus, hDelos*), divinities growing into their maturity (*hZeus, hAp, hArt*); virgin goddesses (*hArt, hAth*); goddesses punishing transgressors (*hArt, hAth, hDem*). Maternity is a strong theme in the last three; fathers and sons to a lesser extent in *hZeus* and *hDem*.

The hymns show a large number of unique verbal repetitions between one another. These have been most recently studied by Ukleja 2005: 21–108, and many are indicated in the notes below.

The Hymns and the Ptolemies

When Ptolemy I Soter became king of Egypt, he was required to rule two distinctly different populations: ethnic Greeks and Greek-speakers immigrating into the new city of Alexandria and the much larger native Egyptian population of the *chora*. He solidified his hold externally by engaging in strategic alliances and occasional wars with his fellow Diadochs, while internally he supported native priesthoods in the building of Egyptian temples and engaged in the rituals that were essential to Egyptian belief. The pharaoh was the liaison between the human and divine spheres and responsible for cosmic and social order. That the Ptolemies ruled their Egyptian subjects as pharaohs is abundantly clear from trilingual inscriptions like the Pithom Stele and the Rosetta Stone. The city of Alexandria incorporated Egyptian cults, such as that of Isis, and Egyptian artifacts seem to have been imported to adorn it. Ptolemy II, for example, imported an obelisk for his sister-wife's funerary temple and the foundations of the Serapeium had inscriptions in hieroglyphics as well as Greek. Callimachus' hymns (and Theocritus' *Idylls* 15, 17, and 24) include references not only to the Ptolemies in their role as Greek sovereigns but also elements that parallel myths central to pharaonic ideology (these are indicated in the notes on individual hymns). Below is a list of those Ptolemies who figure in discussion of the hymns, whether in Greek or Egyptian historical context.

Ptolemy I (Soter) c.367–283, the son of Lagus.   He was one of Alexander's generals, who claimed Egypt as his portion in the division of the empire at Alexander's death in 323 BCE. He had a number of children by Eurydice, the daughter of Antipater, including several sons. However, he divorced Eurydice and married Berenice I, who gave him at least four children, three of whom are important for the hymns: Arsinoe II, Ptolemy II, and Philotera. He was deified with Berenice I as *Theoi Soteres* after his death.

Ptolemy II (Philadelphus) 308–246.   He was the son of Ptolemy I and Berenice I. The youngest of Ptolemy's sons, he inherited the throne in preference to his older brothers. He first married Arsinoe I, the daughter of Lysimachus of Thrace. The marriage produced a number of children, including Ptolemy III (Euergetes) and Berenice Syra. He then married his full sister, Arsinoe II. He and Arsinoe were deified after 270 as *Theoi Adelphoi.*

Arsinoe II 316–270.   She was daughter of Ptolemy I and Berenice I. She was first married to Lysimachus of Thrace from 300/299 until his death in 281. Then briefly, and disastrously, to her half-brother Ptolemy Ceraunus (the son of Ptolemy I and Eurydice, and sometime king of Macedon), who was instrumental in killing her children by Lysimachus. After these events she returned to Egypt and married her full brother sometime between 279 and 274. She died in 270 and was deified. The temple at Cape Zephyrium, about 15 miles east of Alexandria, was built in her honor; there she was worshipped as Arsinoe-Aphrodite. She was widely worshipped throughout Egypt proper, being co-templed with native gods. During her brother-husband's reign a number of cities throughout the Mediterranean were renamed "Arsinoe" in her honor.[15]

Philotera d. 272?   She was the full sister of Ptolemy II and Arsinoe II. She died shortly before Arsinoe II and was deified, and perhaps co-templed with her sister in Alexandria (see Fraser 1972: 2.377n314). She is associated with Demeter in Callimachus' *Ektheosis of Arsinoe* (fr. 228.43–45 Pf.). A number of towns were named after her.

Magas of Cyrene c.317 to 250.   The son of Berenice I and a Philip of Macedon, he ruled Cyrene as regent for his stepfather, then Ptolemy II, before he revolted to become its sole ruler around 275 BCE. His daughter, Berenice II, was betrothed to Ptolemy III Euergetes and, after Magas' death, was finally married to him in 246.

Ptolemy III (Euergetes) c.284–222.   He was associated with his father as co-regent and was sole ruler of Egypt from 246 to 222. He was betrothed to Berenice II for several years before the marriage in 246.

Berenice Syra c.280–246.   The daughter of Ptolemy II and Arsinoe I, she was called "Syra" because of her marriage to the Seleucid king, Antiochus II, who had

---

15. For a recent biography of this queen see Carney 2013.

divorced his first wife Laodice in order to marry her. Antiochus was murdered shortly after the death of Ptolemy II in 246. Berenice claimed the regency for her son, but they were quickly murdered. Posidippus has written a number of epigrams for her victories in chariot-racing at the Panhellenic games.[16]

Berenice II 267/266–222.   The daughter of Magas of Cyrene, she married Ptolemy III. She is featured in two of Callimachus' poems—the *Victory of Berenice* (celebrating her chariot victory at the Nemean games) and the *Lock of Berenice* (a dedication for the safe return of her husband from the Syrian war). These poems open the third and close the fourth book of the *Aetia*. She was murdered at the instigation of her son, Ptolemy IV.[17]

Dating the Hymns

If the hymns were an authorially organized collection, they do not appear to have been written at the same time. At a conservative estimate, there seems to be a range of five to ten years between *hZeus* and *hDelos*, and possibly as much as a forty-year span between *hZeus* and *hAp*. Dates for individual hymns have been assigned by three different criteria: (1) internal stylistic considerations; (2) events or people mentioned in the hymns for which an external date can be established; and (3) textual borrowings by or from Callimachus or self-referentiality between one and another of Callimachus' poems. All three are problematic, but (1) and (3) especially so, since they often are based on scholarly preferences rather than demonstrable facts.

Internal stylistic criteria include arguments about maturity of style and more objective comparison of metrical phenomena. The criterion of maturity of style, when applied to this or that hymn, founders on the fact that much of Callimachus' truly mature work, books 3-4 of the *Aetia*, is now too fragmentary to underpin the discussion. Arguments from predictable metrical features have similar drawbacks. Although Callimachus has clearly defined metrical preferences for both his hexameters and his elegiac couplets, the corpus of the hexameter hymns is only 942 lines; the now fragmentary *Hecale* would have been at least as long, and there were other hexameter and elegiac poems that have not survived. Therefore, the metrical data from the hymns are only partial and insufficient to gauge the validity of apparent trends. G. Kaibel's (1877: 327) argument for an

16. I follow the scholarly consensus (but note that Clayman 2014: 146–58, following Huss 2008, argues that the Berenice in question is Berenice II).

17. For a recent biography of this queen, see Clayman 2014.

order based on increasing presence of the bucolic dieresis, for example, results in an ordering of *hDem, hArt, hAth, hZeus, hAp, hDelos*. However, the apparent linear progression includes a large gap between the first five (bucolic dieresis omitted once in every 11, 13, 17, 32, 40 lines) and *hDelos* (omitted once in 108 lines) that does not fit well with (2) external criteria. If external criteria are factored in, the early date for *hZeus* would require the first three hymns to have been written before or around 280 and all six to have been composed by *c.* 270. While in principle there is nothing wrong with this early assignment of the hymns, apart from the criterion of increasing bucolic diereses, there is little to support it. Moreover, observation of a different metrical phenomenon, incidence of spondaic lines, yields a different order: the frequency decreases from *hZeus* (15 per cent) to *hDelos* (3 per cent), though this too is unlikely to correlate with compositional order.

External events provide a slightly more reliable tool, though this criterion also suffers from editorial subjectivity. Of the six hymns, those featuring gods, *hZeus, hAp,* and *hDelos,* all mention contemporary kings. While many scholars have dismissed these references in *hZeus* and *hAp* as conventional and see no need to identify which king lies behind the remark (see, e.g., Williams p.1), the reference in *hDelos* is undeniably specific, and this fact would militate against these other references being generic. Further, whether a poem was ever performed or simply circulated, its issuance, *ipso facto*, must have coincided with the reign of one or another monarch whose existence would have conditioned a local audience's response, a response of which Callimachus could hardly have been unaware, since he capitalized on it in *hDelos.* Thus when the **Hymn to Zeus** draws an explicit parallel between the swiftness with which Zeus accomplishes his deeds and "our king" (86: ἡμετέρῳ μεδέοντι), the identity of the sitting monarch will necessarily form part of the reception. Allusions in the text, in fact, point to two: according to Justin (13.4.10) "Egypt... fell to Ptolemy by lot" (*Ptolemaeo Aegyptus... sorte evenit*), an event to which Callimachus seemingly alludes in lines 62–64 (Carrière 1969). He declares the story that Zeus and his brothers drew lots for their domains to be an implausible fiction, which in turn undermines any tale that Ptolemy I got Egypt by chance as opposed to capability or conquest. But a few lines before (58–59) Callimachus claimed that Zeus's siblings "although they were older, did not begrudge you heaven to hold as your allotted home." This is a unique and pointed comment on the mythological division but would not apply to Ptolemy I. It does to Philadelphus. The youngest of Soter's sons, he acceded to the throne while his older brothers lived. The goodwill among them did not last much beyond Soter's death, which gives a narrow window for the allusion to be appropriate and thus for the composition of the hymn (roughly 285–280). Moreover, the explicit discussion of youth, growth, and coming-of-age makes sense for Ptolemy II, who would have been 23 at the beginning of his co-regency, but hardly sustainable for Soter, who was 44 at the division of Alexander's empire in Babylon and 61 when he declared himself king of Egypt in 306 BCE. A solution that accounts for both allusions is to locate the hymn at the time of the co-regency between father and son (285–283); allusive conflation of the two monarchs would then suggest continuity of rule.

The **Hymn to Delos** includes an explicit reference to the living monarch, Ptolemy II. The as yet unborn Apollo prophesies this king's future birth on Cos (162–70). It is also the only one of the six hymns that mentions a contemporary military event (162–95). Ptolemy II had hired four thousand Celtic mercenaries for his war against Magas, the king of Cyrene. However, Magas was forced to retreat because of a rebellion of Libyan nomads, and Ptolemy's mercenaries subsequently mutinied. According to Pausanias (1.7.2) and the scholiast on this hymn, they were lured onto an island in the Delta and either burned or starved to death (Hölbl 2001: 39 and n18). These events took place around 275 BCE. A *terminus ante quem* for the hymn is the reference to Phoenician Corsica. This island could only have been "Phoenician" before the decisive battle of the First Punic War, waged for the island by Cornelius Scipio in 259 BCE. In addition, the poem must have been written when Ptolemaic influence or control of Delos was strong, and this provides another *terminus*—the Ptolemies' power waned with the defeat of their forces in the battle of Cos at the end of the Chremonidean war (*c*.261 BCE). Although Ptolemaic interest in Delos continued well into the reign of Ptolemy III Euergetes, the broadest time frame for the hymn is 275–262, with a strong bias for an earlier date, when the episode of the mutiny would have been fresh in the minds of Callimachus' audience.

In the **Hymn to Apollo** the narrator speaks of "our kings" at 68 (who are the Battiads, the historical line of the kings of Cyrene), but "my king" at 26–27 (who in the context should be the reigning king of Cyrene). Between 275 and his death *c*.250, Magas ruled Cyrene; before and after that a Ptolemy would have held that title, Philadelphus until Magas' revolt, and Euergetes when his marriage to Magas' daughter, Berenice II, around 246 reunited the kingdoms. At line 26 the scholiast identified the king as Euergetes (246–222 BCE), but by calling him *philologos* he has muddied the waters, because this epithet would have been much more appropriate for his father Philadelphus.[18] Fraser (1972: 1.652), following an earlier suggestion of Ehrlich, would place the hymn in 246, seeing the marriage of Apollo and Cyrene as a mythological correlative for that of Euergetes and Berenice II. But Cameron (1995: 407–9) raises the cogent objection that we should, if this is true, expect to have some indication of Berenice

18. A papyrus commentary on the hymns also identifies the king as Euergetes (POxy 20.2258 A fr.2d).

II, or at the very least mention of *two* rulers. (Callimachus, after all, is not shy about mentioning this Cyrenean queen in the *Aetia*.) Following Laronde (1987: 362), Cameron suggests rather that the king is Magas, an identification strengthened by the fact that Magas was the eponymous priest of Cyrenean Apollo, and that Callimachus apparently celebrates Magas in a now quite fragmentary elegy (fr. 388 Pf.). A scenario that would account for the single king and the strong emphasis on marriage is that the poem was written before Magas' death in 250, at the time when his daughter was betrothed to Euergetes, but before they became the ruling couple in 246. A further indication of date may be the reference to ζωστῆρες (85). If the word was selected to recall the cult title Apollo *Zoster* and his sanctuary in Attica, the fact that Zoster was fortified at the time of the Chremonidean war (267–261), when the Ptolemaic empire was closely allied with Athens, would locate the hymn no earlier than 267. However, these arguments are speculative; the dating of this hymn is by no means secure.

Arguments predicated on the assumption that similarities between the *sphragis* of this hymn and the *Aetia* prologue require them to have been written at the same time are not cogent. Despite the fact that both passages contain rebarbative statements about poetic practice, if the *Aetia* prologue is late (after 246), there is no inherent reason why Callimachus could not have written the hymn with its *sphragis* much earlier. Apollo as Callimachus' patron in both texts should not affect the date: he was the divinity who oversaw poetry, and he was the patron deity of Callimachus' home city, Cyrene.

None of the three hymns addressed to goddesses (Artemis, Athena, Demeter) mentions contemporary queens, though Callimachus does so in the *Aetia*. A simple inference from this is that these hymns were written when there were no queens—Ptolemy II married his sister, his second wife, between 279 and 274, but after her death in 270 he did not remarry. Egypt had no queen until Euergetes married Berenice II in 246 BCE. There are, however, good reasons to suspect female members of the royal house may stand behind the goddesses in these hymns.

The very close structural parallels between *hDelos* and *hArt* suggest that they are conceived as a pair (despite the different treatment of bucolic dieresis). Nothing precludes the **Hymn to Artemis** being written well before or well after *hDelos*, but the fact that the hymn ends with so much attention to Ephesus points to a contemporary context. Ephesus was closely connected to Arsinoe II. When she was sixteen years old, she was first married to Lysimachus, the Diadoch who ruled Thrace and Asia Minor. The marriage lasted until Lysimachus' death. During the period when he controlled Ephesus, he built a new town to the west of the Artemision, which he named Arsinoe, though the name did not long survive his death (Strabo 14.1.21). The connection of Apollo with Ptolemy II is overt in *hDelos*; therefore it is worth considering whether Arsinoe II is to be identified with Artemis, via her close association with Ephesus.[19] If *hDelos* can only have been written after 275, *hArt* might well have been earlier, belonging to the period of her marriage to Lysimachus and before his death (Ragone 2006: 74–77).[20] If the poem was written after the death of Arsinoe II, a suitable time period would be between 262, when Ephesus came under Ptolemaic control, and 255, when it reverted to the Seleucids. A decade later the relationship was not so positive. In the 250s Berenice Syra, the sister of Ptolemy III, was married to Antiochus II, who died in Ephesus in 246 under dubious circumstances, while Berenice Syra herself was murdered shortly thereafter. Ptolemy III then established a garrison at Ephesus, and it served as his base against the other dynasts for the duration of his reign (Hölbl 2001: Appendix 262–246 BCE).

No external evidence exists for dating the last two hymns, which also seem to have been a tightly constructed pair, despite the fact that they are in different meters. For the dating of the **Hymn to Athena** we must turn to (3) textual borrowings either by or from Callimachus. These are of limited reliability because the relative chronologies for poets writing in early Alexandria are not secure (see pp. 7–8). Still, with respect to *hAth* 2, it seems clear that the phrase ἄρτι φρυασσομενᾶν was subsequently imitated in an epigram (*AP* 5.202) attributed either to Asclepiades of Samos or Posidippus of Pella, in which two *hetairai* engage in sexual combat. The overtly sexual epigram dictates the direction of the borrowing: despite the repressed sexual energy that surrounds Callimachus' portrait of Athena, allusion to the explicit sexual behavior of prostitutes is unlikely to belong to the hymn. In the epigram Athena's mares become "colts of the evening," i.e., the young men being "ridden" by the contending *hetairai*. Of the two epigrammatists, the only secure evidence for dating Asclepiades comes from the 270s (Sens 2011: xxvi), which would dictate an even earlier date for the hymn. If the author of the epigram was Posidippus, he was the recipient of a proxeny decree in 263 or 262 at Thermon in Aetolia. His recently discovered collection of epigrams celebrates the equestrian victories of Berenice I, Arsinoe II, and Berenice Syra, but apparently not Berenice II, whose victory at the Nemean games in 245 or 241 was the subject of Callimachus' *Victory of Berenice*. Cameron (1995: 241–45) has argued that the epigram in which the imitation occurred was a poem for Bilistiche, the mistress of Ptolemy II, who won Olympic victories in chariot racing

19. A signet ring from Egypt seems to show Artemis with the features of Arsinoe (see Pfrommer 2001: 38–39), and coin issues from Ephesus show a head that appears to be Arsinoe on the obverse, with Artemis' bow and quiver on the reverse (see Müller 2009: 345–48 and for illustrations, 451).

20. Meillier 1979: 114 objects to an early date for the hymn because Callimachus does not allude to the destruction that the city suffered around 290. It was rebuilt between 287 and 281.

in 268 and 264, and if he is correct, *hAth* must precede 264. However, Sens (2011: 235–36) disagrees, suggesting rather that Posidippus may be indulging in insouciant self-referentiality, since one of his own equestrian epigrams celebrates the triumph of Berenice I in a chariot victory over a much earlier female contender, Cynisca of Sparta (87 A-B). Certainty is impossible, but if Posidippus is the author, a date for the hymn in the 260s is the most reasonable guess, and the borrowing into a context of horse racing might have resulted from the implicit association of the Athena of the hymn with one of the Ptolemaic royal ladies who had recently won an equestrian victory in a Panhellenic game.

Bulloch (p. 41 and notes ad loc.) argues that in *hAth* Callimachus imitates Theocritus' epithalamium for Helen and Menelaus (*Id.* 18), specifically 22–24: ἄμμες δ' αἱ πᾶσαι συνομάλικες, αἷς <u>δρόμος</u> ωὑτός | <u>χρισαμέναις ἀνδριστὶ παρ' Εὐρώταο</u> λοετροῖς, | <u>τετράκις ἑξήκοντα</u> κόραι... ("We are all age-mates, who have this place for running, having anointed ourselves in manly fashion by the bathing-places of the Eurotas, four times sixty maidens..."). At *hAth* 23–30 Athena runs a δὶς ἑξήκοντα course along the Eurotas (παρ' Εὐρώτᾳ) and anoints herself with manly olive oil (ἄρσεν ἔλαιον... χρίεται). If the direction of the allusion is correct, we may be able to make some headway on a date. Some scholars have thought that *Id.* 18 was written for the marriage of Ptolemy II and Arsinoe II (between 279 and 274). If so, the hymn should be later, and if a female Ptolemy is to be imagined behind the chariot-driving Athena, then the previous association of the language with Arsinoe would make her the most likely candidate, and the hymn could be no later than 270. These assumptions about the priority of Theocritus' poem (and its relationship to a royal marriage) do not have the ring of inevitability, but they do fit the traditional chronologies for the two possible authors of the epigram.

The **Hymn to Demeter** cannot be dated by external evidence. However, Philotera, the sister of Arsinoe II and Ptolemy II, was closely associated with Demeter in cult, as we learn from the *Ektheosis of Arsinoe*. The *Ektheosis* must have been composed at the time of Arsinoe's death in 270, and in that poem Philotera is already dead. If *hDem* has Philotera in the background (or as the hymnic pretext), it would have been composed after her death and deification, but probably not too much later, thus probably before the *Ektheosis*. Moreover, there are distinctive verbal echoes between the *Ektheosis* and *hDem*. Lines 45–46 of the former read: Δηοῦς ἄπο νεισομένα· σέο δ' ἦν <u>ἄπ[υστος]</u>, | ὦ δαίμοσιν <u>ἁρπαγίμα</u>... ("[by Philotera] having returned from visiting Deo. She was unaware of you [sc. Arsinoe II], O carried off [i.e., in death] by the gods"). These same two rare words appear at *hDem* 9: <u>ἁρπαγίμας</u> ὅκ' <u>ἄπυστα</u> μετέστιχεν ἴχνια κώρας. Then at 47–48 Philotera urges her companion to sit upon the lofty (ὑπά[τ]αν) peak and gaze (αὔγασαι), while *hDem* 3–4 urges the βέβαλοι... μηδ' ὑψόθεν αὐγάσσησθε. D' Alessio p. 34

argues, I think correctly, that the direction of these verbal reminiscences cannot be determined, but that both poems probably belong to the end of the 270s.

Finally, Apollonius alludes to *hAth* and *hDem* in a way that suggests he received them as a pair. His narrative of Phineus (2.178–93, 444–47) parallels that of Tiresias, while the neighboring tale of Paraebius (2.456–89), who suffered because his father had chopped down an oak against the protests of its resident Hamadryad, is too close to that of Erysichthon to be a coincidence. Poetic economy would dictate that the allusive direction runs from Callimachus to Apollonius, and not that Callimachus set out to write two distinct hymns in response to Apollonius' text.[21] Still, this does not help with dating, since the dating of the *Argonautica* is around 240, or around the time that we have our last datable evidence for Callimachus' life. But it may have implications for the hymn collection as a whole. Paired hymns suggest a collection by Callimachus, not a later editor.

Language and Style

Callimachus composed his poetry in third-century BCE North Africa, in Cyrene or Alexandria or in both locations. As a Cyrenean, Callimachus would have been a Doric speaker, and Cyreneans in Alexandria, if early immigration into the rest of Ptolemaic Egypt is an accurate indicator, were likely to have been 30–40 per cent of the city's native Greek population. In addition many immigrants from other locations would have retained their regional dialect preferences,[22] although the official city and the army would have used a *koine* that was an admixture of Attic and Ionic.[23] It is also important to note that Homer and Homeric language would have occupied a unique place in the consciousness of those who possessed an education sufficient for entrance into Ptolemaic administration. The prevailing educational system depended heavily on Homer, which guaranteed that Homeric Greek itself functioned as a literary *koine* for all Greek speakers, whatever their individual dialectal affiliations. Thus it is unsurprising that in his writing of hymns, Callimachus adapts a language and diction based primarily on Homer. About 80 per cent

---

21. Bulloch pp. 41–42 argues that Callimachus imitates Apollonius on the basis of the placement of the proclitic οὐ before the main caesura (only at *hDem* 103, but three times in Apollonius, including the passage in question, 2.444). There is no doubt that one poet imitated the other, but the value of this metrical evidence is questionable because there are four times as many extant hexameters of Apollonius. Bulloch does not factor in the Paraebius vignette.

22. See, e.g., Theoc. 15.92, where the ladies assert their right to "speak Peloponnesian."

23. See Colvin 2011 for the constitution of various *koinai* in the early Hellenistic world; see Parsons 2011 for Callimachus' *koinai*.

of his vocabulary occurred previously in Homer; in this he is not unique—the Homeric hymns also have a ratio of 80 per cent of their vocabulary coincident with previous epic to 20 per cent that is new. Pervasive epic features include vocabulary, forms, diction, and occasionally syntax, all of which contribute to an atmosphere of inherited seriousness and link the new compositions to a familiar literary past. The opening of the *Hymn to Zeus* provides an example of how Callimachus achieves this:

> Ζηνὸς ἔοι τί κεν ἄλλο παρὰ σπονδῇσιν ἀείδειν
> λώϊον ἢ θεὸν αὐτόν, ἀεὶ μέγαν, αἰὲν ἄνακτα,
> Πηλαγόνων ἐλατῆρα, δικασπόλον Οὐρανίδῃσι;
> πῶς καί νιν, Δικταῖον ἀείσομεν ἠὲ Λυκαῖον;
> 5   ἐν δοιῇ μάλα θυμός, ἐπεὶ γένος ἀμφήριστον.
> Ζεῦ, σὲ μὲν Ἰδαίοισιν ἐν οὔρεσί φασι γενέσθαι,
> Ζεῦ, σὲ δ᾽ ἐν Ἀρκαδίῃ·

The underlined items are either common Homeric words or forms (κεν, -δῇσιν, -οισιν, λώϊον, αἰέν), words that occur frequently but not exclusively in Homer (ἀείδειν, ἄναξ, θυμός, οὔρεσι), or rarely but in significant contexts (ἐν δοιῇ, δικασπόλον, ἀμφήριστον). Even words that are not particularly marked as Homeric take on a Homeric idiom: for example, φασι and γενέσθαι are hardly exclusive to epic, yet with φασι γενέσθαι Callimachus has written a phrase that occurs four times in the *Iliad* and *Odyssey* at verse end. Αἰέν and ἄνακτα never occur together in Homer, but each word does occur several times in Homer in the metrical position in which Callimachus places them.

Callimachus and Homer

Callimachus' practice with respect to Homeric language may be categorized in four distinct ways:

1. It provides the linguistic background and sonorities that connect the poems to a familiar, collective Greek cultural experience, an experience reinforced by the educational system and the practice of public recitation of Homer. Thus it allows the poet to position his hymnic subjects, gods for a new place, within (and at times against) the epic past.

2. The developing interest in the status of Homer's texts in early Hellenistic Alexandria meant that numerous Homeric expressions were questioned or debated; Callimachus' text, therefore, will occasionally reflect either

his understanding of a disputed Homeric passage or his own determi-
nation of a form.[24] In *hZeus* 11–13, for example, Callimachus describes
the sacred place where Rhea gives birth, after which copious rivers flow:

ἔνθεν ὁ χῶρος
ἱερός, <u>οὐδέ τί μιν</u> κεχρημένον Εἰλειθυίης
ἑρπετὸν οὐδὲ γυνὴ ἐπιμίσγεται…

The phrase οὐδέ τί μιν occurs seven times in the *Iliad* and *Odyssey*. At *Il.*
17.749–51 in particular it describes the sudden flow of rivers:

ὅς τε καὶ ἰφθίμων ποταμῶν ἀλεγεινὰ ῥέεθρα
ἴσχει, ἄφαρ δέ τε πᾶσι ῥόον πεδίονδε τίθησι
πλάζων· <u>οὐδέ τί μιν</u> σθένεϊ ῥηγνῦσι ῥέοντες·

[a wooded ridge] which checks the grievous streams of mighty
rivers, and straightway for all of them turns the flow to wandering over the plain; nor do they, though flowing in strength,
break through it (μιν) at all.

But in this passage Hellenistic scholars debated the exact meaning of οὐδέ τί
μιν. According to a scholium on the passage, Aristophanes of Byzantium objected to μιν and proposed emending to οὐδέ τι μήν. Although earlier than
Aristophanes, Callimachus' use of the phrase οὐδέ τί μιν in the context of
flowing rivers does seem to have signaled his preferred reading of Homer.[25]

3. Homeric diction provided a number of predictable derivatives and
forms upon which Callimachus was able to model his coinages. For
example, *hAth* 91 has δόρκας, from δόρξ, δορκός. The usual form is
δορκάς, δορκάδος, but Callimachus has apparently modeled his noun
on another Homeric word for deer, πρόξ, προκός, that has the doublet
προκάς. (The variant ζόρξ occurs in *hArt* 97.)[26] These neologisms are
occasionally discussed in the notes to each poem, but since this material
is much more thoroughly handled in the commentaries on individual
hymns, interested readers will be directed to the relevant editions.

24. For Callimachus' interpretation of Homeric words see Rengakos 1992; for the Hellenistic
poets' views on the text of Homer see Rengakos 1993.

25. This argument is based in part on McLennan p. 41n12.

26. This example is based on Bulloch pp. 201–3nn91–92.

4. Scholars have frequently commented on Callimachus' predilection for rare or *hapax* words in Homer, which they sometimes characterize as recherché or even as a display of learned obscurity. In fact, the Homeric context of such marked borrowings almost always lends a significant intertextual resonance to Callimachus' own text, as if the earlier poet's voice could be heard in the distance. ἀμφήριστον, quoted above, provides an example. The word occurs twice, in *Il.* 23.382 and 527, in reference to chariots racing in a dead heat. In the first occurrence the tie is broken by the intervention of Apollo. In *hZeus* someone—the god?—interrupts to break the dead heat at line 8. Of course, Callimachus does not restrict this specific type of intertextual voice to Homer. He appropriates Hesiod, the Homeric hymns, lyric, tragedy, and even prose writers in a similar way.

Other Linguistic Influences

In addition, Callimachus had at his disposal a wide variety of previous poetic models that came with generically marked dialects. His linguistic texture is enriched with words familiar from the lyric poets (which may be Doric), particularly in *hAp* and *hDelos*; tragedy (which may be Attic or Doric), particularly in the speeches in *hDelos* and the inserted story of Tiresias in *hAth*; and later epicists like Antimachus of Colophon and Callimachus' immediate poetic predecessor, Philitas of Cos, who wrote in both hexameters and elegiacs. Very often borrowing a unique word or phrase from an earlier poet brings with it specific poetic connotations, though, as is often the case with the lyric poets and later poets like Antimachus and Philitas, the fragmentary nature of a predecessor may obscure the full extent of the borrowing.

In contrast to the familiarity of Homer and his linguistic practice, a very high proportion of Callimachus' non-Homeric words are not found in previous poetry. Many occurred previously only in prose, others have been found in contemporary documents and the *koine*; some describe objects or events for which we have no other poetic testimony (though it may well have existed); some are introduced for a particular effect; some words are new coinages. Since so little poetry has survived between the end of the fifth century BCE and Callimachus' time, it is not easy to assess the extent to which words appearing in his texts for the first time are truly novel, belong to a now lost poetic substratum, or the *koine*. For example, at *hDem* 110 the manuscripts read αἴλουρον, which the scholiast glosses as "cat," but the papyrus has μάλουριν (which is now generally accepted). Hesychius glosses the unique word (μάλουρις) as "white-tailed"; did Callimachus coin it, was it colloquial Greek, or simply unattested in earlier literature?

Callimachus' lexicon has been well studied: F. Lapp (1965: 155–72) lists eighty-six neologisms or variants of previously known words that occur only in Callimachus' hymns and another ninety-six that first occur there. An innovator, Callimachus coined new nouns or alternative forms in -τειρα (e.g., ἀράτειρα, ἐπιθυμήτειρα, θηρήτειρα); -τύς (e.g., ἁρπακτύς, γελαστύς, διωκτύς); -ίς (e.g., ἀμβολαδίς, λεχωίς, σαρωνίς); -ίη (e.g., κυνηλασίη, ῥυηθενίη); adjectives in -σιος and -τιος (e.g., ἐπιδαίσιος, εὐέστιος, παννστάτιος), matro- and patronymics in -ιάς (e.g., Λητωιάς, Πελασγιάς), as well as evocative compounds like ἐλλοφόνος, "fawn-slaying" of Britomartis (hArt 190), μουνόγληνος, "one-eyed" of the Cyclops (hArt 53), or ψευδοπάτωρ, "false father," addressed to Poseidon by Triopas (hDem 98). While many of these may have been coined to allow greater metrical flexibility, they simultaneously impart a sense of linguistic innovation and freshness to the otherwise traditional Homeric language.

A final aspect of Callimachus' language has been his influence on later poets: later epigrammatists, Dionysius the Periegete,[27] Nonnus, Oppian, and Triphiodorus clearly imitated his vocabulary and metrical refinements (see De Stefani and Magnelli 2011). There is, of course, also considerable linguistic overlap with contemporaries like Theocritus, Aratus, Asclepiades, Posidippus, and Apollonius, but with these poets it is much harder to decide the direction of the borrowing.

Callimachus' Doric

The first four hymns are written in epic Ionic and dactylic hexameter; hDem is in hexameters as well. However, hAth and hDem are written in the Doric dialect, though epic-Ionic forms also occur. Doric dialects were spoken in West Greek city-states like Argos and Sparta, and as a result of colonization they were found in Sicily and South Italy, Crete, Cos, Rhodes, Thera, and African Cyrene.[28] Ruijgh (1984) has argued that the Doric of Theocritus (and Callimachus) reflected the dialect as spoken by Cyrenean immigrants to Alexandria, but his theory has not been widely embraced (see Parsons 2011: 142–43). Most scholars believe that Callimachus did not adhere to any one Doric dialect in these hymns, but employed what is usually described as "literary" Doric, by incorporating the most recognizable features of Doric speakers: long α for η; -τι in third person verbal endings; -μες for -μεν; athematic infinitives in -μεν; λης for θέλης; πρᾶτος for πρῶτος; τῆνος for (ἐ)κεῖνος; -οκα for -οτε (e.g., ποκα = ποτε); μέστα for μέσφα; -ευ as a contraction of Ionic -εο; -ω for -ου in masculine

27. J. L. Lightfoot's 2014 commentary now makes the full extent of Dionysius' debt to Callimachus accessible, on whom see her general index s.v. Callimachus.

28. For characteristics of individual Doric dialects see Buck §§242–73.

genitive singular (see further pp. 36–38). Doric forms are sometimes found in his other hymns, for example, οἰκιστήρ ("founder") appears in place of the Attic οἰκιστής in *hAp* 67, where it accurately represents the Cyrenean dialect form.

A complicating factor in assessing Callimachus' practice in the Doric hymns is the manuscript tradition itself: as the hymns were copied and recopied, how often were the forms Callimachus originally wrote replaced, either his Doric by more familiar Attic or Ionic forms or the reverse? Modern scholars tend to make the following assumptions: (1) Callimachus would not have randomly varied Doric and non-Doric forms in the same hymn, so if ποτε and its Doric equivalent ποκα both appear in *hAth* or *hDem*, the non-Doric ποτε should be corrected to Doric. (2) If a Doric form occurs in a papyrus or in ancient testimonia, it is reasonable to assume that this is the correct reading (for example, POxy 2226's Doric μέστα where the medieval mss. have μέσφα). (3) "Organic" consistency dictates that if specific Doric features occur in one word (e.g., μῶνος), it is reasonable to correct -ου to -ω in another word, if the Doric variant is known (so Bulloch p. 74). Thus almost all non-Doric forms found in the mss. of these two hymns have been altered to Doric forms whenever metrically feasible (over 40 such alterations have been made to the inherited manuscript tradition of *hAth*, and even more to *hDem*).[29] But the highly allusive character of Callimachus' text complicates the picture. Cuypers 2004: 108, for example, makes an excellent case for the retention of νιν in the non-Doric *hZeus* 4 "as a pointer to the *Homeric Hymn to Apollo*" (528: πῶς καὶ νῦν); and see below note on *hAth* 4: σοῦσθε... σοῦσθε. In such cases I have chosen to keep the dialect form of what seems to have been an allusion.

Callimachus' Poetic Effects

The structure and organization of Callimachus' verses is carefully balanced. For example, in the opening of *hZeus* 1–7, Zeus, his designations, or his epithets occur in every line but 5 (Ζηνός, θεόν, ἄνακτα, ἐλαρτῆρα, δικασπόλον, Δικταῖον, Λυκαῖον, Ζεῦ, πάτερ). As singer, the narrator occupies the exact center of these seven lines (ἀείσομεν) surrounded by Zeus. The opening seven verses are organized around three questions: Ζηνὸς ἔοι τί κεν ἄλλο... ἀείδειν λώϊον; πῶς καί νιν... ἀείσομεν; πότεροι, πάτερ, ἐψεύσαντο; The two sections between these questions are shaped by a series of doublets: Zeus himself is ἀεὶ μέγαν, αἰὲν ἄνακτα, and Πηλαγόνων ἐλατῆρα, δικασπόλον Οὐρανίδῃσι. The four epithets are in asyndeton, and each is progressively longer, 4, 5, 8, and 9 syllables, which creates a mounting intensity; in line 3 the phrases are arranged in chiasmus with the proper nouns on

---

29. These changes may be found in Bulloch's (*hAth*) and Hopkinson's (*hDem*) apparatus.

the outside, the common nouns within. Between the second and third question another set of doublets occurs: Δικταῖον or Λυκαῖον (again similarity of sounds), varied as Ἰδαίοισιν ἐν οὔρεσί or ἐν Ἀρκαδίῃ in lines 6–7. In line 4 the two adjectives fall on either side of the verb (Δικταῖον ἀείσομεν ἠὲ Λυκαῖον), while in line 5 the two central nouns, θυμός, γένος, are flanked, now by variations on doubt, ἐν δοιῇ, ἀμφήριστον.

Sound is a particularly important feature of the hymns: at the opening of hZeus the ἀεί of ἀείδειν is repeated in the ἀεὶ μέγαν, αἰὲν ἄνακτα of the next line and comes back in 4: ἀείσομεν (thus "eternal" is built into the act of singing). Anaphora and other types of repetition are common in hymns in general, and Callimachus uses it in his hymns very frequently and to great effect. A form of the god's name, Ζηνός, Ζεῦ, opens lines 1, 6, and 7, the last two with anaphora and similarity of sounds (paronomasia) in Ζεῦ, σὲ μέν, Ζεῦ, σὲ δ' ἐν. Similarly, note the opening of the first two lines of hAp: οἷον ὁ τὠπόλλωνος, οἷα δ' ὅλον, and throughout that hymn the frequent play on Apollo and forms of πολύς (see notes ad loc.). In hArt 6–18, the young goddess's demands are constructed around a repeated δός μοι, "gimme." In hDelos 70–75 the flight of the landscape from Leto is punctuated with repeated φεῦγε. HZeus 55 opens and closes with similar sounds: καλά...ἠέξευ, καλά...-ιε Ζεῦ. At hAp 101–2 Apollo rapidly shoots his arrows: ἄλλον ἐπ' ἄλλῳ | βάλλων.

In addition to his aural effects Callimachus' word order often creates word pictures that reinforce sense, a phenomenon more frequent in Latin than in Greek poetry. At hAp 54: ἡ δέ κε μουνοτόκος διδυμητόκος αἶψα γένοιτο, the juxtaposition of the two rare nouns (μουνοτόκος, διδυμητόκος) shows us the one "suddenly" becoming the other. (This is also a good illustration of the generative skills of Callimachus' lexical imagination.) At hAp 88–89: οἱ δ' οὔπω πηγῇσι Κύρης ἐδύναντο πελάσσαι | Δωριέες, the Dorians are separated as far as possible from the "streams of Cyre," to which they were not yet able to draw near (ἐδύναντο πελάσσαι). At hDelos 91–93: ...ὄφις μέγας, ἀλλ' ἔτι κεῖνο | θηρίον αἰνογένειον ἀπὸ Πλειστοῖο καθέρπον | Παρνησὸν νιφόεντα περιστέφει ἐννέα κύκλοις, the great serpent (ὄφις μέγας) with its nine coils (ἐννέα κύκλοις) stretches over three lines as it encloses snowy Parnassus (Παρνησὸν νιφόεντα). At hArt 192: ἡ δ' ὁτὲ μὲν λασίῃσιν ὑπὸ δρυσὶ κρύπτετο νύμφη, the nymph (Britomartis) is positioned at the end of the line, hiding under the shrubs, as far away as possible from Minos (named at the end of 190), who pursues her. At hDem 120–21: χὡς αἱ τὸν κάλαθον λευκότριχες ἵπποι ἄγοντι | τέσσαρες, the anomalous position of the object (τὸν κάλαθον) within the article-noun group (αἱ...ἵπποι) creates the word picture by locating Demeter's basket behind the horses that lead it forward.

Callimachus was a master of polyphony. In the hymns he deploys a wide and sometimes deceptive range of poetic voices. On the surface the non-mimetic hymns (*hZeus, hArt,* and *hDelos*) seem to have one authoritative narrating I, who introduces the divine subject (πῶς καί νιν... ἀείσομεν; Ἄρτεμιν... ὑμνέομεν, τὴν ἱερὴν, ὦ θυμέ,... ἀείσεις | Δῆλον) and relates his/her birth and deeds. However, there are frequent intrusions of other, sometimes ambiguous voices: in *hZeus* 8, for example, who utters the statement "Cretans always lie"? Is it the poet? Zeus himself? Or the ancient sage Epimenides to whom the line was attributed in antiquity? The heavy borrowing of specific language from Hesiod that leads up to the quotation of *Th.* 96 (ἐκ δὲ Διὸς βασιλῆες) at *hZeus* 79 makes it seem as if Hesiod has intruded into his successor's poem. The exchange of Artemis and Zeus at the opening of *hArt* seems to move directly out of a Homeric scene; the exchange of Leto and Peneius in *hDelos* is colored with tragic language, particularly that of Euripides; Apollo, speaking from the womb in *hDelos,* assumes a vatic persona. The situation of the mimetic hymns (*hAp, hAth, hDem*) is even more complex. In all three the speaker is anonymous and his/her connection to the rite is not transparent. Is there one narrator in *hAp* who exhorts the unclean to depart before the god appears, who exhorts the chorus to sing, then narrates the god's biography? Or does the speaker exhort the chorus, who then sing the lines that follow as a paean to the god? In *hDem* the narrator is a woman (see 124); in *hAth* the gender is ambiguous. As a result, considerable scholarship has been devoted to studying the narrative voice in Callimachus (for recent treatments see Morrison 2007: 105–78, Fantuzzi 2011).

The Hexameter Hymns

Five hymns (*hZeus, hAp, hArt, hDelos, hDem*) are written in dactylic hexameter, the meter of Homeric epic, which was said to express a dignified and elevated style and to be more tolerant than others of rare words and metaphor (Arist. *Poet.* 1459b32–36). By the third century hexameter had extended its generic reach to include didactic, hymns, and even bucolic, and as the writing (as opposed to oral performance) of poetry came to assume greater importance, Homer's rhythmical and prosodic practices were distilled and refined, a tendency that reached its apex in the hexameters of Callimachus.

Homer avails himself of twenty-two different arrangements of dactyls and spondees within his hexameter line, Callimachus restricts himself to seven, which greatly increases rhythmic regularity. He also smooths out the hexameter line by limiting the number of short words, incidence of hiatus, and unusual rhythms. Callimachus' verses feel lighter than Homer's, an effect achieved by a slightly higher average number of dactyls per line, but mainly by careful management of the placement of spondees. For example, Callimachus tends to avoid two spondees in succession. If we exclude the final metron, he has a distinct preference for lines with four dactyls + one spondee, and he never writes a line with four spondees.[30]

	Homer	Homeric Hymns	Callimachus
5 dactyls	19%	20%	23%
4 dactyls + 1 spondee	42%	42%	49%
3 dactyls + 2 spondees	30%	28%	25%
2 dactyls + 3 spondees	8%	9%	3%

A Homeric hexameter is generally understood to be organized into a series of four units, called cola; these are marked off by word boundaries and/or semantic pauses.[31] Colon-breaks occur most frequently at caesurae, diereses, and verse end, but additional locations of colon-breaks, especially in the first half of the line, yielded a number of uneven cola, and not all lines are cleanly divisible into four. Callimachus epitomized the tendency, found in other Hellenistic poets, to regularize the dimensions of the Homeric colon, which results in considerable restriction of his sense-pauses to certain locations in the line (see below for examples) and of words (or word-groups) with specific metrical shapes within the hexameter line (called the inner metric). This has generated what Fantuzzi calls "a network of 'prohibitions' of word end at various points in Callimachus' verse, which were identified by scholars (particularly) in the second half of the nineteenth century."[32]

This schematic, numbered for each place where a word break may occur in a hexameter line, will be useful to illustrate the observations that follow:[33]

1st metron | 2nd metron | 3rd metron | 4th metron | 5th metron | 6th metron

— | ◡ | ◡ | — | ◡ | ◡ | — | ◡ | ◡ | — | ◡ | ◡ | — | ◡ | ◡ | — | ◡ |

1   1½   2   3   3½   4   5   5½   6   7   7½   8   9   9½   10   11   12

1. Callimachus usually restricts his sense-pauses to certain locations in the line: at 2, 3, 5, 5½, 8, and 12 or verse-end. For example, in *hZeus* 4: πῶς

30. Taken from Mineur pp. 35–36, these numbers are expressed as percentages, excluding the final metron. They have been adjusted and rounded.

31. The idea originated with H. Fränkel and has been modified by subsequent scholars, see Kirk's helpful discussion of Homer (1985: 18–23).

32. Fantuzzi and Hunter 2004: 36. For these "prohibitions," see below.

33. For comparison of word shape and metric position organized by hexameter poet, see O'Neill 1942: 156; Hagel 2004 has refined O'Neill by adjusting for the presence of enclitics and proclitics, which should be treated as a unit with the word to which they adhere.

καί νιν, / Δικταῖον / ἀείσομεν / ἠὲ Λυκαῖον; the colon breaks occur at 3, 5 ½, 8, 12. The first and last colon breaks coincide with a pause in sense. Four-word lines like *hZeus* 3: Πηλαγόνων / ἐλατῆρα, / δικασπόλον / Οὐρανίδῃσι are the extreme example of this tendency.

2. Hexameters usually have a main word end (**caesura**), often with a sense break, in the third metron, either at 5 (called masculine) or at 5½ (called feminine). All of Callimachus' hexameters have a caesura in the third metron, and he showed a marked preference for the feminine, which occurs in 74 per cent of his lines in comparison to 57 per cent in Homer.[34]

3. Coincidence of word end with the end of a metron was normally avoided except in certain locations: it was frequent at the end of the fourth metron (8, called the **bucolic dieresis**). This pause occurs in 63 per cent of Callimachus' lines, in comparison to 47 per cent in Homer.

4. **Spondees in the fourth metron** are rare; when they do occur, Callimachus does not allow a word end to coincide with the end of the metron (this is called **Naeke's Law**; for an example see *hZeus* 1 below).

5. Although **spondees in the fifth metron** (σπονδειάζοντες) became a fashion in some writers of hexameter poetry (for example, they occur in 22 per cent of Antimachus' verses, and in 24 per cent of Eratosthenes'), they occur in only 7 per cent of Callimachus' and with considerable variation between hymns. When Callimachus does write σπονδειάζοντες, the fourth metron will always be a dactyl, and often the first four metra are dactyls, which again alleviates the weight of the verse. He prefers four-syllable words or occasionally six-syllable words to end these lines. Like other Hellenistic poets, he sometimes writes two σπονδειάζοντες in succession (*hZeus* 46–47, *hArt* 97–98, 170–71, 237–38, 251–52; *hDelos* 65–66) and once three in succession (*hArt* 222–34).[35]

6. Callimachus shows a strict practice with respect to **elision**. He almost always avoids elision at certain positions in the line: at 3½ (called **Meyer's bridge**); at the caesura (5, 5½); at 7½ (called **Hermann's bridge**); and at the bucolic dieresis (8, called **Naeke's bridge**). Prepositions, adverbs, correlatives, conjunctions, and particles that end in a short vowel are normally elided; but elision of endings on nouns, adjectives, and verbs is far less common.[36]

7. Callimachus does not introduce **hiatus** between metra. Within the metron hiatus is normally allowed only after ἤ or before prepositions in

---

34. West 1982: 36 (Homer, recalibrated as a percentage) and 154 (Callimachus).

35. See Hollis pp. 16–18; he observes that Romans probably got their taste for σπονδειάζοντες from poets like Euphorion, not Callimachus.

36. See Silva Sanchez 2003: especially 75, 77–78.

anastrophe (but see *hArt* 176, 233, 237). Words that in Homer appear in hiatus because they originally began with a digamma are sometimes, but not always, treated the same way in Callimachus (especially ϝοι).

8. Other restrictions, named for the scholars who first observed them, are: **Meyer's First Law** (words of the shape × - ◡ rarely end in the second metron; the exceptions are *hAp* 41 and *hDem* 91); **Meyer's Second Law** (words of the shape ◡ - are usually avoided before a caesura); **Giseke's Law** (words of the shape × - ◡ ◡ never end with the second metron); **Hilberg's Law** (a word break rarely occurs after a spondaic second metron); **Naeke's Law** (a word break does not follow a spondaic fourth metron); **Bulloch's Law** (a word break after the third metron will be accompanied by either a masculine or feminine caesura and a bucolic dieresis, with syntactical cola that break at the caesura or dieresis or both).[37]

9. **Epic correption**, or the shortening of a long vowel or diphthong when it precedes a vowel, may occur at 1½, 5½, 8 (the bucolic dieresis), and 9½. It tends to be avoided at 3½, 4, and 7½. The diphthongs -αι and -οι are the most commonly affected. καί, for example, is correpted about 50 per cent of the time.

10. **Crasis** and **synizesis** follow epic usage.

11. **Monosyllabic final words** (excluding the enclitics τε, τοι, περ, τι) in Callimachus' hymns occur at *hZeus* 55; *hAp* 83, 100; *hArt* 77, 120, 157; *hDelos* 193, 228, 259; *hDem* 57, 98. A plausible case can be made for the very close adherence of the word group mitigating the effect in *hArt* 77, 120, 157, *hDelos* 193, 228, and *hDem* 98 may allude to a very specific intertext (see note ad loc).

A characteristic feature of sentence construction within the hexameter is **enjambment**, or the running of the syntactical unit over more than one verse. This practice is usually divided into necessary enjambment (where the sentence or clause is grammatically incomplete unless continued into the next line) and unperiodic enjambment (where the sense unit is complete, but modifying clauses are appended). For example, in the opening lines of *hZeus*, quoted below, lines 1–2 show necessary enjambment—λώϊον is required to complete the thought—and lines 2–3 show unperiodic enjambment—the phrase Πηλαγόνων ἐλατῆρα is grammatically dependent on what precedes, but is not grammati-

---

37. See West 1982: 152–57 for further details. These "Laws" (and "Bridges") are not prescriptive, but describe actual practice. So-called violations are very often the result of looking at a word, not the word-group, that is, a word with its appositives and prepositives (e.g., proclitics, articles, prepositions, relative pronouns, negatives, enclitics); see, e.g., the discussion in Magnelli 1995. When a violation does occur, it may be for some special effect (see, e.g., *hDem* 91n).

cally necessary; lines 4 and 5 show no enjambment; the thought is complete at the end of each. In the hymns, 34 per cent of the lines show necessary enjambment (as compared with Homer's 27.6 per cent and Apollonius' 49 per cent); another 25 per cent show unperiodic enjambment (which is about the same as Homer, and more than Apollonius at 16 per cent). There is also considerable variability among the hexameter hymns, with *hDem* showing the lowest frequency of necessary enjambment (21.6 per cent) and *hArt* the highest (48.9 per cent).[38]

Callimachus very frequently avails himself of **variations in orthography and morphology** to facilitate his metrical preferences. Compare the following treatment of the same phrase in *hZeus*:

6: Ζεῦ, σὲ μὲν Ἰδαίοισιν | ἐν οὔρεσί ‖ φασι γενέσθαι,
51: Ἰδαίοις ἐν ὄρεσσι, | τά τε κλείουσι Πάνακρα.

In line 6 the variant (Ἰδαίοισιν ἐν οὔρεσι) allows both a feminine caesura and a bucolic dieresis; in line 51 the alternative (Ἰδαίοις ἐν ὄρεσσι) permits the feminine caesura. Opening 51 with Ἰδαίοισιν ἐν οὔρεσι, while theoretically possible, would lead to an undesirable dieresis after the third metron and an undesirable word shape (a dactyl) filling the third metron. Frequently occurring orthographic or dialect variants, most of which will be familiar from epic practice, include: ἐν/ἐνί/εἰν, ἕως/ἠώς, ἤ/ἠέ, θεά/θεή, ὀλοός/οὐλοός, ὄρος/οὖρος, πολύς/πουλύς, χειρί/χερί, χρύσειος/χρύσεος (and their compounds), alternative declensions of Ζηνός/Διός, Ζηνί/Διί. Callimachus also alternates between single and double consonants (e.g., ὀσ/ὀσσ-, ὀτ/ὀττ-, ὀκ/ὀκκ-), employs both epic-Ionic and Attic pronominal forms, declensional endings, and verb forms within the same hymn and very often in close proximity (e.g., *hZeus* 42–43: Κνωσοῖο and Κνωσοῦ; *hAp* 34–35: πολυ- and πουλυ-; *hDem* 75, 79: καλέοντες and κικλήσκοισα). For a full list see Lapp 1965: 120–35. Absence of verbal augment follows tragic and later Hellenistic usage, with omission or inclusion to suit metrical needs.

Comparison of Homeric and Callimachean Hexameter
In light of these observations, consider the opening lines of the *Iliad*. (| designates the end of a metron, and ‖ a bucolic dieresis; to the right are the number of dactyls|spondees, omitting the final metron):

Μῆνιν ἄ|ειδε θε|ὰ Πη|ληϊά|δεω Ἀχι|λῆος   4|1
οὐλομέ|νην, ἥ | μυρί' Ἀ|χαιοῖς ‖ ἄλγε' ἔ|θηκε,   3|2

---

38. McLennan 137. Enjambment in Homer has been well studied (see, e.g., Higbie 1990); it is much more complex than the simple division into "necessary" and "unperiodic," but the distinction is sufficient to illustrate the differences between Callimachus and Homer. For enjambment in elegy see below, p. 36.

πολλὰς | δ' ἰφθί|μους ψυ|χὰς Ἄϊ|δι προΐ|αψεν   2|3
ἡρώ|ων, αὐ|τοὺς δὲ ἑ|λώρια ‖ τεῦχε κύ|νεσσιν   3|2
οἰω|νοῖσί τε | πᾶσι, Δι|ὸς δ' ἐτε|λείετο | βουλή,   4|1
ἐξ οὗ | δὴ τὰ | πρῶτα δι|αστή|την ἐρί|σαντε   2|3
Ἀτρεΐ|δης τε ἄ|ναξ ἀν|δρῶν καὶ ‖ δῖος Ἀ|χιλλεύς.   3|2

Lines 1, 3, 4, and 7 have a masculine caesura; lines 2, 5, and 6 have a feminine
caesura; lines 2, 4, and 7 have a bucolic dieresis. Unperiodic enjambment occurs
over lines 1–2, 3–4, 4–5, 5–6, and 6–7; there is no enjambment at 2, 7. There are
no spondaic lines. There are four elisions (μυρί' Ἀχαιοῖς; ἄλγε᾽ ἔθηκε; δ' ἰφθίμους;
δ' ἐτελείετο). There is apparent hiatus at δὲ (Ϝ)ἑλώρια, τε (Ϝ)ἄναξ. Synizesis occurs
at Πηληϊάδεω (scanned - - ⏑ ⏑ -).

Compare the opening of *hZeus*:

Ζηνὸς ἔ|οι τί κεν | ἄλλο πα|ρὰ σπον|δῆσιν ἀ|είδειν   4|1
λώϊον | ἢ θεὸν |αὐτόν, ἀ|εὶ μέγαν, ‖ αἰὲν ἄ|νακτα,   5
Πηλαγό|νων ἐλα|τῆρα, δι|κασπόλον ‖ Οὐρανί|δῃσι;   5
πῶς καί |νιν, Δικ|ταῖον ἀ|είσομεν ‖ ἠὲ Λυ|καῖον;   3|2
ἐν δοι|ῇ μάλα | θυμός, ἐ|πεὶ γένος ‖ ἀμφή|ριστον.   3|2
Ζεῦ, σὲ μὲν | Ἰδαί|οισιν ἐν | οὔρεσί ‖ φασι γε|νέσθαι,   4|1
Ζεῦ, σὲ δ' ἐν | Ἀρκαδί|ῃ· πότε|ροι, πάτερ, ‖ ἐψεύ|σαντο;   4|1

Lines 1–6 have a feminine caesura in the third metron; line 7 has a masculine
caesura. All lines but the first have a bucolic dieresis. Within these seven lines
there is considerable variety in the use of enjambment, which undercuts the otherwise regular patterns of his hexameter. Lines 1–2 show necessary enjambment;
2–3, 6–7 show unperiodic enjambment; 4, 5, and 7 show no enjambment; the
thought is complete at line end. Lines 5 and 7 have spondaic endings (ἀμφήριστον,
ἐψεύσαντο). There is one elision (7: δ' ἐν). There is no hiatus.

Callimachus' Elegiac Hymn

The *Hymn to Athena* is the only hymn in the transmitted corpus of hymns (including
the Homeric, Callimachus', and Proclus' hymns) that is not in hexameters. It is also
the one hymn for which no papyrus fragments have survived and which has a distinctly different title in the mss.[39] These differences raise a question about whether it
was originally included in an ancient collection. However, the close similarity in style
and content of *hAth* and *hDem* would seem to indicate that the two were composed

---

39. It is named εἰς λοῦτρα Παλλάδος or a variant; the others are εἰς + a single name.

as a pair despite metrical differences. Callimachus did compose double *aitia* in the *Aetia* (though in the same meter), so hymns constructed as a pair have precedent.

The reasons for the shift in dialect and meter have long been debated. In *hAth* and *hDem* Callimachus employs an amalgam of Doric forms (see pp. 36–38). A Doric dialect was spoken in Argos, which alone could justify its use in the hymn, but a Doric dialect was also spoken in Callimachus' own city of Cyrene, and if not actually spoken by Alexandria's Macedonian elite, it seems to have been used as a mark of the royal house, whose claims to Greekness depended on an ancestral connection with Argos (see Bulloch pp. 12–13). For example, one of the epigrams in the recently discovered papyrus of Posidippus celebrates the chariot-racing victory of Berenice Syra (the sister of Ptolemy II) at the Olympic games. It was written in Doric, and it emphasized the Macedonian lineage of the Ptolemaic line (87 A-B). Elsewhere in Callimachus' poetry Doric occurs in his lamentation for the death of Arsinoe II (*Ektheosis for Arsinoe*), and in *ep.* 51 Pf. = 15 G-P on Berenice as the fourth Grace, which would support a connection between the dialect and the royal house. Also, the deified Philotera seems to have been identified with or co-templed with Demeter, and it is possible that the use of Doric in *hDem* is a reminder of the connection. However, it is important to acknowledge that Callimachus does use Doric in three very fragmentary *Iambi* (6, 9, 11) and in a number of epigrams that bear no connection to the royal house; in these cases it may be intended to reflect local dialects.[40]

There are two plausible reasons why Callimachus might have chosen to write *hAth* in elegiac meter: (1) to reflect a local Argive practice, the evidence for which is now mostly lost.[41] In his commentary on this hymn Bulloch (37) cites a parallel, either a brief elegiac hymn or an epigram preserved in Aelian (*NA* 11.4 = *SH* 206) for a festival of Demeter (the *Chthonia*) celebrated by the Argive town of Hermione. Although the date is not certain, according to Bulloch "language and dialect suggest that it is not later than the third century BCE." There is good reason to believe that Callimachus was interested in regional performance practices: for example, in his *aition* on Linus and Coroebus (frr. 26-31a Pf.) his information about the Argive Lamb festival was probably drawn from the Argive material of

---

40. Sens 2004: 73 points out that Posidippus uses Doric in his epigrams on Olympic victors, which may have been intended to evoke the Doric tradition of choral lyric. But see also Sens 2011: lxxi–lxxii, where he suggests that in Asclepiades of Samos Doric is associated with Macedonian royalty.

41. For example, the sixth-century aulete Sacadas of Argos was said to have composed elegiacs as well as lyrics, and to have been instrumental in the establishment of the Argive festival known as the *Endymata* ([Plut.] *De mus.* 9.1134A-C). Athenaeus (13.610c) attributes a *Sack of Troy* to Sacadas (where the name is a conjectural restoration). In an unpublished paper Ewen Bowie suggests that the *Endymata*, which must have something to do with clothing (ἐνδύματα), may have stood behind the festival of *hAth*; he further argues that Sacadas' Trojan poem is likely to have been in elegiacs and quite possibly known to Callimachus. See also Cameron 1995: 151.

Agias and Dercylus. (2) The second possibility, which Bulloch (33–34) rejects but others have found attractive (McKay, Hunter 1992: 20–22), is the ancient idea that elegy was to be associated with threnody, and thus the meter sets an appropriate tone for the lamentation of Chariclo in the Tiresias narrative. McKay 1962b: 79–90 makes the case for the most persistent features of the Doric dialect—long α for η and ω for ου—being harnessed to create the sonorities of lamentation.

While the elegiac hymn shares many features of the hexameter hymns, the elegiac hexameter differs in a number of ways from the epic hexameter, because it was conceived as forming, with its pentameter, a single long syntactical and rhythmic unit. Differences include much greater necessary enjambment between the hexameter and its pentameter, and concomitant reduction of enjambment between a pentameter and the following hexameter. The larger unit also affects the inner metric: the spondaic ending is avoided in the hexameter, and there is a tendency to avoid ending the pentameter with an accented syllable. The pentameter breaks into two halves (hemistichs) of the shape - ⏖ - ⏖ - ‖ - ᴗ ᴗ - ᴗ ᴗ -. The first hemistich admits spondees, but the second does not. The reduced number of pure dactyls in the opening metra of the hexameter is probably to avoid repeating the rhythmic and syntactical units that would naturally fill the second hemistich of the pentameter (discussed in Barnes 1995).

Epic-Ionic and Doric Forms in Callimachus

Doric elements in the hymns include generally West Greek characteristics as well as a few restricted to specific Doric-speaking regions (several of which are also found in Homer). The following are the epic-Ionic and Doric forms of the pronoun that appear in Callimachus' hymns:

		EPIC-IONIC		DORIC	
PRONOUNS		singular	plural	singular	plural
1st person					
	N.				ἀμές
	G.	ἐμεῖο, ἐμέθεν			
	D.			ἐμίν	ἀμίν, ἄμμιν
2nd person					
	N.	τύνη			
	G.	σεῦ, σεῖο, σέο		τεῦ, τεοῦ	
	D.	τοι, τεΐν		τίν	
3rd person					
	G.	οὗ			
	D.	οἱ	σφι(ν), σφισι(ν)		φιν
	A.	ἑ, μιν	σφε, σφέας	νιν	

Epic-Ionic and Doric forms of the noun that appear in Callimachus' hymns:

		EPIC-IONIC		**DORIC**	
NOUNS		singular	plural	singular	plural
1st declension	N.			-α (= -η)	
	G.	-αο, -εω	-άων, -έων	-ας	-ᾶν (= -αων)
	D.		-ῃσι, -ῃς	-ᾳ	-αις, -αισι
	A.			-αν	
2nd declension	G.	-οιο		-ω (= -ου)	
	A.				-ως (= -ους)
					-ος (= -ους)
3rd declension	G.	-ιος (= -εως)			
	D.	-ει, ηι	-εσσι(ν), -σσι(ν)		
	A.	-ηα			

Forms of πόλις: πόληος, πόληες , πόληας should be distinguished from
forms of πολύς: πολέος, πολέες, πολέας.

Epic-Ionic and Doric forms of the verb that appear in Callimachus' hymns:

	EPIC-IONIC	**DORIC**
VERBS		
3rd singular of -μι verbs	-τι	
1st plural indicative		-μες (= -μεν)
3rd plural active indicative		-ντι (= -ουσι)
3rd plural perfect indicative		-καντι (= -κασι)
Present active infinitive		-εν (= -ειν)
Athematic infinitives	-μεν, -μεναι, -εναι	
2nd singular aorist middle		-α (= -ω)
Future tenses	-έω (= Attic -ῶ)	All futures are contract
Feminine nominative singular and plural active participles		-οισα (= -ουσα) -οισαι (=-ουσαι)

Verbs in -άω may show -έω forms

Epic-Ionic and Doric forms of the verb εἰμί ("to be") that appear in Callimachus' hymns:

	EPIC-IONIC				DORIC
	Present	Future	Imperfect	Optative	Present
Singular					
1st		ἔσσομαι			
2nd	ἐσσί, εἷς, εἶ				
3rd		ἔσσεται	ἔην, ἦεν ἔσκε(ν)	ἔοι	ἧς (= ἦν)
Plural					
1st					
2nd					
3rd			ἔσαν		
Infinitive	ἔμεναι				
Participle	ἐών, ἐοῦσα, ἐόν				Fem. ἔσσα

The Manuscript Tradition

Callimachus' hymns were not all composed at the same time, but when and by whom they were organized into the collection we know remains a mystery. Callimachus certainly edited other of his poems. He added the independent elegies for Berenice to books 3 and 4 of the *Aetia*, and the epilogue to the *Aetia* suggests that the *Iambi* were also an authorially arranged group.[42] It is therefore inherently probable that he ordered the hymns. Unfortunately, the history of the hymns from the end of Callimachus' lifetime to the first papyrus evidence (from the second century CE) is a blank. The hymns were certainly known to later Hellenistic poets and to Virgil, Propertius, and Ovid, though again there is no direct evidence that they knew the hymns as a collection.[43] The first known editor of Callimachus was Theon of Alexandria, who worked in Rome from around 50 BCE to 20 CE. He edited the *Aetia*, *Iambi*, and possibly the *Hecale* and is likely to have worked on the hymns, even though direct evidence is lacking.[44] The grammarian Sallustius wrote a commentary on the *Hecale* which is widely cited by later lexi-

42. On the assumption that fr. 112.9 Pf.: πεζὸν ... νομόν refers to the *Iambi*.

43. Though Apollonius may have known *hAth* and *hDem* as a pair (see p. 22).

44. He also commented on Pindar, Theocritus, Apollonius, and other Alexandrians and is probably the source of much of what is cited from or said about Callimachus in later scholia (see Pontani 2011: 106–13 for Callimachus' poetry in the commentators and grammarians).

cographers, and he was probably responsible for an edition of the hymns; he is also thought to have been the source of the scholia on the hymns that appear in the manuscript tradition (Pontani 2011: 113; Hollis pp. 37, 42). His *floruit* is uncertain, but not likely to be before the third or after the fifth century CE. Verses or vocabulary from the hymns are cited in scholia to Apollonius of Rhodes, Theocritus, Dionysius the Periegete, Aristophanes, Lycophron, Homer, and Pindar, in Herodian, and the later lexicographers Hesychius, Stephanus of Byzantium, and the *Etymologicum genuinum* and *Etymologicum Gudianum*.[45] While the information derived from these sources is unsystematic, it has proved enormously helpful in supplementing the text as transmitted in the manuscript tradition.

The earliest papyrus evidence for a collection of hymns comes from the *Diegeseis*, prose summaries of Callimachus' poetry dating from the early second century CE (see Falivene 2011). In addition to the *Aetia* and *Iambi*, this work cites by first line and epitomizes the first two hymns in the order in which we now have them before it breaks off. Two fourth fifth century codices from Antinoe provide further indications of a hymn collection: PAnt 1.20 contains scholia for *hAp* and *hArt*, while PAnt 3.179 contains lines from *hArt* and *hDem*. POxy 20.2258, assigned to the fifth-sixth century, contained at least five of the hymns (there are no fragments of *hAth*) in the order in which we have them along with the *Hecale*, *Aetia*, *Iambi*, and minor lyrics. It also included marginal commentary. The fragments of this codex are so small that finding none attributable to *hAth* does not necessarily indicate that the hymn was omitted, though, if it was, the fact of its eccentric meter (elegiacs) may have been a factor. Bulloch (p. 79) points out that it was cited less often in the scholarly tradition than the other hymns.

All of Callimachus' poetry seems to have circulated in Byzantium until the end of the seventh century, and at least one copy of his works was available to Michael Choniates, the archbishop of Athens, who died in 1220. After the fall of Byzantium, manuscripts of the *Aetia* and the *Hecale* disappeared, and these poems survive now only in fragments found in quotations by ancient authors or on papyri. Only the hymns and epigrams escaped the same fate. The majority of the extant epigrams were collected in the *Palatine Anthology*, while sometime in the twelfth or thirteenth century an anonymous editor made a collection of hymns, including the Orphic hymns, the hymns of Proclus, the Homeric hymns,[46] and the hymns of Callimachus with their scholia, along with the Orphic *Argonautica*. This manuscript, designated **Ψ**, is thought to have been a paper codex, brought

---

45. See Dickey 2006: 87–101 on these lexica.

46. Another ms. of the Homeric hymns survives (the Codex Mosquensis), written in Constantinople after 1439. It contains a portion of *HhDion* and *HhDem* (now numbered 1 and 2), both missing in **Ψ**. See Gelzer 1994.

to Italy from Constantinople in 1423 by Johannes Aurispa. The damage to *hDelos* 177 and 200–1, *hAth* 61 and 136, and *hDem* 23 and 118 is found in all extant mss., and this guarantees that they are all descended from this common ancestor. It has not survived, but has been reconstructed from its eight main descendants, all copied in the fifteenth century. The first printed edition was that of Janus Lascaris, published in Florence by Lorenzo di Alopa between 1494 and 1496. Angelo Poliziano (Politian) printed a text of *hAth* only in a miscellany in 1489, which was subsequently reprinted in the Aldine edition of his collected works in 1498 (see Bulloch pp. 58–59).

The first attempt at a systematic collation of the extant codices and earlier editions of the hymns appeared in the 1761 Leiden edition of J. A. Ernesti, for which he had the considerable help of David Ruhnken.[47] Advances in the establishment of the text came one hundred years later in Berlin, when A. Meineke produced a critical revision of Ernesti's work in which he attempted to reconstruct the relationships of the extant codices. Otto Schneider's 1870 Leipzig edition was the first to make use of collations of all the manuscripts in preparing his texts, and his apparatus contains extensive and fascinating information about scholarly attempts to heal the obvious errors accrued in the process of transmission. It also provides insight into the chaotic state of affairs before Ulrich von Wilamowitz-Moellendorf, who in his 1882 and 1897 editions established the texts more systematically, eliminating many useless variants and via new collations made great strides in establishing the *stemma codicum*.[48] The final stage in the creation of the modern text was M. T. Smiley's systematic and detailed collation of all the important mss. and *editiones principes*, which he presented in a series of articles in *Classical Quarterly* in 1920 and 1921. Like most previous editors of the *Hymns*, Rudolf Pfeiffer worked originally on Callimachus' fragments, which appeared in his 1949 Oxford edition. Urged by Oxford Press, he added a second volume of the *Hymns* and *Epigrams* in 1953. For the hymns he relied heavily on Smiley's work, but also recollated most of the mss. himself. His *Callimachus* is a monument of modern classical scholarship,[49] and although subsequent editors of individual hymns differ occasionally in a reading, in general they all depend on the collations of Smiley and Pfeiffer.[50]

---

47. See Lehnus 2011: 24n4, and in general for early editions.

48. See Smiley's evaluation of Schneider's and Wilamowitz's work (1920: 1–3).

49. See, e.g., Barber's assessment (1954: 227).

50. The most readable account of the history of the text in English is to be found in Bulloch pp. 55–83, with the caveat that *hAth* is anomalous in some respects in its transmission. Thanks to N. G. Wilson's redating of the Athos ms., Bulloch (pp. 64–65) was able to refine one branch of the stemma, though the essential Smiley-Pfeiffer structure remains in place.

Pfeiffer's stemma (2.lxxxiii and modified in Bulloch p. 66) sets out four main family groups of mss. (**αβ(ε)ζ**) descended from **Ψ**. These mss. no longer exist but are posited on the basis of the common traits of their descendants. Apart from Callimachus, manuscripts descending from these hyparchetypes may vary in the material they include or omit. The principal extant mss. for each hyparchetype are given below with the *siglum* used in the apparatus criticus.[51]

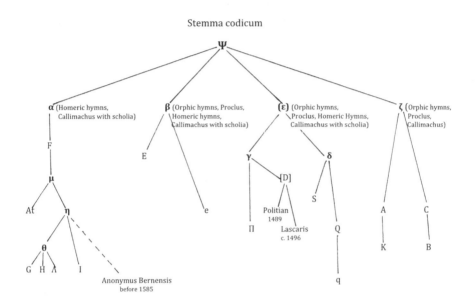

Stemma codicum

α (Homeric hymns and Callimachus with scholia; Smiley 1921a; Pfeiffer 2.lvi–lxiii):

F = Milan, Ambrosianus 120, the Callimachean section probably copied by George Chrysococces in Constantinople between 1420 and 1428. Now the only primary witness for **α**.

μ = Bulloch (p. 65) posits an intermediary on the basis of errors shared by **At** and **η** that are not shared with **F**.

At = Athos, Vatopedi cod. gr. 671 (formerly 587). Previously thought to have belonged to the fourteenth century, but now assigned to the late fifteenth century (Wilson 1974, Bulloch pp. 64–66). It is a *gemellus* of **η**.

Descendants of **η**:

51. These are described in detail in Smiley and Pfeiffer, as noted; more briefly in Bulloch pp. 55–63 and in Bornmann pp. LVI–LIX. What follows is also taken from Smiley and Pfeiffer.

I = Vaticanus gr. 1379, a miscellany written by George Moschus in 1496.

G = Vienna, Austrian National Library, Phil. gr. 318. Late fifteenth century miscellany.

H = Leiden, Vossianus 59. Late fifteenth-early sixteenth century.

Λ = Florence, Laurentianus suppl. 440 (formerly Ashburnamianus 1440). Copied by George Moschus around 1500.

Anon. Bern. = anonymus Bernensis, readings from an unknown ms. and annotator's own conjectures preserved in the margin of Vascosan's Paris edition of 1549; now in Bern.

β (Orphic *Argonautica*, Orphic hymns, Proclus, Homeric hymns, Callimachus with scholia; Smiley 1920c: 112–22; Pfeiffer 2.lxiii–lxv):

E = Paris, Bibliothèque nationale gr. 2763. Fifteenth century miscellany. Hymns appear in the order *hZeus, hAp, hArt, hDelos, hDem, hAth.*

e = Milan, Ambrosianus 734. Fifteenth century.

(ε) (Orphic hymns, Proclus, Homeric hymns, Callimachus with scholia). Reconstructed from the *gemelli* **γ** and **δ**. Pfeiffer 2.lxxx.

γ (Smiley 1920c: 105–12; Pfeiffer 2.lxv–lxviii):

Π = Paris, Bibliothèque nationale gr. suppl. 1095. The primary witness for **γ**.

[D] = Florence, Laurentianus 32.45. The Callimachean portion was apparently removed. (Schneider suggested that Lascaris may have removed it when preparing his own edition of the hymns.)

Lasc. = *Callimachi Cyrenaei hymni*, edited by Janus Lascaris between 1494 and 1498.

Politian = Angelo Poliziano (1454–1494) was the first editor of the *Hymn to Athena* (see p. 40).

δ (Smiley 1920b; Pfeiffer 2.lxviii–lxx):

S = Madrid, Biblioteca Nacional gr. 4562 (= N 24); miscellany with marginal additions, corrections, and supplements made by Constantinus Lascaris apparently based on Politian's first edition, which are designated as S^2; 1464.

Q = Modena, Estensis 164 (= W5.16, formerly III E.II). Written by George Valla before May, 1492. Valla's marginal and supralinear annotations and corrections are designated as Q^2.

q = Ambrosianus 11 (A63 sup.), dated 1509.

ζ (Orphic hymns, Proclus, Callimachus; Smiley 1920a: 6–15; Smiley 1921b; Pfeiffer 2.lxx–lxxii):

A = Vatican, gr. 1691.

K = Vatican, Urbinas gr. 145; a copy of **A**, made by George of Crete.

C = Venice, Marcianus 480. Fifteenth century miscellany. The hymns portion was copied by George of Crete before 1468.

B = Vatican, gr. 36; a copy of **C**, made by George of Crete.

Codices now lost (Smiley 1920a: 4–5; Pfeiffer 2.lxxiv)

N = the codex that F. Robortelli used for his *Locorum variorum annotationes*, 1543, and in his edition of the *Hymns* (Venice, 1555).

O = the ms. used by H. Stephanus, *Poetae Graeci principes heroici carminis et alii nonnulli*, 1566.

R = Madrid codex gr. 122 seems to have disappeared from the Biblioteca Nacional (see Bulloch p. 63).

T = Turin, Biblioteca Nazionale B.v.26 (previously CCLXI.B.VI.21), with marginal notes made by the same hand that copied the text. It was destroyed by fire in 1904.[52]

The Hymns in the Papyri

Within the last two centuries the manuscript tradition of the *Hymns* has been enhanced by information transmitted in papyrus rolls and codices that have come to light from Graeco-Roman Egypt. Currently there are fourteen separate papyrus witnesses for one or another hymns and three fragments of commentaries or word lists.[53]

1. **POxy 20.2258** = Pfeiffer 37. Fifth-sixth century CE codex containing *Hymns, Hecale, Aetia*, minor lyrics with marginal commentary. Fragments from five hymns, but not *hAth*. The majority of the fragments do not even contain full words.

HZeus

POxy 20.2258 contains two small fragments from *hZeus* 53–60, 76–83; line 59 was apparently miscopied.

2. **PSI 15.1477**. Second century CE papyrus roll containing parts of lines 32–41. Not in Pfeiffer.

52. Pfeiffer 2.lxxii–lxxiv also describes a few very late copies unimportant for his stemma. These are designated *codices recentissimi* in the footnotes and are relevant only for their conjectures on *hDelos* 178 and 200.

53. The online resource CEDOPAL (Centre du Documentation de Papyrologie Littéraire) maintains the list of all Callimachean papyri with complete and current bibliographies. Interested readers should consult the site.

HApollo

POxy 20.2258 contains 1–19, 24–40. A number of the recorded variants have generally been adopted, see 8, 35, 36.

3. **PAnt 1.20** = Pfeiffer 44. Fourth-fifth century CE papyrus codex from Antinoe containing scholia on *hAp* 38-76 and also *hArt* 37-94. A few errors: σ for σσ, -οις for -οισιν, -ει for -εται. Only rarely do its scholia coincide with the medieval tradition, but entries sometimes coincide with material found in the lexicographers and in scholia on other authors.

HArtemis

POxy 20.2258 contains very small parts of 2–4, 12–14, 28–29, 36–39. The fragments appear to have an unusual line arrangement.

PAnt 1.20 = Pfeiffer 44. It contains scholia on 37–94 with a few good readings.

4. **PMilVogl 2.42** = Pfeiffer 38. First century BCE papyrus roll from Tebtunis containing parts of lines 1–6, 16, 22–54.

5. **POxy 47.3328**. Second century CE papyrus roll from Oxyrhynchus containing an elementary glossary with words from 1–12. There are no errors and one correct reading (αρχμενοι) not in the medieval mss. Not in Pfeiffer.

6. **PGen inv. 209** = PLG Carlini 3. Fourth-fifth century papyrus codex containing parts of 31–61, 62–92. A number of errors. Not in Pfeiffer.

7. **PCairo inv. 47993B** = Pfeiffer 39. First century CE papyrus roll from Oxyrhynchus containing parts of 46–54, 78–84 with scholia.

8. **PFayumColes**. Second century CE papyrus roll from the Fayum, containing fragments from 67–80. There are no variations from Pfeiffer's text. Not in Pfeiffer.

9. **PAmh 2.20** = Pfeiffer 43. Fourth century CE. Papyrus codex commentary on 107–63, 172–78. Some coincidence with medieval scholia.

10. **PAnt 3.179**. Fourth-fifth century papyrus codex from Antinoe containing two small scraps of *hArt* 162–65, 189–192 and *hDem*. Not in Pfeiffer.

HDelos

POxy 20.2258 contains 130–34, 158–62, 169–74, 196–99, 232–35, 240–45, 260–63, 268–73, 282–83, 307–9.

11. **POxy 19.2225** = Pfeiffer 42. Mid-second century CE papyrus roll from Oxyrhynchus on the back of an account. It contains bits from 11 25, 38–40, 68–75, 81–92, 102–10, 141–46, 156–81, 186–205, 209–18, 230–43. It had the opening of lines 176–80 missing in the medieval mss. and apparently an extra line; it also has 199–201 missing in medieval ms. tradition, but greatly mutilated.

12. **PBodlLibr inv. Ms. gr.cl.f.109(P)** = Pfeiffer 45. Fifth-sixth century
papyrus codex with parts of 52–69, 80–97 with marginalia.

13. **PAlex inv. 547** (= **PLG Carlini 12**) = PMusAlex 5 = Pfeiffer 40.
First century CE papyrus roll with parts of 84–94. It has a number of
variations, none of value.

14. **PMontserrat inv. 145.** Mid- to late-second century CE papyrus roll
with parts of 138–49. Not in Pfeiffer.

15. **PMontserrat inv. 198.** First-second century CE papyrus roll. This is
a very small scrap with beginnings of *hDelos* lines 199–206. It confirms
the opening words of lines 200–1 found in POxy 19.2225, but breaks off
without offering new information. Not in Pfeiffer.

16. **BKT 9.73 (= PBerol inv. 21170).** Early fifth century papyrus codex.
Parts of 271–88, 307–20. Not in Pfeiffer.

HDemeter

POxy 20.2258 contains portions of 125–34 of *hDem* without apparent
variation from the medieval mss., in contrast to POxy 19.2226.

PAnt 3.179 contains portions of 10–12, 37–39.

17. **POxy 19.2226** = Pfeiffer 41. Second century CE papyrus roll. Parts of
32–37, 41–43, 54–63, 79–117, 138 followed by an otherwise unattested
line. The text omits 118–37.

The evidence from papyri is mixed. (1) The hymns do not appear in equal
number: *hArt* appears in nine papyri; *hDelos* in seven; the others in two or three;
hAth is absent entirely. (2) If we factor out itacisms and obvious scribal errors, it
is clear that the earlier transmission sometimes preserved better readings or offered solutions to confusion in the medieval manuscript tradition. For example,
the correct reading at *hArt* 4 (ἄρχμενοι) is not found in the medieval mss., but
was preserved in POxy 47.3328. For this reason editors have tended to prefer
papyrus readings when they differ from the medieval mss. (3) However, papyri
need to be approached with caution. They often contain errors, and because they
are often very fragmentary, the value of their readings can be difficult to assess
(see, e.g., *hDem* 138n). (4) The evidence of the hymns papyri reinforces what we
know from papyri of Callimachus' other poems. Commentaries and marginalia
were an important part of the transmission, and they present various hierarchies
of information. Some are no more than basic aids for reading; others provide
details of mythology or geography. Only rarely do these scholia coincide with
the medieval tradition, but they do overlap with information found in the later
lexicographers. (5) Finally, although the sample is small, the Doric of *hDem* does
not necessarily provide a clearer idea of what forms Callimachus actually wrote.
Perhaps the greatest lesson to be learned from the papyri is the fragility of textual

transmission and to respect even more those who have labored for centuries to provide us with the poems as we now have them.

A Note on the Text

In light of these observations I have been deliberately conservative in the text I present. It differs little from Pfeiffer's: in *hArt* and *hDem* I include more Doric forms than he does, though fewer than Bulloch and Hopkinson have proposed. Problematic passages and attempts to heal them are discussed in the commentary. I have not indicated itacistic spelling variants, editorial changes in *hAth* and *hDem* of Ionic or Attic to Doric, or corrections of the many errors found in the manuscript and papyrus transmissions, unless they are useful in assessing the quality of a papyrus witness or in indicating the direction of an emendation. Readings of the papyri are given in the form in which they occur, normally without accent or word break. In the following, "medieval manuscripts" is a shorthand for "medieval tradition carried by Renaissance manuscripts."

1

The Hymn to Zeus

THE FIRST HYMN IN THIS COLLECTION OPENS WITH THE QUESTION "would anything else be better to hymn at libations for Zeus than the god himself?," and fittingly the god's name (Ζηνός) stands as the first word of the poem. It continues: "How shall we hymn him, as Dictaean or Lycaean?," asking a traditional question in a way that implicitly acknowledges the range in cult locations where the god was worshipped before going on to privilege the specific local cult or occasion for which the hymn was written, and in the process to justify its claim to primacy. Callimachus chooses to narrate the Arcadian genealogy of the god, on the grounds that "Cretans always lie," then describes the god's birth on Mt. Lycaeon at some length (10–32). But just as his audience has settled into his Arcadian tale, Rhea hands the newborn to a nymph (Neda) who transports him to Thenae. At this juncture Callimachus exploits the fact that there were two places named Thenae, one in Arcadia, another in Crete (43), allowing us to imagine for a moment that we are still in Arcadia. However, it is to Crete that the nymph carries the baby, hiding him in order to keep his birth a secret from his father Cronus. Callimachus next narrates Zeus's growth to adulthood on Crete (46–57), the way in which he assumed power as king of the Olympian gods (58–67), and Zeus's divine prerogatives in comparison to other Olympians (70–84). After Zeus becomes the divine patron of kings, Callimachus again shifts geographies, now to the new city of Alexandria. If Zeus presides over the best part of power, or kings—and this is stated in Hesiodic terms with the borrowing ἐκ δὲ Διὸς βασιλῆες (79)—then Ptolemy is the best of all kings and more powerful than the rest, accomplishing at evening what he thought of in the morning (85–88). As a reinforcement of the geographic change, these lines no longer imitate Hesiod, but paraphrase a traditional Egyptian formula for kingship (see 87). The movement from Arcadia, the oldest part of Greece, to Crete, and finally to Alexandria, is complete. Callimachus makes explicit the role he assigns to his Zeus: it is to oversee the well-being and success of one local king in particular, Ptolemy of Egypt. The formulaic concluding prayer (91–96) asks the god for prosperity and virtue.

The Deity and His Relevant Cults

As head of the Olympian pantheon Zeus was widely worshipped throughout Greek-speaking lands under many cult titles and assimilated to many local non-Greek divinities such as Ammon in Libya. In this hymn Callimachus emphasizes Zeus's connections to three locations: Arcadia, Crete, and Alexandria. There was a cult devoted to him on the slopes of Mt. Lycaeon, revived in the fifth and fourth centuries as an affirmation of a collective Arcadian identity (Polignac 2002: 119–22), and he was worshipped at many sites in Crete, among which is the Dictaean cave in eastern Crete and the Idaean cave in central Crete (Chaniotis 2001). Hesiod locates Zeus's birthplace at Lyctus, slightly to the northwest of the Dictaean cave. Hesiod's version of the Cretan birth story is usually taken to be the norm, the Arcadian as the more obscure version of the myth (e.g., Hopkinson 1984b: 143). However, Callimachus was from Cyrene, where, according to Herodotus (4.203), one of the earliest precincts outside the city was that of Zeus *Lycaeus*, probably because many of the city's earliest settlers were from the Peloponnese. In this context E. Maass (1890: 401–2) made the attractive suggestion that the hymn's distinctive blending of Arcadian and Cretan stories reflected or paid tribute to one of the three Cyrenean phylitic units, namely, the Peloponnesian-Cretan. Moreover, the Arcadian and Cretan versions had such similar characteristics that Pausanias (8.38.2) in his discussion of the Arcadian location goes so far as to state that the Arcadians had a place named Cretea and they "claim that the Crete, where the Cretan story holds Zeus to have been reared, was this place and not the island."

In early Alexandria, the most frequent references are to Zeus *Soter*. He was very likely the divinity whose statue stood atop the Pharos lighthouse that was completed around 285 (Fraser 1972: 1.194; McKenzie 2007: 42). Ptolemy I Soter may have been associated with Zeus *Soter* after his death in 283, and somewhat later Zeus *Olympios* appears in dedications with Ptolemy II and Arsinoe II, who were deified as the *Theoi Adelphoi*. Even if these dedications are later than the hymn, they certainly suggest that the association of god and king in the hymn belonged to mainstream Alexandrian cultic behaviors. Local audiences would have been neither confused nor astonished by Callimachus' link of monarch and divinity.

Also, Macedonians worshipped Zeus under the cult title of *Basileus*, and Alexander is said to have celebrated the Macedonian *Basileia* in Egypt at the time he was crowned (Arrian 3.5.2). The early Alexandrians celebrated a *Basileia* that commemorated the birthday of the king, but whether it evolved from or continued elements of the older Macedonian *Basileia* is not clear.

The Sources and Intertexts

Cultic and rhapsodic hymns to Zeus are scarce. The *Homeric Hymn to Zeus* (23) contains only four lines from an invocation. Pindar's now fragmentary first hymn, traditionally thought to have been addressed to Zeus, with its priamelic listing of possible themes, may have been a model for Callimachus (e.g., Hunter and Fuhrer 2002: 170–72); however, D'Alessio's recent reconstruction (2009) makes a strong case for that hymn being addressed to Apollo (of course, the similarities remain). The hymn to Zeus embedded in the first stasimon of Aeschylus' *Agamemnon* bears a general resemblance, but nothing that requires us to posit it as an intertext. The Palaikastro hymn to Zeus of Mt. Dicte (Furley and Bremmer 2001:1.68–76, 2.1–20) mentions Rhea and the Curetes, but is otherwise tangential to Callimachus'. However, lines 2–6 of the now fragmentary *Hymn to Dionysus*, which apparently opened the collection of Homeric hymns in the Codex Mosquensis (see West 2001), provide a good parallel for the opening of Callimachus' hymn: "...Some say it was at Dracanus, some say it was on windy Icaros, and some on Naxos [where Semele bore you]...all speak falsely (ψευδόμενοι)." If this hymn did head a collection of Homeric hymns that predated Callimachus, then his imitation of it in h*Zeus* provides a prima facie argument that he is announcing the opening of his own collection (Hunter and Fuhrer 2002: 172–73).

Callimachus also depends on the *Hymn to Hermes*, as J. J. Clauss has demonstrated (1986). In addition to a series of important verbal links (ἐλατήρ, λίκνον, οἶμος, κήριον, ἀγγελιώτης) there are significant structural parallels: (1) both poems feature lies and their truthful resolution; (2) Hermes' prodigious feats of inventing the lyre and stealing his brother Apollo's cattle on the very day he was born parallel 88–89, where Zeus accomplishes by evening what he thinks in the morning; and (3) the strife between the younger (Hermes) and older brother (Apollo) mirrors that of Philadelphus and his older brother Ceraunus (see below).

By the early Hellenistic period hymns to Zeus had taken a philosophical turn. Cleanthes of Assos (331–232 BCE), who headed the Stoic school in Athens after Zeno, wrote a *Hymn to Zeus* allegorizing him as the Stoic first principle ordering the universe, while Aratus of Soli (late fourth-early third century BCE), who was also a pupil of Zeno, opened his hexameter poem on astral phenomena (*Phaenomena*) with a hymn to Zeus also with Stoic contours. Aratus' and Callimachus' poems are clearly interrelated, though which is prior is debated. Certainly, Callimachus' own hymn shows awareness of philosophical trends. Line 8: 'Κρῆτες ἀεὶ ψεῦσται' was attributed to the sixth-century shaman, Epimenides of Crete, who represents a type of pre-philosophical wisdom. Line 5: ἐν δοιῇ μάλα θυμός, ἐπεὶ γένος ἀμφήριστον is a slightly altered version of the opening of the *Hymn to Eros* of Antagoras of Rhodes: ἐν δοιῇ μοι θυμός, ὅ τοι γένος ἀμφίσβητον (fr. 1.1 Powell, who accepts Meineke's conjecture for ἀμφίβοητον of the mss.). Cuypers 2004: 96–102 makes an attractive argument that Antagoras' own hymn was in part an Academic response to Stoic cosmogonic theories, and by varying the opening line with the rare ἀμφήριστον ("contested on both sides") Callimachus is calling attention to this important philosophical debate about the nature of the divinity being hymned. Elsewhere in the hymn (46–54) Callimachus produces a rationalizing explanation for familiar details of Zeus's birth story that align him with his older contemporary Euhemerus, whose *Sacred Register* speculated that the Olympian deities were originally men whose heroic deeds led to their being worshipped as gods after death (Stephens 2003: 36–39, 89–90; Cuypers 2004: 104–5). This narrative evolution of speculation on the nature of divinity both lends authority to and paves the way for the linking of god and king at the end of the poem.

In this hymn Hesiod's poems provide the most extensive of Callimachus' intertexts, a detailed account of which may be found in Reinsch-Werner 1976: 24–73. *Works and Days* opens with the praise of Zeus as one who makes men famous or not, sung or unsung as he wills; he easily straightens the crooked (7: ῥεῖα τ' ἰθύνει σκολιόν), a sentiment that Callimachus paraphrases at line 83, while the *Theogony*, in relating the order of creation through Zeus's coming to power, shares many features of a hymn to Zeus. The Hesiodic penumbra is pervasive, especially in the Cretan sequence and the discussion of kingship: it culminates with a quotation of *Th.* 96: ἐκ δὲ Διὸς βασιλῆες at line 79.[1]

Callimachus imitates Hesiod (*Th.* 468–80) in the Cretan section to make a very specific poetological point. In the *Theogony*, when Rhea was pregnant with Zeus, she persuaded her parents to send her away from her husband, Cronus, in order to thwart his habit of eating his young. Rhea accordingly goes to Lyctus in Crete, a location near to the Dictaean cave, where she gives birth and then presents Cronus with a swaddled stone (instead of Zeus). Subsequently when Zeus comes to power, he forces Cronus to regurgitate his siblings and along with them the deceptive stone, which he placed in Delphi to mark his reign. Delphi was the center of the old Greek world. In his version of the divine birth, Callimachus provides a new center: lines 44–45 describe how Zeus's umbilical cord (a rationalizing account of the ὀμφαλός) fell off as he was carried over Crete, where the "Plain of the Omphalos" now is.

---

1. For the various "origins" concentrated in this first hymn see Ambühl 2005: 235–45.

Another Hesiodic imitation reinforces a sense of cults in motion. After giving birth, Rhea hands the newborn to her mother, Gaia. This is Callimachus' model for Rhea handing the baby to Neda. But Gaia keeps the child on Crete (*Th.* 477–84). In contrast, Callimachus breaks up and reforms the old order. The Greek god not only moves from Arcadia, a place that boasted the original Greeks, to the southern Mediterranean, but as he does so, the Hesiodic tradition is eclipsed: the center (ὀμφαλός) of the Greek universe has been relocated. It is no longer at Delphi on the mainland, but a new physical space now located roughly halfway between the old center (Delphi) and the cities of Libyan Cyrene and Egyptian Alexandria: thus a fitting proclamation for a hymn collection that celebrates gods for a new world.

Theocritus' *Encomium for Ptolemy* (17) has significant points of overlap with *hZeus*, especially in its opening (Stephens 2003: 148–51), though compositional priority cannot be established. Lines 31–35 of Aratus' *Phaenomena* have an alternative version of Zeus's nurture on Crete with verbal and conceptual similarities to this hymn (see Kidd's notes ad loc.); and Apollonius' description of the establishment of a cult to Rhea on Mt. Dindymon in *Argonautica*, book 1 (1132–52) contains impressionistic details that call this hymn to mind: Rhea produces water on a mountain; young men dance in armor to cover up the sounds of mourning; the bursting forth of water brings with it fertility; and the location is called "Bear mountain" (see Clauss 1993: 169–72).

The Ptolemaic Connections

The festival of the *Basileia* in Alexandria apparently coincided with the celebration of Ptolemy II's birthdate as well as his ascendancy to the co-regency with his father in 285/284 BCE (Koenen 1977: 43–49, 51–55). A co-regency would effectively have excluded Ptolemy Ceraunus, Ptolemy I's oldest son, from the succession, and he remained estranged from Ptolemy II until his death. These historical circumstances have led to a growing consensus that this hymn was written to commemorate the occasion of the *Basileia* (see Clauss 1986; Koenen 1993: 78–79; Perpillou-Thomas 1993: 152–53; Cameron 1995: 10).

Given the certain connection to Ptolemaic kingship, one element of the birth-myth that Callimachus relates, namely that the region of Arcadia was dry before the birth of Zeus and that waters flowed as a consequence, has a ready correlative in Egyptian myths of kingship. The god Horus, who was the divine analogue to the human pharaoh, was born on a "primeval hill" at the beginning of creation, to which the annual rise of the Nile was connected. Callimachus exploits this idea in *hDelos* as well: the Inopus on Delos is linked undersea with the Nile, and it is in spate when Apollo is born (*hDelos* 206–11).

ΕΙΣ ΔΙΑ

Ζηνὸς ἔοι τί κεν ἄλλο παρὰ σπονδῇσιν ἀείδειν
λώϊον ἢ θεὸν αὐτόν, ἀεὶ μέγαν, αἰὲν ἄνακτα,
Πηλαγόνων ἐλατῆρα, δικασπόλον Οὐρανίδῃσι;
πῶς καί νιν, Δικταῖον ἀείσομεν ἠὲ Λυκαῖον;
5   ἐν δοιῇ μάλα θυμός, ἐπεὶ γένος ἀμφήριστον.
Ζεῦ, σὲ μὲν Ἰδαίοισιν ἐν οὔρεσί φασι γενέσθαι,
Ζεῦ, σὲ δ' ἐν Ἀρκαδίῃ· πότεροι, πάτερ, ἐψεύσαντο;
'Κρῆτες ἀεὶ ψεῦσται'· καὶ γὰρ τάφον, ὦ ἄνα, σεῖο
Κρῆτες ἐτεκτήναντο· σὺ δ' οὐ θάνες, ἐσσὶ γὰρ αἰεί.
10   ἐν δέ σε Παρρασίῃ Ῥείη τέκεν, ἧχι μάλιστα
ἔσκεν ὄρος θάμνοισι περισκεπές· ἔνθεν ὁ χῶρος
ἱερός, οὐδέ τί μιν κεχρημένον Εἰλειθυίης
ἑρπετὸν οὐδὲ γυνὴ ἐπιμίσγεται, ἀλλά ἑ Ῥείης
ὠγύγιον καλέουσι λεχώϊον Ἀπιδανῆες.
15   ἔνθα σ' ἐπεὶ μήτηρ μεγάλων ἀπεθήκατο κόλπων,
αὐτίκα δίζητο ῥόον ὕδατος, ᾧ κε τόκοιο
λύματα χυτλώσαιτο, τεὸν δ' ἐνὶ χρῶτα λοέσσαι.
Λάδων ἀλλ' οὔπω μέγας ἔρρεεν οὐδ' Ἐρύμανθος,
λευκότατος ποταμῶν, ἔτι δ' ἄβροχος ἦεν ἅπασα
20   Ἀζηνίς· μέλλεν δὲ μάλ' εὔυδρος καλέεσθαι
αὖτις· ἐπεὶ τημόσδε, Ῥέη ὅτε λύσατο μίτρην,
ἦ πολλὰς ἐφύπερθε σαρωνίδας ὑγρὸς Ἰάων
ἤειρεν, πολλὰς δὲ Μέλας ὤκχησεν ἁμάξας,
πολλὰ δὲ Καρνίωνος ἄνω διεροῦ περ ἐόντος
25   ἰλυοὺς ἐβάλοντο κινώπετα, νίσσετο δ' ἀνήρ
πεζὸς ὑπὲρ Κρᾶθίν τε πολύστιόν τε Μετώπην
διψαλέος· τὸ δὲ πολλὸν ὕδωρ ὑπὸ ποσσὶν ἔκειτο.
καί ῥ' ὑπ' ἀμηχανίης σχομένη φάτο πότνια Ῥείη·
'Γαῖα φίλη, τέκε καὶ σύ· τεαὶ δ' ὠδῖνες ἐλαφραί.'
30   εἶπε καὶ ἀντανύσασα θεὴ μέγαν ὑψόθι πῆχυν
πλῆξεν ὄρος σκήπτρῳ· τὸ δέ οἱ δίχα πουλὺ διέστη,
ἐκ δ' ἔχεεν μέγα χεῦμα· τόθι χρόα φαιδρύνασα,
ὦνα, τεὸν σπείρωσε, Νέδῃ δέ σε δῶκε κομίσσαι
κευθμὸν ἔσω Κρηταῖον, ἵνα κρύφα παιδεύοιο,

---

3 πηλαγόνων Et. gen.: πηλογόνων Ψ   4 νιν Ψ: μιν Wilamowitz   10 Παρρασίη Lasc.: Παρνασίη
Ψ   τέκεν, ἧχι μάλιστα Ψ: τέκεν εὐνηθεῖσα Origen.   20 Ἀζηνίς sch. Dion. Per.: Ἀρκαδίη Ψ
24 Καρνίωνος Arnaldus: Καρίωνος Ψ   33 κομίσσαι αβγδ: κομίζειν ζ, Hopkinson

35   πρεσβυτάτη Νυμφέων, αἵ μιν τότε μαιώσαντο,
     πρωτίστη γενεῇ μετά γε Στύγα τε Φιλύρην τε.
     οὐδ' ἁλίην ἀπέτεισε θεὴ χάριν, ἀλλὰ τὸ χεῦμα
     κεῖνο Νέδην ὀνόμηνε· τὸ μέν ποθι πουλὺ κατ' αὐτό
     Καυκώνων πτολίεθρον, ὃ Λέπρειον πεφάτισται,
40   συμφέρεται Νηρῆϊ, παλαιότατον δέ μιν ὕδωρ
     υἱωνοὶ πίνουσι Λυκαονίης ἄρκτοιο.
     εὖτε Θενὰς ἀπέλειπεν ἐπὶ Κνωσοῖο φέρουσα,
     Ζεῦ πάτερ, ἡ Νύμφη σε (Θεναὶ δ' ἔσαν ἐγγύθι Κνωσοῦ),
     τουτάκι τοι πέσε, δαῖμον, ἀπ' ὀμφαλός· ἔνθεν ἐκεῖνο
45   Ὀμφάλιον μετέπειτα πέδον καλέουσι Κύδωνες.
     Ζεῦ, σὲ δὲ Κυρβάντων ἑτάραι προσεπηχύναντο
     Δικταῖαι Μελίαι, σὲ δ' ἐκοίμισεν Ἀδρήστεια
     λίκνῳ ἐνὶ χρυσέῳ, σὺ δ' ἐθήσαο πίονα μαζόν
     αἰγὸς Ἀμαλθείης, ἐπὶ δὲ γλυκὺ κηρίον ἔβρως.
50   γέντο γὰρ ἐξαπιναῖα Πανακρίδος ἔργα μελίσσης
     Ἰδαίοις ἐν ὄρεσσι, τά τε κλείουσι Πάνακρα.
     οὖλα δὲ Κούρητές σε περὶ πρύλιν ὠρχήσαντο
     τεύχεα πεπλήγοντες, ἵνα Κρόνος οὔασιν ἠχήν
     ἀσπίδος εἰσαΐοι καὶ μή σεο κουρίζοντος.
55   καλὰ μὲν ἠέξευ, καλὰ δ' ἔτραφες, οὐράνιε Ζεῦ,
     ὀξὺ δ' ἀνήβησας, ταχινοὶ δέ τοι ἦλθον ἴουλοι.
     ἀλλ' ἔτι παιδνὸς ἐὼν ἐφράσσαο πάντα τέλεια·
     τῷ τοι καὶ γνωτοὶ προτερηγενέες περ ἐόντες
     οὐρανὸν οὐκ ἐμέγηραν ἔχειν ἐπιδαίσιον οἶκον.
60   δηναιοὶ δ' οὐ πάμπαν ἀληθέες ἦσαν ἀοιδοί·
     φάντο πάλον Κρονίδῃσι διάτριχα δώματα νεῖμαι·
     τίς δέ κ' ἐπ' Οὐλύμπῳ τε καὶ Ἄϊδι κλῆρον ἐρύσσαι,
     ὃς μάλα μὴ νενίηλος; ἐπ' ἰσαίῃ γὰρ ἔοικε
     πήλασθαι· τὰ δὲ τόσσον ὅσον διὰ πλεῖστον ἔχουσι.
65   ψευδοίμην, ἀΐοντος ἅ κεν πεπίθοιεν ἀκουήν.
     οὔ σε θεῶν ἑσσῆνα πάλοι θέσαν, ἔργα δὲ χειρῶν,
     σή τε βίη τό τε κάρτος, ὃ καὶ πέλας εἴσαο δίφρου.
     θήκαο δ' οἰωνῶν μέγ' ὑπείροχον ἀγγελιώτην
     σῶν τεράων· ἅ τ' ἐμοῖσι φίλοις ἐνδέξια φαίνοις.
70   εἵλεο δ' αἰζηῶν ὅ τι φέρτατον· οὐ σύ γε νηῶν
     ἐμπεράμους, οὐκ ἄνδρα σακέσπαλον, οὐ μὲν ἀοιδόν·

---

36 πρωτίστη γενεῇ Ψ: πρωτίστη γενεή Schneider, Pfeiffer   μετά γε Blomfield: μετά τε Ψ   51 τά τε
Ψ: ἅ τε Steph. Byz.   53 πεπλήγοντες Lasc. η: πεπληγότες Ψ   68 οἰωνῶν H. Stephanus: οἰωνόν Ψ

ἀλλὰ τὰ μὲν μακάρεσσιν ὀλίζοσιν αὖθι παρῆκας
ἄλλα μέλειν ἑτέροισι, σὺ δ' ἐξέλεο πτολιάρχους
αὐτούς, ὧν ὑπὸ χεῖρα γεωμόρος, ὧν ἴδρις αἰχμῆς,
75   ὧν ἐρέτης, ὧν πάντα· τί δ' οὐ κρατέοντος ὑπ' ἰσχύν;
αὐτίκα χαλκῆας μὲν ὑδείομεν Ἡφαίστοιο,
τευχηστὰς δ' Ἄρηος, ἐπακτῆρας δὲ Χιτώνης
Ἀρτέμιδος, Φοίβου δὲ λύρης εὖ εἰδότας οἴμους·
'ἐκ δὲ Διὸς βασιλῆες', ἐπεὶ Διὸς οὐδὲν ἀνάκτων
80   θειότερον· τῷ καί σφε τεὴν ἐκρίναο λάξιν.
δῶκας δὲ πτολίεθρα φυλασσέμεν, ἵζεο δ' αὐτός
ἄκρησ' ἐν πολίεσσιν, ἐπόψιος οἵ τε δίκῃσι
λαὸν ὑπὸ σκολιῇσ' οἵ τ' ἔμπαλιν ἰθύνουσιν·
ἐν δὲ ῥυηφενίην ἔβαλές σφισιν, ἐν δ' ἅλις ὄλβον·
85   πᾶσι μέν, οὐ μάλα δ' ἶσον. ἔοικε δὲ τεκμήρασθαι
ἡμετέρῳ μεδέοντι· περιπρὸ γὰρ εὐρὺ βέβηκεν.
ἑσπέριος κεῖνός γε τελεῖ τά κεν ἦρι νοήσῃ·
ἑσπέριος τὰ μέγιστα, τὰ μείονα δ', εὖτε νοήσῃ.
οἱ δὲ τὰ μὲν πλειῶνι, τὰ δ' οὐχ ἑνί, τῶν δ' ἀπὸ πάμπαν
90   αὐτὸς ἄνην ἐκόλουσας, ἐνέκλασσας δὲ μενοινήν.
    χαῖρε μέγα, Κρονίδη πανυπέρτατε, δῶτορ ἐάων,
δῶτορ, ἀπημονίης. τεὰ δ' ἔργματα τίς κεν ἀείδοι;
οὐ γένετ', οὐκ ἔσται· τίς κεν Διὸς ἔργματ' ἀείσει;
χαῖρε, πάτερ, χαῖρ', αὖθι· δίδου δ' ἀρετήν τ' ἄφενός τε.
95   οὔτ' ἀρετῆς ἄτερ ὄλβος ἐπίσταται ἄνδρας ἀέξειν
οὔτ' ἀρετὴ ἀφένοιο· δίδου δ' ἀρετήν τε καὶ ὄλβον.

80 σφε POxy 2258: σφι Ψ   87 νοήσῃ Lasc.: νοήσει Ψ   93 κεν Ψ: καί Wilamowitz   ἀείσει Lasc.
α: ἀείσοι Ψ   94 ἀρετήν τ' ἄφενός τε Ψ: ἀρετὴν ἀφενόν τε Et. gen.

To Zeus

Would anything else be better to hymn at libations of Zeus than the god himself, ever great, ever lord, router of the Titans, dispenser of justice for the sons of Uranus? But how shall we hymn him, as Dictaean or Lycaean? (5) My heart is in doubt, for the birth is contested. Zeus, some say you were born in the Idaean mountains; Zeus, others say in Arcadia. Which of them is telling falsehoods, father? "Cretans always lie." And indeed, Lord, the Cretans built a tomb for you; but you are not dead, you live forever.

(10) In Parrhasia Rhea bore you, where the mountain was especially dense with thickets. Afterwards the place was sacred; nothing in need of Eileithyia, neither crawling thing nor woman approaches it, but the Apidaneans call it the primeval childbed of Rhea. (15) From the moment when your mother produced you from her great womb, immediately she searched for a stream of water in which she might cleanse the afterbirth, and therein might wash your body. But the mighty Ladon was not yet flowing nor was the Erymanthus, the whitest of waters, and the whole of (20) Azenis was not yet irrigated. But thereafter it was to be called well irrigated. For at the time when Rhea loosened her sash, the watery Iaon bore many oaks above it, and the Melas provided a course for many wagons, (25) many serpents made their lair above the Carnion (although it is now wet), and a man was accustomed to walk upon the Crathis and the stony Metope, thirsty. But abundant water lay under his feet. In the grip of helplessness, lady Rhea spoke: "Dear Gaia, you too give birth; your birth pangs are light." (30) She spoke and the goddess, lifting up her great arm, struck the hill with her staff; it was split wide apart for her and a great stream of water poured forth. There she washed your body, O Lord, and swaddled you, and gave you to Neda to carry to a Cretan hideaway, to rear you in secret. (35) She was the eldest of the Nymphs who attended her [Rhea] as midwives in the earliest generation after Styx and Philyra. Nor did the goddess reward her with an empty favor, but named that flow, Neda. This great stream somewhere by the very city of the Caucones (which is called Lepreion) (40) mingles with Nereus, and this most ancient water, the descendants of the bear, the daughter of Lycaon, drink. When the nymph left Thenae carrying you to Cnossus, Father Zeus, (for Thenae was near Cnossus) in that place your umbilical cord fell from you, Daimon, and afterwards the Cydones call it the (45) Omphalian plain. Zeus, you the companions of the Curbantes took into their arms, the Dictaean Meliae, and Adrastea laid you to rest in a golden cradle, and you suckled at the rich breast of the goat, Amalthea, and ate sweet honeycomb. (50) For suddenly the work of the Panacrian bees appeared in the Idaean mountains, which they call Panacra. And the Curetes danced the war dance around you with vigor, beating on their shields so Cronus would hear the clash of the shield and not your infant crying.

(55) Fairly you grew and fairly you were nourished, heavenly Zeus, and growing up quickly, down came swiftly to your cheeks. But when you were still a child you devised all things in their completion. And so your siblings, although they were older, did not begrudge you heaven to hold as your allotted home. (60) Ancient poets are not always completely truthful: they claim that a lot assigned homes in a threefold division to the sons of Cronus, but who would cast lots for Olympus and Hades, unless he was utterly foolish? For one casts lots, it seems, for things that are of equal value, but these are very far apart. (65) I would tell fictions of the sort that would persuade the ear of the listener. Lots did not make you king of the gods, but the deeds of your hands; your force and might, which you have set beside your throne. And you made the most distinguished of birds the messenger of your omens (may those omens you show to my friends be favorable). (70) And you chose what is most excellent among men; you did not choose the skilled in ships, nor the shield-wielding man, nor the singer, but you immediately ceded them to lesser gods, other spheres for others to look after, but you chose the rulers of cities themselves, under whose authority is the farmer, the skilled in the spear, (75) the oarsman, all things. What is not within the power of the ruler? For example, we say that bronze workers belong to Hephaestus, warriors to Ares, huntsmen to Tunic-clad Artemis, and to Phoebus those who are accomplished at the lyre, but "from Zeus are kings"; for nothing is more divine than Zeus's kings. (80) Therefore you chose them for your portion. You gave them cities to guard, and sat yourself in their cities' high places, vigilant for who rules the people with crooked judgments and who does the opposite. You have bestowed wealth on them, and abundant prosperity, (85) to all, but not very evenly. One can infer this from our king, for he far outstrips the rest. At evening he accomplishes what he thinks of in the morning; at evening the greatest things, the lesser, immediately he thinks of them. Others accomplish some things in a year, other things not in one; of others you (90) yourself cut short their accomplishment and thwart their desire.

Fare very well, loftiest son of Cronus, giver of wealth, giver of safety. Who would sing of your deeds? There has not been, there will not be; who shall sing of the deeds of Zeus? Hail, father, again hail. Grant virtue and prosperity. (95) Without virtue, wealth cannot increase men, nor virtue without wealth. Grant virtue and wealth.

Commentary

1–7. For the structure and organization of these lines see pp. 27–28. Both Aratus' *Phaenomena* and Theocritus 17 begin with Zeus (ἐκ Διὸς ἀρχώμεσθα). The scholiast notes that the syntax of these lines is ambiguous: either Ζηνός belongs with the closer παρὰ σπονδῇσιν, "at libations for Zeus," or with λώϊον, "would anything else be better than Zeus to hymn at libations than the god himself." (For the latter the distance between Ζηνός and ἢ θεὸν αὐτόν might mitigate the redundancy and the shift in construction after the comparative.) "Libations for Zeus" should indicate a specific occasion honoring Zeus (as I understand the line), while the alternative may be no more than a generic reference to sympotic practice (see Lüddecke 1998: 12–13). Athenaeus 15.692F-93C records the habit of pouring the first libation at a symposium to Zeus *Soter*, while a scholium to Aratus claims that the first libation was to Zeus *Olympios*, the second to the Dioscuri and the heroes, and the third to Zeus *Soter* (see Kidd's full discussion, p. 163).

3. Πηλαγόνων: the manuscript tradition preserves Πηλογόνων ("Mud-born"), while the variant Πηλαγόνων, glossed as "Giants," occurs in ancient quotations of this line. According to Strabo (7 fr. 40) the Titans were called Πηλαγόνες, though Giants and Titans were often indistinguishable. Steph. Byz. s.v. complicates the picture: he states that Πηλαγονία was a region of Macedon and the name of the natives Πηλαγόνες. This has given rise to the conjecture that Πηλαγόνων was an allusion to the struggles of Ptolemy I with the Macedonian dynasts, particularly in light of 61 below.

ἐλατῆρα: Pindar (*Ol.* 4.1) applies this epithet to Zeus as driver of a chariot of thunder, Homer to a charioteer (*Il.* 4.145, 11.702), and in *HhHerm*, it describes Hermes as a driver away of cows (βοῶν ἐλατῆρα, 14, 265, 377). Certainly in Hesiod (*Th.* 820) Zeus Τιτῆνας ἀπ᾽ οὐρανοῦ ἐξέλασεν, to which incident the phrase might allude (see the discussion in Hunter and Fuhrer 2002: 170n67). Nonnus (18.266) later imitates the phrase as Γηγενέων ὀλετῆρα, where Γηγενέων ("Earth-born") may gloss the ms. reading of Πηλογόνων.

δικασπόλον: the word occurs twice in Homer (*Il.* 1.238, *Od.* 11.186). In the *Odyssey* passage Telemachus acts as a judge (δικασπόλος) in his father's stead in Ithaca; as an intertext it might allude to Ptolemy II as the younger member of a co-regency. For Stoic Zeus as a lawgiver see Cleanthes, *Hymn to Zeus* 24–25.

4. καί "in fact"; when it follows an interrogative, καί "denotes that the question cuts at the foundations of the problem under consideration" (Denniston, 313–14).

νιν: editors tend to preserve the ms. reading, though Wilamowitz proposed emending the Doric νιν to Ionic μιν (cf. 12 below). Cuypers 2004: 108 argues for the retention of νιν on the grounds that it is an echo of *HhAp* 528: <u>πῶς καὶ νῦν</u>

βιόμεσθα. In that passage the Cretan speakers address Apollo as "Lord, who have brought us far from our dear ones and native land, how shall we live?" The allusion would be especially attractive in the context of Alexandria's immigrant community.

5. See p. 50.

6–8. Callimachus asks Zeus himself to adjudicate the dispute over his birth. But the ostensibly formulaic question is unexpectedly answered by Κρῆτες ἀεὶ ψεῦσται ("Cretans always lie"), a famous paradoxical expression that was attributed to the archaic sage, Epimenides of Crete (see Cuypers 2004: 102–5). The logic of what follows is that, since Cretans are known for lying, you cannot trust their claims that Zeus was born in Crete, especially since they had a famous site said to be the tomb of Zeus. But who is the speaker? Is this Zeus, Callimachus, or Epimenides himself? If it is Zeus who answers, his rejection of Hesiod authorizes the hymnic realignment to follow, as the choice the god is given is between the Hesiodic version of his birth (Crete) and the one that Callimachus will go on to prefer (Arcadia). (For the ambiguities in the passage see Goldhill 1986.)

6. Ἰδαίοισιν ἐν οὔρεσι: the plural may be a reminder that in addition to Mt. Ida on Crete, a Mt. Ida also existed in Phrygia. Both locations were claimants for the birthplace of Zeus.

φασι γενέσθαι: four times in Homer, and used twice in this *sedes* of heroic fathers of heroes (*Il.* 4.375, of Tydeus ≈ *Od.* 4.201, of Antilochus): "For I never met or saw him, but they say he was preeminent among others." The intertext would seem to locate Zeus with heroes of a former generation, thus preparing for his identification with "my king" below.

7. Ζεῦ...πάτερ: addressing Zeus as "father" here and again at 43 in the context of his birth may be intended to call into question traditional natal mythologies. The vocative occurs again in the final prayer (see 94 below).

8. ὦ ἄνα: the hiatus is normal and explained by digamma; at 33 the crasis of ὦ + ἄνα (= ὦνα) is unusual. In Callimachus' hymns only Zeus (*hZeus* 8, 33) and Apollo (*hAp* 79) are addressed as ἄνα.

9. ἐτεκτήναντο: the unaugmented epic aorist is much more common, and used at *HhHerm* 25 of Hermes constructing the lyre. τεκταίνομαι often implies deceit (e.g., Eur. *IT* 951), as here.

10. Παρρασίη: Parrhasia was the region of Arcadia associated with Zeus *Lycaeus*.

Ῥείη: the spelling of Rhea alternates between Ῥείη and Ῥέη (21), as Callimachus explores the etymology of the name as from ῥεῖα (= easy) and from the verb ῥέω (= flow); the variants also allude to passages in Hesiod (Hopkinson 1984a).

11–13. Callimachus employs sacral language—the decree that pregnant creatures of any sort, human or animal, may not approach—to mark the holiness that the site takes on from its association with Zeus's birth. For such prohibitions see Parker 1983: 48–50 and 344–46 (Cyrenean cathartic law).

11. περισκεπές "covered all around"; first in Callimachus (also *hDelos* 23); adjective formed from περί + σκέπας.

12–13. μιν... ἐπιμίσγεται: the construction of this verb with the accusative is unusual (Bentley and Schneider emend to οἱ); a parallel may be Hesiod *Th.* 803–4 (see West ad loc.), and the meaning not the more common "mingling with" but "come close to," implying motion towards. In addition, the case may be intended to call attention to the phrase οὐδέ τί μιν: discussed above p. 24.

12. Εἰλειθυίης: Eileithyia was the goddess of childbirth. Naming her in this context hints at multiple traditions about her birth. One version makes her older than Cronus, and a daughter of Gaia; this goddess was associated with Crete. Hesiod (*Th.* 922) makes her the daughter of Zeus and Hera; this Eileithyia would be distinctly anachronistic at Zeus's birth.

14. Four-word lines are exceptional in Callimachus. Here it closes the section and concludes the *aition* (again at 41, and for the thought see 45).

ὠγύγιον "primeval"; Homer seems to treat Ὠγυγίη as a proper name, and uses it always with νῆσος (e.g., for Calypso's island at *Od.* 7.244). In *hDelos* 160 Callimachus describes Cos, the birthplace of Ptolemy II as ὠγυγίην... νῆσον. The symbolism of birth on a primeval hill or island was central in Egyptian creation myth (Stephens 2003: 95–96).

λεχώϊον "place of giving birth"; a Callimachean *hapax*, following a common pattern of treating an adjective as if it were a substantive (see McLennan ad loc. for further examples).

Ἀπιδανῆες: Apidaneans were the earliest Arcadians, said to have lived before the moon. The scholiast on A.R. (4.263–64a) derives the name from Apis, the son of Phoroneus, who was in turn the son of Inachus (the local river). The name *Apidanees*, therefore, conveys not only antiquity, it encapsulates an ancestral relationship: the Inachid line produced Io, her son Epaphus, and his descendants Libya, Danaus, and Aegyptus on the one hand, and Cadmus and Oedipus on the other. The former were significant for the Ptolemies (see p. 238), the latter Callimachus in *hAp* claims as ancestors of Cyrene. A second derivation is from ἀ + πίνω = without drink, or dry (see Hopkinson 1984a).

15–20. Arcadian rivers dried up in the summer and autumn, but Callimachus presents the local rivers—Ladon, Erymanthus, Iaon, Melas, Carnion, and Crathis—as still subterranean, only bursting forth after Zeus has been born. Puns on Rhea, as "flow," and on Azenis (Arcadia), as ἀ-Ζήν or "without Zeus," link names to this condition. Such etymologizing was a feature of Stoic philosophy, though articulated even earlier in Plato's *Cratylus*, where the essence of divine names is explained (e.g., 396a1–b5).

15. ἀπεθήκατο κόλπων: ἀποτίθημι with the genitive "to give birth" (lit. "lay aside from her lap"); cf. *HhHerm* 20: ἀπ᾽... θόρε γυίων; also at *hArt* 25.

16. δίζητο: from δίζημαι, "seek out"; Callimachus also uses the alternate form, δίζομαι. The lengthening of the final syllable before ῥόον is Homeric (cf. *Il.* 17.264, 21.258) and reflects initial digamma; also at *hDelos* 159, 206, *hAth* 77.

17. χυτλώσαιτο: from χυτλόω. This form occurs once in Homer (*Od.* 6.80), when Nausicaa's mother sends her off to the seashore with a flask of oil to anoint herself (χυτλώσαιτο) after bathing, then once here in Callimachus, where it means "wash." Apollonius 4.1311 probably imitates this passage to describe Athena being washed immediately after she was born from the head of her father.

χρῶτα: like Homer and Hesiod, Callimachus uses both forms of the accusative of χρώς (see 32).

λοέσσαι: from λοέω, the uncontracted form of λούω, a third singular aorist optative (so Griffiths 1981: 160). McLennan ad loc. takes as a "final-consecutive" infinitive, though δ' suggests a construction parallel to the preceding optative. The verb occurs once in Homer at *Od.* 19.320, of servants bathing Odysseus.

18–32. For these lines Griffiths 1981: 159 points to the parallel of Aratus 218–20: οὐ γάρ πω ... "for not yet was the peak of Helicon flowing with streams, but the horse struck it with its foot and on that spot water poured forth" (ἀθρόον ... ὕδωρ | ἐξέχυτο).

18. For these rivers see map 2.

19–20. The phrase ἄβροχος ἦεν ἅπασα | Ἀζηνίς makes the equation clear: without rain, ἀ-βροχή = without Zeus, ἀ-Ζήν, without life, ἀ-ζῆν. (J. J. Clauss makes the attractive suggestion that ἅπασα too may be attracted to this privative environment—"not anything.")

19. ἄβροχος points to Egypt: it is a technical term used in Egyptian documents for land that has not been inundated by the Nile flood (cf. Eur. *Hel.* 1485 of the Libyan desert).

20. Ἀζηνίς was the northwestern section of Arcadia bordering on Elis. The mss. read Ἀρκαδίη, but this is almost certainly a gloss on the more specific, though less familiar Ἀζηνίς, found in a scholium on Dionyius the Periegete 415.

21. αὖτις "hereafter" (see LSJ s.v. αὖθις II 2).

ὅτε: the postponed temporal conjunction is frequent in the hymns (*hArt* 150, *hDelos* 229, 309, *hDem* 9).

22–27. Callimachus indicates the absence of the rivers with a number of images: oaks grow above the Iaon; wagons travel above the Melas; snakes have their lairs above the Carnion; and men walk over the Crathis. The anaphora of forms of πολύς in these lines serves to contrast the extreme dryness above ground with the abundant water beneath.

22–23. ἐφύπερθε ... ἤειρεν: the phrase has been taken to indicate Callimachus' preference for reading ἐφύπερθεν ἀειρθείς at *Od.* 9.383; the reading was later questioned by Aristarchus, who preferred ἐρεισθείς (Rengakos 1993: 162–63).

22. σαρωνίδας: first in Callimachus; according to the scholiast the word means "oak trees." Pliny (*HN* 4.18.4–6) claims that the Saronic gulf was so named from its oak trees.

23. Μέλας: more than one river was so named because of the darkness of its waters, though none is attested for Arcadia; here "Black river" contrasts with "whitest" Erymanthus.

ὤκχησεν: from ὀκχέω, a metrically lengthened form of ὀχέω that occurred previously only in Pindar (*Ol.* 2.74, 6.24).

24. Καρνίωνος: the emendation is that of Arnaldus, based on Paus. 8.34.5 (for the Carnion, see map 2); mss. read the otherwise unattested Καρίωνος.

διεροῦ: twice in Homer (*Od.* 6.201, 9.43), where the meaning was debated; the meaning is either "living" or "swift" (see Rengakos 1992: 26). Here it seems to mean "wet," though in light of 19–20 above, "living" may be implicit (as at *hAp* 23).

25. κινώπετα: here for the first time: according to the scholiast "animals that move on the ground." Later in Nicander (*Ther.* 27) it is restricted to venomous creatures like snakes.

26. πολύστιον: according to the scholiast, "with many pebbles"; a Callimachean coinage from πολύ + στίον. The scholiast on A.R. 2.1172 states that στία is what the Sicyonians call "a pebble." Possibly Callimachus chose the Sicyonian word to allude to the mythology of the river Metope.

Μετώπην: the location of this river is not certain, but apparently near Stymphalus, and possibly identical with what Pausanias identifies as the river Stymphalus (Ael. *VH* 2.33.5–8, Paus. 8.4.6, 22.2). Metope was said to have been the daughter of Ladon (18) and the wife of Asopus, the main river of Sicyon (Pi. *Ol.* 6.84).

27. διψαλέος "thirsty" or "parched"; first here, then again of the river Peneius' lament in *hDelos* 130. Later found at *Batrach.* 9 and in the medical writers. Crossing over a river without wetting one's feet is a description of inferior rivers spoken with contempt by the Nile in Callimachus' *Victory of Sosibius* (fr. 384.32–34 Pf.).

29–30. Rhea's invocation of her mother both personifies Gaia and calls attention to the fact that she is the ground beneath her daughter's feet. This begins a section that is heavily dependent on Hesiod's description of the birth of Zeus on Crete. See p. 51.

29. Γαῖα φίλη, τέκε καὶ σύ: cf. *Il.* 21.106 and 119, in which Achilles kills Lycaon, a son of Priam, first telling him: ἀλλά, φίλος, θάνε καὶ σύ. "But, friend, you die too." When he strikes him with his sword, copious amounts of blood flow (ῥέε) and soak the ground (γαῖαν). The imitation may result from the homonym with the Lycaon who was an early king of Arcadia and from whom the local mountain took its name (so Griffiths 1981: 160). But more importantly, Callimachus transforms a typical Homeric moment of war and death into the production of life and water that sustains life (so Hopkinson 1989: 125).

τέκε: aorist imperative from τίκτω. Gaia (Earth) is exhorted to give birth, i.e., to provide water.

ὠδῖνες: usually in plural; it occurs only at *Il.* 11.271 and *HhAp* 92 (of Leto) in the sense of "pangs of childbirth"; in both earlier texts they are bitter or prolonged, in contrast to Rhea's parturition.

30. ἀντανύσασα: aorist participle from ἀνατανύω; a rare verb that combines ἀνά + Homeric τανύω on the model of ἀνατείνω, "stretch out"; also at A.R. 1.344.

θεή: mss. read θεά here, but elsewhere θεή; editors usually emend to bring into conformity with the rest of the hymn. The -α suffix could have arisen under the influence of the previous word.

31. πουλύ = πολύ: Callimachus regularly uses both forms of this adverb, often in close proximity, in the Homeric fashion.

32. χρόα φαιδρύνασα: the phrase may have been taken from Hes. *Op.* 753: μηδὲ γυναικείῳ λουτρῷ χρόα φαιδρύνεσθαι ("[a man] should not wash his skin with a woman's bathwater").

33. ὦνα: see 8n.

σπείρωσε: from σπειρόω, first in Callimachus; according to the scholiast, it is a variant of σπαργανόω. It occurs again at *hDelos* 6 of Delos swaddling Apollo.

34. κευθμόν "hiding place" or "covert"; the singular is formed from the Homeric *hapax* (*Il.* 13.28, ἐκ κευθμῶν); the variant, κευθμών, -μῶνος occurs at *Od.* 10.283, 13.367).

Κρηταῖον: that Zeus was reared in a Cretan cave is a traditional part of the birth myth, though according to Pausanias (8.38.2) there was a "Cretan cave" located on Mt. Lycaeon in Arcadia.

35. πρεσβυτάτη Νυμφέων: Neda is here said to be oldest of the nymphs in attendance, along with Styx and Philyra. For her service the Arcadian river that flowed from Mt. Lycaeon to the Cyparissian gulf was named for her.

μαιώσαντο: from μαιόομαι, "acted as midwives" in Hellenistic and later Greek.

According to Pausanias (8.47.3), the altar in the sanctuary of Athena at Arcadian Tegea represented Rhea, a nymph holding the infant Zeus, eight attending nymphs, including Neda, with figures of the Muses and Memory. Cf. *HhAp* 92–94 for divine attendants at Leto's accouchement, where Eileithyia is also absent.

36. Στύγα: Styx was the name given to the oldest of the daughters of Ocean and to a small river that flowed into the Crathis in northern Arcadia. In Hesiod she is also identified with the Styx of the underworld (*Th.* 775–79). West ad loc. notes that the mythological Styx bears a resemblance to Nonacris, an Arcadian waterfall that was called "Styx" by ancient writers.

Φιλύρην: Philyra was the mother of the Centaur Chiron; in A.R. 2.1231–41 while Zeus was still a child, Rhea surprised her husband Cronus as he was making love to Philyra; he turned himself into a horse. The resulting child was a Centaur, half-man, half-horse.

37. ἀλίην: here "idle" or "empty," though its placement immediately following the names of two Ocean nymphs momentarily suggests the homonym (ἅλιος = "of the sea") and that we will be getting further information about the Oceanids.

39. Καυκώνων πτολίεθρον: the Caucones, according to Homer (*Od.* 3.366), were named for their ancestor Caucon, a son of Lycaon. Their city, Lepreum, is in southern Elis very close to the river Neda's exit to the sea.

πεφάτισται: the perfect passive of φατίζω is not found before the Hellenistic period.

40. Νηρῆι: Nereus was an older sea god, the son of Gaia, whose mythology resembles that of Proteus. Here Nereus is a metonymy for the sea, and naming him reinforces the pre-Olympian time of these events. But Callimachus also anthropomorphizes him with his choice of συμφέρεται, perhaps implying a sexual mingling with Neda.

41. The Arcadian section of the hymn closes with a second four-word spondaic line.

υἱωνοί: the usual meaning of υἱωνός is "grandson," but here clearly "descendant."

Λυκαονίης ἄρκτοιο: Callimachus follows Hesiod (fr. 163 M-W) in making Callisto the daughter of Lycaon. Zeus fell in love with her, and she was subsequently turned into a bear (ἄρκτος), either by Zeus himself, or by Artemis or Hera, and was placed in the night sky as a constellation (Ursa Major, or the Great Bear). Her son by Zeus, Arcas, was an early king as well as the eponymous ancestor of the Arcadians; he also ends up as a constellation (Ursa Minor). Aratus 31–35 makes these constellations originally bears who nursed Zeus when he was reared in a Cretan cave (see Kidd ad loc.).

42–45. These lines create a moment of disorientation for the reader: suddenly, we are no longer in Arcadia (see p. 47).

42. For Cretan Thenae in Hellenistic cult, see Chaniotis 2001: 215–16.

42–43. The variation in the genitive forms of Κνωσοῖο and Κνωσοῦ is also found in Homer.

44. τουτάκι: poetic equivalent of τότε; the form occurs first in Pi. *Py.* 4.28, 255. Callimachus uses it here and again in the Doric hymns at *hAth* 115 and *hDem* 32. Bulloch (on *hAth* 115) conjectures that it may be a Doricism.

πέσε... ἀπ(ο): the preposition of the compound in tmesis here follows its verb. ἀποπίπτω occurs only once in Homer, *Il.* 14.351: στιλπναὶ δ' ἀπέπιπτον ἐέρσαι. After Zeus and Hera make love, they lie upon a cloud from which falls "glistening dew."

45. Ὀμφάλιον... πέδον: the Omphalion plain was located near Cnossus; cf. Diodorus 5.70, whose account of Zeus's birth may owe some features to Callimachus, but also expands on traditional elements like the Curetes, honey, and the she-goat that suckled Zeus.

Κύδωνες: the Cydones, who lived in northwest Crete, are a metonym for the Cretans as a whole; according to Pausanias (8.53.4), they were the descendants of the sons of an Arcadian (Tegeates). Their city, Cydon, is modern Chania.

46–54. Zeus is secretly brought up in Crete, attended by the Ash nymphs. Apart from these nymphs, the rest of the figures would appear to be human (Curetes, Corybantes) and/or demythologized natural phenomena (goats, bees) in contrast to the convergence of divinity and landscape in the Arcadian portion of the poem (e.g., Gaia, Neda, Nereus). The Curetes, who were the Cretan attendants of Zeus, here dance the war dance (πρύλιν: 52) to keep Cronus from hearing the baby's cries. The details of Zeus's nurture align Callimachus' narrative with Euhemerus and earlier rationalizing interpretations of myth (on which see Kirichenko 2012: 188–200) and pave the way for the later linking of god and king.

46. Κυρβάντων: a variant of Κορυβάντων. The Corybantes were servants of Phrygian Cybele. Euripides (*Bacch.* 120–25) is Callimachus' precursor in locating the Corybantes in Crete, where they are said to invent the tambourine (cf. 53: τεύχεα πεπλήγοντες).

προσεπηχύναντο "take into one's arms"; the verb is unique to Callimachus (cf. the simplex πηχύνω, which is also a Hellenistic poeticism).

47. Δικταῖαι Μελίαι: the "Ash nymphs" were said to have sprung from the blood of the castrated Uranus (*Th.* 187). Μελία was also the name of the ash tree, so called because it oozed a honey-like sap (μέλι). Ἀδρήστεια was the sister of the Curetes, and their father was Melissus; and the word for honey bee (μέλισσα) occurs in 50 (see Haslam 1993: 121–22 on this convoluted set of verbal associations).

48. ἐθήσαο: second singular aorist middle indicative of θῆσαι, "to suckle." The verb occurs once in Homer at *Il.* 24.58, where Hera claims that Hector suckled (θῆσθαι) at a human breast in contrast to Achilles, who was the child of a goddess.

48–49. μαζόν | αἰγὸς Ἀμαλθείης: the earliest information on Amalthea is from Pherecydes of Athens (*FGrH* 3 F49, cited in Apollod. 2.7.5). She was a nymph who had a bull's horn that supplied food in abundance (a literal "horn of plenty"). Callimachus and Aratus (163) make Amalthea a goat who suckles Zeus at her "breast." Since μαζόν implies a human breast, not a goat's udder, he calls attention to his own rationalizing variant of the myth. For Amalthea see Frazer's detailed notes (1921: 1.7n3, 257n4).

49 ἐπὶ...ἔβρως: second singular aorist active. While βιβρώσκω is common, the compound ἐπιβιβρώσκω appears here for the first time (in tmesis). The meaning must be "ate after" (as at Dioscorides, *Euphorista* 2.140), referring to the natural progress of a newborn from breast milk to more solid food, the honeycomb. Clauss (1986: 165) points to *HhHerm* 558–62 as a parallel, where the Bee Maidens who live on Mt. Parnassus tell the truth and are able to bring events to fulfillment after eating honeycomb.

50. γέντο: here the equivalent of ἐγένετο (= "was born"), found only at Hes. *Th.* 199 (of Aphrodite) and 283 (of Pegasus). In Homer γέντο always occurs after the bucolic dieresis, and it is the equivalent of ἔλαβεν (as at *hDem* 43).

Πανακρίδος: the location of a mountain named Panacra is unknown (Steph. Byz. s.v. Πάνακρα does no more than cite this passage). Πανακρίδος is formed from πᾶν + the noun ἄκρις ("mountain peak"); Πάνακρα (51) from πᾶν + the adjective ἄκρος. "Mt. Tiptop" may have been a joke invented by Callimachus.

ἔργα μελίσσης: The phrase ἔργα + genitive is modeled on Homeric phrases like ἔργα γυναικῶν (*Il.* 6.289, *Od.* 7.97, and see below 66: ἔργα…χειρῶν). The idea of "manufacture" necessarily humanizes the bees' contribution, as does μαζόν above.

The presence of bees carries another signification: the bee was the hieroglyph used to write "king of Lower Egypt," or the region in which Alexandria was located (see 66).

51. τά τε κλείουσι (= καλέουσι): epic τε marks a digression, usually describing a permanent characteristic, but epic τε could be omitted from the sentence without altering the syntax and is thus closer in use to an adverb than a conjunction. Callimachus uses it about one third as much as Homer (see Ruijgh 1971: 967–71). Also at 69.

52. οὖλα: the adjective is Homeric, and its meanings were debated in antiquity (see Rengakos 1992: 24); the adverbial use is first found in Callimachus, here and again at *hArt* 247 of dancing; the meaning is either "vigorously" or "with quick or rapid steps."

Κούρητες: Strabo 10.3.19 provides the fullest account of the Curetes, citing Hesiod (= fr. 123 M-W), in which they are said to have been the children of Hecaterus and the daughter of Phoroneus (a descendant of Inachus) along with the mountain nymphs and satyrs. They are described as φιλοπαίγμονες ὀρχηστῆρες ("playful dancers"). Strabo goes on to give different versions, including their close connection with Crete and the rearing of Zeus, the tradition that they were the first to wear bronze armor, and that they were identified with the Corybantes in Phrygia.

σε περὶ πρύλιν ὠρχήσαντο: the phrase occurs again at *hArt* 240. The preposition is either in tmesis (and this would be the first occurrence of περιορχέομαι) or following its object σε (and thus should be accented πέρι). Whatever the exact syntax, the meaning is clear.

πρύλιν: the Cretan equivalent of the Athenian πυρρίχη, the dance was performed in armor as a demonstration of manhood (see Ceccarelli 1998: 116–19). Performing it to drown out the sound of Zeus's infant cries reduces the Curetes to the status of baby-sitters, but it may have a significant point in that the war dance had lost some of its cultural luster by the Hellenistic period. For Curetes dancing see also the Palaikastro hymn (Furley and Bremmer 2001: 2.12–13).

53. πεπλήγοντες: either a reduplicated strong aorist (in which case the accent should be πεπληγόντες) or a perfect stem with present endings (thus πεπλήγοντες), which is a feature of Syracusan Doric (Hunter 1999: 225). See also *hArt* 61 for a similar form. The form and accent for such words in Homer was a matter of dispute (see Rengakos 1993: 121). The phrase makes clear that these are the armor-wearing Curetes that Strabo mentions (see 52n).

54. κουρίζοντος: here, "making babyish noises," though κουρίζω normally means to be a child (κοῦρος). Callimachus thus constructs an etymology for Κούρητες.

55–57. Echoed in 85–88, where Zeus's swift growth to maturity and his ability to accomplish his goals even as a child are reflected in Ptolemy's ability to execute his plans as soon as he conceives them. The thought is reinforced by the parallel language: (Zeus) ὀξὺ δ' ἀνήβησας and (Ptolemy) εὐρὺ βέβηκεν, and (Zeus) ἀλλ' ἔτι παιδνὸς ἐὼν ἐφράσσαο πάντα τέλεια and (Ptolemy) ἑσπέριος κεῖνός γε τελεῖ... εὖτε νοήσῃ.

55. καλὰ... κᾰλά: καλός with long α is common in Homer, reflecting digamma after lambda (see Chantraine 1.159); κᾰλός is found in Hesiod, the Homeric hymns, and the lyric poets. Callimachus also changes quantities of a word within the same line at *hAp* 2, 25, 80, 103. For further examples of this kind of metrical variation in Greek poets, see McLennan ad loc.

ἤέξευ: this second singular imperfect middle of ἀέξω ("grow," "increase") is not found elsewhere; Callimachus uses the aorist middle (also unattested elsewhere) at *Hecale* fr. 48.9 Hollis.

ἔτραφες: second singular epic aorist active of τρέφω; in Homer used in a passive sense, as here (see LSJ s.v. τρέφω B).

οὐράνιε Ζεῦ: for Zeus at line end, cf. *Il.* 1.508: μητίετα Ζεῦ, and see Bühler on Mosch. *Eur.* pp. 103–4n5.

56. ταχινοί: late poetic form of ταχύς, first in Callimachus (also at *hArt* 158, *hDelos* 95, 114).

57. The precocity of child gods is a constant theme in Callimachus' hymns: compare Apollo's slaying of the Python in *hAp*, Artemis' strength and acquisitiveness in *hArt*, and the prophecies of the unborn Apollo in *hDelos*. *HhHerm* may have started the trend in Greek poets, but Horus the child was a prominent feature of pharaonic iconography (as adapted by the Ptolemies) as well (see Selden 1998: 386–92).

58. τῷ "therefore"; both orthography and accent were debated in antiquity (see LSJ s.v.).

προτερηγενέες: the word occurs first in Antimachus (fr. 41a.7, and see Matthews ad loc.) to describe the Titans. It next appears here and in A.R. 4.268 (of "Egypt, mother of men of an earlier generation"); Callimachus uses it for Zeus's siblings who are born earlier, but in the same generation, cf. *Il.* 15.166: γενεῇ πρότερος. In Hesiod (*Th.* 478) Zeus is the youngest of the children of Cronus, though in Homer (*Il.* 13.355, 15.166) Zeus is older than Poseidon.

59. οὐρανόν: the object, with ἐπιδαίσιον οἶκον in apposition.

ἐμέγηραν: cf. *HhHerm* 464–65: αὐτὰρ ἐγώ σοι | τέχνης ἡμετέρης ἐπιβήμεναι οὔ τι μεγαίρω. ("Yet I do not grudge you entering into my art").

ἐπιδαίσιον: the word is unique to Callimachus, glossed in the *Suda* s.v. as ὁ ἐπίκοινον καὶ οὐ μεριστόν, ὁ ἐξ ἴσου καταλειφθεὶς δύο τισίν "shared equally and not divided; that which is left equally to two." McLennan ad loc. argues that *pace* *Suda* Callimachus must have meant that the owner did *not* share property with another. But if behind the coinage stands an allusion to a co-regency, the *Suda's* definition has merit: a property allotted in common (i.e., with his father) but undivided (i.e., with his brothers). Another aspect of Callimachus' coinage that must have struck a contemporary audience: Daisios was a Macedonian month name used in early Alexandria.

60–64. Callimachus aligns himself with poets like Hesiod (*Th.* 881–85, where Zeus is elevated by divine consensus) and against previous poets who claimed that the Olympians cast lots for their respective territories (e.g., Homer at *Il.*15. 187–93, *HhDem* 84–87, and Pi. *Ol.* 7.54–56). Because of the tight linking of Zeus and Ptolemy, most scholars have seen this passage as an allusion to contemporary history. See pp. 17–18 and below 61.

60. δηναιοί: here in the sense "ancient," a meaning that first occurs in the tragedians.

ἀληθέες … ἀοιδοί: for poets speaking truths see below 65. This is the second inherited falsehood that Callimachus sets out to contradict. For the first see 6–8 above.

61. διάτριχα "divided into three portions." The word is rare and may recall *HhDem* 85–86: αὐτοκασίγνητος καὶ ὁμόσπορος· ἀμφὶ δὲ τιμὴν | ἔλλαχεν ὡς τὰ πρῶτα διάτριχα δασμὸς ἐτύχθη ("[Hades], your own brother and from the same seed; with regard to privilege, he has the portion he received at first in the threefold division."

62. ἐρύσσαι: epic aorist optative from ἐρύω, "draw."

63. The use of μή with the adjective is generic; see Smyth §2735.

νενίηλος: another coinage, not found elsewhere. Hesychius glosses it ἀνόητος ("without sense"), so appropriate for those who tell foolish stories.

ἰσαίη: a variant of ἴσος, first found here. ἴση with ellipse of μοῖρα or ψῆφος is common for "equal share," cf. *Od.* 9.42. For forms in -αιος see McLennan ad *loc.*

64. πήλασθαι: aorist middle infinitive of πάλλω, "draw lots."

τὰ δὲ τόσσον ὅσον διὰ πλεῖστον ἔχουσι: lit., "these things (τά) [i.e., heaven and Hades] are such (τόσσον) as (ὅσον) differ (διὰ … ἔχουσι) the most."

65. Callimachus' wish to tell more plausible fictions belongs to a long line of poetic statements about the relationship of poetry to truth that begins with Hesiod's programmatic exchange with the Muses at *Th.* 26–28 (see Fantuzzi 2011: 445–48 for a discussion of this passage in light of Hesiod's). Note also Hermes' outrageous declaration at *HhHerm* 368–69: Ζεῦ πάτερ, ἤτοι ἐγώ σοι ἀληθείην ἀγορεύσω· | νημερτής τε γάρ εἰμι καὶ οὐκ οἶδα ψεύδεσθαι ("Father Zeus, I shall tell you the truth, for I am honest and do not know how to lie"). The philosophers also took up the question: both Plato and Aristotle characterize fiction as the ability to καλῶς ψεύδεσθαι, to tell stories that are untrue in a fitting way. Pl. *Rep.* 377e7 points specifically to Hesiod telling the story about Cronus swallowing his children (the story Callimachus does not tell) as an example of a poet who οὐ καλῶς ἐψεύσατο.

66. ἐσσῆνα: most ancient texts have ἐσ-, but ἑσ- is written in a papyrus of the *Aetia* (fr. 178.23 Pf.), hence it is conventional to print the rough breathing here. According to *SIG* 352.6 (fourth century BCE), the term was used for the priests of Artemis at Ephesus (see also Paus. 8.13.1). Callimachus uses it here to mean "king." According to the *Etymologicum magnum*, the king of the Ephesians was called *Essên* by analogy with the king of the bees, so called from residing ἔσω ("inside"). "Bee king" would have an obvious local reference: one of the hieroglyphic signs for the king of Lower Egypt (and used by the Ptolemies) was a bee (Stephens 2003: 107–8).

1. Hieroglyphic for king of Upper and Lower Egypt

67. εἴσαο: second singular aorist middle of ἵζω.

68–79. This section is also heavily dependent on Hesiod, but now *Op.*, where Hesiod delineates the prerogatives of kings. The relationship of Zeus and Ptolemy is first constructed within patterns of Greek kingship.

68. θήκαο: a rare second singular aorist middle of τίθημι.

ἀγγελιώτην "messenger"; previously only at *HhHerm* 296. See Clauss 1986: 166.

69. ἐνδέξια: lit., "things on the right," but here "propitious," since omens that occurred on the right side were deemed auspicious.

70–71. Callimachus lists three professions: sailor, soldier, poet here and at 74–75 farmer, soldier, sailor. Farmers, soldiers, and sailors made up an important portion of Ptolemaic Egypt's immigrant community; Callimachus inserts himself into this essential company.

71. ἐμπεράμους: variant of ἔμπειρος, "skilled in," followed by a genitive; the word first appears here, and is copied by later poets. The adverb occurs at *hAth* 25.

σακέσπαλον "shield brandisher"; first in Homer at *Il.* 5.126 (used of Diomedes' father Tydeus); later much imitated by Nonnus. For the form of the compound cf. 3: δικασπόλον.

72. ὀλίζοσιν: this comparative of ὀλίγος occurs only once in Homer (*Il.* 18.519, ὀλίζονες), of people on the shield of Achilles figured as "smaller" than the soldiers marching out to battle like gods.

αὖθι: here (and 94) as the equivalent of αὖθις; either "straightway" or "in turn." Callimachus' usage was criticized in antiquity (see Hollis on *Hecale*, fr.17.4 and Rengakos 1992: 39).

74–75. The categories that fall under the rulers' power (ὑπὸ χεῖρα) are emphasized by the anaphora of ὧν (γεωμόρος, ἴδρις αἰχμῆς, ἐρέτης), a specificity that concludes with the inclusive πάντα.

74. αὐτούς: note the emphatic placement of the pronoun (also at 81 and 90).

ἴδρις αἰχμῆς may be intended to recall Choerilus' ἴδρις ἀοιδῆς (fr. 2.1 Bernabé), part of his complaint that poets of old were blessed because they wrote before his time, when all topics had already been divided up.

76–78. There is an implicit contrast of the four Olympians mentioned: Hephaestus, Ares, Artemis, and Apollo. Hephaestus and Ares appear only briefly in these hymns, the former as a chthonic figure in *hArt*, the latter as hostile and destructive in *hDelos*. Apollo in *hAp* and *hDelos* brings light and song; Artemis in *hArt* is a protector of women and cities.

76. ὑδείομεν: a metrical variant of ὑδέω, "say," "call"; it is not used before the Hellenistic period. The skill-sets praised are in the accusative: χαλκῆας, τευχηστάς, ἐπακτῆρας, λύρης εὖ εἰδότας οἴμους; the god under whose province they fall is genitive.

77. τευχηστάς: found previously only in Aesch. *Sept.* 644, where it describes a figure on Polyneices' shield.

Χιτώνης: apparently a cult title referring to Artemis' role as a huntress (see *hArt.* 225).

78. λύρης ... οἴμους "pathways of the lyre [i.e., song]"; οἶμος with this meaning is first in Pi. *Py.* 4.247–48 and *Ol.* 9.47; οἴμους ἀοιδῆς occurs in *HhHerm* 451 in a passage on the wonders of Hermes' invention, the lyre.

79. 'ἐκ δὲ Διὸς βασιλῆες': a quotation from Hes. *Th.* 96. See p. 50.

80. λάξιν "portion"; first in Herodotus, and common in prose; it has the legal sense of "assigned by inheritance."

81–83. The description of Zeus's characteristic behavior, sitting in the highest place in cities and watching (ἷζεο δ' αὐτός | ἄκρησ' ἐν πολίεσσιν, ἐπόψιος) occurs just before the mention of "my king." Alexandria was alluvial, and its highest point was Pharos, which was probably dedicated to Zeus *Soter*; Posidippus 115.3 A-B even likened Pharos to σκοπαὶ οὔρεος of the Greek islands. It was built some time between 297 and 285 BCE, so Callimachus could be alluding to Zeus "watching" from that high place.

82. ἐπόψιος: cf. A.R. 2.1123, where it is a cult title for Zeus (*Epopsios*), to whom Argus prays after being shipwrecked.

83. Callimachus borrows the oxymoron from Hes. *Op.* 7, where Zeus, who thunders, is described as seated aloft, where he "straightens the crooked" (ἰθύνει σκολιόν).

84. ῥυηφενίην: *hapax* in Callimachus, from ῥέω + ἄφενος, meaning "flowing wealth," perhaps in contrast to the dry landscape of Arcadia before Zeus's birth. The coinage is literally accurate for the Ptolemies, who depend on the wealth from the Nile flood. Cf. *hDem* 126n and Schmitt 165 (12.5.7).

85–88. Callimachus breaks with the hymnic tradition by introducing one specific monarch, Ptolemy, and the importation of this local king necessarily moves Zeus to Egypt. In his choice of language Callimachus now turns away from Hesiod to use an Egyptian formula for kingship—whatever the king thinks he accomplishes as soon as he conceives the thought (Stephens 2003: 112–13).

86. περιπρό "especially"; *hapax* at *Iliad* 11.180, of Agamemnon's prowess in battle.

87. The best Greek parallel for this sentiment is *HhHerm* 17–18, describing newborn Hermes. The more exact parallel is found in Egyptian royal inscriptions describing the powers of the pharaoh. Theocritus uses similar language in the *Encomium of Ptolemy* (17.13–15) of the deified Soter. Here the choice of language makes sense for a king who is also a pharaoh (Stephens 2003: 108–9), while parallels from *HhHerm* serve as a reminder that this king is also a younger brother.

89. πλειῶνι: in the Hellenistic poets, "period of a full year." It is first found in *Op.* 617, where the meaning is unclear; Callimachus' use may be an interpretation of the earlier text.

89–90. ἀπό ... ἐκόλουσας: tmesis over two lines; κολούω occurs in Homer (*Il.* 20.370; *Od.* 8.211, 11.340,), but the compound may be first in Callimachus.

90. The initially ambiguous αὐτός (= Zeus) immediately following lines about Ptolemy momentarily collapses the distinction between king and god.

ἄνην: previously only in Aesch. *Sept.* 713 and Alcman (*PMG* fr. 1.82–84: ἀλλὰ τᾶν [.]..., σιοί, | δέξασθε· [σι]ῶν γὰρ ἄνὰ | καὶ τέλος ("But receive... gods, for accomplishment and fulfillment are matters for the gods").

ἐνέκλασσας: from ἐγκλάω, variant of the Homeric *hapax*, ἐνικλάω (*Il.* 8.408), of Hera attempting to frustrate whatever Zeus devises. Callimachus may use it here as a gloss on Homeric κολούω, compounded in 89–90 (see Rengakos 1992: 40).

μενοινήν "desire"; first in Callimachus and Apollonius, then much imitated in Nonnus. The noun seems to be a Hellenistic coinage from the epic and lyric μενοινάω.

91–96. The envoi is both a traditional hymnic closing and one that stresses the wealth of the king whom the god favors. Compare the ending of *hDem* with its emphasis on the wealth of herds and crops.

91. χαῖρε μέγα: also at *hArt* 44 and 268, a variant of μέγα χαῖρε (*Od.* 24.402, *HhAp* 466), which Callimachus uses at *hDem* 2, 119.

πανυπέρτατε: previously, once in Homer (*Od.* 9.25), of Ithaca. The adjective was the subject of debate in the Homeric scholia: was the island "last in line" or "furthest west"? But at A.R. 1.1122 it refers to the "highest" trees. For Zeus (and for Ptolemy II) "last in line" would be appropriate as well as "highest."

δῶτορ ἐάων: the phrase occurs in Homer (*Il.* 8.335) and the Homeric hymns 18.12 (to Hermes) and 29.8 (of Hermes), and in Hesiod (*Th.* 46) of the gods.

ἐάων: irregular genitive plural of epic ἐΰς.

92. ἀπημονίης "freedom from harm"; *hapax*, an abstract counterpart of Homeric ἀπήμων.

ἔργματα: poetic variant of ἔργα found in lyric and tragedy; for ἔργματα in the context of song, see Pi. *Nem.* 4.6, 84.

93. ἀείσει: the construction κεν + future indicative is Homeric, though ἄν with the future occurs in later Greek as well (see Moorhouse 1946 for an analysis of this passage). For a similar question see *hAp* 31.

94. χαῖρε, πάτερ: this salutation for Zeus occurs in Aratus 15: χαῖρε, πάτερ, μέγα θαῦμα, μέγ' ἀνθρώποισιν ὄνειαρ ("Hail, Father, great marvel, great boon to humankind"). For Aratus, Zeus is the Stoic first cause, which may be behind Callimachus' choice of epithet here, but in Homer (*Od.* 18.122, 20.199) the salutation is used of Odysseus, and this again suggests a selection of intertexts that positions Ptolemy between gods and men.

ἄφενος is here treated as neuter accusative of an athematic declension; in contrast the genitive form ἀφένοιο (96) must derive from a masculine form of the thematic noun. The variants are as old as Hesiod (see *Op.* 24 with West's note ad loc.).

2

The Hymn to Apollo

T HE SECOND HYMN IN THIS COLLECTION IS MIMETIC. AS THE POEM OPENS, the anonymous speaker recreates the moment of the god's epiphany, describing a series of events for the chorus and reader: the god's approach marked by the shaking of the Delphic laurel, the shaking of the sanctuary itself, the nodding of the Delian palm, and the door bolts opening of their own volition. The speaker admonishes the sinful (2: ἀλιτρός) to be gone from the rite.

The initial section concludes with an instruction to the chorus of youths to make ready the song and dance in honor of the god. Lines 9–31 recap and expand the opening and provide examples of the power of Apollo's song as it quells the lamentations of two mothers (Thetis and Niobe); song even quells the sounds of the sea. Lines 25–31 link "my king" and Apollo, not in the context of kingship, as "our king" and Zeus are linked in *hZeus*, but in song. Next follows a physical description of the god (32–41), his areas of oversight, a number of his cult titles, and selected moments that trace his life from a child to a married adult (see Calame 1993: 40–43). In narrative order we learn of his apprenticeship to Admetus as a young god (47–54), his building of the horned altar on Delos shortly after his birth with the help of his sister (55–64), his role in the colonization of Cyrene (65–90), his marriage to Cyrene (90–96), and finally his slaying of Pytho at Delphi as a young boy (97–106). Lines 65–96 of the hymn describe the leading out of colonists at Apollo's instruction, the foundation of Cyrene, and the first celebration of the *Carneia* at Cyrene, as observed by Apollo and his "bride" the eponymous nymph Cyrene.

The hymn concludes with an exchange between Apollo and Phthonos ("Envy") about the kind of poetry the god prefers, couched as an evaluation of various types of waters: the sea, the Assyrian river, and drops from pure springs. This famous *sphragis* has been understood, like the *Aetia* prologue, as a literary manifesto—pure drops of water equate to small, perfect poems, which are better than the sea or the Assyrian river. The river seems to equate with longer poems that necessarily have flaws because of their vastness, just as the river carries impurities upon its surface. The third body of water in the comparisons is the sea, which Phthonos proposes as his preferred poetic model, even though the sea had previously silenced itself before hymns to Apollo (18). Williams (pp. 87–89) makes the case that the sea must be understood as Homer, and this identification makes sense since Apollo does not directly reject the sea, but alters the terms of comparison to pure springs and the Assyrian river. But to what the Assyrian river refers and who Phthonos and Momos (113) might be has led to considerable debate. The scholium maintains that the latter are Callimachus' contemporaries who mock him for not writing a long poem, but Phthonos might also represent Apollo's own potential ill-will, so that the concluding lines of the hymn function appropriately as a prayer that the god receive the rite favorably. No definitive answer is possible, but it is important to note that the opposition of the sea versus pure fountains also has parallels in cultic language and that models of pollution and purity return us to the poem's opening where those who are not "without sin" are banished from Apollo's presence (Petrovic 2011: 273–75). Cheshire 2008: 354–55n2 reviews the scholarship on this passage.

A central question in this hymn, as in the other mimetic hymns, is "who speaks?" Is the unidentified narrator the "singer" of the whole hymn, or are we to imagine the chorus of youths singing the middle section as a paean to Apollo (see Bing 2009: 33–48, Cheshire 2008)? The paean was a class of hymns usually addressed to Apollo or Asclepius for the well-being of a city or some constituent group and characterized by the ritual cry ἱή, ἱή, παιῆον (21, 97, 103); normally it was sung and danced by a young male chorus (Furley and Bremmer 2001: 1.90–91). The hymn's narrative includes both the foundation of the city and the celebration of Apollo's festival, and among his *aretai* there is a stress on healing (41–42, 45–46). Even the *sphragis*, which is an unusual feature of hymns in general, has parallels in Hellenistic and later paeans (Petrovic 2011: 279–81).

The Deity and His Relevant Cults

Apollo is among the most widely worshipped deities of the Greek pantheon, and in this hymn Callimachus focuses on three of his cult-sites—Delos and Delphi, which are the most important and already linked in the *Homeric Hymn to Apollo*, and Cyrene, Callimachus' native city. He devotes the longest narrative unit to Cyrene and Apollo *Carneius* (65–95). The narrator's stress on "my king" and his statement in 71 that "I call you *Carneius*; thus is my ancestral custom" suggests prima facie that the hymn is for Cyrene and the opening address to the chorus is in reference to a contemporary celebration of the *Carneia*, also in Cyrene. Apollo was the patron deity of the city, with a large, central temple. His sister Artemis had a nearby temple, and on its altar was a relief depicting the slaying of Niobe's children (Bonacasa and Ensoli 2000: 189). Thus the reference to the punishment of Niobe could recall the local monument, just as Mt. Myrtussa and the pure springs of Deo recall local geography.

However, the presence of Delphic laurel (1) and the nodding Delian palm (4) as the hymn opens have made commentators reluctant to identify the *mise en scène* as Cyrene, although explanations for both have often been suggested (e.g., Maass 1890: 403, on which cf. Williams ad loc.). The practice of transplanting shoots from the supposedly original Delphic laurel was widespread, and one might easily have been planted in Cyrene (an analogue for this occurs in the *Branchus* [fr. 229 Pf.], where Apollo himself transplants a laurel shoot from Delphi at his shrine in Mitylene). The Delian palm actually had a specific local presence: apparently a bronze replica stood in an *exhedra* before the temple of Apollo and the nearby Letoion at Cyrene (Bonacasa and Ensoli 2000: 107). Further, Callimachus' description of Apollo (32–34) coincides with features of a colossal cult statue of Apollo that actually belonged to his temple in Cyrene. That statue, now housed in the British Museum, is thought to be a Roman copy of an earlier Hellenistic work belonging probably to the late second century BCE. Obviously even this earlier Hellenistic statue would not have been known to Callimachus, but the coincidence of this statue's details with the description of Apollo in this poem suggests that this Hellenistic work had preserved elements of an even earlier statue. Apollo is androgynous with long curls, wearing a full cloak-like garment draped just below his genitals but fastened at the shoulder, very elaborate sandals, and leaning on a lyre. His quiver is next to the lyre and around it is entwined the Delphic snake, which has a ready hymnic parallel in Callimachus' final excursus on the slaying of the Pytho. The type is known from elsewhere as well (Higgs 1994); the Apollo Belvedere, for example, which is thought to have been a marble copy of a bronze by Leochares *c*.325 BCE, possesses the same features, though the style is more classical.

Delos is featured in lines 55–64, where Apollo builds a horned altar. The altar was a central tourist attraction on the island, mentioned in the *Odyssey* (6.162–65) and occasionally listed among the seven wonders of the ancient world (Plutarch, *De soll. anim.* 983E). It was said to have been constructed with horns taken from the right side of goats' heads and held together entirely without glue or mortar.

In Callimachus the vignette gives us Apollo's first effort in building as a prelude to the foundation of Cyrene. Delphi is the location of the final vignette, where Apollo as a child slew the Pytho. This provides an *aition* for the paean cry and, like the story of Niobe, is another mythological example of Apollo's swift punishment of his enemies. The poem comes full circle in the final lines with their verbal echoes of the opening.

Sources and Intertexts

The *Homeric Hymn to Apollo* provides a model of sorts for this hymn as well as for *hArt* and *hDelos*. The Homeric hymn fell into a Delian and a Pythian section, which Callimachus reprises in two brief vignettes (respectively, 55–64, 97–104): the lengthy narrative of the slaying of the Pytho in the earlier hymn (300–74) is condensed to eight lines, while the sailors at the end of the Pythian section who sing a paean at Apollo's behest (514–19) may have influenced the choice of paean for this hymn. Also, Bing (2009: 41–43) has argued that the ventriloquism of the Delian maidens in the Homeric hymn (162–64) influenced Callimachus' experimentation with narrative voices in *hAp*. Williams (on 61: βωμόν) makes the attractive suggestion that Callimachus may have included the description of the horned altar of Delos because in the *Certamen* it was the location where "Homer" recited his hymn to Apollo.[1] Other important influences were Pindar's Cyrenean odes, particularly *Py.* 5.54–93, with its description of the foundation of the city (on which see Morrison 2007: 131–33), and *Py.* 9, with its narrative of Apollo's courtship of Cyrene. Finally, the closest parallel to the *sphragis* is the end of Timotheus' *Persae* (202-40), in which Timotheus appeals to Apollo to protect him against the Spartans' accusation that he offended the older Muse (παλαιοτέραν...Μοῦσαν: 211–12) with his innovative poetry. Ancient anecdotes related that the Spartan ephors objected to Timotheus' use of a lyre with more than the usual number of strings during his performance at the Spartan *Carneia* (see Hordern 2002: 7–9 and notes on 202–36), which may also have been relevant for Callimachus, whose own paean seems to be an innovation putatively for the Cyrenean *Carneia*.

The Ptolemaic Connections

See the discussion above, pp. 18–19.

---

1. On the *Certamen* see West 2003: 297–300 and 350–51, and cf. fr. 357 M-W.

ΕΙΣ ΑΠΟΛΛΩΝΑ

Οἷον ὁ τὠπόλλωνος ἐσείσατο δάφνινος ὅρπηξ,
οἷα δ' ὅλον τὸ μέλαθρον· ἑκὰς ἑκὰς ὅστις ἀλιτρός.
καὶ δή που τὰ θύρετρα καλῷ ποδὶ Φοῖβος ἀράσσει·
οὐχ ὁράᾳς; ἐπένευσεν ὁ Δήλιος ἡδύ τι φοῖνιξ
5   ἐξαπίνης, ὁ δὲ κύκνος ἐν ἠέρι καλὸν ἀείδει.
αὐτοὶ νῦν κατοχῆες ἀνακλίνασθε πυλάων,
αὐταὶ δὲ κληῖδες· ὁ γὰρ θεὸς οὐκέτι μακρήν·
οἱ δὲ νέοι μολπήν τε καὶ ἐς χορὸν ἐντύνασθε.
ὡπόλλων οὐ παντὶ φαείνεται, ἀλλ' ὅτις ἐσθλός·
10   ὅς μιν ἴδῃ, μέγας οὗτος, ὃς οὐκ ἴδε, λιτὸς ἐκεῖνος.
ὀψόμεθ', ὦ Ἑκάεργε, καὶ ἐσσόμεθ' οὔποτε λιτοί.
μήτε σιωπηλὴν κίθαριν μήτ' ἄψοφον ἴχνος
τοῦ Φοίβου τοὺς παῖδας ἔχειν ἐπιδημήσαντος,
εἰ τελέειν μέλλουσι γάμον πολιήν τε κερεῖσθαι,
15   ἑστήξειν δὲ τὸ τεῖχος ἐπ' ἀρχαίοισι θεμέθλοις.
ἠγασάμην τοὺς παῖδας, ἐπεὶ χέλυς οὐκέτ' ἀεργός.
εὐφημεῖτ' ἀΐοντες ἐπ' Ἀπόλλωνος ἀοιδῇ.
εὐφημεῖ καὶ πόντος, ὅτε κλείουσιν ἀοιδοί
ἢ κίθαριν ἢ τόξα, Λυκωρέος ἔντεα Φοίβου.
20   οὐδὲ Θέτις Ἀχιλῆα κινύρεται αἴλινα μήτηρ,
ὁππόθ' ἰὴ παιῆον ἰὴ παιῆον ἀκούσῃ.
καὶ μὲν ὁ δακρυόεις ἀναβάλλεται ἄλγεα πέτρος,
ὅστις ἐνὶ Φρυγίῃ διερὸς λίθος ἐστήρικται,
μάρμαρον ἀντὶ γυναικὸς ὀϊζυρόν τι χανούσης.
25   ἰὴ ἰὴ φθέγγεσθε· κακὸν μακάρεσσιν ἐρίζειν.
ὃς μάχεται μακάρεσσιν, ἐμῷ βασιλῆι μάχοιτο·
ὅστις ἐμῷ βασιλῆι, καὶ Ἀπόλλωνι μάχοιτο.
τὸν χορὸν ὡπόλλων, ὅ τι οἱ κατὰ θυμὸν ἀείδει,
τιμήσει· δύναται γάρ, ἐπεὶ Διὶ δεξιὸς ἧσται.
30   οὐδ' ὁ χορὸς τὸν Φοῖβον ἐφ' ἓν μόνον ἦμαρ ἀείσει,
ἔστι γὰρ εὔυμνος· τίς ἂν οὐ ῥέα Φοῖβον ἀείδοι;
χρύσεα τὠπόλλωνι τό τ' ἐνδυτὸν ἥ τ' ἐπιπορπίς
ἥ τε λύρη τό τ' ἄεμμα τὸ Λύκτιον ἥ τε φαρέτρη,
χρύσεα καὶ τὰ πέδιλα· πολύχρυσος γὰρ Ἀπόλλων

---

1 δάφνινος **Ψ**: δαφνικος *Diegesis*   2 οἷα δ' Lasc.:]ον^(αδ)ολον POxy 2258: οἶο δ' **Ψ**: οἷον Valckenaer
5 ὁ δὲ **Ψ**: οτε POxy 2258   6 ἀνακλίνασθε sch. Theoc.: ἀνακλίνεσθε **Ψ**   πυλάων **Ψ**: θυράων POxy
2258, sch. Theoc.   7 ὁ γὰρ **Ψ**: επει POxy 2258   8]ντυνασθε POxy 2258: ἐντύνεσθε **Ψ**   10 ἴδῃ **Ψ**:
]δεν POxy 2258, ἴδεν Blomfield   31]ισαν, ουρεα divisit POxy 2258: ἀν' οὔρεα **Ψ** (οὐ ῥέα divisit **T**
in marg.)

35 καὶ πουλυκτέανος· Πυθῶνί κε τεκμήραιο.
   καὶ μὲν ἀεὶ καλὸς καὶ ἀεὶ νέος· οὔποτε Φοίβου
   θηλείαις οὐδ᾽ ὅσσον ἐπὶ χνόος ἦλθε παρειαῖς,
   αἱ δὲ κόμαι θυόεντα πέδῳ λείβουσιν ἔλαια·
   οὐ λίπος Ἀπόλλωνος ἀποστάζουσιν ἔθειραι,
40 ἀλλ᾽ αὐτὴν πανάκειαν· ἐν ἄστεϊ δ᾽ ᾧ κεν ἐκεῖναι
   πρῶκες ἔραζε πέσωσιν, ἀκήρια πάντ᾽ ἐγένοντο.
      τέχνῃ δ᾽ ἀμφιλαφὴς οὔτις τόσον ὅσσον Ἀπόλλων·
   κεῖνος ὀϊστευτὴν ἔλαχ᾽ ἀνέρα, κεῖνος ἀοιδόν
   (Φοίβῳ γὰρ καὶ τόξον ἐπιτρέπεται καὶ ἀοιδή),
45 κείνου δὲ θριαὶ καὶ μάντιες· ἐκ δέ νυ Φοίβου
   ἰητροὶ δεδάασιν ἀνάβλησιν θανάτοιο.
      Φοῖβον καὶ Νόμιον κικλήσκομεν ἐξέτι κείνου,
   ἐξότ᾽ ἐπ᾽ Ἀμφρυσσῷ ζευγίτιδας ἔτρεφεν ἵππους
   ἠιθέου ὑπ᾽ ἔρωτι κεκαυμένος Ἀδμήτοιο.
50 ῥεῖά κε βουβόσιον τελέθοι πλέον, οὐδέ κεν αἶγες
   δεύοιντο βρεφέων ἐπιμηλάδες, ᾗσιν Ἀπόλλων
   βοσκομένῃσ᾽ ὀφθαλμὸν ἐπήγαγεν· οὐδ᾽ ἀγάλακτες
   οἴιες οὐδ᾽ ἄκυθοι, πᾶσαι δέ κεν εἶεν ὕπαρνοι,
   ἡ δέ κε μουνοτόκος διδυμητόκος αἶψα γένοιτο.
55 Φοίβῳ δ᾽ ἑσπόμενοι πόλιας διεμετρήσαντο
   ἄνθρωποι· Φοῖβος γὰρ ἀεὶ πολίεσσι φιληδεῖ
   κτιζομένῃσ᾽, αὐτὸς δὲ θεμείλια Φοῖβος ὑφαίνει.
   τετραέτης τὰ πρῶτα θεμείλια Φοῖβος ἔπηξε
   καλῇ ἐν Ὀρτυγίῃ περιηγέος ἐγγύθι λίμνης.
60 Ἄρτεμις ἀγρώσσουσα καρήατα συνεχὲς αἰγῶν
   Κυνθιάδων φορέεσκεν, ὁ δ᾽ ἔπλεκε βωμὸν Ἀπόλλων,
   δείματο μὲν κεράεσσιν ἐδέθλια, πῆξε δὲ βωμόν
   ἐκ κεράων, κεραοὺς δὲ πέριξ ὑπεβάλλετο τοίχους.
   ὧδ᾽ ἔμαθεν τὰ πρῶτα θεμείλια Φοῖβος ἐγείρειν.
65 Φοῖβος καὶ βαθύγειον ἐμὴν πόλιν ἔφρασε Βάττῳ
   καὶ Λιβύην ἐσιόντι κόραξ ἡγήσατο λαῷ,
   δεξιὸς οἰκιστῆρι, καὶ ὤμοσε τείχεα δώσειν
   ἡμετέροις βασιλεῦσιν· ἀεὶ δ᾽ εὔορκος Ἀπόλλων.
   ὤπολλον, πολλοί σε Βοηδρόμιον καλέουσι,

---

35 καιπου[POxy 2258: καί τε πολυκτέανος Ψ 36 καιμεν POxy 2258: καί κεν Ψ 54 διδυμητόκος anon. ap. L. van Santen: διδυμοτόκος Ψ: διδυματόκος H. Stephanus, Asper 60 καρήατα Ψ: κεράατα PAnt 67 οἰκιστῆρι Bentley: οἰκιστήρ Ψ

70   πολλοὶ δὲ Κλάριον, πάντη δέ τοι οὔνομα πουλύ·
        αὐτὰρ ἐγὼ Καρνεῖον· ἐμοὶ πατρώϊον οὕτω.
        Σπάρτη τοι, Καρνεῖε, τόδε πρώτιστον ἔδεθλον,
        δεύτερον αὖ Θήρη, τρίτατόν γε μὲν ἄστυ Κυρήνης.
        ἐκ μέν σε Σπάρτης ἕκτον γένος Οἰδιπόδαο
75   ἤγαγε Θηραίην ἐς ἀπόκτισιν· ἐκ δέ σε Θήρης
        οὖλος Ἀριστοτέλης Ἀσβυστίδι πάρθετο γαίη,
        δεῖμε δέ τοι μάλα καλὸν ἀνάκτορον, ἐν δὲ πόληι
        θῆκε τελεσφορίην ἐπετήσιον, ᾗ ἔνι πολλοί
        ὑστάτιον πίπτουσιν ἐπ' ἰσχίον, ὦ ἄνα, ταῦροι.
80   ἰὴ ἰὴ Καρνεῖε πολύλλιτε, σεῖο δὲ βωμοί
        ἄνθεα μὲν φορέουσιν ἐν εἴαρι τόσσα περ Ὧραι
        ποικίλ' ἀγινεῦσι ζεφύρου πνείοντος ἐέρσην,
        χείματι δὲ κρόκον ἡδύν· ἀεὶ δέ τοι ἀέναον πῦρ,
        οὐδέ ποτε χθιζὸν περιβόσκεται ἄνθρακα τέφρη.
85   ἦ ῥ' ἐχάρη μέγα Φοῖβος, ὅτε ζωστῆρες Ἐνυοῦς
        ἀνέρες ὠρχήσαντο μετὰ ξανθῇσι Λιβύσσης,
        τέθμιαι εὖτέ σφιν Καρνειάδες ἤλυθον ὧραι.
        οἱ δ' οὔπω πηγῇσι Κύρης ἐδύναντο πελάσσαι
        Δωριέες, πυκινὴν δὲ νάπησ' Ἄζιλιν ἔναιον.
90   τοὺς μὲν ἄναξ ἴδεν αὐτός, ἑῇ δ' ἐπεδείξατο νύμφῃ
        στὰς ἐπὶ Μυρτούσσης κερατώδεος, ἧχι λέοντα
        Ὑψηὶς κατέπεφνε βοῶν σίνιν Εὐρυπύλοιο.
        οὐ κείνου χορὸν εἶδε θεώτερον ἄλλον Ἀπόλλων,
        οὐδὲ πόλει τόσ' ἔνειμεν ὀφέλσιμα, τόσσα Κυρήνῃ,
95   μνωόμενος προτέρης ἁρπακτύος. οὐδὲ μὲν αὐτοί
        Βαττιάδαι Φοίβοιο πλέον θεὸν ἄλλον ἔτισαν.
            ἰὴ ἰὴ παιῆον ἀκούομεν, οὕνεκα τοῦτο
        Δελφός τοι πρώτιστον ἐφύμνιον εὕρετο λαός,
        ἦμος ἑκηβολίην χρυσέων ἐπεδείκνυσο τόξων.
100   Πυθώ τοι κατιόντι συνήντετο δαιμόνιος θήρ,
        αἰνὸς ὄφις. τὸν μὲν σὺ κατήναρες ἄλλον ἐπ' ἄλλῳ
        βάλλων ὠκὺν ὀϊστόν, ἐπηΰτησε δὲ λαός·
        'ἰὴ ἰὴ παιῆον, ἵει βέλος, εὐθύ σε μήτηρ
        γείνατ' ἀοσσητῆρα· τὸ δ' ἐξέτι κεῖθεν ἀείδη.
105   ὁ Φθόνος Ἀπόλλωνος ἐπ' οὔατα λάθριος εἶπεν·
        'οὐκ ἄγαμαι τὸν ἀοιδὸν ὃς οὐδ' ὅσα πόντος ἀείδει.'
        τὸν Φθόνον ὡπόλλων ποδί τ' ἤλασεν ὧδέ τ' ἔειπεν·

72 τόδε Ψ: τό γε Ernesti: πολύ Meineke: τίθει vel δέμε Kuiper: πόρε Williams   80 πολύλ(λ)ιτε Lasc.
η: πολύλλιστε Ψ   88 πηγῇσι Κύρης Schneider: πηγῆς κυρῆς Ψ: πηγαῖσι Κυρήνης sch. Pi.   91 ἧχι
Ψ: ἔνθα sch. Pi.   94 ἔνειμεν Lasc.: ἔδειμεν Ψ, Williams

Ἀσσυρίου ποταμοῖο μέγας ῥόος, ἀλλὰ τὰ πολλά
λύματα γῆς καὶ πολλὸν ἐφ' ὕδατι συρφετὸν ἕλκει.
110 Δηοῖ δ' οὐκ ἀπὸ παντὸς ὕδωρ φορέουσι μέλισσαι,
ἀλλ' ἥτις καθαρή τε καὶ ἀχράαντος ἀνέρπει
πίδακος ἐξ ἱερῆς ὀλίγη λιβὰς ἄκρον ἄωτον.'
  χαῖρε, ἄναξ· ὁ δὲ Μῶμος, ἵν' ὁ Φθόνος, ἔνθα νέοιτο.

113 φθόνος **I**, ed. Aldina, sch. Greg. Naz.: φθόρος **Ψ**

To Apollo

How Apollo's laurel branch shakes! How the whole edifice shakes! Begone, begone, whoever is sinful! It surely must be Apollo kicking at the doors with his fair foot. Do you not see? The Delian palm gently nodded its head, (5) of a sudden, and the swan sings beautifully in the air. Now you door-fastenings open of your own accord, and you bolts! The god is no longer far away. Young men, make ready for the song and the dance.

Apollo does not shine upon everyone, but upon whoever is good. (10) Whoever sees him, this man is great; whoever does not see him, he is of no account. We shall see you, O One Who Acts From Afar, and we shall never be of no account. The young men should not keep the cithara silent or the dance step noiseless when Apollo is present, if they are going to celebrate a marriage, or live long enough to dedicate a lock of gray hair, (15) and if the city is to remain firm upon its ancestral foundations. I do admire the boys, seeing as the tortoise shell is no longer idle.

Be silent while you listen to the song for Apollo. The sea too is silent when the singers celebrate either the cithara or the bow, the implements of Lycoreian Apollo. (20) Nor does Thetis, his mother, mourn for Achilles, whenever she hears the paean cry. And the weeping rock postpones its grief, the moist stone that is fixed in Phrygia, a marble rock in place of a woman uttering some lament. (25) Give the ritual cry (*hie, hie*). It is a bad thing to quarrel with the Blessed Ones. Whoever quarrels with the Blessed Ones, let him quarrel with my king. Whoever quarrels with my king let him quarrel with Apollo. The chorus that sings what is pleasing to his heart, Apollo will honor. He is able to do this because he sits at the right hand of Zeus. (30) Nor will the chorus hymn Phoebus for one day only, since he is a copious subject for song. Who would not readily sing of Apollo?

Apollo's garment is golden, and his cloak fastening, and his lyre, and his Lyctian bow and quiver. His sandals too are golden; Apollo is rich in gold (35) and rich in flocks. You would find proof of this in Pytho [i.e., Delphi]. And indeed he is ever fair and ever young. Never so much as a beard has come to Phoebus' tender cheeks. His hair drips fragrant oils upon the ground. Apollo's hair does not drip the oils of fat, (40) but the essence of healing. And in whatever town those drops might fall to the ground, everything is free from harm.

No one has as many skills as Apollo. That one has received the archer as his lot, and the singer (45) (for to Apollo is entrusted the bow and song), and his are diviners and prophets. And from Phoebus doctors have learned the postponement of death. Phoebus we also call *Nomios* from the time when, by the Amphryssus, he tended the yoked mares, burning with passion for the youth Admetus. (50) Effortlessly would the herd increase, and the nanny goats pastured with the sheep would not lack young, if Apollo cast his eyes upon them while they were grazing. The ewes would not lack milk, nor were they barren, but all would have lambs beneath them. And whoever was the mother of one offspring would soon produce twins.

(55) Men lay out the foundations of cities following Phoebus. For Phoebus always takes pleasure in cities being built, and Phoebus himself weaves together foundations. Phoebus was four years old when he first fitted together foundations in fair Ortygia near the round lake. (60) Hunting continually, Artemis brought him the heads of Cynthian goats, and Apollo wove an altar; he constructed the foundations with horns, and fitted the altar from horns, and he built up walls of horn around it. In this way Phoebus first learned to raise foundations.

(65) Phoebus also instructed Battus about my city with its fertile soil, and as a raven—an auspicious omen for the founder—he led the people entering Libya and swore to give walls to our kings. Apollo always honors his oaths. O Apollo, many call you *Boedromios*, (70) many *Clarius*, and indeed everywhere many a name is yours. But I call you *Carneius*, for thus is my ancestral custom. Sparta, indeed, this was your first shrine, Carneian, then Thera was second, and third was the city of Cyrene; from Sparta the sixth generation from Oedipus (75) led you to their colony at Thera; from Thera baneful Aristoteles established you in the Asbystian land, built you a very beautiful shrine, and established a yearly festival in the city, at which many bulls fall upon their haunches for the last time, O Lord. (80) *Hie, hie*, Carneian, you of many prayers, your altars wear as many colorful flowers in the spring as the Hours gather when Zephyr breathes out his dew, but in winter the sweet saffron. Always your fire is everlasting, and never do ashes feed around yesterday's coal. (85) Indeed Phoebus greatly rejoiced when the men girt for War danced with the fair-haired Libyan women, when the appointed time for the *Carneia* came for them. But the Dorians were as yet unable to draw near to the streams of Cyre, but lived in thickly wooded Azilis. (90) These did the god himself see, and he showed his bride, standing upon horned Myrtussa, where the daughter of Hypseus killed the lion that was the plunderer of Eurypylus' cattle. Apollo has seen no other dance more divine, nor to a city has he allotted so much good fortune as he allotted Cyrene, (95) mindful of his earlier carrying off of the nymph. And the descendants of Battus do not worship another god more than Phoebus.

We hear *hie, hie, paiêon*, because the people of Delphi first devised this refrain, when you demonstrated the launching of your golden weapons. (100) When you were going down to Pytho a demonic beast met you, a dire serpent. You slew him, shooting one swift arrow after another, and the people cried: "*hie, hie paiêon*, shoot your arrow, a savior from the time when your mother gave birth to you." And from that point you are hymned in this way.

(105) Envy spoke secretly into Phoebus' ear: "I do not admire the singer who does not sing even as much as the sea." Phoebus pushed Envy off with his foot and spoke the following: "The flow of the Assyrian river is vast, but it draws along much refuse from the land and much garbage on its waters. (110) Not from any sources do bees carry water to Demeter, but from what comes up pure and undefiled from a holy fountain, a small drop, the choicest of waters."

Hail, Lord. But Blame, let him go where Envy is.

Commentary

1. The scene is outside of Apollo's temple; the narrator is addressing a chorus of young men in breathless anticipation of the god's epiphany. Probably the epiphany is that of the cult statue, though described as if the divinity himself were arriving. Artemidorus 2.35 remarks that "whether the gods appear in the flesh (σάρκινοι) or as a statue made of wood, they have the same force." Callimachus also collapses the actual goddess and the cult statue at the opening of *hAth*.

οἷον: The neuter is exclamatory; it is varied in 2 as οἷα (and see 3n).

τὠπόλλωνος = τοῦ Ἀπόλλωνος. Crasis with the god's name occurs three other times in the hymn (lines 9, 28, 107: ὡπόλλων).

ἐσείσατο: this aorist middle of σείω occurs once only in Homer (*Il.* 8.199, of Hera, shuddering at Hector's boasts). By shifting the subject from a person to a sapling Callimachus conveys the spontaneous action of nature in response to the god. A parallel shift occurs with ἐπένευσεν (4): normally used of a god "nodding assent," its subject here is the Delian palm.

δάφνινος: the adjective ("made of bay," i.e., laurel) is not found elsewhere in poetry, but frequent in medical writing, where laurel is mentioned for its therapeutic properties; here it anticipates Apollo's healing powers (see 40). The laurel was Apollo's sacred tree at Delphi, as was the palm at Delos (4).

ὄρπηξ: a "sapling" or "offshoot" suggests a living tree, not a cut branch. For a discussion of the presence of these trees at the opening of the hymn see p. 74.

2. The speaker commands that those marked by sin or stain (ἀλιτρός) be gone from the rite. Purity regulations banning those who were unholy in some way are common in Greek temples, see Petrovic 2011 and Petrovic 2007: 154–61 for parallels to this language in other Greek sources on divine epiphany. Throughout, the hymn exploits both the punitive and the beneficent aspects of Apollo (Bassi 1989).

ἑκὰς ἑκάς: *sc.* ἔστω. Imitated by Virg. *Aen.* 6.258: *procul, o procul este, profani*. For the ritual repetition see *hAth* 1–2: ἔξιτε, 4: σοῦσθε.

ἀλιτρός: familiar from Homer and archaic poetry. Callimachus uses the word in the *Aetia* (fr. 75.68 Pf.) for the hubris of the Telchines, and at fr. 85.14 Pf. a god with the cult title of *Epopsios* cannot look upon the sinful (ἀλιτρούς). At the end of the poem, Phthonos and Momos, because of their preference for waters that are impure, become examples of ἀλιτροί banished by the god himself.

3. καὶ δή που: this associated string of particles is very rare (Denniston 268). The speech of Justice in Aratus 123–26 opens with οἵην (123) and 125 begins with καὶ δή που, thus parallel to the opening of lines 1 and 3 of this hymn. In Aratus Justice berates men for their wickedness and leaves their presence, claiming that they will not see her again; similarly in Callimachus the wicked will not see Apollo. Callimachus praises Aratus in *ep.* 24 Pf., which suggests that

Callimachus is imitating Aratus rather than the reverse. See also *hZeus* nn18–32, 41, 48–49, 94.

τὰ θύρετρα: only once in Homer with the definite article (*Od.* 18.385), in a passage that also suggests sudden arrival combined with punishment for malefactors: Odysseus in disguise tells Eurymachus that if Odysseus were suddenly to return, the doors would be too narrow for their flight.

καλῷ ποδί: the image returns in the *sphragis* where Apollo spurns Phthonos with his foot (107). The reference to Apollo's "fair foot" is likely to have both poetological and metrical implications (see Bassi 1989: 228–31). καλῷ ποδί may also refer to Apollo and dance; he dances in *HhAp* 514–16, and the chorus of youths is exhorted to dance below (12–13; Cheshire 2008: 363). For the scansion (κᾰλῷ) see *hZeus* 55n.

4. ἐπένευσεν: see 1n.

ὁ Δήλιος … φοῖνιξ: the Delian palm plays a role in Apollo's birth (*e.g.*, *HhAp* 117, *hDelos* 210). As Williams observes ad loc., the shape of the line creates an expectation that it is the divinity who nods, and the first syllable (φοῖ) maintains the fiction; only -νιξ makes it clear that it is in fact the palm tree.

5. Swans are always connected to song in Callimachus, and specifically with the moment of Apollo's birth in *hDelos* 249–54 and in the opening of the shorter *Homeric Hymn to Apollo* (21.1): Φοῖβε, σὲ μὲν καὶ κύκνος ὑπὸ πτερύγων λίγ' ἀείδει ("Phoebus, you even the swan hymns clearly from its wings").

ἠέρι: Homeric form of the dative (from ἀήρ).

καλὸν ἀείδει: similar phrases occur five times in Homer, each heavily weighted (*Il.* 1.473: καλὸν ἀείδοντες παιήονα κοῦροι Ἀχαιῶν; 18.570: λίνον δ' ὑπὸ καλὸν ἄειδε; *Od.* 1.155 of Phemius; 8.266 of Demodocus; 19.519 of the nightingale).

6. αὐτοί = αὐτόματοι. Repetition of the intensive pronouns αὐτοί, αὐταί emphasizes the spontaneity of the door opening as the divinity approaches and contributes a heightened sense of expectation. The standard study of this phenomenon is Weinreich 1929.

κατοχῆες: probably a Callimachean coinage on the model of Homeric ὀχεύς (see Schmitt 52n13), and with a similar meaning, "door bolts."

ἀνακλίνασθε: the nature of the action would seem to require the aorist middle imperative rather than the present of the mss. (also with ἐντύνασθε below).

πυλάων: the reading of the medieval mss. The variant θυράων is earlier, found in POxy 2258 and a scholium to Theocritus. The choice is ostensibly between "gates" or "doors" of the temple, though Williams ad loc. provides good evidence that πυλάων might refer to the more substantial doors of a temple as well.

7. κληῖδες: in Homer the singular of κλείς is usual to describe this mechanism: the hooks that pass through the door to catch the strap holding the bolts (LSJ I 2). Cf. *hDem* 44.

8. οἱ δὲ νέοι μολπήν τε καὶ ἐς χορὸν ἐντύνασθε: direct address to the young men of the chorus. The preposition should be taken in common with both μολπήν and χορόν.

μολπήν: in epic and tragedy, a "lyric song," thus appropriate to designate a paean. Cf. *Il.* 1.472–74: οἳ δὲ πανημέριοι μολπῇ θεὸν ἱλάσκοντο | καλὸν ἀείδοντες παιήονα κοῦροι Ἀχαιῶν | μέλποντες ἑκάεργον ("During the whole day the sons of the Achaeans appeased the god with song, singing a fair paean, hymning the far-working god [sc. Apollo]").

9–11. These lines, arranged chiastically, repeat and condense the thought of the opening eight lines. The sequence οὐχ ὁράᾳς (4), ὅς μιν ἴδῃ (10) culminates in ὀψόμεθ(α) (11). The speaker and the chorus will see the god, since they are without sin. This statement prepares for Apollo's epiphany at the end of the poem, where he spurns Envy in support of Callimachus. Whom the god loves—cities, kings, poets—prosper. Others do not.

9. φαείνεται: a poetic variant of φαίνω; Homer uses the active of φαείνω for the sun shining (e.g., *Od.* 3.2), and for the middle used actively see, e.g., Aratus 619, 713 (so Williams ad loc.). "Shine" is appropriate for Apollo, but the following ἴδῃ also requires that "appear" be implicit.

10. ὅς μιν ἴδῃ: the conditional relative in a generalizing clause occurs without ἄν in Homer and occasionally in lyric (see Smyth §2567b).

λιτός "insignificant"; a prose word, meaning "simple," "frugal," and of persons, "poor."

11. Ancient commentators derive Apollo's epithet, Ἑκάεργε ("Far-worker"), either from his prowess as an archer, shooting arrows from afar (ἑκάς), or to the fact that as the sun god his life-giving rays work from afar. Callimachus exploits both meanings as the hymn continues: Apollo is the god of abundant nature (47–54) and the slayer of the Delphic Pytho with his arrows (97–104).

12–16. The choral performance by young boys, whom the unnamed narrator enjoins to sing and dance, is appropriately on behalf of the city's well-being. The presence and benefaction of Apollo, encouraged by the choral song, will lead to their accomplishment of marriage and a long life, as well as the continued prosperity of the city.

12–13. The infinitive with accusative subject, μήτε… | …τοὺς παῖδας ἔχειν, expresses a wish for the future, a construction confined to poetry (Goodwin, *MT* §785). The word order surrounds the chorus (τοὺς παῖδας) with the god's presence (τοῦ Φοίβου… ἐπιδημήσαντος).

12. σιωπηλήν: also at *hDelos* 302. The adjective occurs in earlier poetry only at Eur. *Med.* 320, though common in later prose.

ἄψοφον ἴχνος: both words occur in tragedy, though ἄψοφος is rare. Eur. *Troad.* 887–88 provides a particularly interesting parallel: Hecuba claims that Zeus, whether he is Necessity or a projection of the human mind, directs all mortal affairs towards justice "on a silent path" (δι' ἀψόφου...κελεύθου), a phrase that later comes to be quoted in philosophical writings. Although the meaning is different—ἄψοφον ἴχνος must mean "silent footstep"—the intertext, if it is one, would fitly link song and dance with just behavior and divine punishment, which is the theme of the hymn's opening.

13. ἐπιδημήσαντος: the aorist describes an act prior to the boys' singing. According to the scholiast, when the god is within his shrine (ἐπιδημεῖν), the prophecies are true, when he is away (ἀποδημεῖν), the prophecies are false.

14. πολιήν (*sc.* κόμην): the grey hair of old age.

κερεῖσθαι: the future of κείρω is frequent in poetry for cutting hair as either a dedication or in mourning. The latter is a common theme in epigram (see Williams ad loc. for examples). Here the trope reverses expectation: instead of mourning, dedicating one's grey hair indicates that one has led a long life.

15. ἑστήξειν: the intransitive future perfect infinitive of ἵστημι with a simple future sense.

τὸ τεῖχος (*sc.* μέλλει): either the city wall, or more likely synecdoche for the city itself.

ἐπ' ἀρχαίοισι θεμέθλοις: an allusion to Pi. *Py.* 4.14–16, where the foundation of Cyrene is described as Ἐπάφοιο κόραν | ἀστέων ῥίζαν φυτεύσεσθαι μελησιμβρότων | Διὸς ἐν Ἄμμωνος θεμέθλοις ("the daughter of Epaphus [= Libya] will be planted with a root of famous cities on the foundations of Zeus Ammon").

θεμέθλοις: see also 57n.

16. ἠγασάμην: the speaker interjects his own voice, expressing his admiration for the chorus. The verb returns in 106 (in the same *sedes*), where Phthonos says οὐκ ἄγαμαι, "I do not admire".

The aorist indicative is used as here for a sudden event that is just happening (see Goodwin *MT* §60) and above ἐσείσατο (1), ἐπένευσεν (4).

χέλυς: Hermes invented the "lyre" by stretching strings over a χέλυς, a "tortoise shell" (see *HhHerm* 47–51). The poet exploits both meanings.

ἀεργός: the shell was "idle" (i.e., did not make sounds) when it housed the tortoise; as the instrument, it is no longer silent when it is played to accompany the chorus. Note also σιωπηλὴν κίθαριν (12) = χέλυς.

17–31. This section opens by calling for ritual silence before the song begins, a common feature of hymns. It then describes the effect of songs in praise of Apollo, so potent that they not only quiet the sea but also two famous mourners: Thetis, who weeps for Achilles, and Niobe, who weeps for her children. The sea as a metaphor for poetry that is boundless occurs again at the conclusion of the hymn (106). Pindar in *Paean* 6.79–80 and the *Aethiopis*, according to Proclus' epitome, make Apollo, in the guise of Paris, the slayer of Achilles. Thetis, then, is aptly paired with Niobe. Apollo has slain the sons of both. Niobe bragged that she was better than Leto because she had seven times as many sons and daughters;

Leto's divine children avenged the insult to their mother by slaughtering all of Niobe's children. The gods took pity on her insatiable mourning by turning her into a rock (essentially a cliff-face), which was variously located in the ancient world. The story occurs again in *hDelos* 95–99, though there she is located in Thessaly.

17. εὐφημεῖτ(ε): the primary meaning of the verb is to refrain from inauspicious utterance, hence "be silent." The mourning mothers would distract from the ritual, and their silence testifies to the potency of songs for Apollo. As a paean, it appropriately heals their grief, at least for the duration of the song.

18. ὅτε κλείουσιν: ὅτε with the present indicative in the causal sense (see LSJ s.v. B).

19. Λυκωρέος ... Φοίβου: Lycoreia (either the nearby town or mountain) is a metonymy for Delphi. The town was said to have been founded by Lycoreus, a son of Apollo.

ἔντεα: used of military equipment in Homer, but of musical instruments in Pindar (*Ol.* 4.22, *Py.* 12.21). Both are appropriate for Apollo at Delphi, where his slaying of the Pytho with his arrows was celebrated with accompanied song.

20. οὐδὲ Θέτις: the final syllable of Thetis is, unusually, long; probably in imitation of Homer's practice (e.g., at *Il.* 18.385: τίπτε, Θέτι τανύπεπλε). According to the scholiast on the Homeric passage, Zenodotus objected to the lengthening and emended to Θέτις.

κινύρεται: first in Ar. *Eq.* 11 with the sense of "lament"; it is rare before the Hellenistic period.

αἴλινα: the plural is adverbial, "mournfully." The ancients derived the word from the cry for Linus: αἲ Λίνον (cf. Aesch. *Ag.* 121); for Linus and mourning see Paus. 9.29.6–9. The αἲ Λίνον cry is silenced by another cry—ἰὴ παιῆον in the following line, the origins of which will be etymologized in 103 (I am indebted to M. Fantuzzi for this observation). Note that μήτηρ ends both 20 and 103.

21. ἰὴ παιῆον: the first indication of the type of ritual song. A scholium on a poem of Bacchylides (POxy 23.2368 = *SH* 293) seems to claim that Callimachus regarded that poem as a paean because it included this cry. By introducing it, Callimachus thus marks his own hymn as a paean.

22. δακρυόεις: even when transformed, Niobe continues to grieve, or so the moisture on the rock is interpreted. The nominative masculine occurs once in Homer, *Il.* 22.499 in Andromache's proleptic lamentation for her son Astyanax, who will come weeping to his widowed mother. As an intertext, this passage adds pathos and contrast: unlike Niobe, Andromache (and her son) were blameless victims of war.

23–25. Niobe is not named, her human identity erased: she is first a weeping rock (δακρυόεις ... πέτρος), then a διερὸς λίθος, where the sense of διερός is both "wet" and "living" (see *hZeus* 24), and finally a μάρμαρον ἀντὶ γυναικός. The apparent phrase, μάρμαρον ... ὀϊζυρόν, is a deception: ὀϊζυρόν modifies not μάρμαρον, but τι. Cf. *Il.* 24.596–614, where Achilles consoles Priam on the loss of his son with the example of the mourning Niobe.

23. ὅστις = ὅς: for this form of the relative following a definite antecedent see LSJ s.v. II, Chantraine 2.241, and *hDelos* 8, 229; *hDem* 46. λίθος is in apposition to the relative.

ἐστήρικται: perfect passive of στηρίζω, "to be fixed immovably."

24. μάρμαρον: the neuter noun first occurs here; in apposition to πέτρος.

χανούσης: from χάσκω, "open one's mouth wide"; with an object meaning to "utter."

25–31. In this section the speaker exhorts the chorus to the ritual paean cry before the hymn proper begins. Just as earlier the chorus was tightly linked with Apollo (13), here it is "my king."

26–27. Note the careful word order—the blessed, my king, my king, Apollo are arranged chiastically and the four clauses are 8-9-8-8 syllables respectively.

26. ὃς μάχεται: for the use of the indicative in a general statement see Goodwin, *MT* §534.

ἐμῷ βασιλῆι: the reigning king of Cyrene. There are three potential candidates: Ptolemy II, Magas, the half-brother of Ptolemy II who declared himself king and broke off relations with Egypt in 275 BCE, or Ptolemy III, who married Magas' daughter, Berenice II, and assumed the kingship of Cyrene in 246. See pp. 19–20.

μάχοιτο: a wish (Smyth §1814). Cf. *hArt* 136–37 for a similar expression.

28–29 and **30–31** show balances similar to 26–27. τὸν χορὸν ὠπόλλων is reversed in οὐδ᾿ ὁ χορὸς τὸν Φοῖβον, while the dependent clause (28) and question (31) both end with song (ἀείδει / ἀείσει).

28. τι οἱ: the memory of the digamma (ϝοι) makes its presence felt in this line.

29. ἐπεὶ Διὶ δεξιὸς ἧσται: the right hand side is the favored position. A number of scholars have argued that, if the first hymn identified Zeus with the Ptolemies, this line alludes to the younger partner in the co-regency either of Ptolemy I and II (ending in 283/282) or of Ptolemy II and III (ending in 246). Fantuzzi suggests that the line refers not just to Apollo's place in the Olympian hierarchy, or a Ptolemy with respect to his royal father, but more concretely to the position of this hymn in a book roll since it would immediately follow (sit to the right) of the previous hymn to Zeus (2011: 450–51).

30–31. Apollo as a copious subject for song sets the stage for the narration of the god's biography. In addition, Callimachus includes a number of cult names of the god and experiments with a number of etymologies for his names (see 43–45 below).

31. This line recalls *HhAp* 19: πῶς τ᾿ ἄρ σ᾿ ὑμνήσω, πάντως εὔυμνον ἐόντα; ("How shall I hymn you seeing you are abounding in hymns?").

32–34. Callimachus often described statues in his poems, and there is a strong likelihood that his description of Apollo reflects a real cult statue (see p. 74).

Gold (πολύχρυσος) marks Apollo as the sun god, which in turn accounts for his beneficence to flocks in the following lines, but the statues were often painted with gold, and here the drape, pin, bow, quiver, lyre, and sandals are all objects that might easily have been gilded.

2. Cyrene Apollo

32. τὸ ... ἐνδυτόν: a loose garment or wrap (related to ἐνδύω, "put on clothes"); POxy 2258 glosses as χιτών.

ἡ ... ἐπιπορπίς: a *hapax*; according to the scholiast, it means "clasp" (περόνη, πόρπη). Danielsson 1901: 78n4 takes it as the equivalent of ἐπιπόρπαμα, a cloak worn by musicians.

33. τὸ ... ἄεμμα: an epic form of prose ἄμμα = anything tied or knotted. ἄεμμα occurred previously in Philitas' *Demeter* (fr. 16b Spanoudakis: γυμνὸν ἄεμμα), then only in Callimachus, here and again in *hArt* 10 (εὔκαμπὲς ἄεμμα). According to the scholiast it means "bowstring", probably as a synecdoche for "bow."

τὸ Λύκτιον: probably a metonym for Cretan, since Cretan archers were well known (e.g., Arrian 2.9.3, Curtius 3.9.9), but Pausanias (4.19.4) mentions archers specifically from Lyctus and a Lyctian archer dedicates his bow in *ep.* 37.1 Pf.

35. πουλυκτέανος "with many possessions"; πολυκτέανος first occurs at Pi. *Ol.* 10.36. Callimachus often juxtaposed πολυ- and πουλυ- compounds; see πολύχρυσος above and *hArt* 225, *hDem* 2, 119.

Πυθῶνι: Pytho (= Delphi) can substantiate the poet's statement because the location was famous for the richness of its treasuries.

τεκμήραιο: τεκμαίρομαι + dative, "judge from the evidence," is found in lyric and tragedy.

36–38. The description of Apollo as beardless, and with youthful locks that drip healing balm, concludes his distinctive physical characteristics and forms a bridge to his role as a healer.

37. θηλείαις "soft" or "tender," i.e., his beard has not yet coarsened (cf. Theoc. 16.49). The adjective also suggests the androgynous quality of many representations of Apollo.

ἐπὶ ... ἦλθε: for ἐπέρχομαι + dative see LSJ I 2.

χνόος "down," or the first growth of a beard on the cheeks.

38. πέδῳ: dative used in a locative sense, found at *HhDem* 455 and in tragedy.

39. λίπος "oil." Apollo's hair does not drip the usual oil that was customary in grooming, but a healing balm.

ἀποστάζουσιν "drip drop by drop." The word occurs first in Aesch. *Supp.* 578–79; Callimachus uses it in *Hecale* fr. 74.5 Hollis and in *hArt* 118. Cf. the *Homeric Hymn to Hestia* (24.3): αἰεὶ σῶν πλοκάμων ἀπολείβεται ὑγρὸν ἔλαιον ("always from your locks drips liquid oil"), where Hestia is addressed as one who tends Apollo's shrine at Delphi (1–2).

ἔθειραι: in Homer always plural, for "horsehair," but used of human hair in lyric and tragedy (as here).

40. πανάκειαν "cure-all" was a common term in the medical writers, and personified as the goddess Panacea, a daughter of Apollo.

41. πρῶκες: a rare word for "dew drops"; elsewhere only at Theoc. 4.16. The form is said to be Doric.

ἔραζε: synonym for πέδῳ.

ἀκήρια "unharmed," as at, e.g., *Od.* 12.98, *HhHerm* 530.

ἀκήρια πάντ᾽ ἐγένοντο: an etymological gloss on πανάκειαν (40), see Cheshire 2008: 364. For a neuter plural as subject of a plural verb, see Chantraine 2.17–18 (and *hArt* 182, *hDelos* 142).

42–46. These five lines state the spheres of Apollo's patronage: archery and song are entwined and first expressed as objects (ὀϊστευτὴν... ἀοιδόν), then repeated as subjects (τόξον... ἀοιδή). The next two are separated, each one to a line: θριαὶ καὶ μάντιες, ἰητροί. The whole framed by τέχνη δ᾽ ἀμφιλαφής and ἀνάβλησιν θανάτοιο.

Plato in the *Cratylus* lists Apollo's spheres of oversight as μουσική, μαντική, ἰατρική, and τοξική (405a1–3). Socrates goes on to derive versions of Apollo's name from each of these. Because he is a healer he is called Ἀπολούων (purifier); because prophets seek truth, which is "one," he is called Ἅπλουν; as an archer he is Ἀειβάλλων; as a musician he is Ὁμοπολῶν, because he brings everything into harmony (405b9–406a2). Callimachus adds a fifth sphere: care of flocks as a subset of healing. Callimachus also experiments with etymologies of Apollo's name: the opening lines οἷον ὁ τὠπόλλωνος | οἷα δ᾽ ὅλον produce a sound effect that links Apollo and "whole," while at 101–2 ἐπ᾽ ἄλλῳ | βάλλων is said of Apollo the archer. Elsewhere Callimachus seems to connect Apollo to πολύς, both in the positive sense (as in 69–70) and in the privative sense, as not (ἀ-) for the many (πολλῶν) in the sphragis. Cf. *hZeus* 10, 15–20nn for etymologies of Rhea and Zeus. See also Pi. *Py.* 5.60–69 for Apollo's powers particularly in respect to Cyrene.

42. ἀμφιλαφής: Apollo is "abundant" or "copious" in his *techne*; cf. Pi. *Ol.* 9. 80–83: εἴην εὑρησιεπὴς ἀναγεῖσθαι | πρόσφορος ἐν Μοισᾶν δίφρῳ· | τόλμα δὲ καὶ ἀμφιλαφὴς δύναμις | ἕσποιτο, where its occurrence is connected to the skill of the poet: "May I be creative in speech and drive forth fittingly in the chariot of the Muses; may boldness and abundant power accompany me." ἀμφιλαφής occurs also at *hArt* 3 and *hDem* 26.

43. ὀϊστευτήν: a Callimachean coinage, imitated by Nonnus. The double noun formation ὀϊστευτὴν... ἀνέρα is common when the second element is ἀνήρ, see below 86 and *hDem* 51. On the form see Schmitt 162 (12.5.4).

ἔλαχ(ε): λαγχάνω is the verb of choice for the allotment of the spheres of divine authority (e.g., *Il.* 15.190–92), and see *hArt* 22–23n.

ἀοιδόν: cf. *hZeus* 71.

45. θριαί: the common noun refers to pebbles used in divination; also, according to Philochorus, the Thriai were nymphs on Mt. Parnassus who nursed Apollo (see Jacoby's very detailed discussion of Philochorus, *FGrH* 328 F 195 in 3b2 Suppl. 449–51). *HhHerm* 552–66 may refer to these nymphs (see Richardson 2010: 219–20).

μάντιες: the prophets who uttered sacred oracles. Apollo's temples at Delphi and Delos regularly used both pebbles and oral communications to respond to petitioners.

46. δεδάασιν: from *δάω ("learn"); first here as present indicative; Homer uses the reduplicated form only in aorist. See Williams' very full discussion.

ἀνάβλησιν "delay"; the noun occurs previously only in Homer (*Il.* 2.380, 24.655), then in later prose.

47. Νόμιον: One of Apollo's cult titles was *Nomios*, or god of the flocks. *Nomios* was also a title of Aristaeus, the son of Apollo and Cyrene, and thus closely connected to Cyrene (Pi. *Py.* 9.64–65). Callimachus links this epithet with Apollo's homoerotic servitude to Admetus, a version of the story previously unattested. Like the cities that prosper because he drips healing balm, the flocks prosper under his watchful gaze.

ἐξέτι: this preposition with the genitive is Homeric: "from the time that" (cf. 104). Note that this line begins with Φοῖβον and ends with κείνου, while line 45 begins with κείνου and ends with Φοίβου. After the earlier anaphora of κεῖνος (= Φοῖβος), the change in meaning to an expression of time is unexpected.

48. Ἀμφρυσσῷ: a river in Thessaly (Str. 9.5.14); it is near Itone (*hDem* 74) and Othrys (*hDem* 86).

ζευγίτιδας: ζευγῖτις (feminine equivalent of ζευγίτης) seems to be a Callimachean coinage, here describing a yoked pair of mares.

49. ἠιθέου: an unmarried youth. The noun is probably a play on Admetus' name: ἄδμητος means "unbroken" with respect to horses and "virgin" when used of women.

Ἀδμήτοιο: objective genitive. Admetus was a king of Thessaly, whom Apollo was required to serve. In the earliest versions of the myth his servitude was a punishment for killing the Cyclopes (or their children) after they, at the order of Zeus, had killed Apollo's son, Asclepius, because he returned the dead to life. A later version, said to be from Anaxandrides of Delphi (*FGrH* 404 F3–5), has Apollo punished for killing the Delphic Python. The relationship between Admetus and Apollo does not seem to have been erotic before the poetry of Callimachus and his contemporary, Rhianus (fr. 10 Powell). The young Apollo seems to be the *erastes* (so Fantuzzi 2011: 436).

50. βουβόσιον: in Aratus 1120 the word means "cattle pasture" (see Kidd ad loc.), but in Callimachus the sense is closer to "herd of cows." Williams ad loc. posits the influence of *Il.* 11.679: συβόσιον, "herd of swine." (For Apollo as a cowherd see Eur. *Alc.* 8.)

τελέθοι: the verb occurs in Homer, though the optative is first found here; with πλέον, "increases"; cf. *HhDem* 241.

51. ἐπιμηλάδες: in apposition to αἶγες. This coinage is found only here, and its meaning is contested: the scholia (and Griffiths 1981: 160) understand as goats "pastured with sheep," while Williams ad loc. understands as "protectresses of their own offspring," pointing out that the variant, ἐπιμηλίδες, was a title for nymphs as "guardians of the flocks" (see also Schmitt 74n10). Griffiths further observes that Callimachus tends to place a "recherché" adjective of the shape ◡◡-◡◡, followed by a relative clause, at this point in the line (so *hAp* 78, 91, *hArt* 94, 179, and *hDelos* 308), an observation that militates against emendation.

52. βοσκομένησ(ι): the passive participle of βόσκω, with the sense found, e.g., at *Od.* 11.108, of cattle "grazing."

ἀγάλακτες "giving no milk"; a variant, unique to Callimachus, of the adjective ἀγάλακτος.

53. ἄκυθοι "unfruitful"; unique to Callimachus and much discussed in the ancient lexicographers (see Williams ad loc.).

ὕπαρνοι "with lambs under them" (i.e., those ewes who have just given birth and are suckling lambs). The word is rare, but does occur in documentary papyri.

54. While tending Admetus' flocks, all the cows dropped twins (Apollod. 3.10.4). Frazer suggests that Apollo may have been able to bring about twin births in cattle because he was a twin himself (1921: 2.376–82).

55–64. Apollo was born on Delos and is presented at the precocious age of four building the island's famous horned altar. The imposition of the structures of civilization on Delos prefigures Apollo's role in the foundation of Cyrene and contrasts with Apollo's laying out of the foundations for his temple at Delphi in *HhAp* (254–55 repeated at 294–95). Callimachus characterizes Apollo's act as weaving (ὑφαίνει, ἔπλεκε), a familiar metaphor for composing poetry (e.g., Pi. *Py.* 4.275, *Nem.* 4.44, 94, Sappho fr. 188 V). This has prompted some scholars (e.g., Wimmel 1960: 65–70) to consider Apollo's building activities at Delos, in tandem with the choice of waters at the end of the hymn, as a statement of poetic values. In *HhAp* 255 Apollo builds foundations that are εὐρέα καὶ μάλα μακρὰ διηνεκές; in Callimachus Apollo painstakingly weaves together animal horns into a seamless construction, allusively likened to fitting strings to the lyre (see below 58n).

55. διεμετρήσαντο: διαμετρέω is the normal word for measuring out the area of a new foundation; here the middle is used in an active sense, a common stylistic feature in Hellenistic poets (see *hArt* 36n).

56. φιληδεῖ "take pleasure in"; first attested in Ar. *Pax* 1130 and found in prose.

57. κτιζομένησ(ι): with πολίεσσι, cities "as they are being founded."

θεμείλια: variant of θέμεθλα (15); it occurs at *HhAp* 254 ≈ 294, where Apollo lays the foundations for his temple at Delphi. In *hArt* 248 he coins θέμειλον, probably for metrical reasons (see Schmitt 166).

58. τὰ πρῶτα: in Homer often adverbial (e.g., *Il.* 1.6, 17.612), and editors so take it here and at 64, but implicit also is that these are Phoebus' *first* foundations.

ἔπηξε: used at *HhHerm* 47 of Hermes constructing the lyre. Apollo's precocity and, by extension, that of his twin, Artemis, may have been inspired by the feats of the newborn Hermes.

59. καλῇ ... λίμνης: a variation of *HhAp* 280.

Ὀρτυγίη: a name for Delos, see p. 102.

περιηγέος ... λίμνης: the round lake near the sanctuary of Apollo, see *hDelos* 261 (and map 7).

60. The theme of Artemis as a hunter is expanded in *hArt* 80–109.

ἀγρώσσουσα: epic for ἀγρεύω, "catch." Once in Homer (*Od.* 5.53), then Callimachus and Lycophron.

καρήατα: Homeric plural of κάρα, "heads."

61–63. Horns are mentioned three times in these lines (κεράεσσιν, ἐκ κεράων, κεραούς) in connection with ἐδέθλια, βωμόν, and τοίχους. It is not clear if Apollo constructs a separate horned shrine, altar, and walls, or whether the ἐδέθλια and τοίχους are parts of the altar (i.e., ἐδέθλια = base and τοίχους = its sides). The latter makes better sense in view of what is known of the site: no evidence for a shrine or walls constructed of horns exists. (For further details see Williams ad loc.)

61. Κυνθιάδων: Cynthus was a mountain on Delos, often identified as the birthplace of Apollo and Artemis. The term "Cynthian" is here applied to the goats grazing on that mountainside. Adjectives, particularly of place, formed in -άς, -άδος are frequent in Callimachus (see Schmitt 73–74 and below 87, 96).

φορέεσκεν: Homeric iterative imperfect of φορέω.

ἔπλεκε: Plutarch (*De soll. anim.* 983C-E), in describing the way in which the halcyon builds her nest, likens it to weaving and draws a parallel with the interlacing of the horns of the Delian altar. Williams ad loc. suggests that the resemblance of the halcyon's nest and the altar may have belonged to pre-Callimachean paradoxology of which the poet availed himself. See also Selden 1998: 399–402, who finds an analogy in Egyptian cosmology, and above 55–64.

62. δείματο: Homeric aorist middle of δέμω, with an active sense; the active form occurs at 77 and see below 94.

ἐδέθλια: a variant of ἔδεθλον (72), first attested in Callimachus. Both forms occur in A.R., at 4.331 (ἔδεθλον) and 4.630 (ἐδέθλια); see Schmitt 35–36n18, 71n1. For a similar variation see 57n.

63. ἐκ κεράων, κεραούς: Callimachus shifts from the noun (κέρας) to the adjective (κεραός), the latter with the sense "made of horns."

65–96. The longest sequence in the poem, it rehearses the history of the colonization of Cyrene, which is also told in Pi. *Py.* 4 and 9 (written respectively for Arcesilas and Telesicrates of Cyrene) and in Herodotus (4.145–205), but here the focus is the festival of the *Carneia*. The colonization myth was unusual because Apollo not only provided the oracle (which is normal), he also seems to have taken direct action in the colony's establishment.

65. βαθύγειον "fertile"; previously only in Theophrastus, though βαθύγαιος occurs at Hdt. 4.23.

Βάττῳ: Battus ("Stutterer") was the founder of the colony. His formal name is given later as Aristoteles (76), though his descendants called themselves the Battiadae (on Battus' speech see Pi. *Py.* 5.57–59).

66. κόραξ: Apollo in the guise of a raven led the colonists to the new foundation. The story is already told in Hesiod (fr. 60 M-W), and a late sixth-century inscription from Cyrene indicates that Apollo was honored there with the epithet Κόραξ (Gasperini 1995: 5–8).

67. οἰκιστῆρι "founder"; the form is known from Cyrenean texts (see Dobias-Lalou 2000: 94, 235); Hdt. 4.153.3 and Pi. *Py* 4.6 apply it to Battus as the founder of Cyrene.

68. ἡμετέροις βασιλεῦσιν: i.e., the Battiad line; "my king" in line 27 refers to a specific, and current, king, for whose identity see pp. 18–19.

69. Βοηδρόμιον: a cult title of Apollo found in a number of places; the Athenians held a festival in honor of Apollo Βοηδρόμιος and even named a month Βοηδρομίων (see Deubner 1932: 202). According to the *Etymologicum magnum* s.v., the title is accounted for as the shout of the army running to the city after a victory (ἀπὸ οὖν τῆς τοῦ στρατεύματος βόης τῆς ἐπὶ τῷ ἄστει δραμούσης).

70. Κλάριον: Claros was the location of a very well-known oracular shrine of Apollo near Colophon and Ephesus; it existed from at least the Archaic period, but came to particular prominence in the Hellenistic period (see Parke 1967: 122, 138).

71. Καρνεῖον: Apollo *Carneius* was worshipped in Sparta, where the festival of the *Carneia* was long celebrated (see Pettersson 1992: 57–72). Cyrene, as a Spartan-Theran colony, venerated him as city patron. The temple precinct of Apollo *Carneius* was the largest in Cyrene.

72–74. The movement from Sparta (the first foundation) to Thera to Cyrene retraces the trajectory of colonization for this portion of North Africa. The story goes that one of the Argonauts was given a clod of Libyan earth (or a tripod) by the god Triton as a promise that the land belonged to Greeks. In Pindar (*Py.* 4) the clod of earth is washed into the sea and only after seventeen generations do the Greek colonizers return to claim their heritage (see also the prophecy at A.R. 4.1749–54). Battus, one of the Spartans who had settled on Thera, consulted Delphi about his stutter and was told to emigrate to Libya (Hdt. 4.155). In fact, Laconian and Arcadian settlers were the largest group in Cyrene, and the city spoke a Doric dialect (see pp. 26–27).

72. τόδε: Williams and others before him have taken exception to the deictic pronoun, but if it is spoken by the poet in the context of πατρώϊον "this ancestral one I just mentioned," the usage seems acceptable (see Smyth §1242).

ἔδεθλον: Hellenistic; also at A.R. 4.331, of the temple of Artemis in the land of the Brugi.

73. γε μέν: see Denniston 386–89; the combination usually has an adversative or a progressive sense; either can apply to this passage, where the third iteration is emphatic. "but *third* is the city of Cyrene."

74. ἕκτον γένος: the sixth generation from Oedipus refers to the settlement of Thera by a descendant of Polyneices (see Hdt. 4.147 and Pi. *Py.* 5.72–75).

75. ἀπόκτισιν: the "founding of a colony"; probably a Callimachean coinage (see Schmitt 72n7).

76. οὖλος: Homer uses this adjective in several senses ("destructive" of heroes, "curly" of hair, "compact" of wool), and the various meanings were much discussed in antiquity. Callimachus' usage at various places in the hymns reflects this Homeric variety (see Rengakos 1992: 24). As an attribute of Aristoteles οὖλος is best taken as "baneful" to follow Homeric usage with heroes (e.g., *Il.* 21.536). However, Williams ad loc. raises the intriguing possibility that since Callimachus calls Aristoteles by his real name, instead of the usual Battus ("stutterer"), here οὖλος has the non-Homeric sense "concise in his speech" (according to Plut. *De garr.* 510E-F, a characteristic of Spartans).

Ἀσβυστίδι... γαίῃ: the Asbystians were one of the indigenous tribes in the Cyrenaica; thus Callimachus regularly named the region the "Asbystian land."

πάρθετο (= παρέθετο): in the middle, "place beside" or "entrust," with accusative of thing/person entrusted. "Aristoteles entrusted you [i.e., set up Apollo's temple] to the Asbystian land."

77. ἀνάκτορον: dwelling for a king or a god; used, e.g., of Apollo's temple at Delphi (Eur. *Ion* 55).

78. τελεσφορίην: according to the scholia, the meaning here is "festival" (cf. *hDem* 129). First here and in A.R. 1.917 (of the Samothracian Mysteries); for the word in its Cyrenean context see Dobias-Lalou 2000: 209–10. In Cyrene the τελεσφόροι were apparently responsible for the ritual slaughter of bulls (Fraser 1972: 2.918n304), which occurs in the next two lines.

ἐπετήσιον: with τελεσφορίην the meaning will be "annual" or "yearly"; it occurs first at *Od.* 7.118 with a different meaning (and see below 81–84).

78–79. πολλοὶ... ταῦροι: apparently not an exaggeration; a fourth-century Cyrenean inscription commemorates the sacrifice of 120 oxen to Artemis (see Gallavotti 1963: 454–55).

79. ὑστάτιον (= ὕστατον): the adjective modifies ἰσχίον ("haunch"), "fallen on its last haunch," i.e., fallen on its haunches for the last time.

80. πολύλλιτε "much prayed for"; a correction for the unmetrical πολύλλιστε found in a number of mss. The line seems to have been imitated in a very fragmentary papyrus of Euphorion (*SH* 428.12); also at *hDelos* 316.

81–84. Cyrene was known for its flowers, and this passage, like the description of the health of cities and of flocks, links Cyrene's fruitfulness to Apollo's favor; based on the description of Alcinous' gardens at *Od.* 7.118–21.

81. τόσσα: here = ὅσσα; also at 94, probably to avoid hiatus; the antecedent is ἄνθεα...ποικίλ(α).

Ὧραι: the personified Seasons; a shrine of the Horae was located next to the temple of Apollo in Cyrene (Chamoux 1953: 268, 364).

82. ἀγινεῦσι: epic form of ἄγω, "bring"; also in *Iamb.* fr. 194.55 Pf. and Herodas 4.87.

ζεφύρου πνείοντος: a variation of *Od.* 7.119: ζεφυρίη πνείουσα.

83. κρόκον ἡδύν: Cyrene was noted for the fragrance of its saffron (e.g., Theophr. *HP* 6.6.5).

84. περιβόσκεται "graze around"; the image from the flocks is carried over into the description of eternal hearth fires. The word is first found in Callimachus and imitated by Nicander.

τέφρη: epic, used in the plural for "ashes."

85–87. The "men girt for War" are the Spartan (Theran) colonists—they are called Dorian in 89—whose dancing (ὠρχήσαντο) with the native women enacts the first *Carneia* on Cyrenean soil. Coupling in the dance is equally a reference to standard colonial behavior—marrying native women. In fact, the passage may be of contemporary relevance because in his constitution for Cyrene (*c.*325 BCE), Ptolemy I allowed children of men who were Cyrenean citizens and local Libyan women to be entered into the citizen rolls for the first time (see Bagnall 1976: 28).

85. ζωστῆρες: in Homer ζωστήρ usually describes a warrior's belt, but the primary meaning of the noun seems simply to be a "belt" or "cincture"; it could be worn by either men or women. Here the addition of Ἐννοῦς makes the context of war clear. ζωστήρ itself is either an agent noun ("men wearing belts") or synecdoche, where "belts" equals "men wearing belts." Theoc. 15.6 provides a parallel for the latter: παντᾷ κρηπῖδες, παντᾷ χλαμυδηφόροι ἄνδρες, in which κρηπῖδες is synecdoche for "men wearing soldier's boots," though the subsequent phrase "cloak-wearing men" clarifies the earlier usage. For the addition of ἀνέρες (86), see above 43n.

Callimachus' phrase highlights two elements: ζωστήρ and war. There was an ancient sanctuary at Zoster in Attica (see Steph. Byz. s.v. Ζωστήρ) with a cult temple dedicated to Apollo, Artemis, Leto, and Athena, where Leto is said to have loosened her ζωστήρ, in preparation for delivering her twins, though she did not give birth there (Paus. 1.31.1). During the Chremonidean war (267–261), in which the Ptolemies were supporters of Athens against Macedon, the location was fortified. Possibly the word was chosen to allude to both the myth of Leto and the historical context.

Ἐννοῦς: Ἐννώ is the goddess of war (*Il.* 5.333, 592 and *hDelos* 276); metonymy for "war" or "battle."

87. τέθμιαι "appointed"; Doric forms of θέσμιος are frequent in Callimachus: in the hymns, here, *hArt* 174, and *hDem* 18 (all are in Doric-speaking contexts). See Buck §164.4, Schmitt 31n10, and Harder on *Aetia* fr. 43.20.

Καρνειάδες "for the Carneian festival"; on the form see 61n.

ἤλυθον: epic form of ἤλθον. Like Homer, Callimachus uses both ἤλθ- and ἤλυθ-, varying for metrical reasons.

88. πηγῇσι Κύρης: Cyre is a local spring, from which some ancient writers derived the name of the city, Cyrene (see map 4). The other derivation was from the eponymous nymph, who is not named in this poem, but referred to as the daughter of Hypseus (92).

89. Ἄζιλιν: Azilis was the region near Cyrene where tradition placed the original settlement (see Hdt. 4.157.3, who spells it Ἄζιρις).

90–92. Cyrene caught the eye of Apollo when he was an indentured servant of Admetus in Thessaly. He then carried her from Thessaly to Cyrene. She is figured as his "bride" in this poem. At least one frieze from Cyrene survives in late Roman copy, depicting the nymph conquering a lion (Bonacasa and Ensoli 2000: 186–87). Other versions of the myth have her slaying the lion in Thessaly.

91. ἐπὶ Μυρτούσσης: Bonacasa and Ensoli (2000: 53) have identified "Myrtussa" with the acropolis (cf. A.R. 2.505: Μυρτώσιον αἶπος).

κερατώδεος "horned," before Callimachus only in Arist. *HA* 595a13 and Theophr. *HP* 5.1.6. The choice of this word to describe the contours of the hill recalls the "horned" altar and the close relationship of Apollo the builder with both.

92. Ὑψηίς: the "daughter of Hypseus." Hypseus was the son of the river god, Peneius, and king of the Lapiths.

κατέπεφνε: Homeric, lyric, and tragic second aorist, with no present form in use, "slew."

σίνιν: the lion as σίνις, "ravager" or "plunderer," first occurs in the mss. of Aesch. *Ag.* 717–18, where Conington's emendation, ἴνιν, is widely accepted. However, the fact that σίνιν occurs again in Lycophron 539 (describing Paris) suggests that it was an accepted reading in the third century BCE (so Williams ad loc.).

Εὐρυπύλοιο: Eurypylus was a son of Poseidon and a legendary native king of Libya; he occurs in Pi. *Py.* 4.33, and A.R. 4.1561. His particulars are given in a scholium on the A.R. passage, attributed to Acesander, *On Cyrene* (*FGrH* 469 F 1, 3–4).

93. θεώτερον: previously this comparative form occurred only in Homer (*Od.* 13.111), where it refers to a portal in a cave of the nymphs used only by gods. On the form see Chantraine 1.257–58 and Williams ad loc. It occurs again at *hArt* 249 (of Dawn looking down on the temple of Artemis at Ephesus). The more common θειότερος occurs at *hZeus* 80.

94. τόσ(α)...τόσσα: for repeated τοσ- forms as correlatives, Williams ad loc. compares Pi. *N*. 4.4–5.

ἔνειμεν: the mss. read ἔδειμεν, or "built," which Lascaris emended to ἔνειμεν, "allotted" or "bestowed"; the latter is the preferred reading of most editors. Williams ad loc. strongly defends the mss., pointing to the other moments in the poem where Apollo is a builder (and citing the original reading of Hes. fr. 273.1 M-W). The comparison with other cities, though, would seem to preclude ἔδειμεν; Apollo may have built the Delian horned altar for himself (62), but he does not build cities; at 77 it is Aristoteles who does so.

ὀφέλσιμα: probably a Callimachean coinage for ὠφέλιμος, "beneficial" (see Schmitt 100n5).

95. ἁρπακτύος: Ionic for ἁρπαγή; only here in Callimachus (cf. *hDem* 9).

96. Βαττιάδαι: the Battiads were the founding and ruling house of Cyrene in the sixth-fifth centuries BCE. They had been superseded by an oligarchy in the fourth century.

97–104. The paean was traditionally a poem for Apollo, though in the Hellenistic period other gods and even humans could be so honored. The inclusion of the paean cry marks this poem as a paean (see 21n). Various explanations for the cry were given in antiquity (see Ath. 15.701c-e), though Callimachus' version is a variant of that attributed to Clearchus of Soli (fr. 64 Wehrli). He derived it from ἵε, παῖ ("go on, son"), uttered by Leto to encourage her son to attack the Pytho. In Callimachus' version, it is the bystanders who cry out: ἰὴ παιῆον. Callimachus emphasizes the point with a virtual gloss: ἵει βέλος in 103, as if the cry were: ἵει, παῖ, ἰόν.

98. ἐφύμνιον "refrain of a hymn"; Hellenistic (cf. fr. 384.39 Pf., A.R. 2.713) and in later prose.

99. ἐκηβολίην: *hapax* at *Il*. 5.54, "skilled at hitting the mark" (see Rengakos 1992: 35) and see 11n.

100–1. The story of Apollo slaying Pytho is the subject of the second half of *HhAp*. Apollo kills the serpent that inhabits the area around Mt. Parnassus in order to establish his sanctuary there. The place where the serpent died and rotted in the sun was called Pytho (from the verb πύθω = "rot"), *HhAp* 372.

101. κατήναρες: second aorist active of κατεναίρομαι. The verb occurs once in Homer (*Od*. 11.519), where Neoptolemus kills Telephus' son, Eurypylus (the homonymous Eurypylus at 92 may be the reason for the imitation, if it is one).

102. ἐπηΰτησε: from ἐπαϋτέω; "called out besides"; previously in Hes. *Sc*. 309 and Theoc. 22.91 (see Sens 1997 ad loc.).

104. ἀοσσητῆρα: cf. *Aetia* fr. 18.4 (also of Apollo) and A.R. 1.471, 4.146, 785. The rare noun may be intended as play on the epithet Παιήων that was applied to many gods. Παιήων means "healer" or "helper," and ἀοσσητήρ, according to the scholiast on *Od*. 4.165, means one who is ready to heed a cry (ὄσσα) for help.

ἐξέτι κεῖθεν "ever since then," "from that point"; cf. 47n.

105–113. For a discussion of this famous *sphragis* see p. 73.

105–7. Compare lines 1–3, where the impure are banished as Apollo kicks the doors with his "fair foot." See also Pl. *Phdr.* 247a, where Socrates describes the heavenly processions of the gods; those with the greatest affinity for the divine may follow: ἕπεται δὲ ὁ ἀεὶ ἐθέλων τε καὶ δυνάμενος· φθόνος γὰρ ἔξω θείου χοροῦ ἵσταται ("he follows who is willing and able, for Envy stands apart from the divine chorus").

105. λάθριος "secret"; a variant of λαθραῖος, found first in tragedy and comedy.

106. The interpretation of this line continues to be disputed. (1) Williams (pp. 87–89) made the case for understanding the sea (πόντος) as Homer, though just how the identification should work poetically is unclear. Griffiths 1981: 161 has set out the basic problems with Williams' argument. (2) Traill 1998, following Williams on the syntax of οὐδ' ὅσα (namely, that it does not mean "not as much as," but "not *even* as much as") shifts the comparison from the Homer of the *Iliad* and *Odyssey*, to the Homer of the *Hymn to Apollo*. He takes the sense to be "I do not admire the poet who, when praising Apollo, does not sing even as much as Homer in his *Hymn to Apollo* did."

108–12. Apollo's reply introduces a new element for comparison—the large flow of the Assyrian river in contrast to pure waters carried by bees from the springs of Demeter. The Assyrian river is most likely the Euphrates, which flowed through the heart of the Seleucid Empire.

108. τὰ πολλά: adverbial, cf. τὰ πρῶτα above 58, 64.

109–10. The opening letters of lines 109–10 read λυ-Δη, and the opening letter of 108 is A. The *Lyde* of Antimachus of Colophon was an epic poem much admired by Plato, but generally denigrated by Callimachus and his contemporaries (cf. fr. 398 Pf.: Λύδη καὶ παχὺ γράμμα καὶ οὐ τορόν). If Antimachus' *Lyde* was embedded in an acrostic, then the poetic style that Apollo (as opposed to Phthonos) rejects is the overly grand epic style of Antimachus (so K. Cheshire in a paper presented at the American Philological Association in 2010). See also Morrison 2007: 135–37, who discusses the passage in terms of a traditional "break-off formula" (*Abbruchformel*).

109. λύματα: the refuse from ritual washing, or from a sacrifice (see *hDem* 115, *Aetia* fr. 75.25 Pf.).

συρφετόν: anything swept away, "refuse"; but in Plato, it is the equivalent of οἱ πολλοί, "the mob"; see Acosta-Hughes and Stephens 2012: 80–83.

110. Bees carrying water to Deo have a local reference. There was a sanctuary of Demeter and Persephone in Cyrene, not far from the temple to Apollo that included a spring. It may also be an allusion to Philitas' poem the *Demeter* (see Williams ad loc.) as well as a cultic reference; priestesses of Demeter were called *Melissae*. See further Petrovic 2011: 275–76.

111. ἀχράαντος (= ἄχραντος): the form is a *hapax* in Callimachus; "undefiled," but the combination καθαρὸν καὶ ἄχραντον occurs earlier in Plato, *Alcibiades* I 113e9. Williams ad loc. suggests that the phrase might have belonged to a ceremonial formula.

112. πίδακος ἐξ ἱερῆς: a variation of *Il.* 16.825: πίδακος ἀμφ' ὀλίγης. The passage is a simile of a boar and a lion fighting over a slender spring.

ὀλίγη λιβάς and **ἄκρον ἄωτον** are in apposition to ἥτις καθαρή (111).

ἄωτον "the choicest" or "the flower of"; the word is frequent in Pindar; ἄκρον ἄωτον occurs in *Is.* 7.18–19: ὅ τι μὴ σοφίας ἄωτον ἄκρον | κλυταῖς ἐπέων ῥοαῖσιν ἐξίκηται ζυγέν ("[Mortals forget] what does not reach the steep pinnacle of wisdom, yoked in famous streams of verse").

113. Μῶμος: the personification of criticism. Cf. Pi. *Ol.* 6.74–76: μῶμος ἐξ ἄλ|λων κρέμαται φθονεόντων | τοῖς, οἷς ποτε πρώτοις περὶ δωδέκατον δρόμον | ἐλαυνόντεσσιν αἰδοία ποτιστά|ξῃ Χάρις εὐκλέα μορφάν ("Blame from others who are envious hangs over those who drive first over the twelve-lap track, on them revered Charis sheds a glorious appearance").

Φθόνος: most mss. read φθόρος, "a destructive man"; Φθόνος is preserved in **I**, the Aldine, and a scholium on Gregory of Nazianzus (quoted by Pfeiffer, testimonia ad loc.). Most editors print Φθόνος, who is already personified in 105, 107, rather than introduce a third term, which lacks the specificity and force of the other two.

The Hymn to Artemis

L IKE *hZEUS* AND *hAP*, THE *HYMN TO ARTEMIS* BEGINS WITH THE DEITY
within an older mythic frame, and as the poem progresses, a new set of responsibilities unfolds. Just as Zeus moves from Arcadia to Hesiodic Crete
to Ptolemaic Alexandria and Apollo from Delos to Pherae to Cyrene, Artemis
moves from Homeric Olympus through Arcadia and Crete to Ephesus and Ionia.
Like Zeus and Apollo, Artemis begins as a child, and as she matures her roles
change from πότνια θηρῶν, the goddess primarily of the outside and the young
(both human and animal), to a maturity that connects her with the prosperity of
cities, the correlative of which is cultic dance.

The narrative of Artemis' girlhood, characteristics, and accomplishments has
a trajectory that leads her from her father's lap as a child to join the ranks of the
Olympians as an adult, and is charted with changing addresses: from παῖς (5) to
κούρη (40) to δαίμων (86) to θεή (112) to ἄνασσα (137). The young goddess is
seen first choosing the nymphs to serve as her chorus and attendants, then going
off to the Cyclopes for her weapons, and to Pan for her hounds. She captures the
Cerynian deer to pull her chariot (98–109), thoughtfully leaving one for Heracles. (This will become his third labor and thus a step on his path to Olympus.)
At 110 the hymn seems first to close then begin again with a series of questions
that move her from the natural world to an oversight of cities resembling that
of Zeus in *hZeus* (and Hesiod). Artemis then arrives on Olympus (141), where
Hermes takes her weapons, while Apollo takes her catch. At least Apollo used to,
the poet corrects himself, but after Heracles was elevated to Olympus, he waits

for her instead. In 164–65 Artemis finally enters the halls, where she takes her seat next to Apollo. Her entry combines elements from Apollo's first entry into Olympus at *HhAp* (2–13) and from the Pythian sequence in *HhAp* 186–206, where Apollo enters Olympus, this time accompanied by the dancing of the immortals. The poet himself appeals to the goddess to inspire him with her story so he can tell the others: εἰπέ, θεή, σὺ μὲν ἄμμιν, ἐγὼ δ' ἑτέροισιν ἀείσω (186), an echo of *HhAp* 165–69. The dance of Artemis and her nymphs (170–74) is modeled on the brief *Homeric Hymn to Artemis* (27). After an apparent *recusatio* (175–82) the poet again poses a series of questions that follow earlier hymnic models— what island, mountain, harbor, city, nymphs most please you? These questions are framed to reflect the range and location of Artemis' cult-sites outside and within settled communities and to act as a bridge between the two. The final section on her nymphs is closely connected with the locations of her cultic worship. It consists of two long sections on females, her nymphs Britomartis (189–205) and Atalanta (215–24), with passing mention of Cyrene, Procris, and Anticlea in between (206–14). The next section features men, where Artemis as helper (Neleus, 225–27, Proetus, 233–36, Ephesus, 251–58) is juxtaposed to her role as avenger (Agamemnon 228–32, Lygdamis, 251–58). Her chorus of nymphs is transformed into the Amazons, who dance in her honor where her cult at Ephesus was later established (238–49). The motif of choral dancing from its initial organization to the final chorus in Ephesus forms a structural underpinning for the hymn; as Bing observes, the dancing of the nymphs shifts the focus from Artemis to her cult-sites and then to the rites that honor her (1988: 126n57).

There are very tight correlations within and between the first and second halves of the hymn: Artemis' statement of her desired weapons, the hunt, nymphs, and virginity (5–20) are fulfilled in 40–45 (where she chooses her nymphs); 46–86 (where the Cyclopes make her weapons); 87–97 (where Pan in Arcadia provides her with hunting hounds); and 98–110 (where her first hunt, without weapons, yields the deer for her chariot). Artemis is addressed as *Parthenie* (110), and the theme of virginity is instantiated in the narratives of Britomartis (189–205) and Atalanta (221–24). Her role in the care of cities is first hinted at by Zeus (36), then expanded in a vignette of the cities of the just and unjust (122–36) modeled on Hesiod *Op.* 225–47. It is seen also in her abandoning of the Taurians for Athens (171–74); in guiding Neleus, the founder of Miletus (225–27); and her protection of Ephesus from Lygdamis and his Cimmerians (251–59). Her desire for πολυωνυμίη (7) comes true in the latter part of the hymn, where she is *Dictynna* (198); *Oupis* (204); *Chitone* (225); *Chesias, Imbrasie* (228); *Korie* (234); *Hemere* (236); *Munychie, Pheraie* (259).

HArt 7 introduces a running theme of rivalry with Apollo. Commentators have tended to regard Artemis as the loser in this contest, pointing to the choice of a poem about Apollo (*HhAp*) as a model for the *Artemis* and the fact that she is conspicuously absent from *hDelos* (Plantinga 2004). But it is possible to account for these features more positively. If Callimachus knew a set of Homeric hymns in which Artemis was the subject only in the very brief hymns 9 and 27, it is possible that he constructed his hymn to address this inequity by now giving her a much longer hymn as well as one that proclaims its "Homeric hymn" status by appropriating the formal structure of her brother's great hymn. Thus if the second half of *HhAp* deals with the establishment of Apollo's cult at Delphi, Callimachus, in his staging of the rivalry between the siblings, narrates at the end of Artemis' hymn not the establishment of a single cult but many cults in fulfillment of Zeus's promise to give her τρὶς δέκα...πτολίεθρα (34).

The absence of Artemis from *hDelos* may have its roots in this hymn. There was more than one version of the twins' birth, and Callimachus may depend on a version that locates hers as prior (as in *HhAp* 16), and relatively easy, as she states in 24–25: "my mother did not suffer pain either in carrying me or in giving me birth." This is a pointed contrast to Apollo's birth in *hDelos*, where Leto's labor is prolonged through Hera's wrath. Artemis' birth was usually located on the island of Ortygia (understood as an alternative name for Delos or the island so named in the Syracusan harbor). In the latter case, after giving birth to Artemis on Syracusan Ortygia, Leto fled to Delos, where Apollo was born. However, there are several accounts (Str. 14.1.20, Tacitus *Ann.* 3.61, Pliny *HN* 5.115, sch. Pi. *Nem.* 1b1, Steph. Byz. s.v. Σμύρνης) that place Artemis' birth (with or without Apollo) at an Ortygia located near Ephesus. Strabo's version is particularly full: he states that the river Cenchreus passes through Ephesian Ortygia, and in it Leto cleansed herself after bearing Apollo and Artemis. On a nearby mountain the Curetes clashed their armor to keep the birth of the children from Hera. Just as Arcadia and Crete seem to have had similar narratives about Zeus's birth or Icaros, Naxos, and Nysa claim Dionysus (see opening of *HhDion*), so there seems to have been a local Ephesian tale that resembled the story of the twins' birth on Delos. This story apparently underpinned the rites of Artemis at Ephesus, and it does predate Callimachus since elements of it are mentioned in the Euphronius decree of 302 BCE.[1] This version of her birth at Ephesus may be latent at the end of this hymn, as a parallel for Apollo's on Delos in *hDelos*.

The Deity and Her Relevant Cults

Artemis' cult-sites in mainland Greece and Ionia were exceeded only by those of her twin, Apollo, although his presence in literature greatly overshadows hers, a circumstance that results in part because as a male his various sexual liaisons with

---

1. See Rogers 2012: 41–42, and 42–43 for the obvious parallels with the birth of Zeus on Crete.

semi-divine and human females were significant in genealogical lines of descent, and because he was the patron of song, while Artemis was closely connected to the dance. She is a virgin goddess of the outside, the hunt, wild creatures, including human young—boys and girls who have yet to be initiated into their roles in adult society. She was also an important city goddess, whose favor (like that of her brother) brought prosperity to citizens, domestic animals, and crops. As the goddess of the outdoors, she is frequently assimilated to Near Eastern divinities like Astarte and Cybele (also called the Berecynthian Mother or Magna Mater). The cult of Artemis *Bendis*, newly introduced into Athens, is featured at the opening of Plato's *Republic*, and even earlier Herodotus identified Egyptian Bast with Artemis (2.156.5). Greeks often identified her with Eileithyia, the goddess of childbirth, and with Hecate.[2] She was worshipped at multiple sites in Arcadia, Boeotia, Laconia, and Thessaly; her most famous cults included Artemis *Orthia* in Sparta, with its violent initiation ritual for boys,[3] and Artemis *Brauronia* at Athens, to whom girls dedicated their toys before marriage. As Artemis *Tauropolos* she was worshipped in the Attic deme of Halae Araphenides, to which her cult statue was said to have been transported from the Tauric Chersonese (Eur. *IT* 1449–61). She also had cults in the Piraeus (Artemis *Munychia*) and according to Pausanias a cult outside the city as *Agrotera* (1.19.6).[4] In the third century BCE Artemis' temples and cults were a significant feature of Crete and the Greek-speaking East, including Perge, Miletus, and above all Ephesus (her temple at Ephesus was reckoned one of the Seven Wonders of the ancient world). Despite her absence in *hDelos*, she had an important sanctuary on Delos that was older than Apollo's, and she was venerated at Delphi. All were areas central to Ptolemaic interest, and Callimachus' section on Cretan Britomartis (189–205) and the closing section on the origins of her cult at Ephesus (237–45) reflect this interest. In Cyrene an Artemision stood next to the great temple to Apollo, and her rites figured prominently in the Cyrenean purity laws. C. Meillier (1979: 45) thinks the hymn was in fact composed for the Cyrenean *Artamitia*, a festival that had many features of mystery cult (see Chamoux 1953: 318–19). There is little evidence for Artemis-worship in early Alexandria, but there was a dedication made by Apollonius, the chief financial officer of Ptolemy II, to Apollo, Artemis (as *Phosphorus* and *Enodia*), Leto, and Heracles. While probably made in southern Egypt, the dedication is unlikely to have been a unique type for that Egyptian location (Fraser 1972: 1.195 and notes).

2. Petrovic 2007: 249–64 (Eileithyia), 5–10 (Hecate).

3. See Calame 1997: 142–74 for a discussion of these cults and Artemis' choruses.

4. For Artemis in Attica see Deubner 1932: 204–10 and for a list of cult locations elsewhere see Petrovic 2007: 305.

Sources and Intertexts

As the subject of only two very brief hymns (9 and 27), Artemis is marginal in the Homeric hymns. In 9, she drives her chariot from Smyrna to Claros (sites on the Turkish Aegean coastline near Ephesus) to meet her brother; in 27, after she finishes her hunting, she hangs up her bow and arrows, then goes to Apollo's "rich house" at Delphi to lead the Muses and Graces in the dances. In *HhAphr* there is a similar balance between Artemis as huntress and her importance in the dance, and the hymn also mentions her care for cities: καὶ γὰρ τῇ ἅδε τόξα καὶ οὔρεσι θῆρας ἐναίρειν | φόρμιγγές τε χοροί τε διαπρύσιοί τ' ὀλυλυγαί | ἄλσεά τε σκιόεντα δικαίων τε πτόλις ἀνδρῶν (18–20: "for the bow and arrow pleases her and to hunt beasts in the mountains and lyres, dances, piercing cries, shady groves, and the city of just men").

The broad structure of Callimachus' hymn is modeled on the *Homeric Hymn to Apollo*. It is the only one of Callimachus' hymns to depend so closely on a Homeric hymn, and on a hymn that is anomalous because it seems to stitch together a hymn to Delian Apollo with another to Pythian Apollo. It is clear that Callimachus knew the Homeric hymn in more or less the same form in which it has come down to us because he imitated its two discrete sections; and he seems to have understood the two parts as moving from birth on Delos to the maturity of divine accomplishment (the slaying of Pytho and the establishment of his cult at Delphi). The Artemis hymn is also the only one to imitate Homeric hymns by beginning with the name of the deity, followed by a few words of praise in the third person before beginning the mythic narrative. Lines 110–12 at first seem to introduce a hymnic closure with the address Ἄρτεμι Παρθενίη Τιτυοκτόνε, but may only bid farewell to the Homeric Artemis. Via a series of questions the narrative continues and brings the myth up to date with details of her important cult-sites throughout the Mediterranean culminating in Ephesus.

In the *Iliad* Artemis is πότνια θηρῶν and almost never participates in the action. Her relationship to the main struggle is best characterized in a scene at *Il.* 21.479–515, where Hera drives her from the battlefield. Homer emphasizes Artemis' anger and quickness to exact punishment in the inserted tales of the monstrous boar (*Il.* 9.530–49), which she sent to ravage Calydon when the local king, Oeneus, neglected her rites (see *hArt* 215–20, 260–61) or in the death of Niobe's children (*Il.* 24.602–19). When Niobe boasted that she surpassed Leto because she had seven sons and seven daughters to Leto's two, as an object lesson, Artemis killed her daughters, Apollo her sons. (This episode is alluded to in *hAp* 22–23 and forms part of Apollo's first prophecy in *hDelos* 86–99, but is not in *hArt*.) In the *Odyssey* Artemis appears as the bringer of death, especially in Penelope's prayer to her at 20.61–90, but in the extended simile in 6.102–8 Nausicaa is compared to her as the standard for young female beauty; she is linked with Athena in a simile for Penelope (17.37≈19.54).

Callimachus' hymn opens with a close imitation of *Il.* 21.468–512. Poseidon and Apollo are on opposite sides in their aid of the warring factions; Poseidon suggests to Apollo that they both retire from supporting mortal endeavors, and Apollo complies, abashed to have contended with his uncle (468–69). Artemis then taunts her brother for backing down (470–77). Hera enters the scene (479) and rebukes Artemis by calling her a "shameless bitch" and directing her to keep to killing beasts in the mountains rather than engage in battle with her betters (485–86). She then snatches Artemis' bow and quiver and boxes her ears. The young goddess retreats in tears while her mother, Leto, picks up the weapons and follows in the wake of her child (501–5). Callimachus imitates this scene of the goddess upon her father's knees at 506: δακρυόεσσα δὲ π̲α̲τ̲ρ̲ὸ̲ς̲ ἐ̲φ̲έ̲ζ̲ε̲τ̲ο̲ γ̲ο̲ύ̲ν̲α̲σ̲ι̲ κούρη, and transforms it in the following way at 4–5: ὅτε πατρὸς ἐφεζομένη γονάτεσσι | παῖς ἔτι. Note that his Artemis is a child (παῖς ἔτι) in contrast to Homer's young woman. Callimachus' Zeus grants the tearful Artemis all that she asks for and more. Her preference for wild beasts (12) and lack of interest in cities (19–20) corresponds to Hera's rebuke (484–88); the next lines on Artemis' assistance to women in childbirth deliberately undercut Hera's claim that "Zeus made you a lioness to women, and granted that you might kill whomever you wished" (483–84). Zeus's response to Artemis reduces the status of Hera and elevates that of Artemis: why should he fear Hera when goddesses have produced children like this for him? (29–31). Finally, in the awarding of so many cities, Artemis makes a transition from a "mistress of beasts" confined to wild spaces to a city goddess—a necessary updating of Homer to reflect third-century cultic realities (Petrovic 2007: 197–221).

The Artemis of lyric poetry has much in common with Callimachus' goddess. For example, Callimachus seems to have incorporated elements from a hymn to Artemis attributed to Sappho (fr. 44A V), in which she swears an oath of perpetual virginity and expresses the desire to haunt the mountain peaks, to which her father assents:

Ἄρτεμις δὲ θέων] μέγαν ὅρκον ἀπώμοσε
    κεφά]λαν· ἄϊ πάρθενος ἔσσομαι
      ].ων ὀρέων κορύφαισ' ἔπι
        ]δε νεῦσον ἔμαν χάριν·
    ἔνευ]σε θέων μακάρων πάτηρ·
    ἐλαφάβ]ολον ἀγροτέραν θέοι
      ].σιν ἐπωνύμιον μέγα· (4–10)

Artemis swore the great oath of the gods... "[by your head] I shall always be a virgin... upon peaks of the mountains... grant this for my sake."... the father of the blessed gods nodded assent... the gods [call her] deer-shooter, huntress... a great title.

To judge from Menander Rhetor, Alcman also balanced her roles as mistress of
the wild and as a city goddess:

> The length of cletic hymns is greater in poetry, since it is possible for them
> [*sc.* poets] to mention many places, as we find in Sappho and in Alcman. For
> he summons Artemis from countless mountains, countless cities, and from
> rivers too (1.334.29–30 Russell-Wilson).

A fragmentary poem of Anacreon (*PMG* fr. 348) addressed to her indicates how
the two roles might coalesce:

> γουνοῦμαί σ' ἐλαφηβόλε
> ξανθὴ παῖ Διὸς ἀγρίων
> δέσποιν' Ἄρτεμι θηρῶν·
> ἥ κου νῦν ἐπὶ Ληθαίου
> δίνῃσι θρασυκαρδίων
> ἀνδρῶν ἐσκατορᾷς πόλιν
> χαίρουσ', οὐ γὰρ ἀνημέρους
> ποιμαίνεις πολιήτας (1–8).

> I implore you, deer-shooter, blonde daughter of Zeus, mistress of the wild
> beasts, Artemis, who now somewhere by the eddies of the Lethaios look
> upon a city of brave-hearted men and rejoice, for you shepherd citizens who
> are not savage.

Bacchylides 5.97–110 tells of the Calydonian boar sent by Artemis to avenge
insult. Bacchylides 11 tells of the madness of the daughters of Proetus, though in
his version Melampus cured them. In 233–36 Callimachus attributes the cure to
Artemis, and the shrines of Artemis *Koria* and *Hemera* at Lousoi to the grateful
father (on which see Calame 1997: 242). Finally, Timotheus of Miletus (*PMG* fr.
778a) wrote a monody to Artemis, supposedly for the rededication of her temple
at Ephesus.[5]

In Aeschylus, Agamemnon needed to propitiate Artemis because she calmed
the winds that left his fleet stranded at Aulis, unable to sail to Troy. Her actions
seem to have been a proleptic retaliation for the wanton destruction that the
Greeks would inflict on Trojan women and children (*Ag.* 134–39). Sophocles (*El.* 565–74) provides a different reason for Artemis' anger: Agamemnon

---

5. See Hordern 2002: 101–4. *PMG adespota* fr. 955 (= Ath.14.636D) may belong to this poem.
The temple was destroyed in 365 BCE, and rebuilt, but Timotheus was dead by then. If the
source is correct, the monody probably refers to the sixth-century temple.

boasted that he was a better hunter than the goddess. In either case he was required to sacrifice his daughter Iphigenia at Aulis (*Ag.* 123–39). But in Euripides' *IT*, Artemis had secretly substituted a deer, and the girl herself was transported to serve in her temple in the Tauric Chersonese, where the barbarous inhabitants demanded blood sacrifice. Orestes, in disguise, discovers that his sister Iphigenia is alive, and the two escape with Artemis' image (βρέτας) to Athens, where the cult of Artemis *Tauropolos* was established (*IT* 1450–69). Elements of this myth are important at the end of Callimachus' hymn. Euripides' *Hippolytus* includes a choral hymn to Artemis (61–72), and his female choruses often invoke Artemis. A recurring theme in tragedy is the virgin nymph in attendance on Artemis or in the performance of dances who catches the eye of a man who desires her, often with tragic results; that theme is reflected in the stories of Britomartis and Atalanta.

HArt has a number of parallels with Callimachus' other hymns. Like Zeus, Artemis has no major Homeric hymn dedicated to her. Both *hZeus* and *hArt* focus on Arcadian and Cretan myths, which are sometimes interconnected. For example, Britomartis (an avatar of Artemis herself), when pursued by Minos, preserved her virginity by leaping into the sea (189–200). She was saved by fishermen's nets, hence she was called "Dictynna" and the local mountain "Dictaion"—a name related to an epithet (Dictaean) applied to Artemis and to Zeus, who was reared on Mt. Dicte. There the Curetes dance the *prulis* to mask the sounds of the infant Zeus (*hZeus* 52), whereas the Amazons dance the *prulis* in honor of Artemis at Ephesus (*hArt* 240). Like Zeus (*hZeus* 81–84), Artemis (122–36) concerns herself with just and unjust cities.

The central section of *hAp* (91–98) features the nymph Cyrene, who appears as Apollo's bride; in *hArt* 206–8, she is a favorite of Artemis. Apollo, like Artemis, makes the transition from the natural or pastoral world (his service to Admetus) to cities (Cyrene). Artemis' golden accoutrements (110–12) match those of Apollo at *hAp* 32–34 and of Delos at *hDelos* 260–65. Artemis' spheres of influence (the bow, hunting, women in childbirth, and just cities) match Apollo's (archery, song, prophecy, healing: *hAp* 44–47); Apollo's protection for flocks and interest in the foundation of cities (*hAp* 48–63) match Artemis' care for cities (*hArt* 122–36). The establishment of Artemis' temple at Ephesus by the Amazons is a close parallel to the founding of the festival of the *Delia/Apollonia* in *hDelos*. In both there is a hostile migrating group, a mythic rite transformed into cult, and the foundation of a temple. The tale of the Amazons dancing the *prulis* parallels Theseus and his followers dancing the crane dance, while the subsequent threat to the Ephesian temple by the outsider Lygdamis has its parallel in the foundation of Delphi threatened by the Gauls. Both of these events introduce historical circumstances into what had been essentially a mythic narrative.

The Ptolemaic Connections

This hymn's numerous overlaps with *hDelos* permit speculation that it also bears some relationship to the Ptolemaic court. Zeus's promise that Artemis' cities will be μεσσόγεως νήσους τε (37) employs the same language as Apollo's prophecy of the extent of the domain of Ptolemy II: ἀμφοτέρη μεσόγεια καὶ αἳ πελάγεσσι κάθηνται (*hDelos* 168). Artemis' nymphs dance near the streams of the Inopus on Delos (171), a river that was already linked with Egypt and Apollo's birth in *HhAp* 18, and more explicitly in *hDelos* (206–8, 263). Arsinoe's connection with Ephesus was discussed at pp. 19–20. During her marriages to Lysimachus and Ptolemy II many cities throughout the Mediterranean were renamed Arsinoe (see Hölbl 2001: 367 for a list), a fact that may lie behind line 37.

ΕΙΣ ΑΡΤΕΜΙΝ

Ἄρτεμιν (οὐ γὰρ ἐλαφρὸν ἀειδόντεσσι λαθέσθαι)
ὑμνέομεν, τῇ τόξα λαγωβολίαι τε μέλονται
καὶ χορὸς ἀμφιλαφὴς καὶ ἐν οὔρεσιν ἐψιάασθαι,
ἄρχμενοι ὡς ὅτε πατρὸς ἐφεζομένη γονάτεσσι
5   παῖς ἔτι κουρίζουσα τάδε προσέειπε γονῆα·
ʻδός μοι παρθενίην αἰώνιον, ἄππα, φυλάσσειν,
καὶ πολυωνυμίην, ἵνα μή μοι Φοῖβος ἐρίζῃ,
δὸς δ᾽ ἰοὺς καὶ τόξα—ἔα πάτερ, οὔ σε φαρέτρην
οὐδ᾽ αἰτέω μέγα τόξον· ἐμοὶ Κύκλωπες ὀϊστούς
10 αὐτίκα τεχνήσονται, ἐμοὶ δ᾽ εὔκαμπὲς ἄεμμα·
ἀλλὰ φαεσφορίην τε καὶ ἐς γόνυ μέχρι χιτῶνα
ζώννυσθαι λεγνωτόν, ἵν᾽ ἄγρια θηρία καίνω.
δὸς δέ μοι ἑξήκοντα χορίτιδας Ὠκεανίνας,
πάσας εἰνέτεας, πάσας ἔτι παῖδας ἀμίτρους.
15 δὸς δέ μοι ἀμφιπόλους Ἀμνισίδας εἴκοσι νύμφας,
αἵ τε μοι ἐνδρομίδας τε καὶ ὁππότε μηκέτι λύγκας
μήτ᾽ ἐλάφους βάλλοιμι θοοὺς κύνας εὖ κομέοιεν.
δὸς δέ μοι οὔρεα πάντα· πόλιν δέ μοι ἥντινα νεῖμον
ἥντινα λῇς· σπαρνὸν γὰρ ὅτ᾽ Ἄρτεμις ἄστυ κάτεισιν·
20 οὔρεσιν οἰκήσω, πόλεσιν δ᾽ ἐπιμείξομαι ἀνδρῶν
μοῦνον ὅτ᾽ ὀξείῃσιν ὑπ᾽ ὠδίνεσσι γυναῖκες
τειρόμεναι καλέωσι βοηθόον, ᾗσί με Μοῖραι
γεινομένην τὸ πρῶτον ἐπεκλήρωσαν ἀρήγειν,
ὅττι με καὶ τίκτουσα καὶ οὐκ ἤλγησε φέρουσα
25 μήτηρ, ἀλλ᾽ ἀμογητὶ φίλων ἀπεθήκατο γυίων.ʼ
ὣς ἡ παῖς εἰποῦσα γενειάδος ἤθελε πατρός
ἅψασθαι, πολλὰς δὲ μάτην ἐτανύσσατο χεῖρας
μέχρις ἵνα ψαύσειε. πατὴρ δ᾽ ἐπένευσε γελάσσας,
φῆ δὲ καταρρέζων· ʻὅτε μοι τοιαῦτα θέαιναι
30 τίκτοιεν, τυτθόν κεν ἐγὼ ζηλήμονος Ἥρης
χωομένης ἀλέγοιμι. φέρευ, τέκος, ὅσσ᾽ ἐθελημός
αἰτίζεις, καὶ δ᾽ ἄλλα πατὴρ ἔτι μείζονα δώσει.
τρὶς δέκα τοι πτολίεθρα καὶ οὐχ ἕνα πύργον ὀπάσσω,
τρὶς δέκα τοι πτολίεθρα, τὰ μὴ θεὸν ἄλλον ἀέξειν

4 ἀρχμενοι POxy 3328, Blomfield: ἀρχόμενοι **Ψ** ὡς ὅτε **Ψ**: καὶ ὅτε **δ**: ὡς ποτε Hermann, Meineke 16 ἐνδρομίδας Et. gen., Lasc.: ἐνδρομάδας **Ψ** 17 θοοὺς **Ψ**: θοὰς **a** Meineke, Brunck, Blomfield 21 ὀξείῃσιν Pfeiffer: ὀξείησιν **a**: ὀξείαισιν **BCK** Lasc. 22 κ⸤.⸥λεωσι PMilVogl: καλέουσι **Ψ** 29 οτε PMilVogl: ὅτε Lasc.: ὅτι **Ψ** 31 ἀλέγοιμι **Ψ**: aliter PMilVogl, ut vid.

35   εἴσεται, ἀλλὰ μόνην σὲ καὶ Ἀρτέμιδος καλέεσθαι·
     πολλὰς δὲ ξυνῇ πόλιας διαμετρήσασθαι
     μεσσόγεως νήσους τε· καὶ ἐν πάσῃσιν ἔσονται
     Ἀρτέμιδος βωμοί τε καὶ ἄλσεα. καὶ μὲν ἀγυιαῖς
     ἔσσῃ καὶ λιμένεσσιν ἐπίσκοπος.' ὡς ὁ μὲν εἰπών
40   μῦθον ἐπεκρήηνε καρήατι. βαῖνε δὲ κούρη
     Λευκὸν ἔπι Κρηταῖον ὄρος κεκομημένον ὕλῃ,
     ἔνθεν ἐπ' Ὠκεανόν· πολέας δ' ἐπελέξατο νύμφας,
     πάσας εἰνέτεας, πάσας ἔτι παῖδας ἀμίτρους·
     χαῖρε δὲ Καίρατος ποταμὸς μέγα, χαῖρε δὲ Τηθύς,
45   οὕνεκα θυγατέρας Λητωΐδι πέμπον ἀμορβούς.
         αὖθι δὲ Κύκλωπας μετεκίαθε· τοὺς μὲν ἔτετμε
     νήσῳ ἐνὶ Λιπάρῃ (Λιπάρη νέον, ἀλλὰ τότ' ἔσκεν
     οὔνομά οἱ Μελιγουνίς) ἐπ' ἄκμοσιν Ἡφαίστοιο
     ἑσταότας περὶ μύδρον· ἐπείγετο γὰρ μέγα ἔργον·
50   ἱππείην τετύκοντο Ποσειδάωνι ποτίστρην.
     αἱ νύμφαι δ' ἔδδεισαν, ὅπως ἴδον αἰνὰ πέλωρα
     πρηόσιν Ὀσσαίοισιν ἐοικότα (πᾶσι δ' ὑπ' ὀφρὺν
     φάεα μουνόγληνα σάκει ἴσα τετραβοείῳ
     δεινὸν ὑπογλαύσσοντα) καὶ ὁππότε δοῦπον ἄκουσαν
55   ἄκμονος ἠχήσαντος ἐπὶ μέγα πουλύ τ' ἄημα
     φυσάων αὐτῶν τε βαρὺν στόνον· αὖε γὰρ Αἴτνη,
     αὖε δὲ Τρινακρίη Σικανῶν ἕδος, αὖε δὲ γείτων
     Ἰταλίη, μεγάλην δὲ βοὴν ἐπὶ Κύρνος ἄυτει,
     εὖθ' οἵγε ῥαιστῆρας ἀειράμενοι ὑπὲρ ὤμων
60   ἢ χαλκὸν ζείοντα καμινόθεν ἠὲ σίδηρον
     ἀμβολαδὶς τετύποντες ἐπὶ μέγα μυχθίσσειαν.
     τῷ σφέας οὐκ ἐτάλασσαν ἀκηδέες Ὠκεανῖναι
     οὔτ' ἄντην ἰδέειν οὔτε κτύπον οὔασι δέχθαι.
     οὐ νέμεσις· κείνους γε καὶ αἱ μάλα μηκέτι τυτθαί
65   οὐδέποτ' ἀφρικτὶ μακάρων ὁρόωσι θύγατρες.
     ἀλλ' ὅτε κουράων τις ἀπειθέα μητέρι τεύχοι,
     μήτηρ μὲν Κύκλωπας ἑῇ ἐπὶ παιδὶ καλιστρεῖ,
     Ἄργην ἢ Στερόπην· ὁ δὲ δώματος ἐκ μυχάτοιο
     ἔρχεται Ἑρμείης σποδιῇ κεχριμένος αἰθῇ.

42 ἐπελέξατο Ψ: απ[.]λεξαο PGen   45 πέμπον sch. Nic.: πέμπεν PMilVogl Ψ   52 Ὀσσαίοισιν
Meineke: οσσαιοις PAnt: ὀσσείοισιν Ψ   54 ὑπογλαύσσοντα sch. Call., F, Bentley: ὑπογλαύσοντα
Ψ   57]ινακρη PAnt: Τρινακρίη E in marg., η: Τρινακίη Ψ   61 τετύποντες Meineke: τετυπόντες
Ψ   μυχθίσσειαν Meineke: μυχεισειαν PAnt, fort. per errorem pro μυχθισειαν: μοχθίσσειαν Ψ:
μοχθήσειαν a Lasc.   64 γε Meineke: δὲ Ψ   66 τεύχοι Ψ: τεύχει a   69 κεχριμένος E, T in marg.:
κεχρημένος Ψ

70   αὐτίκα τὴν κούρην μορμύσσεται, ἡ δὲ τεκούσης
     δύνει ἔσω κόλπους θεμένη ἐπὶ φάεσι χεῖρας.
     κοῦρα, σὺ δὲ προτέρω περ, ἔτι τριέτηρος ἐοῦσα,
     εὖτ' ἔμολεν Λητώ σε μετ' ἀγκαλίδεσσι φέρουσα,
     Ἡφαίστου καλέοντος ὅπως ὀπτήρια δοίη,
75   Βρόντεώ σε στιβαροῖσιν ἐφεσσαμένου γονάτεσσι,
     στήθεος ἐκ μεγάλου λασίης ἐδράξαο χαίτης,
     ὤλοψας δὲ βίηφι· τὸ δ' ἄτριχον εἰσέτι καὶ νῦν
     μεσσάτιον στέρνοιο μένει μέρος, ὡς ὅτε κόρση
     φωτὸς ἐνιδρυθεῖσα κόμην ἐπενείματ' ἀλώπηξ.
80   τῷ μάλα θαρσαλέη σφε τάδε προσελέξαο τῆμος·
     'Κύκλωπες, κἠμοί τι Κυδώνιον εἰ δ' ἄγε τόξον
     ἠδ' ἰοὺς κοίλην τε κατακληῖδα βελέμνων
     τεύξατε· καὶ γὰρ ἐγὼ Λητωϊὰς ὥσπερ Ἀπόλλων.
     αἰ δέ κ' ἐγὼ τόξοις μονιὸν δάκος ἤ τι πέλωρον
85   θηρίον ἀγρεύσω, τὸ δέ κεν Κύκλωπες ἔδοιεν.'
     ἔννεπες· οἱ δ' ἐτέλεσσαν· ἄφαρ δ' ὡπλίσσαο, δαῖμον.
        αἶψα δ' ἐπὶ σκύλακας πάλιν ἤιες. ἵκεο δ' αὖλιν
     Ἀρκαδικὴν ἔπι Πανός. ὁ δὲ κρέα λυγκὸς ἔταμνε
     Μαιναλίης, ἵνα οἱ τοκάδες κύνες εἶδαρ ἔδοιεν.
90   τὶν δ' ὁ γενειήτης δύο μὲν κύνας ἥμισυ πηγούς,
     τρεῖς δὲ παρουαίους, ἕνα δ' αἰόλον, οἵ ρα λέοντας
     αὐτοὺς αὖ ἐρύοντες, ὅτε δράξαιντο δεράων,
     εἷλκον ἔτι ζώοντας ἐπ' αὔλιον, ἑπτὰ δ' ἔδωκε
     θάσσονας αὐράων Κυνοσουρίδας, αἵ ρα διῶξαι
95   ὤκισται νεβρούς τε καὶ οὐ μύοντα λαγωόν
     καὶ κοίτην ἐλάφοιο καὶ ὕστριχος ἔνθα καλιαί
     σημῆναι καὶ ζορκὸς ἐπ' ἴχνιον ἡγήσασθαι.
     ἔνθεν ἀπερχομένη (μετὰ καὶ κύνες ἐσσεύοντο)
     εὗρες ἐπὶ προμολῇσ' ὄρεος τοῦ Παρρασίοιο
100 σκαιρούσας ἐλάφους, μέγα τι χρέος· αἱ μὲν ἐπ' ὄχθης
     αἰὲν ἐβουκολέοντο μελαμψήφιδος ἀναύρου,
     μάσσονες ἢ ταῦροι, κεράων δ' ἀπελάμπετο χρυσός.
     ἐξαπίνης δ' ἔταφές τε καὶ ὃν ποτὶ θυμὸν ἔειπες·
     'τοῦτό κεν Ἀρτέμιδος πρωτάγριον ἄξιον εἴη.'

78 κόρση **T** in marg., Bentley: κόρσην **Ψ**, Mair   80 προσελέξαο litt. τ deleta in **E**: προσελέξατο **Ψ** 81 κἠμοί Meineke: καιμο[PGen.: κἀμοί **L** in marg.: ἢ ἤ μοι **Ψ**   86 δαῖμον **a**: δαίμων **Ψ**   88 δὲ **Ψ**: μεν PGen.   91 παρουαίους coni. Schneider: παρωαίους M. Haupt: παρουατίους **Ψ**   93 εἷλκον **T** in marg.: εἷλον **Ψ**   100 ὄχθης **αβγ**: ὄχθης **δζη**   101 ἀναύρου Meineke, Wilamowitz, Bornmann: Ἀναύρου sch. Call., Ernesti, Mair, Pfeiffer

105   πέντ' ἔσαν αἱ πᾶσαι· πίσυρας δ' ἕλες ὦκα θέουσα
       νόσφι κυνοδρομίης, ἵνα τοι θοὸν ἅρμα φέρωσι.
       τὴν δὲ μίαν Κελάδοντος ὑπὲρ ποταμοῖο φυγοῦσαν
       Ἥρης ἐννεσίῃσιν, ἀέθλιον Ἡρακλῆι
       ὕστερον ὄφρα γένοιτο, πάγος Κερύνειος ἔδεκτο.

110   Ἄρτεμι Παρθενίη Τιτυοκτόνε, χρύσεα μέν τοι
       ἔντεα καὶ ζώνη, χρύσεον δ' ἐζεύξαο δίφρον,
       ἐν δ' ἐβάλευ χρύσεια, θεή, κεμάδεσσι χαλινά.
       ποῦ δέ σε τὸ πρῶτον κεράεις ὄχος ἤρξατ' ἀείρειν;
       Αἵμῳ ἐπὶ Θρήϊκι, τόθεν βορέαο κατάϊξ
115   ἔρχεται ἀχλαίνοισι δυσαέα κρυμὸν ἄγουσα.
       ποῦ δ' ἔταμες πεύκην, ἀπὸ δὲ φλογὸς ἥψαο ποίης;
       Μυσῷ ἐν Οὐλύμπῳ, φάεος δ' ἐνέηκας ἀϋτμὴν
       ἀσβέστου, τό ῥα πατρὸς ἀποστάζουσι κεραυνοί.
       ποσσάκι δ' ἀργυρέοιο, θεή, πειρήσαο τόξου;
120   πρῶτον ἐπὶ πτελέην, τὸ δὲ δεύτερον ἧκας ἐπὶ δρῦν,
       τὸ τρίτον αὖτ' ἐπὶ θῆρα. τὸ τέτρατον οὐκέτ' †ἐπὶ δρῦν†,
       ἀλλά †μιν εἰς ἀδίκων ἔβαλες πόλιν, οἵ τε περὶ σφέας
       οἵ τε περὶ ξείνους ἀλιτήμονα πολλὰ τέλεσκον.
       σχέτλιοι, οἷς τύνη χαλεπὴν ἐμμάξεαι ὀργήν·
125   κτήνεά φιν λοιμὸς καταβόσκεται, ἔργα δὲ πάχνη,
       κείρονται δὲ γέροντες ἐφ' υἱάσιν, αἱ δὲ γυναῖκες
       ἢ βληταὶ θνήσκουσι λεχωΐδες ἠὲ φυγοῦσαι
       τίκτουσιν τῶν οὐδὲν ἐπὶ σφυρὸν ὀρθὸν ἀνέστη.
       οἷς δέ κεν εὐμειδής τε καὶ ἵλαος αὐγάσσηαι,
130   κείνοις εὖ μὲν ἄρουρα φέρει στάχυν, εὖ δὲ γενέθλη
       τετραπόδων, εὖ δ' οἶκος ἀέξεται· οὐδ' ἐπὶ σῆμα
       ἔρχονται πλὴν εὖτε πολυχρόνιόν τι φέρωσιν·
       οὐδὲ διχοστασίη τρώει γένος, ἥ τε καὶ εὖ περ
       οἴκους ἑστηῶτας ἐσίνατο· ταὶ δὲ θυωρόν
135   εἰνάτερες γαλόῳ τε μίαν πέρι δίφρα τίθενται.
       πότνια, τῶν εἴη μὲν ἐμοὶ φίλος ὅστις ἀληθής,
       εἴην δ' αὐτός, ἄνασσα, μέλοι δέ μοι αἰὲν ἀοιδή·
       τῇ ἔνι μὲν Λητοῦς γάμος ἔσσεται, ἐν δὲ σὺ πολλή,
       ἐν δὲ καὶ Ἀπόλλων, ἐν δ' οἵ σεο πάντες ἄεθλοι,

---

109 ὕστερον sch. A.R.: ὕστατον Ψ κερυνειος PAmh, Ψ: κεραύνιος sch. A.R., Lasc. 112 θεή
Pfeiffer: θεά Ψ 114 κατάϊξ Ψ 121 οὐκέτ' ἐπὶ δρῦν Ψ per errorem? Vide versus 120 finem: οὐκέτι
θήρα Meineke: οὐκέτ' ἔπαισας vel ἔπαιξας Barber, Massimilla 122 nisi versus deest, μιν haud
sanum 125 λοιμὸς **η, E** (ο intra λ et ι insertum): λιμὸς Ψ 131 οἶκος Meineke: ὄλβος Ψ

140 ἐν δὲ κύνες καὶ τόξα καὶ ἄντυγες, αἵ τε σε ῥεῖα
θηητὴν φορέουσιν ὅτ᾽ ἐς Διὸς οἶκον ἐλαύνεις.
ἔνθα τοι ἀντιόωντες ἐνὶ προμολῇσι δέχονται
ὅπλα μὲν Ἑρμείης Ἀκακήσιος, αὐτὰρ Ἀπόλλων
θηρίον ὅττι φέρῃσθα—πάροιθέ γε, πρίν περ ἱκέσθαι
145 καρτερὸν Ἀλκεΐδην· νῦν δ᾽ οὐκέτι Φοῖβος ἄεθλον
τοῦτον ἔχει, τοῖος γὰρ ἀεὶ Τιρύνθιος ἄκμων
ἕστηκε πρὸ πυλέων ποτιδέγμενος, εἴ τι φέρουσα
νεῖαι πῖον ἔδεσμα· θεοὶ δ᾽ ἐπὶ πάντες ἐκείνῳ
ἄλληκτον γελόωσι, μάλιστα δὲ πενθερὴ αὐτή,
150 ταῦρον ὅτ᾽ ἐκ δίφροιο μάλα μέγαν ἢ ὅγε χλούνην
κάπρον ὀπισθιδίοιο φέροι ποδὸς ἀσπαίροντα·
κερδαλέῳ μύθῳ σε, θεή, μάλα τῷδε πινύσκει·
ʼβάλλε κακοὺς ἐπὶ θῆρας, ἵνα θνητοί σε βοηθόν
ὡς ἐμὲ κικλήσκωσιν. ἔα πρόκας ἠδὲ λαγωούς
155 οὔρεα βόσκεσθαι· τί δέ κεν πρόκες ἠδὲ λαγωοί
ῥέξειαν; σύες ἔργα, σύες φυτὰ λυμαίνονται.
καὶ βόες ἀνθρώποισι κακὸν μέγα· βάλλ᾽ ἐπὶ καὶ τούς.ʼ
ὣς ἔνεπεν, ταχινὸς δὲ μέγαν περὶ θῆρα πονεῖτο.
οὐ γὰρ ὅγε Φρυγίη περ ὑπὸ δρυῒ γυῖα θεωθείς
160 παύσατ᾽ ἀδηφαγίης· ἔτι οἱ πάρα νηδὺς ἐκείνη,
τῇ ποτ᾽ ἀροτριόωντι συνήντετο Θειοδάμαντι.
σοὶ δ᾽ Ἀμνισιάδες μὲν ὑπὸ ζεύγληφι λυθείσας
ψήχουσιν κεμάδας, παρὰ δέ σφισι πουλὺ νέμεσθαι
Ἥρης ἐκ λειμῶνος ἀμησάμεναι φορέουσιν
165 ὠκύθοον τριπέτηλον, ὃ καὶ Διὸς ἵπποι ἔδουσιν·
ἐν καὶ χρυσείας ὑποληνίδας ἐπλήσαντο
ὕδατος, ὄφρ᾽ ἐλάφοισι ποτὸν θυμάρμενον εἴη.
αὐτὴ δ᾽ ἐς πατρὸς δόμον ἔρχεαι· οἱ δέ σ᾽ ἐφ᾽ ἕδρην
πάντες ὁμῶς καλέουσι· σὺ δ᾽ Ἀπόλλωνι παρίζεις.
170   ἡνίκα δ᾽ αἱ νύμφαι σε χορῷ ἔνι κυκλώσονται
ἀγχόθι πηγάων Αἰγυπτίου Ἰνωποῖο
ἢ Πιτάνῃ (καὶ γὰρ Πιτάνη σέθεν) ἢ ἐνὶ Λίμναις,
ἢ ἵνα, δαῖμον, Ἀλὰς Ἀραφηνίδας οἰκήσουσα
ἦλθες ἀπὸ Σκυθίης, ἀπὸ δ᾽ εἴπαο τέθμια Ταύρων,

144 γε Blomfield: δέ **Ψ** 145–46 φ[οιβοσαεθλο]ν | τουτον PAmh, ut vid.: τοῦτον ἄεθλον | Φοῖβος
Ψ 150 ὅγε Lasc.: ὅτε **Ψ** 151 φέροι **Ψ**: Pfeiffer dubitat an φέρει scribendum, cf. 66 153 θνητοί σε
I, T in marg.: θνητοῖσι **Ψ** 154 κικλήσκωσιν **a, T** in marg., v.l. **E**: κικλήσκουσιν cett. 155 τί δέ κεν
Lasc.: τί κεν **Ψ**: τί κέ μιν Wilamowitz 165 ὠκύθοον Hesychius: ὠκύθεον PAnt 179, **Ψ**
172 Πιτάνη Valckenaer: Πιτάνης **Ψ** 173 Ἀλὰς Bornmann: Ἀλάς **Ψ**

175 μὴ νειὸν τημοῦτος ἐμαὶ βόες εἵνεκα μισθοῦ
τετράγυον τέμνοιεν ὑπ' ἀλλοτρίῳ ἀροτῆρι·
ἦ γάρ κεν γυιαί τε καὶ αὐχένα κεκμηυῖαι
κόπρον ἔπι προγένοιντο, καὶ εἰ Στυμφαιίδες εἶεν
εἰναετιζόμεναι κεραελκέες, αἵ μέγ' ἄρισται
180 τέμνειν ὦλκα βαθεῖαν· ἐπεὶ θεὸς οὔποτ' ἐκεῖνον
ἦλθε παρ' Ἥλιος καλὸν χορόν, ἀλλὰ θεῆται
δίφρον ἐπιστήσας, τὰ δὲ φάεα μηκύνονται.
    τίς δέ νύ τοι νήσων, ποῖον δ' ὄρος εὔαδε πλεῖστον,
τίς δὲ λιμήν, ποίη δὲ πόλις; τίνα δ' ἔξοχα νυμφέων
185 φίλαο καὶ ποίας ἡρωίδας ἔσχες ἑταίρας;
εἰπέ, θεή, σὺ μὲν ἄμμιν, ἐγὼ δ' ἑτέροισιν ἀείσω.
νήσων μὲν Δολίχη, πολίων δέ τοι εὔαδε Πέργη,
Τηΰγετον δ' ὀρέων, λιμένες γε μὲν Εὐρίποιο.
ἔξοχα δ' ἀλλάων Γορτυνίδα φίλαο νύμφην,
190 ἐλλοφόνον Βριτόμαρτιν εὔσκοπον· ἧς ποτε Μίνως
πτοιηθεὶς ὑπ' ἔρωτι κατέδραμεν οὔρεα Κρήτης.
ἡ δ' ὀτὲ μὲν λασίῃσιν ὑπὸ δρυσὶ κρύπτετο νύμφη,
ἄλλοτε δ' εἰαμενῇσιν· ὁ δ' ἐννέα μῆνας ἐφοίτα
παίπαλά τε κρημνούς τε καὶ οὐκ ἀνέπαυσε διωκτύν,
195 μέσφ' ὅτε μαρπτομένη καὶ δὴ σχεδὸν ἧλατο πόντον
πρηόνος ἐξ ὑπάτοιο καὶ ἔνθορεν εἰς ἁλιήων
δίκτυα, τά σφ' ἐσάωσαν· ὅθεν μετέπειτα Κύδωνες
νύμφην μὲν Δίκτυναν, ὄρος δ' ὅθεν ἧλατο νύμφη
Δικταῖον καλέουσιν, ἀνεστήσαντο δὲ βωμούς
200 ἱερά τε ῥέζουσι· τὸ δὲ στέφος ἤματι κείνῳ
ἢ πίτυς ἢ σχῖνος, μύρτοιο δὲ χεῖρες ἄθικτοι·
δὴ τότε γὰρ πέπλοισιν ἐνέσχετο μύρσινος ὄζος
τῆς κούρης, ὅτ' ἔφευγεν· ὅθεν μέγα χώσατο μύρτῳ.
Οὖπι ἄνασσ' εὐῶπι φαεσφόρε, καὶ δέ σε κείνης
205 Κρηταέες καλέουσιν ἐπωνυμίην ἀπὸ νύμφης.
καὶ μὴν Κυρήνην ἑταρίσσαο, τῇ ποτ' ἔδωκας
αὐτὴ θηρητῆρε δύω κύνε, τοῖς ἔνι κούρη
Ὑψηὶς παρὰ τύμβον Ἰώλκιον ἔμμορ' ἀέθλου.
καὶ Κεφάλου ξανθὴν ἄλοχον Δηϊονίδαο,
210 πότνια, σὴν ὁμόθηρον ἐθήκαο· καὶ δέ σέ φασι
καλὴν Ἀντίκλειαν ἴσον φάεσσι φιλῆσαι.
αἱ πρῶται θοὰ τόξα καὶ ἀμφ' ὤμοισι φαρέτρας

ἰοδόκους ἐφόρησαν· †ἀσύλλωτοι δέ φιν ὦμοι
δεξιτεροὶ καὶ γυμνὸς ἀεὶ παρεφαίνετο μαζός.
215 ἤνησας δ᾽ ἔτι πάγχυ ποδορρώρην Ἀταλάντην
κούρην Ἰασίοιο συοκτόνον Ἀρκασίδαο,
καί ἑ κυνηλασίην τε καὶ εὐστοχίην ἐδίδαξας.
οὔ μιν ἐπίκλητοι Καλυδωνίου ἀγρευτῆρες
μέμφονται κάπροιο· τὰ γὰρ σημήϊα νίκης
220 Ἀρκαδίην εἰσῆλθεν, ἔχει δ᾽ ἔτι θηρὸς ὀδόντας·
οὐδὲ μὲν Ὑλαῖόν τε καὶ ἄφρονα Ῥοῖκον ἔολπα
οὐδέ περ ἐχθαίροντας ἐν Ἄϊδι μωμήσασθαι
τοξότιν· οὐ γάρ σφιν λαγόνες συνεπιψεύσονται,
τάων Μαιναλίη νᾶεν φόνῳ ἀκρώρεια.
225   πότνια πουλυμέλαθρε, πολύπτολι, χαῖρε, Χιτώνη
Μιλήτῳ ἐπίδημε· σὲ γὰρ ποιήσατο Νηλεύς
ἡγεμόνην, ὅτε νηυσὶν ἀνήγετο Κεκροπίηθεν.
Χησιὰς Ἰμβρασίη Πρωτόθρονε, σοὶ δ᾽ Ἀγαμέμνων
πηδάλιον νηὸς σφετέρης ἐγκάτθετο νηῷ
230 μείλιον ἀπλοΐης, ὅτε οἱ κατέδησας ἀήτας,
Τεύκρων ἡνίκα νῆες Ἀχαιίδες ἄστεα κήδειν
ἔπλεον ἀμφ᾽ Ἑλένῃ Ῥαμνουσίδι θυμωθεῖσαι.
ἢ μέν τοι Προῖτός γε δύω ἐκαθίσσατο νηούς,
ἄλλον μὲν Κορίης, ὅτι οἱ συνελέξαο κούρας
235 οὔρεα πλαζομένας Ἀζήνια, τὸν δ᾽ ἐνὶ Λούσοις
Ἡμέρῃ, οὕνεκα θυμὸν ἀπ᾽ ἄγριον εἴλεο παίδων.
σοὶ καὶ Ἀμαζονίδες πολέμου ἐπιθυμήτειραι
ἔν κοτε παρραλίῃ Ἐφέσῳ βρέτας ἱδρύσαντο
φηγῷ ὑπὸ πρέμνῳ, τέλεσεν δέ τοι ἱερὸν Ἱππώ·
240 αὐταὶ δ᾽, Οὖπι ἄνασσα, περὶ πρύλιν ὠρχήσαντο
πρῶτα μὲν ἐν σακέεσσιν ἐνόπλιον, αὖθι δὲ κύκλῳ
στησάμεναι χορὸν εὐρύν· ὑπήεισαν δὲ λίγειαι
λεπταλέον σύριγγες, ἵνα ῥήσσωσιν ὁμαρτῇ
(οὐ γάρ πω νέβρεια δι᾽ ὀστέα τετρήναντο,
245 ἔργον Ἀθηναίης ἐλάφῳ κακόν)· ἔδραμε δ᾽ ἠχώ
Σάρδιας ἔς τε νομὸν Βερεκύνθιον. αἱ δὲ πόδεσσιν
οὖλα κατεκροτάλιζον, ἐπεψόφεον δὲ φαρέτραι.
κεῖνο δέ τοι μετέπειτα περὶ βρέτας εὐρὺ θέμειλον
δωμήθη, τοῦ δ᾽ οὔτι θεώτερον ὄψεται ἠώς

---

213 ἀσύλ(λ)ωτοι **Ψ**: ἀσίλλωτοι tempt. Mair   235 Ἀζήνια Holstenius, Graevius:
ἀξείνια **Ψ**   243 ῥήσσωσιν Jan: πλήσσωσιν **Ψ**

250　οὐδ᾽ ἀφνειότερον· ῥέα κεν Πυθῶνα παρέλθοι.
　　　τῷ ῥα καὶ ἠλαίνων ἀλαπαξέμεν ἠπείλησε
　　　Λύγδαμις ὑβριστής· ἐπὶ δὲ στρατὸν ἱππημολγῶν
　　　ἤγαγε Κιμμερίων ψαμάθῳ ἴσον, οἵ ῥα παρ᾽ αὐτόν
　　　κεκλιμένοι ναίουσι βοὸς πόρον Ἰναχιώνης.
255　ἆ δειλὸς βασιλέων, ὅσον ἤλιτεν· οὐ γὰρ ἔμελλεν
　　　οὔτ᾽ αὐτὸς Σκυθίηνδε παλιμπετὲς οὔτε τις ἄλλος
　　　ὅσσων ἐν λειμῶνι Καϋστρίῳ ἔσταν ἄμαξαι
　　　νοστήσειν· Ἐφέσου γὰρ ἀεὶ τεὰ τόξα πρόκειται.
　　　　　πότνια Μουνιχίη λιμενοσκόπε, χαῖρε, Φεραίη.
260　μή τις ἀτιμήσῃ τὴν Ἄρτεμιν (οὐδὲ γὰρ Οἰνεῖ
　　　βωμὸν ἀτιμάσσαντι καλοὶ πόλιν ἦλθον ἀγῶνες),
　　　μηδ᾽ ἐλαφηβολίην μηδ᾽ εὐστοχίην ἐριδαίνειν
　　　(οὐδὲ γὰρ Ἀτρεΐδης ὀλίγῳ ἐπὶ κόμπασε μισθῷ),
　　　μηδέ τινα μνᾶσθαι τὴν παρθένον (οὐδὲ γὰρ Ὦτος,
265　οὐδὲ μὲν Ὠαρίων ἀγαθὸν γάμον ἐμνήστευσαν),
　　　μηδὲ χορὸν φεύγειν ἐνιαύσιον (οὐδὲ γὰρ Ἱππώ
　　　ἀκλαυτὶ περὶ βωμὸν ἀπείπατο κυκλώσασθαι)·
　　　χαῖρε μέγα, κρείουσα, καὶ εὐάντησον ἀοιδῇ.

253 ἤγαγε Ψ: ἤλασε Et. Gud.　263 ἐπὶ κόμπασε Meineke: ἔπι κόμπασε Wilamowitz,
Mair: ἐπικόμπασε Π: ἐπεκόμπασε Ψ

To Artemis

Artemis (for it is no light matter for singers to pass over her) we hymn; the bow and shootings of hare are her concern and the abundant chorus and to take pleasure in the mountains, beginning from the time when still a little girl, sitting upon her father's knees, (5) she spoke in this childish way to her father: "gimme virginity, Daddy, to preserve forever, and to be called by many names, so that Phoebus may not rival me. And gimme arrows and bows—let me, Father, I do not ask you for a quiver or a large bow: for me the Cyclopes (10) will fashion arrows in an instant, and, for me, a supple bow—and to be a light-bearer and to hitch up my tunic with a fringed border as far as my knees, so that I may kill wild beasts. Gimme sixty Ocean nymphs as my chorus, all nine-year-olds, all girls who have not yet put on the woman's headband. (15) Gimme twenty Amnisian nymphs as attendants, who would take care of my high hunting boots and, whenever I am no longer shooting at lynxes and deer, my swift hounds. Gimme all the mountains, and any city, whichever you wish. For it is rare when Artemis will go down to a town. (20) I'll dwell in the mountains, but mingle with the cities of men only when women who are worn down under the sharp pangs of childbirth call for my aid. The Fates ordained me to help them when I was first being born, because my mother did not suffer pain either in carrying me or giving me birth, (25) but she released me effortlessly from her own womb." When the girl, after speaking in this way, wanted to touch her father's beard, in vain she stretched her hands out several times in order to touch it. But her father laughed and nodded assent, and caressing her he said, "When goddesses would bear me such children as this, (30) I would have little concern for the jealousy of an angry Hera. Take, my child, freely, as much as you ask, and other, still greater things will your father give you. Thrice ten cities and more than one tower shall I grant you; to you thrice ten cities that will not know how to cherish any other god (35) but you alone, and to be called Artemis'. And I shall give you many cities to receive a share in common [*sc.* with other gods], both on land and on the islands. And in all there will be altars and groves of Artemis. And you will be guardian over streets and harbors." Having spoken thus, he confirmed (40) his speech with a nod of the head. Then the girl went to White Mountain in Crete, leafed over with woods, and then to Ocean; she selected many nymphs, all nine-year-olds, all girls who have not yet put on the woman's headband. The river Caeratus rejoiced greatly, Tethys rejoiced, (45) because they were sending their daughters to be companions to Leto's daughter.

And she went in turn to the Cyclopes. She found them on the island of Lipari (Lipari is the new name, but then its name was Meligounis) at Hephaestus' anvil, standing around a red-hot mass of iron. A great work was being hastened along: (50) they were fashioning a horse-trough for Poseidon. The nymphs were terrified when they saw dread monsters resembling the peaks of Ossa (all had, under their brow, a single eye like a shield with four layers of hide, glowering fiercely) and when they heard the thud of (55) the far-sounding anvil, the great blast of the bellows, and the groan of their labored breathing. For Etna cried out, and Trinacria cried out, the seat of the Sicanians, neighboring Italy cried out, and Corsica gave out a great shout, whenever the Cyclopes, having lifted their hammers above their shoulders (60) and struck in turn bronze or iron sizzling from the forge, would snort mightily. Therefore the Oceanids did not bring themselves to look straight at them or to hear the din without fear. They are not to blame. (65) Not even the daughters of the blessed ones (and they are not children) look on those creatures without a shudder. But whenever one of the girls is disobedient to her mother, her mother summons the Cyclopes—Arges or Steropes—to her child. And Hermes comes out from the inner parts of the house smeared with burnt ashes, (70) and immediately plays the part of Mormo to frighten the child, and she gets into her mother's lap, placing her hands over her eyes. Girl, you, even before, when you were only three years old, Leto came carrying you in her arms, at the invitation of Hephaestus, so he might give you a gift. (75) When Brontes placed you on his mighty knees, you grasped the shaggy hair from his great chest, and plucked it out by force. And even up until this day the midmost part of his chest remains hairless, as when mange once it has become established on a man's temple grazes upon the hair. (80) Therefore you addressed them very boldly that day: "Cyclopes, for me too come fashion a Cydonian bow and arrows and a hollow capped quiver for my shafts. For I am a child of Leto, just as Apollo is. If with my bow I hunt some solitary beast or some terrible creature, (85) that the Cyclopes would eat." You spoke and they accomplished the task. Immediately you were equipped, goddess.

Swiftly you went in turn for your hounds; you came to the Arcadian grotto of Pan. He was cutting up the meat of a Maenalian lynx so that his pregnant bitches might eat food. (90) And the bearded one gave you two half-white hounds, three chestnut-colored, and one variegated, which, pulling down even lions, whenever they fastened on their throats, used to drag them still alive to the grotto. And he gave you seven Cynosurian bitches swifter than the wind, who were the fastest at pursuing (95) fawns and the hare that does not close its eyes, and at sniffing out the covert of the stag and where are the lairs of the porcupine, and at following the track of the roe deer.

Leaving there (and your hounds hurried after), you found at the foot of Mt. Parrhasius (100) bounding deer—a great business! They always grazed by the banks of the swift current with its black pebbles, more massive than bulls, and gold flashed out from their horns. You were amazed and spoke to your heart: "This would be a first hunt worthy of Artemis." (105) There were five in all. Four you took by running swiftly without hunting with your hounds, so they might pull your swift chariot. But the one that fled beyond the river Celadon through

Hera's command, so that it might later become a test for Heracles, the Cerynian crag received.

(110) Artemis, Maiden, Slayer of Tityus, golden are your arrows and your girdle, you yoked a golden chariot, and, goddess, you put golden bridles on your deer. Where first did your horned team begin to take you? To Thracian Haemus, whence the sudden squall of Boreas (115) comes, bringing an evil breath of frost to those without cloaks. Where did you cut the pine? From what flame did you light it? On Mysian Olympus, and you placed the breath of unquenchable flame in it that your father's thunderbolts distill. How many times, goddess, did you test your silver bow? (120) First at an elm tree, second you shot at an oak, and third again at a beast. The fourth time no longer... but you shot into a city of the unjust, who to themselves and to strangers did many offensive deeds, scoundrels, on whom you would wreak your harsh anger. (125) On their herds pestilence feeds, on their worked fields, a frost. Old men cut their hair in mourning over their sons, their wives die either stricken in childbirth, or having escaped that fate, breed children none of whom stands on a straight ankle. But those on whom you would gaze smiling and gracious, (130) their field bears abundant corn, abundant their race of four-footed beasts, and abundantly does their household increase. Nor do they go to a tomb, except when they are carrying out something very old. Nor does dissension wound their tribe, which ravages even well-established houses. (135) And wives of brothers take their seats around one table with their sisters-in-law. Mistress, of these let whoever is my true friend be, and I myself, Queen, and have song ever as my care. In it will be the marriage of Leto, and in it you will be prominent, and in it also Apollo, and in it all your exploits, (140) in it your hounds and bow and chariots, which easily carry you in your splendor, when you drive to the house of Zeus. Meeting you there in the forecourt, Hermes *Akakasios* takes your arms, but Apollo takes whatever beast you have brought. At least Apollo did this before mighty Alcides arrived. (145) Now Phoebus no longer has this task, for such as he is the Tirynthian anvil always takes up his place before the gates waiting if you should come bringing some rich edible. The gods all laugh continuously at that one, but especially his own mother-in-law, whenever from your chariot he should carry a very large bull (150) or a wild boar by its hind foot as it writhes. With this very crafty speech, goddess, he admonishes you: "Shoot at evil beasts so that mortals may call you their helper, as they do me; let deer and hares feed in the mountains. (155) What could deer or hares do? Boars destroy tilled fields, boars destroy orchards, and bulls are a great evil for men. Shoot at those too." Thus he spoke, and quickly set to work on the great beast. For even though under a Phrygian oak his limbs had been deified, (160) he had not ceased from his gluttony. He still possessed the stomach with which he once encountered Thiodamas as he was plowing. Your Amnisian nymphs rub down the deer who have been released from the yoke, and for them to graze on they cut and

carry (165) much swift-growing tripetal from Hera's meadow, upon which Zeus's horses also feed. And they fill golden troughs with water so that there would be a heart-pleasing drink for the deer. You yourself enter your father's house, and all invite you to sit with them, but you sit next to Apollo. (170) When the nymphs form a circle around you in the dance near the streams of Egyptian Inopus or Pitane (for Pitane also was yours) or in Limnae, or where, goddess, you came from Scythia to dwell in Halae Araphenides, and you renounced the rites of the Taurians, (175) then may my oxen not plough a four-acre field for a wage under the hand of a foreign plowman, for surely they would come to the byre with their limbs and their necks exhausted, even if they were nine-year-old Stymphaeans, drawing by their horns, which are the best (180) to cut a deep furrow; since the god Helios never goes by that fair chorus but stopping his chariot he watches, and the daylight is lengthened.

Now which of the islands, what mountain is especially favored by you? What harbor, what city? Which of the nymphs do you love above all, and (185) what heroines do you have as companions? Speak, goddess, you to me, and I will sing to others. Of islands, Doliche, of cities, Perge is favored by you. Taÿgetus of mountains, and the harbors of Euripus. Beyond the others you love the Gortyn-ian nymph, (190) Britomartis, the keen-sighted deerslayer. For once upon a time Minos was struck by love of her and wandered the mountains of Crete. But the nymph sometimes used to hide herself under the shaggy oaks, and at other times in the meadows. For nine months he frequented the heights and cliffs and did not cease pursuit until, when nearly captured, (195) she leapt into the sea from a high peak and jumped into the fishermen's nets that saved her. Hence afterwards the Cydonians called the nymph Dictynna, and the mountain from which the nymph leapt they call Dictaion, and they erected altars and (200) performed sac-rifices. The garland on that day is pine or mastic, but hands do not touch myrtle, because once a myrtle branch caught up the girl's peplos, when she was fleeing. For this reason she was very angry at the myrtle. Oupis, queen of the fair visage, bringer of light, and you also do (205) the Cretans name Dictynna after that nymph. And furthermore, you made Cyrene your companion and gave her two hunting hounds, with which the daughter of Hypseus won a prize alongside the Iolcian tomb. And the fair-haired wife of Cephalus, the son of Deioneus, (210) you placed among your companions in the hunt. And they say that you loved the fair Anticlea as much as your own eyes. These for the first time wore swift bows and arrow-bearing quivers over their shoulders... their right shoulders, and their breast always appeared bare. (215) Further, you greatly praised swift-footed Ata-lanta, the boar-slaying daughter of Arcadian Iasius, and you taught her the chase with hounds and marksmanship. Not with her did the hunters summoned for the Calydonian boar find fault, for the tokens of victory (220) came to Arcadia, and it has still the beast's tusks. And not even Hylaeus and foolish Rhoecus, I imagine, even though they hate her in Hades, would fault her archery. For their flanks will not conspire in the falsehood, with whose blood the peaks of Maenalus flowed.

(225) Mistress of many shrines, many cities, hail Lady of the Chiton, dweller in Miletus. For Neleus made you his guide when he set out with his ships from the land of Cecrops. Lady of Chesion, Lady of Imbrasia, first enthroned, to you Agamemnon dedicated his ship's rudder in your shrine, (230) a charm against bad weather, when you subdued the winds for him, at the time when the Achaean ships sailed to harass the towns of the Teucri, angered about Rhamnusian Helen. For surely to you Proetus dedicated two shrines, one to *Koria* [Artemis of Maidenhood] because you gathered up his daughters (235) who were wandering in the Azanian mountains, and the other in Lousoi, to *Hemera* [Artemis the Mild], when you took away the wild spirit from his daughters. And to you the Amazons, who are dedicated to war, once by the shore in Ephesus set up an image beneath an oak trunk, and there Hippo performed the rite for you. (240) They themselves, Oupis, Queen, danced the war dance, first armed with shields, then arranging the broad chorus in a circle. Pipes provided delicate accompaniment with a clear sound, so that their feet might beat in time. (For they did not yet drill holes in the bones of the fawn, (245) a work of Athena, an evil for the deer.) An echo ran to Sardis and to the Berecynthian territory. They stamped their feet rapidly and their quivers rattled. Afterwards around that image a broad foundation was built, and dawn saw nothing more divine than this, (250) nothing richer. It would easily surpass Pytho. For this reason surely as he wandered Lygdamis in his arrogance threatened to destroy it, and he led a force of Cimmerians, who milk their mares, equal in number to the sand, who dwell adjacent to the very Passage of the Cow, daughter of Inachus [Io]. (255) Ah, deluded among kings, how much did he sin! For he was not going to return again to Scythia nor were any other of the great number whose wagons stood in the Caÿstrian plain. For your bow always stands as a defense of Ephesus.

Mistress of Munychia, guardian of harbors, hail Lady of Pheraea. (260) Let no one dishonor Artemis. (For no fair contests came to the city when Oeneus dishonored her altar.) Do not contend with her in the shooting of deer or in marksmanship. (For the son of Atreus boasted at no small price.) Let no one court the maiden. (265) (For neither Otus nor Orion courted her for a happy marriage.) Do not flee her yearly dance. (For not without tears did Hippo refuse to dance around her altar.) Hail greatly, queen, and graciously encounter my song.

Commentary

1. Both Homeric hymns to Artemis begin similarly: (9) Ἄρτεμιν ὕμνει and (27) Ἄρτεμιν ἀείδω. The hymns to Demeter and Hermes also begin with the god's name, though *HhAp* does not. The main thought appears in the first words of lines 1 and 2: Ἄρτεμιν... | ὑμνέομεν, with a parenthetical statement inserted between object and verb.

ἀειδόντεσσι: only here and in Plato *Rep.* 424b9–10 in a passage that condemns musical innovation. Plato "quotes" Homer, *Od.* 1.351–52:... ἀοιδὴν μᾶλλον ἐπιφρονέουσ' [for Homer's ἐπικλείουσ'] ἄνθρωποι | ἥτις ἀειδόντεσσι (for Homer's ἀκουόντεσσι) νεωτάτη ἀμφιπέληται as part of his argument. But he alters the Homeric text, shifting the emphasis from audience (ἀκουόντεσσι) to poets (ἀειδόντεσσι). There are two ways to understand Callimachus' use of this otherwise *hapax* form: (1) he and Plato both knew a text of Homer that read ἀειδόντεσσι or (2) Callimachus deliberately alludes to Plato's "misreading." Since Plato's reading is in a context of debate over musical innovation, (2) seems more likely. The consequences of (2) are that Callimachus is signaling his intention at the opening of his poem to offer a hymn that is an innovation on Homer, an ἀοιδή that is truly νεωτάτη. Further, M. Fantuzzi points out that Callimachus' οὐ γὰρ ἐλαφρὸν...λαθέσθαι would seem to presuppose Plato's emphasis on thoughtful memory (ἐπιφρονέουσι) in his misquotation of Homer, instead of the standard Homeric idea of praise (ἐπικλείουσι).

λαθέσθαι: in middle/passive the verb means "forget" or even "pass over deliberately," here echoing *HhAp* 1: μνήσομαι οὐδὲ λάθωμαι Ἀπόλλωνος ἑκάτοιο. It may be a comment on the relative unimportance of Artemis in the Homeric hymns as well as a sly dig at Plato who did "forget" his Homer.

2. λαγωβολίαι: only in Callimachus, "hare-shootings"; the related λαγωβόλον occurs three times in Theocritus (4.49, 7.128, *ep.* 2.3); ἐλαφηβόλος as a title of Artemis occurs in Sappho and Anacreon (see pp. 105–6) and ἐλαφηβολίην ("shooting of deer") at 262 (see Schmitt 36n22).

2–3. μέλονται has three subjects (τόξα, λαγωβολίαι, χορός) and a dependent infinitive (ἐψιάασθαι). "For whom bows and shooting hares are a care and an abundant chorus and to take pleasure in the mountains [*sc.* is a care]."

3. ἀμφιλαφής: here Artemis' "abundant" choruses; in *hAp* 42, of Apollo's abundant skills.

ἐψιάασθαι: Homeric (*Od.* 21.429) and in A.R. 3.950, of delighting in song. It is clear from compounds that the word is aspirated; the scholia gloss as διατρίβειν, "frequent" and παίζειν, which covers a wide range including to play, to hunt, and to dance.

4. ἄρχμενοι: ἀρχόμενοι of the medieval mss. is unmetrical; the correct reading is preserved in POxy 47.3328 (a glossary of the hymn). The syncopated form occurs at *Aet.* fr. 7.25 and 75.56.

ὡς ὅτε: Pfeiffer accepts this reading of the mss. but Bornmann obelized it on the grounds that in Homer ὡς ὅτε always introduces a simile. However, there is one example of ὡς ὅτε that does not do so; in *Il*. 10 (the authenticity of which is disputed) Diomedes asks Athena for help; cf. 285–86: σπεῖό μοι ὡς ὅτε πατρὶ ἅμ᾽ ἕσπεο Τυδέϊ δίῳ | ἐς Θήβας ("follow me as when you went together with my father, godlike Tydeus, to Thebes").

ἐφεζομένη: see p. 105.

γονάτεσσι: this form occurs again at 75 and in Theoc. 16.11.

5. κουρίζουσα: earlier the verb seems to be used of young men and women (e.g., Hom. *Od*. 22.185, of the youthful Laertes), but in *hZeus* 54 and *hDelos* 324 of an infant, and here of a very small child.

γονῆα: from γονεύς, "parent" or "father"; previously the form occurs only in Hesiod *Op*. 331. In Callimachus it occurs at fr. 41.2 Pf., on which see Harder ad loc., and cf. *hDem* 73.

6–25. Artemis' speech is structured around **δός μοι**, the childish "gimme," repeated five times, lines 6, 8, 13, 15, 18, followed by three futures in lines 19 and 20. The extreme hyperbaton of 8–10 and the convoluted explanation of 21–25 may be intended to mimic the speech patterns of children.

6. παρθενίην αἰώνιον: Artemis asks for perpetual virginity, to which Zeus assents, cf. *HhAphr* 26–28 and Sappho 44A V. The poet addresses her as Παρθενίη at 110.

ἄππα: diminutive for πάππας; according to *Et. mag*. 167.32–35, a Macedonian word for "father."

7. πολυωνυμίην: this rare abstract noun is dependent on δός μοι. Callimachus here and with φαεσφορίην (11) employs abstracts to describe these divine prerogatives in place of the more common adjectives (cf. Sappho, fr. 44A V: ἐπωνύμιον μέγα). The effect may be intended as humorous: "gimme many-named-ness."

ἵνα μή μοι Φοῖβος ἐρίζῃ: the first mention of sibling rivalry.

8. The interruption of the thought is found elsewhere in Callimachus after a feminine caesura (e.g., below 144; *Aet*. fr. 75.4 Pf.), but this is an extreme example, since her main thought is only resumed in 12.

ἔα: imperative of ἐάω, used absolutely.

9. οὐδ᾽ ... μέγα τόξον: Artemis' request for a small bow inverts the usual Homeric μέγα τόξον, perhaps as a metaliterary comment.

10. τεχνήσονται: Artemis has a previous acquaintance with the Cyclopes (72–79), so she can speak with certainty: "they will fashion."

ἄεμμα: see *hAp* 33n.

11. φαεσφορίην (sc. δός μοι) "illumination." Another rare abstract noun that is the equivalent of εἶναι φωσφόρον (see 204 and above 7n). It seems to belong with the abstracts in 6–7, not with requests suited to the hunt. This too goes to characterize Artemis' speech as childish. Artemis' cult title Φαεσφόρος (= Φωσφόρος) is attested at Eur. *IT* 21 and Paus. 4.31.10 (Messenia), and see *LIMC* s.v. Artemis 811–13. The scholiast connects the title with Hecate (for Artemis-Hecate, see Petrovic 2007: 6–8).

ἐς γόνυ μέχρι: the adverbial use of μέχρι modifying a prepositional phrase is found in prose, though here, unusually, it follows its phrase. Cf. *hDelos* 47.

χιτῶνα: Artemis may be represented either with a long gown or with the short chiton for the hunt (see illustrations in *LIMC*, e.g., 411–16). Her title Χιτώνη connects her with the hunt in *hZeus* 77 and is derived from her short dress (so Steph. Byz. s.v. Ἑρμιών).

12. ζώννυσθαι (*sc.* δός μοι) "to tie the waistband," here in such a way that the chiton is kept above the knees.

λεγνωτόν: first in Callimachus; according to Hesychius s.v., it refers to anything having either a fringed or colored border.

καίνω: first in tragedy; here subjunctive in a final clause.

13. χορίτιδας: from χορῖτις, a female member of a chorus; first here and *hDelos* 306; imitated by Nonnus (see Schmitt 26n46).

Ὠκεανίνας "the daughters of Ocean"; first in Hes. *Th.* 364, 389. In Hellenistic poetry, feminine patronymics or matronymics in -ίνη were useful forms to fill out a hexameter (see Hollis on *Hecale* fr. 103.2).

14. εἰνέτεας: Callimachean *hapax* for ἔνατος ἔτος (cf. 179). The Oceanids are all nine years old, which is the usual age for girls' choruses in Artemis' traditional cult worship (see Calame 1997: 29).

ἔτι παῖδας: echoes the παῖς ἔτι of line 5.

ἀμίτρους: a *hapax*: "without the woman's *mitra*" signifies a young girl. The *mitra* was a headband worn by women in lyric and tragedy; it was also a mark of distinction in the Ptolemaic court (see Moyer 2011).

15. ἀμφιπόλους: these are personal servants; Artemis only needs twenty personal servants to care for her clothing and equipment, but sixty Oceanids for the dance (for the size of choruses of young women, see Calame 1997: 21–25).

Ἀμνισίδας: daughters of the Cretan river Amnisus (see map 3), which meets the sea about five miles to the east of Heracleion. See Petrovic 2007: 249–56 for the Amnisides and the Artemis cult on Crete.

16. αἵ τε: for this use of τε see *hZeus* 51n.

ἐνδρομίδας: only here and in *hDelos* 238 (of Iris). According to Pollux (7.93.5), a boot for running characteristic of Artemis (though the information is probably inferred from this passage).

16–17. ὁππότε… βάλλοιμι: the unusual interruption of ἐνδρομίδας τε καὶ… θοοὺς κύνας by a temporal clause, ὁππότε… βάλλοιμι, fits the spontaneous and unstructured speech of a young child. The mood of the verb in a temporal clause following an optative referring to future time is regularly assimilated to the same mood (Smyth §2186b).

16. λύγκας: see below 88n.

17. θοούς: the reading of the mss. that a number of editors have preferred to emend to θοάς on the grounds that most hunting hounds are female, but males appear at 91 (ἕνα, οἵ).

κομέοιεν: future optative in a relative clause of purpose in secondary sequence (Smyth §2554a).

18. οὔρεα πάντα: Artemis' affinity for mountains is reflected in cult titles like "Mountain-walker" (*Oreobatis, Oresiphoitos*), "Mountainy" (*Oreias*), and "Inhabiter of the peaks" (*Koryphaia*). The *Homeric Hymn to Artemis* (27) essentially celebrates her as a goddess of the mountains and the hunt.

18–19. The first ἥντινα is an adjective modifying πόλιν, the second an indefinite relative, which gives the passage a colloquial flavor.

19. λῇς: Doric form of θέλω, frequent in Theocritus, but only here in the hymns.

σπαρνόν (*sc. ἐστί*): according to the scholiast, σπαρνόν = σπάνιον, "rare"; σπαρναί first occurs in a fragment of Hesiod's *Catalogue* (fr. 66.6 M-W), apparently about Hermes.

κάτεισιν: from κάτειμι, here used as a future of κατέρχομαι, as in Attic.

21. Artemis was also identified with Eileithyia, the goddess who protected women in childbirth, who in turn was connected with Crete (hence the Amnisian nymphs and Dictynna).

ὀξείῃσιν ὑπ' ὠδίνεσσι: the phrase may recall *Il.* 11.268.

22. τειρόμεναι: the participle is used to describe the distress of Artemis' own mother in labor at *hDelos* 61 and 211.

καλέωσι: the reading of PMilVogl for indicative of the medieval mss. The generalizing temporal clause without ἄν is Homeric (see Smyth §2412).

βοηθόον: Homeric and lyric, "responding to a call for help." It occurs at *hDelos* 27 of Apollo.

22–23. Two ideas are combined—the Fates spinning the thread of life and the allotment of prerogatives to the individual gods. Plato (*Theaet.* 149b10) even etymologizes the assignment of childbirth to Artemis: ἄλοχος οὖσα τὴν λοχείαν εἴληχε. Artemis was worshipped under the aspect of Λοχία (cf. Eur. *IT* 1097, *Hipp.* 166–68).

23. γεινομένην: at the time of her birth: cf. *hAth* 105.

ἐπεκλήρωσαν "allot"; mainly found in prose. For the thought, see *hZeus* 62–64 (where allotment is specifically rejected for Zeus) and 76–80 (for hunters assigned to Artemis).

ἀρήγειν "aid," though in the *Iliad* usually "aid in war."

24. ὅττι: a common Homeric variation of ὅτι for metrical reasons (also at 144 and *hDelos* 319).

25. ἀμογητί: adverb, "effortlessly"; Homeric *hapax* (*Il.* 11.637), and generally rare in poetry. Leto's ease in giving birth to Artemis contrasts sharply with Apollo's birth in *hDelos*, where parturition is continually delayed (e.g., 162).

φίλων "one's own" (LSJ s.v. φίλος I2c).

ἀπεθήκατο: see *hZeus* 15n.

γυίων: usually the meaning is "limb," but in *HhHerm* 20, "womb," as here.

26. γενειάδος... πατρός: see p. 105. A marble relief (second century CE) in Hierapolis, Phrygia, portrays the infant Artemis with Zeus; Artemis is so small that she cannot reach her father's chin (*LIMC* s.v. Artemis 1262).

27. πολλάς: with χεῖρας, in an adverbial sense, "many times."

ἐτανύσσατο: the form occurs earlier at *HhHerm* 51 of Mercury stretching out the cords on the tortoise shell.

28. μέχρις ἵνα "enough so that she might touch"; the combination of the adverb μέχρις + the final conjunction ἵνα occurs only here in Callimachus.

29–39. Zeus's response differs from Artemis' request, which is to assume the role of the Homeric πότνια θηρῶν. Instead he bestows on her the honors and the responsibilities of a civic deity. The speech is comparable to Apollo's prophecy for Ptolemy II in *hDelos* 162–70.

29. καταρρέζων: epic, "pat" or "caress"; often in the Homeric formula: χειρί τέ μιν κατέρεξεν ἔπος τ' ἔφατ(ο) ("he/she caressed her/him with his hand and spoke" (e.g., *Il.* 1.361, 5.372).

ὅτε: the temporal construction represents future events as uncertain; it is dependent on a leading verb in the optative (LSJ s.v. I2b).

θέαιναι: Callimachus uses this marked epic equivalent of θεαί only here.

30. τυτθόν: epic for (σ)μικρόν; here adverbial as at *hDelos* 236, and cf. 64. The word is common in Hellenistic poetry, and because of its use at *Aet.* fr. 1.5 Pf. as a description of Callimachus' preferred poetic style, it may sometimes have programmatic force.

ζηλήμονος: the form is a *hapax* in Homer (*Od.* 5.118), where Calypso complains about the "jealous" gods who do not allow female divinities human lovers; one of her examples is Artemis killing Orion, the lover of Dawn. On the manuscript variant δηλήμονος in Homer, see Rengakos 1993: 35. ζηλήμων is frequent in Nonnus.

31. χωομένης: epic, "be angry at."

ἀλέγοιμι: epic and lyric; without a negative, ἀλέγω usually requires an accusative object, though here and at *hDelos* 10 it occurs with the genitive. τυτθόν may have lent a virtual negative sense to this passage, which seems modeled on *Il.* 8.477–78: ἐγὼ οὐκ ἀλεγίζω | χωομένης, where Zeus speaks of Hera's anger.

φέρευ: Doric for φέρου; the form is found only here and at Theoc. 1.128.

τέκος: epic and in later poets for τέκνον.

ἐθελημός: a *hapax* in Hesiod (*Op.* 118, see West ad loc.); a rare adjective with the sense of "pleasing yourself"; Heschyius glosses as πρόθυμος.

33. τρὶς δέκα... πτολίεθρα: note the extreme anaphora as the whole phrase is immediately repeated for emphasis.

πτολίεθρα: lengthened epic form for πόλις. I. Petrovic suggests a play on πτολ- and Πτολεμαῖος as a possible reason for this word in the context of possessing many cities (cf. *hZeus* 81).

οὐχ ἕνα πύργον: litotes, "many a tower."

35. ἀλλὰ (*sc.* εἴσεται) **μόνην σέ.**

36. ξυνῇ: Ionic and Homeric adverbial dative = Attic κοινῇ.

διαμετρήσασθαι (*sc.* ὀπάσσω): from διαμετρέω, middle in an active sense here and at *hAp* 55; "receive a share" (on the relationship of the two passages, see Petrovic 2007: 213). The line's spondaic ending confers an oracular solemnity to the statement.

37. μεσσόγεως νήσους τε: similar language occurs again in *hDelos* 168, when Apollo is prophesying the birth and dominions of Ptolemy II.

38. ἀγυιαῖς "streets." Ἀγυιεύς was an epithet of Apollo, as guardian of the streets and highways. As Ἐν(ν)οδία Artemis-Hecate was the guardian of streets (Petrovic 2007: 6, 226). Bornmann ad loc. suggests the assignment of the function to Artemis is another moment in the twins' rivalry.

39. λιμένεσσιν ἐπίσκοπος: cf. 259, where the epithet is associated with Artemis *Munychia*.

40–109. Artemis now travels from Crete to the Lipari Islands and Arcadia. First she chooses her nymphs (40–45), then in their company she goes to the Cyclopes for her weapons (46–86), to Pan for her hounds (87–97), then to capture the deer for her chariot (98–109). The narrative begins in the third person: βαῖνε δὲ κούρη (40), αὖθι…μετεκίαθε (46), then shifts with the address at 72: κοῦρα, σύ and continues in the second person: αἶψα…ἤιες (87), ἔνθεν…εὗρες (98–99).

40. ἐπεκρήηνε: from ἐπικραίνω, "bring to pass": Zeus "brought his word [= his promise] to fulfillment with his head [*sc.* by nodding his head]"; καρήατι puns on the verb, which Hesychius (s.v. ἐπικραᾶναι) glosses as "to nod the head."

41. Λευκὸν ἔπι Κρηταῖον ὄρος: if not the White Mountains of western Crete (so the scholiast), a snow-covered peak (λευκὸν ἐπὶ…ὄρος) near the Caeratus.

κεκομημένον ὕλῃ: the analogy of trees on a mountain to hair on the head is a commonplace in Greek poetry. The second half of the line is modeled on *Od.* 13.351: ὄρος καταειμένον ὕλῃ, which describes the area around Mt. Neriton on Ithaca as sacred to the nymphs.

43. Repeated from 14, the closest Callimachus comes to Homeric formulae. Some scholars wish to excise on the grounds that Callimachus does not repeat whole lines, but it does appear in our earliest witness, PMilVogl.

44. χαῖρε: third singular, epic imperfect from χαίρω. Note the anaphora.

Καίρατος: the Caeratus was a small Cretan river near Cnossus (Str. 10.4.8). It flowed nearly parallel to the much larger Amnisus (Petrovic 2007: 260–61). Note the pun: χαῖρε…Καίρατος.

Τηθύς: Tethys is the wife of Ocean.

45. θυγατέρας: as in epic, the υ may be long (cf. *hDelos* 293, *hAth* 132).

Λητωίδι: this form of the matronymic also occurs at A.R. 2.938, 3.878, but Λητωϊάς occurs at 83. In Hesiod, Leto was the daughter of the Titans Coeus and Phoebe, whose sister was Tethys (see West, *Th*. p. 36); thus Tethys' daughters, the Oceanids, are Artemis' cousins.

ἀμορβούς: first in Callimachus, "follower" or "attendant." Also in *Hec*. fr. 117 Hollis and in other Hellenistic poets.

46–86. The visit to the workshop of the Cyclopes is modeled on Thetis' visit to Hephaestus to procure arms for her son Achilles (*Il*. 18.369ff.). These were not the pastoralists that Odysseus encountered, but the three children of Gaia according to Hesiod; they are named for aspects of the thunderbolt: Brontes = Thunder, Steropes = Lightning, and Arges = Flashing. They also have only one eye (see West on *Th*. 139–40). The section contrasts the nymphs' fear of the Cyclopes (51–71) with Artemis' bravery.

46. αὖθι: see *hZeus* 72n.

ἔτετμε: from the epic aorist τέτμον; "reach."

47–48. The Lipari are volcanic islands off of the east coast of Sicily, one of several locations that ancient sources claimed for Hephaestus' forge. Meligounis is given as the earlier name by Philitas, *Hermes* (fr. 1.1a Spanoudakis; the poem is summarized in Parthenius 2.1), where it figures as the island of Aeolus visited by Odysseus (see also Harder on *Aetia* fr. 93). The point of the name-change in this hymn may be to signal the post-Homeric world (in fact the *Suda* credits Callimachus with a treatise on the *Foundations of Islands and Cities and Their Name-Changes*, an interest that is visible throughout the hymns). The island also may have had contemporary relevance: the first naval battle of the Punic Wars in 260 BCE was fought there, in which Carthage defeated Rome.

49. ἑσταότας: from ἑσταώς, the Homeric perfect participle of ἵστημι; it alternates with the form ἑστηῶτας (134).

μύδρον: either the anvil itself, or a mass of molten metal being worked on the anvil.

50. ἱππείην: see *hAth* 6. Bornmann points to the incongruity of this epic epithet attached to the pedestrian ποτίστρην; the whole is described as a μέγα ἔργον.

τετύκοντο: for the sense of fashioning works of art, cf. *Il*. 14.220 (embroidery), 18.574 (the shield of Achilles).

ποτίστρην "watering trough"; first here and common in documentary papyri: see Parsons 2011: 152.

51. Callimachus imitates *Od*. 10.219 (the reaction of Odysseus' men to Circe's creatures): τοὶ δ᾽ ἔδεισαν, ἐπεὶ ἴδον αἰνὰ πέλωρα ("They were afraid when they saw the dread beasts").

ὅπως ἴδον: Homer's ἐπεὶ ἴδον is varied with another Homeric phrase (cf. *Il*. 11.459, 12.208), where ὅπως is temporal.

52. Note the repeated οσ/οι(σ) sounds, and the implicit play on ὄσσε, "eyes."

πρηόσιν: from πρηών, an epic variant of πρών, "cliff" or "peak"; first in Hes. *Sc.* 437.

Ὀσσαίοισιν: the peaks of Mt. Ossa in Thessaly. Otus and Ephialtes (the Aloadae) attempted to reach Mt. Olympus by piling nearby Mt. Pelion on Ossa, the former to carry off Artemis, the latter Hera. They were killed by Apollo (*Od.* 11.307–20) or Artemis (Apollod. 1.7.4). Otus occurs at 264.

ὑπ᾽ ὀφρύν: a nice detail: "eyebrow" is singular because they have only one eye each.

53. φάεα: Callimachus uses φάος as "light" and as a metonym for "eyes," see below 71 (eyes), 182 (light); the double meaning is a leitmotif in the tale of the blinding of Tiresias in *hAth.*

μουνόγληνα "one-eyed," from γλήνη, "eyeball"; first here, then imitated in later Greek poetry.

τετραβοείῳ "consisting of four bull-hides," first here. The image reflects the work of the Alexandrian doctor Herophilus, who argued for a four-fold layering of the human eye (see Oppermann 1925).

54–56. The nymphs hear three types of sounds: δοῦπον "thud," ἄημα "blast," and στόνον "groan."

54. ὑπογλαύσσοντα: ὑπογλαύσσω, "glance from under," i.e., "glance furtively," according to the scholiast = ὑποβλέπω. First here, then imitated at Mosch. *Eur.* 86.

55. ἠχήσαντος ἐπὶ μέγα "sounding afar" (and see below 62).

56–61. The noise and motion of the Cyclopes resembles the cosmic disturbance at *hDelos* 141–47.

56. φυσάων: from φῦσα; "bellows" is usually plural.

στόνον: epic and tragic for "groan." Presumably the deep groans of the Cyclopes as they labor.

αὖε: again in 57, and a variant (ἀΰτει) in 58. The same cluster, αὖε δέ, ἀΰτει, αὖε occurs in *Il.* 20.48–51, a description of the Olympians joining in the battle at the wall. Here the personified locations "cry aloud," i.e., ring from the noises of the forge.

Αἴτνη: according to Timaeus (*FGrH* 566 F164), Hephaestus' workshop was in a cave under the volcanic Mt. Etna.

57. Τρινακρίη "three-pronged"; according to Thucydides (6.2.1), the earliest settlers of Sicily were the Cyclopes, then the Sicani, after whom the island was named Sicania, its previous name being Trinacria. Callimachus reflects this historical trajectory, though he calls Trinacria the seat of the Sicani (Σικανῶν ἕδος). Sicilian cities were the topic in a long section at the opening of *Aet.* book 2 (fr. 43 Pf.), in which Callimachus also follows Timaeus and Thucydides.

γείτων: here an adjective, as at Pi. *Nem.* 9.43 and Aesch. *Pers.* 66–67.

58. ἐπὶ ... ἀΰτει: in tmesis, no doubt for the anaphora, see above 56.

Κύρνος: the ancient name of Corsica (Hdt. 1.165).

59. οἵγε: emphatic relative = the Cyclopes.

ῥαιστῆρας "hammers"; before Callimachus once in Homer (*Il.* 18.477) of Hephaestus working the shield of Achilles, then in late prose.

60. ζείοντα: ζείω (= Homeric ζέω) is used to describe boiling water or any hot liquid; here of molten metal. Cf. *Il.* 21.362: λέβης ζεῖ, followed by ἀμβολάδην (364), of a river burning with fire.

καμινόθεν: first here; from κάμινος + -θεν, "from the kiln."

61. ἀμβολαδίς: *hapax* modelled on the Homeric adverb ἀμβολάδην (60n). Its derivation from ἀναβολή, "that which is thrown up," suggests it should mean "with uplifted arms," but the scholiast glosses, ἐκ διαδοχῆς, "in succession" (i.e., striking with their hammers in succession).

τετύποντες: see *hZeus* 53n.

μυχθίσσειαν: from μυχθίζω, first in Callimachus, "snort" or "exhale loudly," a conjecture of Meineke that the papyrus confirms (where μυχεισειαν seems to have been an error for μυχθισειαν). ἀναμυχθίζομαι occurs at Aesch. *PV* 743. The medieval mss. read μοχθίσσειαν (from μοχθίζω, "toil").

62. ἐτάλασσαν: epic aorist from *τλάω.

63. ἄντην: epic adverb, with ἰδέειν "to look straight at them [σφέας]"; cf. *Il.* 19.15: οὐδέ τις ἔτλη | ἄντην εἰσιδέειν (of the Myrmidons not daring to look at the shield of Achilles, newly fashioned by Hephaestus).

κτύπον οὔασι δέχθαι: κτύπος οὔατα occurs at *Il.* 10.535, and for the expression cf. Eur. *Bacch.* 1086: ὠσὶν ἠχὴν ... δεδεγμέναι (of the Maenads).

64. οὐ νέμεσις: the expression occurs at *Il.* 3.156 and *Od.* 1.350, in the sense of "no shame." But there is a covert play on names as well: Nemesis was a goddess identified with Artemis/Hecate and worshipped at Rhamnus in Attica (the story is in the *Cypria*); "Rhamnusian Helen" (232) refers to this Nemesis. "Not Nemesis = Not Artemis."

64–65. The extreme hyperbaton of these lines separates the object of fear (κείνους) from θύγατρες as far as possible; as a subject "daughters of the blessed gods" is a surprise.

64. μάλα modifies μηκέτι, "not especially."

μηκέτι: see *hZeus* 63n.

65. ἀφρικτί: *hapax*, adverb formed from φρίσσω, "without shuddering."

ὁρόωσι: the uncontracted form results from diectasis (when the originally contracted -ῶ is expanded as -όω, not -άω); see Chantraine 1.75–83. Callimachus imitates this Homeric practice at *hArt* 142: ἀντιόωντες, 149: γελόωσι, 161: ἀροτριόωντι; *hDelos* 28: περιτροχόωσιν, 174: ἐσχατόωντος, 202: ὁρόωσα; and at *hDem* 38: ἐψιόωντο.

66–71. As an illustration of how terrifying the Cyclopes are, even for divinities, Callimachus includes a vignette of mothers summoning a Cyclops to act as a bogeyman to scare a naughty daughter.

66. κουράων: this form occurs earlier in *Il.* 6.247 (Priam's daughters) and *Od.* 6.122, where it describes Nausicaa's attendants, likened to nymphs.

ἀπειθέα … τεύχοι: Bornmann takes as a periphrasis for ἀπειθέω, "to be disobedient."

67. καλιστρεῖ: from καλιστρέω = καλέω. Previously only in *Against Euergus* 60, a fragment attributed either to Demosthenes or Dinarchus (Harp. s.v. ἐκαλίστρουν, who calls it Ionic). For similar formations, cf. ἐλαστρέω (from ἐλαύνω) or βωστρέω (from βοάω). καλιστρέω occurs again at *hDem* 97, where as here the context seems parodic.

68. Ἄργην ἢ Στερόπην: see above 46–86n.

μυχάτοιο: irregular superlative of μύχιος, "inmost"; first found in Callimachus and A.R.

68–69. ὁ … Ἑρμείης: word order imitates the temporal order of the event; "from the house emerges Hermes," followed by a description of what the viewer would first see.

69. Ἑρμείης: Hermes was the quintessential naughty child: he stole the cattle of his half-brother, Apollo, and when Apollo approached him in anger, he pretended to be sleeping in his cradle. *HhHerm* 235–59 narrates a scene in which Apollo tries to persuade him to reveal where he hid the cattle. The passage opens with a simile of the innocent-looking baby in his crib, like embers concealed under wood-ash (σποδός). Hermes frightening children may be a sly allusion to the *Homeric Hymn to Pan* (19.35–39); Pan is Hermes' son, and his newborn appearance is so startling (with beard, horns, and goat's feet), that his mother jumps up and runs away when she first sees him.

κεχριμένος: from χρίω, "rub," "anoint."

αἰθῇ: the adjective describes the greyish color of burnt ash, cf. Ar. *Thesm.* 246.

70. μορμύσσεται = μορμολύττομαι: cf. *hDelos* 297. Only here and in a late inscription. Greeks used the bogeyman Mormo to frighten children into obedience, and here the verb emphasizes the childish state of the divinity. For the thought, cf. Plato *Crito* 46c4: δύναμις ὥσπερ παῖδας ἡμᾶς μορμολύττηται "a power like the bogeyman that frightens us like children."

71. δύνει ἔσω κόλπους: apparently modeled on *Il.* 18.140: δῦτε θαλάσσης εὐρέα κόλπον, where, after Thetis promises to go to Hephaestus for new armor for her son, she instructs her sister nymphs "to go down into the broad bosom of the sea."

72–79. An example of Artemis' fearlessness: three-year-old Artemis accompanied her mother on a visit to Hephaestus; when she sat on Brontes' knees, she grabbed his chest hairs and pulled them out.

72. κοῦρα: for the vocative with a short α, see *hDelos* 215n (on νύμφα).

προτέρω: the adverb is more common with local signification, but here of time, "before"; cf. A.R. 2.864.

τριέτηρος: first here, "three years old."

73. ἔμολεν: aorist of βλώσκω, poetic for "go" or "come."

ἀγκαλίδεσσι: from ἀγκαλίς in plural, "arms"; the phrase imitates *Il.* 18.555 and 22.503: ἐν ἀγκαλίδεσσι.

74. ὀπτήρια: gifts given when seeing someone for the first time, e.g., a new child, or a bride without her veil; cf. Eur. *Ion* 1126–28.

75. Βρόντεω: see 46–86n.

ἐφεσσαμένου: epic aorist middle participle from ἐφίζω, cf. *Od.* 16.443: γούνασιν οἷσιν ἐφεσσάμενος, "having set [me] on his knees"; cf. the opening of the hymn with Artemis on Zeus's knees.

76. ἐδράξαο: from δράσσομαι, "grasp"; and see below 92n.

χαίτης: epic for loose, flowing hair; a tongue-in-cheek description of the Cyclops' shaggy chest hair.

77. ὤλοψας: from ὀλόπτω, first here: "pluck" or "tear out."

βίηφι: the adverb is usually descriptive of male strength, not infant girls.

ἄτριχον "hairless"; first in Hes. *Cat.* (fr. 204.129 M-W), of a serpent; after Callimachus mainly in medical writers.

78. μεσσάτιον: irregular superlative of μέσσος, "midmost," first here, then in later poets.

79. ἐνιδρυθεῖσα: from ἐν + ἱδρύω. Here with ἀλώπηξ, "when mange has become established."

ἐπενείματ(ο): from ἐπινέμω, to graze cattle on another's land, and by extension, to "encroach" or "spread"; mainly in Hellenistic and later Greek. The verb, properly used of animals, may be intended as a joke, given the double meaning of ἀλώπηξ.

ἀλώπηξ "fox," but came to = ἀλωπεκία, or "mange"; see Herodas 7.71–72 for a similar thought and Headlam's extensive note ad loc. on the medical sources.

80. τῆμος: epic adverb, "then."

81. κἠμοί = καὶ ἐμοί.

Κυδώνιον: Cydon was a city in Crete (see *hZeus* 45), and Crete was noted for archers. Cf. *hAp* 33.

εἰ δ' ἄγε: a common Homeric expression (e.g., *Il.* 1.302, 524); the singular is usual even with a second person plural verb. Callimachus uses it only here in the hymns.

82. κατακληῗδα: Ionic for κατακλείς, which seems to mean "something fitted with a cap" and is here clearly used for Artemis' quiver. I. Petrovic suggests that this might be Callimachus' rewriting of the scene in *Il.* 21.489–92, when Hera snatches up Artemis' quiver to beat her and in the process scatters the arrows. Instead of the open quiver of Homer, Callimachus provides Artemis' quiver with a cap.

βελέμνων: from βέλεμνον, an epic variant of βέλος.

83. ἐγὼ Λητωϊὰς ὥσπερ Ἀπόλλων: this continues the rivalry between the siblings. For Λητωϊάς: see 45n.

84. αἰ δέ κ' ἐγώ: cf. *HhAp* 56: αἰ δέ κ' Ἀπόλλωνος.

μονιόν "solitary," Hellenistic and later Greek. Bornmann ad loc. suggests that "solitary beast" refers to animals like the boar, and thus a tasty meal for the Cyclopes.

πέλωρον: here an adjective with θηρίον.

85. ἔδοιεν: from ἔδω, epic equivalent of ἐσθίω "eat." The repetition of the verb at 89 below aligns Artemis' promise of food for the Cyclopes to eat with Pan feeding his bitches.

86. The goddess orders, they obey. For the relationship of childish speech to accomplishment, see *hZeus* 57n.

δαῖμον: Artemis is addressed as a divinity for the first time.

87–97. After procuring her nymphs and her weapons, the young divinity visits Pan to get suitable hunting dogs. Pan is not usually associated with Artemis, though he is found with Cybele and Hecate (see *LIMC* Suppl. 936); but by connecting the two via the intertext of the *Homeric Hymn to Pan* (19), Callimachus underscores Artemis' liminality in the first half of the hymn (see Faulkner 2013).

87. σκύλακας: in the technical sense of young dogs or puppies that are being trained to hunt (Xen. *Cyn.* 7.6).

πάλιν: here "in turn," cf. Soph. *El.* 371.

αὖλιν: a place of shelter to spend the night, here Pan's grotto; cf. *HhHerm* 71; apparently a variant of αὔλιον, as at 93 (and *HhHerm* 103, 106, 134).

88. Ἀρκαδικὴν ἔπι Πανός: Pan was closely associated with the mountains and untamed landscape of Arcadia; in *HhPan* (32–37) Hermes fathered him there upon the daughter of Dryops. Cf. Theoc. 1.123–26 on Pan's haunts and Aratus' *Hymn to Pan* (*SH* 115), which designates him "Arcadian."

λυγκός "lynx"; the word is not common in poetry, but Pan wears the "hide of a lynx" at *HhPan* 24. Thomas 2011: 158n21 points out that Callimachus is providing the backstory to the skin—before it became a garment, its meat served as food for Pan's hounds.

ἔταμνε: cf., e.g., *Il.* 9.209, for cutting up meat.

89. Μαιναλίης: the region around Mt. Maenalus in Arcadia, sacred to Pan; also at 224.

τοκάδες "breeding bitches"; at *Od.* 14.16 of sows used for breeding. According to Xen. *Cyn.* (7.1–2), pregnant females should be relieved of hunting in the winter in order to produce healthier puppies in the spring.

90. τίν: Doric pronoun, both dative and accusative; here = σοι. The main verb, ἔδωκε, is not expressed in the μέν-clause and only appears in 93.

ὁ γενειήτης: Ionic, "bearded," first here or Theoc. 17.33, of Heracles. The infant Pan is ἠϋγένειον, "full-bearded" in *HhPan* 39.

πηγούς: according to Hesychius, the color the adjective described was disputed: "some say white, others black." Callimachus' ἥμισυ may play on the dispute, since the dogs, whether white or black, will only be half of that color, and the remaining half presumably of the other color (so Rengakos 1992: 24–25 and see Jan 1893: 20–25).

91. παρουαίους: mss. read παρουατίους, a *hapax* that should mean "with hanging ears," but the context demands another color word. Schneider (modifying Haupt) conjectured the otherwise unattested παρουαίους, as a variant of παρώας = "chestnut." This would come close to Xenophon's πυρρός.

αἰόλον "variegated." Xenophon (*Cyn.* 4.7) recommends that hounds not be entirely of one color.

91–92. λέοντας | αὐτούς "even lions." For the hounds' prodigious feat, cf. Pi. *Nem.* 3.44–49, where Achilles as a child kills wild things, including lions, which he drags back half dead to the Centaur.

92. αὖ ἐρύοντες: the phrase is a resolution of Homeric αὐερύω into its components. See, e.g., *Il.* 1.459 ≈ 2.422: αὐέρυσαν μὲν πρῶτα καὶ ἔσφαξαν καὶ ἔδειραν ("they drew back their heads first, cut their throats, and flayed them"), on which this line is partially modelled. Aristarchus and others interpreted αὐερύω as αὖ ἕλκω. The insertion of εἷλκον a line later may be intended to gloss the earlier participle.

δράξαιντο: cf. Theoc. 24.28: δραξάμενος φάρυγος, "having seized them by the throat," of the infant Heracles with the two snakes sent by Hera to destroy him.

δεράων: the uncontracted form is found only here; probably from Aeolic δέρα.

93. εἷλκον: imperfect here for customary action.

ἐπ' αὐλίον: either Pan's cave or the hounds' kennel (see 87n).

94. Κυνοσουρίδας: according to the scholiast a Κυνοσουρίς was a Spartan hunting dog supposedly bred from a dog and a fox.

95. ὤκισται (*sc.* εἰσίν).

μύοντα: from μύω, "shut the eyes"; the first syllable of this verb is occasionally long, as here. The hare was thought to have slept with its eyes open (Xen. *Cyn.* 5.11, Ael. *NA* 2.12, 13.13).

96. ὕστριχος ἔνθα καλιαί: note the shift in syntax to a relative clause.

ὕστριχος: the "porcupine" (ὕστριξ) was hunted in antiquity. Previously the noun occurs in poetry at Aesch. *Diktyoulkoi* (*TrGF* 3 fr. 47a.809 Radt), describing young Perseus' delight in fawns and porcupines and predicting his growth into a fine hunter.

καλιαί "lair"; elsewhere, when used of animals, it is a bird's nest (e.g., Theoc. 29.12, *Anacreontea* 25.7).

97. ζορκός "deer"; see pp. 24–25.

ἡγήσασθαι: the spondaic ending may be intended to imitate the steady course of the tracking hounds. It also closes the section.

98–109. Transition to Artemis' first hunt, when she captures the deer for her chariot.

98. μετά: adverbial with the verb of motion; cf., e.g., *Il*. 23.133.

ἐσσεύοντο: in the middle with active meaning: "hurry" or "rush."

99. προμολῇσ(ι): Hellenistic word for "approach" or "vestibule," plural for singular also at 142 (cf. A.R. 1.1174); here the base of Mt. Parrhasius.

Παρρασίοιο: the mountain is in Arcadia (at *hZeus* 10, where Zeus is born).

100. σκαιρούσας "skip" or "dance." In *Od*. 10.412 of calves.

ἐπ᾽ ὄχθης "on a river bank"; the reading is probably ὄχθης (dative), preferred by Pfeiffer and Wilamowitz over ὄχθης (genitive), preferred by Schneider and Cahen. Since παρ᾽ ὄχθης was preferred by Zenodotus at *Il*. 14.445 in place of παρ᾽ ὄχθας, Callimachus may be expressing his own preference by recalling the Homeric passage (see next note).

101. ἐβουκολέοντο: from βουκολέω, in passive, "graze," as at *Il*. 20.221. The active participle βουκολέοντι occurs at *Il*. 14.445.

μελαμψήφιδος: first in Callimachus, here and at *hDelos* 76, "with black stones." For an analogous formation see Hdt. 1.55.2: πολυψήφιδα παρ᾽ Ἕρμον ("by the Hermus with many stones"); the prophecy is later quoted in Pl. *Rep*. 566c5, and the scholiast on the passage wrote μελαμψήφιδα above πολυψήφιδα.

ἀναύρου: ἄναυρος is a common noun for "mountain torrent," while Anaurus is the name of the river in Thessaly where Hera appeared to Jason as an old woman (e.g., A.R. 3.66–75); editors differ on which form to print. But this is surely intended geographic wordplay, where the "black-stoned torrent" of a different river, probably the Celadon of 107, momentarily suggests the "black-stoned Anaurus" with its rich mythology.

102. μάσσονες: poetic comparative of μακρός.

κεράων: the deer that Artemis seeks are female at 107 (τὴν … μίαν). Whether females had horns was a matter of dispute in antiquity, taken up by Ael. *NA* 7.39, who quotes the poets as his authorities.

103. ἔταφες "be amazed," aorist from epic τέθηπα.

ὅν: the use of the normally third person form for a first or second person reflexive does seem to occur in Homer, though the usage was disputed (see Chantraine 1.273–75). Here = "your."

ποτί: Doric equivalent of πρός, though Callimachus does not restrict its usage to his Doric hymns.

104. πρωτάγριον: first fruits of the hunt; first here, then imitated by Nonnus.

105. πίσυρας: Aeolic for τέσσαρες; it occurs occasionally in Homer (*Od*. 5.70, 16.249). Of the five deer, Artemis takes four for her chariot, leaving the last to be a labor for Heracles. The capture of the Cerynian deer was the third (or sometimes the fourth) of Heracles' twelve labors. Treated in Pi. *Ol*. 3.25–30 and Eur. *HF* 375–79, it was also a frequent subject for the plastic arts. Reference to this event here may serve as a temporal marker—this is very early in Artemis' career. At some future time the divinity will encounter the deified Heracles on Olympus.

ὦκα: Homeric adverb of ὠκύς, "quickly," "swiftly."

106. νόσφι: here a preposition with the genitive: "unaided by." Cf. *HhAp* 314.

κυνοδρομίης: only here and once in later poetry, "hunting with dogs."

107–9. The inverted word order postpones the subject and main verb (πάγος Κερύνειος ἔδεκτο) until the final clause. Callimachus plays off of the normal expectation that the fleeing animal would be captured.

107. Κελάδοντος ... ποταμοῖο: the river Celadon is a tributary of the Alpheus (Paus. 8.38.9).

108. A reminder of Hera's ongoing hostility to Zeus's children by other women. The four-word spondaic hexameter encapsulates the relationship— Hera's orders, Heracles' labor.

ἐννεσίῃσιν: the sole use of this noun in Homer provides a fine intertext: *Il.* 5.894: τῷ σ' ὀΐω κείνης τάδε πάσχειν ἐννεσίῃσιν ("thus I suppose you suffer these things at her suggestions"); Zeus is chastising Ares, who has carried out Hera's commands to his detriment.

ἀέθλιον Ἡρακλῆι: the line is partially imitated in A.R. 1.997.

109. πάγος Κερύνειος: according to the scholiast a ridge or crest of a hill in Arcadia. (Keryneia was a small hill town in Achaea, the region directly north of Arcadia.)

110–41. This section introduces Artemis in her new role as a city goddess. It begins by invoking her as "Virgin," "Slayer of Tityus," describes her accoutrements of gold, then her transition from the outside to city patron.

110. Τιτυοκτόνε: there are various versions of the story of Tityus; in most he tried to rape Leto, and one or both of her children killed him (see *LIMC* s.v. Leto 16). The incident is represented on Jason's cloak (A.R. 1.759–62), where Apollo slays him; in *Od.* 11.576–81 it is Artemis. Another version has him attack Artemis herself (sch. A.R. 1.181, attributed to Euphorion).

110–12. For the anaphora, χρύσεα...χρύσεον...χρύσεια, cf. *hAp* 32–34 and *hDelos* 260–64 (where features of the natural world turn to gold at Apollo's birth). Like Apollo, Artemis has golden armament. She also drives a golden chariot, and her deer have golden bits.

111. ζώνη: Artemis' cincture; as a virgin goddess this remains tied in place; untying the ζώνη signals sexual activity (e.g., *HhAphr* 164).

ἐζεύξαο: from ζεύγνυμι, "yoke"; in middle "putting animals to the bridle."

112. ἐν δ' ἐβάλευ: in tmesis; the phrase occurs again at *hDelos* 265 immediately following a fivefold anaphora of χρύσεος.

θεή: Artemis is now addressed as θεή as Callimachus seems to start again. This address immediately follows the mention of Heracles and his labors (108); she is again so addressed at 152, when she has entered the ranks of the Olympians. The now deified Heracles meets her.

κεμάδεσσι: κεμάς is *hapax* at *Il.* 10.361, and its meaning was debated in antiquity: it was either a deer (ἔλαφος) or possibly an antelope (δορκάς). Callimachus treats it as a synonym for ἔλαφος (see 100, 167). For a discussion of the controversy, see Rengakos 1992: 41.

113–18. The hymn begins again with a series of questions that introduce the characteristics of the divinity being hymned. They are immediately answered in a way that moves Artemis from the Homeric goddess to one who is concerned with justice within states. Each question takes a full line with variation in subject and structure. The second question is a doublet: ποῦ, ἀπὸ … ποίης. The first two have specific geographic answers: Thracian Haemus, Mysian Olympus. The third does not limit the range of the deity's activities in regard to just and unjust cities.

113. κερόεις: lyric and tragic adjective, "horned," here a transferred epithet with ὄχος ("chariot").

114. Αἵμῳ ἐπὶ Θρήϊκι: Mt. Haemus in Thrace. For ἐπὶ + dative following a verb of motion, see LSJ s.v. BI1.

κατάϊξ "sudden squall"; possibly invented by Callimachus and imitated by A.R. 1.1203 (see Schmitt 141n9). The derivation and accent of the word were debated in antiquity; see *Hecale* fr. 18.15 with Hollis' note.

115. ἀχλαίνοισι: from ἄ-χλαινος, an adjective used substantively, "without a cloak" or mantle; first in Simonides, *IEG²* fr. 6.1–3: τήν ῥά ποτ' Οὐλύμποιο περὶ πλευρὰς ἐκάλυψεν | ὠκὺς ἀπὸ Θρήκης ὀρνύμενος Βορέης, | ἀνδρῶν δ' ἀχλαίνων ἔδακεν φρένας ("[the snow] with which swift Boreas rising in Thrace covers the sides of Olympus, and bites the heart of cloakless men"), a passage that Callimachus seems to be imitating.

δυσαέα: Homeric epithet, "ill-blowing," always of winds (e.g., *Od.* 13.99); with κρυμόν, the sense is nicely captured by Mair's "evil breath of frost."

116. πεύκην "pinewood torch."

ἀπὸ δὲ φλογὸς ἥψαο ποίης "from what flame [i.e., from what place] did you light it?," a variation of ποῦ … ἔταμες. The answer is in 117. One of Artemis' many cult titles (which she shared with other goddesses) was "Light-bearer" (cf. above 11: φαεσφορίην).

ἥψαο: aorist middle from ἅπτω used in the active sense.

117–21. These lines evoke the opening of the *Iliad* (1.37–52), where Apollo takes vengeance upon the Greeks in response to the plea of his insulted priest, Chryses.

117. Μυσῷ ἐν Οὐλύμπῳ: Mysian Olympus; Mysia was a region east of the Troad. Μυσῷ may pun on μῦς, "mouse," since Apollo *Smintheus* ("Mouse-slayer"), who had a cult in the Troad, is invoked at *Il.* 1.39. According to Pausanias (3.20.9) Artemis was worshipped under the title of *Mysia* in Laconia.

φάεος δ' ἐνέηκας ἀϋτμήν: a variation of the Homeric πυρὸς ἵκετ' ἀϋτμή ("the breath of fire has reached [them]"). It may also be a reminiscence of *Il.* 10.89, where the rare form of ἐνίημι is in close proximity to ἀϋτμή. The context is Zeus putting troubles upon Agamemnon (and see next note).

118. ἀποστάζουσι "fall drop by drop"; here "which the thunderbolts of your father distill." The goddess has added the unquenchable element of her father's thunderbolt to her torch. Artemis thus appropriates Zeus's own ability to punish wrongdoers.

119. ἀργυρέοιο ... τόξου: in 111 Artemis' bow is golden. Here the phrase may be a reminder of Apollo, whose epithet Ἀργυρότοξος occurs at *Il.* 1.37.

120–21. Artemis practices her archery, first shooting at an elm, then an oak, finally at a beast. Compare *Il.* 1.50–52: Apollo strikes first the mules, then the dogs, and finally the men with his retributive arrows.

121. τὸ τέτρατον οὐκέτ᾽ †ἐπὶ δρῦν†: in similar Homeric priamels the first three are failures, the fourth a success. Previous scholars have found the repetition of oak tree to be a problem, and it could easily be a dittography of the preceding line where ἐπὶ δρῦν occupies the same *sedes*. McKay (1963: 249–56) discusses the various attempts to emend the passage and defends the ms. reading, arguing that Artemis shot at but missed the elm, the oak, and the beast, before aiming at the much broader target of the city and the final "no oak" is meant to be playful. *Aetia* fr. 75.12–20 Pf. provides a Callimachean parallel: thrice the girl got sick, the fourth time ... her father did not wait: τὸ τρίτον αὖτ[ις] ... τέτρατον [ο]ὐκέτ᾽ ἔμεινε πατήρ. Prima facie this suggests the missing word should be a verb, and certainly a verb beginning ἐπ- might be enough to confuse an inattentive scribe. Since the three examples are from the outdoors and hunting, possibly a verb like ἔπαισας was the original reading: "the fourth time no longer did you sport, but..." A potential parallel is Soph. *El.* 567, where Agamemnon hunting (παίζων) offends Artemis. This line of argument was originally suggested by Barber (1954: 229) and more recently by Massimilla (2002: 51–54), and is by far the most reasonable solution to the crux.

121–35. This section is a reworking of Hes. *Op.* 225–47, where the cities ruled by those who give straight judgments flourish, and both the people and the land prosper (on which see Reinsch-Werner 1976: 74–86). The Hesiod passage in turn links *hArt* with *hZeus* 80–85.

122. ἀλλά †μιν: previous editors have noted that τόξου (119) is not a proper antecedent for μιν since it means "bow" at 119, but would need to mean "arrow" here. Barber's ἀλλά τιν᾽ (taken with πόλιν) has merit: "but a city" of the unjust.

122–23. περὶ σφέας | ... περὶ ξείνους: i.e., in regard to their own citizens and strangers; for this use of περί, see Smyth §1693.3c.

123. ἀλιτήμονα: the adjective is found once in Homer (*Il.* 24.157 ≈ 186), where it seems to have the active sense "offending against," instead of "being offensive," as here (also at A.R. 4.1057). So Bornmann ad loc.

124. τύνη: epic nominative = σύ.

ἐμμάξεαι: second singular aorist from ἐμμάσσομαι; with dative, "inflict." Previously it occurred at Ar. *Nub.* 676, but with a different meaning.

125. Artemis, like Apollo at the beginning of the *Iliad*, inflicts plague on sinful men (see above 117–21n).

λοιμός: cf. *Il.* 1.61.

καταβόσκεται: the compound καταβόσκω is first attested here, with the sense "devour" (i.e., "graze down completely"); the active form occurs at Theoc. 15.126, and in a third century BCE document (PSI 4.346.5) with the sense "graze." Cf. περιβόσκεται at *hAp* 84.

ἔργα: here as often in Callimachus with the meaning of "fields" or cultivated land.

πάχνη "hoarfrost" (*sc.* καταβόσκεται): once in Homer, *Od.* 14.476.

126. κείρονται δὲ γέροντες: old men cut their hair in mourning for their sons who have died.

υἱάσιν: Homeric for υἱοῖς.

127. βληταί: verbal adjective (from βάλλω); here "stricken" by Artemis in childbirth; cf. *hDem* 101: "struck down by Apollo." It is found in the medical writers for stricken with disease (e.g., Hippocrates, *Acut.* 17, *Coac.* 394).

λεχωΐδες: from λεχωΐς; first in Callimachus, here and at *hDelos* 56; "woman in childbed" or one who has just given birth; again at A.R. 4.136 and imitated in Nonnus.

φυγοῦσαι: i.e., women who have escapéd death in childbirth.

128. τίκτουσιν [*sc.* τέκνα] **τῶν οὐδέν**: a suppressed inner object; "they breed [children] none of whom stands..."

σφυρὸν ὀρθόν "straight ankle," i.e., one who is not lame. This may be an explanation for Artemis' cult name *Orthia*, i.e., as "Standing Upright." As *Orthia*, she was worshipped at Sparta (in a very well-attested ritual in which ephebes were whipped at her altars) and also in Crete (see Petrovic 2007: 252–53).

129–35. A description of the benefits that the goddess will bestow, emphasized by anaphora in lines 130–33: εὖ μέν... εὖ δὲ... εὖ δ᾽... καὶ εὖ περ, and anticipated by εὐμειδής (129). The adverb occurs only twice elsewhere in the hymns, and its repetition here may be meant to recall Solon, *IEG*² fr. 4.32–39 (= 4.32–39 Noussia, and see her comments ad loc.), where Solon praises the benefits of Εὐνομίη, as εὔκοσμα and εὐθύνει... δίκας σκολιάς, and putting an end to civil strife (διχοστασίη). See also Anacreon, *PMG* fr. 348, quoted above p. 106.

129. εὐμειδής "smiling"; first here and in A.R. 4. 715 (of Circe).

αὐγάσσηαι: a contrast with *hDem* 4 (see note), where the bystanders are instructed not to gaze at Demeter's procession.

130. στάχυν: collective for "ears of corn," cf. *hDem* 136, and A.R. 1.688.

131. ἐπὶ σῆμα "to their tomb"; σῆμα is the grave marker.

132. πολυχρόνιόν τι "something very old"; they only die when they are so old that their bodies have become depersonalized (so Bornmann ad loc.); cf. *hAth* 128: βιότῳ τέρμα πολυχρόνιον, part of Athena's promise to Tiresias.

φέρωσιν: in the sense of ἐκφέρω, carry out for burial.

133. διχοστασίη "dissension," especially civic discord, see 129–35n.

τρώει: epic present of τιτρώσκω: "damage," "injure."

ἤ τε: see *hZeus* 51n and below 140: αἵ τε.

134. ἑστηῶτας: cf. 49n.

θυωρόν: rare biform adjective found first in Pherecydes of Syros 12 D-K as an epithet for τράπεζαν (here omitted); a table that holds offerings, with μίαν πέρι.

135. εἰνάτερες: the term for wives of brothers or of husband's brothers.

γαλόῳ: used for a husband's sister or brother's wife; here nominative plural (contracted from -οοι). Cf. *Il.* 6.378: ἠέ πῃ ἐς γαλόων ἤ' εἰνατέρων εὐπέπλων.

δίφρα: heteroclite plural of δίφρος, first here; the object of τίθενται "take their seats."

136–37. Callimachus articulates a symbiotic relationship with the deity: at first he lists proposed hymnic topics, but with the final element (the chariot that takes her to Olympus), there is a slip between the physical vehicle and his promised song, as if it is the latter that really brings the goddess to Olympus (see Bing and Uhrmeister 1994: 26–28).

The construction is an optative of wish; also at *hAp* 26–27 and *hDelos* 98.

137. μέλοι δέ μοι αἰὲν ἀοιδή: the clausula echoes *HhAp* 188: ἀθανάτοισι μέλει κίθαρις καὶ ἀοιδή. Cf. fr. 494 Pf.

138–40. Callimachus describes his "song" in chronological order: the "marriage of Leto," you (a lot), and Apollo, thus reordering the song of the Delian maidens at *HhAp* 158–59 (Apollo, Leto, Artemis). For the anaphora with ἐν, see *hDem* 27–28. The model is the shield of Achilles, *Il.* 18.483; as elswhere the formula of ἐν δέ is used in ecphrasis of the plastic arts (e.g., Jason's cloak in A.R. 1.730–64). Thus Bing 1988: 18–19 suggests that the anaphora concretizes the song as a papyrus roll (comparing *Aet.* fr. 75.64–66 Pf.).

141. Artemis' arrival at the "house of Zeus" marks the end of her childhood and her maturation into a deity potent enough to be accepted on Olympus. The second half of the hymn begins with an imitation of Apollo's arrival on Olympus in *HhAp* 1–13. Hermes, and later Heracles, greets Artemis; in the Homeric hymn Leto takes Apollo's bow.

θηητήν: Ionic for θεατός, "wondrous," Hesiod and lyric.

142. ἀντιόωντες: see above 65n.

προμολῇσι: see above 99n.

143. Ἑρμείης Ἀκακήσιος: according to Pausanias (8.36.10), Hermes was reared in Arcadia, educated by Lycaon's son, Akakos, where there was also a cult of Artemis *Hegemone* (8.37.1). ἀκάκητα, "gracious," is an epithet of Hermes at *Il.* 16.185 and *Od.* 24.10, on which see Rengakos 1992: 44. Hermes' presence at Artemis' initial reception on Olympus may suggest an earlier moment when Hermes introduced his own son, Pan, to the immortals (*HhPan* 42–47).

143–44. Ἀπόλλων | θηρίον ὅττι φέρῃσθα: cf. *hAp* 60–63, where Artemis brings horned goats to Apollo, from which he builds the Delian altar.

144. πάροιθε: cf. *Il.* 15.227, of Apollo taking Zeus's aegis.

145–61. Heracles is portrayed as a glutton, a characterization familiar from drama (cf. Eur. *Alc.* 787–802, Ar. *Aves* 1574–1693).

145. Ἀλκεΐδην: Heracles. According to Apollod. 2.4.12, he was called Alcides after his grandfather, Alcaeus, the father of Amphitryon. Alternatively, his name was Ἀλκαῖος ("Mighty") before Apollo gave him the name Heracles (sch. Pi. *Ol.* 6.68 [115]). καρτερόν may play on the latter meaning.

146. Τιρύνθιος ἄκμων "the Tirynthian anvil." Heracles' grandfather had been the king of Tiryns, and when his cousin Eurystheus inherited the throne, Heracles was forced to serve him. The metaphor of the anvil first appears in Aesch. *Pers.* 51, describing soldiers impervious to the enemy lance. The scholiast explains as "not wearied by his toils."

147. ποτιδέγμενος: in Homer προσδέχομαι means "await"; cf. *Od.* 23.90–91: ὁ δ᾽ ἄρα πρὸς κίονα μακρὴν | ἧστο κάτω ὁρόων, ποτιδέγμενος εἴ τί μιν εἴποι ("But he sat by a tall column looking down, waiting if she [Penelope] would say something").

148. νεῖαι: from Homeric νέομαι: "come" or "go."

πῖον ἔδεσμα: the Homeric πίων is usually found with goats (αἶγες) or thighbones (μηρία); here with a prosaic word for "edibles," for comic effect.

149. ἄλληκτον: rare Homeric adjective, here used adverbially: "ceaselessly" (cf. ἄσβεστος γέλως at *Il.* 1.599), where the gods laugh at Hephaestus.

γελόωσι: see above 65n.

πενθερή: Heracles' "mother-in-law" was Hera. When Heracles was elevated to Olympus, he married Hebe, the daughter of Zeus and Hera. Here Heracles is attendant on divinities, but cf. Theoc. 17.26–33, where the now deified Alexander and Ptolemy I carry Heracles' bow and club.

150. ὅτ(ε): see *hZeus* 21n.

χλούνην: used as an epithet for a wild boar (as here), or substantively with the same sense; once in Homer (*Il.* 9.539), where Artemis sends a χλούνην σῦν ἄγριον against Oeneus. Cf. the description of Heracles with the Erymanthian boar in A.R. 1.126–29.

151. ὀπισθιδίοιο: a variant of ὀπίσθιος, "belonging to the hind quarters" (modifying ποδός); the form is attested previously in Sophron (*PCG* 1 fr. 49 K-A), then imitated by Nonnus. The pose described is standard for Heracles; he was often represented with a club swung back over his shoulder, and sometimes he holds animals in a similar way: the Cerynian hind (*LIMC*, s.v. Heracles 2177); the Erymanthian boar (*LIMC* 2111, 2147); a lion (*LIMC* 1977); an Egyptian (Caeretan hydria, *LIMC* s.v. Busiris 9); and he even holds a stool by its leg with which he attacks his music teacher Linus (*LIMC* 1667–68, 1671).

ἀσπαίροντα: from ἀσπαίρω, poetic and Ionic; "writhing" (usually of death throes); cf. *Il.* 13.571.

152. κερδαλέῳ μύθῳ: cf. *Od.* 6.148, where Odysseus addresses a κερδαλέον μῦθον ("crafty speech") to Nausicaa, likening her to Artemis. Heracles' crafty speech suggests to Artemis that she can be like him by shooting not at small creatures but at boars and larger beasts that are harmful to men.

152. πινύσκει "admonish"; once in Homer, *Il.* 14.249, where Sleep recalls Heracles sacking Troy.

155. βόσκεσθαι: commonly in the passive of cattle grazing (also at *hAp* 52); here applied to deer and hares.

155–56. τί...κεν...ῥέξειαν: the phrase is modelled on *Od.* 4.649: τί κεν ῥέξειε, "what can one do" when a man like that makes an entreaty? Initially Heracles' statement is consistent with his role as a bringer of civilization by clearing the landscape of wild beasts and monsters, but βόες (157) clarifies Heracles' real concern—tasty meat to eat (though wild bulls like that of Marathon occasionally devastated the landscape).

156. ἔργα: see 125n.

φυτά: cultivated as opposed to wild plants; in the plural "orchard."

157. βάλλ' ἐπὶ καὶ τούς (= αὐτούς): the hyperbaton is emphatic, and the phrase echoes βάλλε κακοὺς ἐπί above 153.

158. ταχινός: see *hZeus* 56; also at *hDelos* 95, 114.

πονεῖτο: in Homer, frequently of servants who prepare a banquet.

159. Φρυγίη...ὑπὸ δρυΐ "under the Phrygian oak," referring to the location of Heracles' funeral pyre.

θεωθείς: from θεόω, "make into a god," first in Callimachus.

160. ἀδηφαγίης "gluttony," first found in Aristotle (fr. 144 Rose), but common in later prose.

πάρα = πάρεστι.

νηδύς: any body cavity, here "stomach"; cf. *Od.* 9.296 of the Cyclops.

161. The story of Thiodamas is compressed into three words. It appears in *Aet.*, book 1, frr. 24–25 Pf., and A.R. 1.1211–14 records a more negative version. In the area of Trachis, Heracles requested food for his son from the old man Thiodamas, who was plowing. Thiodamas refused and Heracles killed him. Thiodamas' son was Hylas, guardianship of whom Heracles assumed. The loss of Hylas in A.R. 1.1221–39 led Heracles to abandon the expedition of the Argonauts.

ἀροτριόωντι "plow," see 65n on the form.

συνήντετο: from συνάντομαι; Homeric, only in present and imperfect, "fall in with," "meet."

162. Ἀμνισιάδες: the twenty attendants Artemis requested in 15.

ζεύγληφι: the form is a *hapax* in Callimachus, and an imitation of *Il.* 24.576: οἳ τόθ' ὑπὸ ζυγόφιν λύον ἵππους ἡμιόνους τε ("they loosed the horses and mules from under the yoke"), where ζυγόφιν = ζεύγληφι.

163. ψήχουσιν: from ψήχω, a technical term for currying a horse.

κεμάδας "young deer," see 112n.

164. ἀμησάμεναι: from ἀμάω; mostly epic, in the middle, "draw," "gather." The nymphs gather fodder for the deer from Hera's meadow.

165. ὠκύθοον: previously only in Eur. *Supp.* 993, of swiftly running nymphs; here of the "swift-growing" grass.

τριπέτηλον "tripetal," only here and in Nic. *Ther.* 522. According to Hesychius s.v., it is clover.

ἔδουσιν: see 85n.

166. ἐν ... ἐπλήσαντο: from ἐμπίμπλημι; for the thought cf. *HhDem* 170.

ὑποληνίδας = ὑπολήνιον: *hapax* in Callimachus; a "trough" for the deer to drink from. (In later Greek ὑπολήνιον is a wine vat.) It is gold in contrast to Poseidon's horse trough above, 50.

167. θυμάρμενον = θυμαρής "delightful," "pleasing to the heart." First in Bacchylides 17.71, of a portent, then here.

168. Artemis' triumphal entry into her father's house imitates the opening of *HhAp* 1–5.

169. σὺ δ᾽ Ἀπόλλωνι παρίζεις: Artemis, as Apollo's twin, was closely associated with him in visual representation. She also had sanctuaries at Delos and at Cyrene that were close to his own, and this line could allude to either (or both). It has also been interpreted as referring to Arsinoe II as sitting next to her brother/husband. Fantuzzi 2011: 451 suggests that it might also indicate the position of *hArt* in the collection as "sitting next to" *hAp*.

170. χορῷ ἔνι: Bornmann ad loc. observes that this type of anastrophe and accompanying hiatus are not uncommon in Callimachus.

κυκλώσονται: unlike those of tragedy, lyric choruses were usually circular; see Calame 1997: 34–38.

171. ἀγχόθι: four times in Homer (e.g., *Od.* 13.103 ≈ 347), then frequent in the Hellenistic poets.

Αἰγυπτίου Ἰνωποῖο: the Inopus on Delos is the location of Apollo's birth (*hDelos* 206–8 and *HhAp* 18), and in both hymns connected to the Nile.

172. Πιτάνη ... Λίμναις: Pitane was one of the five early villages of Sparta; according to Paus. 3.16.9, the rites of Artemis *Limnaea* were conducted there. For Artemis *Limnatis* see Calame 1997: 142–49.

173. Ἀλὰς Ἀραφηνίδας: a coastal deme of Attica, according to Strabo (9.1.22), with a temple dedicated to Artemis *Tauropolos*. Eur. *IT* 1446–61 relates how Orestes and Iphigenia bring the cult statue from the Tauric Chersonese on the Black Sea to Athens at Athena's instruction.

174. Artemis leaves the Taurians, rejecting their practice of human sacrifice as part of her rites.

Σκυθίης: the Taurians were identified with the Scythians, and later with the Cimmerians, see below 253.

ἀπὸ δ᾽ εἴπαο: from ἀπεῖπον, "repudiate" or "reject"; middle forms of -εῖπον in -α occur in compounds (also at 267), but this uncontracted second person is unique.

τέθμια "rites." See *hAp* 87n.

175. τημοῦτος = τῆμος: previously only in Hesiod (*Op.* 576) in the context of lenghtening days of spring; "at that time." The point of the convoluted image (175–82) is that since Helios stops in his course to watch the dancing, daylight is extended, hence the usual time that it would take to plow a field of four γύαι would be greatly lengthened. The passage is an adaptation of *Od.* 18.371–75 in which Odysseus, in disguise, challenges Eurymachus to a contest in plowing.

> εἰ δ᾽ αὖ καὶ βόες εἶεν ἐλαυνέμεν, οἵ περ ἄριστοι,
> αἴθωνες μεγάλοι, ἄμφω κεκορηότε ποίης,
> ἥλικες, ἰσοφόροι, τῶν τε σθένος οὐκ ἀλαπαδνόν,
> τετράγυον δ᾽ εἴη, εἴκοι δ᾽ ὑπὸ βῶλος ἀρότρῳ·
> τῶ κέ μ᾽ ἴδοις, εἰ ὦλκα διηνεκέα προταμοίμην.

If again there were oxen to drive, which were the best, sleek and large, both sated on grass, of the same age, equal yoke-bearers, whose strength was inexhaustible, and there were a four-acre field and its soil would yield under the plow; then you would see me, whether I could cut a furrow straight to the end.

Callimachus inverts his intertext, however, expressing the wish that his oxen not plow a four-acre field. Bing 1988: 83–89 argues that by so doing Callimachus makes a statement about poetic composition, i.e., a preference for smaller hexameter poetry in place of epic. He also notes that plowing was a common metaphor for writing poetry, especially in Pindar (e.g., *Nem.* 6.32, 10.26, *Py.* 6.2). Another version of the Homeric (or Homeric and Callimachean) passage is A.R. 3.1340–44, where Jason is required to plow the field with Aeetes' fire-breathing oxen.

176. τετράγυον: Homeric, four γύαι; the γύης was a measure of land and τετράγυον as a neuter substantive indicates as much as a man can plow in a day, see *Odyssey* above.

ὑπ᾽ ἀλλοτρίῳ ἀροτῆρι: a hireling would be uninterested in the welfare of the oxen, hence would overwork them.

177. γυιαί "limbs," with a play on γύαι.

κεκμηυῖαι: perfect active participle from κάμνω, "wearied from labor."

178. κόπρον "dung," "dunghill," used in Homer for a cattle byre.

προγένοιντο "come into sight"; a *hapax* in Homer, *Il.* 18.525–26, where cattle are described on the shield of Achilles: οἳ δὲ τάχα προγένοντο, δύω δ᾽ ἅμ᾽ ἕποντο νομῆες | τερπόμενοι σύριγξι ("they soon came into sight, and two herdsmen followed, playing upon syrinxes"). If the passage is a *recusatio*, the shield provides an alternative to epic, because on it are found singers performing in smaller, non-heroic venues.

Στυμφαιίδες: Stymphaeum (or Tymphaeum) was a region of Epirus where a number of battles between the Diadochs took place. (Plut. *Pyrrh.* 6; D.S. 20.28.1). According to the scholiast, it was known for the quality of its cattle (cf. Arist. *HA* 522b14–25).

179. εἰναετιζόμεναι: the verb does not occur elsewhere, but the parallel form πενταετίζομαι, "to be five years old," occurs in *IG* xiv.1971. Hesiod recommends nine-year-old oxen as the best (*Op.* 436).

κεραελκέες "drawing by their horns," first in Callimachus, imitated by Nonnus.

180. ὦλκα: twice in Homer (see above 175n): "furrow," only in accusative singular (as here) or plural.

180–82. The word order is unusual, but carefully balanced: ἐπεὶ θεὸς οὔποτ' ἐκεῖνον (*sc.* καλὸν χορόν) is restated in Ἥλιος καλὸν χορόν, with the verb between. The effect is to stop Helios as he passes by, as the next lines state (δίφρον ἐπιστήσας); the spondaic ending to the hexameter (μηκύνονται) also slows down the time.

181. ἦλθε παρ(ά): unusually with the preverb in tmesis following.

183–85. After this transition, Callimachus begins again in proper hymnic fashion by asking a series of questions to establish how he should praise Artemis: what islands, mountain, harbor, city, what special nymph, heroines? Note the variation and balance of the lines: τίς δέ νύ τοι νήσων, ποῖον δ' ὄρος…τίς δὲ λιμήν, ποίη δὲ πόλις, τίνα δ' ἔξοχα νυμφέων…ποίας ἡρωίδας.

183. εὔαδε: epic aorist of ἀνδάνω, "please." Cf. *Il.* 14.340 and 17.647: νύ τοι εὔαδεν.

184–85. τίνα…φίλαο: the question is answered when Callimachus repeats the verb in 189. Cf. *Od.* 4.171–72 (Menelaus about Odysseus): καί μιν ἔφην ἐλθόντα φιλησέμεν ἔξοχα πάντων | Ἀργείων ("and I said that if he returned I would cherish him exceedingly beyond all the Argives").

185. φίλαο: epic aorist middle of φιλέω. Callimachus uses the verb in the hymns only of goddesses' favorite nymphs: see 211 for her love of Anticlea and *hAth* 58 for Athena's love for the nymph Chariclo. On Artemis' "homophilic" relationship with her nymphs, see Calame 1997: 253.

ἡρωίδας: from ἡρωίς = ἡρωίνη (also at fr. 602.1Pf.). Bornmann argues that these are not indigenous goddesses like Cyrene and Britomartis, but locally deified women of myth as in *hDelos* 161. (At Theoc. 13.20 and 26.36 ἡρωίνη refers to famous women—Alcmene and the daughters of Cadmus.) Here ἡρωίς distinguishes Procris and Atalanta from the nymphs Britomartis and Cyrene.

186. εἰπέ, θεή, σὺ μὲν ἄμμιν, ἐγὼ δ' ἑτέροισιν ἀείσω: there is tight binding of poet to subject: "(you) speak to me, I shall sing to others." The poet as an interpreter of the Muse is a commonplace (see, e.g., *Il.* 2.484–86, Pi. *Pae.* 6.6, Pl. *Ion*

534, and Theoc. 16.29, 17.115), but here Callimachus has substituted the goddess for his Muse; for a similar familiarity with the deity, cf. *hZeus* 7.

187. Δολίχη: according to Steph. Byz. (s.v. Ἴκαρος), Dolichos was an alternative name of Icaros, one of the Cyclades; it was also called Macris or Ichthyessa; according to Strabo (14.1.19), this island had a temple to Artemis *Tauropolos*.

Πέργη: Perge was a city in Pamphylia well known for its temple and annual festival to Artemis *Pergaia* (see Petrovic 2007: 194–95).

188. Τηΰγετον: Taÿgetus was a mountain range running the length of the middle peninsula of the Peloponnese (above the Mani, with Sparta lying to the east); it was said to have been named for Taÿgetis, the mother of Europa.

Εὐρίποιο: the strait that separates Euboea and Boeotia; according to Pausanias 9.19.6, nearby Aulis had a temple to Artemis with two statues, one of her holding a torch, another of her shooting an arrow.

189. ἔξοχα δ᾽ ἀλλάων (= ἀλλῶν)**:** see above 184–85.

Γορτυνίδα "Gortynian"; the form occurs only here, a metonym for Cretan.

190–205 relate the story of the Cretan nymph Britomartis, who fled from the attentions of Minos, eventually jumping into the sea. She was saved by a fisherman's net, and for that reason came to be worshipped in Crete as Dictynna. (The story is similar to that of Asteria and Zeus, related in *hDelos*.) According to D. S. 5.76.3, Britomartis was the daughter of Zeus and Carme and invented the hunting net, hence was called Dictynna. He rejects Callimachus' version of the story, which is the earliest attested. Hesychius s.v. claims that βριτύ is the Cretan equivalent of γλυκύ. Her name is attested in Cretan inscriptions. (On Britomartis see Larsen 2007: 177–78, 190.)

190. ἐλλοφόνον "fawn slayer"; a *hapax* in Callimachus, though it is an epithet of Artemis in a second century CE magic text (*PGM* 4.2722). ἐλλός is a young deer or fawn at *Od.*19.228 (also a *hapax*).

ἧς ποτε Μίνως: the introduction of a narrative by means of a relative pronoun is characteristic of epic, see Bornmann ad loc. for Homeric examples (also at *hDelos* 308).

191. κατέδραμεν: here, uniquely, it seems to mean "ran over" the mountains, though forms of κατατρέχω usually mean "overtake" or "overcome"; cf. Theoc. 22.204: κὰδ δ᾽ ἄρα οἱ βλεφάρων βαρὺς ἔδραμεν ὕπνος ("and heavy sleep overcame his eyes"). This more common usage may be implicit, since the verb follows ὑπ᾽ ἔρωτι.

192–93. ὁτὲ... ἄλλοτε: apparently imitating *Il.* 11.64–65: Ἕκτωρ ὁτὲ μέν τε μετὰ πρώτοισι φάνεσκεν | ἄλλοτε δ᾽ ἐν πυμάτοισι κελεύων ("Hector appeared now among the first ranks and then in the last, giving his orders") and cf. *Il.* 20.49–50; in Callimachus Britomartis *dis*appears, first hiding in the thickets, then in the marshes.

192. ὁτέ: indefinite adverb, "now" (see LSJ s.v. ὅτε C).

Notice the position of **νύμφη**, separated from its article, "hiding under the shaggy oaks" and separated from the pursuing Minos by two lines.

193. εἰαμενῇσιν: a riverside pasture or low-lying meadow; twice in Homer (*Il.* 4.483, 15.631), then imitated by Theoc. 25.16 and A.R. 3.1202. The meaning of the word and whether or not it was aspirated were debated in antiquity.

194. παίπαλα: only here, apart from scholia and lexicographers, according to whom these are areas difficult to walk on.

διωκτύν: Ionic for δίωξις, "pursuit"; a *hapax* in Callimachus, surely intended as a pun with the δικτ-words that follow in 197–200.

195. μαρπτομένη "seize," "catch"; Bornmann ad loc. makes the intriguing suggestion that Callimachus' choice of verb may have punned on the Cretan form of the name, Βριτομάρπις (see Larsen 2007: 190).

καὶ δὴ σχεδόν: καί is not copulative; the word order echoes the meaning: "captured... even nearly." For a similar hyperbaton see *hAth* 58.

ἥλατο: aorist of ἅλλομαι "leap"; usually followed by a preposition, but cf. *hDelos* 37.

196. πρηόνος: see 52n.

ἔνθορεν: epic aorist from ἐνθρῴσκω "leap in or among"; in Homer with dative (e.g., *Il.* 24.79).

197. σφ(ε): here for αὐτήν, as occasionally in tragedy.

197–99. Note the interlaced δίκτυα... | νύμφην... Δίκτυναν... νύμφη... | Δικταῖον, progressing from net to nymph to her name to the name of the mountain as Callimachus derives the name of Mt. Dicte from δίκτυα. The Mt. Dicte associated with Britomartis' leap is not the mountain connected with the birth of Zeus (*hZeus* 47), which sits inland, east and below Heracleion. Strabo takes Callimachus to task for the mistake (10.4.12), though the poet is more likely to be playing on known geographic doublets (as he does in *hZeus*). For Κύδωνες... καλέουσιν concluding a similar *aition*, see *hZeus* 45 (and below 205).

200. ἱερά τε ῥέζουσι: cf. *HhAp* 394.

201. σχῖνος "mastic," a small shrub native to the southern Mediterranean from which an elastic resin was extracted.

μύρτοιο δὲ χεῖρες ἄθικτοι: i.e., their hands do not touch myrtle. Callimachus provides an explanation for the ritual exclusion of myrtle in the next lines, though it is more likely to have been excluded because of its connection with other rites, e.g., the Mysteries (Ar. *Ran.* 330), or, as Bornmann ad loc. suggests, its popularity with Aphrodite.

202. δὴ τότε: a Homeric formula found also at *hDelos* 307.

203. χώσατο: from epic χώομαι, "be angry" + dative.

204. Οὖπι: here a cult title for Artemis at Ephesus; it occurs in Alexander the Aetolian (fr. 4.5 Powell, a poem apparently on her temple at Ephesus); at *hDelos* 292 Oupis is a daughter of Boreas.

εὐῶπι "fair of face" (εὖ + ὤψ) may be intended as an etymology of the cult name Οὖπις.

φαεσφόρε: another cult title of Artemis (see 11n); it also appears in *PGM* 4.2722 (see 190n).

205. Κρηταέες: a variant of Κρηταιεῖς, probably for metrical reasons.

206. Κυρήνην: Cyrene was the Thessalian nymph beloved of Apollo and taken by him to Cyrene. Artemis apparently had a prior claim, and one that suggests a competing version of the myth.

ἐταρίσσαο: from ἑταιρίζω; in the sense "take as a companion"; cf. *Il.* 13.456.

207. θηρητῆρε: θηρητήρ seems to be used substantively in Homer (e.g., *Il.* 21.574), but θηρευτής as an adjective (e.g., *Il.* 11.325: κυσὶ θηρευτῇσι). It may be relevant that in this latter passage Aristarchus preferred θηρητῆρσι (so Bornmann ad loc.)

τοῖς ἔνι: the sense of ἔνι is between local "among them" (*sc.* the hounds) and instrumental, "with them."

208. Ὑψηίς: Cyrene, see *hAp* 90–92n.

τύμβον Ἰώλκιον: according to the scholiast, the tomb of Pelias in Thessaly, whose funeral games were well attested.

ἔμμορ(ε): Homeric aorist of μείρομαι, with the genitive, ἔμμορε τιμῆς, "receive as one's due honor"; Callimachus uses the form only here, possibly a reminiscence of *Il.* 1.278, in which Agamemnon reminds the "son of Peleus" that he is not entitled to the same portion as the king.

ἀέθλου: the noun is deceptive: in the context of hunting dogs (207) many scholars take the "prize" to refer to Cyrene's defeat of the lion, which according to Pindar (*Py.* 9) took place in Thessaly (though at *hAp* 91–92 it happens in Cyrene). Equally it could refer to Atalanta's defeat of Peleus in wrestling at the funeral games for Pelias (Apollod. 3.9.2), which was also a subject for vase painting (see *LIMC* s.v. Atalanta for illustrations). See Bornmann ad loc. on the controversy.

209. Κεφάλου ... ἄλοχον Δηιονίδαο: Procris was the daughter of Erechtheus (of Athens) and wife of Cephalus, the son of Deioneus. Cephalus was carried off by Dawn, and Procris spent eight years as a companion of Artemis before returning to her husband. Ov. *Met.* 7.694–755 has the story.

210. ὁμόθηρον: a *hapax* in Callimachus, rare afterwards; "companion in the hunt."

211. Ἀντίκλειαν: the only known mythological figure with this name is the mother of Odysseus, but there is no evidence that she was ever a companion of Artemis.

212–15. An *aition* for the traditional costume of the Amazons; for Artemis as an Amazon, see *LIMC* s.v. Artemis 337–52.

212. αἱ πρῶται: Procris and Anticlea.

212–13. φαρέτρας | ἰοδόκους "arrow-holding quivers"; the expression is Homeric: *Il.* 15.443–44 (of Ajax), *Od.* 21.59–60 (of Penelope with Odysseus' bow and quiver).

213. †ἀσύλλωτοι: the ms. reading is unattested elsewhere; it has been corrected to the rare ἀσύλωτοι, "unassailable," which is scarcely appropriate (the sense should be something like "uncovered"). Mair prints an unattested ἀσίλλωτοι, as if from ἄσιλλα (yoke), translating as "quiver strap."

214. γυμνὸς ... μαζός: the Amazons were frequently portrayed with the right (or left) breast uncovered. However, their name was derived by some ancient scholars from ἀ + μαζός, "without a breast," on the theory that these women removed one breast to allow ease in pulling the bow. By specifying "the bared breast" Callimachus may be writing against that tradition.

παρεφαίνετο: of a body part seen falling past the edge of a garment; first in Hes. *Op.* 734, and see Ar. *Ec.* 94.

215–24. The story of Atalanta. Bornmann ad loc. points out that the sections on Artemis' nymphs, Britomartis, Procris and Anticlea, and finally Atalanta, all conclude with an *aition*, though the section on Cyrene does not; this may be because of Cyrene's close association with Apollo as the eponymous nymph of Callimachus' own city, see *hAp* 90–96.

215. ἔτι πάγχυ: first in Homer, only at *Od.* 14. 338: "utterly," "completely."

ποδορρώρην: according to *Et. mag.* 678.29: παρὰ τὸ πούς καὶ τὸ ὀρούειν. Callimachus' compound is unique, but apt for Atalanta, who was a swift runner.

216. Ἰασίοιο ... Ἀρκασίδαο: Atalanta's father, Iasius, was the son of Lycurgus of Arcadia. (In other versions her father was Iasus, Schoenus, or Maenalus.) According to Apollod. 3.9.2, her father exposed Atalanta at birth because she was not a boy; in the wild, she-bears suckled her until she was discovered by hunters, who raised her. She remained a virgin, dedicated to the hunt. Two Centaurs, Hylaeus and Rhoecus, tried to rape her, but she killed them both (see 221–24). The story is related in Ael. *VH* 13.1.

συοκτόνον "boar-slayer," first here in Callimachus, imitated by Nonnus; for the compound with -κτόνος, cf. 110: Τιτυοκτόνε.

Ἀρκασίδαο: a rare word for Arcadian, previously in Hesiod's *Catalogue* (frr. 129.17, 22; 165.8 M-W).

217. κυνηλασίην: first in Callimachus, "hunting with hounds."

εὐστοχίην: "skill in shooting"; cf. Eur. *IT* 1239 of Apollo (also at 262 below).

218. ἐπίκλητοι: the heroes who were invited to participate in the hunt as distinct from Atalanta (μιν). The adjective may hint at a version of the boar hunt in which the men objected to Atalanta's presence (e.g., Apollod. 1.8.2).

218–19. Καλυδωνίου ... κάπροιο: in the generation that predated the Trojan War, Oeneus, the king of Calydon, failed to honor Artemis when he was sacrificing first fruits; she punished him by sending a fierce boar to destroy his land. He then summoned a number of heroes to hunt the boar, including Atalanta (see Apollod. 1.8.2, where she is the daughter of Schoenus). The story of the boar hunt is related in Bacchylides 5, although there is no mention of Atalanta.

218. ἀγρευτῆρες: rare Hellenistic noun for "hunter" (also at [Theoc.] 21.6), imitated especially by Oppian.

219. σημήια (= σημεῖα) "tokens" of victory would have been the skin and tusks of the slain animal, which Atalanta was allowed to keep.

220. θηρὸς ὀδόντας: Paus. 8.45.4–7 claims the tusks were displayed in a temple of Athena in Tegea. This temple, which was rebuilt in the early fourth century BCE, included a frieze of the boar hunt.

221. See above 216n.

ἔολπα: Homeric perfect of ἔλπω, with present sense: "suppose," "expect"; only here in Callimachus.

222. μωμήσασθαι: from μωμάομαι, "find fault with" (cf. Momus in *hAp* 113). This incident is superficially similar to the preceding, in which the men do not grudge Atalanta the tokens of the hunt; now it is the bodies of the Centaurs whom Artemis has slain that cannot fault the accuracy of her bow. These two incidents, with fortunate and dire outcomes, foreshadow Artemis' behavior in the sequel.

223. τοξότιν "archeress," first in Callimachus.

συνεπιψεύσονται "will join in lying"; first in Callimachus, then in Lucian.

224. τάων: relative, the antecedent is λαγόνες (here feminine).

Μαιναλίη...ἀκρώρεια: the region was associated with Pan (see above 88–89n) as well as Atalanta. She is often called Maenalian (e.g., Eur. *Phoen.* 1162, cf. A.R. 1.769–70).

νᾶεν: from νάω; "drip" or "flow" of liquids. Here "flow" with slaughter.

225–58. In this final section the role of Artemis as a city goddess, assigned by her father at the beginning of the hymn (33–35), is fleshed out. Now Callimachus details her involvement in new foundations (Neleus), protecting the young (Agamemnon, Proetus), and finally in the establishment of her great temple at Ephesus (238–58).

225. πουλυμέλαθρε: a *hapax* in Callimachus, "with many shrines."

πολύπτολι: first in Callimachus, here and again at *hDelos* 266, later in prose: "with many cities."

Χιτώνη: Artemis is so titled in *hZeus* 77. The sanctuary of Artemis *Chitone* was located to the east of Miletus; the Persians destroyed it in 494 BCE; it was later rebuilt inside the new city (see Herda 1998).

226. ἐπίδημε: Callimachus uses the term for divinities who are closely associated with, if not patrons of a place (cf. *hAp.* 13 and of Artemis, fr. 75.26 Pf.)

Νηλεύς: this Neleus was said to have been the son of Codrus, the king of Athens, and the mythical founder of Miletus (Hdt. 9.97, Str. 14.1.3) and other Ionian cities. Cf. *Aet.* fr. 80.16–18 Pf., the *aition* of Phrygius and Pieria, and the festival of the *Neleia* (see Harder ad loc.).

227. ἡγεμόνην: the cult title *Hegemone* is attested in a number of localities, and is connected to Artemis as a guide for the foundation of a colony. See Bornmann ad loc.

Κεκροπίηθεν: Cecropia was the ancient name for Athens (see Hdt. 8.44, *hDelos* 315); the form occurs only here and at A.R. 1.95, 214.

228. Χησιάς: Chesias was one of the two main regions of Samos and also a Samian river.

Ἰμβρασίη: the Imbrasus was another small river on Samos. According to Ath. 7.283D–F, who quotes A.R. (fr. 7 Powell), Chesias was a nymph beloved by the river Imbrasus, who gave birth to Ocyrhoe. Apollo fell in love with the latter, but she fled him and crossed over to Miletus during a festival of Artemis. Hera is the deity most closely connected to Samos, and *Chesia* and *Imbrasie* were Samian cult titles used for her and for Artemis (see Gardner 1882: 17).

Πρωτόθρονε: a cult of Artemis *Protothronios* (a variant of *Protothronos*) existed at Ephesus (Pausanias 10.38.6).

228–32. See pp. 106–7 and 121n for Artemis and Agamemnon.

229. πηδάλιον "a ship's rudder"; this bears a resemblance to ex-voto offerings of ships after a safe voyage (e.g., *AP* 6.69, 70 or Catullus, *c.* 4), but as a μείλιον ἀπλοΐης it is also a reminder of the blood sacrifice of Iphigenia. Note the puns on νηός (from ναῦς) and νηῷ (from ναός).

230. μείλιον: an offering of propiation; in Homer only at *Il.* 9.147 ≈ 289 for the bridal gifts that Agamemnon offers to propitiate Achilles, and thus appropriate for Agamemnon's gift to Artemis to appease her anger (cf. A.R. 4.1190, 1549).

ἀπλοΐης: the "impossibility of sailing"; in Aesch. *Ag.* 188 it describes the calm at Aulis.

κατέδησας ἀήτας: variant of a Homeric formula that describes the calming of the winds (cf. *Od.* 5.383, 7.272, 10.20). Cf. Aesch. *Ag.* 149–50 and 188–204 on the dire effects of adverse winds (ἀντιπνόους) on Agamemnon's fleet delayed at Aulis and unable to sail to Troy.

231. ἄστεα: i.e., the towns surrounding Troy. M. Fantuzzi suggests that Callimachus is alluding to the cities, mainly of the Troad, that Achilles sacked in the years before the events of the *Iliad*, for which a poetic tradition may well have existed (see, e.g., Nagy 1979: 140–41).

232. ἀμφ' Ἑλένῃ "for the sake of Helen," as at *Il.* 3.70.

Ῥαμνουσίδι: Rhamnus was a coastal deme in northeastern Attica, famous for a temple of Nemesis that had been deliberately left unfinished. To flee the attentions of Zeus, she turned herself into a goose, while Zeus, to seduce her, became a gander (Apollod. 3.10.7). Her story is a doublet of Leda's in that Nemesis laid an egg that produced Helen. The site of that seduction was supposedly Rhamnus (Eratos. *Cat.* 1.25). For the connection with Helen, see *Cypria,* fr. 9 Bernabé and sch. Lycophron 88. In historical times, it was a base for the Ptolemies and their allies in the Chremonidean War (267 to 261).

233. ἣ μέν τοι: once in Homer (*Od.* 14.160 ≈ 19.305) and once in A.R. (3.152), where it stresses the truth of the statement.

Προῖτος: Proetus, the son of Abas, was a king of Argos, in the hereditary line of the Argive kings (he occurs at *Aet.* fr. 54a.10 Harder). His daughters were driven mad because they slighted Hera (Bacchyl. 11.44–56) or Dionysus (Hes. fr. 131 M-W) and were condemned to roam the local mountains. See Calame 1997: 116–20.

234. Κορίης: the title is not attested for Artemis, but Pausanias 8.21.4 mentions a temple to Athena *Koria* in Arcadia.

235. Ἀζήνια: see *hZeus* 20n.

τὸν δ' ἐνὶ Λούσοις: cf. Bacchyl. 11.96.

236. Ἡμέρη: Pausanias 8.18.8 mentions the title of Artemis *Hemerasia* in connection with the healing of Proetus' daughters.

237–58. This section provides one last *aition,* on the establishment of Artemis' cult at Ephesus and its defense against the invading Cimmerians. Pliny (*HN* 34.53) describes statues of Amazons dedicated in the temple of Artemis, and Pausanias (7.2.7) claims that according to Pindar (= fr. 174 S-M) the Amazons founded the sanctuary during their campaign against Athens and Theseus. Given the emphasis on Theseus at the end of *hDelos*, this may allude to another moment in the sibling rivalry.

237. ἐπιθυμήτειραι: feminine of ἐπιθυμητής, a *hapax* in Callimachus; "women who long for" (*sc.* war). For a discussion of the form as a comment on Homeric ἀντιάνειραι (*Il.* 3.189, 6.186), see Rengakos 1992: 44–45.

238. ἔν κοτε παρραλίῃ: for the temporal adverb within a locative phrase to mark the beginning of a narrative, see *hAth* 57, *Hecale* fr. 1.1 with Hollis ad loc., fr. 194.6 Pf.

Ἐφέσῳ: Ephesus and Miletus were central areas of devotion to Artemis. See p. 102.

βρέτας: the noun is frequent in tragedy for a wooden image of a god; in Eur. *IT* 1475–85, it is the βρέτας of Artemis that Orestes and Iphigenia bring to Attica from the Tauric Chersonese (cf. A.R. 1.1119).

239. φηγῷ ὑπὸ πρέμνῳ: cf. *hDelos* 210, 322. Either one of the datives is in apposition to the other, or there is an error in the line. An easy correction would be φηγοῦ ὑπὸ πρέμνῳ, but Renehan 1987: 250 on *hDem* 82 provides parallels for two nouns in the same case.

πρέμνῳ: first in *HhHerm* 238; "tree stump," or the bottom part of a living tree (also at *hDelos* 210, 322).

Ἱππώ: Hippo is otherwise unattested as an Amazon (she is an Oceanid in Hes. *Th.* 351). Possibly it is an alternate name for Hippolyte, the queen of the Amazons, who was the mother of Hippolytus by Theseus.

240. Οὖπι ἄνασσα: see 204n.

περὶ πρύλιν: according to Aristotle (fr. 519 Rose), the Cretans call the dance *prulis*, but elsewhere it is the *pyrriche*. The *pyrriche* was danced by girls for Artemis in Eretria. Ceccarelli (2004: 100) makes a strong argument for this dance belonging to the ritual of Artemis *Tauropolos* as well. *HZeus* 52 connects it to the Cretan Curetes, who bore considerable resemblance to the Ephesian Curetes (see Rogers 2012: 100–13).

241. ἐνόπλιον "martial rhythm"; but here used as an equivalent of ἔνοπλος, "in arms."

241–42. Note the circular choral dance above 170 and *hDelos* 313.

242–43. The passage is dependent on *Il.* 18.569–71 (the shield), where a young boy plays his clear-voiced lyre (φόρμιγγι λιγείη | ἱμερόεν κιθάριζε) while he sings a Linos song (or the λίνον sings) sweetly in a delicate voice (λίνον δ' ὑπὸ καλὸν ἄειδε | λεπταλέῃ φωνῇ), while they (*sc.* the harvesters), beating the earth in accompaniment... (τοὶ δὲ ῥήσσοντες ἁμαρτῇ...). Ancient critics disputed the meaning of λίνον: it was either the string of the cithara (so Zenodotus) or the Linos, a genre of song (so Aristarchus). By making σύριγγες the subject of ὑπήεισαν Callimachus would seem to be agreeing with Zenodotus; but at *hDelos* 304 the personal subject with this rare verb suggests the later Aristarchan interpretation (see Rengakos 1992: 46).

242. ὑπήεισαν: third plural, aorist indicative of ὑπᾴδω: "to sing in accompaniment."

λίγειαι: although often translated as "shrill" or "high," the adjective more accurately refers to tones that are cleanly produced by the human voice in singing and by musical instruments in performance (West 1992: 42).

243. λεπταλέον "slender," "delicate," here used adverbially; cf. A.R. 3.872–80, where it describes the chitons of Medea's attendants as she goes to meet Jason (a passage in which she is is likened to Artemis). Callimachus uses λεπταλέης as a stylistic marker at the opening of the *Aetia* (fr. 1.24 Pf.).

ὁμαρτῇ: a variant of the Homeric adverb ἁμαρτῇ, "together."

244. νέβρεια... ὀστέα: pierced fawn bones were used for pipes.

δι(ά)... τετρήναντο: from διατετραίνω, "bore through"; first in Hdt. 3.12 and frequent in later prose; in poetry before Callimachus only at Ar. *Thesm.* 18.

245. ἔργον Ἀθηναίης: Bornmann points out that the phrase is deceptive, since Athena is normally associated with women's handiwork. According to ancient sources, she found the *aulos* in mountain thickets but hurled it away because playing it distorted her face (Ath. 14.616E-F).

ἐλάφῳ κακόν: the comment is ironic: the discovery that pierced fawn bones would make good musical instruments is bad news for the deer, but they are already the prey of Artemis.

ἔδραμε δ᾽ ἠχώ: the verb personifies the natural phenomenon.

246. νομὸν Βερεκύνθιον: apparently the standard title for the region (cf. Pliny *HN* 5.108.6: *Berecynthius tractus*) with a pun on νόμος (melody). Berecynthian flutes were well known (Str. 10.3.17), and the Berecynthian mountain was the home of the Great Goddess Cybele ([Plut.] *De fluviis* 10.4.2), whose worship was accompanied by flutes.

247. οὖλα: here of dancing; see *hZeus* 52n (and cf. *hAp* 76).

κατεκροτάλιζον: the κρόταλον was a kind of castanet used in the worship of Cybele. The verb, which is a *hapax* in Callimachus, transfers the rattling sounds to the dancers: as they dance, their quivers clatter, thus imitating the κρόταλον. For the presence of castanets in the worship of Artemis, see *PMG* fr. 955, which may belong to a hymn of Timotheus (cf. Hordern 2002:102). Pan is φιλόκροτος at *HhPan* 2, which has prompted A. Faulkner (2013: 232) to suggest that the *hapax* serves as a reminder of the connection between the two deities, and the inherently problematic relationship of wilderness and civilization that this hymn negotiates.

ἐπεψόφεον: the compound first in Callimachus, "rattle."

248. θέμειλον: a variant of θεμείλιον, on which see *hAp* 57; for the expression cf. *HhAp* 254–55: θεμείλια... εὑρέα.

249. δωμήθη: from δωμάω, "build"; first here in Callimachus and A.R. 2.531.

θεώτερον: see *hAp* 93n.

ἠώς: Dawn watches here, Hesperus in *hDelos* 303.

250. ἀφνειότερον: the wealth of the Artemision in Ephesus was proverbial; cf. Apollo, who is πολύχρυσος at *hAp* 34.

ῥέα κεν Πυθῶνα παρέλθοι: Delphi was a particularly rich sanctuary because many states kept their treasuries there (hence the reason that the Gauls sacked it), but Ephesus was even richer.

251. ἠλαίνων: variant of ἀλαίνω, first occurring at Theoc. 7.23, of "flitting" birds. Here the scholiast glosses as μωραίνων, "being foolish" or "mad." ἀλαίνω is common in tragedy for wandering, often in madness or of the dead. Since the Cimmerians were nomadic, the word may be deliberately ambiguous—Lygdamis is "wandering" from place to place and in his mind.

ἀλαπαξέμεν: future infinitive from epic ἀλαπάζω, "sack," "plunder."

ἠπείλησε: according to the D-scholium on *Il.* 8.150, the verb has three different meanings; Callimachus uses it in all three ways: here as "boast," at *hDelos* 87 and 125 as "threaten," and at *Aet.* fr. 18.6 Pf. as "promise" (so Rengakos 1992: 33). See also Callimachus' employment of οὖλος (*hAp* 76n) and ὑπᾴδω (*hArt* 242–43n) in various senses.

252. Λύγδαμις ὑβριστής: Lygdamis was a seventh-century king of the Cimmerians whose rise to power led him to attack many of the Ionian coastal cities. He is mentioned in Str. 1.3.21, and according to Hesychius s.v., he burned the temple of Artemis at Ephesus.

ἱππημολγῶν "mare-milkers" were the Scythians or Tartars; a *hapax* in Homer at *Il.* 13.5 and at Hes. *Cat.* fr. 150.15 M-W; cf. Str. 7.3.2–3.

252–53. ἐπὶ … ἤγαγε: the verb in tmesis is unusually broken over two lines.

253. Κιμμερίων: the Cimmerians are first mentioned at 174. Cf. Callinus, *IEG²* fr. 5 (= Str. 14.1.40) on their invasion of Sardis.

ψαμάθῳ ἴσον: cf. *hDelos* 171–76 for a similar description of the invasion of the Celts at Delphi.

253–54. In Homer κεκλιμένοι is normally followed by the dative when it means "bordering on" (e.g., *Il.* 5.709, 15.740), but in later Greek it may occur with πρός or εἰς + accusative. Bornmann ad loc. understands αὐτόν to belong with πόρον to mean "precisely" or "exactly" (citing *Il.* 13.615).

254. βοὸς πόρον Ἰναχιώνης: the Bosporos ("Cow Passage") was named for Io, who wandered across the strait in the form of a cow when she was fleeing Hera. The Inachid line of Argos was promoted as ancestors of the Ptolemies, and Io, of course, was both Egyptian and Greek. The *Suda* attributes a poem on the *Arrival of Io* (i.e., in Egypt) to Callimachus.

255. ἆ δειλὸς βασιλέων: a Homeric exclamation of pity or contempt, e.g., *Il.* 11.816, *Od.* 20.351.

ἤλιτεν: epic aorist, from ἀλιταίνω; the form occurs only at *Il.* 9.375, where Achilles accuses Agamemnon of sinning against him.

256. παλιμπετές "back again"; Homeric adverb, used twice in a context of failed purpose (*Il.* 16.395, *Od.* 5.27).

257. ὅσσων ἐν λειμῶνι Καϋστρίῳ: an imitation of the simile at *Il.* 2.459–68, where Homer likens the swarming Achaean armies to birds gathering in the meadow by the Caÿster. Note 461: ἐν λειμῶνι Καϋστρίου and 467–68: ἔσταν δ' ἐν λειμῶνι … μυρίοι, ὅσσα τε φύλλα … (on the Caÿster see Str. 13.4.5).

ἅμαξαι: conveyance by wagons was typically attributed to Scythian nomads by ancient authors.

259–68. The envoi consists of a series of prohibitions that reprise three of Artemis' principal characteristics—hunting, virginity (which includes the protection of the young), and festival dance—and each prohibition is accompanied by a parenthetical reference to an instructive mythological paradigm. Four of the named examples (Oeneus, Agamemnon, Otus, and Hippo) were treated earlier, but by including Orion and alluding to a story about Hippo that is not told, Callimachus may be suggesting that Artemis' hymn might have been even longer, had he chosen to tell these stories. (On the ending of the hymn see Plantinga 2004: 272–74.)

259. πότνια Μουνιχίη: according to the scholiast, the epithet refers to Artemis' temple in Attica, described by Pausanias (1.1.4) as near the harbor and the sanctuary of Artemis *Bendis* (see Deubner 1932: 204–7). Λιμενοσκόπε ("Watcher of the Harbor") supports this identification. However, our last location was Ephesus. According to Strabo (14.1.20), there was a temple of Artemis Μουνυχία, "a foundation of Agamemnon and inhabited by part of his men" at Pygela on the Ephesian coast, and Agamemnon (Ἀτρεΐδης) is mentioned in 263 and his dedication to her at 228–29. Given the geographic doublets or overlaps elsewhere in the hymns, it is possible Callimachus wishes to call attention to both cult-sites (Athens and Pygela).

Φεραίη: the cult was of Artemis/Hecate (see Petrovic 2007: 199). Pausanias (2.23.5) claims that Artemis was also worshipped as Φεραίη at Argos, Athens, and Sicyon. The Argives apparently claimed that Artemis' cult statue was brought from Pherae in Thessaly. (See p. 235 for multiple claims for possession of Athena's Palladium.)

260. Οἰνεῖ: see 218–19n.

262. ἐλαφηβολίην: first at Soph. *Aj.* 178 of Artemis exacting retribution (cf. Apollod. *Epit.* 3.21). According to Plut. *Mul. virt.* 244D7 (again at *Quaest. conv.* 660D5), the Phocians celebrated a festival called the *Elaphebolia* in honor of Artemis.

μηδ'…ἐριδαίνειν: infinitive in a prohibition (also 264); cf. *Od.* 21.310: μηδ' ἐρίδαινε, where the suitors tell Odysseus not to compete in the trial of the bow.

εὐστοχίην: see 217n.

263. Ἀτρεΐδης: for Agamemnon boasting of his prowess in archery, see 121n.

264. μνᾶσθαι: once in Homer, *Od.* 14.91, of the suitors' unrighteous courting of Penelope.

Ὦτος: one of the Aloadae, see 52n.

265. οὐδὲ μέν: the sense is progressive, see Denniston 362.

Ὠαρίων: according to [Hyginus] (*Astronomica* 2.34), Orion hunted with Artemis in Crete, and either boasted to her of his prowess or attempted to rape her; she killed him, and he was later transformed into the constellation.

266. Ἱππώ: see 239n. Why Hippo refused to dance is not known.

267. ἀκλαυτί "unwept." The adverb is first found in Callimachus; the spelling (-τί or -τεί) was debated by ancient grammarians, see *Hecale* fr. 115.2 (with Hollis' note).

ἀπείπατο: see 174n.

268. εὐάντησον: only here in Callimachus, "meet graciously." Cf. the context of the anaphora of εὖ at 129–35n.

4

The *Hymn to Delos*

T 326 LINES THE LONGEST HYMN IN THE COLLECTION, THE *HYMN TO*
Delos (like *hArt*) matches in size the longer Homeric hymns. Its hymnic
subject is the island of Delos, herself a goddess and famous as the birthplace of Apollo. Much of the hymn is taken up with the early mythical history
of the island, whose original name was Asteria. A minor goddess, Asteria had
chosen to avoid Zeus's advances by leaping into the sea and thus commenced life
as a wandering island. Unlike other islands, she had no fixed location, but floated
throughout the Aegean (thus a correlative in nature to Leto's wandering in search
for a place to give birth). The driving force of the narrative is Hera's anger at
Leto for her liaison with Zeus: Hera and her abettors, Ares and Iris, threaten any
region that attempts to succor the pregnant Leto as she comes near to her term.
As Leto wanders in search of a resting place, the prenatal Apollo prophesies from
her womb on two separate occasions: the first is about the downfall of Niobe and
her children; the second predicts the birth of Ptolemy II on Cos and the Gaulish
attack on Apollo's own shrine at Delphi. Of all the possible locations, it is Asteria,
who is already a nomad and has nothing to risk in defying Hera, who offers herself to Leto. When Apollo is born, she acts as his nurse. At that moment she takes
root in the sea, and her name is changed from Asteria to Delos. The final section
of the hymn narrates the cultic history of the island, from Olen, who according to
myth wrote its first hymns, to Theseus. Upon his return from slaying the Minotaur on Crete, he stops on Delos to dedicate an ancient statue of Aphrodite and,
with the young men and women who accompanied him, to celebrate the crane

dance. The hymn is organized as a series of interlocked sections that may be sche-
matized as follows (adapted from Schmiel 1987 and Bing 1988: 146):

1-10. The prooemium.
    11-27. Praise of Delos as preeminent among islands in contrast to her
    earlier history.
        28-54. Asteria as a wandering island; prediction of her change of name
        at Apollo's birth.
            55-248. The narrative of Leto's wandering.
                55-69. Hera's anger.
                    70-99a. Leto's wandering through Arcadia and Boeotia
                    (interrupted by Apollo's first prophecy).
                    99b-214. Leto's wandering through Achaea and Thessaly and
                    the islands
                    (Peneius episode),
                    (interrupted by Apollo's second prophecy of the birth
                      of Ptolemy on Cos, the Gaulish attack on Delphi, and
                      Ptolemy's defeat of the Gaulish mercenaries).
                215-48. Hera's anger runs its course and is finally mitigated.
            249-74. Birth of Apollo, with the glorification of Delos.
            275-324. The rites of Apollo on Delos in the past and today.
    325-26. Envoi.

The Divinity and Her Cult

Delos was a Panhellenic cult center from at least the sixth century BCE, to which
Mediterranean states sent *theoriai* at times that probably coincided with one
or another of the festivals for Apollo. These included the *Delia*, celebrated on a
four-year cycle, and the *Apollonia*, celebrated annually. Under Athenian control,
the *Delia* probably coincided with the *Thargelia*, a commemoration of Apollo's
birth held in the month of Thargelion. In 477 the island became the center of
the Delian League, a loose federation of 150 to 170 states under the leadership
of Athens, with meetings and treasuries located at Delos. As before, it was a
venue for choruses and artists from many cities throughout the Greek world (see
Furley and Bremer 2001: 1.139–58; Wilson 2007: 175–82). Athens lost control
in 314 BCE, and the island remained quasi-independent until 168 BCE, when the
Romans returned the island's administration to Athens. Between 314 and 168
Delos was an important asset in the struggle between the Antigonids and the
Ptolemies for control of the Aegean. After its "liberation" from Athenian control

by the Antigonids, it became the center of the Nesiotic (i.e., Islanders') League, initially a loose federation of Antigonid supporters. When the Antigonids were defeated by Ptolemy Soter in alliance with Lysimachus of Thrace (who was then married to his daughter, Arsinoe II) and Pyrrhus of Epirus in 286, the League fell under Ptolemaic influence (Bagnall 1976: 151–52, and see now Meadows 2013: 33–36). Around 280 BCE the League passed a decree to hold a festival in honor of Ptolemy Soter (a *Ptolemaia*), and for the individual states to send ambassadors (*SIG* 390). During its history Delos was, as Callimachus says, a frequent subject of songs, many of which could have served him as intertexts. For a discussion of visual representations, see *LIMC* III.1 (s.v. Delos) 368–69 (Bruneau).

The Sources and Intertexts

Callimachus' most straightforward model was the Delian portion of the *Homeric Hymn to Apollo* (19–164), which describes an Ionian festival with choral performance and competitions (*HhAp* 147–50), including the famous performance of the Delian maidens (160–64). Both narratives include Leto's wandering while pregnant, her approach to the island, the description of the island itself as of little consequence, Hera's holding back of Eileithyia, the absence of Artemis (who was born on Ortygia in *HhAp* 16), and finally the birth with concomitant fame, a visible correlative of which is the resulting golden aspect of the island. There is a considerable lyric and tragic presence as well.

The identification of Delos with Asteria, who leapt into the sea to avoid Zeus's advances, is found in Pi. *Pae*. 5.35–48 S-M to Delian Apollo, *Pae*. 7b for Delos, and in fr. 33c S-M. These passages adumbrate the story of Asteria plunging into the ocean.

Ieie, Delian Apollo, they took possession of the scattered islands (the Sporades) rich in flocks and held glorious Delos, seeing as Apollo, the golden-haired, gave them the body of Asteria to dwell upon (Ἀπόλλων δῶκεν ὁ χρυσοκόμας Ἀστερίας δέμας οἰκεῖν, *Pae*. 5.40–42 = fr. 52e.40–42 S-M).

Paean 7b has more of Asteria's story:

.]υνας· τί πείσομα[ι
ἢ Διὸς οὐκ ἐθέλο[ισα
Κοίου θυγάτηρ π[
45   ἄπιστά μ[ο]ι δέδο[ι]κα καμ[
    δέ μιν ἐν πέλ[α]γ[ο]ς
    ῥιφθεῖσαν εὐαγέα πέτραν φανῆναι[·

καλέοντί μιν Ὀρτυγίαν ναῦται πάλαι.
πεφόρητο δ' ἐπ' Αἰγαῖον θαμά·
50   τᾶς ὁ κράτιστος
ἐράσσατο μιχθείς
τοξοφόρον τελέσαι γόνον

What shall I suffer?...she spoke, unwilling...of Zeus, the daughter of
Coeus [sc. Asteria], things unbelievable to me I fear...having been thrown
into the sea she appeared as a bright rock; sailors of old called her Ortygia,
and she was frequently carried upon the Aegean sea. The mighty one [sc.
Zeus] when he lay with her [sc. Leto] desired to beget a bow-bearing offspring (fr. 52h.42–52 S-M).

Another important, though more complex, model is to be found in Pindar's
First Hymn. Now very fragmentary, the hymn was well known in antiquity and
much cited (and apparently imitated). Its reconstruction by Bruno Snell as a *Hymn
to Zeus* has been normative for a generation of Greek scholars, and seen as a precedent for Callimachus' first hymn also being addressed to Zeus, but D'Alessio's
recent reconstruction (2009) raises doubts about Snell's identification of the subject as Zeus. Pindar's hymn was for Thebes, and it opened with a mention of two
sites important to Apollo—Ismenus (a son of Apollo who is also the local river)
and Melia (a nymph "bride" of Apollo and the name of his Theban sanctuary).
Also included were a song of the Muses, which Apollo accompanied while leading
the chorus; a theogony that concludes with the creation of the Muses, Zeus, and
Themis; the marriage of Harmonia and Cadmus (fr. 29 S-M); Heracles attacking
wrongdoers on the island of Cos (fr. 33a S-M); a mention of Delos as Asteria (fr.
33c S-M); and the birth of Apollo on Delos (fr. 33d S-M). D'Alessio 2009 suggests
that the hymn might, in fact, have been for Apollo, a conclusion that would have
made it an even stronger model for Callimachus, and it is possible to discern the
following parallels between the two: the narrative trajectory from the origins of
islands to the birth of Apollo (and song); the intimate link of Apollo, Delos, and
the Muses (see especially the opening of Callimachus' hymn), the sequence of
Cos and Delos, with mention of the Meropes, and finally the fixing of Delos in the
sea at the time of the deity's birth. Consider the following two fragments:

χαῖρ', ὦ θεοδμάτα, λιπαροπλοκάμου
παίδεσσι Λατοῦς ἱμεροέστατον ἔρνος,
πόντου θύγατερ, χθονὸς εὐρεί-
    ας ἀκίνητον τέρας, ἄν τε βροτοί
5   Δᾶλον κικλήσκοισιν, μάκαρες δ' ἐν Ὀλύμπῳ
    τηλέφαντον κυανέας χθονὸς ἄστρον.

Hail, god-built offshoot most desirable to the children of Leto of the anointed locks, daughter of the sea, unshakable wonder of broad earth, whom mortals call Delos, but the blessed ones in Olympus call the far-shining star of dark earth (fr. 33c S-M).

> ἢν γὰρ τὸ πάροιθε φορητὰ
>   κυμάτεσσιν παντοδαπῶν ἀνέμων
> ῥιπαῖσιν· ἀλλ' ἁ Κοιογενὴς ὁπότ' ὠδί-
>   νεσσι θυίοισ' ἀγχιτόκοις ἐπέβα
> 5 νιν, δὴ τότε τέσσαρες ὀρθαί
>   πρέμνων ἀπώρουσαν χθονίων,
> ἂν δ' ἐπικράνοις σχέθον
> πέτραν ἀδαμαντοπέδιλοι
> κίονες, ἔνθα τεκοῖ-
> 10 σ' εὐδαίμον' ἐπόψατο γένναν.

For before it was borne upon the waves by blasts of winds from every direction; but when the daughter of Coeus, frantic with her pangs of approaching birth, stepped on to her, then at that point four straight pillars with adamantine bases rose up from the roots of the earth and support the rock with their capitals. There after giving birth she looked upon her blessed offspring (fr. 33d S-M).

In addition to Pindar, the scholiast cites Bacchylides. His *Dithyramb* 17, which Callimachus identified as a *paean* (see p. 86n21), seems to have been written for a Cean chorus for the *Delia* (see Fearn 2007: 242–56). Its influence is felt at the end of the hymn, where Theseus and his companions dance the crane dance on Delos. Praise of the island appears in Theognis 5–10:

> Φοῖβε ἄναξ, ὅτε μέν σε θεὰ τέκε πότνια Λητώ
>   φοίνικος ῥαδινῆς χερσὶν ἐφαψαμένη
> ἀθανάτων κάλλιστον ἐπὶ τροχοειδέι λίμνῃ,
>   πᾶσα μὲν ἐπλήσθη Δῆλος ἀπειρεσίη
> ὀδμῆς ἀμβροσίης, ἐγέλασσε δὲ Γαῖα πελώρη,
>   γήθησεν δὲ βαθὺς πόντος ἁλὸς πολιῆς.

Lord Phoebus, when the goddess, mistress Leto bore you, grasping the palm tree with her slender arms, fairest of the immortals, beside the circular lake, all Delos was filled with an ambrosial fragrance, and giant Earth laughed, and the deep sea of white foam rejoiced.

Himerius attributes to Alcaeus a *paean* (fr. 307c V) on the subject of Apollo's birth and his later sojourn among the Hyperboreans that probably influenced the final section of the poem (see ad loc.).[1] The island also appears in Euripidean choruses (e.g., *IT* 1095–1105; *Ion* 164–69, 919–22). The influence of tragedy imbues the central section where Leto flees Hera's wrath and the dramatically constructed speeches of Leto, Peneius, and Delos herself, who, in accepting Leto, shows that she is resigned to her fate. The final section on Olen, the Hyperboreans, Theseus, and the first festival on Delos reflects Bacchylides, but may also owe something to historical sources, especially Thucydides, for the origins of the Athenian *theoriai*, and for Theseus, the Atthidographers. Thucydides' account of the Delian festival is as follows (note the parallel with Ephesus):

> There was once long ago a great assembly of the Ionians and the surrounding islanders at Delos. This sacred mission included [choruses of] women and boys, just as now that of the Ionians does at Ephesus, and there was a contest there also of gymnastics and music, and the cities brought choruses.... Later the islanders and the Athenians sent choruses with the sacred offerings. Most of the contests were dissolved apparently as a result of circumstances, until [in 426/425] the Athenians created the current contest and the horse races [at Delos], which were not there before. (3.104.3 and 6)

Delos also figures in *Aet.*, book 3 (frr. 67–75 Pf.): the young lovers Acontius and Cydippe—one from Ceos, the other from Naxos—first meet at a Delian festival.

The Ptolemaic Connections

This hymn is unique among the hymns in its explicit reference to the living monarch, Ptolemy II, via the prophecy of the as yet unborn Apollo. Ptolemy II's future birth on another island (Cos) aligns him so closely with the speaking divinity that what is true of the one seems necessarily true for the other (as in the defeat of the Gauls). Because of the close link of Ptolemy and Delos, Meillier 1979: 180–91 made the attractive suggestion that the hymn was written for the Delian *Ptolemaia*. As in *hZeus*, elements of Egyptian mythologies of kingship are aligned with Greek myth. The explicit markers of this alignment are the prenatal prophecy itself, the island birth, the coincidence of divine birth with the inundation of the Nile, and the movement from cosmic chaos to order that comes into being with the divine birth—all fundamental elements in Egyptian cosmogonic and theogonic thought (Stephens 2003: 114–21; Bing 1988: 128–39). For a discussion of the historical circumstances of the mutiny of Gaulish mercenaries and their deaths at the hands of Ptolemy II, see p. 18.

---

1. For Alcaeus' influence on Callimachus' hymns, see Acosta-Hughes 2010: 123–30.

ΕΙΣ ΔΗΛΟΝ

Τὴν ἱερήν, ὦ θυμέ, τίνα χρόνον †ηποτ† ἀείσεις
Δῆλον Ἀπόλλωνος κουροτρόφον; ἦ μὲν ἅπασαι
Κυκλάδες, αἳ νήσων ἱερώταται εἰν ἁλὶ κεῖνται,
εὔυμνοι· Δῆλος δ᾽ ἐθέλει τὰ πρῶτα φέρεσθαι
5   ἐκ Μουσέων, ὅτι Φοῖβον ἀοιδάων μεδέοντα
λοῦσέ τε καὶ σπείρωσε καὶ ὡς θεὸν ᾔνεσε πρώτη.
ὡς Μοῦσαι τὸν ἀοιδὸν ὃ μὴ Πίμπλειαν ἀείσῃ
ἔχθουσιν, τὼς Φοῖβος ὅτις Δήλοιο λάθηται.
Δήλῳ νῦν οἴμης ἀποδάσσομαι, ὡς ἂν Ἀπόλλων
10 Κύνθιος αἰνήσῃ με φίλης ἀλέγοντα τιθήνης.
    κείνη δ᾽ ἠνεμόεσσα καὶ ἄτροπος οἷά θ᾽ ἁλιπλήξ
αἰθυίης καὶ μᾶλλον ἐπίδρομος ἠέπερ ἵπποις
πόντῳ ἐνεστήρικται· ὁ δ᾽ ἀμφί ἑ πουλὺς ἑλίσσων
Ἰκαρίου πολλὴν ἀπομάσσεται ὕδατος ἄχνην·
15 τῷ σφε καὶ ἰχθυβολῆες ἁλίπλοοι ἐννάσσαντο.
ἀλλά οἱ οὐ νεμεσητὸν ἐνὶ πρώτῃσι λέγεσθαι,
ὁππότ᾽ ἐς Ὠκεανόν τε καὶ ἐς Τιτηνίδα Τηθύν
νῆσοι ἀολλίζονται, ἀεὶ δ᾽ ἔξαρχος ὁδεύει.
ἡ δ᾽ ὄπιθεν Φοίνισσα μετ᾽ ἴχνια Κύρνος ὀπηδεῖ
20 οὐκ ὀνοτὴ καὶ Μάκρις Ἀβαντιὰς Ἐλλοπιήων
Σαρδώ θ᾽ ἱμερόεσσα καὶ ἣν ἐπενήξατο Κύπρις
ἐξ ὕδατος τὰ πρῶτα, σαοῖ δέ μιν ἀντ᾽ ἐπιβάθρων.
κεῖναι μὲν πύργοισι περισκεπέεσσιν ἐρυμναί,
Δῆλος δ᾽ Ἀπόλλωνι· τί δὲ στιβαρώτερον ἕρκος;
25 τείχεα μὲν καὶ λᾶες ὑπὸ ῥιπῆς κε πέσοιεν
Στρυμονίου βορέαο· θεὸς δ᾽ ἀεὶ ἀστυφέλικτος·
Δῆλε φίλη, τοῖός σε βοηθόος ἀμφιβέβηκεν.
    εἰ δὲ λίην πολέες σε περιτροχόωσιν ἀοιδαί,
ποίῃ ἐνιπλέξω σε; τί τοι θυμῆρες ἀκοῦσαι;
30 ἦ ὡς τὰ πρώτιστα μέγας θεὸς οὔρεα θείνων
ἄορι τριγλώχινι τό οἱ Τελχῖνες ἔτευξαν
νήσους εἰναλίας εἰργάζετο, νέρθε δὲ πάσας

1 ἢ πότ᾽ **a e** Lasc. **δ**: ἢ ποτ᾽ **Επζ**: εἴ ποτ᾽ Reiske: εἶπον Lloyd-Jones: ἠύτ᾽ Mineur ἀείσεις **Ψ**: ἀτίσσεις Maas 5 ἀοιδάων Lasc. **η**: ἀοιδέων **Ψ** 7 ἀείσῃ sch. Lyc.: ἀείσει **Ψ** 10 Κύνθιος **I** in marg., Lasc.: Καρνέος Gallavotti 11 ἄτροπος **Ψ**: ἄτροφος Blomfield: ἄτρυγος Meineke: ἄβροχος Mineur οἷά θ᾽ **Ψ**: οἷά γ᾽ Reiske: αἷά θ᾽ Mineur 14 πολλὴν **Ψ**: πολιὴν Ruhnken 15 om. POxy 2225 21 ἐπενήξατο **Ψ**: ἐπεβήσατο vel ἐπενάσσατο Meineke: ἐπεμίξατο Mineur 25 ὑπὸ ῥιπῆς POxy 2225 (coniecerat Meineke): ὑπαὶ ῥιπῆς **Ψ** 30 ἦ **T** in marg., H. Stephanus: χ᾽ ὡς **Ψ**

ἐκ νεάτων ὤχλισσε καὶ εἰσεκύλισε θαλάσσῃ;
καὶ τὰς μὲν κατὰ βυσσόν, ἵν' ἠπείροιο λάθωνται,
35   πρυμνόθεν ἐρρίζωσε· σὲ δ' οὐκ ἔθλιψεν ἀνάγκη,
ἀλλ' ἄφετος πελάγεσσιν ἐπέπλεες· οὔνομα δ' ἦν τοι
Ἀστερίη τὸ παλαιόν, ἐπεὶ βαθὺν ἥλαο τάφρον
οὐρανόθεν φεύγουσα Διὸς γάμον ἀστέρι ἴση.
τόφρα μὲν οὔπω τοι χρυσέη ἐπεμίσγετο Λητώ,
40   τόφρα δ' ἔτ' Ἀστερίη σὺ καὶ οὐδέπω ἔκλεο Δῆλος.
πολλάκι σε Τροιζῆνος ἀπὸ †ξάνθοιο πολίχνης
ἐρχόμενοι Ἐφύρηνδε Σαρωνικοῦ ἔνδοθι κόλπου
ναῦται ἐπεσκέψαντο, καὶ ἐξ Ἐφύρης ἀνιόντες
οἱ μὲν ἔτ' οὐκ ἴδον αὖθι, σὺ δὲ στεινοῖο παρ' ὀξύν
45   ἔδραμες Εὐρίποιο πόρον καναχηδὰ ῥέοντος,
Χαλκιδικῆς δ' αὐτῆμαρ ἀνηναμένη ἁλὸς ὕδωρ
μέσφ' ἐς Ἀθηναίων προσενήξαο Σούνιον ἄκρον
ἢ Χίον ἢ νήσοιο διάβροχον ὕδατι μαστόν
Παρθενίης (οὔπω γὰρ ἔην Σάμος), ἧχί σε νύμφαι
50   γείτονες Ἀγκαίου Μυκαλησσίδες ἐξείνισσαν.
ἡνίκα δ' Ἀπόλλωνι γενέθλιον οὔδας ὑπέσχες,
τοῦτό τοι ἀντημοιβὸν ἁλίπλοοι ‡ὔνομ' ἔθεντο,
οὔνεκεν οὐκέτ' ἄδηλος ἐπέπλεες, ἀλλ' ἐνὶ πόντου
κύμασιν Αἰγαίοιο ποδῶν ἐνεθήκαο ῥίζας.
55   οὐδ' Ἥρην κοτέουσαν ὑπέτρεσας. ἡ μὲν ἁπάσαις
δεινὸν ἐπεβρωμᾶτο λεχωῖσιν αἴ Διὶ παῖδας
ἐξέφερον, Λητοῖ δὲ διακριδόν, οὕνεκα μούνη
Ζηνὶ τεκεῖν ἤμελλε φιλαίτερον Ἄρεος υἷα.
τῷ ῥα καὶ αὐτὴ μὲν σκοπιὴν ἔχεν αἰθέρος εἴσω
60   σπερχομένη μέγα δή τι καὶ οὐ φατόν, εἶργε δὲ Λητώ
τειρομένην ὠδῖσι· δύω δέ οἱ εἴατο φρουροί
γαῖαν ἐποπτεύοντες, ὁ μὲν πέδον ἠπείροιο
ἥμενος ὑψηλῆς κορυφῆς ἔπι Θρήικος Αἵμου
θοῦρος Ἄρης ἐφύλασσε σὺν ἔντεσι, τὼ δέ οἱ ἵππω
65   ἑπτάμυχον βορέαο παρὰ σπέος ηὐλίζοντο·
ἡ δ' ἐπὶ νησάων ἑτέρη σκοπὸς αἰπειάων
ἧστο κόρη Θαύμαντος ἐπαΐξασα Μίμαντι.
ἔνθ' οἱ μὲν πολίεσσιν ὅσαις ἐπεβάλλετο Λητώ
μίμνον ἀπειλητῆρες, ἀπετρώπων δὲ δέχεσθαι.

---

34 βυσσόν Dindorf: βυθόν Ψ   41 πολλάκι σε Reiske: πολλάκι σ' ἐκ T in marg.: πολλάκις ἐκ Ψ   ἀπὸ
ξάνθοιο Ψ: Ξάνθοιο sch. Call.: ζαθέοιο Meineke: ἀλιξάντοιο Ruhnken: ἀποξάντοιο Mineur
57 διακριδόν Ψ: διακριτον PBodl   66]πειαων (αἰπειάων?) PBodl: εὐρειάων Ψ

70 φεῦγε μὲν Ἀρκαδίη, φεῦγεν δ' ὄρος ἱερὸν Αὔγης
    Παρθένιον, φεῦγεν δ' ὁ γέρων μετόπισθε Φενειός,
    φεῦγε δ' ὅλη Πελοπηῒς ὅση παρακέκλιται Ἰσθμῷ,
    ἔμπλην Αἰγιαλοῦ γε καὶ Ἄργεος· οὐ γὰρ ἐκείνας
    ἀτραπιτοὺς ἐπάτησεν, ἐπεὶ λάχεν Ἴναχον Ἥρη.
75 φεῦγε καὶ Ἀονίη τὸν ἕνα δρόμον, αἱ δ' ἐφέποντο
    Δίρκη τε Στροφίη τε μελαμψήφιδος ἔχουσαι
    Ἰσμηνοῦ χέρα πατρός, ὁ δ' εἵπετο πολλὸν ὄπισθεν
    Ἀσωπὸς βαρύγουνος, ἐπεὶ πεπάλακτο κεραυνῷ.
    ἡ δ' ὑποδινηθεῖσα χοροῦ ἀπεπαύσατο νύμφη
80 αὐτόχθων Μελίη καὶ ὑπόχλοον ἔσχε παρειὴν
    ἥλικος ἀσθμαίνουσα περὶ δρυός, ὡς ἴδε χαίτην
    σειομένην Ἑλικῶνος. ἐμαὶ θεαὶ εἴπατε Μοῦσαι,
    ἦ ῥ' ἐτεὸν ἐγένοντο τότε δρύες ἡνίκα Νύμφαι;
    'Νύμφαι μὲν χαίρουσιν, ὅτε δρύας ὄμβρος ἀέξει,
85 Νύμφαι δ' αὖ κλαίουσιν, ὅτε δρυσὶ μηκέτι φύλλα.'
    ταῖς μὲν ἔτ' Ἀπόλλων ὑποκόλπιος αἰνὰ χολώθη,
    φθέγξατο δ' οὐκ ἀτέλεστον ἀπειλήσας ἐπὶ Θήβῃ·
    'Θήβη τίπτε τάλαινα τὸν αὐτίκα πότμον ἐλέγχεις;
    μήπω μή μ' ἀέκοντα βιάζεο μαντεύεσθαι.
90 οὔπω μοι Πυθῶνι μέλει τριποδήϊος ἕδρη,
    οὐδέ τί πω τέθνηκεν ὄφις μέγας, ἀλλ' ἔτι κεῖνο
    θηρίον αἰνογένειον ἀπὸ Πλειστοῖο καθέρπον
    Παρνησὸν νιφόεντα περιστέφει ἐννέα κύκλοις·
    ἀλλ' ἔμπης ἐρέω τι τομότερον ἢ ἀπὸ δάφνης.
95 φεῦγε πρόσω· ταχινός σε κιχήσομαι αἵματι λούσων
    τόξον ἐμόν· σὺ δὲ τέκνα κακογλώσσοιο γυναικός
    ἔλλαχες. οὐ σύ γ' ἐμεῖο φίλη τροφὸς οὐδὲ Κιθαιρών
    ἔσσεται· εὐαγέων δὲ καὶ εὐαγέεσσι μελοίμην.'
    ὡς ἄρ' ἔφη. Λητὼ δὲ μετάτροπος αὖτις ἐχώρει.
100 ἀλλ' ὅτ' Ἀχαιάδες μιν ἀπηρνήσαντο πόληες
    ἐρχομένην, Ἑλίκη τε Ποσειδάωνος ἑταίρη
    Βοῦρά τε Δεξαμενοῖο βοόστασις Οἰκιάδαο,
    ἂψ δ' ἐπὶ Θεσσαλίην πόδας ἔτρεπε· φεῦγε δ' Ἄναυρος
    καὶ μεγάλη Λάρισα καὶ αἱ Χειρωνίδες ἄκραι,
105 φεῦγε δὲ καὶ Πηνειὸς ἑλισσόμενος διὰ Τεμπέων·
    Ἥρη, σοὶ δ' ἔτι τῆμος ἀνηλεὲς ἦτορ ἔκειτο
    οὐδὲ κατεκλάσθης τε καὶ ᾤκτισας, ἡνίκα πήχεις

71 Φενειός Arnaldus: φεναιός Ψ: φανιο[POxy 2225 73 γε καὶ Wilamowitz: τε καὶ Ψ 85 μ[ηκετι
POxy 2225, ut vid.: οὐκέτι Ψ

ἀμφοτέρους ὀρέγουσα μάτην ἐφθέγξατο τοῖα·
Νύμφαι Θεσσαλίδες, ποταμοῦ γένος, εἴπατε πατρί
110 κοιμῆσαι μέγα χεῦμα, περιπλέξασθε γενείῳ
λισσόμεναι τὰ Ζηνὸς ἐν ὕδατι τέκνα τεκέσθαι.
Πηνειὲ Φθιῶτα, τί νῦν ἀνέμοισιν ἐρίζεις;
ὦ πάτερ, οὐ μὴν ἵππον ἀέθλιον ἀμφιβέβηκας.
ἦ ῥά τοι ὧδ' αἰεὶ ταχινοὶ πόδες, ἦ ἐπ' ἐμεῖο
115 μοῦνον ἐλαφρίζουσι, πεποίησαι δὲ πέτεσθαι
σήμερον ἐξαπίνης; ὁ δ' ἀνήκοος. ὦ ἐμὸν ἄχθος,
ποῖ σε φέρω; μέλεοι γὰρ ἀπειρήκασι τένοντες.
Πήλιον ὦ Φιλύρης νυμφήϊον, ἀλλὰ σὺ μεῖνον,
μεῖνον, ἐπεὶ καὶ θῆρες ἐν οὔρεσι πολλάκι σεῖο
120 ὠμοτόκους ὠδῖνας ἀπηρείσαντο λέαιναι.'
τὴν δ' ἄρα καὶ Πηνειὸς ἀμείβετο δάκρυα λείβων·
Λητοῖ, Ἀναγκαίη μεγάλη θεός. οὐ γὰρ ἔγωγε
πότνια σὰς ὠδῖνας ἀναίνομαι (οἶδα καὶ ἄλλας
λουσαμένας ἀπ' ἐμεῖο λεχωΐδας)· ἀλλά μοι Ἥρη
125 δαψιλὲς ἠπείλησεν. ἀπαύγασαι, οἷος ἔφεδρος
οὔρεος ἐξ ὑπάτου σκοπιὴν ἔχει, ὅς κέ με ῥεῖα
βυσσόθεν ἐξερύσειε. τί μήσομαι; ἦ ἀπολέσθαι
ἡδύ τί τοι Πηνειόν; ἴτω πεπρωμένον ἦμαρ·
τλήσομαι εἴνεκα σεῖο, καὶ εἰ μέλλοιμι ῥοάων
130 διψαλέην ἄμπωτιν ἔχων αἰώνιον ἔρρειν
καὶ μόνος ἐν ποταμοῖσιν ἀτιμότατος καλέεσθαι.
ἠνίδ' ἐγώ· τί περισσά; κάλει μόνον Εἰλήθυιαν.'
εἶπε καὶ ἡρώησε μέγαν ῥόον. ἀλλά οἱ Ἄρης
Παγγαίου προθέλυμνα καρήατα μέλλεν ἀείρας
135 ἐμβαλέειν δίνησιν, ἀποκρύψαι δὲ ῥέεθρα·
ὑψόθε δ' ἐσμάραγησε καὶ ἀσπίδα τύψεν ἀκωκῇ
δούρατος. ἡ δ' ἐλέλιξεν ἐνόπλιον· ἔτρεμε δ' Ὄσσης
οὔρεα καὶ πεδίον Κραννώνιον αἵ τε δυσαεῖς
ἐσχατιαὶ Πίνδοιο, φόβῳ δ' ὠρχήσατο πᾶσα
140 Θεσσαλίη· τοῖος γὰρ ἀπ' ἀσπίδος ἔβραμεν ἦχος.
ὡς δ', ὁπότ' Αἰτναίου ὄρεος πυρὶ τυφομένοιο
σείονται μυχὰ πάντα, κατουδαίοιο γίγαντος
εἰς ἑτέρην Βριαρῆος ἐπωμίδα κινυμένοιο,
θερμάστραι τε βρέμουσιν ὑφ' Ἡφαίστοιο πυράγρης

---

108 ἐφθέγξατο E Lasc. **δ**: ἐφθέγξαο **Ψ**   115 μοῦνον anon. Bern.: μοῦνοι **Ψ**   140 ἔβραμεν **βΠδζ**:
ἔβραχεν **a** Lasc.

145 ἔργα θ᾽ ὁμοῦ, δεινὸν δὲ πυρίκμητοί τε λέβητες
καὶ τρίποδες πίπτοντες ἐπ᾽ ἀλλήλοις ἰαχεῦσιν,
τῆμος ἔγεντ᾽ ἄραβος σάκεος τόσος εὐκύκλοιο.
Πηνειὸς δ᾽ οὐκ αὖτις ἐχάζετο, μίμνε δ᾽ ὁμοίως
καρτερὸς ὡς τὰ πρῶτα, θοὰς δ᾽ ἐστήσατο δίνας,
150 εἰσόκε οἱ Κοιηῒς ἐκέκλετο· σώζεο χαίρων,
σώζεο· μὴ σύ γ᾽ ἐμεῖο πάθῃς κακὸν εἵνεκα τῆσδε
ἀντ᾽ ἐλεημοσύνης· χάριτος δέ τοι ἔσσετ᾽ ἀμοιβή.᾽
ἦ καὶ πολλὰ πάροιθεν ἐπεὶ κάμεν ἔστιχε νήσους
εἰναλίας· αἱ δ᾽ οὔ μιν ἐπερχομένην ἐδέχοντο,
155 οὐ λιπαρὸν νήεσσιν Ἐχινάδες ὅρμον ἔχουσαι,
οὐδ᾽ ἥτις Κέρκυρα φιλοξεινωτάτη ἄλλων,
Ἶρις ἐπεὶ πάσῃσιν ἐφ᾽ ὑψηλοῖο Μίμαντος
σπερχομένη μάλα δεινὸν ἀπέτρεπεν· αἱ δ᾽ ὑπ᾽ ὁμοκλῆς
πασσυδίῃ φοβέοντο κατὰ ρόον ἥντινα τέτμοι.
160 ὠγυγίην δ᾽ἤπειτα Κόων Μεροπηΐδα νῆσον
ἵκετο, Χαλκιόπης ἱερὸν μυχὸν ἡρωίνης.
ἀλλά ἑ παιδὸς ἔρυκεν ἔπος τόδε· ᾽μὴ σύ γε, μῆτερ,
τῇ με τέκοις. οὔτ᾽ οὖν ἐπιμέμφομαι οὐδὲ μεγαίρω
νῆσον, ἐπεὶ λιπαρή τε καὶ εὔβοτος, εἴ νύ τις ἄλλη·
165 ἀλλά οἱ ἐκ Μοιρέων τις ὀφειλόμενος θεὸς ἄλλος
ἐστί, Σαωτήρων ὕπατον γένος· ᾧ ὑπὸ μίτρην
ἵξεται οὐκ ἀέκουσα Μακηδόνι κοιρανέεσθαι
ἀμφοτέρη μεσόγεια καὶ αἳ πελάγεσσι κάθηνται,
μέχρις ὅπου περάτη τε καὶ ὁππόθεν ὠκέες ἵπποι
170 Ἥλιον φορέουσιν· ὁ δ᾽ εἴσεται ἤθεα πατρός.
καί νύ ποτε ξυνός τις ἐλεύσεται ἄμμιν ἄεθλος
ὕστερον, ὁππόταν οἱ μὲν ἐφ᾽ Ἑλλήνεσσι μάχαιραν
βαρβαρικὴν καὶ Κελτὸν ἀναστήσαντες Ἄρηα
ὀψίγονοι Τιτῆνες ἀφ᾽ ἑσπέρου ἐσχατόωντος
175 ρώσωνται νιφάδεσσιν ἐοικότες ἢ ἰσάριθμοι
τείρεσιν, ἡνίκα πλεῖστα κατ᾽ ἠέρα βουκολέονται,
177a παιδ[   ]. .   σα[ ].[ ]
177b Δωρι . [.] . [   ] .   οσα[ ]ς

154 εἰναλίας Lasc.: εἰναλίδας Ψ: 158 δεινο[POxy 2225: πολλὸν Ψ]τρεπεν POxy 2225: ἀπέτραπεν Ψ ὑπ᾽ ὁμοκλῆς Ψ: υφομ[…]ης POxy 2225 159 πασσυδίῃ Lasc.: πασσυδι[POxy 2225:]ασσυδ[POxy 2258: πανσυδίῃ Ψ 161 ἵκετο Ψ POxy 2258, ut vid.: [.]ετο POxy 2225: ἵετο coni. Lobel, Pfeiffer 175 ρώσωνται H. Stephanus: ρώσονται Ψ. In codd. post versum 176 nihil nisi φρούρια καὶ relictum, versus 178 sequitur. Sed duorum versuum fragmenta conservat POxy 2225 177a παιδ[POxy 2225: παῖδες δὲ suppl. Pfeiffer 177b δωρι.[.].[POxy 2225: Δωρι.[suppl. Pfeiffer

καὶ πεδία Κρισσαῖα καὶ Ἡφαί[στο]ιο φάρ[αγγ]ες
ἀμφιπεριστείνωνται, ἴδωσι δὲ πίονα καπνόν
180 γείτονος αἰθομένοιο, καὶ οὐκέτι μοῦνον ἀκουῇ,
ἀλλ᾽ ἤδη παρὰ νηὸν ἀπαυγάζοιντο φάλαγγας
δυσμενέων, ἤδη δὲ παρὰ τριπόδεσσιν ἐμεῖο
φάσγανα καὶ ζωστῆρας ἀναιδέας ἐχθομένας τε
ἀσπίδας, αἳ Γαλάτῃσι κακὴν ὁδὸν ἄφρονι φύλῳ
185 στήσονται· τέων αἱ μὲν ἐμοὶ γέρας, αἱ δ᾽ ἐπὶ Νείλῳ
ἐν πυρὶ τοὺς φορέοντας ἀποπνεύσαντας ἰδοῦσαι
κείσονται βασιλῆος ἀέθλια πολλὰ καμόντος.
ἐσσόμενε Πτολεμαῖε, τά τοι μαντήια Φοίβου.
αἰνήσεις μέγα δή τι τὸν εἰσέτι γαστέρι μάντιν
190 ὕστερον ἤματα πάντα. σὺ δὲ ξυμβάλλεο, μῆτερ·
ἔστι διειδομένη τις ἐν ὕδατι νῆσος ἀραιή,
πλαζομένη πελάγεσσι· πόδες δέ οἱ οὐκ ἐνὶ χώρῃ,
ἀλλὰ παλιρροίῃ ἐπινήχεται ἀνθέρικος ὥς,
ἔνθα νότος, ἔνθ᾽ εὖρος, ὅπη φορέῃσι θάλασσα.
195 τῇ με φέροις· κείνην γὰρ ἐλεύσεαι εἰς ἐθέλουσαν.᾽
αἱ μὲν τόσσα λέγοντος ἀπέτρεχον εἰν ἁλὶ νῆσοι·
Ἀστερίη φιλόμολπε, σὺ δ᾽ Εὐβοίηθε κατῄεις,
Κυκλάδας ὀψομένη περιηγέας, οὔτι παλαιόν,
ἀλλ᾽ ἔτι τοι μετόπισθε Γεραίστιον εἵπετο φῦκος·
200 ὡς δ᾽ ἴδες, [ὡς] ἔστης [   ]ιδου[.]α
θαρσαλέη τάδ᾽ ἔλεξας [   ]....ρ[   ]
δαίμον᾽ ὑπ᾽ ὠδίνεσσι βαρυνομένην ὁρόωσα·
᾽Ἥρη, τοῦτό με ῥέξον ὅ τοι φίλον· οὐ γὰρ ἀπειλάς
ὑμετέρας ἐφύλαξα· πέρα, πέρα εἰς ἐμέ, Λητοῖ.᾽
205 ἔννεπες· ἡ δ᾽ ἀρητὸν ἄλης ἀπεπαύσατο †λυγρῆς,
ἕζετο δ᾽ Ἰνωποῖο παρὰ ῥόον ὅν τε βάθιστον
γαῖα τότ᾽ ἐξανίησιν, ὅτε πλήθοντι ῥεέθρῳ

178]ηφαι[...]ιοφαρ[...]ες POxy 2225: Ἡφαί[στο]ιο φάρ[αγγ]ες suppl. Lobel: ἤπειροι tum
spatium relictum Ψ: ἠπείροιο φάραγγες codd. recentissimi: αἱ Πλειστοῖο φάραγγες Bosquet:
Ὑλάθοιο φ. Barber: Ἀμφίσσαο φ. Mineur: αἱ Φαίστοιο Bing 179 ἀμφιπεριστείνωνται anon. Bern.:
-στείνωνται Ψ καπνόν POxy 2225: καρπόν Ψ 181 φαλαγγας POxy 2225: φάλαγγες Ψ 188]ου
POxy 2225: Φοίβ]ου suppl. Lobel: φαίνω Ψ 189 versum om. POxy 2225 192 ἐνὶ χώρῃ
Schneider:]ωρη POxy 2225: ἐνὶ χώρῳ Ψ 195 εἰς ἐθέλουσαν Lasc.: εἰσεθέλουσα Ψ:]θελουσα POxy
2225 197 κατῄεις Ψ:]ηγεις POxy 2225 200 versum om. Ψ: init. ωδιδεσ[.]......[POxy 2225:
ὡς δ᾽ ἴδες [ὡς] ἔστης suppl. Pfeiffer: ἔστης δ᾽ ἐν μέσσῃσι codd. recentissimi fin.]ιδου[.]α POxy
2225: κατοικτείρασα δὲ Λητώ codd. recentissimi 201 init. om. Ψ: θαρσαληταδελεξασ[POxy 2225
fin. φλέξας (τάδ᾽ ἔλεξας Τ in marg.) ἐπεὶ περικαῖεο πυρί (κῆρι Canter) Ψ 202 δαιμον POxy 2225:
τλήμον᾽ Ψ 205 ἀπεπαύσατο λυγρῆς Ψ: ἀπεπαύσατο δηρῆς Mineur: ἀπεπαύσατο πάσης Gigante
Lanzara: ἀπεπαύσατ᾽ ὀλοιῆς Bing 206 aut 207 om. POxy 2225

Νεῖλος ἀπὸ κρημνοῖο κατέρχεται Αἰθιοπῆος·
λύσατο δὲ ζώνην, ἀπὸ δ᾽ ἐκλίθη ἔμπαλιν ὤμοις
210 φοίνικος ποτὶ πρέμνον ἀμηχανίης ὑπὸ λυγρῆς
τειρομένη· νότιος δὲ διὰ χροὸς ἔρρεεν ἱδρώς.
εἶπε δ᾽ ἀλυσθενέουσα· ᾽τί μητέρα, κοῦρε, βαρύνεις;
αὕτη τοι, φίλε, νῆσος ἐπιπλώουσα θαλάσσῃ.
γείνεο, γείνεο, κοῦρε, καὶ ἤπιος ἔξιθι κόλπου.᾽
215 νύμφα Διὸς βαρύθυμε, σὺ δ᾽ οὐκ ἄρ᾽ ἔμελλες ἄπυστος
δὴν ἔμεναι· τοίη σε προσέδραμεν ἀγγελιῶτις,
εἶπε δ᾽ ἔτ᾽ ἀσθμαίνουσα, φόβῳ δ᾽ ἀνεμίσγετο μῦθος·
῾ Ἥρη τιμήεσσα, πολὺ προὔχουσα θεάων,
σὴ μὲν ἐγώ, σὰ δὲ πάντα, σὺ δὲ κρείουσα κάθησαι
220 γνησίη Οὐλύμποιο, καὶ οὐ χέρα δείδιμεν ἄλλην
θηλυτέρην, σὺ δ᾽, ἄνασσα, τὸν αἴτιον εἴσεαι ὀργῆς.
Λητώ τοι μίτρην ἀναλύεται ἔνδοθι νήσου.
ἄλλαι μὲν πᾶσαί μιν ἀπέστυγον οὐδ᾽ ἐδέχοντο·
Ἀστερίη δ᾽ ὀνομαστὶ παρερχομένην ἐκάλεσσεν,
225 Ἀστερίη, πόντοιο κακὸν σάρον· οἶσθα καὶ αὐτή.
ἀλλά, φίλη, δύνασαι γάρ, ἀμύνειν πότνια δούλοις
ὑμετέροις, οἳ σεῖο πέδον πατέουσιν ἐφετμῇ.᾽
ἢ καὶ ὑπὸ χρύσειον ἐδέθλιον ἷζε κύων ὥς
Ἀρτέμιδος, ἥτις τε, θοῆς ὅτε παύσεται ἄγρης,
230 ἵζει θηρήτειρα παρ᾽ ἴχνεσιν, οὔατα δ᾽ αὐτῆς
ὀρθὰ μάλ᾽, αἰὲν ἑτοῖμα θεῆς ὑποδέχθαι ὁμοκλήν·
τῇ ἰκέλη Θαύμαντος ὑπὸ θρόνον ἵζετο κούρη.
κείνη δ᾽ οὐδέ ποτε σφετέρης ἐπιλήθεται ἕδρης,
οὐδ᾽ ὅτε οἱ ληθαῖον ἐπὶ πτερὸν ὕπνος ἐρείσει,
235 ἀλλ᾽ αὐτοῦ μεγάλοιο ποτὶ γλωχῖνα θρόνοιο
τυτθὸν ἀποκλίνασα καρήατα λέχριος εὕδει.
οὐδέ ποτε ζώνην ἀναλύεται οὐδὲ ταχείας
ἐνδρομίδας, μή οἵ τι καὶ αἰφνίδιον ἔπος εἴπῃ
δεσπότις. ἡ δ᾽ ἀλεγεινὸν ἀλαστήσασα προσηύδα·
240 ᾽οὕτω νῦν, ὦ Ζηνὸς ὀνείδεα, καὶ γαμέοισθε
λάθρια καὶ τίκτοιτε κεκρυμμένα, μηδ᾽ ὅθι δειλαί
δυστοκέες μογέουσιν ἀλετρίδες, ἀλλ᾽ ὅθι φῶκαι
εἰνάλιαι τίκτουσιν, ἐνὶ σπιλάδεσσιν ἐρήμοις.
Ἀστερίη δ᾽ οὐδέν τι βαρύνομαι εἴνεκα τῆσδε

---

212 αλ[…]ενεο[POxy 2225: ἀλ[υσθ]ενέο[υσα suppl. Lobel: ἀλυσθμαίνουσα Ψ sed vide infra 217
217 ἔτ᾽ Ψ: αρ POxy 2225 226–27 ἀμύνειν…δούλοις ὑμετέροις Ψ: ἀμύνεο…δούλους ὑμετέρους
Maas 227 ἐφετμῇ Ψ: ἐφετμήν Crönert 231 ὁμοκλήν Pfeiffer: ὁμοκλήν Ψ 234 ἐρείσει Ψ: ἐρείσῃ
Schneider 242–43 μογέουσιν et τίκτουσιν Ψ: μογεο[(μογέο[ιεν?) et τικτοιε[POxy 2258

245   ἀμπλακίης, οὐδ' ἔστιν ὅπως ἀποθύμια ῥέξω.
      τόσσα δέ οἱ (μάλα γάρ τε κακῶς ἐχαρίσσατο Λητοῖ)·
      ἀλλά μιν ἔκπαγλόν τι σεβίζομαι, οὕνεκ' ἐμεῖο
      δέμνιον οὐκ ἐπάτησε, Διὸς δ' ἀνθείλετο πόντον.'
      ἡ μὲν ἔφη· κύκνοι δὲ θεοῦ μέλλοντος ἀοιδοί
250   Μηόνιον Πακτωλὸν ἐκυκλώσαντο λιπόντες
      ἑβδομάκις περὶ Δῆλον, ἐπήεισαν δὲ λοχείῃ
      Μουσάων ὄρνιθες, ἀοιδότατοι πετεηνῶν
      (ἔνθεν ὁ παῖς τοσσάσδε λύρῃ ἐνεδήσατο χορδάς
      ὕστερον, ὁσσάκι κύκνοι ἐπ' ὠδίνεσσιν ἄεισαν)·
255   ὄγδοον οὐκέτ' ἄεισαν, ὁ δ' ἔκθορεν, αἱ δ' ἐπὶ μακρόν
      νύμφαι Δηλιάδες, ποταμοῦ γένος ἀρχαίοιο,
      εἶπαν Ἐλειθυίης ἱερὸν μέλος, αὐτίκα δ' αἰθήρ
      χάλκεος ἀντήχησε διαπρυσίην ὀλολυγήν.
      οὐδ' Ἥρη νεμέσησεν, ἐπεὶ χόλον ἐξέλετο Ζεύς.
260   χρύσεά τοι τότε πάντα θεμείλια γείνετο Δῆλε,
      χρυσῷ δὲ τροχόεσσα πανήμερος ἔρρεε λίμνη,
      χρύσειον δ' ἐκόμησε γενέθλιον ἔρνος ἐλαίης,
      χρυσῷ δὲ πλήμυρε βαθὺς Ἰνωπὸς ἑλιχθείς.
      αὐτὴ δὲ χρυσέοιο ἀπ' οὔδεος εἵλεο παῖδα,
265   ἐν δ' ἐβάλευ κόλποισιν, ἔπος δ' ἐφθέγξαο τοῖον·
      'ὦ μεγάλη, πολύβωμε, πολύπτολι, πολλὰ φέρουσα,
      πίονες ἤπειροί τε καὶ αἳ περιναίετε νῆσοι,
      αὕτη ἐγὼ τοιήδε· δυσήροτος, ἀλλ' ἀπ' ἐμεῖο
      Δήλιος Ἀπόλλων κεκλήσεται, οὐδέ τις ἄλλη
270   γαιάων τοσσόνδε θεῷ πεφιλήσεται ἄλλῳ,
      οὐ Κερχνὶς κρείοντι Ποσειδάωνι Λεχαίῳ,
      οὐ πάγος Ἑρμείῃ Κυλλήνιος, οὐ Διὶ Κρήτη,
      ὡς ἐγὼ Ἀπόλλωνι· καὶ ἔσσομαι οὐκέτι πλαγκτή.'
      ὧδε σὺ μὲν κατέλεξας· ὁ δὲ γλυκὺν ἔσπασε μαζόν.
275   τῷ καὶ νησάων ἁγιωτάτη ἐξέτι κείνου
      κλήζῃ, Ἀπόλλωνος κουροτρόφος· οὐδέ σ' Ἐννώ
      οὐδ' Ἀΐδης οὐδ' ἵπποι ἐπιστείβουσιν Ἄρηος·
      ἀλλά τοι ἀμφιετεῖς δεκατηφόροι αἰὲν ἀπαρχαί
      πέμπονται, πᾶσαι δὲ χοροὺς ἀνάγουσι πόληες,
280   αἵ τε πρὸς ἠοίην αἵ θ' ἕσπερον αἵ τ' ἀνὰ μέσσην
      κλήρους ἐστήσαντο, καὶ οἳ καθύπερθε βορείης

246 τόσσα δέ οἱ **AtηE**: τοσσάδε οἱ **FQS**: τόσσα δέοι Lasc. 249 θεοῦ **Ψ**: θεὸν Ruhnken, D'Alessio
μέλλοντος Dyck: μέλλοντες Wilamowitz: μέλποντες **Ψ** ἀοιδοί **Ψ**: ἀοιδῇ Blomfield: ἀοιδαῖς
Ruhnken: ἀΐσσειν Reiske: ἄοζοι Meineke 255 ἄεισαν **αβ**: ἤεισαν **γ**: ἔβησαν **δ** 266 μεγάλη **Ψ**:
Μεγάλη Leo, Wilamowitz 268 αὕτη Ernesti: αὐτὴ **Ψ**

οἰκία θινὸς ἔχουσι, πολυχρονιώτατον αἷμα.
οἱ μέν τοι καλάμην τε καὶ ἱερὰ δράγματα πρῶτοι
ἀσταχύων φορέουσιν· ἃ Δωδώνηθε Πελασγοί
285   τηλόθεν ἐκβαίνοντα πολὺ πρώτιστα δέχονται,
γηλεχέες θεράποντες ἀσιγήτοιο λέβητος·
δεύτερον Ἴριον ἄστυ καὶ οὔρεα Μηλίδος αἴης
ἔρχονται· κεῖθεν δὲ διαπλώουσιν Ἀβάντων
εἰς ἀγαθὸν πεδίον Ληλάντιον· οὐδ᾽ ἔτι μακρός
290   ὁ πλόος Εὐβοίηθεν, ἐπεὶ σέο γείτονες ὅρμοι.
πρῶταί τοι τάδ᾽ ἔνεικαν ἀπὸ ξανθῶν Ἀριμασπῶν
Οὖπίς τε Λοξώ τε καὶ εὐαίων Ἑκαέργη,
θυγατέρες Βορέαο, καὶ ἄρσενες οἱ τότ᾽ ἄριστοι
ἠϊθέων· οὐδ᾽ οἵγε παλιμπετὲς οἴκαδ᾽ ἵκοντο,
295   εὔμοιροι δ᾽ ἐγένοντο, καὶ ἀκλεὲς οὔποτ᾽ ἔσονται.
ἤτοι Δηλιάδες μέν, ὅτ᾽ εὐηχὴς ὑμέναιος
ἤθεα κουράων μορμύσσεται, ἥλικα χαίτην
παρθενικαῖς, παῖδες δὲ θέρος τὸ πρῶτον ἰούλων
ἄρσενες ἠϊθέοισιν ἀπαρχόμενοι φορέουσιν.
300   Ἀστερίη θυόεσσα, σὲ μὲν περί τ᾽ ἀμφί τε νῆσοι
κύκλον ἐποιήσαντο καὶ ὡς χορὸν ἀμφεβάλοντο·
οὔτε σιωπηλὴν οὔτ᾽ ἄψοφον οὖλος ἐθείραις
Ἕσπερος, ἀλλ᾽ αἰεί σε καταβλέπει ἀμφιβόητον.
οἱ μὲν ὑπαείδουσι νόμον Λυκίοιο γέροντος,
305   ὅν τοι ἀπὸ Ξάνθοιο θεοπρόπος ἤγαγεν Ὠλήν·
αἱ δὲ ποδὶ πλήσσουσι χορίτιδες ἀσφαλὲς οὖδας.
δὴ τότε καὶ στεφάνοισι βαρύνεται ἱρὸν ἄγαλμα
Κύπριδος ἀρχαίης ἀριήκοον, ἥν ποτε Θησεύς
εἵσατο, σὺν παίδεσσιν ὅτε Κρήτηθεν ἀνέπλει.
310   οἱ χαλεπὸν μύκημα καὶ ἄγριον υἷα φυγόντες
Πασιφάης καὶ γναμπτὸν ἕδος σκολιοῦ λαβυρίνθου,
πότνια, σὸν περὶ βωμὸν ἐγειρομένου κιθαρισμοῦ
κύκλιον ὠρχήσαντο, χοροῦ δ᾽ ἡγήσατο Θησεύς.
ἔνθεν ἀειζώοντα θεωρίδος ἱερὰ Φοίβῳ
315   Κεκροπίδαι πέμπουσι τοπήϊα νηὸς ἐκείνης.
   Ἀστερίη πολύβωμε πολύλλιτε, τίς δέ σε ναύτης
ἔμπορος Αἰγαίοιο παρήλυθε νηῒ θεούσῃ;

---

287 Ἴριον Pfeiffer: ἱερὸν PBerol **Ψ**   295 ἔσονται Mineur: κεῖνοι vel ἐκεῖνοι **Ψ**: κεῖναι Wilamowitz: κεῖνται Maas: 296 ἤ τοι **Ψ**: ἤ γὰρ coni. Pf. 298 ἰούλων **E**, **T** in marg.: ἰούλῳ **Ψ** 306 ποδὶ **αγδ**: ποδὸν **β**: ποδιὸν **ζ**: ποδοῖν Meineke

οὐχ οὕτω μεγάλοι μιν ἐπιπνείουσιν ἀῆται,
χρειὼ δ' ὅττι τάχιστον ἄγει πλόον, ἀλλὰ τὰ λαίφη
320   ὠκέες ἐστείλαντο καὶ οὐ πάλιν αὖτις ἔβησαν,
πρὶν μέγαν ἢ σέο βωμὸν ὑπὸ πληγῇσιν ἑλίξαι
ῥησσόμενον καὶ πρέμνον ὀδακτάσαι ἁγνὸν ἐλαίης
χεῖρας ἀποστρέψαντας· ἃ Δηλιὰς εὕρετο νύμφη
παίγνια κουρίζοντι καὶ Ἀπόλλωνι γελαστύν.
325   ἱστίη ὦ νήσων εὐέστιε, χαῖρε μὲν αὐτή,
χαίροι δ' Ἀπόλλων τε καὶ ἣν ἐλοχεύσατο Λητώ.

---

320 αὖτις I: αὖθις Ψ   321 ὑπὸ πληγῇσιν ἑλίξαι Ψ: ὑπὸ πληγῆς ἐλελίξαι Schneider   322 ῥησσόμενον
Ψ: ῥησσομένους Ernesti   326 ἐλοχεύσατο Ψ: ἐλοχεύσαο Wilamowitz, Pfeiffer

To Delos

Holy—O my heart, at what time…will you sing of—Delos, Apollo's nurse? Surely all of the Cyclades, the holiest of the islands that lie in the sea, are well-hymned. But Delos is accustomed to carry off the first fruits from the Muses, (5) because she bathed and swaddled Phoebus, lord of song, and first praised him as a god. Just as the Muses dislike the singer who does not sing of Pimpleia, so Phoebus dislikes the singer who forgets Delos. To Delos now I shall give her allotted song, so that Apollo (10) *Cynthius* might praise me for respecting his dear nurse.

That one—windswept and harsh and wave-beaten as she is, rather more a course for the sea gull than for horses—is fixed in the sea, which strongly surging around her wipes off much foam from the Icarian water. (15) Therefore on her sea-sailing fishermen dwelt. But she causes no indignation to be spoken of among the first, whenever to Ocean and the Titan Tethys the islands gather, and she always leads the chorus. Phoenician Corsica follows behind in her footsteps (20), not to be scorned, and Abantian Macris of the Ellopians and lovely Sardinia and onto whom Cypris first swam from the water and whom she keeps safe in exchange for this embarkation. These are secure because of their sheltering ramparts, but Delos because of Apollo. What defense is more adamant? (25) Stone walls might fall under the onslaught of Strymonian Boreas, but the god is a bulwark forever. Beloved Delos, such is the support that surrounds you.

If a great many songs circle around you, what song shall I weave about you? What is delightful for you to hear? (30) Is it when in the beginning the great god, striking the mountain with the three-pointed spear that the Telchines had fashioned for him, formed the islands of the sea, and from below lifted them all from the foundations and rolled them into the sea? At the sea's bottom he fastened them root and branch, so that they might forget the mainland. (35) But necessity did not constrain you, but freely you sailed upon the open seas. And your name of old was Asteria, since you leapt into the deep trough of ocean from heaven, fleeing a marriage with Zeus, like a shooting star. As long as golden Leto did not draw near you, (40) so long were you still Asteria, and were not yet called Delos. Often did sailors coming from the town of…from Troezen to Ephyra within the Saronic gulf catch sight of you, and returning from Ephyra they no longer saw you there, (45) but you had run along the swift strait of the narrow Euripus, with its loud-sounding flow. On the same day turning your back on the water of the Chalcidian sea you swam up to the Sounian headland of Athens or to Chios or to the well-drenched breast of the island of Parthenia (for it was not yet called Samos), (50) where the nymphs of Mykale, neighbors of Ancaeus, hosted you. But when you offered your soil for Apollo as a gift for his birth, sailors gave you this name in exchange, for you no longer sailed about inconspicuous but into the waves of the Aegean sea you put down the roots of your feet.

(55) You did not tremble at Hera in her wrath, who bellowed in terrible rage against all women in labor who bore children to Zeus, but Leto especially, because she alone was about to bear Zeus a son more beloved than Ares. So in consequence she herself kept watch within the aether; (60) angered greatly and beyond speech, she hindered Leto, who was distressed by her labor pains. Hera set her two guards to keep watch over the land; the one, sitting upon a high peak of Thracian Haemus, bold Ares, in armor, kept watch over the land of the continent, while his two horses (65) he stabled near the cave of Boreas with its seven recesses. And the other established herself as a watcher over the steep islands, the daughter of Thaumas, who had darted on to Mimas. There, as threats to as many cities as Leto approached, they remained and prevented them from accepting her. (70) Arcadia fled, Auge's holy Mt. Parthenion fled, and after her fled aged Peneius. The land of Pelops, all that is joined to the isthmus, fled, except for Aegialus and Argos. For those were not paths that she trod upon, since Hera had been allotted the Inachus. (75) Aonia also fled along the same course, and Dirce and Strophie, holding the hand of their father, black-pebbled Ismenus; far behind followed Asopus, slowed by his knees (for he had been defiled by a thunderbolt). In her trembling she ceased her dance, (80) the earthborn nymph, Melia, and her cheek grew pale as she caught her breath over the oak that was her coeval, when she saw Helicon's hair shaking. My goddesses, Muses, tell me, is it really true that the oaks were born simultaneously with the nymphs? "The nymphs rejoice when rain makes the oaks grow, (85) but they weep when there are no longer leaves on the oaks." With them, Apollo, still in his mother's womb, was extremely angry, and he spoke out threatening Thebe, not without consequence: "Thebe, why, wretch, do you put to the proof your coming destiny? Do not yet compel me to prophesy against my will. (90) The tripod seat of Pytho is not yet my concern; nor yet is the great snake dead, but still that beast with its dire jaws, stretching down from the Pleistus, enwraps snowy Parnassus with its nine coils. But nonetheless I shall say something more clearly than from my laurel. (95) Flee on. Swiftly shall I overtake you, bathing my bow in blood. You have been alloted the children of an evil-tongued woman. You will not be my dear nurse, nor will Cithaeron. I am pure and I would be in the care of those who are also pure." Thus he spoke. Leto turned and came back. (100) But when the Achaean cities refused her as she returned—Helice, the companion of Poseidon, and Bura, the cowstead of Dexamenus, the son of Oeceus—she turned her feet back to Thessaly. Anaurus fled, and mighty Larisa, and Chiron's peaks. (105) Peneius also fled winding through Tempe. Hera, a forgiving heart did not yet lie within you; your anger did not break down and you had no pity when she stretched out both her arms and spoke such things—in vain. "Thessalian nymphs, race of the river, tell your father (110) to calm his great flood. Entwine yourselves in his beard, praying that the children of Zeus be born in his waters. Phthiotian Peneius, why

do you now contend with the winds? O father, you are not mounted on a race-horse. Indeed are your feet always this swift, or (115) are they only nimble in my case and suddenly today you made them fly? But he does not hear. O my burden, where shall I carry you? My unhappy ankles refuse. Pelion, O bridal chamber of Philyra, but you, stay, stay, since in your mountains even wild beasts, lionesses, in labor often (120) drop the raw fruits of their labor." Then Peneius answered her pouring forth his tears: "Leto, Necessity is a mighty goddess. For it is not I, mistress, who refuse your birth pangs. (I know that others, too, have washed the afterbirth in my waters.) But Hera has (125) threatened me abundantly. Look who keeps watch, seated on the mountaintop, who would easily drag me down from the depths. What shall I do? Or is Peneius being destroyed a pleasant thing for you? Let my day of destiny come; I shall risk it for your sake, even if I should wander for eternity, (130) ebbing and thirsty, and alone among the rivers should be called the least honorable. Here I am. What more can I say? Only call upon Eileithyia." He spoke and halted his great flood. But Ares, having lifted the peaks of Pangaeum from their base, was going (135) to hurl them into his eddies and cover up his streams. On high he crashed and struck his shield with the point of his spear, and made it quiver with a warlike beat. The mountains of Ossa trembled and the plain of Crannon and the windswept heights of the Pindus, and all of Thessaly danced in fear. (140) Such a noise rang from his shield. Just as, when the whole interior of Mt. Etna, smoldering with fire, is shaken because the Giant Briareos under the earth moves onto his other shoulder, the furnaces roar under Hephaestus' tongs (145) and likewise his implements; the fire-wrought basins and tripods ring out as they fall upon each other. Just as loud as this then was the clash of his well-rounded shield. Peneius did not draw back, but remained steadfast as before, and stopped his rapid eddies, (150) until the daughter of Coeus called to him: "Farewell, save yourself, save yourself. Do not suffer evil for my sake as a recompense for your pity. Your favor will be rewarded." She spoke and after much effort came to the islands of the sea. But they did not receive her when she approached, (155) not the Echinades, who had a rich harbor for ships, nor Corcyra, who was the friendliest of all to strangers, since Iris on Mimas' peak, terribly angered with them all, turned them away. At Iris' reproach, the islands fled together with the current, whichever Leto approached. (160) Then she arrived at primeval Cos, the island of Merops, the holy inner sanctuary of the heroine Chalciope.

But this utterance of her son held her back. "You should not give birth to me here, mother. I do not blame or grudge the island, seeing as it is rich and thriving in flocks, if any other is. (165) But another god is destined to it from the Fates, the lofty blood of the Saviors. Under whose diadem will come, not unwilling to be ruled by a Macedonian, both lands and the lands that dwell in the sea, as far as the ends of the earth and where the swift horses (170) carry the Sun. He will have the character of his father. And now at some later time a common struggle will come to us, when against the Hellenes later born Titans raising up a barbarian dagger and Celtic war, from the farthest west (175) will rush, like snowflakes or equal in number to the stars, when they graze most closely together upon the aether...and the plain of Crisa and the glens of Hephaestus are hard pressed on all sides, and they shall see the rich smoke (180) of the burning neighbor, and no longer only by hearsay, but already beside the temple they would perceive phalanxes of the enemy, already alongside my tripods the swords and the shameless belts and the hated shields that will line the evil path of the Galatians, a crazed tribe. (185) Some of these shields will be my reward, others will be set by the Nile, having seen the bearers breathe their last in the fire, the prizes of a much laboring king. O Ptolemy who will be, these are Phoebus' predictions for you. You will praise greatly in all the days to come (190) him who prophesied within the womb. But consider, mother. There is a small island to be seen in the water, wandering in the sea. Her feet are not in one place, but she swims with the tide like the asphodel, where the south wind, then the east wind, wherever the sea may carry her. Please carry me there, (195) for you will come to her with her consent."

When he had spoken so many things, the islands ran away into the sea. Asteria, lover of song, you came down from Euboea about to visit the encircling Cyclades— not a long time ago, but Geraestian seaweed still trailed behind...(200) when you see as it [...] bravely you said these things [...] seeing the goddess, heavy in her labor. "Hera, do to me what pleases you. For I have not heeded your threats. Come, come over to me, Leto." (205) You spoke. And she readily put an end to her...wandering. She sat by the stream of the Inopus, which the earth then sends forth at its most abundant, when the Nile in full spate comes down from the Ethiopian highland. She loosed her belt and leaned her shoulders back (210) against the trunk of a palm tree, weakened by her helpless distress. And damp sweat poured over her skin. In her weakened state she said: "Why, child, are you weighing down your mother? Here is your island, dear one, floating on the sea. Be born, be born, child, and gently come forth from my womb." (215) Bride of Zeus, burdened with anger, you were not going to be long uninformed. Such a messenger ran to you, and she spoke still panting, and her report was mingled with fear. "Honored Hera, most preeminent among the goddesses, I am yours, all things are yours, and you sit as the (220) legitimate queen of Olympus, and we fear no other female hand. And you, Queen, will know the reason for your anger. Leto is untying her cincture on an island. All the others loathed her and did not receive her. But Asteria called her by name as she was passing by, (225) Asteria, vile refuse of the sea. You yourself also know her. But dear—for you are able—Mistress, avenge your servants who walk the earth at your command." Thus she spoke and sat beside the golden throne, like Artemis' bitch, which, when it has ceased from the swift hunt, (230) sits, the huntress, by her feet with her ears pricked, ever ready to undertake the goddess's summons.

Like her the daughter of Thaumas sat by the throne. She never forgets her place, not even when sleep presses his wing that causes forgetfulness upon her. (235) But there at the corner of the great throne, leaning her head a bit aslant, she sleeps. She never loosens her sash or her swift hunting boots, in case her mistress might speak some sudden order. And Hera responded exceedingly angered. (240) "So now, you shameful possessions of Zeus, you would even marry secretly and bear hidden creatures, not even where poor mill workers labor in misbegotten childbirth, but where seals of the deep breed in the solitary rocks. I am not at all seriously angered at Asteria for this (245) deed, and it is not possible that I shall act heartlessly. But so many things [*sc.* would I do] to her—she was very wrong to do this favor for Leto. Still I do honor her exceedingly because she did not trample upon my bed, and pre-ferred the sea to Zeus."

She spoke. And the swans, singers of the god about to be, (250) having left Meionian Pactolus circled seven times around Delos, and they accompany the birth in song, birds of the Muses, most melodious of all winged creatures. (And then the child fitted as many strings to the lyre afterwards as the swans that sang at his birth pangs.) (255) But the eighth time they no longer sang. For he had leapt out, and the Delian nymphs with far sounding voice, offspring of an ancient river, sang the holy tune of Eleithyia, and immediately the bronze sky echoed the penetrating cry, and Hera did not hold a grudge, since Zeus had driven away her anger. (260) And then all your foundations became gold, Delos, your round lake flowed with gold all the day, and golden bloomed the shoot of the olive, in response to your birth. And the eddying Inopus flowed deep with gold. And you yourself took up the child from the golden earth, (265) and placed him in your lap, and spoke such a word: "O great earth, many altared, many citied, bearing many things! Rich lands and you islands that dwell around, I am such as this, not amenable to the plow, but from me Apollo shall be called Delian, and no (270) other land shall be as beloved to any other god, not Cerchnis to Poseidon who rules Lechaeum, nor the hill of Cyllene to Hermes, nor Crete to Zeus, as I to Apollo. And I shall no longer wander." Thus you spoke and he suckled at your sweet breast.

(275) And so from that time you are called the holiest of islands, Apollo's childhood nurse. Neither Enyo, nor Hades, nor the horses of Ares set foot upon you; but annually tithes of first fruits are sent to you, all cities lead out choruses, (280) those that cast their lot to the East, and those to the West, and those in the South, and who have their dwellings beyond the northern shore, most ancient blood. These are the first to bring you the stalk and holy sheaves of corn ears, which the Pelasgians from Dodona, (285) stepping out from afar, first receive, servants of the unsilent cauldron, who sleep on the ground. Next they come to the town of Ira and mountains of the Melian land; from there they sail into the fair Lelantian plain of the Abantes. And not far (290) is the journey from Euboea, since their harbors are your neighbors. The first to bring you these things from

the fair-haired Arimaspi were Oupis and Loxo and happy Hecaerge, daughters of Boreas, and those who then were the best of the young men. And they did not go back home again, (295) but their fate was happy, and they will never be without glory. Truly, the Delian girls, when the fair sounding hymeneal threatens to disrupt their girlish habits, bring an offering of their virgin hair to the virgins and the boys offer to the young men the first down of their chins, as first fruits.

(300) Asteria, redolent of incense, the islands have formed a circle around and about you, and surround you as a chorus. Hesperus with his thickly curled hair looks down upon you neither silent nor without noise, but ever sounding on all sides. The men accompany the hymn of the old Lycian, (305) which the seer Olen brought to you from Xanthus. The girls in the choir beat with their feet the secure ground. Then too the holy image is laden with wreaths, the famous one of archaic Cypris, which Theseus once set up, when with the youths he sailed back from Crete. (310) When they fled the harsh bellow and fierce son of Pasiphae and the twisted seat of the crooked labyrinth, mistress, they danced around your altar in a circle, as the cithara-playing began, and Theseus led the chorus. From that time, as ever-living offerings of the envoy ship, (315) the Cecropidae send Phoebus the rigging of that ship.

Asteria, with your many altars, with your many prayers, what merchant sailor of the Aegean passed by you in a swift ship? Mighty winds do not bear so hard upon him and necessity compel the swiftest possible voyage, (320) but they swiftly furled their sails and did not embark again before winding about your great altar, which is buffeted by blows, and biting the holy trunk of the olive with their hands tied behind their backs. These things the nymph of Delos invented as amusing games for the infant Apollo.

(325) O well-hearthed of the islands, hail, you, and hail also Apollo and her whom Leto bore.

Commentary

1–10. In this opening Delos is mentioned four times (2, 4, 8, 9), tightly bound to Apollo (2, 9) and to Φοῖβος (5, 8)—as nurse, swaddler, first to praise, subject for song; the Muses open lines 5 and 7, ending then beginning their constructions chiastically, each with dependent clause: ὅτι Φοῖβον, τὼς Φοῖβος ὅτις. Callimachus as the singer who will please Apollo appears at the beginning and end (1, 9–10) in contrast to the hypothetical singer who does not please the Muses or Apollo (7–8). In line 2 Delos as nurse (Δῆλον... κουροτρόφον) embraces Apollo, and again in lines 9–10 Δήλῳ... τιθήνης embraces Apollo *Cynthius* and the poet (ἀποδάσσομαι... με). Note also frequent polyptoton (Δῆλον, Δῆλος, Δήλοιο, Δήλῳ; ἱερήν, ἱερώταται; ἀείσεις, ἀοιδάων, ἀοιδόν; ἤνεσε, αἰνήσῃ; πρῶτα, πρώτη).

The proem opens with the subject postponed until line 2; in *hArt*, there was a similar hyperbaton and postponement of ὑμνέομεν and in *hDem* the goddess is only addressed in line 2 (though that hymn is mimetic). Callimachus' poetic subject (Δῆλον) is combined with an adjective (ἱερήν) and an epithet (κουροτρόφον) more commonly applied to place than divinities. These are features found in lyric (see, e.g., the opening of the first three Nemean odes); in addition, D'Alessio 2007 ad loc. points out that the ambiguity between the name of a place and the eponymous divinity is a motif frequently used in encomiastic poetry, especially in Pindar.

1. ὦ θυμέ: the vocative θυμέ is not epic, but evokes lyric practice (see Pi. *Ol.* 2.89, *Nem.* 3.26, frr. 123.2, 127.4 S-M), where questions immediately follow θυμέ. This vocative is also found in Theognis (213, 695, 877, 1029, 1070a). Callimachus consults his heart also at the opening of *hZeus* 5 (and in fr. 75.5 Pf.).

τίνα χρόνον †ηποτ†: the mss. reading τίνα χρόνον ἢ πότ' has been questioned on the grounds that a second question (πότ') would be redundant. Attempts to repair include: (1) assuming the redundancy is a form of lyric emphasis (Mair, Cahen), though Mineur ad loc. observes that ἤ would not be used to join two elements that are not truly disjunctive; (2) assuming the meaning of the two expressions to be different (Vahlens takes τίνα χρόνον as "for how long"; Giangrande as the equivalent of ἕνα χρόνον, "once and for all"); and (3) emending the text (Reiske, εἴ ποτ', "if ever"; Maas 1982/Lloyd-Jones τίν' ἐς χρόνον, εἶπον, ἀτίσσεις, "for how long, tell me, will you slight [Delos]"; Mineur, ἠπύτ' ἀείσεις, "loudly will you sing"). The Maas/Lloyd-Jones line is the most promising, and A.R. 1.615 of Aphrodite: οὕνεκά μιν γεράων ἐπὶ δηρὸν ἄτισσαν ("because they had long deprived her of her honors") provides a parallel. All of these emendations are reported in Mineur ad loc., where they are discussed in much greater detail.

ἀείσεις: a form of ἀείδω or ὑμνω is the usual Homeric hymnic opening, though *HhAp* is an exception.

2. κουροτρόφον: once in Homer (*Od.* 9.27), where Odysseus, with similar affection, describes Ithaca as a "good nurse."

ἤ μέν: used for a strong affirmation (Denniston 389).

2–3. ἄπασαι Κυκλάδες: the Cyclades form a rough circle in the Aegean sea to the south and east of Boeotia, hence their name in antiquity. Their number may vary (e.g., Hdt. 5.30, Eur. *Ion* 1583, Theoc. 17.90). They were of central interest to the Ptolemies (e.g., in *OGIS* 54.6 the kingdom of Euergetes is described as Egypt, Libya, Syria, Phoenicia, and the Cycladic islands).

3. The line is a close adaptation of *HhAp* 38: Χίος, ἢ νήσων λιπαρωτάτη εἰν ἁλὶ κεῖται ("Chios, which is the richest of the islands lying in the salt-sea"), and see *Od.* 9.25: πανυπερτάτη εἰν ἁλὶ κεῖται, of Ithaca.

ἱερώταται: the Cyclades are "the holiest" from their association with Delos, but there may have been a more specific topical reference: the islands' participation in the Nesiotic League, which was founded by Antigonus Monophthalmos but came under Ptolemaic control. Whether or not Delos was a member is uncertain, but Nesiotic decrees were regularly set up in the Delian temple of Apollo. By the time of this hymn the League had voted to accept a *Ptolemaia* and was the first to honor Soter as a god (Fraser 1972: 1.224, 2.373–74nn, 279–80, and Merker 1970: 158–59).

4. εὔυμνοι "well-hymned"; the epithet occurs previously of Apollo at *HhAp* 19 (≈ 207) and at *hAp* 31.

τὰ πρῶτα: Pfeiffer indexes as τὰ πρῶτα (*sc.* ἄεθλα) in his *index vocabulorum* (under πρότερον), and compare *Il.* 23.538: τὰ πρῶτα φερέσθω. Reinsch-Werner 1976: 322–23 expands this to understand Callimachus' poem ("Delos") as wishing to take first prize in a contest with the Homeric hymn. D'Alessio follows Pfeiffer, taking as "first fruits of the Muses" (cf. 16: ἐνὶ πρώτῃσι λέγεσθαι).

5. Μουσέων: within the hymns, the Muses are named only in *hDelos* (5, 7, 82, 252). The genitive Μουσέων is found in Hesiod (*Th.* 94, in the context of Apollo), and Μουσάων occurs once in *Il.* 1.604, where Apollo and the Muses sing in responsion. It is possible that the variant spellings are intended to allude to these passages, but both forms do occur regularly in other poetry.

Φοῖβον: Homer almost always employs Φοῖβος as part of the formula Φοῖβος Ἀπόλλων or Ἀπόλλων Φοῖβος, while in lyric and tragedy they serve as alternatives; Callimachus follows the latter practice.

ἀοιδάων "songs"; Ψ reads ἀοιδέων ("singers"), a form that occurs only once (in the *Life of Oppian*), hence Lascaris emended to the more common ἀοιδάων. M. Fantuzzi suggests ἀοιδέων resulted from the influence of Μουσέων.

μεδέοντα: the participle is commonly used for a divinity's sphere of influence or dominion. Apollo is the "master of song" in contrast to Artemis' "abundant chorus," *hArt.* 3.

6. λοῦσέ τε καὶ σπείρωσε: the two homely verbs make it clear that the island is literally a κουροτρόφος; she bathed and swaddled the newborn god.

σπείρωσε: see *hZeus* 33n.

7–8. ὡς … τώς: the correlative adverbs are paired in tragedy (e.g., Aesch. *Sept.* 483–84, *Supp.* 65–69) but not in Homer. They occur only here in the hymns. For the thought cf. Hes. *Th.* 96–97.

7. Πίμπλειαν: an epithet derived from Mt. Pimpleia in Thrace sacred to the Muses (cf. Str. 10.3.17, who calls it Πίμπλα). Orpheus was also associated with the region (Str. 7a.17, 18).

8. ὅτις [= ὅστις] **Δήλοιο λάθηται:** cf. *HhAp* 1: μνήσομαι οὐδὲ λάθωμαι Ἀπόλλωνος ἑκάτοιο and the comments on *hArt* 1.

9. οἴμης "way of song," only here in Callimachus; the word occurs three times in the *Odyssey* of minstrels who are instructed in song by the Muses or the god: *Od.* 8.74, 481 (Demodocus), 22.347 (Phemius). Cf. οἴμους, *hZeus* 78.

ἀποδάσσομαι: epic future of ἀποδατέομαι, which occurs earlier at *Il.* 17.231, 22.118, 24.595, and Pi. *Nem.* 10.86; the meaning is to give out one's allotted share (with genitive).

9–10. ὡς ἄν … αἰνήσῃ με: a final clause (see Smyth §2201). In line 6 ἤνεσε was used of Delos honoring Apollo as a divinity. Here of the divinity honoring the poet and at 189 of Ptolemy II honoring Apollo.

10. Κύνθιος: the reading has been restored by Lascaris from corrupt mss.; others have restored Κάρνεος, but Mt. Cynthus was on Delos, while *Carneius* was a title of Spartan or Cyrenean Apollo. The vocative Κύνθιε occurs at *Aet.*, frr. 67.6 Pf. and 114.8 Pf., the adjective Κυνθιάδων at *hAp* 61.

φίλης … τιθήνης: the image of an island as a nurse is frequent in Hellenistic poetry, see Theoc. 17.58–59 (of Cos), A.R. 4.1758 (of Thera), and 48n.

ἀλέγοντα: see *hArt* 31n.

11–26. This initial characterization of Delos as barren and inhospitable is in contrast to her later abundance of wealth and visitors when she becomes a cult center (316–24).

11. ἄτροπος: the usual meaning is "rigid" or "firm" (as such, it was the name given to one of the Fates). The scholiast explains as "uncultivated" (i.e., "unturned by the plow") or "unshaken." Both fit: the island was too rocky for cultivation, and after Apollo's birth it no longer roamed the Aegean. However, some have objected to the word on the grounds that unlike the other qualities described, its primary meaning is not necessarily negative (although it is formed as an α-privative) and its sense is repeated in the verb. Attempts to emend include Blomfield's ἄτροφος, which Hopkinson (1985: 250–51) points out would be a nice paradox with κουροτρόφος (2); Meineke's ἄτρυγος (cf. *HhAp* 55); or even ἄβροχος (cf. *hZeus* 19).

οἴά θ': the ms. reading has raised concerns. If it stands, it will introduce a comparison ("as one beaten by the sea"), or it will be the equivalent of ὥστε, with causal force (so Ruijgh 1971: 969–70, cf. A.R. 3.618). But in his edition Pfeiffer questioned the reading on the grounds that in Homer οἴά τε introduces a clause of comparison, not a single word. (See Mineur ad loc. and Ukleja 2005: 227–28.)

ἁλιπλήξ: Callimachean variant of ἁλίπληκτος; both words are rare. See Pi. *Py.* 4.14, where Medea prophesies the future settlement of Cyrene from the sea-beaten (ἁλιπλάκτου) island of Lemnos. Later in this hymn Apollo will prophesy the future of Ptolemy II.

12. Callimachus has adapted a Homeric passage where Telemachus explains why he cannot accept Menelaus' gift of horses: *Od.* 4.605–6: ἐν δ᾽ Ἰθάκῃ οὔτ᾽ ἄρ δρόμοι εὐρέες οὔτε τι λειμών· | αἰγίβοτος καὶ μᾶλλον ἐπήρατος ἱπποβότοιο ("In Ithaca there are neither broad runs nor any meadow, lovely for goat-grazing rather more than horse-grazing"). See also *Il.* 10.556–57: ἠέ περ οἴδε | ἵππους ("horses [better] than these").

αἰθυίης: according to Thompson 1895: 18, probably a large seagull.

καὶ μᾶλλον: καὶ is the equivalent of πολύ (so Mineur ad loc.); cf. *Od.* 4.606, quoted above.

ἠέπερ: normally printed as ἠέ περ in Homer, though Zenodotus preferred ἠέπερ (T sch. on *Il.* 1.260).

13. ἐνεστήρικται: from ἐνστηρίζω. Once in Homer, *Il.* 21.168, of driving a spear in the earth, but *HhHerm* 11 provides a closer parallel: it describes the fixing of the moon in heaven in its tenth month as the time when Maia gave birth to Hermes; language from this same passage is also imitated at 225. See also the description in 53–54 of Delos being fixed in the sea.

14. This is one of the two "golden" lines in Callimachus (the other is *hDem* 9)—two adjectives, two nouns with a verb between. The form was popularized in Latin poetry. For a discussion, see McLennan, p. 97 and Hopkinson on *hDem* 9.

Ἰκαρίου: the Icarian Sea was that portion of the Aegean that fell between the Cyclades and the coast of Asia Minor from roughly Chios in the north to Thera in the south. The island of Icaros lay in its center. Both were named for Icarus, the son of Daedalus, who, flying upon waxen wings, fell into this part of the Aegean when he came too close to the sun, which melted the wax.

ἀπομάσσεται: Hellenistic and later, mainly prose; here with the sense of "wipe off on." Callimachus uses the verb in *ep.* 27.3 Pf. = 56.3 G-P with the sense of "mold" or "copy."

ἄχνην "foam," usually of liquids. In Homer of the sea at *Il.* 4.426 and *Od.* 5.403; cf. also A.R. 4.1238: ὕδατος ἄχνη.

15. τῷ: see *hZeus* 58n.

ἰχθυβολῆες: a Callimachean variant of ἰχθύβολος, "fisherman"; later imitated by Nonnus and Oppian.

ἁλίπλοοι "sea-sailing," again at 52. Previously it is *hapax* in Homer (*Il.* 12.26), of walls that Apollo and Zeus reduce to debris "swimming on the sea."

ἐννάσσαντο: from ἐνναίω; ναίω is common in epic, but ἐνναίω is first found in tragedy (Soph. *OC* 788, *Phil.* 472, Eur. *Hel.* 488). The spondaic line ends the geographic description.

16. οὐ νεμεσητόν: construed with an infinitive; "not a cause for retaliation" or "indignation" in others for her to be spoken of among the first; the expression occurs in *Il.* 9.523, of Achilles' righteous anger at Agamemnon, and shortly before the story of Artemis, Oeneus, and the Calydonian boar (527–49), mentioned at *hArt* 215–220. The phrase οὐ νέμεσις occurs at *hArt* 64, where the Oceanids tremble before the Cyclopes.

ἐνὶ πρώτῃσι: cf. Theoc. 17.3: ἐνὶ πρώτοισι λεγέσθω, in praising Ptolemy II.

17–18. The islands form a choral procession as they visit Ocean and his wife Tethys. These two were the parents of various water nymphs, some of whom form Artemis' chorus in *hArt*. Here Callimachus creates a picture of the islands themselves, as a chorus, visiting Ocean. There may have been a literary antecedent to a procession of nymphs to Ocean (see Mineur ad loc.), but it also prefigures the *theoriai* to Delos at the end of the poem.

17. ὁππότ(ε): Callimachus preferred this spelling, useful at line opening or before the bucolic diercsis; in the hymns ὁπότε occurs only at *hDelos* 141 (in Homer ὁππότε is twice as frequent as ὁπότε).

Τιτηνίδα: although the epithet is only applied to Tethys, she and Oceanus were both children of Gaia and Uranus, hence Titans (see Hes. *Th.* 132–36).

18. ἀολλίζονται: from ἀολλίζω, "gather." The verb occurs in the *Iliad* (e.g., 6.270), only here in Callimachus, and is then imitated in later Greek, especially by Nonnus.

ἔξαρχος: a leader, especially of a chorus; once in Homer in this sense (*Il.* 24.721) and frequent in later Greek.

ὁδεύει "travel"; once in Homer (*Il.* 11.569), afterwards mainly in prose.

19–22. Callimachus names four islands as potential rivals for Delos as choral leader: Corsica, Euboea, Sardinia, and Cyprus—two of the largest islands in the far western and the two largest in the far eastern Mediterranean. Commentators have been puzzled by the choice, and the absence of Sicily and Crete, but offer no solutions (Meineke posits two missing lines). Yet the choice is comprehensible, since the four act as a geographical bracket encompassing the whole Greek world, with Libyan connections in the west and mythological models of islands nurturing gods in the east (see notes below).

19. Φοίνισσα... Κύρνος: Corsica was originally colonized by Phocaeans (Hdt. 1.165), but subsequently Tyrrhenians (Etruscans) and Carthaginians took it over (hence it is called "Phoenician" here). Cornelius Scipio invaded it in 259 BCE at the beginning of the First Punic War. The hymn was almost certainly composed before this date; see p. 18. The island is also mentioned in *hArt* 58.

ὀπηδεῖ: Homer uses only in the third singular present (as here) or imperfect: "follow."

20. ὀνοτή: a variant of Homeric ὀνοστός, "scorned"; first in Pi. *Is.* 3/4.68, then here and at A.R. 4.91; note the litotes.

Μάκρις: first here as the name of Euboea. According to A.R. 4.1128–38 Macris was the daughter of Aristaeus (see 21n below), who nursed the infant Dionysus in a cave on Euboea (thus a parallel to Delos and Apollo). Hera found them and banished them to Phaeacia. Macris (i.e., "Large") later came to be one of the many names for the island, which, as M. Giuseppetti observes, serves as a contrast to Apollo's slender nurse Delos (ἀραιή, 191).

Ἀβαντιάς: a Callimachean variant of Ἀβαντίς, another name for Euboea (Hes. fr. 296 M-W); at *Il.* 2.536 Homer calls the people Abantes.

Ἑλλοπιήων: Ἑλλοπιεύς is unattested elsewhere but conforms to Callimachus' practice in generating forms (see Schmitt 51–52 for examples). According to Str. 10.1.3, Ἑλλοπία was another name for Euboea, and the people Ellopians, named for Ellops, the son of Ion.

21. Σαρδώ: according to Paus. 10.17.2, the first non-native settlers to have reached Sardinia were Libyans, led by one Sardus. Subsequently, Aristaeus, the son of Cyrene and Apollo, came there. The close North African connection via Aristaeus may have been the reason for inclusion here.

ἣν ἐπενήξατο Κύπρις: Κύπρις the goddess is the subject of ἐπενήξατο, and the island Κύπρον (or νῆσον) is the suppressed antecedent of ἥν and object of σαοῖ (22). There is implicit word play between Κύπρις and Κύπρος.

ἐπενήξατο: from ἐπινήχομαι; the compound is mainly found in late prose, including Callimachus' paradoxography (fr. 407.88 Pf.); in poetry, at *Batrach.* 107, [Theoc.] 23.61, and Cercidas 17.11 Powell.

Κύπρις: when Cronus castrated his father Uranus, he cast the genitals into the sea, and Aphrodite was born from the white foam exuded from the genitals; she came to land on Cyprus, where she was reared (thus another parallel for Apollo and Delos). After her return to Egypt, Arsinoe II was identified with Aphrodite, and in particular as the Aphrodite who granted safe sailing to those going to sea (see Posidippus 39.5 and 119.6 A-B). Finally, Cyprus was a Ptolemaic naval base from 294 BCE.

22. σαοῖ: from σαόω (= σῴζω). See *hDem* 134n.

ἐπιβάθρων: Homeric *hapax* (*Od.* 15.449) meaning a "passenger's fare," and in papyri (PCairZen 4.59753.34, 36), a "landing fee." Here doubtless meant to be a joke: the "payment" for Aphrodite disembarking onto the island. And see below 28.

23. περισκεπέεσσιν: here in an active sense "surrounding"; at *hZeus* 11 in a passive sense.

ἐρυμναί: prose, "fortified" or "secure."

24. Ἀπόλλωνι: here the first syllable is short; at 86, 269, 276 it is long. The variation is frequent in Callimachus and found already in Homer.

25. τείχεα μὲν καὶ λᾶες: either two examples of strong objects overturned by the force of the winds or hendiadys for "stone walls" (so Schneider, Cahen); Mineur ad loc. considers it an *interpretatio* of *Il.* 12.27–33.

26. Στρυμονίου βορέαο "Strymonian Boreas" was a wind blowing from the northeastern region of Thrace, where the river Strymon was located. The epithet may allude to one of the northern dynasts who controlled the area of Amphipolis at the time of the hymn, either Antigonus Gonatas or Pyrrhus (after 274).

ἀστυφέλικτος: before Callimachus only in Xenophon, *Constitution of Sparta* 15.7, where it describes the condition of the city (unshaken) as long as the kings abide by their oaths.

27. τοῖός σε βοηθόος: note the placement of σε enclosed by "such…a helper" and reinforced by the verb.

ἀμφιβέβηκεν: the verb is used, especially of Apollo, to express divine protection (e.g., *Il.* 1.37).

28–274. The narrative of Leto, her flight, Delos as her refuge, and finally the god's birth. The very length of the narrative functions as a literary correlative to the long process of her parturition.

28. λίην: best taken with πολέες, i.e., "very many."

πολέες: the two-termination adjective is used here (as in *Il.* 10.27). Delos did indeed have very many songs written about it, in part because its great festival in honor of Apollo (the *Delia* or *Apollonia*) featured choral competitions. See pp. 161–62.

περιτροχόωσιν: a variant of -τροχάω (= -τρέχω); on the form see *hArt* 65n. Callimachus may have modelled the verb on the Homeric *hapax* at *Od.* 15.451: ἅμα τροχόωντα, describing a child following his nurse (another *hapax* from this passage occurs at 22). The sense, "encircle," "surround" plays on the image of the choral singing of the islands expressed above.

29. ποίη ἐνιπλέξω σε "into what fabric shall I weave you?'" The metaphor of weaving song is commonplace; the compound first in Aesch. *PV* 610, 1079. However, Callimachus himself uses the verb in *Iamb.* 13 (fr. 203.17 Pf.) for mixing Ionic and Doric, a passage that has some connections with Pl. *Laws* 669d2-5, where the Athenian stranger is complaining about the poets' habits of intermingling sounds inappropriately, but also shapes. Since Delos is both an island and a woman, this might (like the opening of Artemis) allude to Plato's strictures.

θυμῆρες: θυμήρης is found once in Homer (*Od.* 10.362), and the Homeric scholia questioned whether this form, which Callimachus also uses in *hDem* 55, or the more common θυμαρής was correct. For θυμήρης in the envoi of *HhDem* 494, see the helpful note of Richardson (1974).

30–35 describe the birth of islands from the bottom of the sea. Callimachus connects this event allusively to pre-Olympian times with mention of the Telchines, who fashioned Poseidon's trident.

30. ἢ ὡς τὰ πρώτιστα: an adaptation of *HhAp* 25 and 214, the only other place where this phrase ἢ ὡς with a form of πρῶτον occurs (see Bing 1988:112). Mineur ad loc. points out that at *HhAp* 25 this temporal marker introduced the birth of Apollo, here the "birth" of the islands.

μέγας θεός: although the Telchines belong to a pre-Olympian order, the "great god" is surely Poseidon, whose role in island formation and breaking off large chunks from the mainland is well attested (see, e.g., *Od.* 13.162–64, Str. 10.5.16 [on Nisyros and Cos], the Orphic *Argonautica* 1279–83, and Posidippus 19, 20 A-B).

31. ἄορι "sword," or generically, "weapon." The initial alpha may be either long or short at metrical convenience (for the relationship of this passage to the Homeric scholia on ἄορ, see Rengakos 1992: 38).

τριγλώχινι: apparently anything with three prongs; Homer uses it of arrows at *Il.* 5.392–94: τλῆ δ' Ἥρη, ὅτε μιν κρατερὸς πάϊς Ἀμφιτρύωνος | δεξιτερὸν κατὰ μαζὸν ὀϊστῷ τριγλώχινι | βεβλήκει ("And Hera suffered, when the mighty son of Amphitryon struck her over the right breast with a tri-pronged arrow"). The reminder that Hera too had been made to suffer would make a fine subtext to the moment. At *Aet.* fr. 1.36 Pf. Callimachus describes Sicily as τριγλώχιν, "three-cornered." Subsequently the word appears in imitation of these passages or in scholia.

οἱ Τελχῖνες: these were chthonic figures connected with islands, particularly Rhodes and Ceos, earthquakes, and primitive metallurgy. They were destroyed for their hubris when the gods destroyed Ceos at *Aet.* fr. 75.64–69 Pf. (In the *Aetia* prologue Callimachus labels his critics who prefer more traditional poems Telchines.) The long discussion in Diodorus Siculus (5.55) makes them analogues of the Curetes who reared Zeus: they are said to have received Poseidon from Rhea and reared him.

32. εἰναλίας: a variant of ἐνάλιος, frequent in tragedy and prose for anything "in the sea" (also at 243).

33. νεάτων: epic superlative, "from the lowest part."

ὤχλισσε: from Homeric ὀχλίζω, poetic for "lever up" (*Il.* 12.448, *Od.* 9.242, of men of old lifting up gigantic boulders), cf. A.R. 4.962.

εἰσεκύλισε "roll up into," from εἰσκυλίνδω; previously twice in Ar. *Thesm.* 651, 767.

34. βυσσόν: the mss. read βυθός, the υ of which is normally short. Thus W. Dindorf emended to βυσσόν on the basis of the sole occurrence of that noun at *Il.* 24.80. Most editors accept his emendation.

ἵν' ἠπείροιο λάθωνται: a final clause with retained subjunctive in secondary sequence. There are few Homeric parallels, but it is common in later Greek.

35. πρυμνόθεν "from the bottom"; previously in Aesch. *Sept.* 71, 1056; also in Aratus 343 and A.R. 4.911.

ἐρρίζωσε: from ῥιζόω; the allusion is to *Od.* 13.162–64: τῆς δὲ σχεδὸν ἦλθ' ἐνοσίχθων, | ὅς μιν λᾶαν ἔθηκε καὶ ἐρρίζωσεν ἔνερθε | χειρὶ καταπρηνεῖ ἐλάσας ("And the Earthshaker came near her, who turned her [*sc.* the ship] into stone and caused her to take root below, driving down and pressing with his hand"), where Poseidon firmly roots the Phaeacian ship delivering Odysseus to Ithaca in the sea, and it thus becomes an island.

36. ἄφετος: wandering freely, but also with the sense of dedicated to a deity; cf. Eur. *Ion* 822, Pl. *Critias* 119d7. For unstable islands see Pliny *HN* 2.209; Hopkinson 1985: 251 suggests that Callimachus may have included the topic in his *Paradoxa*.

37. Ἀστερίη: readers learn that the original name of the island was Asteria, because "like a star" she leapt from heaven to avoid Zeus's advances. In Hesiod (*Th.* 409, and see West ad loc.) she is Leto's sister, though Callimachus (and Pindar?) makes nothing of the relationship. At the time of Apollo's birth her name is changed to Delos (= "bright," "conspicuous"). Delos, in fact, had many names including Ortygia. For the etymology of Asteria see Pindar fr. 33c S-M (above, pp. 160–61) and Bing 1988: 100–109.

βαθύν: for βαθεῖαν; Callimachus treats this as a two-termination adjective here, but cf. *hArt* 180.

ἥλαο: from ἅλλομαι, "leap." This equivalent of epic ἅλσο is found only in Callimachus—here and at *Aet.* fr. 37.3 Pf. (where Athena leapt from the head of her father). The verb occurs elsewhere in the hymns only at *hArt* 195 of Britomartis leaping into the sea to escape Minos' advances.

τάφρον: trench or ditch; frequent in Homer. Here unusually for the sea itself or possibly for a strait between two islands in the sea (Wilamowitz *HD* 2.65).

39–40. τόφρα... τόφρα: the usual correspondence would be ὄφρα... τόφρα. Either the first τόφρα is the equivalent of ὄφρα or both are adverbial: "until then... then").

41–50. This long, convoluted period mirrors the island's wandering in the course of one day. The island (σε) slowly recedes as sailors running from Troezen to Ephyra within the Saronic gulf first see her; by the time they return she is gone. Lines 42–43 (ἐρχόμενοι Ἐφύρηνδε...ἐξ Ἐφύρης ἀνιόντες) mark the predictable route of the sailors as they come and return; in contrast the island's course seems haphazard. She might run east from the strait of Euripus, and slightly south towards Cape Sounion, then across the Ionian sea to Chios, Samos (Parthenia), and Mykale (opposite Samos on the Turkish mainland)—all on the same day (lines 44–50). There she is the guest of nymphs of Mykale (lines 49–50).

41. πολλάκι σε Τροιζῆνος ἀπὸ †ξάνθοιο πολίχνης: of the two textual problems here, the first is that the mss. read πολλάκις ἐκ, with the marginal correction to πολλάκι σ' ἐκ in **T**. Editors have objected to two prepositions (ἐκ...ἀπὸ) and normally follow Reiske's correction to πολλάκι σε (the corruption of σε into ἐκ would have been easy).

ἀπὸ †ξάνθοιο is more complex: the mss. show an accent on α, which should rule out a form of the adjective ξανθός, though Mair and Mineur accept the adjective. Meineke emended to ζαθέοιο ("sacred"). Others (Giangrande, Ruhnken, Mineur) accept πολλάκις ἐκ and limit the corruption to ἀποξάνθοιο, the best solution for which is Ruhnken's ἁλιξάντοιο, "sea-swept." The second line of repair, following the scholiast, who understood as "Xanthus, a king of Troezen," is to take this as a proper name (so D'Alessio), though this Xanthus is otherwise unattested. Lehnus 2000 provides good support for an earlier conjecture of Schneider's (1.263–65): ἀπὲξ Ἄνθαο (or Ἄνθοιο); Anthes was the founder of the nearby Antheia, which was united with Troezen under Pittheus, the grandfather of Theseus. Anthes from Troezen is mentioned in Steph. Byz. (s.v. Ἁλικαρνασσός) in a context attributed to Callimachus (fr. 703 Pf.). This reading requires emendation to ἀπέξ, a very rare form, though attested in Quintus of Smyrna 4.540 and as a ms. variant at HhAp 110. The phrase would then mean: "out from Troezen, Anthes' town." This seems the best solution, though it does not have the ring of inevitability.

Τροιζῆνος: the city of Troezen was on the coast in the northeastern Peloponnese; it was the birthplace of Theseus, whose mother, Aethra, was the daughter of Pittheus, the king of Troezen.

πολίχνης: common in prose, a "small town"; as a proper name it appears in Hdt. 6.26.11 and Thuc. 8.14.3.

42. Ἐφύρηνδε: Ephyra was an ancient name for Corinth. As Mineur points out, according to Eumelus' Corinthiaca (fr. 1 Bernabé = sch. A.R. 4.1212–14b), Ephyra was the daughter of Ocean and Tethys, and thus Asteria's cousin.

Σαρωνικοῦ... κόλπου: the Saronic gulf is a region of the northern Aegean that falls between Aegina and the isthmus of Corinth. The sailors follow the inner Saronic gulf in a northwesterly direction from Troezen to Corinth and back.

43. ἐπεσκέψαντο: the sailors would have been able to see the island as she moved from Cape Sounion to Ceos; when they returned from Corinth, she must have moved on to Samos.

44. ὀξύν: here referring to the swiftness of the currents through the strait (see LSJ s.v. ὀξύς IV).

45. Εὐρίποιο: the narrow strait that divides Euboea from Boeotia. Also at hArt 188.

καναχηδὰ ῥέοντος: for the phrase see Hes. Th. 367, where it describes the "loud sounding" rivers who are the sons of Ocean (cf. A.R. 3.71 of the Anaurus).

46. Χαλκιδικῆς: according to the scholiast, this is not the peninsula, but Chalkis in Euboea, near the mouth of the strait of Euripus.

ἀνηναμένη: aorist middle participle from ἀναίνομαι. Here with the sense of "turning away from," because the straits were far too small for an island to pass through. But the verb also has the connotation of refusing sexual favors, and coupled with the alternative name of Parthenia for Samos in line 49, this may be an implicit reminder of Asteria's rejection of Zeus's advances.

47. μέσφ' ἐς: the combination is unique, though examples of μέσφα with a preposition denoting motion towards (ἐπί, παρά, ποτί) are found in the Hellenistic period. Str. 8.3.10 quotes Il. 11.756 with μέσφ' ἐπί (in place of the standard reading of ὄφρ' ἐπί), and see Aratus 599, AP 12.97.

προσενήξαο: the compound προσνήχομαι ("swim towards") is found in later prose, but in poetry only here and [Theoc.] 21.18.

Σούνιον ἄκρον: Cape Sounion was the southernmost tip of Attica, with a prominent temple to Poseidon. (Brauron, the site sacred to Artemis, is close by.)

48. Χίον: the island of Chios lies off of the Turkish coastline between Lesbos (north) and Samos (south).

νήσοιο διάβροχον ὕδατι μαστόν: literally, "the breast of the island inundated with water." Land as a nurturing breast is first found in Pi. *Pyth* 4.8, where Battus is told to found his colony and it will be nurtured by the shimmering breast of Libya. That passage is imitated at A.R. 4.1734, where Euphemus nurtures a clod of earth at his own breast. The clod, when thrown into the sea, becomes Thera. In this passage, μαστόν portends Asteria's role as the future nurse of Apollo, as another island, Cos, will become the future nurse of Ptolemy II. Islands emerging from waters (upon which gods are born) are an important feature of Egyptian cosmology, to which the phrase διάβροχον ὕδατι is likely to refer (see Stephens 2008: 111–13). The connection of Apollo's birth and the Nile flood is explicit in 206–8.

49. Παρθενίης: Parthenia was the earlier name of Samos, and the river Imbrasus was called Parthenius (fr. 599 Pf.: ἀντὶ γὰρ ἐκλήθης Ἴμβρασε Παρθενίου, from the scholia on A.R. 2.866). One of Artemis' titles in *hArt* 228 is Ἰμβρασίη.

50. A four-word spondaic line ends the section.

Ἀγκαίου: a king of Samos and one of the crew of the Argo (A.R. 2.865).

Μυκαλησσίδες: the nymphs of Mykale, a mountain in Caria opposite Samos. They are not otherwise attested. However, Μυκαλησσός (see Paus. 1.23.3) was a city in Boeotia (the area from which Asteria had swum) mentioned at *HhAp* 224. This is probably another of Callimachus' deliberate geographic misprisions.

51. γενέθλιον: here probably "for his birth"; cf. 262, where the olive shoot is described as γενέθλιον. In *Iamb*. 12, fr. 202.21 Pf. it refers to a birthday present.

52. ἀντημοιβόν: the adjective is found only here in Callimachus, but ἀνταμείβομαι, "exchange one thing for another," is well attested.

ἁλίπλοοι: cf. Pindar fr. 52h.48 S-M: καλέοντί μιν Ὀρτυγίαν ναῦται πάλαι ("sailors of old call her Ortygia").

53. In exchange for giving Apollo a place to be born, Asteria is no longer ἄδηλος, or inconspicuous, but receives the name of Δῆλος—"clear," "visible." The name is apt for Asteria's brief life as a star and for her new role as the birthplace of the Sun. The idea is implicit already in Pindar, fr. 52h.47 S-M: εὐαγέα πέτραν φανῆναι (see p. 159), sch. A.R. 1.308 (and see Bing 1988: 101–3).

54. ποδῶν ... ῥίζας "roots of your feet," i.e., your feet as roots.

55–69. The wrath of Hera prevents Leto from giving birth. Hera's anger is a feature of *HhAp* 91–101, and it also seems to have appeared in Antimachus' *Lyde* (see Matthews 1996: 259–62).

55. οὐδ' ... κοτέουσαν ὑπέτρεσας: the participle and the verb emphasize the heroic quality of the island; in Homer the former is used for divine anger (e.g., *Il.* 23. 391), the latter of trembling before the enemy.

56. ἐπεβρωμᾶτο: a Callimachean *hapax*. βρωμάομαι occurs at Ar. *Vespae* 618 of a braying ass and in Arist. *HA* 579a of a bellowing stag. There have been attempts to emend to a form of ἐπιβριμάομαι, which according to Hesychius means to "be angry at," but it is also possible that the verb reflects metapoetic play. Callimachus' poetic enemies bray like asses in the *Aetia* prologue (fr. 1.30–31 Pf.); if Bing's argument (1988: 94–96) that Delos represents Callimachus' poetry is correct, then Hera, like the Telchines of the prologue, may be figured as a "braying" enemy.

λεχωΐσιν: cf. *hArt* 127 and below 124.

57. διακριδόν: adverb, "distinctly" or "especially"; twice in Homer (*Il.* 12.103, 15.108, the phrase is the same), then A.R. and later hexameter poets. PBodl's διάκριτον, "preeminently," also has merit as a reading (it occurs in Posidippus 85.1 A-B and Theoc. 22.163).

58. ἤμελλε: the double augment on ἤμελλε occurs already in Hesiod and Theognis and becomes common after the fourth century. For the following aorist, see Hes. *Th.* 478: ἤμελλε τεκέσθαι (of Zeus's birth) and West ad loc.

φιλαίτερον: this irregular comparative form of φίλος occurs first in Xenophon (*Anab.* 1.9.29), then in Hellenistic poetry. See Theoc. 7.98, Philitas fr. 23.3c Spanoudakis.

Ἄρεος υἷα (= υἱόν): Ares was Hera's son from Zeus. Commentators have long suspected that the competition of the two "wives" and their sons reflected contemporary politics, since the sons of Ptolemy I by his earlier wife, Eurydice, were passed over in favor of his son (Ptolemy II) by Berenice I (also see 78n).

59. τῷ ῥα καί: the phrase occurs four times in Homer, twice of tensions between the siblings Poseidon and Zeus. It occurs again at *hArt* 251 of Lygdamis' threats against Ephesus.

61. εἴατο: third plural epic imperfect of ἧμαι.

φρουροί "guards"; found in Euripides, but mainly prose.

62–67. Hera sets her two henchmen—Ares and Iris—to watch over the mainland and the islands to prevent Leto from finding a resting place. These lines are constructed as parallels (and both with spondaic endings): Ares (ὁ μὲν...ἥμενος) observes the land (πέδον ἠπείροιο), Iris (ἡ δ'...ἧστο) the islands (ἐπὶ νησάων... αἰπειάων).

63. Θρήϊκος Αἵμου: the Haemus range spanned northern Thrace, from the Adriatic to the Euxine sea. Mt. Haemus was said to be its highest point (cf. *hArt* 114). For Ares and Thrace, cf. *Il.* 5. 460–62, *Od.* 8.361.

64. θοῦρος Ἄρης: a Homeric formula found either in nominative or accusative (see, e.g., *Il.* 5.30, 35, 507), "furious," "rushing Ares."

τὼ...ἵππω: the dual is found only three times in the hymns: here, *hArt* 207 (hunting dogs) and *hAth* 70 (Athena and Chariclo).

65. ἑπτάμυχον...σπέος: the cave of the North wind, with "seven recesses" (cf. the Minotaur's lair, 311). According to the *Suda* (s.v. Φερεκύδης) Pherecydes of Syrus wrote a cosmogonic history entitled: Ἑπτάμυχος ἤτοι Θεοκρασία ἢ Θεογονία (*Heptamuchos, or Divine Mingling or Theogony*, on which see Schibli

1990: 14–26). Given the rarity of the word, Callimachus is likely to be alluding to Pherecydes, possibly as a reminder that we are in primordial time, before the coming of Apollo.

66. ἐπί: the grammatical function of ἐπί has been questioned: (1) Pfeiffer understood it to be in tmesis with ἧστο; (2) Giangrande (1967: 153–4) takes as a rare example of a noun in tmesis playing on Homeric ἐπίσκοπος; and (3) Mineur argues for Schneider's interpretation of ἡ…ἐπὶ νησάων reminiscent of a title, translating as "set over the islands." The last gives the best sense.

νησάων: the form is unique to Callimachus (here, at 275, and fr. 67.8 Pf.); ancient as well as modern scholars have suspected the form because νῆσος is not an α-stem (though similarly formed genitives are attested in epic). Mineur suggests the influence of *Od.* 14.199: Κρητάων… εὐρειάων.

αἰπειάων: the medieval mss. read εὐρειάων; PBodl apparently αἰπειάων. The former occurs twice, at *Od.* 14.199, 16.62 (of Crete); for the latter see *Od.* 3.293 and Α.R. 1.936 (with νῆσος). Both give acceptable sense: either Iris sits on Mt. Mimas where she can observe the islands far-reaching (εὐρειάων) on either side or the islands are described as αἰπειάων, "steep." The papyrus reading has the edge, since it also conveys their inhospitable terrain (see Giuseppetti 2007: 53).

67. κόρη Θαύμαντος: according to the scholiast, Iris was the "daughter of Thaumas" (also in Hes. *Th.* 780). Since Thaumas had more than one daughter (including the Harpies), Mineur suggests that the ambiguous phrase is meant momentarily to deceive the reader, since her name does not occur until 157 (see below).

Μίμαντι: a promontory in Asia Minor lying opposite the island of Chios (again at 157, and cf. *hDem* 91).

69. μίμνον: poetic; the form provides an etymology for the name of the mountain: where "they remained."

ἀπειλητῆρες: *hapax* in Homer, *Il.* 7.96, with the meaning of "braggart"; here the sense is those who make threats. After Callimachus, imitated especially by Nonnus.

ἀπετρώπων: from ἀποτρωπάω, a frequentative of ἀποτρέπω; for the construction with an infinitive, see *Il.* 18.585; here "they were deterring [*sc.* the cities] from receiving [*sc.* Leto]."

70–72. φεῦγε μὲν … φεῦγεν δ᾽ | … φεῦγεν δ᾽ | … φεῦγε δ᾽: the repetition of the simple verb at the beginning of four clauses mimics the effect and the urgency of Leto's plight as each place she approaches flees before her. The repeated verbs also personify the locations—blurring the distinction between a locality and its nymph or associated divinity.

70–71. ὄρος ἱερὸν … | Παρθένιον: Parthenion was a mountain sacred to Athena in the region between Arcadia and the Argolid.

70. Αὔγης: Auge was the daughter of Aleus, the king of Tegea, and a priestess of Athena. She bore Telephus to Heracles on Mt. Parthenion. Since this was against her father's will (and a subject for tragedy—Euripides' *Auge* and *Telephus*) it serves as a parallel for Leto. Also there is an implicit joke in giving birth on "Virgin mountain."

71. This line atypically contains both penthemimeral and hepthemimeral caesurae, and elision at the caesura, which caused Maas (1956: 23) to question it, but the effect may be deliberate— the double caesurae conveying the halting steps of the old man.

μετόπισθε: characteristic of a slow old man.

Φενειός: Arnaldus' correction of the mss., but the reading remains problematic. According to the scholiast, a city in Arcadia, in which case, it should be a variant of Φενεός (attested at Paus. 8.13.6). But γέρων requires a personification; the preferred solution is to understand the form -ειός as referring to a river and a doublet for the city (cf. e.g., Ἀλφεός, Ἀλφειός); alternatively with γέρων referring to the city's founder, whom Pausanias (8.14.4) calls Φενεός and describes as an autochthon.

72. Πελοπηΐς (*sc.* γῆ): not the whole Peloponnese, but the Argolid, as the qualifying phrase (ὅση etc.) makes clear.

73. ἔμπλην: a strengthend form of πλήν, here with the following genitives. The use is post-Homeric.

Αἰγιαλοῦ: according to Pausanias (7.1.1), Aegialus was the region between Elis and Sicyonia, now called Achaea, but originally named for Aegialeus, and the people Aegialians (cf. *Il.* 2.575, from the catalogue of ships). Aegialeus was a son of Inachus in some Argive genealogies (see Hall 1997: 83–88, especially 85).

Ἄργεος: the city of Argos was sacred to Hera; hence Leto avoids it.

74. ἀτραπιτούς "paths," cf. *HhAp* 227–28, and see Chantraine *DE* s.v. ἀτραπός. Leto's avoidance of trodden paths parallels Callimachus' expressed poetics (see *Aet.* fr. 1.25–28 Pf.).

ἐπεὶ λάχεν … Ἥρη: for Argos as Hera's allotment, see *Aet.* fr. 55.2 with Harder ad loc. For divine allotments elsewhere in the hymns, see *hZeus* 62–64, *hAp* 43, *hArt* 22–23, and 97 below.

Ἴναχον: the Inachus was the main river in the Argolid. He was personified in myth and was said to have been the first king of Argos. For his genealogy and the importance of the line for the Ptolemies, see p. 238.

75–80. φεῦγε resumes the flight of islands and territories, begun in 70–72, as they run from Leto. The narrative turns to Boeotia and presents a three-generational portrait of flight: Dirce and Strophie clutching the hands of their father Ismenus, with his father Asopus tottering after on aged knees.

75. Ἀονίη: a name for Boeotia, not attested before Callimachus (see also fr. 572 Pf.); citing Statius (*Theb.* 9.95 for the patronymic Aonides), Mineur ad loc. suspects the source may have been Antimachus' *Thebaid.*

τὸν ἕνα δρόμον: ἕνα here with the meaning of "same" (LSJ s.v. εἷς 2).

76. Δίρκη: here Dirce seems to be a river, though a spring near Thebes was also so named. According to Eur. *Bacch.* 519–33, another son of Zeus (Dionysus) was washed in the Dirce after being taken from Semele's scorched body (she had asked Zeus to appear to her with his thunderbolt, the power of which destroyed her). The chorus asks Dirce: τί με φεύγεις; (533). For Theban Dirce in myth, see Berman 2007.

Στροφίη: otherwise unknown, but with its στροφ- root, "winding," is a good name for a river.

μελαμψήφιδος "black-pebbled," see *hArt* 101n.

77. Ἰσμηνοῦ: the Ismenus was the central river in Thebes, either a son of Asopus (Apollod. 3.12.6) or of Apollo and Melia (Pi. *Py.* 11.4, Paus. 9.10). Pindar's first hymn (fr. 29 S-M), written for Thebes, begins: Ἰσμηνὸν ἢ χρυσαλάκατον Μελίαν, "[Shall we hymn] Ismenus or Melia, with her golden spindle." (Melia is named at 80 below.) By including these names and locations from Pindar's hymn (and *Py.* 11) Callimachus recalls his predecessor, but implicitly requires different genealogies, since Apollo is yet to be born.

78. Ἀσωπός: there were several rivers so named, but this Boeotian river and another near Sicyon were the most famous (and their respective myths were often conflated or confused). According to the scholiast ad loc., the Asopus was struck by a thunderbolt when he pursued Zeus, who was carrying off his daughter Aegina. (Apollod. 3.12.6 tells the same story of the homonymous river in Sicyon.)

βαρύγουνος: Asopus' "knees are heavy" either from old age (see 75–80n) or because his waters were made turbid when struck by a thunderbolt. The word occurs both here and at Theoc. 18.10 and is later imitated by Nonnus.

πεπάλακτο: unaugmented pluperfect from παλάσσω, the normal meaning of which in the passive is "be bespattered" or "defiled" (e.g., *hAth* 7, *Od.* 22.402). If this is correct, the waters were made turbulent by the lightning strike, thus impeding the river's flight; this interpretation stresses the effect of lightning on the Asopus as a river, not the river's personification. Alternatively some editors have assumed that it is here the equivalent of ἐπέπληκτο (πλήσσω), "struck" as at *Il.* 8.455: πληγέντε κεραυνῷ (the meaning accepted by LSJ s.v. παλάσσω II). Mineur ad loc. prefers Naber's emendation (1906: 234) to πεπάτακτο, from πατάσσω = strike. The ambiguity may be deliberate (see Rengakos 1992: 43). It is also possible that these peculiar details allude to the victory of Ptolemy Ceraunus ("Thunderbolt") over Antigonus Gonatas (= "Knees") in 281 BCE (see Mineur ad loc.).

79. ὑποδινηθεῖσα: only here as a compound. The scholiast glosses as "quivering" or "being shaken"; either she is shaking in fear or because the mountain shook under her feet (82) (*pace* LSJ s.v. ὑποδινέομαι, who define as "becomes dizzy").

χοροῦ ἀπεπαύσατο: the effect of hiatus is metrically to stop the dance.

80. αὐτόχθων Μελίη: Melia, a daughter of Ocean, was beloved of Apollo and associated with his Theban sanctuary (see above 76–77), though here she seems to have been an indigenous tree-nymph (see Hes. *Th.* 187). Callimachus mentions the Meliae at *hZeus* 47, Ash-tree nymphs associated with Crete. Cf. fr. 598 Pf. = sch. A.R. 2.4.

ὑπόχλοον: a unique Callimachean variant of ὑπόχλωρον, "greenish," "pale."

81. ἥλικος: the Hamadryads were born at the same time as their tree (see 82n).

ἀσθμαίνουσα: the verb means "panting for breath" (as at 217 of Iris), and may also be used for the gasps of the dying (as at *HhAp* 359). Here the nymph pants in fear at the fate of her tree; but because she is coeval with her tree ἀσθμαίνουσα may also include the second sense.

δρυός: originally δρῦς seems to have had the broader meaning of "tree," but later came to be applied specifically to oaks. Since nymphs were associated with a variety of trees, Callimachus must be using δρῦς in its generic sense.

χαίτην: cf. *hArt* 41n.

82–83. Lobel (and noted in Pfeiffer's apparatus) posits the omission of 83 in POxy 2225 with the substitution of an unattested line reading]χωδεση.[; upon inspecting the papyrus I find the trace after η fits ν; thus εσην might belong to δρύ]ες ἥν[ικα of 83. The traces before are broken, but might fit]κων[. Possibly the scribe copied σειομενηνελι]κων from line 82 again, then either corrected himself or dropped his eye to finish with the end of 83: εςην[ικανυμφαι.

82. σειομένην Ἑλικῶνος: Mt. Helicon's hair (= head) shakes either because he is refusing refuge to Leto or because he too is fleeing (so McKay 1962a: 177). Gigante Lanzara ad loc. suggests that, insofar as Helicon was the traditional seat of the Muses, the shaking leaves were meant to register disquiet at the regional rejection of Apollo.

ἐμαὶ θεαὶ εἴπατε Μοῦσαι: Muses are normally invoked at the beginning of a hymn (or other poem) in a request for inspiration or assistance in singing the appropriate song. But here Callimachus interrupts his narrative in a manner that is not unlike his encounter with the Muses in the *Aetia*, where after being transported to Helicon in a dream he asks them a series of questions (see, e.g., fr. 7 Pf. or fr. 43.46–55 Pf.). The proximate cause for the interruption is Leto moving past the Muses' mountain (Helicon), but the effect is as if the poet were in motion as well. The question (like the allusions to Asopus, Ismenus, and Melia) foregrounds the competing versions of local myths and raises issues of truth/falsity that were embedded in poetic discourse as early as Hesiod's *Theogony*. Some poetic sources treat the Dryads and Hamadryads as coeval with their trees (*HhAphr* 264–72, Pi. fr. 165 S-M, A.R. 2.477–80), others like Plutarch (*De def. or.* 415C-D), quoting Hesiod (fr. 304 M-W) in contrast to Pindar (fr. 165 S-M), claim that nymphs lived much longer. Bing 1988: 40–44 suggests this is a textual response to oral poetic traditions. Of course, competing traditions are already built into the Homeric hymns (see, e.g., the opening of the *HhDion*), but what Callimachus desires for his poetry in *hZeus* 65 ("may I tell more plausible fictions") becomes increasingly critical in an enviroment where the truth-claims of philosophy and history were competing with the traditional role of the poets.

83. ἤ ῥ᾽ ἐτεόν: the sequence is first attested here and may have been used elsewhere in Callimachus, since it also occurs at *AP* 7.42.2, an epigram on Callimachus' *Aetia*. Elsewhere only in Gregory of Nazianzus. Hesychius glosses as ὄντως ἀληθῶς.

δρύες ἡνίκα Νύμφαι: see above 81.

84–85. Pfeiffer, following Wilamowitz (*HD* 2.67), treats these lines as a response of the Muses, though *hZeus* 7 suggests that the identification of the respondent, if there is one, is deliberately ambiguous. The formal shape of the lines, in which the pleasure or sorrow of the nymphs is directly dependent on the growth or loss of their tree, suggests a poetic answer that is not rational but an exercise in linguistic sympathetic magic. (M. Fantuzzi compares Theoc. 8.33–40 for a similar incantatory effect on the growth of herds.) Both lines have 15 syllables and the same word breaks; Νύμφαι μέν responds to Νύμφαι δ᾽ αὖ; the two verbs are equal in number of syllables and similar in sound; the temporal clauses both begin with an oblique case of δρῦς. (See Bing 1988: 41–43, following McKay 1962a: 117.)

85. μηκέτι: this reading of POxy 2225 (for οὐκέτι of the medieval mss.) is preferable for a generalizing statement.

86–99. Apollo's first prophecy from the womb is addressed to Thebe (the eponymous nymph of Thebes). It begins with his baroque description of the Pytho at Delphi before he kills it, followed by a prophecy on the destruction of Niobe's children. Niobe was the daughter of Tantalus and married to Amphion, the king of Thebes. She had seven sons and seven daughters and boasted therefore that she surpassed Leto, who had only one of each. Apollo and Artemis subsequently killed all fourteen of her children (see *LIMC*, s.v. Apollo 1172–79). She fled to Mt. Sipylon in Asia Minor; in pity for her unquenchable lamentations, the gods turned her into a weeping rock. Callimachus alludes to the story at the opening of *hAp* 22–24.

86. ὑποκόλπιος: Meiller 1979: 314n82 suggests an allusion to Herophilus' theory of fetal position. One of Apollo's titles was *Delphinius*, which was connected, among other things, with δελφύς, "womb."

αἰνά "exceedingly," the neuter plural as an adverb occurs four times in Homer, twice (*Il.* 1.414, 22.431) in the context of mothers and sons. It is common with verbs of anger (as here) or mourning.

87. ἐπὶ Θήβῃ: Thebe was another daughter of Asopus (Pi. *Is.* 8.16a-20, Bacchyl. 9.53–54) and the wife of Amphion's brother Zethus, hence Thebe and Niobe were sisters-in-law.

88. "Why, wretch, do you put to the proof your coming destiny?" Apollo's prenatal speech is startling enough, but it is apparently addressed to one of the nymphs/landscape passing by in flight.

τὸν αὐτίκα πότμον: the scholiast glosses τὸν ἐσόμενόν σοι πότμον. Thebes had so many doomed moments in its myth-history (e.g., the death of Pentheus at the hand of his own mother, Oedipus, and his sons' undying enmity that led to war) that Apollo needs the adverb αὐτίκα to clarify: the death of Niobe's children is the immediate disaster that Thebes will now endure.

89. μήπω μή μ᾿ ἀέκοντα βιάζεο μαντεύεσθαι: cf. *Od.* 21.348. Note the solemnity of spondaic beginnings of 89–90 and the spondaic ending of μαντεύεσθαι, the sounds, μή... μή, μ᾿ ἀέ..., μα-, and the anaphora of οὐ- at 90–91. These effects reinforce Apollo's reluctance to utter prophecies.

90. τριποδήϊος: an epicizing form in -ήϊος, common in the Hellenistic period (see Schmitt 42–43). With ἕδρη Mineur ad loc. suggests parallels from tragedy (Eur. *Ion* 130: μαντεῖον ἕδραν) and lyric (Pi. *Ol.* 5.8: νέοικον ἕδραν). Apollo's "tripodial" seat at Delphi was the locus from which the priestess uttered her prophecies.

91. ὄφις μέγας: cf. *hAp* 101; the beast is masculine in this hymn, but feminine in *HhAp* 300. Since he speaks from the womb, Apollo's prophecy asserts the temporal priority of Callimachus' hymn over the Homeric hymn.

92. αἰνογένειον "with dire jaws," a *hapax* in Callimachus.

Πλειστοῖο: the Pleistus was a small river near Parnassus that flowed below Delphi (Paus. 10.8.8, sch. A.R. 2.711).

καθέρπον: neuter participle with θηρίον. Best taken not as "creeping down" but as "stretching down" (so Mineur ad loc.).

93. Παρνησόν: Mt. Parnassus is in central Greece above the Corinthian gulf; it sits above Delphi and was also sacred to Apollo. Callimachus imagines the snake as sufficiently long to stretch down the length of the mountain and encircle Delphi with its coils.

ἐννέα κύκλοις: Statius *Theb.* 1.563–65 mentions a snake with seven coils. Dion. Per. 441–43 (see Lightfoot 2014: 362–63) and Menander Rhetor 2.441 (Russell and Wilson 1981: 214–15) talk of a dragon that obscured Parnassus with its coils, but a pre-Callimachean source is not attested.

94. ἐρέω: Apollo returns to his main point.

τομώτερον: τομός means "sharp" or "cutting," which has occasioned concern in this passage. The sense must be that Apollo will say something less ambiguous, "sharper" in meaning than his later Delphic prophecies will be. PBodl has the marginal note: τορώτατον, "most clearly," whether a gloss or an alternative reading cannot be ascertained (see Giuseppetti 2007: 54–55).

ἀπὸ δάφνης "from the laurel" is the equivalent of "from the tripod," Delphi's prophetic center; cf. *HhAp* 396: χρείων ἐκ δάφνης.

95. ταχινός: also of Zeus's swift growth to maturity (*hZeus* 56n).

95–96. αἵματι λούσων | τόξον ἐμόν "washing my bow with blood." The thought has occasioned concern; washing one's arrow in the enemy's blood is attested, but not the bow; most explain τόξον as a metonym for arrow (for which there are no parallels), though at *Il.* 21.502 Homer uses τόξα for bow and arrows.

96. κακογλώσσοιο γυναικός: Niobe, see 86–99n. Legrand (1894: 276) was the first to suggest that Niobe and her children were an allusion to Ptolemy II's historical circumstances. His first wife was Arsinoe I, probably the daughter of Lysimachus of Thrace and the mother of Ptolemy III and several other children. She was banished around 276 to Coptus in the Thebaid on the grounds that she had conspired against her husband (she died there in 247). If the hymn was composed around 275, her banishment will have been a recent event. However, the parallel can only be partial: her children seem not to have suffered any adverse effects from their mother's disgrace.

97. ἔλλαχες: with double λ first in *HhDem* 86–87 (of Aidoneus receiving Hades by lot, a version of the distribution of powers that Callimachus explicitly denies in *hZeus* 63–64); then frequent in Hellenistic poetry.

Κιθαιρών: Apollo killed Niobe's sons on Mt. Cithaeron, and Pentheus was killed by his mother and aunts in the same location.

98. εὐαγέων δὲ καὶ εὐαγέεσσι μελυίμην: a variant of Theoc. 26.30: αὐτὸς δ' εὐαγέοιμι καὶ εὐαγέεσσιν ἄδοιμι ("May I be pure and be pleasing to the pure"). Though priority cannot be established, the passages are clearly related. *Idyll* 26 is a brief narrative of the death of Pentheus as merited for his opposition to Dionysus. Since Dionysus was claimed as a divine ancestor of the Ptolemies, especially prominent in the Grand Procession, scholars have been tempted to see some contemporary event behind the poem. That impression is strengthened by Callimachus' passage, which also seems to allude to recent events, though to what exactly remains obscure (see F. Griffiths 1979: 101–5). The optative without ἄν expresses a wish (Smyth §1814). See *hAp* 26–7, *hArt* 136–37.

99. μετάτροπος: Leto reverses direction. The word is rare before Callimachus—once in Hesiod (*Th.* 89) and in drama, then much imitated by Nonnus.

100. ἀπηρνήσαντο: here middle with active sense and construed with an accusative of person, "refuse," "reject"; ἀρνέομαι occurs in Homer, but this compound is first attested in tragedy and comedy (usually in passive with active sense). Also at *hDem* 75, 106.

101–2. Helice was a coastal city of Achaea with a well-known cult of Poseidon (see, e.g., *Il.* 20.404, Paus. 7.24.5) and Bura, a bit further inland, was often linked with it, since both were destroyed by an earthquake and tidal wave in 373 BCE.

102. Δεξαμενοῖο … Οἰκιάδαο: Dexamenus was the son of Oeceus, the king of the city of Olenus in Achaea, who entertained Heracles at his court (Paus. 7.18.1, D.S. 4.33.1, Apollod. 2.5.5). A. Griffiths 1988: 231 points out the pun: "Dexamenos son of Oikeus brought in because Boura did not *receive* Leto in its *houses*?"

βοόστασις: an "ox-steading," previously in Aesch. *PV* 653, in a passage urging Io to go to an ox-steading where she would encounter Zeus and his amorous desires.

103–52. These lines detail Leto's encounter with the personified geography of Thessaly, its rivers, cities, and mountains. All of Thessaly flees from Leto, except for the river Peneius, who offers to let Leto give birth by his streams, despite the threats from Ares. But Leto herself takes pity on him and turns towards the coastline and the islands of the Aegean. The whole is suffused with tragic language, with Leto and Peneius constructed as characters ensnared in a tragic web. But the effect of the landscape running away from the pregnant woman is necessarily humorous, and the address to Peneius seems to invoke both tragic and comic traditions, see 112n.

103. ἂψ δ' ἐπί: previously only at *Il.* 17.543, where conflict resumes over the body of Patroclus.

103, 105 resume the earlier anaphora of φεῦγε δέ.

103. Ἄναυρος: a Thessalian river, over which Jason carried Hera when she was disguised as an old woman (see A.R. 3.67 and cf. 1.9). In contrast, see *hArt* 101n.

104. μεγάλη Λάρισα: Larisa was a fortified town on a tributary of the Peneius. It was the major city of the Pelasgiote district. Like Thebe, Larisa is the eponymous nymph. She was said to have been the daughter of Pelasgus.

αἱ Χειρωνίδες ἄκραι "the Cheironian heights," i.e., Mt. Pelion, where the nymph Philyra gave birth to the Centaur Chiron. After her liaison with Cronus, she had fled there in fear of Rhea. Cf. *HhAp* 33, and see 118n.

105. Πηνειός: the river god was the grandfather of Cyrene, the eponymous nymph who "marries" Apollo in *hAp*. This long and favorable account of the river who will risk his existence to aid Leto is set in contrast with Thebe in the previous episode.

ἑλισσόμενος: descriptive either of Peneius' flight or the course of his river or both.

Τεμπέων: Tempe (τὰ Τέμπη) is the valley that lies between Mt. Olympus and Mt. Ossa; the river Peneius flows through it (see Hdt. 7.173 and the long description in Aelian *VH* 3.1 and below 177b n).

106–8. The narrator first addresses Hera, the source of nature's hostility to Leto, as still implacable, then quickly sketches the scene, as Leto speaks, stretching out her hands in a gesture of supplication.

106. ἀνηλεές "pitiless"; the earliest occurrences of the form seem to be in Aeschines (*De falsa leg.* 163) and Menander (*Epitr.* 899).

107. κατεκλάσθης: passive from κατακλάω with the meaning "break down" or "degenerate." ἀνηλεές ἦτορ ... κατεκλάσθης seems to be a play on the Homeric formula: κατεκλάσθη φίλον ἦτορ ("my heart is broken"), see, e.g., *Od.* 4.538, 9.256.

109–20. Leto begins by supplicating the Thessalian nymphs, who are imagined as the children of the river, to intercede for her, then addresses Peneius himself, her unborn son (ὦ ἐμὸν ἄχθος), and finally Mt. Pelion.

110. μέγα χεῦμα: cf. *hZeus* 32.

περιπλέξασθε: here the aorist middle imperative of περιπλέκω, "entwine," "enfold," is construed with the dative, though the aorist passive is more common. Normally one touches the beard in supplication (see, e.g., *hArt* 26–28 and Herodas

Mim. 3.72 with Headlam's note) or embraces the knees (Timotheus *Pers.* 145–46). Callimachus seems to conflate the two, fittingly for a family of rivers or streams, whose "embrace" would require them to flow around each other.

γενείῳ: a common metonym for beard.

111. τὰ Ζηνὸς … τέκνα: the plural seems to indicate that Artemis has not yet been born, though see discussion at p. 102.

τέκνα τεκέσθαι: the *figura etymologica* occurs at *HhDem* 136 in the context of Demeter's wandering and at *Od.* 22.324.

112. Πηνειὲ Φθιῶτα: the line, with its epichoric vocative (Φθιῶτα) combined with a question, seems to have been modelled on a passage in Aeschylus' now fragmentary *Myrmidons*: Φθιῶτ' Ἀχιλλεῦ, τί ποτ' ἀνδροδάϊκτον ἀκούων, "Phthian Achilles, why when hearing of the slaughter of men" (*TrGF* 3 fr. 132.1 Radt). "Euripides" quotes the line in Ar. *Ran.* 1264–65, adding the tag: οὐ πελαθεὶς ἐπ' ἀρωγάν; ("not drawing near for the rescue?"), which suggests that it was very well known.

τί νῦν ἀνέμοισιν ἐρίζεις: the river flees so quickly that he appears to be "competing" against the winds (cf. *Il.* 10.437: θείειν δ' ἀνέμοισιν ὁμοῖοι, of Rhesus' horses). Another joke: according to Aelian (*VH* 3.1), the Peneius normally flowed slowly "like olive oil."

113. ὦ πάτερ: a term of respect; elsewhere in the hymns the vocative is used only for Zeus (*hZeus* 7, 43, 94; *hArt* 8). It is a reminder to Peneius that he too is a parent.

ἀμφιβέβηκας: the unseemliness of the river's haste is likened to one riding in a horse race.

114. πόδες: Mineur suspects a pun, since πούς refers to the mouth of a river at fr. 384.48 Pf.

115. μοῦνον: the mss. read μοῦνοι, but the sense demands not "your feet alone" but "only in my case."

ἐλαφρίζουσι: from ἐλαφρίζω, "lighten," "lift up." Before Callimachus, attested in Archilochus (*IEG*² fr. 176) a and fragment of Euripides' *Meleager* (*TrGF* 5.1 fr. 530.8 Kannicht), and much imitated by Nonnus and later Greek poets.

πεποίησαι: best taken as transitive with πόδας understood; "you have made (your feet) to fly."

116. ὁ δ' ἀνήκοος: either part of Leto's speech, as a concession of despair, or an interjection of the narrator. See above 82–85 for the narrator's question and the response. In general, ambiguity of voice is a persistent feature of these hymns (see pp. 28–29).

117. ἀπειρήκασι: from ἀπεῖπον, "refuse," but with body parts, "sink in exhaustion"; see, e.g., Eur. *Hipp.* 1353.

τένοντες: here, "tendons" of the foot or ankle.

118. νυμφήϊον: epicizing form of νυμφεῖον, first here, then Moschus *Eur.* 159, and Nonnus; the usual meaning is "bridal chamber," but since Philyra was delivered of Chiron on Mt. Pelion (see above 104n), Kuiper suggested the sense should be "delivery room," as a sly comment on Homeric νύμφη τέκε (e.g., *Il.* 14.444, 20.384) and the frequent pregnancies of nymphs; νυμφεῖον as a substantive occurs first in Soph. *Ant.* 891, 1205.

118–19. μεῖνον | μεῖνον: the doubling of the imperatives, like the vocatives, is a mark of tragic style.

120. ὠμοτόκους: the compound is first found in Callimachus, here of birth pangs (ὠδῖνας), but at *hDem* 52 of the lioness herself (on which see Hopkinson's detailed note). The meaning is disputed especially since there should be a correlation between the lioness and Leto. Later the adjective refers to "premature birth" (Soranus 3.47), which does not seem applicable to a Leto well past her due date. Alternatively the adjective refers to a lioness's difficult parturition: Hdt. 3.108 claims that the cubs damaged the uterus at birth; alternatively the newborn cubs were small and blind at birth (Arist. *HA* 579b2, Ael. *NA* 4.34). The last may be the sense here, with the idea that Mt. Pelion in the past has provided shelter for lionesses which, after giving birth, will need protection to nurture their cubs. The sense will then be "the lioness deposited the raw fruits of her labor." Other potential points of comparison for a lioness in this location include Thetis and Cyrene. The former had the ability to tranform herself into a lion. Peleus subdued her on Mt. Pelion in Pi. *Nem.* 4.62–65. Cyrene, Peneius' granddaughter, defeated a Thessalian lion, cf. Pi. *Py.* 9. 1–30. For giving birth in wild, secret places, see *hZeus* 10–14.

ἀπηρείσαντο: the compound ἀπερείδω occurs in Attic prose; here in the middle with the sense of "deposit" or "leave."

121. Peneius finally responds to Leto's plea *cum* accusation, shedding tears as he does so, emphasizing the dynamic between the anthropomorphized and actual river.

122–26. Peneius' agitation is reinforced by the meter; each line is enjambed with a break at the bucolic dieresis, four times with vowel against vowel to create the effect of gasping. When Peneius describes the threat to the flow of his waters (124–35), Hopkinson 1985: 251 notes an "elaborate word play, especially at line end" of words in -ρα, -ρει, -ρη, -ρο: Ἥρη, ἔφεδρος, ῥεῖα, ῥοάων, ἔρρειν, ἡρώησε, ῥόον, Ἄρης, ἀείρας, ῥέεθρα.

122. Ἀναγκαίη μεγάλη θεός: apparently a variant of the proverb: Ἀνάγκη οὐδὲ θεοὶ μάχονται (Zenobius 1.85, and cf. 3.9), and see Plato, *Laws* 741a3–4, 818b2–3.

123–24. Peneius replies that others have "washed their afterbirth in my waters." The reference is obscure unless to Creusa, who gave birth to Hypseus, the father of Cyrene. She was the "bride" of Peneius himself.

125. ἀπαύγασαι: aorist middle imperative from ἀπαυγάζω, "see at a distance." First here in Callimachus and again at 181 below, then in later Greek prose. (Forms of αὐγάζω occur at *hArt* 129 and *hDem* 4.)

126. The construction is epic; for κε(ν) with the optative in a relative clause, see Chantraine 2.249.

127. βυσσόθεν: the sense is either from the bottom of the riverbed or from the river's source, and in contrast to ἐξ ὑπάτου (126). Before Callimachus, only at Soph. *Ant.* 590, of ruin swelling from the deep to overtake a whole family.

τί μήσομαι: Peneius' questions are again tragic in style: see Soph. *Trach.* 973, Eur. *Hipp.* 593.

128. ἡδύ τι: construed with the infinitive as in tragedy.

ἴτω: editors are divided between contruing the third person imperative with πεπρωμένον ἦμαρ: "Let the fated day come" (so Wilamowitz, Pfeiffer, Mair, Mineur, Asper) or as independent: "Let it come" (so Meineke, Kuiper, D'Alessio, Gigante Lanzara). In the latter case, πεπρωμένον ἦμαρ will be the object of τλήσομαι.

πεπρωμένον: from aorist πορεῖν (no present); epic and tragic. See, e.g., Eur. *Alc.* 147.

130. διψαλέην: see *hZeus* 27n.

ἄμπωτιν "ebb," normally in prose, but once in Pi. *Ol.* 9.52 as the full form (ἀνάπωτιν) in the context of Zeus contriving an ebbtide after the flood that left only Deucalion and Pyrrha.

132. Peneius' speech ends with a spondaic line.

ἠνίδ(ε): an interjection ("here") frequent in Theocritus and found in Callimachus' epigrams, then imitated in later Greek, probably conveying the immediacy of spoken language.

τί περισσά (*sc.* ἐστί;): the expression is found earlier in an unassigned fragment of Euripides (*TrGF* 5.2 fr. 924 Kannicht: τί περισσὰ φρονεῖς;), and later in *AP* 7.335.

133. μέγαν ῥόον: μέγας ῥόος occurs at *hAp* 108 of the Assyrian river, but it is not clear if the phrase has programmatic force here as well.

134–47. The sequence begins with Ares about to hurl a mountaintop onto the river to staunch its flow, but he halts in order to sound his shield menacingly, at which all of Thessaly quakes. Lines 140–47 introduce a double simile: the quaking mountains are likened to the shaking induced when the Giant Briareos, lying under the earth, turns over on his shoulder, and Ares' shield-rattling is like the noise of Hephaestus' forge. Peneius stands his ground, but Leto turns away to save him. Despite the logic of the sound-inspired terror, Giuseppetti (2013: 154–58) observes that Briareos undermines the potency of Ares and prefigures his defeat later in the hymn, since the Giant was overthrown and confined to the underworld; it should also be noted that in *hArt* the noise produced in Hephaestus' smithy only frightens the young nymphs, the goddess herself is unaffected.

134. Παγγαίου: Mt. Pangaeum is in Thrace about 140 miles from Mt. Haemus, where Ares originally stationed himself (63).

προθέλυμνα: here, "from their foundations," epic and comic (e.g., *Il.* 10.15; 9.541, Ar. *Eq.* 528). For the word as an interpretation of Homeric usage, see Rengakos 1992: 42 and Mineur ad loc.

καρήατα: here "peaks" of mountains.

135. ἀποκρύψαι δὲ ῥέεθρα: the phrase echoes *HhAp* 383: ἀπέκρυψεν δὲ ῥέεθρα, where Apollo blocks Telphusa's stream. The threat is more serious than simply blocking the river's flow; according to Hdt. 7.130, Xerxes' plan to dam the Peneius would have submerged all of Thessaly.

136. ἐσμαράγησε: from Homeric σμαραγέω, "crash," "resound," used of the Titans in Hes. *Th.* 679.

137–39. Mt. Ossa, the plain of Crannon, and the Pindus form a line between Ares' perch and the location of the Peneius (see map 6).

137. ἐλέλιξεν: from ἐλελίζω; the verb has two distinct derivations: (LSJ A) an epic reduplicated form of ἐλίσσω, "turn around," "cause to vibrate," and (LSJ B) related to ἐλελεῦ, "raise a cry." LSJ enters this passage under (B), and most editors take the sense as "rang with a warlike noise," but D'Alessio's "e quello (*sc.* lo scudo) marziale vibrò" is attractive (see next note). See also *Homeric Hymn to Athena* (28) 9. Note that the verb onomatapoetically vibrates.

ἐνόπλιον = ἔνοπλον "armed," "in a warlike manner," but ἐνόπλιος could also specify a martial rhythm, which Ares' beating on the shield sounded out, and to which all of Thessaly danced in fear (139–40). Cf. *hArt* 241: ἐνόπλιον of the dance of the Amazons.

138. δυσαεῖς "ill-blowing," usually of winds, though here transferred to the furthest regions of the Pindus from which harsh winds blow (cf. *hArt* 115). Mineur ad loc. suggests that the phrase might be an allusion to the battle between Antigonus and Pyrrhus in the region in 275 BCE.

140. ἔβραμεν is common to the majority of the mss., although one hyparchetype (α) and Lascaris in his 1496 edition read ἔβραχεν. (ἔβραχεν was also said to be the reading of PMont inv. 145, but in the photograph published with the re-edition of that papyus by A. López 1993 the χ clearly belongs to ἦχος.) ἔβραχεν is frequent in Homer (e.g., *Il.* 5.859, 863 of Ares), while ἔβραμεν (as a variant of ἔβρεμεν) would be unique to this passage of Callimachus. The arguments for retaining it are that it is the *lectio difficilior* and possibly plays on ἔδραμε δ' ἠχώ (*hArt* 245, so Reinsch-Werner 1976:177n3). In the *Dionysiaca* Nonnos writes ἔβρεμεν Ἥρη (6.201) and ἔβρεμεν ἠχώ (28.317) in passages that seem to imitate Callimachus.

ἦχος: the form is late; earlier poetry uses ἠχή (which occurs at *hZeus* 53).

141–47. The syntax of the simile is complex. Instead of the usual Homeric ὡς ὁπότε, Pfeiffer punctuates after ὡς δ', separating the comparison from the temporal clause; thus ὡς δ' responds to τόσος in 147. The temporal clause then falls into subordinate (ὁπότ'... σείονται μυχὰ πάντα) and main clauses (θερμάστραι τε βρέμουσιν, ἔργα θ᾽ ὁμοῦ, and λέβητες… ἰαχεῦσιν). The reason for the periodic shaking is stated in the long genitive absolute: κατουδαίοιο… κινυμένοιο. Callimachus may be imitating the peculiar syntax of Hes. *Th.* 702–5: ὡς ὅτε… τόσσος δοῦπος ἔγεντο ("as when… so great a crash there was…"), on which see West ad loc. That passage describes the clash of the Olympians and Titans as if Earth and Sea had come together, with attendant earthquakes; Briareos is mentioned at 714.

141. τυφομένοιο: Aeschylus (*PV* 351–65) and Pindar (*Ol.* 4.7, *Py.* 1.15–20, fr. 92 S-M) locate Typhon (or Typhoeus) under Mt. Etna, to which Callimachus doubtless alludes with τυφομένοιο (from τύφω, "smoke"), a play on the name Typhon, although Callimachus names the Giant as Briareos (see 143).

142. μυχά: heteroclite plural from μυχός; "inmost part." Cf. 65, also of the earth's inmost recesses.

κατουδαίοιο: the adjective is rare; it first occurs in *HhHerm* 112, where Hermes contains his newly discovered fire in a pit dug "into the earth." (Hes. *Cat.* fr. 150.9, 18 M-W mentions Katoudaioi as an ethnic group along with Pygmies, Ethiopians, and Egyptians.)

142–43. γίγαντος… Βριαρῆος: Briareos was one of the Hundred-Handers according to Hes. *Th.* 149–50, but was later identified as a Giant. Callimachus locates him under Etna in this passage, a place he gives to Enceladus in the *Aetia* prologue (fr. 1.36 Pf.); see 141n.

143. ἐπωμίδα: first in the medical literature; here, "shoulder."

κινυμένοιο: Homeric and later epic, κίνυμαι: "move."

144. θερμάστραι: first in Callimachus; according to Hesychius s.v., the meaning is "oven" or "furnace."

πυράγρης: previously, twice in Homer for "fire-tongs" (*Il.* 18.477, *Od.* 3.434).

145. πυρίκμητοι: "wrought with fire," a Callimachean neologism, modelled on Homeric -μητος words (see Schmitt 61n12).

146. ἰαχεῦσιν: from ἰαχέω, found in Homer, *HhDem* 20, but mainly tragedy, though used of persons.

147. At last the point of the simile—Ares clashing his shield to frighten Peneius. Note the sound effect of -ος repeated five times. A spondaic line marks the conclusion of the simile.

ἄραβος: here with the meaning "clash," as in later Greek.

148–49. Peneius stops the flow of his waters, so that Leto may give birth safely.

150. εἰσόκε: epic, "until," with the subjunctive or optative in Homer, but later with the indicative, as here (see, e.g., A.R. 1.820, 1001).

Κοιηΐς: Leto, the daughter of Coeus.

σῴζεο "save yourself."

151–52. Cf. Plato, *Crat.* 406a6–10 for Leto's gentleness (ἥμερόν τε καὶ λεῖον) as the source of her name. On the text: if ἐμεῖο depends on εἵνεκα ("for my sake"), there will be a word + sense break after the tenth element, which is usually avoided in Callimachean hexameter. Metrically preferable would be to construe τῆσδε with the personal pronoun (see LSJ s.v. ὅδε I 3), with the meaning of "for the sake of me here" or εἵνεκα with the following τῆσδε...ἐλεημοσύνης. But in the former case the sense is banal, in the latter the position and function of ἀντ(ί) makes no sense. Gigante Lanzara considers reading an unattested ἀντελεημοσύνης (i.e., "your corresponding pity"), while D'Alessio 2007 proposes the more radical emendation of ἀντ' to σῆς (but without much enthusiasm). However, the metrical anomaly in conjunction with the unusual separation of ἐμεῖο and εἵνεκα may be signaling an intertext: εἵνεκα with an earlier object separated by two words occurs only once in Homer (*Od.* 11.438: Ἑλένης μὲν ἀπωλόμεθ' εἵνεκα πολλοί, and cf. *Od.* 4.145). Leto by turning away from Peneius shuns the role of Helen in bringing disaster upon others.

151. μὴ σύ γ' ἐμεῖο πάθῃς: with the emphatic pronoun (σύ γ') the sense is best taken as a prohibition (cf. 162) rather than dependent on σῴζεο.

152. ἀντ(ί): normally not elided, but see above v. 22, and for the difficulties of interpretation see above 151–52n.

ἐλεημοσύνης: first in Callimachus. Though this has been suggested as his own coinage, Schmitt 113 can cite only one other example in -σύνη. The noun is so common in later Christian writings that it seems more likely to be a feature of *koine* rather than a literary refinement.

ἀμοιβή "recompense" for Peneius' goodwill. He was the grandfather of Cyrene, the nymph whom Apollo carried off to Libya. The promised reward may be this later event and/or his cult in Cyrene.

153. Leto now turns away from inland water sources to the islands, first in the west (Echinades at the mouth of the Acheloüs, which empties into the Ionian sea, and Corcyra) and then Cos in the east. Her lengthy journey from west to east is narrated in nine lines (153–61) in contrast to the long section on Thessaly.

ἦ καί: the Homeric formula marks the end of a speech, often at this position in the line.

πολλὰ πάροιθεν ἐπεί: the word order is unusual: the object πολλά begins the clause, followed by a temporal adverb (πάροιθεν), only then does the temporal conjunction ἐπεί occur. There may be word play with the juxtaposition of "before" and "after."

154. εἰναλίας: the mss. read the unattested εἰναλίδας; Lascaris corrected to εἰναλίας, though Mineur ad loc. defends the ms. reading on the grounds that such variation is frequent in Callimachus.

154–56. Note the anaphora of οὐ with the ellipse of ἐδέχοντο in 155–56. The triple anaphora echoes that of φεῦγε (70–72), though here the repeated negative is ironically ambiguous. With the second and third repetitions of οὐ, ἐδέχοντο/ ἐδέχετο must be understood, but word order encourages misreading, namely, οὐ λιπαρόν ("not rich") and οὐ...φιλοξεινοτάτη ("the least friendly to strangers").

155. Ἐχινάδες: the Echinades were scattered small islands near the mouth of the Acheloüs; they occur in the catalogue of ships (*Il.* 2.625–30) and at Eur.

Alcmene (*TrGF* 5.1 fr. 87b.9 Kannicht) as a base of the Taphian pirates. On this passage A. Griffiths 1988: 231 points out the parallel of Alcmaeon, who was instructed by Apollo to kill his mother Eriphyle because she accepted the bribe of a necklace to betray Thebes. After wandering to Arcadia, Psophis, Calydon, and the Thesprotians, he was finally purified by the river Acheloüs, after which he colonized the small islands at its mouth (Apollod. 3.7.5). The allusion culminates in the pun on λιπαρόν... ὅρμον. By the classical period these small islands had silted up, so that they no longer would have had a "smooth-surfaced harbor" (see, e.g., Hdt. 2.10), but the phrase could describe Eriphyle's "rich necklace" that Alcmaeon brought with him in his exile and flight.

156. φιλοξεινωτάτη: Corcyra is "friendliest to strangers" because it is identified with the Odyssean Scheria, the homeland of the Phaeaceans (see *Od.* 6.121), but the epithet is ironic because even this most hospitable of islands rejects Leto.

157. Ἶρις: first named here, though she appears at 67. Iris here is the abettor of Hera in contrast to *HhAp* 102–6, where Iris is bribed by the other goddesses with a necklace (μέγαν ὅρμον) to ignore Hera's wishes; it is Iris who cajoles Eileithyia into attending Leto so she can give birth.

158. σπερχομένη: here "angry with" followed by the dative πάσῃσιν (cf. above 60, where it is used of Hera).

δεινόν: the reading of POxy 2225 against πολλόν of the medieval mss. A similar variant occurs at Hes. *Th.* 582, on which see West ad loc.

ἀπέτρεπεν: POxy 2225 records the imperfect against the aorist (ἀπέτραπεν) of the mss.

ὑπ' ὁμοκλῆς: the expression is used of horses "under the shouted command" of their chariot driver. It creates the image of the islands fleeing Leto with Iris driving them like a chariot-team. ὑπ' ὁμοκλῆς is the reading of the medieval mss. (as at *HhDem* 88 and Hes. *Sc.* 341 with smooth breathing), though POxy 2225 reads υφομ[. Wackernagel 1916: 207n1 suggests that the aspirate for this word in Homer has no etymological basis, but was later introduced into the ms. tradition. For this reason Pfeiffer prints ὁμοκλήν against the mss. at 231.

159. πασσυδίη "with all speed"; the medieval mss. have πανσυδίη, the papyri apparently πασσυδίη. Ancient grammarians also disagreed about about the form of this Homeric word: Zenodotus preferred the spelling -σσ-, while Aristarchus later preferred -νσ-. Callimachus in general seems to have readings that coincide with Zenodotus, but then Aristarchus lived a century later (see Rengakos 1993: 72 and n4).

τέτμοι: iterative optative in relative clause, from τέτμον, epic aorist (there is no present in use): "overtake," "reach."

160. ὠγυγίην ... νῆσον: for Callimachus and primeval islands, see Stephens 2008: 111–14.

δήπειτα = δὴ ἔπειτα. Editorial practice in representing this combination differs: the choices are to print δὴ ἔπειτα with synizesis or δήπειτα with crasis. Editors of Callimachus usually print the latter since it is common in mss. of Homer (see also West, *Th.* p. 100).

Κόων: this form of the accusative is found earlier only in Hes. *Cat.* fr. 43a.66 M-W. Cos was one of the Sporades, situated opposite Halicarnassus and Cnidos. It seems to have been an independent ally of the Ptolemies during the first three decades of the third century, before falling briefly under Antigonus Gonatas' control. Cos had close ties with Delos, and when the attack against Delphi was repelled, Cos celebrated the event (Fraser 1972: 1.660 and *SIG* 398). The island also had close literary ties with Alexandria: Philitas of Cos was the tutor of Ptolemy II, and Theocritus and Herodas write about it in their poetry. Ptolemy II was born there in 308.

Μεροπηΐδα: Cos was named for the daughter of Merops (Thuc. 8.41, Steph. Byz. s.v. Κῶς), and one of the island's many names was Meropis; for multiple names see above *hArt* 47–48n.

161. ἵκετο: the reading of the medieval mss. and POxy 2258; ἵετο is the restoration of Lobel, based on POxy 2225, which reads]ετο with only space for one letter in the lacuna. Pfeiffer preferred ἵετο on the basis of meaning:"hastened towards" as opposed to "arrived at," but either would make sense in the context, and the former is better supported.

Χαλκιόπης: Chalciope was the daugther of Eurypylus, who was the king of Cos, and the bride of Heracles.

ἱερὸν μυχόν: possibly a variation of μυχῷ νήσων ἱεράων (cf. Hes. *Th.* 1015, with West ad loc). The Hesiodic phrase refers to Telegonus, the son of Odysseus (another wanderer through the Mediterranean) and Circe, who ruled islands in the far west.

ἡρωίνης: before Callimachus at Ar. *Nub.* 315 (of the clouds); also at Theoc. 13.20 (of Alcmene) and 26.36 (of the daughters of Cadmus).

162–90. Apollo prophesies a second time, now predicting the birth of Ptolemy II on Cos, a future attack of the Gauls on his sanctuary at Delphi, and the subsequent defeat of Gauls by this same Ptolemy. The parallels drawn between divinity and king (called θεὸς ἄλλος) are obvious. Fantuzzi and Hunter (2004: 356) point out that in this section Callimachus has inserted a "Pythian" hymn into his larger "Delian" one, thus varying the structure of the archaic *HhAp*. In both there is an assertion of Olympian order over the forces of chaos, whether primordial serpents or attacking Gauls. This prophecy from Leto's womb is a tour-de-force not easily paralleled in previous or later Greek poetry. While commentators regularly cite the precocity of the newborn Hermes in inventing the lyre and stealing his brother's cattle, P. Bing (1988: 133–35) has correctly located the stimulus in Egyptian kingship ideology. Only in this context is *post eventum* prophecy routine (see Stephens 2003: 120–21). On this passage as a whole, see now Giuseppetti 2013: 146–64.

162–63. μὴ...τέκοις: for the optative as a virtual command, see Smyth §1820.

163. τῇ: i.e., on the island of Cos. Apollo hastens to explain that he rejects Cos for his birthplace, not because the island is at fault, but promised to another "god," namely, Ptolemy II.

164. εὔβοτος: a *hapax* at *Od.* 15.406, of the island of "Syria... above Ortygia"; also at A.R. 3.1086.

165. οἱ = Cos. For the idea of "owed by the Fates," see McKay 1962b: 94.

θεὸς ἄλλος: Ptolemy II. He was alive at the time of the writing and depending on the date of the hymn may already have been deified (see Müller 2009: 262).

166. Σαωτήρων ὕπατον γένος "the lofty race of the Saviors" refers to Ptolemy's parents, the now deified Soter and Berenice I. Their official cult title was Θεοὶ Σωτῆρες.

ᾧ ὑπὸ μίτρην "under whose diadem." The noun is used for several types of royal headgear—here probably an allusion to the diadem worn by Alexander and taken up later by the Ptolemies (see Stephens 2005: 237–40).

167. οὐκ ἀέκουσα: the notion of willing Egyptian subjects is not entirely accurate. Egyptians revolted from Ptolemaic rule on a regular basis, in southern Egypt especially.

Μακηδόνι: Callimachus uses the noun only here to describe the Ptolemies, in contrast to Posidippus, who uses it frequently in his epigrams. The whole passage moves from Macedon, to Cos, and finally Egypt, just as in the Zeus hymn the newborn moved from Arcadia in old Greece, to Crete, to Alexandria (see map 1).

κοιρανέεσθαι: best understood as dependent on οὐκ ἀέκουσα.

168. ἀμφοτέρη μεσόγεια: μεσόγεια "interior lands" is in contrast to "those that dwell in the sea" or the islands that were subject to Ptolemy. ἀμφοτέρη has two points of reference: both continents, Europe and Asia, and the "two lands" of Egypt proper. The latter was regularly conceptualized as Upper and Lower, and royal power was marked with a set of double symbols—crowns, birds, flowers (see Stephens 2003: 238–41, and see fig. 1). Thus Ptolemy will rule the whole world.

169. μέχρις ὅπου: the combination is first found here, but occurs in later prose.

περάτη: the "furthest boundary" whether of east or west: the western horizon here and in Homer (*Od.* 23.243), the eastern in Aratus (670, 821) and A.R. (1.1281).

170. The idea that a son reflects the character of his father is expressed at *Od.* 2.276–77 and Hes. *Op.* 182 (see West ad loc.); with explicit reference to the Ptolemies, see Theoc. 17.63–64 and Eratosthenes fr. 35.13 Powell. The physical likeness of the heir apparent to his father was also a cliché of Egyptian kingship, where each pharaoh could be imagined as a reincarnation of his father (Stephens 2003: 151–59).

εἴσεται: the future of οἶδα; with ἤθεα, "have the disposition of"; the use is Homeric (cf. *Il.* 16.73, *Od.* 2.231).

171–89. Apollo then narrates an incident from the future, when Ptolemy will defeat the Κελτοί (i.e., the Gauls), the "late-born Titans." They were a collection of migratory tribes that over a period of several centuries moved from what became Roman Gaul to modern Bulgaria, then into northern Greece. The Gauls attacked Delphi in 279 BCE. Although they often served as mercenaries, these tribes were also a nuisance to all of the reigning Hellenistic kings. The Successors of Alexander each promoted his war(s) against these groups, and defeating them came to occupy an analogous symbolic space to Greeks of an earlier time defeating the Persians. This is made explicit in Pausanias' discussion of the Gaulish invasion (10.19.5–10.23). Defeating Gauls was commemorated in monuments and poetry as well: see Mitchell (2003: 285–86) on monuments dedicated by the Attalids, and for the poetry Bing 1988: 129n64. On the Gauls in general, see Mitchell 2003.

171. ἄμμιν aligns Apollo with either Ptolemy II in his later struggles, or more likely with the Greeks (cf. ἐφ' Ἑλλήνεσσι in the next line), who waged a number of wars against the Gauls.

172. οἱ μέν (*sc.* ὀψίγονοι Τιτῆνες): the delay of the noun creates suspense.

ἐφ' Ἑλλήνεσσι: i.e., the attack is against Delphi. Callimachus uses the collective Ἕλληνες only here and at fr. 379 Pf., about the Gaulish invasions, in direct contrast to βαρβαρικήν in 173. For this use of ἐπί + dative, see LSJ s.v. B II c.

173. βαρβαρικήν: the adjective is normally confined to prose, and in fact much of the language in the passage echoes that of contemporary inscriptions (see Fantuzzi and Hunter 2004: 357).

ἀναστήσαντες: the zeugma links instrument and event: "raising their barbarian knives and Celtic war."

Ἄρηα "Ares"; like "Enyo" in *hAp* 85, the name of the god/goddess of war is a metonym for "war."

174. ὀψίγονοι Τιτῆνες: the Titans made war against the Olympian gods, and in the *Theogony* defeating them brought Zeus to power. By naming the Gauls "late-born Titans" Callimachus imparts a cosmic status to the contemporary conflict.

ἐσχατόωντος "lying on the edge"; for the form see *hArt* 65n.

175–87. These lines refer to the attack on Delphi in 279/278 BCE led by Brennus (described at length in Pausanias, see above 171–89n). Callimachus links that event with the later annihilation of the Gaulish mercenaries who had revolted from the armies of Ptolemy II (see p. 18 for details). According to the *Suda*, Callimachus wrote at least one other poem on the subject, the *Galatea*. She was the eponymous ancestor of the *Galatai*, and one of the fragments assigned to the poem by Pfeiffer (fr. 379 Pf.) includes the Gaulish leader, Brennus: οὓς Βρέννος ἀφ' ἑσπερίοιο θαλάσσης | ἤγαγεν Ἑλλήνων ἐπ' ἀνάστασιν. ("Whom Brennus led from the western sea to displace the Greeks").

175. ῥώσωνται: from Homeric ῥώομαι, "rush"; the mss. read ῥώσονται, which Lascaris corrected to the subjunctive, dependent on ὁππόταν (172). See Mineur ad loc. for a defense of the ms. reading.

νιφάδεσσιν ἐοικότες: the comparison occurs at *Il.* 3.222, describing Odysseus' words. The Homeric phrase was frequently quoted in later Greek sources.

ἰσάριθμοι: a prose word, first found in the philosophers, e.g., Pl. *Tim.* 41d8: ψυχὰς ἰσαρίθμους τοῖς ἄστροις (cf. τείρεσιν below).

176. τείρεσιν: lengthened form of τέρας; at *Il.* 18.485 τείρεα are constellations, so also at Aratus 692; here more likely "stars." LSJ s.v. βουκολέω understands them as meteors, but since meteors are quite rare, they would not suit the earlier comparison with snowflakes.

κατ᾽ ἠέρα βουκολέονται: the introduction of this pastoral image contrasts with the destructive path of the Gauls in the next lines.

177a–b. These verses were mutilated in transmission at either the top or bottom of a codex page (and lines 200–1, which would have fallen on the opposite side, were also affected). Unfortunately, POxy 2225, which includes this section of the hymn, does not preserve more than a few letters from the lines. From the letters that survive on the papyrus it is clear that not one but two lines are missing, hence the numbering. On the basis of the papyrus readings, Pfeiffer conjectured that the lines must have referred to the *S(t)epterion*, a festival celebrated every eight years in commemoration of Apollo's slaying of Pytho. As part of the festival a procession carried laurel for the victors' crowns in the Pythian games from the valley of Tempe (see his apparatus on 177b, Plut. *De def. or.* 417E–18D, and the long description in Ael. *VH* 3.1). The laurel in *Iamb.* 4 (fr. 194.34–36 Pf.) boasts of this festival. See further Bing 1988: 129–31 (especially n46) on the timing of the festival and the Gaulic invasion.

178. πεδία Κρισσαῖα καὶ Ἡφαί[στο]ι̣ο φάρ[αγγ]ες: the medieval mss. are defective in this line, giving only πεδία Κρισσαῖα καὶ ἤπειροι. On the basis of POxy 2225, Lobel and Pfeiffer tentatively filled it out Ἡφαί[στο]ι̣ο φάρ[αγγ]ες ("glens of Hephaestus"), though Pfeiffer expressed doubt, since there was no trace of a cult of Hephaestus in this region. Mineur points to Aesch. *Eum.* 12–16, where παῖδες Ἡφαίστου (the Athenians, said to be descended from Erichthonius, the son of Hephaestus) built a road to the sanctuary, though he doubts the glens would have been so named. Still, this suggests that there might have been some local connection to Hephaestus; certainly enough to retain the reading in the absence of more compelling options. (For a discussion of the many alternatives proposed, see Bing 1986.)

179. ἀμφιπεριστείνωνται: a Callimachean coinage, only here in Greek: "crowded round and about." The mss. have the indicative, but the surrounding subjunctives require the correction. The effect of the neologism, which fills a half-line, is to mirror the hoards of Gauls as they swarm into the region.

ἴδωσι: the subject is likely to be παῖδ[ες from the damaged line 177a.

180. γείτονος αἰθομένοιο: either sacrificial offerings burning on the altars at Delphi in celebration of the victory or, as Mineur ad loc. suggests, smoke from the neighboring towns that have been set on fire by the invading Gauls.

ἀκουῇ "by hearsay"; i.e., they will not simply hear a report but the enemy will be close enough to be seen advancing.

181–85. These lines collapse the temporal framework: the invading army— phalanxes, swords, shields, baldrics—are imagined as menacing and simultaneously captive (i.e., ἐμοὶ γέρας, 185). See Stephens 2003: 138–40.

181. ἀπαυγάζοιντο: Danielsson 1901: 95 connects the shift from subjunctive to optative with the oracular style; similarly at *Aet.* fr. 1.33–35 Pf., though there a final clause. For the verb see 125n.

φάλαγγας: medieval mss. read φάλαγγες, which is suspect; POxy 2225 confirms the accusative.

181–82. The anaphora of ἤδη reinforces the immediate presence of the enemy.

182. δυσμενέων: epic and tragic for "enemy." Cf. Theoc. 24.100, and for the implications of the term see Stephens 2003: 138–40.

παρὰ τριπόδεσσιν: these are the tripods within the sanctuary from which the prophet prophesies, thus an image of the most sacred space violated (as well as triumphant).

183–84. φάσγανα καὶ ζωστῆρας ἀναιδέας ἐχθομένας τε | ἀσπίδας: the Gauls had distinctive armor and weaponry, and their shields had been hung on display at Delphi (see Paus. 10.19.4).

184. Γαλάτῃσι: Timaeus (*FGrH* 566 F69) was apparently the first to refer to these migrating groups in the east as *Galatai*. Callimachus also calls them *Keltoi* (see above 173).

κακὴν ὁδόν: Gigante Lanzara suggests that the expression is an inversion of the ἱερὴ ὁδός, "the sacred way" as the route to the sanctuary was called (e.g., Hdt. 6.34). It probably refers to Brennus' path as he began the attack (Paus. 10.22.10).

ἄφρονι φύλῳ: in apposition to Γαλάτῃσι.

185–86. The shields are imagined in two groups and thus from two distinct events: the first (αἱ μὲν ἐμοὶ γέρας) Apollo takes as his reward, and these are hung in Delphi; the second (αἱ δέ) are personified as seeing (ἰδοῦσαι) their owners destroyed in Egypt.

185. στήσονται: the subject is the shields, and the meaning seems again to telescope time—the shields "will forge an evil path" for the *Galatai* as they attack, but the shields will also line the path of their destruction.

τέων: the scholiast takes as ὧντινων; others as a demonstrative τῶν.

186. ἐν πυρὶ τοὺς φορέοντας ἀποπνεύσαντας: these are the mercenaries (around 4,000) who revolted against Philadelphus; they were confined on an island in the Delta and killed. Versions of their destruction vary, but here clearly

Callimachus represents them as being burned to death, "breathing out their last in the fire." Burning the enemy was a traditional means in Egyptian mythology of destroying the forces of chaos, often personified as Seth (see Koenen 1993: 83–84).

187. κείσονται: with ἐπὶ Νείλῳ above: "they will be placed by the Nile." The actual fate of these shields is unknown.

βασιλῆος: Ptolemy II.

188. Apollo now directly addresses Ptolemy II, as one who will be born in the future on Cos. The point is not just to name the king, but to adumbrate his future accomplishments, capped by his defeat of the Gauls, an act that will mirror Apollo's own victory a few years earlier.

ἐσσόμενε: the vocative of the future participle of εἰμί occurs only here. Virgil famously imitates the line at *Aeneid* 6.883: *tu Marcellus eris*. Though in Virgil Marcellus, unlike Ptolemy II, is unable to complete his destiny.

τά τοι μαντήια Φοίβου (sc. ἐστί).

Φοίβου: the reading of the medieval mss. is φαίνω, which is acceptable metrically and makes sense, "I reveal my prophecies for you." However, POxy 2225 shows the termination -ου, (although the preceding letters are now missing) which supports the earlier conjecture of Lascaris (Φοίβου); cf. Eur. *Andr.* 926 and *Ion* 66.

189. αἰνήσεις: for Ptolemy and Delos see pp. 159, 162. There was no formal cult of Apollo in Alexandria, so Mineur suggests this line foreshadowed Ptolemy's devotion to Apollo as patron of the Muses via the Museum. Since Apollo seems to have been Callimachus' choice as patron god (as well as the chief deity in Cyrene), this may be a subtle request for artistic patronage. On the intercultural level, this may reflect Ptolemaic support for native Egyptian Horus cult, since Horus was equated with Apollo, and the Ptolemies, as pharaohs, styled themselves "Horus" (see Koenen 1993: 59). Use of this verb throughout also tightly binds Delos, Apollo, Ptolemy, and the poet (see above 9–10n).

190. ξυμβάλλεο: from συμβάλλω, "consider"; Apollo now turns his attention to his mother Leto with a form of address that may be connected to the interpretation of oracles; cf. ἀλλὰ συμβαλεῦ | τὦνιγμα, "but interpret the riddle," addressed to Pittheus in *Iamb.* 5 (fr. 195.32–33 Pf.).

191. διειδομένη: this form is restricted to the Hellenistic period (cf. A.R. 1.546). LSJ and Pfeiffer assign to διεῖδον, "being seen"; Mineur connects it rather with Homeric δια-ϝείδω, "appear" (though δια- seems always to appear with this verb); the scholiast glosses as φαινομένη.

ἀραιή: the scholiast glosses as λεπτή, "slender." The word is appropriate because Delos was a long, narrow island. But slenderness was also a prized characteristic of Hellenistic poetry. The word thus supports a metaliterary reading of this poem (see Bing 1988: 119–20).

192. πλαζομένη πελάγεσσι: cf. 36n. Callimachus again collapses nymph and island; Asteria floated on the sea, so her feet (πόδες) were not rooted in the ground (ἐνὶ χώρῃ).

193–95. An imitation of *Od.* 5.327–32, where Odysseus' raft is compared to thistles that the winds carry in all directions.

193. παλιρροίη: mainly a prose word that seems to mean "back against the tide." **ἐπινήχεται** "swim to" or "float to"; see 21n.

ἀνθέρικος ὥς: the asphodel or thistle down was a plant common to the area of Cyrene, and it was given as an offering to Apollo on Delos (Plut. *Sept. sap. conv.* 158A). See Bing 1988: 121–22 on the simile; for details of the plant, see Mineur ad loc.

194. ὅπη: variant of the adverb ὅπῃ; "to whatever place," with τῇ below.

195. τῇ με φέροις: Apollo's response to Leto's plaintive question to her embryo in 116–17: ποῖ σε φέρω; at the same position in the line.

εἰς ἐθέλουσαν: Lascaris corrected from the ms. reading εἰσεθέλουσαν. The word order is unusual, but the postponed ἐθέλουσαν emphasizes that at least one place is willing to receive her. Mineur cites *Od.* 6.175–76: σὲ γὰρ κακὰ πολλὰ μογήσας | ἐς πρώτην ἱκόμην ("for to you after suffering many evils I have come first") of Odysseus to Nausicaa (whom he has just compared to the Delian palm).

196–214. With the closure of Apollo's prophetic speech (τόσσα λέγοντος), the hymn now proceeds to the Delian birth of the god. While the other islands flee, Asteria perceives Leto's distress and changes course to offer her a place to give birth.

197. φιλόμολπε: the epithet is used earlier in the lyric poets; cf. Pi. *Nem.* 7.9 of the island Aegina.

κατῇεις "you returned." Asteria's route as a wandering island was discussed above 41–50n. Here she is imagined as visiting her sister islands, collecting seaweed as she goes.

198. Κυκλάδας: the Cyclades were mentioned earlier, though only two of the islands are named: Chios (48) and Samos (49).

περιηγέας "circular" or "surrounding"; a pun on the name of the Cyclades.

199. Γεραίστιον: a promontory in southern Euboea with a famous temple of Poseidon (cf. *Od.* 3.177–79). See Posidippus 20.5 A-B.

φῦκος "seaweed," earlier only at *Il.* 9.7, of seaweed stirred up by the winds; here trailing in Asteria's wake.

200–201. These lines describe the first encounter of Asteria and Leto. Unfortunately, they share the damage to the hyparchetype visible earlier in lines 177a-b. A few late codices attempt to supplement the text, but the supplements only partially coincide with the reading of POxy 2225.

201. θαρσαλέη τάδ' ἔλεξας[: cf. *hArt* 80: θαρσαλέη...τάδε προσελέξαο. The supplement in the medieval mss. for the end of the line, which earlier editors printed, ἐπεὶ περικαίεο πυρί, does not fit the traces of the papyrus.

202. δαίμον(α): so POxy 2225; the medieval mss. read τλῆμον'.

ὑπ' ὠδίνεσσι βαρυνομένην "heavy with birth pangs." The verb is standard for pregnant women and animals. Cf. Eur. *IT* 1228, in a temple prohibition. The verb occurs also at 212, 244, 307.

ὁρόωσα: for the form see *hArt* 65n; the subject of the participle is Asteria, upon seeing Leto.

203–4. Asteria's carefully structured two-line speech contrasts with Peneius' longer lament. Ἥρη begins, Λητοῖ ends the speech; the sounds of Ἥρη τοῦτό με are repeated in πέρα εἰς ἐμέ; and the pattern of vocative, με, imperative in Ἥρη … με ῥέξον reverses itself in πέρα … ἐμέ, Λητοῖ.

203. ῥέξον: imperative from ῥέζω; construed with a double accusative as at *hAth* 85.

204. πέρα: imperative from περάω: "pass over"'or "pass through."

205. ἔννεπες: the verb often concludes a speech in Callimachus, see, e.g., *hArt* 86, *Aet.*, frr. 177.15, 178. 27.

ἀρητόν: a verbal adjective (from ἀράομαι) used adverbially. The meaning seems to be "something prayed for" (or against). The latter sense occurs in Homer (e.g., *Il.* 17.37), the former is the sense of the proper name Ἄρητος.

†λυγρῆς: the reading of the medieval mss. The papyrus reads]αυσατο…ης, with space for at most three letters before ης at the end of the line and no traces compatible with what should be the descenders of υ and ρ. In fact, λυγρῆς is probably a copyist's error, under the influence of 210. The missing word is likely an adjective modifying ἄλης: Mineur suggests δηρῆς; Gigante Lanzara πάσης; and Bing 1986 ὀλοιῆς, citing as an intertext *Od.* 15.342: μ' ἔπαυσας ἄλης καὶ ὀϊζύος αἰνῆς ("you ended my wandering and grievous hardship"). His conjecture is the most attractive; it would require a rare elision of the verb termination, but Callimachus does elide the verb at this position.

206–8. The Inopus was a river on Delos that seems to have been part of the legend of Leto's parturition (see *HhAp* 18: ὑπ' Ἰνωποῖο ῥεέθροις). Probably because it is a dry watercourse most of the year the river was said (erroneously) to have a subterranean connection to the Nile (see *hArt* 171, Lycophron 575, Paus. 2.5.3), its increase in flow thought to depend on the Nile's annual rising from Ethiopia. In Egyptian myth the rise of the Nile was imagined as an annual replication of the original creation and coincident with the birth of Horus, the first divine king, and Horus was identified with Apollo as early as Herodotus. The rise of the Inopus at the time of the god's birth links Greek myth with Egyptian ideologies of kingship (Stephens 2003: 117–18).

206. ἕζετο: note the emphatic placement of the verb—Leto finally is allowed to rest.

ὅν τε: see *hZeus* 51n.

207. ἐξανίησιν: from ἐξανίημι; cf. A.R. 4.293, of the Acheloüs flowing forth into the sea (in a context of instructions given to the Argonauts by the Colchians, who are figured as descendants of Egyptians).

πλήθοντι ῥεέθρῳ "in full spate"; cf. *HhAp*. 18: ὑπ᾽ Ἰνωποῖο ῥεέθροις. The Nile began to rise in July around the time of the first sighting of Sirius; these events fell at the beginning of the Egyptian New Year.

208. ἀπὸ κρημνοῖο κατέρχεται Αἰθιοπῆος: the river "flows down from the Ethiopian highland." The details are correct, though the source of the Nile's waters was a well-known topic of debate in antiquity (see, e.g., Hdt. 2.19–28).

Αἰθιοπῆος: genitive from the Hellenistic variant Αἰθιοπεύς.

209. λύσατο δὲ ζώνην: women typically untie their garments for sleep (as Iris at 209), sexual activity, or in preparation for giving birth, as here and at *hZeus* 21.

ἀπὸ δ᾽ ἐκλίθη: from ἀποκλίνομαι. Leto's posture, with her back braced against the palm tree is parallel to *HhAp* 17, where she is leaning against Mt. Cynthus, but the opposite of *HhAp* 117–18, where she kneels on the ground and embraces the palm. Most 1981: 183–86 suggests that Callimachus' birthing posture here reflects the innovative views of the Alexandrian doctor Herophilus on the best position for giving birth.

210. φοίνικος: the Delian palm was a permanent feature of Apollo's birth. Leto is usually represented as touching or holding it while kneeling in labor. The iconic value of the tree is confirmed by the habit of planting shoots from it in other sanctuaries of Apollo; apparently a bronze replica of the Delian palm stood near the Letoion in Cyrene (see *hAp* 1).

πρέμνον: the "base or trunk of a tree." Callimachus has a different version at *Iamb.* 4 (fr. 194.83–84 Pf.): τεῦ γ]ὰρ τὸ πρέμνον Δήλιοι φυλάσσουσι; | [τὸ τ]ῆς ἐλαίης ἢ ἀν[έπαυσ]ε τὴν Λητώ ("the trunk of what tree do the Delians preserve? The trunk of the olive that gave rest to Leto"). The Delian olive appears below at 262.

ἀμηχανίης ὑπὸ λυγρῆς: as a description of women in childbirth, cf. Eur. *Hipp.* 163–64: δύστανος ἀμηχανία... ὠδίνων.

211. νότιος: with ἱδρώς: "damp," because southerly winds were thought to bring rain. For the phrase compare *Il.* 11.811≈ 23.715 : κατὰ δὲ νότιος ῥέεν ἱδρώς ("damp sweat poured down").

212. ἀλυσθενέουσα "in her weakened condition"; the medieval mss. read ἀλυσθμαίνουσα, which is otherwise unattested, glossed by the scholiast as πνευστιῶσα, ἀσθμαίνουσα, "gasping for breath." Lobel read the traces on the papyrus as αλ[..].ν..[, which allows insufficient space for the medieval reading (and the traces that are visible are of rounded letters). In its place he conjectured ἀλ[υσθ]ενέο[υσα, which is unattested as a verb, though the *Etymologicum magnum* glosses ἀλυσθένειαν as ἀσθένειαν.

212–14. Leto addresses her unborn child (κοῦρε... φιλε... κοῦρε) in an attempt to hasten the process (γείνεο, γείνεο... ἔξιθι κόλπου).

212. βαρύνεις: here with the sense of burden, "weigh down."

213. ἐπιπλώουσα: epic and Ionic variant of ἐπιπλέω.

214. γείνεο, γείνεο: the morphology is uncertain: Pfeiffer assigns to γείνομαι "be born," but Mineur observes that it could equally be from γίγνομαι, lengthened for metrical purposes. In either case, the imperatives addressed to Apollo ("be born!") are unique.

ἔξιθι: Callimachus employs the language of divine epiphany with humorous effect (cf. *hAth* 55, and *hAth* 1, 2: ἔξιτε).

215–17. The narrator introduces Iris' speech by addressing Hera as "bride of Zeus" with transparent irony. While Hera is the official νύμφα Διός, Leto's stature as the mother of Apollo makes her also νύμφα Διός. Hera, unproductively βαρύθυμος, contrasts with Leto, weighed down by her pregnancy (212: βαρύνεις).

215. νύμφα: the vocative with short α occurs in Homer (*Il.* 5.130) and in Callimachus at *Aet.* fr. 54.2 (see Harder ad loc.), fr. 228.5 Pf., and fr. 788 Pf. (on which see Pfeiffer's note).

βαρύθυμε: previously only at Eur. *Med.* 176, where the chorus expresses the wish that they might mitigate Medea's "heavy" anger. Since Medea's wrath led to the destruction of her children, the word continues the ominous, tragic tone of this section.

215–16. Cf. *Il.* 5.205: τὰ δὲ μ' οὐκ ἄρ' ἔμελλον ὀνήσειν ("but this is not going to benefit me"); if deliberate, a fine, ironic parallel.

215. ἄπυστος: a rare Homeric adjective, here with the sense of "not hearing," i.e., without knowledge of; cf. *Od.* 5.127–28, where Zeus is not long ἄπυστος of Demeter lying with Iasion. Also at *hDem* 9.

216. δήν: epic and poetic temporal adverb, "for a long while." Here and at *Hecale* 49.3 Hollis.

ἔμεναι: epic infinitive of εἰμί.

ἀγγελιῶτις: a feminine equivalent, unique to Callimachus, of ἀγγελιώτης.

217. ἀσθμαίνουσα: the detail of Iris "panting" in her rush to tell Hera prefigures the later comparision with a hound.

ἀνεμίσγετο "mixed with"; the verb commonly occurs in the middle for A mixing with B (in dative), often of opposites (cf. *Aet.* fr. 24.3 and Harder ad loc.).

218–27. Iris' speech to Hera is carefully contrived to deflect blame from herself onto Asteria. She begins with flattery (218–21), two lines of report, two more lines on Asteria's perfidy, and finishes with a fawning prayer that Hera now take over. The opening emphasis on Hera's powers reflects the style of hymnic address: σὴ μὲν ἐγώ, σὰ δὲ πάντα, σὺ δὲ κρείουσα κάθησαι | γνησίη Οὐλύμποιο ("I am yours, all things are yours, you are the legitimate queen of Olympus"). It is calculated to flatter, but γνησίη in its emphatic position at the opening of the line goes to the heart of the matter—Hera's fear for her own status.

221. θηλυτέρην: the stipulation of "female" power is necessary, since Zeus reigns supreme.

ἄνασσα: the honorific is normally used of goddesses (see *hArt* 137, 204, 240; cf. *hDem* 121), but also of Ptolemaic queens (see *Aet.*, fr. 112.2 Pf.)

εἴσεαι: second person singular future of οἶδα. As Mineur points out, the tense is important: Hera does not yet know about Leto and Asteria, because she has been sitting on her throne on Olympus (κάθησαι); but she soon will.

222. μίτρην ἀναλύεται "she is untying her cincture" (in the same sense at *hZeus* 21). The present indicates the swiftness of Iris' report, but also the urgency of the matter. At 166 above, μίτρη is a fillet tied around the head (probably a diadem) and occurs at *hArt* 14 (ἀμίτρους) in the same sense.

ἔνδοθι νήσου: Callimachus' narration of events contrasts with *HhAp* 89–101, where all the goddesses are in attendance on Leto (92: θεαὶ δ' ἔσαν ἔνδοθι πᾶσαι), except Hera, who "was seated in the halls of Zeus," and Eileithyia, whom Hera had kept unaware. The other goddesses then bribe Iris to fetch Eileithyia without Hera's knowledge.

223. ἀπέστυγον "hate utterly" (see fr. 178.11 Pf. for loathing deep drinking). First in tragedy and Herodotus.

224–25. The repetition of Ἀστερίη is calculated to redirect Hera's anger— Asteria, who had the temerity to call out to Leto by name as she was passing by, i.e., deliberately supporting Hera's enemy; thus Asteria is "scum."

225. σάρον: related to σαίρω, "sweep," hence the meaning of "sweepings" or "rubbish." For the insult compare the *sphragis* in *hAp* 106–9.

οἶσθα καὶ αὐτή "you yourself also know." Iris' tactful way of calling Hera's attention to Asteria's history as another nymph who attracted Zeus's attention, but unlike Leto refused his bed. Cf. the infant Hermes to Zeus in *HhHerm* 382–83: οἶσθα καὶ αὐτὸς | ὡς οὐκ αἴτιός εἰμι ("you yourself also know that I am not to blame"), where Hermes is lying.

226. The extreme hyperbaton of the line mimics Iris' breathlessness (and fear) by breaking into six parts, none of which is syntactically contiguous with what proceeds or follows.

φίλη: vocative with πότνια.

δύνασαι γάρ: the thought is parenthetical, "for *you* can," a subtle indication of status—as queen of Olympus she is better placed to bring about the desired result than her servants (Iris and Ares), who have failed.

226–27. ἀμύνειν ... δούλοις | ὑμετέροις: this reading of the mss. was emended by Maas (1958: 28–31) to ἀμύνεο ... δούλους | ὑμετέρους (a solution accepted by Pfeiffer) on the grounds that ἀμύνειν violated Naeke's Law (when a word-end coincides with the end of the fourth metron, its final syllables should not be spondaic); the middle ἀμύνεο also required a change to accusative of person. Maas's conjecture thus requires three changes to the transmitted text, none of them palaeographically plausible. Moreover, ἀμύνειν does occur in this metrical position in Homer (e.g., *Il.* 6.463, 13.814) with dative of person (as here). Finally,

Maas's ἀμύνεο requires a shift from the active sense of "aid your servants [i.e., Ares and Iris], who walk the earth by your command" to middle, "take revenge on" or "punish your servants [who must therefore be Asteria and Leto], who trample upon your command." If the reading of the mss. is retained, the infinitive will function as an imperative (see, e.g., *hAp* 12–13, *hDem* 129, *epp.* 10.3 Pf. = 33.3 G-P, 54.3 Pf. = 24.3 G-P); but given Iris' tortured syntax, the force of δύνασαι might still be felt ("but, dear—for you are able—to aid—mistress, etc."). Recent editors (Asper, D'Alessio, Gigante Lanzara, and Mineur) retain the ms. reading (*pace* Hopkinson 1985: 251–52), and M. Fantuzzi observes that the violation of Naeke's law may convey the rhythm of Iris' broken sobs.

227. πέδον πατέουσιν: the combination occurs elsewhere only at Aesch. *Ag.* 1357 and *Ch.* 643, where the sense is "trample upon" justice or convention. Fraenkel in his note on 1357, quoting Conington, regards the phrase as "almost a compound verb." There are many verbal echoes of Aeschylus in the hymns, but if Iris is speaking of herself and Ares, the overt sense should be closer to "walk the earth."

ἐφετμῇ: the mss. have ἐφετμῆ (or -ῇ), emended by Crönert to ἐφετμήν to bring the relative clause in line with Maas's changes in the main clause, which require a shift in the identity of the servants. The noun is normally used for commands or requests of divinities or one's parents (e.g., *Il* 1.495, Pi. *Ol.* 3.11).

228–39. A detailed description of Iris crouched at the base of Hera's throne to await her orders. She is likened to one of Artemis' hounds in her alertness. Callimachus' choice of simile is ironic on two levels: it is a reminder of Apollo's twin, who is otherwise absent from this hymn, but also of Artemis' elevation to the ranks of Olympians—the very thing that Hera seeks to prevent (note Zeus's remark at the opening of *hArt* 29–31). It may also be intended to recall the narrative in *hArt* 87–97 of the young Artemis going to Pan to select her hounds, if *hArt* is prior.

228. ἐδέθλιον: here, "throne," but in *hAp* 62, "foundation."

ἷζε: properispomenon is Aristarchus' preferred accent for the imperfect of ἵζω, but mss. of Homer as well as of Callimachus show it accented ἷζε (see Chantraine 1.482).

κύων ὥς "like a dog," as at *Il.* 15.579. For the postpositive ὥς at line end, see Mineur, introduction 4.4.5 (p. 45). For dogs as agents of the gods, see LSJ s.v. III.

229. ἥτις τε: see *hZeus* 51n and Ruijgh's comment (1971: 969).

ὅτε: see *hZeus* 21n and below 309.

230. θηρήτειρα: a *hapax*, a Callimachean coinage based on Homer's θηρητήρ (so Schmitt 29n32); "huntress."

παρ' ἴχνεσιν: here a metonym for "foot"; punning on the meaning of the word as the "traces" or "tracks" that a hunting dog would follow. Iris sits "at her [= Hera's] feet."

230–31. οὔατα . . . ὀρθὰ μάλ(α) "with her ears pricked up," ever on the alert.

231. θεῆς: Ionic feminine, also at *hZeus* 37, *hArt* 119.

ὁμοκλήν: see 158n.

232. τῇ ἰκέλη "like her," i.e., Artemis' hound.

Θαύμαντος … κούρη: cf. 67n.

ἵζετο: here middle; active and middle forms are interchangeable, as in Homer.

233–39. The description of Iris, ever ready, seated at the corner of Hera's throne is framed by κείνη (Iris) and δεσπότις (Hera) and built around the repetition of οὐδέ ποτε … οὐδὲ … ἀλλ᾽ … μή.

233. σφετέρης: cf. *hArt* 229; for examples of the use of σφέτερος with the third person singular, see LSJ s.v. I 2. It is a feature of Homeric but also later poetic language.

ἐπιλήθεται ἕδρης: the root of the verb λήθ- appears in ληθαῖον in the next line; while ἕδρα echoes ἐδέθλιον above 228. The sense must be "she does not forget her physical place" beside Hera's throne, to which she returns even for sleep.

235. γλωχῖνα: according to the scholiast, "an angle" or "leg"; here probably the angled corner of a square-based throne (for the controversy over its Homeric meaning, see Rengakos 1993: 35).

236. τυτθόν: here an adverb, "a little"; used elsewhere in Callmachus with programmatic effect (see *Aet.* fr. 1.5 Pf).

λέχριος "aslant"; Xenophon (*Cyn.* 4.3) describes the proper way for hunting dogs to track, with heads down and aslant.

237. ζώνην ἀναλύεται: an ironic reminder that Iris is a female while it also calls to mind Leto's preparation for giving birth, above 209 and 222.

238. ἐνδρομίδας: cf. *hArt* 16n.

μή … εἴπη: a virtual expression of fearing.

239. δεσπότις: tragic and later Greek for "mistress." Hera's status, placed in an emphatic position, contrasts with her frustration and the impotence of her anger.

ἀλεγεινόν: accusative singular of the Homeric adjective used adverbially, "grievously."

ἀλαστήσασα: from ἀλαστέω, "be distraught with wrath"; twice in Homer. At *Il.* 15.21 it expresses the indignation of the gods at Zeus's punishment of Hera for devising harm to Heracles.

240–48. Hera responds to Iris with a face-saving speech, first directing her vitriol to Zeus's liaisons generically, then mollifying her anger by "forgiving" Asteria, who at least did not "trample upon" Hera's bed by sleeping with Zeus.

240. ὦ Ζηνὸς ὀνείδεα: rarely used of persons; the plural, ὀνείδεα, encompasses all of Zeus's girlfriends, though Leto is the object of her address.

γαμέοισθε: in the middle, of women marrying. The verb is almost never used for illicit unions. The choice of verb indicates Hera's insecurity over her own position and elevates the status of Leto's liaison. This passage supports the view that Berenice I (the mother of Ptolemy II), who became the

wife of Soter after being his mistress for many years, stands behind the por-
trayal of Leto.

241. κεκρυμμένα: the neuter perfect passive participle from κρύπτω, used adverbially, "in secret."

242. δυστοκέες "ill-begotten"; first here in Callimachus; the morphology is
murky: either a compound of τοκεύς (so LSJ s.v.) or τόκος (see Schmitt 120n37).

μογέουσιν: from Homeric μογέω, "suffer with pain or trouble."

ἀλετρίδες "women who grind corn"; slave women at *Od.* 20.105, though at
Ar. *Lys.* 643 describing well-born Athenian girls who prepared the offering cakes.

φῶκαι: cf. *HhAp* 77, where Delos fears that after he is born Apollo will spurn
her, and she will become a home for the octopus and seals.

243. σπιλάδεσσιν: Homeric, "rocks over which the sea dashes" (*Od.* 3.298,
5.401).

245. ἀμπλακίης: lyric and tragic, "fault," "misdeed."

οὐδ' ἔστιν ὅπως: the idiom is common in prose and a nice contrast to the Homeric adaptation of ἀποθύμια ῥέξω.

ἀποθύμια: a *hapax* in Homer at *Il.* 14.261: μὴ...ἀποθύμια ἔρδοι, "lest he do
something displeasing"), where Zeus checks his anger against Night (who had
participated in a deceptive scheme of Hera's).

246. τόσσα δέ οἱ "and such things to her—"; there are two possible articula-
tions for this phrase, neither unproblematic. (1) The majority of editors accept
Lascaris' emendation τόσσα δέοι, and construe with the preceding οὐδ'... ῥέξω
to mean "nor shall I do to her as much as I should," i.e., the continuation of
Hera's speech of reconciliation. But the emendation is syntactically anomalous: no good parallels exist for τόσσα instead of ὅσσα or for the omission of
ἄν with δέοι (though Mineur ad loc. makes a case for acceptance). (2) Lloyd-
Jones (1982) and Gigante Lanzara, following him, argue for the reading of **At
η E**: τόσσα δέ οἱ, which they understand as aposiopesis. Support for the reading is found in Nonnus' *Paraphrase of the Gospel of John* (12.149), in which he
appears to imitate this otherwise unattested phrase: τόσσα δέ οἱ τελέσαντι ("to
him having accomplished so many things"). If (2) is correct, then Hera will
begin in 244 to express her willingness to forgive Asteria, interrupt herself in
a burst of anger (246) to express what she would like to do to her for her of-
fenses, before recalling her reason for forgiveness (247). In this case, though,
the parenthesis introduced by μάλα γάρ τε is confusing, and must be explained
as simulating a speech of considerable agitation. Nonnus' imitation has in-
clined me towards (2).

μάλα γάρ τε: the expression is Homeric, but this is the only example in Callimachus; here it lacks the usual generalizing force (see Ruijgh 1971: 970).

κακῶς ἐχαρίσσατο: for "doing a favor for appropriately" (καλῶς) or "basely"
(πονηρῶς) see Pl. *Sym.* 183d7, 184b6.

247. σεβίζομαι: for the middle of σεβίζω in the active sense cf. Aesch. *Supp.* 815, 922.

248. δέμνιον οὐκ ἐπάτησε: cf. 227n. MacKay 1962a: 163 would connect this passage with 227. He accepts the Maas-Crönert emendations (226–27n) and argues that in that passage Iris complained of Asteria and Leto "trampling on Hera's command," while Hera now replies that Asteria at any rate had not "trampled on her bed" (while this is an attractive parallel, other problems with the emendations persist, e.g., δούλους is hardly an appropriate term for Asteria and Leto).

ἀνθείλετο: from ἀνθαιρέομαι, "prefer" one thing (accusative) to another (genitive). The verb is not common in poetry.

249–59. With the close of Hera's speech the "tragic" conflict in the hymn is resolved, and the forces of disruption and chaos now disappear. Music, harmonious accord, and light predominate at the moment of birth.

249. κύκνοι: the belief that swans were sacred to Apollo was widespread. According to Himerius, *Or.* 48.200 (= fr. 307c V), Alcaeus wrote a hymn in which Zeus gave Apollo a lyre at his birth and a chariot driven by swans. Plato, *Phaedo* 85b1–2 claims that swans are the mantic birds of Apollo, and in Ar. *Aves* 769–84 swans sing a hymn to the god.

θεοῦ μέλλοντος ἀοιδοί: the ms. reading θεοῦ μέλποντες ἀοιδοί has been questioned on a number of grounds: (1) the redundancy of "singers singing," (2) the fact that they are called both "singers of the god" and a few lines later "birds of the Muses," (3) that singing at this point makes little sense in light of the expanded discussion in 251–52 (especially ἀοιδότατοι), and (4) the god is not yet born. Emendations include changing (1) the case of θεοῦ to θεόν, or (2) μέλποντες to μέλλοντες, with the sense of "future," and/or (3) ἀοιδοί to the rare ἄοζοι, "servants" (see Aesch. *Ag.* 231). A. Dyck proposes the elegant solution adopted here, namely to emend μέλποντες to μέλλοντος; Apollo as θεὸς μέλλων would be parallel to ἐσσόμενε Πτολεμαῖε (188).

250. Μηόνιον: Maeonia was more or less coextensive with Lydia (e.g., Strabo 13.4.5).

Πακτωλόν: the Pactolus ran from Mt. Tmolus by ancient Sardis to empty into the river Hermus. It is very near the Caÿster, a river that Homer (*Il.* 2.459–65) claims was filled with swans and cranes (see *hArt* 257n). The Pactolus contained electrum and gold dust and was a source of wealth for local kings (Hdt. 1.93.1), thus proleptic of 263.

250–51. The swans circle Delos seven times in flight. Seven is a sacred number for Apollo—he was born on the seventh day (Hes. *Op.* 770 with West ad loc.). His festivals were often celebrated on the seventh day of the month. Seven also matches the number of strings in the lyre he invents in the next lines.

251. ἑβδομάκις: a *hapax* in Greek, and its origins have been much discussed; see Mineur ad loc. He makes the attractive suggestion that it is deliberately modelled on other ἑβδομ- words that are connected to Apollo. The sense must be that the swans circled "seven times." The scholiast on the passage offers the insight that "Apollo was born in the seventh month" (though Leto might not agree).

ἐπήεισαν: from ἐπαείδω, "sing so as to charm," also at 254 (in tmesis). First in Hdt. 1.132.14 (of a magus chanting), Eur. *El.* 864; frequent in Plato.

λοχείη "child-birth"; see Plato's comment in the *Theaetetus* quoted at *hArt* 22–23n. Since one of Artemis' titles was Λοχεία, the choice of word may be intended to recall the absent twin (see Eur. *IT* 1097).

252. Μουσάων ὄρνιθες: cf. Eur. *IT* 1104–5: ἔνθα κύκνος μελῳδὸς Μούσας θεραπεύει ("there [*sc.* at Delos] the melodious swan serves the Muses").

ἀοιδότατοι πετεηνῶν: the superlative with πετεηνῶν is found in Homer (e.g., *Il.* 8.247, 15.238, 22.139). Note the chiastic arrangement of cases in this line.

253–54. These lines seem to steal the thunder of *HhHerm* 51, where Hermes invents the lyre; cf. *HhAp* 131–32, where the precocious Apollo escapes his leading strings to demand the lyre (εἴη μοι κίθαρις).

255. ἔκθορεν: aorist of ἐκθρῴσκω; for the verb used of infants springing from the womb, cf. *HhAp* 119 and *HhHerm* 20.

255–56. αἱ... νύμφαι Δηλιάδες: cf. *HhAp* 157–63, where the κοῦροι Δηλιάδες first hymn Apollo, Leto, and Artemis, before mimicking the voices of other singers (cf. *hArt* 138–40).

255. ἐπὶ μακρόν: either temporal ("for a long time") or local ("with a far-sounding voice").

256. ποταμοῦ γένος ἀρχαίοιο: these also seem to be nymphs of the river Inopus. See McKay 1962b: 167n5.

257. Ἐλειθυίης ἱερὸν μέλος: Eileithyia is present at Apollo's birth in *HhAp* (115–16), though she does not appear obviously in this hymn. In fact, the potential allusions to Artemis *Lochia* may substitute. For Eileithyia and local women singing at Apollo's birth, see Pi. *Pae.* 12.16–19 S-M (where the spelling is also Ἐλ-, as elsewhere in Pindar).

258. ἀντήχησε: from ἀντηχέω. Previously in Euripides (*Alc.* 423, *Med.* 427) for "sing in response."

διαπρυσίην ὀλολυγήν: the expression appears in *HhAphr* 19 of Artemis, who is said to love "piercing cries."

259. For Zeus's interest in Apollo's birth, see Pi. *Pae.* 12.10–11 S-M. Here his resolution of the conflict with Hera has an element of the *deus ex machina* that is not untypical of his behavior in the *Iliad* and fitting for the quasi-tragic style of much of the hymn. For the phrase χόλον ἐξέλετο Ζεύς, cf. *Il.* 6.234 (≈ 19.137, Hes. *Sc.* 89): φρένας ἐξέλετο Ζεύς.

νεμέσησεν: for the line cf. *Il.* 8.198: νεμέσησε δὲ πότνια Ἥρη, where Hera's anger sets Olympus quaking (cf. 16: οὐ νεμεσητόν).

260–64. χρύσεα...χρυσῷ...χρύσειον...χρυσῷ...χρυσέοιο: the fivefold anaphora with polyptoton ends Leto's term of trial (begun with the fivefold anaphora of φεῦγε at 70–75) and begins the next phase—the triumph of Apollo and Delos. And cf. *HhAp* 135, where Delos is all golden.

260. θεμείλια: see *hAp* 57n.

γείνετο: the form appears to be variation of the epic γείνατο. It occurs at Mosch. *Eur.* 79; see Bühler ad loc.

Δῆλε: at Apollo's birth Asteria's name is changed to Delos; she is now so addressed for the first time; lines 251 and 256 prefigured this moment.

261. τροχόεσσα...λίμνη: one of the well-attested features of the Delian sanctuary was its round lake, cf. Theog. 7, Eur. *IT* 1103–4, *hAp* 59 (see map 7).

262. The sudden introduction of the olive tree (ἔρνος ἐλαίης) has caused concern since only the palm was mentioned at 210. But in Eur. *IT* 1099–1102 the palm, the laurel, and the olive are all mentioned in connection with Apollo's birth, and according to Hdt. 4.34 there was an olive tree growing to the left of the entry of the sanctuary of Apollo on Delos.

γενέθλιον: see 51n.

263. πλήμυρε: πλημύρω ("overflow") is rare, but occurs in papyri for the Nile inundation.

βαθύς: the adjective may be taken either with the river itself, which is joined to the Nile in spate—"the Inopus becoming deep"—or with χρυσῷ—"becoming deep with gold."

ἑλιχθείς: from ἑλίσσω, describing the meandering bed of the river.

264. χρυσέοιο ἀπ' οὔδεος: the very earth on the island is golden.

εἵλεο: Asteria is addressed in her new role as wetnurse; "you took up" the newborn.

265. ἐν δ' ἐβάλευ: cf. *hArt* 112.

ἔπος δ' ἐφθέγξαο τοῖον: Mineur compares the speech formula at Hdt. 5.106.3: κοῖον ἐφθέγξαο ἔπος (again at 7.103.1–2). The phrase is imitated at *Batrach.* 12.

266–73. Delos now boasts of her own exalted state. Cf. the speech of Cos at the birth of Ptolemy II in Theoc. 17.66–70.

266. ὦ μεγάλη: from the sequel the addressee is obviously Earth. Cults of *Gaia Megale* are attested (e.g., Paus. 1.31.4), but none is known for Delos. However, the island did have a Metroon, and numerous inscriptions to *Mater Megale* and *Mater Theon* have been found there (see Bruneau 1970: 431–35), who may be the deity to whom Callimachus refers.

πολύβωμε, πολύπτολι: these compounds first occur here in Callimachus, the latter also in *hArt* 225. The piling up of adjectives with or without asyndeton is often found in epic descriptions (see Hopkinson on *hDem* 66).

267. πίονες ἤπειροί τε καὶ αἳ περιναίετε νῆσοι "rich lands and you islands that dwell around me"; cf. 168n.

268. αὕτη ἐγὼ τοιήδε: αὕτη, Ernesti's emendation of αὐτή of the mss., aligns with 213: αὕτη τοι, φίλε, νῆσος.

δυσήροτος "unplowable," found only in Callimachus. The tiny island was not suitable for agriculture, which is why it may have been dedicated as a cult-site. The form seems to be modelled on *Od.* 9.123: ἀνήροτος, of the untilled land of the Cyclopes (see Schmitt 163).

269. Δήλιος: henceforth Apollo will be called "Delian" for his cult-site on the island.

κεκλήσεται: the future perfect passive from καλέω is common in tragedy in aetiological contexts, e.g., Aesch. *PV* 734, 840.

270. πεφιλήσεται: future perfect passive of φιλέω; the form occurs only here. It is construed with the dative of agent, which extends to the examples below.

271. Asteria goes on to cite other locations dear to divinities in a negative priamel: "Cenchreae will not have been loved by Poseidon, nor the Cyllenian district by Hermes, nor Crete by Zeus as much as I by Apollo." Hermes and Zeus fit the model of Apollo, since these deities were considered to have been born in Cyllene and Crete respectively. Poseidon was not born in Cenchreae, which is located on the eastern coast of the isthmus, but was closely associated with nearby Corinth (he was the deity to whom the Isthmian games were dedicated). According to Pausanias (2.1.6) Poseidon and Helios quarreled over possession of the isthmus; Briareos settled the dispute by awarding it to Poseidon.

Κερχνίς (*sc.* γῆ): the adjective is unique to Callimachus, but will refer to the region around Cenchreae, one of the two harbors of Corinth on the Saronic gulf.

Λεχαίῳ: according to Paus. 2.2.3, the Corinthian harbors bore the names Λέχης and Κεγχρίας, after two sons of Poseidon and Peirene, the daughter of the river god Acheloüs. Apparently the source of the story was Hesiod's *Megalai Ehoiai* (fr. 258 M-W). There was a sanctuary to Poseidon at Lechaeum, but Pausanias notes only the existence of a bronze image of the god at Cenchreae.

272. Ἑρμείῃ: this rare form of the dative is otherwise found only at Hes. *Cat.* fr. 66.4 M-W: Ἑρμείηι ... [Κυλλη]γίωι.

Κυλλήνιος: Cyllene in Arcadia is the birthplace of Hermes, see *HhHerm* 2, Pi. *Ol.* 6.77–80.

Κρήτη: according to Hes. *Th.* 468–80, Zeus was born in Crete, and in *hZeus*, Zeus is reared in Crete (see 42–54).

273. ἔσσομαι οὐκέτι πλαγκτή: for the fixing of Delos in the sea, see above 51–54. For the phrase compare *hAp* 11.

274. The island as wetnurse is a theme also in Theoc. 17 and again in A.R., of Thera (see 48n). Cf. *HhAp* 123–25, where Apollo is not nursed, but Themis feeds him on nectar and ambrosia, the proper food of the gods.

ἔσπασε: from σπάω; the verb is commonly used for "suckle" (see LSJ s.v. III).

275–324. The remainder of the hymn narrates the legendary events that underpin the Delian festival(s): the first time that first fruits (ἀπαρχαί) were sent and origins of the various choruses. The practice of sending first fruits (consisting of bound stalks of wheat) was attributed to the Hyperboreans, who initially accompanied them with a chorus of young women. The most important festival on the island was the *Delia*, apparently Athenian in origin, with a foundation myth connected to Theseus' return from killing the Minotaur. When the hymn was composed, this festival was under the control of the Ptolemies. See p. 159.

275. νησάων: see 66n.

ἐξέτι κείνου: temporal, see *hAp* 47n.

276. Ἀπόλλωνος κουροτρόφος: the title appears at the hymn's opening (2) and now serves to close the frame.

276–77. Delos was exempt from war (Ἐννώ | …ἵπποι…Ἄρηος), and burials (Ἀΐδης) were not allowed. These details do not belong to the early history of Delos, but to the purification of the island by the Athenians in 426/425: the graves were removed, and for the future no one was allowed to die or to give birth on the island; pregnant women were sent to a neighboring island (Thuc. 3.104.2).

276. Ἐννώ: cf. *Il.* 5.592 and *hAp* 85n.

277. ἵπποι…Ἄρηος: see 64n.

ἐπιστείβουσιν: from ἐπιστείβω, "tread on"; before Callimachus found only in Soph. *OC* 56, of walking on sacred ground.

278–300. This passage reflects the information found in Hdt. 4.32–34, who states that originally the Hyperboreans had sent two girls to accompany their offerings, but when the girls did not return, they were afraid to send others. Instead they bound their offerings into stalks of wheat, which were passed in succession to the Scythians, the peoples in the far west, then south to Dodona, and from there to the Malian gulf and Euboea, then the islands of Carystos, Andros, Tenos, and finally Delos (Hdt. 4.33.1–2). Callimachus devotes one of his *Aetia* to the Hyperboreans as well (fr. 186; see Harder ad loc.). For the route of the offerings, see map 8.

278. ἀμφιετεῖς: only here and in later Orphic hymns: "celebrated annually."

δεκατηφόροι "bearing a tenth," that is, a tithe of first fruits; the adjective occurs only here; elsewhere, according to Pausanias (1.42.5), a cult title of Apollo at Megara.

279. Athens and many island cities (including Cos) sent embassies consisting of choruses of young men and women as part of the annual festival; other cities may have availed themselves of local choruses of Delian girls. Again this telescopes time by overlaying contemporary custom onto cultic beginnings. For a discussion of the Delian chorus, see Calame 1997: 104–10.

280–82. Cities from east, west, south, and north all converge on Delos for its festival.

280. ἠοίην "towards the dawn," "easterly" (cf. *Od.* 8.29: ἠὲ πρὸς ἠοίων ἢ ἑσπερίων ἀνθρώπων).

αἵ τ᾽ ἀνὰ μέσσην: cf. Soph. *OC* 1247: αἱ δ᾽ ἀνὰ μέσσαν ἀκτῖν(α), where αἱ is also repeated with four different directions. The scholiast glosses ἐν μεσημβρίᾳ "the South," as is clear also from the parallel.

281. κλήρους: the word has two potentially relevant meanings: "lot" and "allotment of land." Thus with ἐστήσαντο, "obtained by lot" or "as their lot," but equally "established their plot of land." Since many of the cities sending annual gifts to Delos were originally colonies, *kleros* as allotted land is appropriate, and may also evoke the large-scale settlement of veterans on *kleroi* in the Fayum under Ptolemy II (see *hAth* 142n).

281–82. οἱ καθύπερθε βορείης ... θινός: the Hyperboreans, whose name was etymologized as living beyond (ὑπέρ) the North Wind (Boreas). The Hyperboreans first appear in Hes. *Cat.* fr. 150.21 M-W and in a *paean* of Alcaeus (fr. 307c V). Apollo is said to have lived among them, while Pi. *Py.* 10.29–44 describes their utopian way of life without war. They often play host to the gods and are thus a suitable, holy people to initiate tribute to Apollo.

282. πολυχρονιώτατον αἷμα: at *hArt* 132 and *hAth* 128 πολυχρόνιον refers to length of life. The superlative may refer to the longevity of the Hyperboreans, but also implicit may be their antiquity. Callimachus was interested elsewhere in the oldest of Greeks—the Arcadians in *hZeus*, the Pelasgians in *hAth*.

283–84. καλάμην ... ἀσταχύων: in Homer (*Il.* 19.222) καλάμη is collective; according to Hdt. 4.33, the corn stalks were bound in stalks of wheat (ἐν καλάμῃ πυρῶν), presumably to protect them. The phrase occurs also at *hDem* 19–20.

284. φορέουσιν: frequentative of φέρω; here and again at 299 it records customary or repeated action as first-time events are becoming ritual.

Δωδώνηθε "from Dodona"; Dodona was an important oracle of Zeus in northwestern Greece.

Πελασγοί: the Pelasgians were the oldest Greeks of the region.

285–89. Callimachus marks the passage of the offerings with temporal adverbs, πρώτιστα, δεύτερον, κεῖθεν, οὐδ᾽ ἔτι μακρός, that balance his directional markers in 280–81.

286. γηλεχέες: γη-λεχής is a gloss on the Homeric χαμαι-εύνης (*Il.* 16.234–35), a passage in which Achilles prays to Zeus of Dodona, mentioning the local attendants: ἀμφὶ δὲ Σελλοὶ | σοὶ ναίουσ᾽ ὑποφῆται ἀνιπτόποδες χαμαιεῦναι "and around you dwell the Selloi, interpreters with unwashed feet who lie upon the ground." Callimachus' coinage is a good example of one of his allusive techniques: paraphrasing a unique and memorable Homeric expression (see Schmitt 123n84).

ἀσιγήτοιο λέβητος: the "unsilent cauldron" is the bronze tripod from which the prophecies at Dodona were uttered. These were so well known that they served as a proverb for talkative people (see Zenobius 6.5 and Cook 1902).

287. Ἴριον ἄστυ: mss. read ἱερὸν ἄστυ, which makes little sense in the context of cities through which the tribute is passing; Pfeiffer's conjecture of Ἴριον resolves the problem. The town of Ira (or Iros) was in southeastern Thessaly near the Malian gulf; it is mentioned at Lycophron 905.

Μηλίδος αἴης: the "Malian land."

288. διαπλώουσιν: Ionic form of διαπλέω, occurring only in Hellenistic poetry.

Ἀβάντων: see 20n.

289. πεδίον Ληλάντιον: the Lelantine plain lay between Chalkis and Eretria. Cf. *HhAp* 220. This adjectival form is first found in Callimachus.

290. Εὐβοίηθεν: Callimachus omits the final stages recorded in Herodotus, Carystos, Andros, and Tenos, and moves directly to Delos (see map 8).

ἐπεὶ σέο γείτονες ὅρμοι "since their harbors are your neighbors"; the phrase is imitated in *Batrach.* 67 and Nonnus.

291–99. Callimachus next describes the women who first brought the gifts: Oupis, Loxo, and Hecaerge, the daughters of Boreas. Herodotus gives two versions of the story: at 4.33.3, he claims the Hyperborean girls were Hyperoche and Laodice, but in 4.35.1–5 he names Arge and Opis as prior and says that their gifts were a thank-offering to Eileithyia for ease of delivery in childbirth. At 293–94 Callimachus mentions without name the men who accompanied them.

291. ἔνεικαν: Ionic aorist from φέρω.

ἀπὸ...Ἀριμασπῶν: according to Hdt. 4.27, the Arimaspi were a one-eyed people (from Scythian *arima* = "one" and *spou* = "eye") who lived just to the south of the Hyperboreans (4.13). Occasionally they are identified with the Hyperboreans. They next receive the offerings in *Aet.* fr. 186.12 Pf. (see Harder ad loc.).

292. Οὖπις: = Herodotus' Ὦπις. The name is also a cult title of Artemis. The scholium on *hArt* 204 derives the cult titles of Artemis *Oupis* and Apollo *Loxias* and *Hekaergos* respectively as tributes to these girls.

Λοξώ: Loxo occurs only here and later in Nonnus.

εὐαίων "happy in life"; the word occurs in tragedy before Callimachus; also at *hAth* 117.

Ἑκαέργη: a female equivalent of *Hekaergos*, a cult title of Apollo. According to Pausanias 5.7.8, Melanopus of Cyme wrote a hymn to Opis and Hecaerge claiming that they were the first to come to Delos from the Hyperboreans. (Opis and Hecaerge are named also in the spurious Pl. *Axioch.* 371a5–6.)

294. παλιμπετές: the neuter used adverbially, "back again," cf. *Il.* 16.395. The reason they do not return is never given, though scholars have conjectured that Callimachus treated the subject in fr. 186 Pf. of the *Aetia*.

295. εὔμοιροι "alloted good fortune"; Mineur ad loc. understands as a euphemism for their death, and surely that is correct since 296–99 detail grave offerings.

ἀκλεὲς οὔποτ᾽ ἔσονται: ἔσονται is an emendation proposed by Mineur for ἐκεῖνοι of the mss., which has been questioned on the grounds that it is banal and unnecessary. The change to ἔσονται allows a pointed contrast of past and future as at *hZeus* 93: οὐ γένετ', οὐκ ἔσται (and for final ἔσονται, see *hArt* 37). The line itself may be a reworking of Hector's famous remark at *Il.* 22.303–5: "now my fate (μοῖρα) has caught up to me…but let me not die ἀκλειῶς."

296. ἤτοι: the Homeric expression occurs only here in Callimachus, which led Pfeiffer to suggest emending to ἤ γάρ (p. 167 of his *index vocabulorum*). Mineur, following Ruijgh 1981, regards it as an intensification of μέν (see Denniston 554). For the accent of ἤτοι, see Denniston 553.

Δηλιάδες: here young women on Delos of marriagable age; at 256 it denotes nymphs, who are daughters of Inopus; and in *HhAp* 157 local girls who form the choirs in honor of the god.

εὐηχής "fair-sounding," previously only at Pi. *Py.* 2.14.

297. ἤθεα κουράων: either "maidens' quarters" (so Mair), or "the feelings of young girls"; with the verb ("frighten"), the latter seems more likely. For the former, cf. *hArt* 70, where divine mothers are said to frighten their naughty daughters by having Hermes enter the women's quarters in disguise and act the bogeyman (μορμύσσεται). Thus the idea of the hymeneal being a fearsome intruder into female space will also be part of the equation. The point is "when the girls are ready for marriage."

ἤλικα: dependent on χαίτην: "hair, of equal age to the virgins," i.e., hair that has never been cut. The dedication of hair before marriage was a widespread cultural practice, though Hdt. 4.34 relates that on Delos boys and girls cut their hair in honor of the Hyperborean maidens who died there.

298. θέρος: here in the sense of "harvest." The young men's dedication of the first growth of their beards is analogous to the girl's dedication of a lock of hair.

299. ἄρσενες: for ἄρσην as a qualifier of παῖς, see *Aet.* fr. 75.3 Pf. (cf. *ep.* 40.5 Pf.), though not strictly necessary here since the participle is masculine.

ἠιθέοισιν: i.e., the young men described in 293–94.

ἀπαρχόμενοι: the verb has two related meanings: to "cut something off in offering" and to "dedicate as first fruits."

φορέουσιν: see 86n.

300. θυόεσσα: cf. *HhAp* 87, where Apollo's altar is θυώδης, "fragrant" with sacrifices.

σὲ μὲν περί τ' ἀμφί τε: here prepositions follow their object. For the expression cf. Aesch. *Pers.* 475, Hes. fr. 150.28 M-W.

300–1. νήσοι | κύκλον ἐποιήσαντο: now that Delos is stationary, the nearby islands express their sympathy for her by reshaping the geography to form a permanent circle around her; according to Dion. Per. 525–26, the name "Cyclades" derives from the fact that the other islands of the group encircle Delos (see Lightfoot 2014: 381–82 and above 2–3n). At 312–13 Theseus and his companions will dance in a circle around Asteria/Delos.

301. καὶ ὡς χορὸν ἀμφεβάλοντο "they surrounded you like a chorus." The circular shape of the chorus was standard (see Calame 1997: 34–38 and *hArt* 170,

241–42). The theme of the chorus of the islands was anticipated at 17–18 and 198. (See Mineur's note at 17f. for a discussion of literary and visual representations of islands as choruses.)

302–3. These lines provide a vivid image of the Evening Star (Hesperus) looking down upon the choruses performing even into the night. There is an implicit contrast of the normal silence of the night sky—Hesperus usually marks the end of human activities and the time for rest—and the music "ringing on all sides" (ἀμφιβόητον) far into the night. *Nocturnal Feast* (Παννυχίς, fr. 227 Pf.) was the title of one of Callimachus' *mele*.

302. οὔτε σιωπηλὴν οὔτ᾽ ἄψοφον (*sc.* σε = Δῆλον): cf. *hAp* 12, where, as Williams has made clear, the phrase refers to choral song and to dance. The hyperbaton of 302–3 guarantees that Delos (σε) is in fact surrounded by sound (οὔτε σιωπηλὴν … ἀμφιβόητον).

οὖλος: the word had a range of meanings, and Callimachus seems to use them all; see *hZeus* 52n and *hAp* 76n. With hair (ἐθείραις), the sense is usually "thick" or "curly" (cf. Bacchyl. 17.113 of Theseus). Why Callimachus includes this detail is not clear. Jan 1893: 12, referring to *Od.* 6.231 and μέλας Hesperus at *Od.* 1.423, thought it connoted blackness.

303. καταβλέπει: first here as a compound: "look down on."

ἀμφιβόητον: the reading of the mss. in the hymn to Eros of Antagoras of Rhodes (fr. 1.1 Powell); if correct, the sense must have been "disputed on both sides" (see p. 50). The meaning here is closer to "surrounded with sound."

304–15. Callimachus constructs his "historical" narrative out of several different elements of Delian tradition: (1) men singing the nome composed by Olen; (2) a female chorus dances (possibly to be connected with the Delian maidens of *HhAp*); (3) a holy and ancient statue of Aphrodite, dedicated by Theseus when he returned to Crete (Paus. 9.40.3; Plut. *Thes.* 21); (4) Theseus and his companions perform a circular dance around the altar; (5) these events are commemorated in an annual *theoria* sent by Athens (Pl. *Phaedo* 58a-c, Xen. *Mem.* 4.8.2). Of these, (2) and (4) continue the emphasis on circular dance (stressed again at 306 and 313) that unites nature (the chorus of islands) and the human world.

304. ὑπαείδουσι: cf. *hArt* 242 (based on *Il.* 18.570) and Calame 1997: 81. The verb refers to musical accompaniment for a chorus. The alpha is long, exceptionally, but Callimachus so treats it in *Aet.* fr. 26.8 Pf. and *Hec.* fr. 74.25 Hollis.

νόμον "nome" is a term applied to the melodies that accompany various verse forms (hexameter, lyric, elegy, dithyramb) for specific occasions, and they could be performed by a variety of instruments. See West 1992: 215–17 and Calame 1997: 80–82 and 222n for the citharodic nome at Delos.

Λυκίοιο γέροντος: the "Lycian old man" was Olen (named in the next line). According to Hdt. 4.35, Olen composed the first hymns to be sung by maidens' choirs as the offerings were presented.

305. ἀπὸ Ξάνθοιο: Xanthus was the name both of a river and of an important town in Lydia; the town was under Ptolemaic control at the time of the hymn. (If Ξάνθοιο is correct at 41, it refers to a person, not a place.)

θεοπρόπος: the adjective has two potentially appropriate meanings: "prophetic" or, as a substantive, someone sent to an oracle. Paus. 10.5.8 claims that Olen was the first prophet of Apollo at Delphi.

306. χορίτιδες: a Callimachean coinage, here and at *hArt* 13, for female members of a chorus (on the form see Schmitt 26n46).

ἀσφαλὲς οὖδας: the ground is "secure" because Delos now has been given fixed foundations.

307. βαρύνεται: the statue "is laden" with wreaths. Callimachus first used βαρύνω of Leto's pregnancy (202, 212), then of Hera's anger (244), now in the celebratory context of "being burdened" with offerings.

308. Κύπριδος ἀρχαίης: according to Pausanias 9.40.3, this archaic statue of Aphrodite was a small wooden image with a square base instead of feet; it is said to have been the work of Daedalus, and Ariadne brought it with her when she left Crete. Theseus later dedicated it at Delos. ἀρχαίης may simply refer to the antiquity of the statue, but Mineur suggests that it might also have been a reminder that there is a younger Aphrodite—the Aphrodite identified with Arsinoe II in her temple at Cape Zephyrium. For Aphrodite in Delian cult, see Calame 1997: 123–28 and Bruneau 1970: 334.

ἀριήκοον: the adjective occurs first here in a passive sense, "much heard of," though in A.R. 4.1707 in an active sense, "quick to hear."

ἥν ποτε Θησεύς: see *Od.* 11.321–23: Ἀριάδνην | ... ἥν ποτε Θησεύς | ἐκ Κρήτης, the only mention of Theseus in the Homeric poems. Callimachus alludes to these same Homeric lines at the opening of his *Hecale*, his hexameter treatment of Theseus' capture of the Marathonian bull, an event that predates the adventure with the Minotaur (Fantuzzi and Hunter 2004: 198–99).

309. εἴσατο: first aorist middle of ἵζω, common for "dedicate," "set up"; see A.R. 4.119, with Livrea's note ad loc.

σὺν παίδεσσιν ὅτε Κρήτηθεν ἀνέπλει: the story of Theseus leading out seven youths and seven maidens as a tribute to Minos of Crete in expiation for the death of his son Androgeos was a staple of Athenian self-fashioning. Plato recounts the story at *Phaedo* 58a10-b4 and *Laws* 706a4-c7; see also Plut. *Thes.* 17–21 (parts of which may be dependent on this hymn, if they are not both derived from a common source such as one of the Atthidographers).

310–15. The *aition* of the famous crane dance around the horned altar. The first instance of the dance was attributed to Theseus and his companions on their triumphant return after escaping the labyrinth of the Minotaur.

310–13. Wilamowitz *HD* 2.75n3 provides an elegant explanation for the complex word order. Elements occur as the young men and women would have experienced them: first the "dire bellow," then the "son of Pasiphae," i.e., the Minotaur himself, and finally the twistings of the labyrinth as they escape it.

310. μύκημα: first in Aesch. *PV* 1062, of the roar of thunder, and Eur. *Bacch.* 691, of the bellowing of cows.

ἄγριον υἷα (= υἱόν): the Minotaur.

311. Πασιφάης: Pasiphae was the daughter of Helios and wife of Minos, king of Crete. Poseidon gave Minos a fine bull to sacrifice, but the king decided to keep it. In punishment, Pasiphae was afflicted with an erotic passion for the bull; hence Daedalus, the resident artist, was induced to design a wooden cow by means of which she coupled with the bull. The resulting offspring was half-man, half-bull. Minos then confined him to the labyrinth. According to Apollod. 3.1.4 and Paus. 2.31.1 the name of the Minotaur was Asterius.

γναμπτόν "twisted" or "bent"; Homeric, in Pi. *Is.* 1.57 of the course for chariot racing. It is a virtual synonym for σκολιοῦ (used at Pi. *Py.* 2.85 of ὁδοῖς). The two words mimic the structure of the Cretan labyrinth by twisting and winding into ἕδος and out again.

λαβυρίνθου: Callimachus is the first to apply the term to the Minotaur's lair on Crete; Hdt. 2.148 uses the word first to describe an extensive palace compound in Egypt (in the Fayum).

312. πότνια: Asteria is addressed by a term that pays tribute to her newly acquired status; earlier πότνια was addressed to Leto (123), then to Hera (226).

κιθαρισμοῦ: only here in Callimachus; it is generally taken to be a variant of the unique Homeric κιθαριστύς (*Il.* 2.600 of Thamyris). For the form see Schmitt 99n30; for the "citharodic" nome, see above 304n.

313. κύκλιον ὠρχήσαντο: according to Dicaearchus (fr. 85 Wehrli), this dance was called the γέρανος, or "crane"; it supposedly originated from the participants mimicking their twisted path through the labyrinth (Plut. *Thes.* 21, see Calame 1997: 123–28).

ἡγήσατο: ἡγέομαι + genitive is usual for acting as leader of the chorus, e.g., Alcman's Ἁγησιχόρα (*Partheneion*, 53, 57, 77, etc.). See Calame 1997: 56–58 for a discussion of Theseus as choral leader.

314–15. These lines refer to the ship upon which Theseus sailed. According to Plutarch, *Theseus* 23, it was preserved by the Athenians until the time of Demetrius of Phalerum, who was the ruler of Athens from 317 to 307 BCE. The ship was dispatched annually to the Delian festival with its ambassadors and choruses. As parts of the ship wore out they were continually replaced; it thus stimulated discussion among philosophers about sameness vs. change. The word order is confusing: although placed forward, ἀειζώοντα θεωρίδος ἱερά is in apposition to τοπήια νηὸς ἐκείνης, which is the object.

314. ἀειζώοντα: the ἱερά may be "ever-living" because they are celebrated annually, but equally because of the continual replacement of the ship's parts.

θεωρίδος: the sacred ship that carried the *theoria* (Hdt. 6.87: τὴν θεωρίδα νέα), without the addition of ναῦς. Though some have questioned whether it makes better sense to understand here as = θεωρίης, the *Theoria*; see Danielsson's full discussion 1901: 100–6.

315. Κεκροπίδαι: the Athenians, so named from Cecrops, an ancestral king of the city.

τοπήϊα: a variant of τοπεῖον, probably for metrical reasons, only here in Callimachus; see Schmitt 42n3, 49 (3.16.3); according to the scholiast: ὅπλα νεώς, "ship's tackle." (There is no external evidence for this kind of dedication at Delos, but it does provide a parallel in this hymn for Agamemnon's dedication of a ship's rudder at Ephesus in *hArt* 229–30.)

316–26. The envoi is framed with the names of Asteria at the beginning and Leto at the end, inserted between which (316–24) is one final *aition*.

316. πολύβωμε: above 266, of Earth.

πολύλλιτε: see *hAp* 80n.

316–17. Earlier (41–44) sailors were barely able to catch sight of the island as she wandered the Aegean. Now every passing ship will stop to participate in her rites. Hence the question: "what sailor passed by...?"

317. ἔμπορος Αἰγαίοιο: for the importance of Delos in Ptolemaic Aegean trade see Fraser 1972: 1.169–73; Bagnall 1976: 151–56.

νηὶ θεούσῃ: a Callimachean recasting of Homeric formulae. At verse end it reflects νηὶ μελαίνῃ, in thought νηὶ θοῇ.

318. μιν = ναύτην.

319. χρειώ: epic variant of χρέω; here subject of ἄγει; "necessity compels the fastest possible course."

320. ἐστείλαντο: Callimachus shifts to the plural as he proceeds from the question: "what sailor passed you by?" to the answer that all sailors furled their sails and did not embark again before completing the rites described.

321. πρὶν... ἤ: although particles may occupy the space between πρὶν and ἤ, the intrusion of an adjective (μέγαν) has led to attempts to emend (see Mineur ad loc. for details). But *Od.* 24.430: πρὶν τοῦτον ἢ ἐς Πύλον ὦκα ἱκέσθαι ("before this one [Odysseus] hastens off to Pylos") provides a parallel.

μέγαν... σέο βωμόν: which Delian altar is never made clear, but surely that of Apollo, as the scholiast assumes; it must be the equivalent of σὸν περὶ βωμόν at 312.

ἑλίξαι: when ἑλίσσω takes an object it usually means "roll" or "twist" something, or it is used with a preposition (as at 13). It is usually absolute when describing motions of the dance, i.e., "turning" or "dancing around"; cf. Eur. *HF* 687–90: παιᾶνα μὲν Δηλιάδες | <ναῶν> ὑμνοῦσ' ἀμφὶ πύλας | τὸν Λατοῦς εὔπαιδα γόνον, | εἰλίσσουσαι καλλίχοροι ("the Delian maidens hymn a paean to Leto's fair child around the temple doors as they turn, beautiful in the dance"). But if ἑλίξαι is absolute here, it is difficult to account for the case of βωμόν. This is no doubt why LSJ (s.v. ἐλίσσω) regards it as transitive (i.e., "twisting around the altar").

322. ῥησσόμενον (*sc.* βωμόν): the passage has occasioned considerable discussion. ῥήσσω may describe dancers whose feet "beat" the ground (see *hArt* 242–43n, where *Il.* 18.571 is cited; cf. *HhAp* 516 and A.R. 1.539); this has led to the interpretation that the altar is "shaken by the stomping" of the dancers' feet (thus expressing a thought similar to ποδὶ πλήσσουσι at 306). Alternatively the altar itself is "beaten by blows" as the men wind around it (so the scholiast). Finally, Hesychius (s.v. Δηλιακὸς βωμός) explains as "to run around the altar at Delos in a circle and be beaten" (i.e., the men). Because ritual of beating of an altar is unattested, while the rites of Artemis *Orthia* in Sparta involved beating the participants as they stood before an altar, Hesychius' explanation of the rite is attractive, but no help with the syntax unless one follows Ernesti and emends to ῥησσομένους. Mineur ad loc. provides considerable bibliography on attempts to identify the rite.

πρέμνον: see 210n.

ὀδακτάσαι: from ὀδακτάζω, only here and at A.R. 4.1608, "bite." The rite seems to require the itinerant sailors to bite at the olive tree while circling with "their hands behind their backs" (χεῖρας ἀποστρέψαντας). It is otherwise unattested and has occasioned considerable discussion with meager results.

ἁγνὸν ἐλαίης: the palm is the tree always associated with Delos, but the olive seems to have maintained a presence there as well, see above 262n.

323. Δηλιὰς ... νύμφη: this is an unlikely designation for Asteria/Delos, so it must be one of the Deliades mentioned at 255–56 above.

324. κουρίζοντι: see *hZeus* 54n.

γελαστύν: only here in Callimachus; Ionic for γέλως, "something to provoke laughter."

325. ἱστίη ὤ: the address is to Delos, as center or "hearth" of the islands, and possibly of the Ptolemaic empire in a wider sense; see the discussion of movement from the center in the introduction to *hZeus*. For the correption, see *HhAphr* 22: Ἱστίη, ἥν.

εὐέστιε: the word occurs only here and in a third-century funerary epigram (*GLP* 106.5 = *SH* 980.5); the scholiast glosses as εὔοικος, "convenient to inhabit." It is a pun hinting at etymology, and quite likely a coinage of Callimachus.

326. χαίροι: cf. *HhAp* 165 for an example of the optative in a salutation.

ἐλοχεύσατο: the reading of the mss. suggests Artemis, i.e., "she whom Leto bore." For a parallel see Eur. *Ion* 921–22: ἔνθα ... ἐλοχεύσατο | Λατὼ Δίοισί σε κάποις ("there Leto gave birth to you in the Zeus-sent bower"). However, since Artemis is otherwise absent in this hymn apart from allusion, Pfeiffer accepted Wilamowitz's emendation and printed ἐλοχεύσαο, i.e., "Leto, for whom you [= Asteria] acted as a midwife." Mineur suggests retaining the reading of the mss. but taking the subject as Apollo, "Leto, whom he delivered," since Apollo is not in need of a midwife but spontaneously leaps from his mother's womb (255). See Fantuzzi 2011: 451–52 for an editorial explanation of the phrase.

5

The Hymn to Athena
On The Bath of Pallas

THIS IS A MIMETIC HYMN WRITTEN IN DORIC AND IN ELEGIAC COUPLETS.[1] The unidentified narrator creates an aura of anticipation, exhorting the female worshippers to come forward since Athena is drawing near. They are celebrating a well-documented type of festival in which selected members of the community engage in the ritual purification of a cult statue. Callimachus' female celebrants will carry the Palladium, the ancient cult statue of Athena that Diomedes was said to have captured from Troy (33–42), to the river Inachus for this purpose. Its talismanic power had guaranteed the safety of the Trojan citadel, which fell when the object was taken. In addition to the Palladium, the shield of Diomedes is also ritually cleansed; the narrator includes a brief vignette of Eumedes, the priest who taught the Argives the rite (35–42). The theme of cleansing is introduced by the narrator's remarks on Athena's bathing habits: the warrior goddess is described as having just returned from battle intent upon caring for her horses before attending to her own hygiene (4–11). Her lack of concern for feminine beauty continues in a brief, slyly humorous version of the judgment of Paris at which Athena arrived, disdaining mirrors and any ointments except her own olive oil, after having run "twice sixty double stades" (19–26). The audience will know, of course, that she lost the contest. These details provide mythological analogues for the events of the ceremony: the statue would have

---

1. See pp. 26–27 (for Doric) and pp. 34–35 (for elegiacs and the form of the title). See also Manakidou's very detailed history of the dialect and meter in question (2013: 118–30).

been transported by a horse-drawn wagon or chariot and the statue anointed with oils after the ritual bathing.

Within his mimetic frame Callimachus' narrator inserts a long sequence on the blinding of Tiresias, who is the son of Everes and the nymph Chariclo. She is the favorite attendant of Athena. Her son is punished for accidentally seeing Athena as she emerged naked after bathing in a spring (55–136). Although Athena cannot alter his fate, she gives him the gift of prophecy and long life in compensation. He subsequently served as a priest of Apollo for Cadmus as well as his descendants down through Oedipus (120–26). A doublet of his fate is provided in the vignette of Actaeon, another young man who, while hunting, inadvertently came upon Artemis as she was bathing; he was ripped apart by his own hounds for the sacrilege. Actaeon was Cadmus' nephew, hence also connected to Thebes, and Athena recounts his harsher fate (107–18) by way of consolation to Chariclo, when she complains of the goddess's cruel punishment of her son. Functionally, the blinding of Tiresias provides a mythological exemplum of the consequences for men who would ignore the narrator's exhortation to avert their eyes from the statue, the procession, and the bathing. The hymn concludes with an urgent assertion that Athena is near and a prayer to her to care for Inachan Argos and the whole legacy of the Danaans (142).[2]

The Deity and Her Relevant Cults

Athena was a second-generation Olympian, a daughter of Zeus. There are two versions of her birth: without a mother, she sprang from the head of her father, or she was the daughter of Metis (Intelligence) and Zeus. Lines 134–45 allude to the former version, rationalized to explain her close association with her father's honors (133). She was widely worshipped in the Greek world, but most prominently as the patron goddess of Athens, as *Parthenos* (Virgin) and *Polias* (City Goddess). This hymn is set in Argos and its environs, where Athena had a number of temples dedicated to her: within the city, she was worshipped as Athena *Oxyderkes* "Sharp-eyed" and as Athena *Polias*. The shield of Diomedes (35) was probably kept in the temple of Athena *Oxyderkes*. Pausanias claims that Diomedes dedicated it to honor the goddess, because she once removed the mist from his eyes while fighting at Troy (*Il.* 5.127, Paus. 2.24.2–3). Apart from this hymn, evidence for the Argive possession of the Palladium depends upon recovered statues of an armed goddess, the image of the Palladium on a few Argive coins, and a comment in Pausanias (2.23.5), who states that the Argives claim to have the Palladium along with the tombs of Deianeira and Helenus, the son of Priam. But he discounts this, stating that the Palladium "was brought by Aeneas

2. For the relationship of this hymn to *hDem*, see Hopkinson 13–17 and Ambühl 2005: 204–24.

to Italy." In Argos, the Palladium would have been housed either in the temple of Athena *Oxyderkes* or that of Athena *Polias*.[3]

More than one ancient city claimed to possess the Palladium: more prominent claims were made especially by Athens, Rome, and even Sparta (see Frazer's long note on Apollod. 3.12.3). Apart from this hymn, the ritual washing at Argos is unattested; however, similar rites were widely practiced throughout Greece. Some Ionian *poleis* even had months named *Plynterion* designating the period for this ceremonial washing (Parker 1983: 26–27). There was a well-attested bathing ritual of the Palladium at Athens, during which ephebes carried the statue annually to Phalerum. The mythic rationale for the Athenian *Plynteria*, as it seems to have been presented in the Atthidographers, involved a contest between Diomedes, who took the original and brought it to Athens, and a claim to it by Agamemnon, for whom Diomedes had an imitation of the original made (Cleidemus *FGrH* 323 F20, Phanodemus *FGrH* 325 F16, and see Paus. 1.28.8–9). The story of the two statues and the involvement of the Argive Diomedes and Agamemnon, with his clear connections to the Argolid, seem to indicate that the dispute over the Palladium was very old, and at the same time they reinforce the claim that Athens possesses the original. Callimachus clearly gives the nod to Argos. (For the relationship of the *Plynteria* to the ephebic procession and the tradition of two Palladia, see Sourvinou-Inwood and Parker 2011: 225–61).

Athena was also important in Cyrene (see, e.g., Pi. *Py* 9.98) and the Cyrenaica. According to Herodotus (4.180), a native goddess identified with Athena was worshipped near lake Tritonis, where she was said to have been born; the ritual involved choosing a young woman dressed in full armor to drive a chariot around the circuit of the lake. Callimachus refers to Athena's Libyan birthplace in *Aetia* fr. 37 Pf., and according to Pliny (*HN* 5.28.4–5) Callimachus called lake Tritonis "Pallantian," i.e., "of Pallas" (see 42n). Manakidou (2009: 372–79) suggests that aspects of Athena in this hymn are meant to recall Libyan Athena and to strengthen the Dorian connections between the two spaces (see *hAp* 74n). This is particularly attractive in light of the potential link to Cyrene in the Tiresias episode.

In contrast, there is very little evidence for Athena cult in early Alexandria, but when she does appear, she is the equivalent of Egyptian Neith (Fraser 1972: 1.195). This goddess had her principal cult center in Saïs, a town only a few kilometers south of Alexandria, and like the temple of Zeus Ammon in the Siwah oasis, it was very well known to the Greek world. Ptolemy II apparently rebuilt her temple there in the 260s and introduced a statue of his late sister-wife as Isis-Arsinoe (Quack 2008: 284–85). At this temple precinct in an earlier period Herodotus saw the rites he calls the mysteries, claiming that "it was the daughters of Danaus who brought this rite from Egypt and taught it to Pelasgian women" (2.170–71). In this context, it may

---

3. For the complex relationship of Callimachus' geography to the archaeological evidence, see Billot 1997–98: 28–38.

be relevant that Aristophanes (*Thesm.* 1136–59) links Athena and Demeter with respect to the Eleusinian Mysteries, since both are so closely connected to Athens (Furley and Bremer 2001: 1.360–64), and that Callimachus' hymns to Athena and Demeter are also tightly connected. Later Plato in the *Timaeus* (22–24) claimed that Saïs and Athens were founded by the same goddess—Athena/Neith (Martin Bernal's "Black Athena"). In addition, Pausanias (2.36.8–37.1) claims that Danaus dedicated the temple of Athena *Saïtis* in the region outside of Argos, while a local river was named for his daughter, Amymone. Although these sources are diffuse, it is safe to conclude that more than one Greek writer imagined close cultic connections between the Egyptian goddess and Athenian and Argive Athena; Ptolemaic support for the Neith cult in Saïs is likely to have capitalized on this link.

The Sources and Intertexts

Athena is the subject of two minor Homeric hymns (11, 28), and she appears in the *Homeric Hymn to Aphrodite* (8–15). In hymn 28 she bursts forth from the head of Zeus dressed in shining armor, an event that causes trepidation among the immortals until she sets her armor aside. Callimachus mentions the same birth story at the end of his hymn (135–36), and his Athena is equally dangerous, but only to those who violate taboos. In *HhAphr* Athena is introduced as one of three goddesses (along with Artemis and Hestia) impervious to the sweet longings sent by Aphrodite, preferring war and teaching household skills to girls (8 15); Aphrodite's encounter with the mortal Anchises in the Homeric hymn has a close analogue to the encounter of the goddess (Athena) and a mortal male (Tiresias). What leads to sexual relations in the earlier hymn infuses the latter with a sexual tension and contributes to the sexual ambiguity of the portrait of Athena (see Hadjittofi 2008: 15–18).

The story of the Palladium was first recounted in the *Little Iliad*, and variations of the story are to be found in numerous sources (for which see Sourvinou-Inwood and Parker 2011: 227–41). About the shield of Diomedes, nothing beyond Callimachus' text is known. According to the scholiast (37), "when the Heracleidae were coming against the Oresteidae, Eumedes, the priest of Athena, was suspected by the Argives on the grounds that he wished to betray the Palladium to the Heracleidae. In his fear he took the Palladium and brought it to so-called Mt. Ipheion." The scholiast's Mt. Ipheion is otherwise unknown, but is likely to have been a copyist's error for Kreion, the mountain that Callimachus mentions in connection with the story (40–41).

Elements in Callimachus' presentation of the judgment of Paris (14–32) coincide in detail with the *Krisis*, a satyr play by Sophocles. The plot is briefly summarized in Athenaeus (15.687c and 12.510c = *TrGF* 4 fr. 361.1–2 Radt): "Sophocles…stages Aphrodite as being a goddess of pleasure, anointing herself with myrrh and looking into her mirror [κατοπτριζομένην], while Athena is the goddess of wisdom and good sense and, further, virtue, rubbing down with olive oil and exercising [ἐλαίῳ χριομένην καὶ γυμναζομένην]."

The story of the blinding of Tiresias as a result of seeing Athena in her bath first occurred in the fifth-century mythographer, Pherecydes of Athens (reported in Apollod. 3.6.7 and the T scholium on *Od.* 10.493 = *FGrH* 3 F92). The usual story was that Zeus and Hera turned Tiresias into a woman for a period so that he could settle their dispute about whether men or women had the greater pleasure in sex. When Tiresias said women, Hera took away his eyesight (this is the version in Ov. *Met.* 3.316–38). The ps.-Plutarchan *Parallela minora* (309F) claims that when the shrine of Athena in Troy was in flames, Ilus touched the statue in order to rescue it and was blinded (though later cured). The source of the tale, we are told, is Dercyllus' *Foundations of Cities.* The *Parallela minora* are a series of parallel Greek and Roman anecdotes with what are generally taken to have been invented "sources" (Cameron 2004: 127–34). But the connection of loss of sight with violating the boundaries of the Palladium may have a kernel of authenticity, especially if the source, named Dercyllus, was based on or meant to be the Dercylus who wrote the *Argolica* from which Callimachus culled other Argive lore (e.g., *Aet.* frr. 26–31 Pf., Linus and Coroebus, and frr. 65–66 Pf., the Fountains of Argos). The hymn itself is filled with word play on sight (φάος, δέρκομαι, δόρξ, ὄψις, ἐσοράω, Ὀξυδέρκης). Another suggestive anecdote, found in Aelian (fr. 44 Hercher), records that Battus, the founder of Cyrene, violated the *Thesmophoria* when it was being celebrated there, and the female worshippers castrated him for his sacrilege. Provided it is not a later fiction, this story is so conspicuously linked to Cyrene that Callimachus would certainly have known it (see Bing 2009: 62). Tiresias himself was associated with the Cadmids, the line from whom Callimachus traces the descent of the Battiads of Cyrene in *hAp* 74. Also, there are obvious genealogical connections between Actaeon, whose fate is introduced by way of parallel to that of Tiresias, and Cyrene. Actaeon was the son of Aristaeus and the grandson of Cyrene, and Autonoe, the daughter of Cadmus.

The version of Actaeon's story narrated in this hymn and subsequently imitated in Ovid (*Met.* 3.138–252) has no extant parallel. However, a papyrus fragment assigned to Hesiod's *Catalogue of Women* provides a tantalizing glimpse of a potential intertext.[4] In it a goddess, most probably Athena (αἰγιόχοιο Διὸς κούρη μεγ[άλοιο), is consoling Chiron and his wife for the death of Actaeon. Actaeon was raised by Chiron, and his wife, according to Pindar (*Py.* 4.103), is almost certainly named Chariclo. This suggests the possibility that Callimachus has constructed Athena's consolation to Tiresias' mother, who is a different Chariclo, to

---

4. POxy 2509, which, however, is not accepted by West; see Depew 1994: 413n24 for a discussion of the attribution. For the most recent discussion, see Manakidou 2013: 75–79.

recall an earlier (Hesiodic?) Actaeon story. Such a deliberate juxtaposition of disparate myths with homonymous characters would mark as ironic his assertion that: μῦθος δ' οὐκ ἐμός, ἀλλ' ἑτέρων (56).

The Ptolemaic Connections

The most concrete link to contemporary Alexandria is the fact that Argive ancestors were important for the Ptolemies in their self-fashioning as Greek kings of Egypt. The movement of the Inachid Io to Egypt, and her descendants' subsequent return to Argos was prominent in Callimachus' poetry (the *Suda* lists a *Foundation of Argos* and an *Arrival of Io* among his lost poems). In the beginning of his elegiac epinician for the victory of Berenice II in chariot racing at the Nemean games in 245 or 241, which now opens *Aetia*, book 3, Callimachus exploited the Argive-Egyptian dimensions of the Danaid line. Within the city itself, names of Alexandria's civic units (or demes) included *Inacheios*, *Autodikeios* (named for a daughter of Danaus), and *Andromacheios* (named for a son of Aegyptus) (see Acosta-Hughes and Stephens 2012: 185–87, Manakidou forthcoming).

This fits well with the emphasis in the hymn on the daughters of Danaus as bringers of water to an arid land. The narrator exhorts the female celebrants "today, you, the slave women, carry your pitchers to Physadeia or to Amymone, the daughter of Danaus" (47–48). The Danaids' discovery is first mentioned in Hesiod, but Strabo gives the most detailed account: "while [Argos] is situated in an arid location, there is an abundance of wells, which they ascribe to the daughters of Danaus, on the grounds that they discovered them" (8.6.8).[5]

By reminding his audience that Danaus' daughters were discoverers of water, Callimachus moves Argos into the imaginary realm of Egypt (as constructed by previous Greek literature). Egypt was famously a dry land, rescued from aridity by the inundating Nile, and it may be that the girls' Egyptian origin was the associative link that generated the earlier myth of their discovery of water for thirsty Argos (Stephens 2003: 99). The hymn ends: "Hail, Goddess, look with favor on Inachan Argos...protect the whole estate of the Danaans." Callimachus' Argos is evoked in terms of the river Inachus, who is Io's progenitor, Danaus her descendant, and his daughters, who are Egyptian before they return to the land of their forebears.[6]

5. For a detailed discussion of Argive cults and their mythological links with Egypt, see Billot 1997–98: 47–51.

6. In her 2013 commentary on this hymn F. Manakidou provides considerable evidence to support her argument that Callimachus is coopting Athena (as the symbol of Athens) in a strategy to subsume an Athenian literary heritage under Doric traditions and to legitimate the Doric origins of both Cyrene and the Ptolemaic line. Shorter versions of her arguments may be found in her 2009 and forthcoming articles.

ΕΙΣ ΛΟΥΤΡΑ ΤΗΣ ΠΑΛΛΑΔΟΣ

Ὅσσαι λωτροχόοι τᾶς Παλλάδος ἔξιτε πᾶσαι,
    ἔξιτε· τᾶν ἵππων ἄρτι φρυασσομενᾶν
τᾶν ἱερᾶν ἐσάκουσα, καὶ ἀ θεὸς εὔτυκος ἔρπεν·
    σοῦσθέ νυν, ὦ ξανθαὶ σοῦσθε Πελασγιάδες.
5   οὔποκ' Ἀθαναία μεγάλως ἀπενίψατο πάχεις,
    πρὶν κόνιν ἱππειᾶν ἐξελάσαι λαγόνων·
οὐδ' ὅκα δὴ λύθρῳ πεπαλαγμένα πάντα φέροισα
    τεύχεα τῶν ἀδίκων ἦνθ' ἀπὸ γαγενέων,
ἀλλὰ πολὺ πράτιστον ὑφ' ἅρματος αὐχένας ἵππων
10   λυσαμένα παγαῖς ἔκλυσεν Ὠκεανῶ
ἱδρῶ καὶ ῥαθάμιγγας, ἐφοίβασεν δὲ παγέντα
    πάντα χαλινοφάγων ἀφρὸν ἀπὸ στομάτων.
ὦ ἴτ' Ἀχαιιάδες, καὶ μὴ μύρα μηδ' ἀλαβάστρως
    (συρίγγων ἀίω φθόγγον ὑπαξόνιον),
15   μὴ μύρα λωτροχόοι τᾷ Παλλάδι μηδ' ἀλαβάστρως
    (οὐ γὰρ Ἀθαναία χρίματα μεικτὰ φιλεῖ)
οἴσετε μηδὲ κάτοπτρον· ἀεὶ καλὸν ὄμμα τὸ τήνας.
    οὐδ' ὅκα τὰν Ἴδᾳ Φρὺξ ἐδίκαζεν ἔριν,
οὔτ' ἐς ὀρείχαλκον μεγάλα θεὸς οὔτε Σιμοῦντος
20   ἔβλεψεν δίναν ἐς διαφαινομέναν·
οὐδ' Ἥρα· Κύπρις δὲ διαυγέα χαλκὸν ἑλοῖσα
    πολλάκι τὰν αὐτὰν δὶς μετέθηκε κόμαν.
ἀ δὲ δὶς ἑξήκοντα διαθρέξασα διαύλως,
    οἷα παρ' Εὐρώτᾳ τοὶ Λακεδαιμόνιοι
25   ἀστέρες, ἐμπεράμως ἐτρίψατο λιτὰ λαβοῖσα
    χρίματα, τᾶς ἰδίας ἔκγονα φυταλιᾶς,
ὦ κῶραι, τὸ δ' ἔρευθος ἀνέδραμε, πρώιον οἵαν
    ἢ ῥόδον ἢ σίβδας κόκκος ἔχει χροϊάν.
τῷ καὶ νῦν ἄρσεν τι κομίσσατε μῶνον ἔλαιον,
30   ᾧ Κάστωρ, ᾧ καὶ χρίεται Ἡρακλέης·
οἴσετε καὶ κτένα οἱ παγχρύσεον, ὡς ἀπὸ χαίταν
    πέξηται, λιπαρὸν σμασαμένα πλόκαμον.

ἔξιθ', Ἀθαναία· πάρα τοι καταθύμιος ἴλα,
    παρθενικαὶ μεγάλων παῖδες Ἀρεστοριδᾶν·

3 ἔρπεν Schneider: ἔρπει Ψ 4 σοῦσθε Ψ: σώσθε Bulloch 14 ὑπαξόνιον **ESQ** Politian.: ὑπαξονίων
aeΠ Lasc. **ζ** 18 Ἴδᾳ Bentley, Stanley: ἴδαν Ψ 19 οὔτ'…οὔτε Meineke: οὐδ'…οὐδὲ Ψ
25 ἐτρίψατο Ψ: ἐνετρίψατο Meineke λαβοῖσα Π Politian.: βαλοῖσα **αβ** Lasc. **δ**, v.l. in mss., ut vid.
27 οἵαν H. Stephanus: οἷον Ψ 29 τι Bergk: τε Ψ 34 Ἀρεστοριδᾶν Valckenaer: ἀκεστοριδᾶν Ψ

35   ὠθάνα, φέρεται δὲ καὶ ἁ Διομήδεος ἀσπίς,
       ὡς ἔθος Ἀργείως τοῦτο παλαιοτέρως
   Εὐμήδης ἐδίδαξε, τεΐν κεχαρισμένος ἱρεύς·
       ὅς ποκα βωλευτὸν γνοὺς ἐπὶ οἱ θάνατον
   δᾶμον ἑτοιμάζοντα φυγᾷ τεὸν ἱρὸν ἄγαλμα
40   ᾤχετ' ἔχων, Κρεῖον δ' εἰς ὄρος ᾠκίσατο,
   Κρεῖον ὄρος· σὲ δέ, δαῖμον, ἀπορρώγεσσιν ἔθηκεν
       ἐν πέτραις, αἷς νῦν οὔνομα Παλλατίδες.
   ἔξιθ', Ἀθαναία περσέπτολι, χρυσεοπήληξ,
       ἵππων καὶ σακέων ἁδομένα πατάγῳ.
45   σάμερον, ὑδροφόροι, μὴ βάπτετε—σάμερον, Ἄργος,
       πίνετ' ἀπὸ κρανᾶν μηδ' ἀπὸ τῶ ποταμῶ·
   σάμερον αἱ δῶλαι τὰς κάλπιδας ἢ 'ς Φυσάδειαν
       ἢ ἐς Ἀμυμώναν οἴσετε τὰν Δαναῶ.
   καὶ γὰρ δὴ χρυσῷ τε καὶ ἄνθεσιν ὕδατα μείξας
50   ἡξεῖ φορβαίων Ἴναχος ἐξ ὀρέων
   τἀθάνᾳ τὸ λοετρὸν ἄγων καλόν. ἀλλά, Πελασγέ,
       φράζεο μὴ οὐκ ἐθέλων τὰν βασίλειαν ἴδῃς.
   ὅς κεν ἴδῃ γυμνὰν τὰν Παλλάδα τὰν πολιοῦχον,
       τὦργος ἐσοψεῖται τοῦτο πανυστάτιον.
55   πότνι' Ἀθαναία, σὺ μὲν ἔξιθι· μέστα δ' ἐγώ τι
       ταῖσδ' ἐρέω· μῦθος δ' οὐκ ἐμός, ἀλλ' ἑτέρων.

   παῖδες, Ἀθαναία νύμφαν μίαν ἔν ποκα Θήβαις
       πουλύ τι καὶ περὶ δὴ φίλατο τᾶν ἑτᾱρᾶν,
   ματέρα Τειρεσίαο, καὶ οὔποκα χωρὶς ἔγεντο·
60   ἀλλὰ καὶ ἀρχαίων εὖτ' ἐπὶ Θεσπιέων
   – ‿‿ – ‿‿ –‿ ἢ εἰς Ἁλίαρτον ἐλαύνοι
       ἵππως, Βοιωτῶν ἔργα διερχομένα,
   ἢ 'πὶ Κορωνείας, ἵνα οἱ τεθυωμένον ἄλσος
       καὶ βωμοὶ ποταμῷ κεῖντ' ἐπὶ Κουραλίῳ,
65   πολλάκις ἁ δαίμων νιν ἑῶ ἐπεβάσατο δίφρω,
       οὐδ' ὄαροι νυμφᾶν οὐδὲ χοροστασίαι
   ἁδεῖαι τελέθεσκον, ὅκ' οὐχ ἁγεῖτο Χαρικλώ·
       ἀλλ' ἔτι καὶ τήναν δάκρυα πόλλ' ἔμενε,
   καίπερ Ἀθαναίᾳ καταθύμιον ἔσσαν ἑταίραν.

---

36 Ἀργείως anon. Bern.: ἀργείων Ψ   παλαιοτέρως anon. Bern.: παλαιότερον Ψ   46 τῶ ποταμῶ anon. Bern.: τῶν ποταμῶν Ψ   55 σὺ Ψ: τὸ Meineke   μέστα coni. Pfeiffer: μέσφα Ψ   58 περὶ Ψ: πέρι Pfeiffer   61 lacunam indicavit Wilamowitz: ἢ 'πὶ Κορωνείας Ψ (= 63 init.): ἢ 'πὶ Ἀλαλκομένειον Livrea

70   δή ποκα γὰρ πέπλων λυσαμένα περόνας
       ἵππω ἐπὶ κράνᾳ Ἑλικωνίδι καλὰ ῥεοίσᾳ
           λῶντο· μεσαμβρινὰ δ' εἶχ' ὄρος ἀσυχία.
       ἀμφότεραι λώοντο, μεσαμβριναὶ δ' ἔσαν ὧραι,
           πολλὰ δ' ἀσυχία τῆνο κατεῖχεν ὄρος.
75   Τειρεσίας δ' ἔτι μοῦνος ἁμᾶ κυσὶν ἄρτι γένεια
           περκάζων ἱερὸν χῶρον ἀνεστρέφετο·
       διψάσας δ' ἄφατόν τι ποτὶ ῥόον ἤλυθε κράνας,
           σχέτλιος· οὐκ ἐθέλων δ' εἶδε τὰ μὴ θεμιτά.
       τὸν δὲ χολωσαμένα περ ὅμως προσέφασεν Ἀθάνα·
80   'τίς σε, τὸν ὀφθαλμὼς οὐκέτ' ἀποισόμενον,
       ὦ Εὐηρείδα, χαλεπὰν ὁδὸν ἄγαγε δαίμων;'
           ἁ μὲν ἔφα, παιδὸς δ' ὄμματα νὺξ ἔλαβεν.
       ἑστάκη δ' ἄφθογγος, ἐκόλλασαν γὰρ ἀνῖαι
           γώνατα καὶ φωνὰν ἔσχεν ἀμαχανία.
85   ἁ νύμφα δ' ἐβόασε· 'τί μοι τὸν κῶρον ἔρεξας
           πότνια; τοιαῦται, δαίμονες, ἐστὲ φίλαι;
       ὄμματά μοι τῶ παιδὸς ἀφείλεο. τέκνον ἄλαστε,
           εἶδες Ἀθαναίας στήθεα καὶ λαγόνας,
       ἀλλ' οὐκ ἀέλιον πάλιν ὄψεαι. ὦ ἐμὲ δειλάν,
90   ὦ ὄρος, ὦ Ἑλικὼν οὐκέτι μοι παριτέ,
       ἦ μεγάλ' ἀντ' ὀλίγων ἐπράξαο· δόρκας ὀλέσσας
           καὶ πρόκας οὐ πολλὰς φάεα παιδὸς ἔχεις.'
       ἁ μὲν <ἄμ'> ἀμφοτέραισι φίλον περὶ παῖδα λαβοῖσα
           μάτηρ μὲν γοερὰν οἶτον ἀηδονίδων
95   ἄγε βαρὺ κλαίοισα, θεὰ δ' ἔλέησεν ἑταίραν.
           καί νιν Ἀθαναία πρὸς τόδ' ἔλεξεν ἔπος·
       'δῖα γύναι, μετὰ πάντα βαλεῦ πάλιν ὅσσα δι' ὀργάν
           εἶπας· ἐγὼ δ' οὔ τοι τέκνον ἔθηκ' ἀλαόν.
       οὐ γὰρ Ἀθαναίᾳ γλυκερὸν πέλει ὄμματα παίδων
100   ἁρπάζειν· Κρόνιοι δ' ὧδε λέγοντι νόμοι·
       ὅς κε τιν' ἀθανάτων, ὅκα μὴ θεὸς αὐτὸς ἕληται,
           ἀθρήσῃ, μισθῶ τοῦτον ἰδεῖν μεγάλω.
       δῖα γύναι, τὸ μὲν οὐ παλινάγρετον αὖθι γένοιτο
           ἔργον, ἐπεὶ Μοιρᾶν ὧδ' ἐπένησε λίνα,

75 μοῦνος **Ψ**: μῶνος Ernesti, Bulloch ἁμᾶ Brunck, Pfeiffer: ἁμᾷ Bulloch: ἅμαι vel ἅμαι **Ψ**
82 ἔλαβεν anon. in marg. Ald. ap. Ernesti: ἔβαλεν **Ψ**, defendit Renehan 83 ἑστάκη Buttmann:
ἑστάθη **Ψ** 87 ἀφείλεο **E** in marg.: ἀφείλετο **Ψ** 93 ἄμ' suppl. Schneider 94 γοερὰν in marg. Ald.
ap. Ernesti: γοερῶν **Ψ** οἶτον **Ψ**: οἶκτον H. Stephanus: οἶμον Svarlien 100 ἁρπάζειν **Ψ**: ἁρπάζεν
Bulloch 104 ἐπένησε Bentley: ἐπένευσε **Ψ**

105   ἁνίκα τὸ πρᾶτόν νιν ἐγείναο· νῦν δὲ κομίζευ,
            ὦ Εὐηρείδα, τέλθος ὀφειλόμενον.
       πόσσα μὲν ἁ Καδμηὶς ἐς ὕστερον ἔμπυρα καυσεῖ,
            πόσσα δ᾽ Ἀρισταῖος, τὸν μόνον εὐχόμενοι
       παῖδα, τὸν ἁβατὰν Ἀκταίονα, τυφλὸν ἰδέσθαι.
110   καὶ τῆνος μεγάλας σύνδρομος Ἀρτέμιδος
       ἔσσεται· ἀλλ᾽ οὐκ αὐτὸν ὅ τε δρόμος αἵ τ᾽ ἐν ὄρεσσι
            ῥυσεῦνται ξυναὶ τᾶμος ἑκαβολίαι,
       ὁππόκα κ᾽ οὐκ ἐθέλων περ ἴδῃ χαρίεντα λοετρά
            δαίμονος· ἀλλ᾽ αὐταὶ τὸν πρὶν ἄνακτα κύνες
115   τουτάκι δειπνησεῦντι· τὰ δ᾽ υἱέος ὀστέα μάτηρ
            λεξεῖται δρυμὼς πάντας ἐπερχομένα·
       ὀλβίσταν δ᾽ ἐρέει σε καὶ εὐαίωνα γενέσθαι
            ἐξ ὀρέων ἀλαὸν παῖδ᾽ ὑποδεξαμέναν.
       ὦ ἑτάρα, τῷ μή τι μινύρεο· τῷδε γὰρ ἄλλα
120   τεῦ χάριν ἐξ ἐμέθεν πολλὰ μενεῦντι γέρα,
       μάντιν ἐπεὶ θησῶ νιν ἀοίδιμον ἐσσομένοισιν,
            ἦ μέγα τῶν ἄλλων δή τι περισσότερον.
       γνωσεῖται δ᾽ ὄρνιχας, ὃς αἴσιος οἵ τε πέτονται
            ἄλιθα καὶ ποίων οὐκ ἀγαθαὶ πτέρυγες.
125   πολλὰ δὲ Βοιωτοῖσι θεοπρόπα, πολλὰ δὲ Κάδμῳ
            χρησεῖ, καὶ μεγάλοις ὕστερα Λαβδακίδαις.
       δωσῶ καὶ μέγα βάκτρον, ὅ οἱ πόδας ἐς δέον ἀξεῖ,
            δωσῶ καὶ βιότω τέρμα πολυχρόνιον,
       καὶ μόνος, εὖτε θάνῃ, πεπνυμένος ἐν νεκύεσσι
130   φοιτασεῖ, μεγάλῳ τίμιος Ἀγεσίλᾳ.᾽
       ὣς φαμένα κατένευσε· τὸ δ᾽ ἐντελές, ᾧ κ᾽ ἐπινεύσῃ
            Παλλάς, ἐπεὶ μόνᾳ Ζεὺς τόγε θυγατέρων
       δῶκεν Ἀθαναίᾳ πατρώϊα πάντα φέρεσθαι,
            λωτροχόοι, μάτηρ δ᾽ οὔτις ἔτικτε θεάν,
135   ἀλλὰ Διὸς κορυφά. κορυφὰ Διὸς οὐκ ἐπινεύει
            ψεύδεα – ‿‿ – ‖ – ‿‿ αι θυγάτηρ.
       ἔρχετ᾽ Ἀθαναία νῦν ἀτρεκές· ἀλλὰ δέχεσθε
            τὰν θεόν, ὦ κῶραι, τὦργον ὅσαις μέλεται,
       σύν τ᾽ εὐαγορίᾳ σύν τ᾽ εὔγμασι σύν τ᾽ ὀλολυγαῖς.
140   χαῖρε, θεά, κάδευ δ᾽ Ἄργεος Ἰναχίω.
       χαῖρε καὶ ἐξελάοισα, καὶ ἐς πάλιν αὖτις ἐλάσσαις
            ἵππως, καὶ Δαναῶν κλᾶρον ἅπαντα σάω.

---

113 ὁππόκα κ᾽ οὐκ Bulloch: ὁππόκα κοὐκ (= καὶ οὐκ) Wilamowitz: ὁππόταν οὐκ **Ψ** 117 δ᾽ **Ε**,
suppl. Bergk: om. **Ψ** 124 ἄλιθα Bulloch: ἤλιθα **Ψ** 136 init. ψεύδεα α: ψευ β fin. αἱ θυγάτηρ **Atη**
(θυγάτηρ **γ**): om. **β**: ἁ θυγάτηρ **F** Bulloch totum versum om. **δξ** 138 τὦργον Boissonade: τὦργος **Ψ**

On the Bath of Pallas

As many of you who are bath-pourers of Pallas, all come out, all come out. Just now I heard her sacred mares neighing. And the goddess is ready to come. Now hasten, you fair-haired Pelasgian women, hasten. (5) Athena never washed her mighty arms before removing the dust from her mares' flanks. Not even when carrying her equipage completely spattered with gore she came from the lawless Earth-born ones, but the very first thing after freeing the necks of her horses from their harness (10) she rinsed off their sweat and grime with the streams of Ocean, and cleaned all the compacted foam from their bit-biting mouths. Oh, come, Achaean women, and neither myrrh nor perfume jars (I hear the sound from under the axle naves), (15) you bath-pourers, bring neither myrrh nor perfume jars for Pallas (for Athena is not fond of mixed ointments), do not even bring her a mirror. Her looks are ever fair. Not even when on Ida the Phrygian was judging the contest did the great goddess glance into the orichalc or (20) into the transparent eddies of the Simois. Neither did Hera. But Cypris having frequently taken up the shining bronze twice rearranged the same lock of hair. But Athena having run twice sixty double lengths of the course just like the Lacedaemonian stars [*sc.* Castor and Pollux] along the Eurotas, (25) and taking a simple oil, the product of her own planting, skillfully rubbed herself down, girls, and a blush suffused her, like the early rose or the seed of the pomegranate has on its surface. Therefore bring some manly olive oil only, (30) with which Castor, with which Heracles too anointed himself. Bring her also a comb, all gold, that she may comb her hair, having cleansed her shining tresses.

Come forth, Athena, a band pleasing to your heart is at hand, virgin daughters of the mightly line of the Arestoridae. (35) O Athena, the shield of Diomedes too is being carried, as Eumedes, the high priest most favored by you, taught this custom to the Argives of old. Who, when he perceived death being plotted for him, took your sacred image (40) and hastened in flight, and settled on Mt. Kreion, Mt. Kreion; and you, goddess, he placed on the precipitous rocks, which now have the name Pallatides. Come forth, Athena, City-sacker, golden-helmeted, delighting in the clash of horses and of shields. (45) Today, do not dip your pitchers, water-carriers—today, Argos, drink from the fountains and not from the river [*sc.* the Inachus]. Today, you slave women, carry your pitchers to Physadeia or to Amymone, the daughter of Danaus. For indeed having mingled his waters with gold and blossoms, (50) Inachus will come from the nourishing mountains bringing Athena a bath that is fair. But, Pelasgian, take care lest inadvertantly you catch sight of the queen. Whoever sees Pallas naked, the guardian of the city, he will look upon this city of Argos for the last time. (55) Lady Athena, you come forth, and meanwhile I shall say something to these women here. The story is not mine, but others'.

Girls, once upon a time in Thebes Athena loved one nymph far beyond her other companions, the mother of Tiresias, and they were never apart. (60) But even when she would drive her horses to ancient Thespiae...or to Haliartus, traversing the tilled fields of the Boeotians, or to Coroneia, where she had a grove redolent with sacrifices and altars situated upon the river Couralius, (65) the goddess often placed her upon her chariot, and the whisperings of the nymphs and their dances were not sweet when Chariclo was not leading them, but still even for her many tears remained, although she was a companion dear to Athena's heart. (70) For once, having loosened the pins from their robes, the two were bathing by the fair-flowing spring of the Heliconian horse. The midday quiet had fallen upon the mountain. Both were bathing, the hour was midday, and deep quiet had taken possession of that mountain. (75) Yet Tiresias only, with his hounds, his cheeks just darkening with a beard, came to that holy place. With an unspeakable thirst he came to the flow of the spring, poor wretch. Inadvertently he saw that which is not permitted. In her rage, nevertheless, Athena spoke to him: (80) "What daimon has led you down this harsh path, child of Everes, who never shall get back your eyesight?" She spoke and night took possession of the boy's eyes. He stood speechless, for distress struck his limbs and helplessness took hold of his voice. (85) But the nymph cried out: "What have you wrought for my boy, Lady? Are you these sorts of friends, divinities? You have taken my son's eyes. O accursed child, you saw Athena's chest and thighs, but you shall not again see the sun. O wretched me. (90) O mountain, O Helicon, no longer to be trodden by me! Ah, you have exacted a great price for a small infraction, deprived of deer and roe—not many—you have my son's eyesight." And having embraced her dear son with both arms, his mother kept up the lament of mournful nightingales, (95) weeping from the depths of her heart; the goddess took pity on her companion. Athena spoke the following words to her: "Shining lady, take back again all that you have said in anger. I did not make your son blind. It is not sweet for Athena to snatch away the eyes of children. (100) But Cronus' laws proclaim this: whoever catches sight of an immortal, where the god himself does not choose, this one sees at a great price. Shining lady, this deed will not be reversible in the future, for so the thread of the Fates has spun, (105) when first you gave him birth. Now receive, child of Everes, the payment that is owed. How many offerings will the daughter of Cadmus burn in a later time, how many Aristaeus, praying to see their only son, the youthful Actaeon, blind! (110) And he will be the co-hunter of great Artemis. But neither the hunting course nor their common skill in archery in the mountains shall save him, when, even though inadvertantly, he sees the fair bath of the goddess. But his own bitches shall dine upon their former master. (115) And his mother shall collect her son's bones traversing all the coverts. She will declare you to be utterly happy and blessed, since you got your son back from the mountains blind. O companion, then do not lament.

(120) For this one here, because of you, from me, many other gifts will remain, since I shall make him a prophet, famous among posterity. Indeed greater by far beyond the others. He will know birds: which is auspicious, which fly without significance, and whose flights are not well-omened. (125) Many prophecies to the Boeotians, many to Cadmus will he give, and later to the mighty Labdacids. I shall also give him a great staff, which will direct his feet as necessary; I shall also give a limit to his life that is very long, and alone, when he dies, he will go sentient among the dead, (130) honored by the mighty Leader of Men." Having spoken thus, she nodded assent. What Pallas nodded assent to was fulfilled, since Zeus gave this to Athena alone of his daughters, to bear all honors belonging to her father. Bath-pourers, no mother bore the goddess, (135) but the head of Zeus. The head of Zeus does not nod assent to falsehoods...daughter.

Athena is now certainly coming. Come, receive the goddess, girls, you to whom the task falls, with salutations, with prayers, with joyous cries. (140) Hail, goddess, have a care for Inachan Argos. Hail, having driven out, and as you drive your mares back again, protect the whole estate of the Danaans.

Commentary

1. Most editors assume that there is a single unnamed narrator, but Hunter 1992: 15–16 raises the possibility of "excited observations by more than one speaker... establishing the choric nature of the poem at the very outset," or alternatively that the narrator addressed first the celebrants (1–2), then turned to the audience with explanatory mythological material (5–12). The speaker in *hDem* is female, but in this hymn the gender is indeterminate, which Morrison (2005: 30–36) would link with the ambiguous sexuality of Athena herself. Throughout the opening, two different logics are collapsed: the myth and the real time event of washing the ancient statue.

Ὅσσαι (sc. ἐστέ) **... πᾶσαι**: males would have been excluded from the bathing ceremony itself, though the excursus on Eumedes (35–42) seems to indicate the presence of male priests or perhaps a male escort for the passage to the river, as happened with the Athenian ephebic escort of the Palladium.

λωτροχόοι are technically those who pour water for a bath; here the female celebrants who will bathe the statue. The Doric form is not elsewhere attested, but the forms λωτρόν and λωτήριον do occur; the former Hesychius claims is Laconic, the latter is attested in Argive inscriptions (see Bulloch for details).

Παλλάδος: the origin of this epithet of Athena is unknown, but some ancient etymologies derived it from Pallas, a Giant defeated by Athena during the Gigantomachy alluded to at 7–8 (see Renehan 1987: 244–45 for details); here the epithet is appropriate since the focus of the ceremony is the Palladium, the name of which was derived from Pallas. The epithet is repeated at 15, 53, and 132, each time in a different case.

1–2. ἔξιτε ... ἔξιτε: the imperatives are addressed to the female celebrants; the singular (ἔξιθι) is addressed to Athena at lines 33, 43, and 55. Either the speaker is urging the female celebrants to gather the proper equipment for the ritual as they emerge from their own homes or simply to come forth to begin the procession. In the latter case the procession is already in motion with the women leading off and the wagon with the statue of Athena and the shield of Diomedes following. Kleinknecht 1939: 303–4 takes the verb as a technical term that marks the beginning of the procession.

2–3. The description of the horses refers both to the present-time wagon that will carry the statue and to the mythological time of Athena's horses described in 5–6. This remark and line 14 serve as asides by means of which the speaker mediates to the audience the kinds of sounds that must be audible, though not perhaps at the precise moment when they are mentioned.

2. τᾶν ἵππων: Athena's chariot is drawn by mares. It is possible that the ritual prohibited anything male; note that the horses carrying the κάλαθος at *hDem* 120 are also mares.

φρυασσομενᾶν "whinny"; the rare φρυάσσομαι is imitated in an epigram attributed to Asclepiades or Posidippus, but in an obscene context. See p. 20.

3. καί: Bulloch ad loc. recommends the punctuation and translation, pointing out that the link between ἐσάκουσα and εὔτυκος is awkward, while treating the phrase independently suits the asyndeton and urgency of the passage.

εὔτυκος (*sc.* ἐστίν) "ready," a rare form found earlier in Aesch. *Suppl.* 974, 994 to describe the fluency with which the Danaids spoke a foreign tongue. Verbal echoes from the *Suppliants* suit this hymn's Argive context well. The return of Danaus and his fifty daughters to Argos from Egypt is the subject of Aeschylus' play, and for Callimachus a useful reminder of the hereditary connections between Greece and Ptolemaic Egypt.

ἔρπεν: an explanatory infinitive dependent on εὔτυκος; in Doric the verb is used as an unmarked equivalent to ἔρχομαι.

4. σοῦσθε: this middle imperative form is found previously in Aeschylus and in Ar. *Vesp.* 458. According to the scholiast, it is from σεύω, though Bulloch ad loc. notes that its etymology may have been disputed in antiquity. Cf. the repeated σοῦσθε at Aesch. *Suppl.* 836 and again at 842, addressed by the Egyptians to the Danaids; here by the narrator to their descendants. Although Bulloch emends to Doric σῶσθε, the intertext suggests retaining the reading of the mss.

Πελασγιάδες: the Argive celebrants are addressed as "daughters of Pelasgus," and "Pelasgian" was one of the names used for the original Argives (cf. Hdt. 1.56–58; Aesch. *Suppl.* 249–53). This form of the name in -ιάς first appears in Callimachus (see p. 26).

5–12. The description of Athena caring for her horses before she turns to her own ablutions characterizes her as a good horsewoman (see Xen. *De re eq.* 4.1). The description is one long sentence in four clauses, each covering a couplet, introduced by οὔποκ(α) ("never"), οὐδ(ὲ) ὅκα ("not even when"), ἀλλά...πράτιστον ("but...first"), and δέ ("and"); it is balanced by the next block of eight lines (also introduced by negatives) that describe her own grooming practice. Wilamowitz's suggestion (*HD* 2.16) that Callimachus included this detail because the horses carrying the Palladium would have been ritually washed before the ceremony is attractive.

5. Ἀθαναία: Doric variant of Ἀθήνη used throughout this hymn.

μεγάλως ... πάχεις: cf. Rhea in *hZeus* 30: μέγαν...πῆχυν.

6. ἱππειᾶν: genitive plural; this epic adjective suits the martial background; cf. *hArt* 50n.

7. πεπαλαγμένα: from παλάσσω. Possibly recalling *Il.* 6.268: αἵματι καὶ λύθρῳ πεπαλαγμένον where Hector returning from battle pours his libation to Zeus, "bespattered with blood and gore," then instructs his mother to go to the temple of Athena (where the Palladium was kept) to pray for success in the war (and see below 9–11).

πάντα: adverbial.

8. ἦνθ(ε) = ἦλθε: the change of λτ, λθ to ντ, νθ is not a general feature of West Greek; it occurs in Argolic, Cyrenean, Arcadian, and in writers like Epicharmus and Theocritus (see Buck §72). Callimachus uses the form here and in *hDem* (26, 74, 77) and fr. 197.48 Pf.

γαγενέων "Earth-born"; the term is applied to both Titans and Giants, who were Gaia's children. The battle of the Gods and Giants was usually located in the Phlegraean plain near Pallene in the Chalcidice. Athena's role in their defeat was a subject for the *peplos* that Athenian girls wove to adorn the goddess's cult statue (see, e.g., Eur. *Hec.* 466–74, sch. Pl. *Rep.* 327a). Cf. *hZeus* 3n.

11. ἱδρῶ καὶ ῥαθάμιγγας: the two words occur in *Il.* 23.502–8 (on the horses of Diomedes). ῥαθάμιγγες usually designates drops of liquid, though here and in the Homeric passage (502: κονίης ῥαθάμιγγες), it seems to mean "particles" of dust (see Renehan 1987: 245).

ἐφοίβασεν: from the rare verb φοιβάω. The sense seems to be a formal or ritual cleansing (e.g., Theoc. 17.134). At A.R. 2.302 the Argonauts cleanse the accumulated filth from the blind seer Phineus.

παγέντα: from πήγνυμι, "congealed."

12. χαλινοφάγων: a Callimachean coinage, only here; literally, "bit-eating," i.e., "champing at the bit." The formation is analogous to other -φάγος compounds, which are fairly common: Callimachus coins γηφάγος (fr. 55 Hollis) and ποιηφάγος (fr. 56 Hollis) in the *Hecale*.

13. ὦ ἴτ᾽ Ἀχαιιάδες: again the women are urged to come forth, this time with oil for anointing. Argive women are here called "Achaean women" just as they were "Pelasgian women" above. Though technically Achaea was in the north-western Peloponnese, Bulloch ad loc. suggests it is used in the Homeric sense of Ἄργος Ἀχαιϊκόν, in deliberate contrast to a Pelasgian Argos, which in Homer (*Il.* 2.681) is in Thessaly.

ἀλαβάστρως: the alabastron was a small jar that held unguents or perfume.

14. συρίγγων: technically, any groove, but here the naves of the axle.

ὑπαξόνιον: mss. vary between -ίων and -ιον: the *hapax* ὑπαξόνιον, if correct, modifies φθόγγον, i.e., "the-under-axle sound of the naves"; the reading of ὑπ᾽ ἀξονίων should mean "sound of the naves from under the axles."

16. χρίματα: the reading is confirmed by the papyrus. Though rare, this variant of χρίσματα occurs at Aesch. *Ag.* 94 and Xen. *Anab.* 3.6, 4.4.13. Callimachus uses it in *Iamb.* 4 (fr. 194.45 Pf.) of the olive: ἡ τέκουσα τὸ χρῖμ[α ("she who bore oil").

μεικτά: verbal adjective from μείγνυμι, "mix" or "blend"; cf. 25–26 λιτὰ...| χρίματα and 29 ἄρσεν τι...ἔλαιον; Athena, like male athletes, prefers to anoint herself with olive oil unmixed with myrrh or other scents. Also, unmixed oils were apparently appropriate for unmarried girls (see 25n).

17. οἴσετε: an aorist imperative form based on the future stem of φέρω, found in Homer and Attic comedy, according to Chantraine (1.417–18) for metrical reasons. Also below 31, 48, and *hDem* 136 (οἶσε).

ἀεὶ καλὸν ὄμμα "her eye/visage is always fair" is not only a tribute to Athena's beauty, but the choice of noun foreshadows Tiresias' fate and may also allude to her cult title *Oxyderkes*. The shape and sound of the phrase is reflected in κάτοπτρον.

18–32. This series of instructions to the celebrants is illustrated by the example of Athena's preparations for the judgment of Paris and concludes with reference to two heroes with whom she was closely associated—Castor and Heracles (both were important for the Ptolemies).

18. τὰν Ἴδᾳ Φρὺξ ἐδίκαζεν ἔριν: by placing the location, subject, and verb within τὰν ... ἔριν ("the on-Ida-Phrygian-judged quarrel") Callimachus encapsulates the whole event, which may be intended to allude to Sophocles' satyr play, the *Krisis* (see pp. 236–37).

Φρὺξ "the Phrygian" is Paris, who, as a shepherd on Mt. Ida, was given the task of judging which of the three goddesses, Hera, Athena, or Aphrodite, was the fairest. Bulloch ad loc. suggests that referring to Paris only as "the Phrygian" (an ethnic often associated with effeminacy) may have implied contempt, implicitly undermining the award to Aphrodite.

19. ὀρείχαλκον: a mirror made from orichalchum, an imaginary alloy of rare metals.

Σιμοῦντος: the river Simoeis near Troy, though some distance from Mt. Ida.

20. δίναν ... διαφαινομέναν: the surface flow of the water was so clear that the goddess could have used it as a mirror.

21. οὐδ' Ἥρα· Κύπρις: the two other contestants were Hera and Aphrodite. Aphrodite won by promising Paris the most beautiful woman in the world—Helen. The word order encapsulates the judgment itself—not Hera, Cypris.

διαυγέα χαλκόν: the phrase occurs at *AP* 6.210.3–4, an epigram attributed to Philitas of Samos (a mistake for Philitas of Cos? See G-P 2.476–77), in which a *hetaira*, upon retirement, dedicates her equipment to Aphrodite. If this epigram predates Callimachus, then his own allusion to a *hetaira* may have prompted the tenor of the later epigrammatic imitation of Posidippus or Asclepiades; see p. 20.

22. For this line as an echo of Heraclitus' dictum that δὶς ἐς τὸν αὐτὸν ποταμὸν οὐκ ἂν ἐμβαίης ("you cannot step into the same river twice") and the repetition of δι- and δίς (22–23), see Heyworth 2004: 142–44. Aphrodite twice rearranges her hair; in contrast, Athena runs her course twice sixty times.

μετέθηκε κόμαν: Aphrodite arranging her hair may owe something to the popularity of the Aphrodite Anadyomene type of sculptural representation in the

Hellenistic period. The goddess is usually standing, partially draped and wringing out her wet hair with her hands (see, e.g., Bieber 1961: 98).

κόμαν: usually hair of the head; rarely for the singular "lock," though cf. *Aetia* fr. 110.51 Pf. and Latin *coma* (and below 32: πλόκαμον).

23–28. These lines imitate Theocritus' epithalamium for Helen and Menelaus discussed on p. 21. Callimachus transfers the simple health regimen of Helen's female attendants (running, anointing in manly fashion) to Athena; other correspondences to the hymn include mention of the Eurotas (24) and Athena bathing with her attendants (70–72). However, Theocritus goes on to inform us that none of these girls is the equal of Helen, just as in the contest Athena, however healthy, is no match for Aphrodite.

23. ἁ δέ = Athena.

διαθρέξασα: aorist from διατρέχω, "run across"; an alternative to ἔδραμον, forms of ἔθρεξα occur in Homer and in Attic comedy. Possibly here used in contrast to ἀνέδραμε below.

διαύλως: the *diaulos* (or double stade) was a standard race in which the course was run from the starting posts to the terminus and then back.

24. παρ' Εὐρώτᾳ: the Eurotas was the principal river of Laconia in the Peloponnese.

24–25. Λακεδαιμόνιοι | ἀστέρες: the Dioscuri were Spartan Helen's twin brothers who were translated into stars, the constellation of Gemini (see Arat. *Phaen.* 147 and Kidd ad loc.). They were worshipped in Alexandria and may have been identified with the *Theoi Soteres* of the Lighthouse (Fraser 1972: 1.18–19, 207). According to the *Diegesis* of the *Ektheosis of Arsinoe*, the Dioscuri carry the dead queen to the heavens (Pf. 1.218).

25. ἐμπεράμως: cf. *hZeus* 71n.

ἐτρίψατο "rubbed herself down." Meineke emended this ms. reading to the compound, ἐνετρίψατο (on the grounds that the simplex verb does not mean "rub in," but "rub" or "wear down"), and this has been accepted by most editors. But Renehan 1987: 247 provides considerable evidence for the simplex in the context of athletic rubdowns (compare, e.g., παιδοτρίβης), which is thus thoroughly appropriate for Athena, particularly given the technical term, *diaulos*.

λιτά "simple" or inexpensive. Cf. fr. 110.78 Pf. of the simple hair oil used by unmarried girls.

26. ἔκγονα: in apposition to χρίματα. Athena's very own tree (τᾶς ἰδίας … φυταλιᾶς) was the olive, which she gave to Athens; olive oil is described as its "offspring."

φυταλιᾶς: a place full of plantings in Homer, later the planting itself, whether tree or vine. Callimachus has reversed the usual comparison of the planted shoot to a child (see Theoc. 7.44 with Gow ad loc., and see below).

27–28. The likening of Athena's healthy skin tone to a rose or a pomegranate plays off of Helen's skin as ῥοδόχρως (Theoc. 18.31).

27. ἔρευθος: a healthy glow from exercise suffuses her skin, so she needs no further cosmetics. The word is rare before the Hellenistic period, then common in the medical writers.

ἀνέδραμε: lit., "ran up"; the verb reinforces the source of Athena's glow, her recent running of sixty *diauloi*, but is also a reminder of the likening of Helen to a tall cypress that has sprung up (Theoc. 18.29–30: ἀνέδραμε... κυπάρισσος).

πρώϊον: the adjective conveys the freshness of the bloom: whether "early" because it is the rose that blooms at sunrise or early in the year. Hopkinson (1989: 114) suggests "perhaps we should rather read πρώκιον, 'dewy'."

28. σίβδας: the Doric form σιβδ- is found only here; the scholiast glosses as ῥοιᾶς, "pomegranate" (cf. *HhDem* 372, 412: ῥοιῆς κόκκον). This fruit is commonly associated with Argive Hera, who holds it in her hand in some cult statues, and also with Demeter's daughter Persephone, who was required to spend six months of the year in the underworld because while Hades' captive she ate six seeds from the fruit.

29. ἄρσεν... ἔλαιον: cf. Soph. *Trach.* 1196–97, where Heracles specifies ἄρσεν(α)... ἄγριον ἔλαιον for his funeral pyre, and Theoc. 18.23: ἀνδριστί. Heracles, who is mentioned in the next line, was also closely connected to the olive, which he introduced into Olympia (see Pi. *Ol.* 3.13, Paus. 5.7.7).

30. The repetition of ᾧ after ᾧ Κάστωρ leads the audience to expect Castor's twin, Pollux, not Heracles, who is not named until the end of the line.

χρίεται: although the iota was normally long, late poets shortened it before a vowel. See LSJ s.v. χρίω.

31–32. See *Il.* 14.175–76, where Hera prepares to seduce Zeus: χαίτας | πεξαμένη χερσὶ πλοκάμους ἔπλεξε φαεινούς ("having combed her hair, she braided her shining locks with her hands"). Hera had borrowed a dress woven by Athena and a sash from Aphrodite. The allusion reminds Callimachus' audience of the other (failed) contestant, who, unlike Athena, gave heed to her appearance.

ἀπὸ... πέξηται: from ἀποπέκω, "comb out."

32. σμασαμένα: aorist middle from σμάω, "cleanse" with soap or, as here, with oil.

33–56. The speaker now turns to the ceremony with an invocation of the goddess (ἔξιθ', Ἀθαναία) that echoes the opening words to the celebrants (1–2); a narrative of the shield (35–42) that parallels that of Athena as a warrior goddess (5–12); and a concluding section, introduced by the repeated ἔξιθ', Ἀθαναία, instructing the celebrants where to fetch water and warning men to turn away (43–56) that matches the instructions in 18–28.

33. πάρα τοι = πάρεστί σοι.

καταθύμιος: this adjective may have either two or three terminations. Callimachus chooses to treat it as having two, instead of using a special feminine form; he pairs it with a feminine noun (Doric ἴλα) that usually denotes a masculine group (a military band) but is here explicitly identified as female. This seems a deliberate play on gender indeterminacy, fitting for Athena herself and for the liminal status of the παρθένοι that attend her cult.

34. Ἀρεστοριδᾶν: genitive plural. Arestor was an early member of the Argive royal line, either the son-in-law of Inachus (the river and first king) and father of Argus, the guardian of Io (Pherecydes, *FGrH* 3 F67), or a grandson of Argus and the father of Pelasgus and Io (Charax, *FGrH* 103 F13, F15). Like Πελασγιάδες (4), Ἀρεστοριδᾶν is a synonym for Argive. See Hall 1997: 879–85 and Manakidou 2013: 46–65 for various Argive genealogies.

35. ὠθάνα = ὦ Ἀθάνα; cf. 51: τἀθάνᾳ.

ἁ Διομήδεος ἀσπίς: the Trojan hero Diomedes was from Argos, so it is unsurprising to find some relic of his venerated there, but apart from the scholium on this line, nothing further about the shield, its cult, or its location is known. The fact that he was a favorite of Athena in the *Iliad*, and that at 5.127 she lifts the mist from his eyes, makes him a fit counterexample for Tiresias.

36. ἔθος ... τοῦτο "this custom," i.e., the practice of carrying the shield in the procession of the Palladium.

37. Εὐμήδης: known only from this passage and the scholium ad loc.

τεῖν (= σοί) **κεχαρισμένος ἱρεύς**: the combination of these three markedly Homeric words imparts a formulaic feel (cf. *Il.* 5.243: ἐμῷ κεχαρισμένε θυμῷ, "dear to my heart").

ἱρεύς: the rare form is thrice used in Homer for priests attached to a divinity (*Il.* 5.10, 16.604, *Od.* 9.198).

38. βωλευτόν: the verbal adjective is common in prose; in poetry first at Aesch. *Ch.* 494, in the same sense as here: "something plotted."

39. τεὸν (= σὸν) **ἱρὸν ἄγαλμα**: the Palladium; cf. *hDelos* 307, of the *xoanon* of Aphrodite.

40. Κρεῖον δ' εἰς ὄρος: the mountain is otherwise unknown, but restating the name marks it as important. Some commentators have argued that the lines explaining the location must now be missing, but the fact that we no longer understand the reference is dangerous grounds for positing a lacuna.

ᾠκίσατο: the verb suggests a settlement or at least a shrine for the statue.

41. ἀπορρώγεσσιν: from ἀπορρώξ, "precipitous"; with πέτρα, cf. Xen. *An.* 6.4.3, Polyb. 5.59.6, 10.48.5.

42. Παλλατίδες: the location is not otherwise attested; the scholiast informs us that the name is derived from Pallas (but this may be no more than an obvious inference).

43. περσέπτολι "city-sacker"; this rare epithet of Athena occurs previously only at Ar. *Nub.* 967 in a line from a well-known song taught to the boys by Κρείττων Λόγος. The author of the song is disputed (see *PMG* s.v. Lamprocles 1[a] and Dover 1968: 215).

χρυσεοπήληξ: vocative, "golden-helmeted"; previously χρυσοπήληξ occurs in Aesch. *Sept.* 106, as an epithet of Ares. For the form (χρυσεο-), see West 1986: 29, who observes that these forms here and above 31 (παγχρύσεον) are metrical coinages rather than dialect variants.

44. πατάγῳ: a "clash" of horses and shields, i.e., the sounds of battle.

45–48. Note the anaphora (σάμερον) and the careful balances: ἀπὸ...μηδ᾽ ἀπό, ἤ (ἐ)ς...ἤ ἐς, μὴ βάπτετε...πίνετ(ε)...μηδ᾽ [*sc.* πίνετε]...οἴσετε. The subjects alternate between plural ὑδροφόροι, the collective Ἄργος, and another plural, δῶλαι.

45. σάμερον: Doric (= Attic τήμερον).

45–46. Ἄργος | πίνετ(ε): singular substantives denoting a group of persons may take a plural verb as also at *hDem* 42–43 (see Smyth §950).

47. κάλπιδας: the κάλπις is the traditional pitcher that women used for collecting water from communal sources.

47-48. Physadeia and Amymone were daughters of Danaus, after whom two of the city's central springs were named; the location of the Physadeia is unknown, but the Amymone was a major water source for Argos located near Lerna; see, e.g., Eur. *Phoen.* 187–88 and sch. ad loc. Callimachus (*Aet.* frr. 65–66 Pf. with Harder ad loc.) also treats these springs. The scholiast on that *aition* claims Agias and Dercylus, the authors of a regional history of *Argos*, as his source (see 56n).

50. φορβαίων: a *hapax*; LSJ s.v. connects it with φορβή, "pasture," thus defining it as "pasture-giving," but Bulloch ad loc. suggests "nourishing" (from φέρβειν) as more appropriate. φέρβω occurs in the envoi of *hDem* 136–37.

Ἴναχος: the Inachus was the central river in the Argolid; personified as a river god, he was the ancestor of the Danaid line (cf. *hDelos* 74, where he is Hera's by divine lot).

51. Note the emphatic placement of Athena (τἀθάνᾳ) at the beginning of the line, and separated as far as possible from Πελασγέ.

Πελασγέ: Pelasgus was an early king of Argos, whom Danaus replaced. Here the vocative singular is used for any citizen male.

52. φράζεο μή: μή + subjunctive following a verb of caution (see Smyth §2220b).

οὐκ ἐθέλων "unwittingly," i.e., without deliberate intent.

τὰν βασίλειαν "queen"; the term can be used for a goddess (as here).

53. πολιοῦχον "city protector"; an epithet of Athena in Pi. *Ol.* 5.10 and in Ar. *Nub.* 602, *Eq.* 581, *Lys.* 345. The phrase Παλλάδα...πολιοῦχον refers to Athena, but also recalls the Palladium and its protective qualities. Callimachus again collapses the two—if a Pelasgian looks at the rites, of course he will see the statue unveiled, not the goddess herself.

54. τὦργος (= τὸ Ἄργος): the crasis is usual in Doric. West 1966: 158 proposed reading τὦργον (= τὸ ἔργον), but Bulloch is surely right that τὦργος "is protreptic to τοῦτο" and the sense "this city of Argos."

παννστάτιον: Callimachean variant of the more common πανύστατον, "for the very last time"; ὑστάτιον occurs at *hAp* 79.

55. μέστα "while"; found in Cretan and Cyrenean Doric for μέσφα; the medieval mss. read μέσφα, but Pfeiffer's conjecture of μέστα was inspired by the occurrence of the word in POxy 2226. (See *hDem* 111.)

56. μῦθος δ᾽ οὐκ ἐμός, ἀλλ᾽ ἑτέρων: the phrase indicates that Callimachus is telling an unfamiliar story which he took from specific sources (in contrast to the judgment of Paris, which is related without comment). The plural ἑτέρων may refer to the historians of the Argolid, Agias and Dercylus, whom he used elsewhere (see 47–48n). A distinctive feature of Callimachus' poetic technique was the inclusion of references to earlier sources, and even the claim that he sang nothing without witness (ἀμάρτυρον οὐδὲν ἀείδω, fr. 612 Pf.). Another potential source for this story was Pherecydes of Athens (see p. 237).

57–130. The blinding of Tiresias falls into four sections: the affectionate relationship of Athena and the nymph Chariclo (57–74); the inadvertent encounter with Tiresias (75–84); Chariclo's anguished complaint to Athena (85–92); and the goddess's reply (92–130). Callimachus' narrator begins fittingly: "Girls, once upon a time in Thebes..." The episode is suffused with tragic language and allusions, especially to Sophocles' Oedipus plays. For the "literary geography" see Ambühl 2005: 113–60.

57–58. The word order juxtaposes Athena and νύμφαν μίαν, but separates the two as far as syntactically possible from the rest of their companions (τᾶν ἑταρᾶν).

57. νύμφαν: Chariclo is described for eight lines before being named at the end of 67. She is called νύμφαν, ματέρα Τειρεσίαο, and finally Chariclo. This strategy leaves open the possibility of alternative versions of the story until the final name. The name may, in fact, have been a surprise, especially if another Chariclo (the wife of Chiron) was already associated with the Actaeon story (see pp. 237–38). She is also unusual in that she has borne a child; most female attendants of virgin goddesses are virgins themselves (though not Procris in *hArt* 209).

ἔν ποκα (= ποτε) **Θήβαις**: see *hArt* 238n.

58. περί: Bulloch follows H. Stephanus in treating περί as an adverb (on the accent see his note ad loc.) to be understood with πουλύ τι καί ("quite exceedingly well"); he points to the dieresis following δή, which separates περί from τᾶν ἑταρᾶν and takes τᾶν ἑταρᾶν as dependent on μίαν. But West's observation that τᾶν ἑταρᾶν could not stand without περί is surely correct (1986: 29).

φίλατο: as in Homer and Hesiod, the aorist middle is used of a divinity's love for a mortal.

ἑταρᾶν: the form occurs previously only at *Il.* 4.441 (ἑτάρη), the famous description of Strife, the companion of Ares.

59. ἔγεντο (= ἐγένετο): see Bulloch ad loc.

60–64. The towns of Thespiae, Haliartus (61), and Coroneia (63), as well as the river Couralius (64), are on the northern and eastern slopes of Mt. Helicon. Cults of Athena existed in all three cities, though the sanctuary to Athena *Itonia* at Coroneia, the site of the Panboeotian festival, was the best known. Thespiae and Haliartus had much smaller shrines (see Schachter 1981: 114–26, 133).

60. Θεσπιέων: by the third century, the name of the town was Θεσπιαί, here formed with the epic-Ionic genitive plural -έων in place of -άων.

61. The first half of the line is corrupt; the mss. either omit the line entirely or begin it with ἡ 'πὶ Κορωνείας, which seems to be an intrusion from 63. Bulloch ad loc. sets out two metrical arguments for not retaining ἡ 'πὶ Κορωνείας: (1) if it stands, the following ἡ would normally be shortened by correption, thus requiring -ας to be short and (2) "the masculine caesura after Κορωνείας in v. 61 requires a secondary caesura" after the seventh (here a proclitic) or eighth element. (His other arguments are less cogent.) Livrea 1987: 34–36 reviews previous attempts to remedy the line and suggests an emendation that meets the metrical criteria: ἡ 'πὶ Ἀλαλκομένειον has a feminine caesura and -ον is short. Further, according to Pausanias (9.33.5), Alalcomenae boasted an ancient temple marking the location where Athena was reared; at Strabo 9.2.27, the town is linked with Haliartus, and a tomb of Tiresias is said to have been nearby (see Schachter 1981: 111–13 on Alalcomenae and 1994: 38–39 on Tiresias). If Livrea is correct, then Athena and her nymphs travel not in a more or less northwesterly direction from Thespiae to Haliartus to Coroneia, but back and forth in a zigzag pattern.

61. ἐλαύνοι: an iterative optative. The subject is Athena (either from 55 or ἁ δαίμων at 65), who is also the subject of διερχόμενα.

62. ἔργα: tilled fields, as at *hArt* 125, 156.

63. 'πὶ Κορωνείας: for Athena and Coroneia see Alcaeus (fr. 325 V): ὤνασσ' Ἀθανάα πολεμάδοκε | ἅ ποι Κορωνήας μεδ[| ναύω πάροιθεν ἀμφι[| Κωραλίω ποτάμω πὰρ ὄχθαις ("Lady Athena, war-sustaining…, who perhaps as protector [?] of Coroneia…in front of the temple…by the banks of the river Couralius…").

65. ἁ δαίμων νιν ἑῷ ἐπεβάσατο δίφρῳ: the word order reflects meaning as the goddess (δαίμων) and the possessive (ἑῷ) surround the nymph (νιν), while the hiatus after ἑῷ isolates the two. Also, Bulloch suggests that the transitive use of the middle "may emphasize the closeness of Athena and Chariclo (Athena acts with her own interest in view)."

ἐπεβάσατο: Hellenistic poets occasionally inflect otherwise athematic verbs as if a sigmatic aorist with normal -σα endings (see Bulloch ad loc.).

66. ὄαροι: the whispered speech of girls; see, e.g., Hes. *Th.* 205, *HhAphr* 249 (see Faulkner 2008: ad loc.), Posidippus *ep.* 55.2 A-B. Cf. fr. 500.2 Pf., where it seems to mean "discussions."

χοροστασίαι: first in Hermesianax (fr. 7.58 Powell) and here, then imitated in late Greek. Literally, the setting up of the chorus; here "choruses."

67. ἀδεῖαι τελέθεσκον: an iterative imperfect of τελέθω; it has two senses: "happen" or simply "to be." Mair and Bulloch understand it in the former sense, with ἀδεῖαι as attributive. Alternatively, the verb serves as a copula, ἀδεῖαι as predicate: "the dances were not sweet, when…" (so Asper, D'Alessio).

Χαρικλώ: see 57n.

68. ἔμενε: for the transitive use in the context of an ill fate awaiting someone, cf. Aesch. *Ag.* 1277, *Ch.* 103.

69. ἔσσαν = οὖσαν. The form occurs in some Doric writers and inscriptions and possibly in Sappho (fr. 121.2 V). Callimachus uses it only here.

70. λυσαμένα: by the Hellenistic period the dual was rare even in poetry apart from natural pairs, which may be the point: to emphasize the closeness of the deity and Chariclo. (A dual subject with a plural verb is common even in Homer; see Chantraine 2.26–27.)

περόνας "fastening pins"; Oedipus blinds himself with περόνας from Jocasta's garment (Soph. *OT* 1269); the choice of noun here may prefigure Tiresias' blinding.

71. ἵππω ἐπὶ κράνᾳ Ἑλικωνίδι: the fountain of the Hippocrene is located on Mt. Helicon. Cf. the opening of Hesiod *Th.* 1–8, where the Muses bathe in the spring and dance. The mention of Helicon in combination with 72–74 creates an expectation of divine epiphany that is brutally inverted.

καλὰ ῥεοῖσα "fair flowing"; the Doric form of the participle (from ῥέω) is found only here.

72. λῶντο = λούοντο, the imperfect middle of λούω. The variant λώοντο occurs in 73.

72–74. The scene is carefully prepared: μεσαμβρινά ("midday") is the traditional time of danger in the country, when the local divinities might be present. The time, the preternatural calm, and the repetitions create the effect: μεσαμβρινά (72, 73) ἀσυχία (72, 74) and εἶχ' ὄρος…ἔσαν ὧραι…-εἶχεν ὄρος, where the mountain (ὄρος) and the hour of enchantment (ὧραι) fade into each other.

75. Τειρεσίας δ' ἔτι μοῦνος: McKay 1962b: 39 takes this to mean "still an only child" as parallel to Actaeon (108–9: τὸν μόνον…παῖδα). However, ἔτι μοῦνος is a *hapax* in Homer (*Il.* 2.212) in a similarly shaped phrase that describes Thersites (Θερσίτης δ' ἔτι μοῦνος), who alone continues to talk when the others are quiet; this parallel suggests that only Tiresias had continued to hunt in this dangerous midday hour. μοῦνος presents an interesting challenge for editors: the mss. read ἔτι μοῦνος, which makes the Homeric intertext clear; would it still be heard with Ernesti's universally accepted change to the Doric μῶνος? Cf. 4n.

75–76. ἄρτι γένεια | περκάζων: "ripening with respect to his beard"; the verb is common for the ripening of fruit, and in an erotic context is often applied to young men at the time when their beards first appear, a sign that their beauty is at its peak (see, e.g., *Theoc.* 7.120, where Philainos is described as ἀπίοιο πεπαίτερος, "riper than a pear"). For the trope see Tarán 1985.

77. ἄφατόν τι: ironically used as an adverbial accusative with διψάσας, and more appropriate for Tiresias' "unspeakable" mistake. Note ἄφθογγος in 83 and φωνὰν ἔσχεν ἀμαχανία in 84. Tiresias himself has no speaking lines in the hymn.

78. εἶδε τὰ μὴ θεμιτά: similar phrases occur elsewhere with respect to those areas of a goddess's body (the groin) that may not be seen or represented naked in art; cf. *Anacreontea* 57.10: ὅσα μὴ θέμις δ' ὁρᾶσθαι with West's note.

79. περ ὅμως: the combination of this emphatic particle and conjunction is first found in Hes. *Op.* 20 (see West ad loc.).

80–82. The confusing word order (the interrogative τίς is separated from δαίμων by two full lines) may be intended to reflect Athena's agitation. The question τίς σε … δαίμων is familiar from tragedy; see Aesch. *Ag.* 1174–75, Eur. *Hel.* 669.

80. τὸν ὀφθαλμὼς οὐκέτ' ἀποισόμενον: in apposition to σε.

ἀποισόμενον: in the middle, "get back for oneself." This participial form is first found here, then occasionally in late Greek.

81. Εὐηρείδα: Tiresias was the "son of Everes" (for his lineage see Apollod. 3.6.7). He is also addressed as Εὐηρείδα at Theoc. 24.71.

δαίμων: frequently in the sense of fate or chance.

82. νὺξ ἔλαβεν: see Renehan 1987: 248 for a justification of the alternative reading ἔβαλεν.

83. ἐστάκη (= Attic ἐστήκει): this unaugmented Doric pluperfect is not found elsewhere in literary texts; it is Buttmann's correction of a problematic ms. reading and universally accepted. See Bulloch ad loc.

ἐκόλλασαν: from κολλάω, "glue" or "fasten together." The word is not used in epic and is rare in lyric and tragedy. A possible intertext is Aesch. *Ag.* 1566: κεκόλληται γένος πρὸς ἄτᾳ ("the clan is stuck in ruin"), describing the Atreidae; it would be equally applicable to the Cadmid house that Tiresias will serve, whose descendants included Actaeon and Pentheus.

84. γώνατα καὶ φωνάν: the zeugma provides a graphic image of Tiresias' terror; he can neither run away nor speak.

84–85. Tiresias' speechlessness (φωνὰν ἔσχεν ἀμαχανία) is juxtaposed to his mother's outcry (ἐβόασε). While he does not know what has happened to his eyes, his mother is all too aware of the cause and effect.

86. Chariclo softens the accusation by generalizing: "divinities, are you these sorts of friends?"

87. ἄλαστε: Homeric and tragic, "accursed." The adjective is masculine vocative by attraction to the gender of the subject (Tiresias), not the neuter vocative (τέκνον). Cf. Soph. *OC* 1483, where the chorus asks mercy from the deity for caring for an ἄλαστον ἄνδρα (*sc.* Oedipus).

88. λαγόνας: at the opening of the hymn λαγόνων (6) is used of horses' flanks; but with women it usually specified the space from the base of the ribs through the groin, thus with στήθεα, two intimate portions of female anatomy. While there is no doubt that Callimachus is creating an erotically charged scene, the repetition of the noun is jarring. (See also λυσαμένα in both contexts [10, 70]).

89. ἀέλιον: the form is common to Pindar and tragedy (and see Buck §41.3); here possibly for the sound effect with ἐμὲ δειλάν.

ὤ: Chariclo's exclamation of woe is repeated three times, in the fashion of tragic lament. For the accent, see Bulloch ad loc.

ἐμὲ δειλάν "wretched me"; a rare exclamatory accusative, found in ritual lament. Cf. Bion, *Adonis* 28 (on which see Reed's helpful note). Chariclo first addresses her son (87), then herself, and finally the mountain (90).

90. παριτέ: vocative with Helicon; from παριτός (verbal adjective from πάρειμι), only here in Callimachus: "traversable."

91. ἐπράξαο: πράττω in aorist middle = "exact payment." Chariclo shifts her complaint to the region, Mt. Helicon; it has exacted a great penalty for a small matter (ὀλίγων). The mountain may have lost a few deer to Tiresias as he hunted, but it took the boy's eyes in compensation.

δόρκας "gazelles" were supposedly named from their large eyes (cf. δέρκομαι), thus a punning exchange of one type of eyes (δόρκας) for another (φάεα).

92. φάεα: from φάος; here metonymy for "sight." Cf. *hArt* 53, 71, 211.

93–95. The long μέν-clause describing Chariclo's lament is starkly contrasted with the δέ-clause, expressing Athena's response in a half line and an aorist (ἐλέησεν). There are four difficulties with these lines: (1) The opening of 93 in the mss. (ἁ μὲν ἀμφοτέραισι) lacks a syllable. (2) ἁ μέν is separated from μάτηρ μέν by a full line. (3) The usual meaning of οἶτον is "fate," not, as is required here, "lament." (4) How to understand ἄγε? Resolutions of these difficulties include: (1) Schneider's emendation to ἁ μὲν <ἄμ'>, presupposing haplography. (2) Bulloch ad loc. explains μάτηρ as "almost predicative," translating it as "being as she was, his mother...," and the repeated μέν an emphatic contrast to θεὰ δ(έ). Note also that the word order allows ἁ... μάτηρ to embrace her son: παῖδα is surrounded by ἀμφοτέραισι (*sc.* χερσί)...περὶ...λαβοῖσα. (3) Attempts to fix include emending to οἶκτον, οἶμον (see *hZeus* 78), or changing ἄγε to εἶχε (e.g., "had the fate"). For a full discussion of the attempts to repair, see Svarlien 1991. (4) Mair understands ἄγε with a suppressed παῖδα ("she led her son away"); alternatively with κλαίοισα ("she led her life weeping"), or with οἶτον ("kept up the lament," so Bulloch). The latter two make better sense with the contrasting tenses of ἄγε and ἐλέησεν.

93. περὶ...λαβοῖσα: in tmesis for effect, see above; cf. A.R. 1.1197. The verb is rare in poetry.

94–95. Callimachus is imitating *Il.* 9.563–64: μήτηρ ἀλκυόνος πολυπενθέος οἶτον ἔχουσα | κλαῖεν ("the mother, having the fate of the halcyon of many sorrows, wept," because Apollo had taken away her son).

94. γοερᾶν: the adjective is common in tragedy (e.g., Eur. *Hec.* 84, *Phoen.* 1567a) for the sounds of mourning.

ἀηδονίδων: from Doric ἀηδονίς; first at [Eur.] *Rhes.* 550, then found in Hellenistic epigram. The song of the nightingale was identified with the mourning of Procne and a common image in tragedy for a mother's mourning (e.g., Aesch. *Suppl.* 58–65).

98. ἀλαόν "blind"; the word is not common: it is applied to Tiresias in *Od.* 10.493 and 12.267 and to Oedipus at Soph. *OC* 150, Eur. *Phoen.* 1531.

100. Κρόνιοι... νόμοι: the first and best example of the just lawgiver, Cronus ruled over the Golden Age (see, e.g., Plato, *Laws* 713a-14a). The label may be ironically applied here, where the punishment does not fit the circumstances.

101–2. These lines echo the language of law codes: the indefinite relative clause states the crime, and the penalty is recorded with accusative and infinitive (τοῦτον ἰδεῖν), as if ἔδοξε were understood (see Smyth §2013b). Athena, by "quoting" Cronus' law code, displaces her responsibility for the act.

102. ἀθρήσῃ: from ἀθρέω, "gaze at"; cf. Soph. *OT* 1305, *OC* 1032.

103. παλινάγρετον: a *hapax* in *Il.* 1.526, of the irreversible nature of divine decisions (and see below 131). It occurs once in A.R. 2.444 (Αἰσονίδη, τὸ μὲν οὐ παλινάγρετον, where Phineus describes his own blindness) and only here in Callimachus. One poet is clearly imitating the other; see p. 22.

γένοιτο: for the optative see *hAp* 26n.

104. Μοιρᾶν ὧδ᾽ ἐπένησε λίνα "thus did the threads of the Fates spin out." Behind the passage stands the exchange of Hecuba and Priam in *Il.* 24. She begs her husband not to come into the sight of savage Achilles (206–8: εἰ... ἐσόψεται ὀφθαλμοῖσιν | ὠμηστὴς καὶ ἄπιστος ἀνὴρ ὅ γε, οὔ σ᾽ ἐλεήσει ("If he shall see you with his eyes, savage and untrustworthy man, he will not pity you"); she continues about Hector: ὥς ποθι <u>Μοῖρα</u> κραταιή | γειγνομένῳ <u>ἐπένησε λίνῳ</u>, ὅτε μιν τέκον αὐτή, | ἀργίποδας κύνας ἆσαι... (209–11: "Thus once upon a time mighty fate spun the thread at his birth, when I myself bore him, to sate swift-footed dogs..."). In *hDem* 102 Callimachus again turns to *Il.* 24, recollecting the scene with Priam and Achilles. In this hymn the relationship of mothers and sons is positioned against the backdrop of Homeric pathos, while in *hDem*, it is the plight of fathers.

105. ἐγείναο: second person aorist from γείνομαι, "you gave birth to."

106. τέλθος: most probably a Doric form of τέλος, which the scholiast glosses as χρέος ("payment" or "debt"); it is found only only here and at *hDem* 77.

107–18. The story of Actaeon is related as a consolation to Chariclo. In previous versions, Actaeon is killed by Artemis because he boasts that he is the better hunter (Eur. *Bacch.* 337–40) or because he aspires to marriage with Semele (Stesichorus, *PMG* fr. 236; Acusilaus of Argos, *FGrH* 2 F33; Apollod. 3.4.4). See Guimond, *LIMC* (s.v. Aktaion) and Lacy 1990.

107–8. πόσσα … πόσσα: West 1986: 30 points out that exclamatory πόσσα for ὅσσα is mainly a *koine* usage.

107. ἁ Καδμηΐς: the "daughter of Cadmus" was Actaeon's mother, Autonoe; his father, Aristaeus (108), was the son of Apollo and Cyrene, who are featured at the end of *hAp*. These are further links in the genealogical chain between Cyrene and Argos.

ἔμπυρα: these are "burnt offerings," and the term is often used in the context of divination (e.g., Pi. *Ol.* 8.3). The term is surely ironic with reference to Tiresias, who will spend his life as a blind prophet, hence be unable to read the auguries for himself.

109. ἀβατάν (i.e., ἡβητήν) "in his prime," scanned - - -, with an implied pun on ἄβατος, scanned ◡ ◡ ×, that which is "not to be trodden upon."

τυφλὸν ἰδέσθαι: the juxtaposition is ironic: prima facie, praying "to see their son blind" (but at least alive), but equally possible that Chariclo hears praying for "her blind son to see."

110. σύνδρομος: the word has two meanings, both relevant: Callimachus reinforces the meaning of "running with," in the sense of "companion," with δρόμος and ξυναί in 111–12, but it more commonly means "running into," "meeting," thus suggestive of the event that led to Actaeon's death.

111. ἔσσεται: the future is used because Actaeon postdates Tiresias.

112. ῥυσεῦνται: third plural future from (ἐ)ρύομαι (LSJ s.v. ἐρύω D). The form is not attested elsewhere.

ἐκαβολίαι: once in Homer (*Il.* 5.54), where Scamandrius, whom Artemis herself taught to hunt, is killed. Neither Artemis nor his skill in archery (ἐκαβολίαι) was of any avail in warding off death.

113. ὁππόκα κ' οὐκ: the mss. read ὁππόταν οὐκ, the objection to which is that within his fully Doric poems Callimachus only uses the modal κε (κεν), not ἄν (as at *hDelos* 172). Thus Wilamowitz emended to ὁππόκα κοὐκ (= καὶ οὐκ), without modal; Bulloch, arguing that the modal is necessary in a temporal clause referring to a specific situation, articulated as κ' οὐκ (= κε οὐκ), though West (1986: 28) remains skeptical, pointing to the absence of modal at 129.

περ lends concessive force to the participle, which takes account of Tiresias' circumstance (see 78).

115–18. The two couplets set the two mothers in stark contrast: the one will scour the thickets to collect her son's bones, while the other, happy in comparison, will still have a son to lead home, even though he is now blind.

115. τουτάκι: see *hZeus* 44n.

δειπνησεῦντι: the incongruity of the verb, which more commonly refers to human feasting, heightens the horror: "his bitches will dine on their former master."

116. λεξεῖται: Doric future of λέγω, "gather." Bones of the dead are normally gathered after cremation, though here the dogs have done the work of removing the flesh.

117. ὀλβίσταν: a poetic superlative of ὄλβιος.

119–20. The word order juxtaposes Chariclo (μινύρεο) and her son (τῷδε) and separates Chariclo (τεῦ) from Athena (ἐμέθεν); elsewhere they (or their pronouns) are together.

119. μινύρεο: second person imperative, from μινύρομαι, a tragic/comic variant of μινυρίζω. It seems to describe a low whimper or hum, characteristic of birds, especially the nightingale, thus a sound of mourning.

τῷδε: μένω (120) does not normally take a dative object; given the distance between τῷδε and the verb, the deictic pronoun is best taken as a dative of interest or respect and μενεῦντι as absolute in the sense of "will be lasting" (cf. LSJ s.v. I 4) and see 131n.

121. ἐσσομένοισιν: cf. Homer, *Il.* 6. 357–58: οἶσιν ἐπὶ Ζεὺς θῆκε κακὸν μόρον, ὡς καὶ ὀπίσσω | ἀνθρώποισι πελώμεθ᾽ ἀοίδιμοι ἐσσομένοισι ("on whom Zeus has brought an evil fate, so that we will be a subject for song even to men in the future").

122. μέγα... δή τι: with περισσότερον "very much superior" to the others.

123. ὄρνιχας, ὃς αἴσιος: Soph. *OT* 52: ὄρνιθι... αἰσίῳ, of the propitious (bird) omen that brought Oedipus to power. The recently discovered roll of Posidippus' epigrams contains a number of poems on bird augury (21–29, 31 A-B), and Callimachus himself wrote a prose work on the subject (frr. 414–28 Pf.).

124. ἄλιθα: Doric for ἤλιθα. The adverb has two meanings: "exceedingly" and "in vain" (for examples see Livrea on A.R. 4.177); here in the latter sense.

πτέρυγες "wings," metonym for "flight."

125. θεοπρόπα: either with the ellipse of a noun (*sc.* ἔπη) or the plural adjective = θεοπρόπια, "prophecies."

126. Λαβδακίδαις "the sons of Labdacus"; he was the grandson of Cadmus and the grandfather of Oedipus.

128. πολυχρόνιον "lasting a long time"; cf. *hDel* 282n.

129. πεπνυμένος: from epic πέπνυμαι; perfect with present sense. It means "to be sentient" but more commonly "to be wise." For Tiresias maintaining his cognitive functions and vatic powers in the underworld, see *Od.* 10.494–95.

130. Ἀγεσίλᾳ "leader of the people," a euphemistic epithet of Hades, previously only in Aesch. *TrGF* 3 fr. 406 Radt.

131. A reworking of Zeus to Athena at *Il.* 1.524–26: εἰ δ᾽ ἄγε τοι κεφαλῇ κατανεύσομαι, ὄφρα πεποίθῃς· | τοῦτο γὰρ ἐξ ἐμέθεν γε μετ᾽ ἀθανάτοισι μέγιστον | τέκμωρ· οὐ γὰρ ἐμὸν παλινάγρετον... ("Come now, I shall nod my head to you, so that you may be certain; for this from me is the greatest sign among the immortals; for my assent may not be recalled... "). The language of the passage occurs at 103 (παλινάγρετον) and 120 (ἐξ ἐμέθεν). Athena, like Zeus, nods an assent that cannot be undone. The explanation for her participation in Zeus's divine authority is given in the next lines. For Artemis' participation in Zeus's authority, see *hArt* 118.

τὸ ... ἐντελές (*sc.* ἐστίν): τό is the demonstrative antecedent of ᾧ.

ἐπινεύσῃ: the shift from κατανεύω to ἐπινεύω with virtually the same meaning "nod assent" may reflect an ancient discussion about the two verbs. See Bulloch ad loc. and Rengakos 1993: 140.

132. τόγε: defined by the following πατρώϊα πάντα φέρεσθαι.

135. Διὸς κορυφά: cf. Aesch. *Supp.* 92 for the phrase and a similar sentiment; if this is deliberate allusion, it is also a reminder of the Danaid connection to Egypt.

136. ψεύδεα - ‾ˇ - || - ˇˇ αι θυγάτηρ: all mss. have a lacuna in this line, but the thought is clear: the head of Zeus does not nod assent to falsehoods, nor does his daughter.

137–42. The formal close of the hymn. As the goddess's statue finally arrives, the girls are exhorted to greet her with prayers for the city.

137. ἀτρεκές: adverbial accusative. Athena is now "really" coming.

139. εὐαγορίᾳ "fair speech" in the sense of well spoken of; the noun occurs only here and at Pi. *Pae.* 2(fr. 52b).67 S-M.

εὔγμασι: εὔγμα is rare; with the meaning of "prayers" it is found in tragic and comic lyrics; cf. Soph. *Ant.* 1185, where Eurydice is on her way to address prayers to Athena.

ὀλολυγαῖς: usually female cries of invocation to a divinity; it is a *hapax* in Homer at *Il.* 6.301, where the aged women of Troy cry out to Athena, but Athena does not heed their prayers to stop Diomedes' rampage against the Trojans (though cf. *hDelos* 258).

140. Ἰναχίω: genitive; the Inachus is both the river in which the statue will be cleansed and the ancestor of the line that led to Danaus.

141–42. ἐξελάοισα ... ἐς ... ἐλάσσαις | ἵππως: the close echoes language of the opening (6: κόνιν ἱππειᾶν ἐξελάσαι).

142. κλᾶρον: the sense of "estate" or "inheritance" seems to be poetic. κλᾶρος occurs in the elegiac hymn for the town of Hermione in the Argolid, preserved in Aelian (= *SH* 206) and discussed above p. 35: καὶ πάντων θάλλοι κλᾶρος ἐν Ἑρμιόνᾳ. In *hAth* κλᾶρον refers to the land of Argos, but it would have resonance in the land of the Ptolemies as well, since Ptolemy II had given allotments of land (κλῆροι) to his veterans.

6

The Hymn to Demeter

L IKE *HATH*, THIS HYMN IS MIMETIC AND WAS COMPOSED IN LITERARY
Doric (see pp. 26–27). It also has a similar narrative frame with an inserted
cautionary tale, and while Tiresias' story has strong tragic contours in *hAth*,
the story of Erysichthon in this hymn has elements of social comedy. The temporal frame is the return of a sacred procession to the temple at the approach of
evening; the celebrants, who have been fasting, are accompanying a κάλαθος conveyed by four white mares (120). The unidentified female narrator (see 124) recreates the atmosphere of a festival for Demeter that in detail seems somewhere
between the Athenian *Thesmophoria* and the Mysteries at Eleusis. The narrator
exhorts the female celebrants and warns observers not to look at the contents of
the sacred basket as it passes by. After the story of Demeter's search for her ab-
ducted daughter is rehearsed and then abandoned, the narrator launches into the
apotropaic tale of Erysichthon, an event that takes place in Thessaly (25–117).
The young man was cutting down trees sacred to the goddess, when Demeter
assumed the guise of her own priestess to deter him from the sacrilege. In his
insolence he refused to heed her, claiming that the felled trees would make an
appropriate space for continual banqueting (54–5). The punishment suits the
crime: he is visited with a gargantuan hunger and insatiable thirst. Boundaries
of propriety and measure are transgressed as his appetite demands twenty slaves
to prepare enough food for his banquet, twelve more to pour sufficient drink. Of
course, he cannot be allowed to attend common banquets (72) since he would
disgrace his family by eating everything in sight. When he has literally eaten them

out of house and home, having consumed all their stores, oxen and horses, and even a small domestic animal, he is last seen wasting away at a crossroads begging for crusts (110–15). Lines 118–38 return to the ritual frame, with further cautions before the final salutation and prayer for prosperity.

The embedded tale has features in common with fourth-century comedy. The excesses of kings and aristocrats were easy comic targets because of their conspicuous consumption in symposia as well as other forms of luxury. Athenaeus, for example, in a section on gluttony, quotes from Sositheus' satyr play, *Lityersis* (a bastard son of Midas and the king of the Celaenians in Phrygia): "He eats three loaves and three pack mules in one short day; and he drinks down a ten-amphora jar, calling it one measure" (10.415B-C = *TrGF* 1, 99 Sositheus F 2.6–8 Snell). It is possible to read Callimachus' hymnic insert in the context of this topos, and with a similarly serious purpose: to be a mirror held up to those in power that reflects their own egregious behavior, executed in a mode that is closer to comedy than the kind of earnest philosophical instruction to kings found in, for example, Plato's *Seventh Letter*.

In topic and detail Erysichthon's story is a humorous inversion of the serious cult frame: fasting and abstinence pay service to the goddess, in return for which she provides humankind with her bounty. Erysichthon abuses Demeter's bounty in service of his own excess: a suitable space for his indulgence requires no less than an act of sacrilege. But his punishment takes on a kind of narrative excess as he consumes everything in sight including the "white tail." Callimachus' narrative itself is a boundary transgression that incorporates elements of iambic and comic lampoon into the framework of the Homeric hymn. After all, it was Iambe (a feminine embodiment of iambic) telling rude tales who finally made Demeter laugh, break her fast, and restore her gifts to mankind. A now fragmentary hymn to Demeter (in choriambic hexameters) written by Callimachus' Alexandrian contemporary Philicus mentions the arrival of Iambe, who proclaims: for the solemn ([τοῖσι δὲ] σεμνοῖς) a humorous tale is not without advantage (ἀκερδή[ς]).[1] Callimachus' hymn both recreates the solemnity of the festival and incorporates elements of the comic revival of the goddess, and via the comic elements provides a potent criticism of aristocratic excess in a form calculated to amuse as well as instruct.

The Deity and Her Relevant Cults

Demeter was worshipped throughout the Greek-speaking world in two translocal rituals: the *Thesmophoria*, which was a civic festival performed by citizen women

1. *GLP* 90.8 = *SH* 680.55. For the role of iambic within Demeter festivals, see Rosen 2007: 47–56.

to guarantee the city's agricultural and human fertility; and the Mysteries, which involved personal devotion without regard to social status or gender and held out the promise of benefits for eternity. The same myth subtended both—Demeter's loss of her daughter, Demeter's wandering, followed by the girl's return—and was closely connected to the cycle of the seasons: Demeter's bountiful gifts of agriculture ceased while she searched for and mourned her daughter, thus bringing on winter. The girl's return led to the rebirth of vegetation in the spring. The best known examples of these festivals were at Athens, but similar festivals were celebrated throughout the Greek-speaking world, and Demeter herself was assimilated to other local divinities, particularly Isis in Egypt. The ritual elements that Callimachus mentions seem to divide between these two known cult types: in being exclusively female, with the fasting, and night procession, the festival described by Callimachus resembles the *Nesteia*, the second day of the *Thesmophoria*, but the mention of initiates (128–29) and the procession of the κάλαθος with sacred objects resembles the Eleusinian Mysteries. In the mysteries at Andania in the southern Peloponnese both men and women participated, with specific dress codes, but in separate groups, while "sacred virgins" chosen by lot accompanied the cart with the sacred implements (see Connelly 2007: 86, 106–7, 314n3). It is possible, therefore, to imagine that Callimachus was addressing only women in a mixed-gender mystery rite. But since the κάλαθος, λίκνα, and the language of initiation and exclusion would suit either festival (see 3n, 129n), it is more likely that his ritual is a civic *Thesmophoria*.

Unlike the middle four hymns, *hDem* mentions no particular cult-site, but it is the only one for which the scholiast records an Alexandrian context:

> Ptolemy Philadelphus in imitation instituted Athenian customs in Alexandria, in which there was a procession of the basket (καλάθου). For it was the habit in Athens on a designated day for the basket to be borne on a vehicle in honor of Demeter.

There is also excellent evidence for Demeter cult in Alexandria. Papyrus evidence seems to indicate that a *Demetria* and a *Thesmophoria* were being celebrated in the city as early as 258 BCE (Perpillou-Thomas 1993: 78–81). Polybius (15.29.8) mentions a Thesmophorion, in the vicinity of the Inner Palace of the city, in connection with the events of 203/202, but not when it was built. Alexandria had a suburb named Eleusis, which Satyrus, writing on the *Demes of Alexandria* in the second century BCE, claims was named for Athens' Eleusis and that a festival was celebrated there with contests. Fraser (1972: 1.201 and 2.338n82) doubts that these were true Mysteries but "recitations, perhaps even dramatic scenes, concerning the Eleusinian story." Recitations and dramatic scenes would well suit Callimachus' hymn. Finally, an image of a large basket mounted on a *quadriga* appears on Alexandrian coins from the time of Trajan, which looks very like what Callimachus describes at 120 (see 1n).

In addition to Alexandria, the hymn has often been claimed for Cyrene. That city had a well-established Demeter sanctuary within the walls and an extramural sanctuary, at which, from the archaeological remains of pig bones, it is clear that a *Thesmophoria* was celebrated (see Kane 1998). Archaeologists have attempted to use Callimachus' hymn to trace a processional route between the two, though with inconclusive results.[2] Fraser 1972: 2.916–17n290 and Sherwin-White 1978: 306–11 also make a case for Cos. The inability of scholars to agree on a location combined with the confusing ritual details led Hopkinson (pp. 32–39) to argue against any real performance context or known rite, and his views have largely been accepted. In this regard a few points seem worth making: (1) *HZeus* and this hymn flank the collection, and they are the only ones that do not identify a specific cultic location. For reasons outlined above p. 51 *hZeus* is surely for Alexandria—and probably for a festival of Zeus *Basileus*. It is worth considering, therefore, if the final hymn is also to be assigned to Alexandria, since it had a region (Eleusis) where some kinds of rites for Demeter were being celebrated. Finally, the hymn ends with the deictic τάνδε σάω πόλιν, the same prayer closing the three-line *Homeric Hymn to Demeter* (13), about which Calame 2011: 335–36 remarks:

> The request for safeguarding the city is accompanied by an act of verbal *deixis*, which consists of τάνδε σάου πόλιν 'save *this* city'. The self-referential act of singing (aedic-rhapsodic) is located in both time and space: it takes place *hic et nunc*. Whatever its length, the *Homeric Hymn*, in its role as a hymnic song addressed to a divinity as a musical offering, has the function of introducing the rhapsodic recitation into the series of ritual acts honouring this divinity. The hymn therefore makes the performance of the rhapsodic song itself a ritual act and an activity of cult.[3]

(2) All of the elements that Callimachus alludes to in *hDem* have known correlations in cultic activities throughout Greece and the Greek East, and since we know very little about real cultic activities outside of Athens, there is no inherent reason to assume that these details were a fictional admixture. (3) Finally, whether or not these hymns were performed on the occasion of a specific ritual event, in the context of ancient ritual behaviors (and poetic coherence) it seems highly unlikely that a poet would write a hymn that contaminated ritual

2. The case for Cyrene is made by Chamoux 1953: 265–68 and Laronde 1987: 362–66; White 1984: 47–48 thinks the evidence is inconclusive.

3. Cf. Calame's discussion of the ending of *hDem* (2004: 440–41).

behaviors. It is much more likely that a specific festival stood behind Callimachus' hymn even if its location and cultic particulars now elude the modern critic. Given the fact that Demeter was well represented with cults in early Alexandria, even if the hymn was not written to reflect a specific Alexandrian festival, it would have had considerable resonance for local audiences (as it did for the scholiast).

The Sources and Intertexts

Callimachus obviously drew on *HhDem*, which was probably the most popular of the Homeric hymns and well attested in the Hellenistic period. That hymn begins by narrating Demeter's futile search for her daughter, then turns to the origins of the Eleusinian Mysteries. The goddess in disguise as an old woman comes to be the nurse for a male infant in an elite Athenian household. She begins a process to make the child (Demophoön) immortal by placing him in the fire by night to burn away his mortality; when she is detected by the not unreasonably hysterical mother, Metaneira, she assumes her full divine aspect and both exacts a punishment and bestows a favor. Demophoön remains mortal, but the goddess gives the city the Mysteries that promise a better life after death, and the hereditary priests of the cult are to be Demophoön's descendants. The story of Demeter's wrath in *HhDem* has obvious parallels with the Erysichthon episode: Demeter disguises herself as an old priestess of her own cult; the domestic space is a central feature; and Erysichthon himself, while not a newborn, seems to be no more than an adolescent. Erysichthon's transgressions, however, are of a different order from Metaneira's. Further, Callimachus deliberately rejects the narrative of Demeter's wandering (17: μὴ μὴ ταῦτα λέγωμες), and the *aition* of the Eleusinian Mysteries has no parallel in his hymn.

The story of Erysichthon, the son of Triopas, who in turn is the son of Poseidon and Canace, has tantalizing antecedents that do not quite dovetail with Callimachus' version. Hesiod's *Catalogue* (fr. 43 M-W) records the story of Mestra, who can change her form. She is the daughter of Erysichthon (called Aethon, for his "flaming" hunger). To support her father's needs she is married off to various suitors for a bride-price. Once married, she changes into animal form, abandons her spouse, and returns to her father to repeat the sequence. Callimachus clearly maintains the feature of all-consuming hunger and alludes to the name Aethon at 66–67, but other elements of Hesiod's tale (e.g., Mestra) are missing. Ovid's version of the story in *Met.* 8.738–878 fuses elements of Hesiod (Mestra) and Callimachus (Erysichthon felling the oak in a sacred grove and being punished by all-consuming hunger). The story of Mestra and Aethon appears in Lycophron (1391–96), and Diodorus (5.61) recounts a version that makes Triopas, not Erysichthon, the transgressor. Since he is writing after Callimachus, it is reasonable to assume that he knows a version that differs from both Hesiod and Callimachus. Then there is the Coan Tale, a nineteenth-century folktale recorded from Cos and published by R. M. Dawkins in 1950; it includes a king's son who cuts down trees, one of which is inhabited by a female spirit. She curses him with eternal hunger. Scholars continue to debate the nature and importance of this folktale: is it an artifact of the ancient tale that both Callimachus and Ovid drew on, or is it a relatively recent popular tale that resulted from contact with literary sources such as Ovid? See Hopkinson pp. 26–29 for a discussion of the topic and Robertson 1984 on the various versions of the Erysichthon story.

The Ptolemaic Connections

The introduction of the Demeter cult in Alexandria was attributed to the first Ptolemies (variously Soter or Philadelphus). Fraser (1972: 1.201) thinks that they were capitalizing on the link already made in Herodotus between Isis and Demeter and the historian's claim that the Mysteries were imported to the Greek world by the daughters of Danaus. Philotera, the sister of Ptolemy II, seems to have been associated with Demeter in cult; see pp. 15, 21.

ΕΙΣ ΔΗΜΗΤΡΑ

Τῶ καλάθω κατιόντος ἐπιφθέγξασθε, γυναῖκες·
'Δάματερ, μέγα χαῖρε, πολυτρόφε πουλυμέδιμνε.'
τὸν κάλαθον κατιόντα χαμαὶ θασεῖσθε, βέβαλοι,
μηδ' ἀπὸ τῶ τέγεος μηδ' ὑψόθεν αὐγάσσησθε
5   μὴ παῖς μηδὲ γυνὰ μηδ' ἃ κατεχεύατο χαίταν,
μηδ' ὅκ' ἀφ' αὐαλέων στομάτων πτύωμες ἄπαστοι.
Ἕσπερος ἐκ νεφέων ἐσκέψατο—πανίκα νεῖται; —
Ἕσπερος, ὅς τε πιεῖν Δαμάτερα μῶνος ἔπεισεν,
ἁρπαγίμας ὅκ' ἄπυστα μετέστιχεν ἴχνια κώρας.
10 πότνια, πῶς σε δύναντο πόδες φέρεν ἔστ' ἐπὶ δυθμάς,
ἔστ' ἐπὶ τὼς Μέλανας καὶ ὅπα τὰ χρύσεα μᾶλα;
οὐ πίες οὔτ' ἄρ' ἔδες τῆνον χρόνον οὐδὲ λοέσσα.
τρὶς μὲν δὴ διέβας Ἀχελώϊον ἀργυροδίναν,
τοσσάκι δ' ἀενάων ποταμῶν ἐπέρασας ἕκαστον,
15 τρὶς δ' ἐπὶ Καλλιχόρῳ χαμάδις ἐκαθίσσαο φρητί
αὐσταλέα ἄποτός τε καὶ οὐ φάγες οὐδὲ λοέσσα.
μὴ μὴ ταῦτα λέγωμες ἃ δάκρυον ἄγαγε Δηοῖ·
κάλλιον, ὡς πολίεσσιν ἑαδότα τέθμια δῶκε·
κάλλιον, ὡς καλάμαν τε καὶ ἱερὰ δράγματα πράτα
20 ἀσταχύων ἀπέκοψε καὶ ἐν βόας ἧκε πατῆσαι,
ἁνίκα Τριπτόλεμος ἀγαθὰν ἐδιδάσκετο τέχναν·
κάλλιον, ὡς (ἵνα καί τις ὑπερβασίας ἀλέηται)
π – ‿‿ – ‿‿ – ‿‿ – ‿‿ –‿ ἰδέσθαι
     οὔπω τὰν Κνιδίαν, ἔτι Δώτιον ἱρὸν ἔναιον,
25 †τὶν δ' αὐτᾷ† καλὸν ἄλσος ἐποιήσαντο Πελασγοί
δένδρεσιν ἀμφιλαφές· διά κεν μόλις ἦνθεν ὀϊστός·
ἐν πίτυς, ἐν μεγάλαι πτελέαι ἔσαν, ἐν δὲ καὶ ὄχναι,
ἐν δὲ καλὰ γλυκύμαλα· τὸ δ' ὥστ' ἀλέκτρινον ὕδωρ
ἐξ ἀμαρᾶν ἀνέθυε. θεὰ δ' ἐπεμαίνετο χώρῳ
30 ὅσσον Ἐλευσῖνι, Τριόπᾳ θ' ὅσον ὀκκόσον Ἔννᾳ.
ἀλλ' ὅκα Τριοπίδαισιν ὁ δεξιὸς ἄχθετο δαίμων,
τουτάκις ἁ χείρων Ἐρυσίχθονος ἅψατο βωλά·
σεύατ' ἔχων θεράποντας ἐείκοσι, πάντας ἐν ἀκμᾷ,
πάντας δ' ἀνδρογίγαντας ὅλαν πόλιν ἄρκιος ἆραι,

---

10 πόδες φέρεν Ψ: φερεν]ποδ[ες PAnt, ut vid. 15 τρὶς δ' Ψ: πρίν γ' coni. West 23 init. π[et fin.
] ἰδέσθαι Ψ: π[αῖδα κακὸν Τριόπα σκιοειδέα θῆκεν] ἰδέσθαι tempt. Wilamowitz 25 τὶν δ' αὐτᾷ Ψ:
τῇ δ' αὐτᾷ Wilamowitz: τὶν δ', Ἀγνά Barber (ἀγνᾷ Schadewaldt): τᾷ δ' αὐτεῖ Hopkinson 34 ἄρκιος
Reiske: ἄρκιος Ψ

35 ἀμφότερον πελέκεσσι καὶ ἀξίναισιν ὁπλίσσας,
ἐς δὲ τὸ τᾶς Δάματρος ἀναιδέες ἔδραμον ἄλσος.
ἧς δέ τις αἴγειρος, μέγα δένδρεον αἰθέρι κῦρον,
τῷ ἔπι ταὶ νύμφαι ποτὶ τῶνδιον ἐψιόωντο·
ἁ πράτα πλαγεῖσα κακὸν μέλος ἴαχεν ἄλλαις.

40 ᾄσθετο Δαμάτηρ, ὅτι οἱ ξύλον ἱερὸν ἄλγει,
εἶπε δὲ χωσαμένα· 'τίς μοι καλὰ δένδρεα κόπτει;'
αὐτίκα Νικίππᾳ, τάν οἱ πόλις ἀράτειραν
δαμοσίαν ἔστασαν, ἐείσατο, γέντο δὲ χειρὶ
στέμματα καὶ μάκωνα, κατωμαδίαν δ' ἔχε κλᾷδα.

45 φᾶ δὲ παραψύχοισα κακὸν καὶ ἀναιδέα φῶτα·
'τέκνον, ὅτις τὰ θεοῖσιν ἀνειμένα δένδρεα κόπτεις,
τέκνον ἐλίνυσον, τέκνον πολύθεστε τοκεῦσι,
παύεο καὶ θεράποντας ἀπότρεπε, μή τι χαλεφθῇ
πότνια Δαμάτηρ, τᾶς ἱερὸν ἐκκεραΐζεις.'

50 τὰν δ' ἄρ' ὑποβλέψας χαλεπώτερον ἠὲ κυναγόν
ὤρεσιν ἐν Τμαρίοισιν ὑποβλέπει ἄνδρα λέαινα
ὠμοτόκος, τᾶς φαντὶ πέλειν βλοσυρώτατον ὄμμα,
'χάζευ', ἔφα, 'μή τοι πέλεκυν μέγαν ἐν χροῒ πάξω.
ταῦτα δ' ἐμὸν θησεῖ στεγανὸν δόμον, ᾧ ἔνι δαῖτας

55 αἰὲν ἐμοῖς ἑτάροισιν ἄδην θυμαρέας ἀξῶ.'
εἶπεν ὁ παῖς, Νέμεσις δὲ κακὰν ἐγράψατο φωνάν.
Δαμάτηρ δ' ἄφατόν τι κοτέσσατο, γείνατο δ' ἁ θεύς·
ἴθματα μὲν χέρσω, κεφαλὰ δέ οἱ ἅψατ' Ὀλύμπω.
οἱ μὲν ἄρ' ἡμιθνῆτες, ἐπεὶ τὰν πότνιαν εἶδον,

60 ἐξαπίνας ἀπόρουσαν ἐνὶ δρυσὶ χαλκὸν ἀφέντες.
ἁ δ' ἄλλως μὲν ἔασεν, ἀναγκαίᾳ γὰρ ἕποντο
δεσποτικὰν ὑπὸ χεῖρα, βαρὺν δ' ἀπαμείψατ' ἄνακτα·
'ναὶ ναί, τεύχεο δῶμα, κύον κύον, ᾧ ἔνι δαῖτας
ποιησεῖς· θαμιναὶ γὰρ ἐς ὕστερον εἰλαπίναι τοι.'

65 ἁ μὲν τόσσ' εἰποῖσ' Ἐρυσίχθονι τεῦχε πονηρά.
αὐτίκα οἱ χαλεπόν τε καὶ ἄγριον ἔμβαλε λιμόν
αἴθωνα κρατερόν, μεγάλᾳ δ' ἐστρεύγετο νούσῳ.
σχέτλιος, ὅσσα πάσαιτο τόσων ἔχεν ἵμερος αὖτις.
εἴκατι δαῖτα πένοντο, δυώδεκα δ' οἶνον ἄφυσσον.

71 καὶ γὰρ τᾷ Δάματρι συνωργίσθη Διόνυσος·
70 τόσσα Διώνυσον γὰρ ἃ καὶ Δάματρα χαλέπτει.
οὔτε νιν εἰς ἐράνως οὔτε ξυνδείπνια πέμπον

---

37 ἧς Lasc.: ἥν Ψ   38 τῶ δ' Ψ, PAnt, ut vid.: δ' del. Schneider   ἔπι E Lasc.: ἐπὶ Ψ   55 ἄδην Ψ: ἄδαν
Hopkinson   57 ἁ POxy 2226 Ψ : αὖ Bergk, Hopkinson   70–71 ordinem correxit Reiske

αἰδόμενοι γονέες, προχάνα δ᾽ εὑρίσκετο πᾶσα.
ἦνθον Ἰτωνιάδος νιν Ἀθαναίας ἐπ᾽ ἄεθλα
75 Ὀρμενίδαι καλέοντες· ἀπ᾽ ὦν ἀρνήσατο μάτηρ·
῾οὐκ ἔνδοι, χθιζὸς γὰρ ἐπὶ Κραννῶνα βέβακε
τέλθος ἀπαιτησῶν ἑκατὸν βόας.᾽ ἦνθε Πολυξώ,
μάτηρ Ἀκτορίωνος, ἐπεὶ γάμον ἄρτυε παιδί,
ἀμφότερον Τριόπαν τε καὶ υἱέα κικλήσκοισα.
80 τὰν δὲ γυνὰ βαρύθυμος ἀμείβετο δακρύοισα·
῾νεῖταί τοι Τριόπας, Ἐρυσίχθονα δ᾽ ἤλασε κάπρος
Πίνδον ἀν᾽ εὐάγκειαν, ὁ δ᾽ ἐννέα φάεα κεῖται.᾽
δειλαία φιλότεκνε, τί δ᾽ οὐκ ἐψεύσαο, μᾶτερ;
δαίνυεν εἰλαπίναν τις· ῾ἐν ἀλλοτρίᾳ Ἐρυσίχθων.᾽
85 ἄγετό τις νύμφαν· ῾Ἐρυσίχθονα δίσκος ἔτυψεν᾽,
ἢ ῾ἔπεσ᾽ ἐξ ἵππων᾽, ἢ ῾ἐν Ὄθρυϊ ποίμνι᾽ ἀμιθρεῖ.᾽
ἐνδόμυχος δἤπειτα πανάμερος εἰλαπιναστάς
ἤσθιε μυρία πάντα· κακὰ δ᾽ ἐξάλλετο γαστήρ
αἰεὶ μᾶλλον ἔδοντι, τὰ δ᾽ ἐς βυθὸν οἷα θαλάσσας
90 ἀλεμάτως ἀχάριστα κατέρρεεν εἴδατα πάντα.
ὡς δὲ Μίμαντι χιών, ὡς ἀελίῳ ἔνι πλαγγών,
καὶ τούτων ἔτι μέζον ἐτάκετο, μέστ᾽ ἐπὶ νεύρας
δειλαίῳ ῥινός τε καὶ ὀστέα μῶνον ἐλείφθη.
κλαῖε μὲν ἁ μάτηρ, βαρὺ δ᾽ ἔστενον αἱ δύ᾽ ἀδελφαί
95 χὠ μαστὸς τὸν ἔπωνε καὶ αἱ δέκα πολλάκι δῶλαι.
καὶ δ᾽ αὐτὸς Τριόπας πολιαῖς ἐπὶ χεῖρας ἔβαλλε,
τοῖα τὸν οὐκ ἀίοντα Ποτειδάωνα καλιστρέων·
῾ψευδοπάτωρ, ἴδε τόνδε τεοῦ τρίτον, εἴπερ ἐγὼ μέν
σεῦ τε καὶ Αἰολίδος Κανάκας γένος, αὐτὰρ ἐμεῖο
100 τοῦτο τὸ δείλαιον γένετο βρέφος· αἴθε γὰρ αὐτόν
βλητὸν ὑπ᾽ Ἀπόλλωνος ἐμαὶ χέρες ἐκτερέϊξαν·
νῦν δὲ κακὰ βούβρωστις ἐν ὀφθαλμοῖσι κάθηται.
ἢ οἱ ἀπόστασον χαλεπὰν νόσον ἠέ νιν αὐτός
βόσκε λαβών· ἁμαὶ γὰρ ἀπειρήκαντι τράπεζαι.
105 χῆραι μὲν μάνδραι, κενεαὶ δέ μοι αὔλιες ἤδη
τετραπόδων· οὐδὲν γὰρ ἀπαρνήσαντο μάγειροι.
ἀλλὰ καὶ οὐρῆας μεγαλᾶν ὑπέλυσαν ἁμαξᾶν,

---

79 ἀμφότερον Ψ: ἀμφοτέρως Maas 80]ρυοισα POxy 2226: δακρυχέουσα Ψ 84 αλλοτ[..]αι POxy 2226: ἀλλοτρίοις Ψ 86 αμιθρει POxy 2226: ἀμιθρεῖ coni. Ruhnken et Valckenaer: codd. om. vel suppl. ἀμέλγει 90 πάντα Ψ: πολλα POxy 2226 92 μεζ[POxy 2226: μείζον Ψ μεστεπι POxy 2226: μέσθ᾽ ἐπὶ Ψ 93 ρινος POxy 2226: ἶνες Ψ ελειφθη POxy 2226: ἐλείφθεν Ψ, Hopkinson 94 ἀδελφαί Ψ: ἀδελφαί Meineke, Hopkinson 97 ποτ[POxy 2226: ποσειδάωνα Ψ 106 ουδεν POxy 2226: ἤδη Ψ 107 μεγαλᾶν Ernesti: μεγάλαν Ψ

καὶ τὰν βῶν ἔφαγεν, τὰν Ἑστίᾳ ἔτρεφε μάτηρ,
καὶ τὸν ἀεθλοφόρον καὶ τὸν πολεμήϊον ἵππον,
110 καὶ τὰν μάλουριν, τὰν ἔτρεμε θηρία μικκά.'
μέστα μὲν ἐν Τριόπαο δόμοις ἔτι χρήματα κεῖτο,
μῶνον ἄρ' οἰκεῖοι θάλαμοι κακὸν ἠπίσταντο.
ἀλλ' ὅκα τὸν βαθὺν οἶκον ἀνεξήραναν ὀδόντες,
καὶ τόχ' ὁ τῶ βασιλῆος ἐνὶ τριόδοισι καθῆστο
115 αἰτίζων ἀκόλως τε καὶ ἔκβολα λύματα δαιτός.
Δάματερ, μὴ τῆνος ἐμὶν φίλος, ὅς τοι ἀπεχθής,
εἴη μηδ' ὁμότοιχος· ἐμοὶ κακογείτονες ἐχθροί.
–͝͝͝ παρθενικαί, καὶ ἐπιφθέγξασθε, τεκοῖσαι·
'Δάματερ, μέγα χαῖρε, πολυτρόφε πουλυμέδιμνε.'
120 χὼς αἱ τὸν κάλαθον λευκότριχες ἵπποι ἄγοντι
τέσσαρες, ὣς ἁμὶν μεγάλα θεὸς εὐρυάνασσα
λευκὸν ἔαρ, λευκὸν δὲ θέρος καὶ χεῖμα φέροισα
ἡξεῖ καὶ φθινόπωρον, ἔτος δ' εἰς ἄλλο φυλαξεῖ.
ὡς δ' ἀπεδίλωτοι καὶ ἀνάμπυκες ἄστυ πατεῦμες,
125 ὣς πόδας, ὣς κεφαλὰς παναπηρέας ἔξομες αἰεί.
ὡς δ' αἱ λικνοφόροι χρυσῶ πλέα λίκνα φέροντι,
ὣς ἁμὲς τὸν χρυσὸν ἀφειδέα πασεύμεσθα.
μέστα τὰ τᾶς πόλιος πρυτανήια τὰς ἀτελέστως,
†τὰς δὲ τελεσφορίας† ποτὶ τὰν θεὸν ἄχρις ὁμαρτεῖν,
130 αἵτινες ἑξήκοντα κατώτεραι· αἱ δὲ βαρεῖαι,
χἄτις Ἐλειθυίᾳ τείνει χέρα χἄτις ἐν ἄλγει,
ὡς ἅλις, ὡς αὐταῖς ἱθαρὸν γόνυ· ταῖσι δὲ Δηώ
δωσεῖ πάντ' ἐπίμεστα καὶ †ὡς ποτὶ ναὸν ἴκωνται.
    χαῖρε, θεά, καὶ τάνδε σάω πόλιν ἔν θ' ὁμονοίᾳ
135 ἔν τ' εὐηπελίᾳ, φέρε δ' ἀγρόθι νόστιμα πάντα·
φέρβε βόας, φέρε μᾶλα, φέρε στάχυν, οἶσε θερισμόν,
φέρβε καὶ εἰράναν, ἵν' ὃς ἄροσε τῆνος ἀμάσῃ.
ἵλαθί μοι, τρίλλιστε, μέγα κρείοισα θεάων.

108 βῶν Ψ: βουν POxy 2226 110 μαλουριν POxy 2226: αἴλουρον Ψ 111 μεσταμενεν POxy 2226: μέσφ' ὅτε μὲν Ψ ἔτι Lobel: ἐνὶ Ψ 112 μωνον POxy 2226: μῶνοι Ψ 113 ἀλλ' ὅκα Schneider: αλλοκο POxy 2226: ἀλλ' ὅτε Ψ ἀνεξήραναν Ernesti: ἀνεξήραινον Ψ 114 τόχ' ὁ coni. Brunck: τοχο POxy 2226: τότ' ὁ Ψ 117 κακογείτονες Ψ: κακοδαίμονες Meineke 118–37 om. POxy 2226 118 init. lacuna in Ψ 120 χὼς, ut divisit II. Stephanus. χ' ᾦσι Ψ 126 ὥς, δ' ut Meineke. ὣς αἱ Ψ 127 πασεύμεσθα Meineke: πασσαίμεσθα Ψ 128 μέστα Pfeiffer: μέσφα Ψ POxy 2258 129 τὰς Ψ:]ᾷις POxy 2258: ταῖς coni. Pfeiffer τελεσφορίας Ψ: τελεσφοριαῖς coni. Pfeiffer: τελεσφορέας anon. Bern., Th. Bentley, Hopkinson θεὸν CB: θεῦν Ψ (cf. v. 57) 130 αἱ δὲ Ernesti: αἵ τε Ψ 132]ιςϊθαρον POxy 2258: αὐτὰν ἱκανὸν Ψ 133 ἐπίμεστα καὶ ὡς Ψ (αἷς sch. Call., ut vid.): καὶ αἷς Barber: καὶ αἶ Danielsson: ἐπίμεσθ' ἇ καὶ αἷς Hermann ποτὶ Ψ: ποκα Meineke 134 ἔν θ' ed. Vascos. (1549): ἐν δ' Ψ 135 ἔν τ' Ψ: ἐν δ' Et. gen. 137 ἄροσε τῆνος Brunck: ἄροσε κεῖνος Lasc.: ἄρ...κεῖνος vel ἔκεινος Ψ, ut vid. 138 init. conservatur in POxy 2226. Infra 138 init. δῳ[..]ασιδ[legit Lobel.

To Demeter

As the basket returns, speak out, women: "a great welcome, Demeter, the nurturer of many, the provider of much corn." You will watch the returning basket
from the ground, uninitiated, (5) not from the roof, nor from above let any child
or woman gaze, not even one who has let her hair down, not even when we spit
from parched mouths in our fasting. Hesperus has watched from the clouds—
When will it arrive? Hesperus, who alone persuaded Demeter to drink, when she
followed the undetectable tracks of the girl who was carried off. (10) Mistress,
how could your feet carry you as far as the sun's setting, as far as the Black Men,
and where the golden apples are? You did not drink, you did not eat during
that time, you did not even bathe. Three times indeed you crossed the silver
eddy of the Acheloüs, as many times you crossed each of the ever-flowing rivers;
(15) three times you sank to the ground by the well of Callichoron, parched and
thirsty, and you did not eat or bathe. Do not, do not speak things that bring a tear
to Deo. Better, say how she gave fair laws to cities; better, how she first (20) cut
sheaves and holy corn ears and placed them for oxen to tread upon, when Trip-
tolemus was instructed in the beneficial art; better, how (so that one may avoid
going too far) . . . to see.

They still lived in holy Dotium, not yet the Cnidian land, (25) and to you
yourself? the Pelasgians there made a fair grove, abundant with trees. An arrow
scarcely penetrated it. In it were pines, great elms; in it were pears; in it were beautiful
sweet apples. The water like amber boiled up from the watercourses. The goddess
was mad for the place as (30) much as she was for Eleusis; and as much as she was
mad for Triopas, as much as she was for Enna. But when their good daimon grew
angry with the Triopidae, then a bad plan took hold of Erysichthon. He rushed out
with twenty attendants, all in the prime of life, men like Giants fit to lift a whole city,
(35) having armed them with both double-axes and hand-axes; and shameless, they
ran into Demeter's grove. There was a poplar, a great tree reaching to the sky; near it
the nymphs used to play about noontime. The tree when first struck cried out a dire
note to the rest. (40) Demeter sensed that her sacred wood was in pain, and spoke
in her anger: "Who is cutting my beautiful trees?" Immediately, she assumed the
likeness of Nicippe, whom the city had appointed as her public priestess, and she
took a garland and a poppy in her hand, and held a key against her shoulder. (45)
She spoke soothingly to the base and shameless man: "Child, you who are chopping down trees dedicated to the gods, child, cease, child much prayed for by your
parents, stop, and dismiss your attendants, so that Mistress Demeter does not at all
grow angry; you are devastating her sacred place." (50) Glaring at her more fiercely
than the lioness who has given birth gazes at a hunter in the Tmarian mountains
(they say her eyes are then the fiercest), "Go away," he said, "lest I stick my great axe in
your flesh! These will make my hall securely roofed, in which I shall provide savory
banquets (55) for my companions in abundance." The boy spoke, and Nemesis kept

the account of his evil speech. Demeter was unspeakably angry, and she became the goddess. Her feet were on the ground, but her head touched Olympus. The attendants, half-dead when they saw the lady, (60) suddenly fled and left their bronze in the trees. And she let the rest go, for they followed by necessity under a despotic hand, but she replied to their overbearing master: "Yes, yes, build your chamber, dog, dog; and in it you will make feasts. In the future your banquets will crowd upon each other." (65) When she had spoken these words she contrived evil for Erysichthon. Immediately she cast a cruel and fierce hunger upon him, a mighty burning, and he was afflicted with a great sickness. Wretched one, as much as he ate, the desire for as much immediately took him. Twenty labored for his feasting, twelve drew his wine. (70) What angered Demeter also angered Dionysus. For Dionysus grew angry along with Demeter. His parents, in their shame, did not send him to feasts or common banquets; every excuse was found. The Ormenidae came, inviting him to the games in honor of Itonian Athena. (75) His mother put them off. "He is not in; yesterday he went to Crannon, collecting a hundred oxen in payment of a debt." Polyxo came, the mother of Actorion, for she was arranging a marriage for her child, inviting both, Triopas and his son. (80) The woman answered her weeping and with a heavy heart: "Triopas will attend, but a boar has wounded Erysichthon in the fair dales of the Pindus, and he has been lying sick for nine days." Wretched mother, who loves her son, what lies did you not tell? Someone invited him to a feast: "Erysichthon is out of town." (85) Someone was getting married: "A discus struck Erysichthon," or "He fell from his chariot," or "He is counting the flocks on Othrys." In the inmost part of the house, then, an all-day banqueter, he consumed a myriad of things. His evil belly leapt up as he always ate more, and everything he ate flowed down as into the depths of the sea, (90) vainly and without appreciation. Like the snow on Mt. Mimas or a wax doll in the sun, even more than these he wasted away down to the sinews. Only skin and bone was left to the wretched one. His mother wept, his two sisters groaned deeply, (95) as did the breast that was accustomed to nurse him, and often the ten slave women. Triopas himself threw his hands on his gray hairs and cried out to Poseidon (who wasn't listening) such things as this: "False father, behold this one here, third in descent from you, if I am by birth from you and Canace, the daughter of Aeolus, (100) and this wretched offspring is mine. If only, struck down by Apollo, my hands had buried him. But now evil ox-hunger sits in his eyes. Either remove this dire sickness from him, or take him and feed him yourself. For my tables refuse. (105) My sheepfolds are widowed, my pens are empty of four-footed beasts, for the cooks have refused him nothing. But they even unhitched the mules from the great wagons, and he ate the heifer that his mother was rearing for Hestia; he ate the racehorse and the warhorse, (110) and the white tail at which small beasts were accustomed to tremble." As long as there was money in Triopas' halls, only his private chambers knew of the evil, but when his teeth had drained the house's deep pockets, then the son of the king sat in the crossroads, (115) begging for morsels and refuse cast out from the feast. Demeter, do not let that one be a friend to me who is hateful to you nor be a neighbor. Bad neighbors are hateful to me.... maidens and mothers repeat the cry: "Demeter, a great welcome, the nurturer of many, the provider of many bushels of grain." (120) And when four white-haired mares lead forth the basket, then the great, wide-ruling goddess will come to us bringing a propitious spring, a propitious summer, winter, and autumn, and will protect us for another year. When we walk barefooted and bareheaded in the city, (125) so shall our feet and our heads be always free from harm. As the basket-bearers bring the baskets full of gold, so shall we get gold without limit. The uninitiated should follow [*sc.* the procession] as far as the city's prytaneion, but for the rites [i.e., those attending the rites?] all the way to the shrine of the goddess, (130) whoever is under sixty. But those who are burdened, whoever reaches out her hand to Eileithyia or who is in pain, as far as her knee is able. For these Deo shall give all good things...they come to her temple.

Farewell goddess, and protect this city in concord (135) and prosperity, provide every return in the fields. Nourish the cattle, bring forth fruit, bring forth corn, bring forth the harvest; also nourish peace, so that who sows may reap. Be gracious to me, thrice called upon, most powerful of the divinities.

Commentary

1–7. The hymn opens with the vivid recreation of a religious ritual in honor of Demeter. The narrator initially addresses two groups: urging the female participants to sing the hymnic refrain and those excluded to look only from the ground. Those on the rooftops are instructed to look away as the procession with the open basket carrying sacred objects reaches the temple at the approach of evening. The participants have been fasting throughout the day.

1. καλάθω: an open basket that contained the ritual implements. Knowledge of the contents was restricted to specific hierophants, and for others to see the contents was forbidden. Clement mentions the κάλαθος as part of the Eleusinian Mysteries (*Prot.* 2.21.2), but such containers are attested for other cults as well. From the end of the hymn (120–21) it seems that the basket was mounted on a chariot pulled by four white mares. An image of a large basket mounted on a *quadriga* and driven by an Egyptian priest appears on Alexandrian coins from the time of Trajan. Burkert 1985: 99 and 387n9 connects the scene with this passage, aligning it with the Mysteries, though Cahen 1930: 249–50 takes the image as symbolic and not connected to a real ceremony.

ἐπιφθέγξασθε "give the ritual refrain"; the compound is common in prose; in poetry only at Aesch. *Ch.* 457 and here.

3. Coin image of chariot carrying *kalathos*

γυναῖκες: the address specifically to women participants suggests that only females were allowed to participate, but unlike *hAth*, men are nowhere specifically excluded. See p. 265.

2. μέγα χαῖρε: the phrase occurs at *Od.* 24.402 (Dolius to Odysseus) and *HhAp* 466 (of the Cretan leader to Apollo) as part of a greeting: οὖλέ τε καὶ μέγα χαῖρε. μέγα χαῖρε is repeated at the close of the hymn (119).

πολυτρόφε: the adjective first occurs in Matro of Pitane (fr. 1.1 Olson-Sens). They observe that it is "a witty adaptation of the Homeric πολύτροπον" and active ("much-nourishing"), rather than passive ("well-fed"), hence the accent is paroxytone.

πουλυμέδιμνε "provider of much corn" (the μέδιμνος was a corn measure), unique to Callimachus. Both epithets underscore the province of the goddess. πολυ- compounds are particularly relevant to Demeter as the provider of abundance. (On the variation πολυ-/πουλυ-, see p. 33.)

3. χαμαί: those spectators "on the ground"; sitting or lying on the ground was a central feature of the second day of the *Thesmophoria* (the *Nesteia*, see Burkert 1985: 243–44), but it is difficult to find a connection here.

θασεῖσθε: Doric contract future of θεάομαι. The verb is frequent in Homer, with the meaning of "gaze at," often with a sense of wonder, but in later prose and poetry "view as a spectator"; both are appropriate for bystanders at the procession. The future indicative has an imperative cast.

βέβαλοι: either "uninitiated," which is appropriate for the Mysteries, or, as in the Cyrenean cathartic regulation, "unclean" or "profane," i.e., those who are ineligible to participate in the ritual (*SEG* IX.72.1, 9, and 21, and see Dobias-Lalou 2005: 205). The etymology of the form is uncertain (see Schmitt 92n1), but it seems to be connected to βαίνω: "permissible to walk upon." (The addition of χαμαί may hint at this derivation.) Since the adjective has only two terminations, it is unclear whether it refers to men, men and women, or women who are distinct from those in 4–6. Certainly men would normally be outside and (if present) watching from the ground, while women would be inside, either on the rooftops or within buildings looking out from above.

4. μηδ' ἀπὸ τῶ τέγεος μηδ' ὑψόθεν: viewing from the rooftops (which were flat) is common, especially for women whose quarters seem to have been located above the ground floor (for women on the rooftops during female festivals, see Ar. *Lys.* 395, Men. *Sam.* 45–46).

ὑψόθεν: apparently a third group, which must be those viewing from upper chambers.

αὐγάσσησθε: cf. the Homeric *hapax* at *Il.* 23.458. Idomeneus, who first spots the returning horses in the horse race, says: οἷος ἐγὼν ἵππους αὐγάζομαι ἦε καὶ ὑμεῖς; ("do I alone see the horses or do you as well?"). If deliberate, this is a nice reminder that horses were conveying the κάλαθος (120–21), thus the first thing the participants would see. The aorist subjunctive is usual in prohibitions: "you should not glimpse" (cf. *hArt* 129).

5–6. Editors divide between (1) two groups, children and women—the latter qualified by μηδ(ὲ) . . . χαίταν—or (2) three groups, girls, married women, and those who have either cut their hair or let their hair down, i.e., young women who have left childhood but are as yet unmarried. Hopkinson is surely right that there are only two, with 5–6 describing women who have followed the ritual practice—loosening their hair (as if in mourning) and fasting.

6–9. Callimachus alludes to the following passage from *HhDem* 200–3 while providing an alternative version: "But [Demeter] not laughing, not tasting food or drink [ἄπαστος ἐδητύος ἠδὲ ποτῆτος], sat keening in sorrow for her deep-bosomed daughter, until cherished Iambe diverted her."

6. αὐαλέων "parched" from the ritual fast; the aspiration of this word was disputed, but it is guaranteed by the preceding ἀφ' of the mss. (See Hopkinson ad loc. for details.)

πτύωμες: spitting from a dry mouth would be an irrelevant detail unless it belonged to a ritual connected with fasting or breaking fast. Ritual spitting was normally apotropaic (cf. Theoc. 6.39, where Polyphemus spits thrice into the water reflecting his image to avert the evil eye).

ἄπαστοι "untasted." Many Greek rituals demanded fasting, and in those dedicated to Demeter, ritual fasting supposedly mimicked Demeter's own refusal to eat or drink while she searched for her daughter. The *Nesteia*, the second day of the *Thesmophoria*, was a day of fasting, though fasting was also required in the Eleusinian Mysteries (as at *Aet.* fr. 21.10 Pf., and see the full discussion of Richardson 1974 on *HhDem* 47).

7. Ἔσπερος ἐκ νεφέων ἐσκέψατο: Hesperus looking out from the clouds marks the beginning of evening, the normal time for breaking the fast. As in *hAth* the narrator interweaves "real" time and the mythic time of Demeter's wanderings (see 10–16n). For this kind of ritual mimicry, see Connelly 2007: 104–15.

πανίκα: πηνίκα is common in prose and the comic poets to introduce either a direct or an indirect question. Hopkinson, following Schneider, takes it to be a direct question contributing to the *enargeia* of the passage. Mair (also Pfeiffer) understands as indirect: "Hesperus from the clouds marked the time of its coming."

8. ὅς τε: see *hZeus* 51n.

πιεῖν: epic aorist infinitive of πίνω, see also πίες (12).

μῶνος: by making Hesperus "alone" the one to persuade Demeter to break her fast, Callimachus seems to reject the version in *HhDem* 202–4 that it was Iambe (see 6–9n).

9. ἁρπαγίμας: the adjective is rare; its sense seems to be "carried off" in death or to the underworld (e.g., *AP* 7.186.6, 11.290.4), thus it is appropriate for Kore. For its use in fr. 228 Pf. see pp. 21–22.

ὅκ(α): see *hZeus* 21n.

ἄπυστα: here in a passive sense: ἴχνια, about which "nothing is known" (see also *hDelos* 215n).

10–16. Callimachus compresses Demeter's wandering in search of Kore into seven lines. The clauses are broken into three groups: (1) the temporal conjunction ἔστ' ἐπί in combination with the local adverb ὅπα indicates the distance the goddess travelled (as far as the setting sun, the Black Men, the golden apples); (2) the triple negatives (the mythological rationale for ritual prohibitions), οὐ, οὔτ', οὐδέ ("you did not drink, you did not eat, you did not even bathe"); and (3) the three numbers that open lines 13–15: τρὶς μέν, τοσσάκι δ', τρὶς δ'. The outer elements, 13–15, contrast the large river (Acheloüs) and a small water source, the spring at which Demeter sits; between are "each of the ever-flowing rivers." As the lines unfold, they bear a similarity to the *sphragis* of *hAp*, where Apollo preferred the pure drops from Demeter's spring to the Assyrian river. Line 12 is repeated at 16 with variation: οὐ πίες = ἄποτος; οὔτ' ἔδες = οὐ φάγες; the final element is the same.

10–11. Demeter travels to the west (ἐπὶ δυθμάς) to the Melanes and on to the golden apples. Hopkinson ad loc. takes τὼς Μέλανας as Ethiopians, whom Greeks divided into two groups—those in the east and those in the west near Libya (see Hdt. 7.69–70); he also assumes that the golden apples are in the west, understanding the lines as three different designations for the same direction. West 1986: 30 rather argues that the Melanes are Hesiod's κυάνεοι ἄνδρες (*Op.* 527 and note ad loc.) located in the south and that Callimachus is placing τὰ χρύσεα μᾶλα in the far north, in the land of the Hyperboreans (see Apollod. 2.5.11). Thus Demeter's wandering would have taken her west, south, and north, more or less traversing the known world.

10. πότνια: in contrast to Artemis, who is not addressed as πότνια until *hArt* 136, Demeter is always marked as a potent divinity.

φέρεν: unmarked Doric equivalent of φέρειν.

δυθμάς "sunset"; this Doric form occurs first in Pi. *Is.* 3/4.83: ἐν δυθμαῖσιν αὐγᾶν; Callimachus uses it also at *Aet.* fr. 54c.6 Harder (see Schmitt 98n15).

11. ἔστ(ε) ἐπί: the conjunction + preposition function adverbially to mark time or (as here) space: "as far as"; previously only at Xen. *Anab.* 4.5.6, it occurs at A.R. 2.789, 4.1611 (on which see Livrea ad loc.), and Theoc. 7.67.

12. ἔδες: epic imperfect of ἔδω, "eat." The form occurs only here.

λοέσσα: second person singular aorist middle indicative of λοέω (see *hZeus* 17n).

13. Ἀχελώϊον: the Acheloüs in Aetolia was the largest river in Greece and was often identified with Ocean, the source of all waters (see D'Alessio 2004).

ἀργυροδίναν "with silver eddies," an epithet of Acheloüs first at Hes. *Th.* 340 (see West ad loc.). That passage lists the rivers that Tethys bore to Ocean, which is appropriate to Callimachus' context of ποταμῶν... ἕκαστον (14).

14. ἀενάων ποταμῶν: the phrase appears formulaic; first at Hes. *Op.* 737, then Aesch. *Suppl.* 553.

15. τρὶς δ': thrice crossing the rivers suggests some kind of ritual, but West 1986: 30 makes the attractive suggestion that τρὶς δ' might have been an early corruption of πρίν γ' (cf. *HhDem* 202).

Καλλιχόρῳ ... φρητί: in *HhDem* 270–72 the well of Callichoron was the site over which Demeter commanded her Eleusinian temple to be built (see Richardson 1974: 326–30).

16. αὐσταλέα: rare variant of more common αὐαλέος (6). Renehan 1987: 252 points out that it refers to skin that has not been lubricated (see *Od.* 19.327 of Odysseus in disguise), and that the sentence is arranged chiastically—"αὐσταλέα responds to οὐδὲ λοέσσα, ἄποτος to οὐ φάγες."

17. μὴ μή: emphatic repetition of the negative is reinforced by the anaphora of κάλλιον, ὡς (18, 19, 22).

Δηοῖ: Deo, a variant name for Demeter. Callimachus deploys the two in contexts that hint at their derivation: Demeter (2) as the all-nourishing provider of cereal crops suggests Γῆ Μήτηρ, while Deo, in the context of the rape of her daughter, suggests the etymology of the Derveni papyrus (col. 22.13 Betegh): Δηὼ ὅτι ἐδη[ώθ]ει ἐν τῇ μείξει ("Deo, because she was ravaged in sexual intercourse"). See West 1986: 30.

18–20. These lines celebrate Demeter's most important gifts to humankind— as *Thesmophoros*, or Lawgiver, and as the teacher of agriculture to men. They have been understood to point to the *Thesmophoria* as the cult model for the hymn. Demeter as Lawgiver may have owed something to her connection in Egypt with Isis, who was also a goddess of justice (so Fraser 1972: 1.199). Justice and just behavior is a central theme in what follows.

18. κάλλιον (*sc.* ἐστὶ λέγειν): repeated in 19 and 22.

ἐαδότα: perfect active participle of ἀνδάνω; *hapax* at *Il.* 9.173 ≈ *Od.* 18.422: ἐαδότα μῦθον ("a pleasing word").

τέθμια: here "laws" (see *hAp* 87n).

19–20. An adaptation of *HhDem* 455–56: ἦρος ἀεξομένοιο, πέδῳ δ᾽ ἄρα πίονες ὄγμοι | βρισέμεν ἀσταχύων, τὰ δ᾽ ἐν ἐλλεδανοῖσι δεδέσθαι ("As spring progressed, on the ground the rich furrows would be laden with ears of corn, while others were being bound into sheaves"). Callimachus makes Demeter the first to harvest grain, and ἱερὰ δράγματα imply the first fruits that were dedicated to a divinity; see also *hDelos* 283–84n.

19. πράτα: Demeter was often praised as the first to give agriculture to men, see, e.g., Isoc. *Pan.* 28–29.

20. ἐν...ἧκε: from ἐνίημι.

πατῆσαι: an infinitive of purpose, "for treading" (see Smyth §2008).

21. Τριπτόλεμος: an ancient king of Eleusis, connected with Demeter and the Eleusinian Mysteries at Athens; she taught him agriculture so that he could teach the rest of the Greeks; see Richardson 1974: 194–96 for a detailed discussion of his myth.

22. ὑπερβασίας: a variation of the last line (828) of Hes. *Op.*: that man is happy who knows how to do his work, not offending the deathless gods, and . . . "avoiding transgressions" (ὑπερβασίας ἀλεείνων).

23. This line, which fell at the bottom of a verso in the archetype, was damaged irreparably; *hAth* 136, the corresponding line of the recto, was also damaged. The single word ἰδέσθαι in some mss. has not been successfully explained; Smiley 1921b: 120–22 even suggests that it has crept in from another source. When the text resumes, the inserted tale of Erysichthon has begun.

24. Κνιδίαν (*sc.* γῆν): Cnidos was located at the tip of a southern peninsula on the Ionian coast, slightly south of Cos. It was part of the Dorian hexapolis (later pentapolis), the six cities supposedly founded by the Dorians (along with Halicarnassus, Cos, and three Rhodian cities). The sanctuary of Apollo established by Triopas was located there (Hdt. 1.144). According to Diodorus (5.61), Triopas came to Thessaly, where he expelled the earlier population of Pelasgians and settled on the plain of Dotium. Later he was expelled after he cut down Demeter's sacred grove; afterwards he settled in Cnidos. Callimachus tells a different story: it is not Triopas but his son who commits the sacrilege, but he may be alluding to the alternative version with the information provided in 24: "not yet in the Cnidian land, but they still lived in holy Dotium." The Ptolemies had interests in this region (see Bagnall 1976: 98), and it is mentioned in Theocritus' *Encomium of Ptolemy* (17.68, and see below 30n).

Δώτιον: Dotium was a region in Thessaly, through which the Peneius river flowed (see *hDelos* 105). It is "holy" because it was an ancient center of Demeter cult.

25–29. Demeter's sacred grove is essentially a bucolic *locus amoenus* and, as Hopkinson observes on 27–29, reminiscent of Alcinous' gardens (*Od.* 7.114–32). It is populated with a thick growth of trees and a spring. But the trees named in 27–28 are unlikely to have grown together in nature: two are fruit-bearing and two are tall shade trees.

25. †**τὶν δ' αὐτᾷ**†: the objection to this phrase ("to you yourself") is that the last address to Demeter (16) is too far away to sustain the dative pronoun without an intervening vocative. Hopkinson ad loc. discusses the attempts to emend, though none has been sufficiently persuasive for editors to adopt it.

ἄλσος: usually a sacred grove; cf. *Il.* 20.8 and *HhAphr* 97: ἄλσεα καλά, where nymphs dwell.

Πελασγοί: the Pelasgians were the pre-Dorian peoples of mainland Greece, thought to have been autochthonous. The Greek myth has them being displaced by the Dorians. Triopas is a Dorian.

26. ἀμφιλαφές "abundant"; see *hAp* 42n. A πλάτανος ... ἀμφιλαφής also opens the *locus amoenus* adopted as ideal setting of the philosophical discussion in Plato's *Phaedrus* (230b3).

διά ... ἤνθεν = διῆλθεν: for the form see *hAth* 8n.

27. πίτυς ... πτελέαι ... ὄχναι: pine, elm, and pear trees. See above 25–29n.

28. γλυκύμαλα: before Callimachus "the sweet-apple" is known only from Sappho (fr. 105a V) and Theoc. 11.39 (which is based on the Sappho). The tree was said to be an apple grafted onto a quince.

ὥστ(ε): Ruijgh 1971: 970 explains the force of ὥστε as not so much a comparison as an expression of quality.

ἀλέκτρινον "like amber." Electron had two different meanings: (1) the fossilized resin, amber, and (2) an alloy of gold and silver. Callimachus uses it to describe the color of the water in the filtered light of the grove. The scholiast glosses with the adjectives διαυγές, "translucent" or "shining," that would suit either meaning of electron (cf. *hAth* 21 used of a bronze mirror). Adjectives formed in -ινος denote the material from which something is made or which it resembles (cf. *hAp* 1: δάφνινος, *hArt* 202: μύρσινος).

29. ἀμαρᾶν: Doric genitive plural; ἀμάρης ("irrigation channel") is a *hapax* at *Il.* 21.259.

ἀνέθυε: imperfect from ἀναθύω; this compound of θύω, "rage," appears to have the sense of "bubble up with force."

ἐπεμαίνετο "was mad with love for," a *hapax* in *Il.* 6.160, then found in the epigrammatists and late Greek.

29–30. Either there are four places: the grove in Dotium (= χώρῳ), Eleusis, the Demeter sanctuary in Cnidos established by Triopas, and Enna in Sicily; or two places (Dotium, Eleusis) and two people (Triopas, Enna). The difficulty is Τριόπᾳ, which should be the personal name, not the place; if it is to stand, then Ἔννᾳ is also likely to be the name of the eponymous (though unattested) nymph, with the sense that Demeter loved this grove as much as Eleusis, and as much as she loved the individuals Triopas and Enna. There have been a number of attempts to emend Τριόπᾳ to a place name, though without a satisfactory result (for details see Hopkinson ad loc.)

30. ὅσσον . . . ὅσον ὀκκόσον: the repetition of "as much as" is colloquial, cf. Theoc. 4.39. The spelling ὀκκόσον occurs only in Callimachus (also at *Aet.* fr. 64.1, *Hec.* fr. 109.1 Hollis); cf. Euphorion fr. 84.2 Powell.

Ἐλευσῖνι: Eleusis was the site of Demeter's sanctuary outside of Athens where the Mysteries were celebrated. *HhDem* is associated with that site (see Richardson 1974: 326–30).

Τριόπᾳ: Callimachus must be compressing time since Triopas only established the Cnidian sanctuary after leaving Dotium. The place is mentioned at Theoc. 17.68 in a similar statement: the island of Cos speaking to Ptolemy II asks "may you honor me as much Phoebus Apollo honored dark-circled Delos. In equal honor may you hold the hill of Triops [Τρίοπος . . . κολώναν] . . . equally did lord Apollo love Rheneia."

Ἔννᾳ: the location of a temple of Demeter in Sicily, sometimes identified with the scene of Kore's abduction by Hades. In fr. 228.43–45 Pf., the dead Philotera has been visiting the place just before she learns of the death of her sister Arsinoe II.

31–32. The lines are parallel in structure to reinforce the cause-effect relationship of divine favor and good judgment. ὁ δεξιὸς . . . δαίμων parallels ἁ χείρων . . . βωλά; ἄχθετο, ἅψατο; two names; and two temporal adverbs.

31. ὁ δεξιὸς . . . δαίμων: Fraser 1972: 2.355–56 suggests the phrase was modeled on ἀγαθὸς δαίμων, the cult of which was popular in early Alexandria.

32. τουτάκις: see *hZeus* 44n.

Ἐρυσίχθονος: the first mention of the subject of the story.

34. The line contains three anomalies that have led editors to suspect its authenticity: the *hapax* ἀνδρογίγαντας, ἀρκίος, and ἄραι. Hopkinson ad loc. defends the line.

ἀνδρογίγαντας: only here in Greek; the sense is probably "men with the strength of Giants." It seems to have been modeled on Eur. *Phoen.* 1131–32, describing the device on Capaneus' shield as γίγας ἐπ᾿ ὤμοις γηγενὴς ὅλην πόλιν

| φέρων ("an earthborn Giant bearing a whole city on his shoulders"); this comes from a passage that has been thought to be an interpolation in the text of Euripides, though Mastronarde (1994: 456–58 and 468n2) seems inclined to accept it as authentic. Since the Giants were the offspring of *Ge*, "man-Giants" attacking Demeter (= *Ge Meter*) is doubly sacrilegious.

ἄρκιος "sufficient to" or "capable of" + infinitive; an emendation of Reiske for ἄρκιος of the mss. Masculine accusative plural in -ος was a feature of Thessalian, Arcadian, and Cyrenean Doric, and is also found in Theocritus (for the morphology see Buck §78). ἄρκιος is nominative at *Hec.*, fr. 10.2 Hollis, "when the boy Theseus is capable of lifting [ἀγκάσσασθαι ἄρκιος] the hollow stone."

ἄραι: aorist active infinitive of αἴρω, "to raise," though elsewhere Callimachus prefers forms of ἀείρω. This has contributed to editorial suspicions about the line, but morphological variation is common in Callimachus.

35. ἀμφότερον: neuter singular used adverbially: "both together" (cf. 79n).

πελέκεσσι καὶ ἀξίναισιν: cf. *Il.* 13.612 and 15.711; the distinction between the two types of axes is not clear (see Janko 1992 on *Il.* 13.612).

37. αἴγειρος "black poplar." Hopkinson points out ad loc. that the phrase ἦν δέ τις always introduces a person in Homer (cf. *Il.* 5.9, 10.314) and is thus appropriate here since the tree is alive (39).

κῦρον: neuter participle from κύρω (variant of κυρέω), "reach to"; cf. *HhDem* 188–89 of Demeter herself (μελάθρου | κῦρε κάρη); for κυρέω + dative in this sense Renehan 1987: 250 cites Aesch. *Tantalus* (οὐρανῷ κυρῶν, *TrGF* 3 fr. 159 Radt). It is also found with the dative at A.R. 2.363, 4.945, though probably imitating this passage.

38. τῷ ἔπι: anastrophe, "near which."

τῶνδιον: Tiresias' encounter with Athena also happens at midday (see *hAth* 73).

ἐψιόωντο: see *hArt* 3n and for the form see *hArt* 65n.

39. μέλος: the basic meaning is "member," thus a body part, but also a phrase of song (e.g., *hDelos* 257). With ἴαχεν, the sense is "cry out a cry," but with "struck" (πλαγεῖσα), Callimachus may be exploiting the first meaning as well.

ἴαχεν "cry out"; used twice in *HhDem* (20, 81) of Kore's cry as she is being carried off by Hades; and cf. the *Homeric Hymn to Artemis* (27.7).

40–41. These lines are constructed in parallel like 31–32 above. Finite verbs begin and end each line, with a contrast between aorist (Demeter's actions) and the continuing force of the pain and the chopping (ἄλγει, κόπτει). Demeter opens both lines, first perceiving (ἄσθετο) then acting (εἶπε); οἱ ξύλον ἱερὸν equates with μοι καλὰ δένδρεα; the indirect (ὅτι) with direct (τίς).

40. ἄσθετο: the mss. read ἤσθετο; editors consistently emend on the grounds that Doric did not augment verbs that began with a diphthong. αἰσθάνομαι creates a psychic link between the goddess and her nymphs (she senses their pain).

οἵ = Demeter, and again in 42.

41. χωσαμένα: aorist middle participle of χώομαι, "angered"; imitated at Euphorion fr. 9.14 Powell, where Demeter punishes Ascalaphus for knowing about the pomegranate seed that Kore ate.

42. Νικίππα: the publicly appointed priestess of Demeter, whose aspect Demeter initially assumes to reason with Erysichthon. Nicippe is not known from other extant versions of the myth. Clayman 2014: 87 makes the intriguing suggestion that the elements of the name, *nike* and *hippe* ("she who is victorious with horses"), are similar to those of Berenice: *phere-* and *nike* ("she who brings victory").

ἀράτειραν "priestess." ἀράτειρα is the feminine equivalent of Homeric ἀρητήρ, probably coined by Callimachus and then imitated at A.R. 1.312, 3.252.

42–43. πόλις . . . ἔστασαν: for the syntax see *hAth* 45–46n.

43. ἐείσατο: from εἴδομαι; form and meaning are Homeric, "seem," "be like."

γέντο "she took"; see *hZeus* 50n.

43–44. χειρί | στέμματα: for the phrase cf. the description of Chryses, the priest of Apollo, at *Il.* 1.14. Bulloch 1977: 102–3 discusses the similarities between Chryses' encounter with Agamemnon and Nicippe's with Erysichthon.

44. μάκωνα: Doric form of μήκων, "poppy"; it was an emblem of Demeter, cf. Theoc. 7.157.

κατωμαδίαν: before Callimachus, it occurs only in Homer (*Il.* 23.431), to describe the placement of a discus before the throw. Hesychius s.v. understands the Homeric word to mean being cast "from the shoulder"; here it makes better sense as "against the shoulder" (see below).

κλᾷδα: Doric for κλεῖδα; a temple key was a standard mark of the priestess's office, many of which were quite large; illustrations often show them resting on the priestess's shoulder (for a discussion with illustrations, see Connelly 2007: 92–104).

45. παραψύχοισα "console" or "soothe"; first here or Theoc. 13.54, of the nymphs soothing Hylas. At first the goddess speaks mildly to Erysichthon; τέκνον ("child") occurs three times in 46–47, emphasizing his youth and Demeter's motherly concern.

46–47. The syntax reflects Demeter's agitation as the second element in the apparent tricolon introduced by τέκνον . . . τέκνον . . . τέκνον is broken by a command.

46. ὅτις = ὅστις: for the indefinite used of a definite subject, see LSJ s.v. ὅστις II. The relative is masculine by attraction to the gender of the subject (Erysichthon), as with the vocative in 47 and at *hAth* 87.

ἀνειμένα: from ἀνίημι, "dedicated to."

47. ἐλίνυσον "cease," aorist imperative from ἐλινύω; before Callimachus the verb is found in Ionic prose and in tragedy.

πολύθεστε "much prayed for"; a *hapax*; the word is thought to be Callimachus' interpretation of the contested Homeric *hapax* ἀπόθεστος ("despised":

Od. 17.296); Callimachus apparently derived it from ἀπό + θέσσασθαι ("prayed against") instead of ἀ + ποθεῖν ("not desired"). (See Rengakos 1992: 38–39.)

48. χαλεφθῇ: from χαλέπτω, "provoke"; Homeric *hapax* at *Od.* 4.423: θεῶν ὅς τίς σε χαλέπτει ("who of the gods is angry with you").

49. ἐκκεραΐζεις: ἐκκεραΐζω, "plunder"; first in Callimachus, possibly as a variation of Homeric κεραΐζω (see Hopkinson ad loc). Cf. *AP* 9.312.2 (echoing Callimachus).

50–52. Epic similes are very rare in the hymns; this passage is modeled on *Il.* 17.133–36, where Ajax, standing guard over a fallen comrade, is likened to a male lion with his young. Callimachus transposes this to the more common example of the lioness, and in so doing ironizes the simile. Erysichthon is no Ajax, and the angered lioness protecting her young is more appropriate for Demeter, whose wrath erupts a few lines later, and with dire results.

50. ὑποβλέψας: the lion's fierce glare was one of its most noted characteristics (see Ael. *NA* 4.34).

51. ὤρεσιν ἐν Τμαρίοισιν: the Tmarian mountains were located in Epirus near the shrine of Zeus at Dodona. They occur again in *Aet.* fr. 23.3 Pf. as an example of a remote place.

ἄνδρα: in apposition to κυναγόν. The attachment of a form of ἀνήρ to a noun occurs also at *hAp* 43.

λέαινα "lioness." The feminine form is first found in prose, then Hellenistic poetry.

52. ὠμοτόκος: Callimachus may have coined this form. The cognate words (ὠμός, τόκος) refer to bringing forth immature offspring, which might make sense here, since lion cubs are weak at birth, but it is problematic in *hDelos* 120 (see ad loc.). The existence of cubs makes the lioness more protective and thus more dangerous, as in Eur. *Med.* 187–89.

βλοσυρώτατον "dire," "fearful," of lions at Hes. *Scut.* 175. Renehan 1987: 252 suggests that with ὄμμα it is an allusion to *Il.* 11.36–37: βλοσυρῶπις, the gaze of the Gorgon. For Callimachus' understanding of Homeric βλοσυρός, see Rengakos 1992: 34.

53. ἔφα: the use of parenthetic ἔφη to introduce direct speech is common in Plato, but not found in poetry before the Hellenistic period. It is a feature of everyday speech patterns (which Plato affects) inserted into a more elevated hymnic context. It is in keeping with the mundane details of Erysichthon's punishment.

πάξω: from πήγνυμι, "stick." μή + future indicative produces an expression amounting to a threat.

54. ᾧ ἔνι: anastrophe, "in which."

55. ἄδην "in abundance" (see Renehan 1987: 250).

56. Νέμεσις: Nemesis was the daughter of Night (Hes. *Th.* 223) and assigned the role of punishing mortals for lack of piety. She had an important sanctuary at Rhamnus in northeastern Attica (see *hArt* 232n).

ἐγράψατο "make a note of," "cause to be written down" for the purposes of judgment. The middle is often used for "indict."

57. γείνατο … ἁ θεύς (= θεός): the sense should be "Demeter … became the goddess," i.e., returned to her normal divine aspect, but there are two difficulties: (1) the aorist γείνατο seems always to be transitive in epic usage, and (2) there are no good parallels for the definite article used in this way. On the options for resolving (1) see Hopkinson's full but inconclusive discussion. For (2) most editors let the transmitted text stand, though Hopkinson accepts Bergk's emendation to αὖ, "she became a goddess again".

θεύς (= θεός): the form is unique to Callimachus, here and again at fr. 731 Pf. (on which see Pfeiffer ad loc.). For the contraction of εο > ευ, see Buck §42.5.

58. The line clearly echoes the language of divine epiphany at *HhDem* 188–89 and *HhAphr* 173–74. Bornmann 1992 argues that Eur. *Phoen.* 1184 (κόμαι μὲν εἰς Ὄλυμπον, αἷμα δ' ἐς χθόνα) also underpins the line (see 34n). Because *Phoen.* 1184 is now considered spurious, he considers this evidence that the interpolation must have antedated Callimachus. Mastronarde (1994: 478n2) is not convinced that Callimachus does imitate Euripides, but all other adduced parallels lack the specificity of the head reaching to Olympus. However, both Callimachus and the interpolator (if there was one) may have imitated a now lost source.

ἴθματα: a *hapax* in Homer, *Il.* 5.778 (a variant of which appears at *HhAp* 114), of Athena and Hera, who went "with steps like timorous doves." The meaning of the word was discussed in antiquity (see Rengakos 1992: 36).

59. ἡμιθνῆτες "half-dead," i.e., the men nearly fainted when the goddess manifested herself.

62. βαρύν "overbearing," rather than "angry" (*pace* Hopkinson).

63. Demeter's fury is conveyed by the repetition of ναί and κύον (cf. the narrator's μὴ μή at 17).

τεύχεο: the abrupt command is echoed in 65, where Demeter "prepares" evils for Erysichthon.

64. θαμιναί: before Callimachus only in *HhHerm* 44 for "frequent" thoughts.

εἰλαπίναι: formal feasts or banquets, often conflated with symposia.

67. αἴθωνα "fiery," "burning"; an allusion to Aethon, an alternative name for Erysichthon (see p. 267).

ἐστρεύγετο: from στρεύγω, "to be distressed." The word occurs in Homer, *Il.* 15.512 and *Od.* 12.351. See Bulloch 1977: 104–7 for parallels to the story of the cattle of the Sun.

68. σχέτλιος: at *hArt* 124, of the unjust who have come to Artemis' attention, and at *hAth* 78, of Tiresias, just before he sees Athena.

πάσαιτο: optative, from πατέομαι, Homeric for "eat."

69. εἴκατι: Doric for εἴκοσι; the number of the servants.

71–70. Functionally these two lines display the complete accord between Demeter and Dionysus as the deities responsible for corn (food) and wine (drink). However, their order in the mss. introduces Dionysus first without a clear transition from 69. Proposed solutions are to reverse the order (as in this text) or to delete one or the other line. Given the elegance of the chiasmus Δάματρι, Διόνυσος, Διώνυσον, Δάματρα, and the number of duplicated thoughts elsewhere in the poem, the simple reversal seems the best solution, especially since they act as a close for the section. Renehan 1987: 250 provides a simple explanation for the transposition: in an ancestor to the archetype one line (now 71) was omitted, then later added in the margin; a subsequent copyist inserted it, but in the wrong place.

71. Διόνυσος: cf. 70, Διώνυσον. Both forms occur in the *Iliad*, the *Odyssey*, and the Homeric hymns, varied for metrical reasons.

70. τόσσα Διώνυσον γάρ: the postponement of γάρ is not easily paralleled in epic, but it is a feature of comedy (see Denniston 96–98), and what follows is clearly comedic in style.

72–110 comprise a narrative of increasing parental embarrassment as the family makes a series of inventive excuses for why Erysichthon cannot attend any social occasion. The section begins with two specific invitations, from the sons of Ormenus and from Polyxo, followed by generic requests (83–86) that illustrate the increasing frustration and despair of his parents. His mother and other females are foregrounded in 74–95, his father in 97-110.

72. ξυνδείπνια: the word first occurs here, where it seems to mean "common meals"; in PCairZenon 59764.45 (third century BCE), the meaning is "dining-room."

73. προχάνα: only found in Callimachus; here the Doric form, in contrast to *Aet.* fr. 72 Pf. προχάνησιν. According to the scholion the meaning is "pretext," but the derivation is unclear. The mss. accent προχανά, though modern editors follow Heschyius and others in accenting προχάνα.

74–76. The festival of the *Itonia* and Crannon are associated not with Demeter but Athena (see Graninger 2011: 50–51), and in fact Demeter is not prominent in Thessalian civic cult.

74. Ἰτωνιάδος: Itone was a city in Thessaly, and Athena *Itonia* an important Thessalian divinity. This patronymic (-ιάς) is previously unattested, but it follows the pattern for Callimachean innovation (see Schmitt §5.12).

75. Ὀρμενίδαι "sons of Ormenus"; Ormenium was a town near Mt. Pelion, the eponymous king of which was Ormenus. He was the grandfather of Phoenix (Str. 9.5.18).

ὦν: Doric for οὖν; the insertion of this particle between a preposition and the verb compounded with it (here ἀπ'... ἀρνήσατο) is a feature of Ionic prose and of popular speech (see Denniston 429–30).

76. ἔνδοι: this variant of ἔνδοθι is not generically Doric but localized in Syracusan and Cyrenean and a few other dialects (see Buck §133.4, Dobias-Lalou 2000: 119).

Κραννῶνα: a city in Thessaly (Str. 9.5.20); also at *hDelos* 138; an *Itonia* was celebrated there (Graninger 2011: 54–55).

77. τέλθος: see *hAth* 106n. Here in apposition to ἑκατὸν βόας.

77–78. Πολυξώ, | μάτηρ Ἀκτορίωνος: Polyxo is otherwise unknown, as is the identity of her son, Actorion. West 1986: 30 points out that one of Ormenus' sons was Tlepolemus, who was married to a Polyxo (Paus. 3.19.9–10), which might have inspired the name here.

79. ἀμφότερον: Hopkinson takes as the adverb, but Renehan (1987: 253), citing the parallel of Pl. *Soph.* 248d4–5 (τὸ γιγνώσκειν ἢ τὸ γιγνώσκεσθαί φατε ποίημα ἢ πάθος ἢ ἀμφότερον; ["Do you say that knowing and being known is doing or experiencing, or both?"]), takes as a masculine accusative substantive with Τριόπαν τε καὶ υἱέα in apposition.

Τριόπαν: Triopas, Erysichthon's father, is named here for the first time.

80. τάν: Polyxo.

βαρύθυμος: see *hDelos* 215 (of Hera) with note.

82. εὐάγκειαν: a *hapax*; on the analogy of other -άγκεια compounds (e.g., *Il.* 4.453, μισγάγκεια = συνάγκεια in later writers), this should be a noun (so Hopkinson: "fair valleys"). However, the masculine ἐν εὐάγκεῖ λόφῳ (a *hapax* at Pi. *Nem.* 5.46) suggests that it could also be a feminine form of the adjective εὐαγκής, "with sweet glades" (so Schmitt 2n7). For a double noun construction see *hArt* 239 and *hDelos* 63 and Renehan 1987: 250.

φάεα: here, "days"; accusative of duration of time.

83. φιλότεκνε: common in prose; also in Euripides in aphorisms: cf. *HF* 636, *Phoen.* 356, 965, expressing the sentiment that all parents love their children, and *TrGF* 5.2 adespota fr. 1015 Kannicht: "mothers love their children more than fathers."

84–86. The excuses are made so often that they become routinized: 84 corresponds to the specific event of 74–77; 85 corresponds to 77–81. The two mentioned—feasts and weddings—are linked at *Il.* 18.491 (the shield) and *Od.* 1.226 as standard and recurring events in ancient social life.

84. δαίνυεν: imperfect, a variant of Homeric δαίνυμι. The line seems modeled on *Il.* 23.201: εἰλαπίνην δαίνυντο.

ἐν ἀλλοτρίᾳ (*sc.* γῇ): "out of town." The following hiatus is unusual, but may be intended to reflect his mother's anguish at telling another lie.

86. Ὄθρυϊ: Mt. Othrys is in Phthiotis in north central Greece; Hes. *Th.* 632 places the Titanomachy nearby (cf. *hAth* 8).

ἀμιθρεῖ: Ionic form of ἀριθμέω, "count"; see Buck §88 on this type of consonant transposition.

87. Four-word lines are rare in Callimachus, and normally the thought is complete with the line, but here it spills over, like Erysichthon's hunger, to consume part of the following line.

ἐνδόμυχος "inmost part of the house"; first in Soph. *Phil.* 1457 (of Philoctetes' cave), here, then very popular with Nonnus (cf. *hDelos* 65: ἑπτάμυχον).

δήπειτα: see *hDelos* 160n.

εἰλαπιναστάς: an ironic use of a Homeric *hapax* (*Il.* 17. 577, where it is used of a good "companion at the feast").

88. ἦσθιε: imperfect for Erysichthon's constantly recurring need to eat.

μυρία πάντα: the phrase is rare; first at Alcaeus fr. 121.1 V, which seems to contrast the poor with the wealthy. Note also Aratus 113: μυρία πάντα παρεῖχε Δίκη; in the Golden Age "Justice provided all their countless needs," on which Kidd ad loc. states that μυρία expresses the number and πάντα the variety.

ἐξάλλετο: the sense is probably "was leaping up," *sc.* in eagerness for food (so Wilamowitz *HD* 2.32–33), despite the scholiast's gloss as ηὐξάνετο ἐπὶ τῷ ἐσθίειν ("it increased from eating," i.e., his stomach was swollen or bloated), which is the meaning recorded in LSJ s.v. II 2. Callimachus seems to allude to Melanthius' insult to Odysseus at *Od.* 17.228: βούλεται αἰτίζων βόσκειν ἣν γαστέρ' ἄναλτον ("He wishes by begging to feed his insatiable belly"). For a more detailed discussion see Hopkinson ad loc.

90. ἀλεμάτως: first in Sappho (fr. 26.5 V) and Alcaeus (fr. 70.4 V), then in the Hellenistic poets (Theoc. 15.4, *A.R.* 4.1206); "in vain."

91–92. Two further similes describe Erysichthon's wasting away from hunger: snow and a wax doll that melts in the sun. The passage has features in common with Theoc. 7.76–77, where Daphnis "was wasting away like a snow [χιὼν ὥς τις κατετάκετο] under Haemus or Athos or Rhodope."

91. The line has been suspected because it has two metrical anomalies: (1) Callimachus normally does not allow a word break after the second foot trochee in a word that begins in the first foot as Μίμαντι does (i.e., -⏑⏑|-⏑⏑); (2) he tends to avoid iambic words before a masculine caesura (as χιών here). Given the elegance of its shape otherwise and the sentiment, the anomalies are likely to be deliberate (e.g., M. Fantuzzi notes that ὡς δὲ Μίμαντι χιών gives the impression of a hemistich). Could it be intended to simulate melting?

Μίμαντι: Two mountains bear this name. Probably Callimachus refers to the more famous Mt. Mimas in Ionia (opposite Chios, called "snowy" at Ar. *Nub.* 273) rather than the homonymous mountain in Thessaly (Alexander of Myndus, *FGrH* 25 F 4).

ἀελίῳ: see *hAth* 89n.

πλαγγών: according to the scholiast, a wax doll. Melting dolls in the context of Demeter's punishment suggest ritual magic: such a doll could be used for inflicting harm. The context was often erotic, which might recall the circumstances of Theocritus' Delphis (*Id.* 2.28–29, if Callimachus is the imitator), but wax images also occur in the Cyrene Foundation Decree for cursing those who do not abide by oaths (Faraone 1993: 60–61).

92. μέζον: POxy 2226 has μέζον for μεῖζον of the mss., a form common to Ionic and Arcadian.

μέστ(α) = μέχρι; the adverb is often followed by a preposition, as here. Callimachus uses it in this hymn again at 111, 128. See also *hAth* 55n.

93. ῥινός τε καὶ ὀστέα "skin and bone," a colloquial expression that can be paralleled in many cultures; the phrase also occurs at A.R. 2.201 of Phineus.

ἐλείφθη: medieval mss. have ἐλ(ε)ιφθεν, epic third plural; POxy 2226 has ἐλείφθη, third singular from its closer subject, neuter ὀστέα. Hopkinson prints ἐλειφθεν on the grounds that it occurs at *HhHerm* 195 and A.R. 1.1325. I have preferred the papyrus reading.

94–95. Callimachus portrays the females of the household in a crescendo of weeping, employing the language of tragic mourning. However, the rapid piling up of weeping women—mother, two sisters, wetnurse, and ten servants—has elements of comedy, especially when Callimachus describes the wetnurse as "the breast from which he was accustomed to drink." It is an incongruous reminder that women typically bared their breasts in mourning and at the same time of Erysichthon's consuming need for food.

95. ἔπωνε: πώνω is an Aeolic present of πίνω, found first in Alcaeus fr. 376 V; the imperfect emphasizes the continuous action of the past as a defining characteristic of the present (so Renehan 1987: 251).

πολλάκι: most likely the adverb should be construed with the verb (cf. Theoc. 2.88), though Hopkinson ad loc. prefers as intensifying the number, "many tens."

96–110. After the women, Erysichthon's father appears tearing his hair out and supplicating his father Poseidon for aid. The funeral imagery reaches a climax as Triopas expresses the wish that his son had been struck dead by Apollo before such a fate as he now endures. But the tragic tone is undercut by the bathos of the speech's conclusion—Erysichthon has consumed all the stores, the warhorse, and even the "white tail." Callimachus alludes to two sets of fathers and sons, which also point, as does this whole narrative, to the opposite directions of tragedy/ epic and comedy: Priam plucking out his hair in frustration that he cannot deter Hector from fighting (*Il.* 22.77–78) and the Cyclops' prayer to his father Poseidon (*Od.* 9.528–30). There are a number of indications of the speaker's agitation: his bitter address to Poseidon as "false father"; the command to "look at this one here"; εἴπερ ἐγὼ μέν, with the unusual line ending of the monosyllable μέν; the μεν-clause with no answering δέ.

96. πολιαῖς: the gray hair of age, cf. *hAp* 14.

97. Ποτειδάωνα: medieval mss. read Ποσειδάωνα, the papyrus has ποτ[(a high trace after the omicron rules out Ποσ[). The form is probably a Doricization of epic Ποσειδάων (see Buck §41.4, §61.4).

καλιστρέων: see *hArt* 67n.

98–100. Compare the Cyclops' prayer to his father, Poseidon (*Od.* 9.528–29): κλῦθι, Ποσείδαον, … | εἰ ἐτεόν γε σός εἰμι ("Hear me, Poseidon, … if I am truly yours"). Poseidon does answer his son by attempting to destroy Odysseus, though the ultimate fate of Erysichthon is not revealed in the hymn. These three lines adumbrate the familial relationship with the three subjects: ψευδοπάτωρ … ἐγὼ … βρέφος. τόνδε τεοῦ τρίτον and τοῦτο τὸ δείλαιον … βρέφος surround Triopas' two enjambed lines.

98. This line has a rare monosyllabic ending and is the only one in the hymns to end in μέν; surely an allusion to *HhAp* 233: οἳ δὲ τέως μέν, from a description of Poseidon's sacred grove at Onchestus in Boeotia (the only line in the Homeric hymns to end with μέν).

ψευδοπάτωρ: the compound is found only here in Greek literature. Hopkinson ad loc. suggests the Homeric *hapax* ψευδάγγελος (*Il.* 15.159) may have served as a model, but ψευδ- compounds are not restricted to Homer, e.g., ψευδόμαντις, Soph. *OC* 1097, Eur. *Or.* 1667, or ψευδομάρτυς, Pl. *Gorg.* 472b4–5.

τόνδε: the deictic pronoun implies the presence of Erysichthon as Triopas addesses his divine father (cf. τῷδε of Tiresias at *hAth* 119).

τεοῦ: Doric and Aeolic = σοῦ (cf. Antimachus fr. 191 Matthews); this form is found only here in Callimachus and was possibly chosen for its alliteration. A genitive of origin: "third from you" (cf. Pl. *Rep.* 391c1–2).

98–99. εἴπερ ἐγὼ μέν … γένος (*sc.* εἰμί).

99. **Αἰολίδος Κανάκας**: Triopas was the son of Poseidon and Canace, the daughter of Thessalian Aeolus in some versions (cf. Apollod. 1.7.4).

100. **βρέφος**: normally, an infant, though Erysichthon was at least an adolescent. It fits with the description of the nurse in 95, and what may stand behind both is the Homeric hymn, in which Demeter served as the nurse for the infant Demophoön.

αἴθε = εἴθε: with aorist indicative for an unattainable wish (cf. LSJ s.v. εἰ B I3b).

101. **βλητόν**: the sudden death of women was attributed to Artemis (cf. *hArt* 127), of men to Apollo. Triopas wishes his son had died quickly before his ravening appetite led to the slow wasting of his body.

ἐκτερέϊξαν "bury with due honors." Cf. *Il.* 24.657, where Achilles agrees to stay the fighting so that Priam may bury Hector.

102. **βούβρωστις**: a *hapax* at *Il.* 24.532, where it seems to mean grinding poverty, though its etymology is disputed (see Richardson 1993: 331). Callimachus' choice of word inserts the plight of Triopas and his son into a moment of great epic pathos that is shared between Priam and Achilles, but Triopas is grieving for a son who has not died, and the pervasive sadness of the *Iliad* sequence is undercut by Callimachus using βούβρωστις as if derived from βοῦς and βιβρώσκω, since at 108 Erysichthon will have even eaten the βοῦς that was destined for sacrifice.

For the relationship of Callimachus' hymn to Socrates' objection to this Homeric passage, see Acosta-Hughes and Stephens 2012: 19–20. See also *hAth* 104–5n, where Chariclo's lament takes on contours of Hecuba's grief.

ἐν ὀφθαλμοῖσι "in his eyes" (*sc.* Erysichthon's); so Renehan 1987: 251.

104. βόσκε "feed" or "tend flocks"; when applied to feeding persons, it is pejorative; with βῶν below, a pun on βούβρωστις.

ἀμαί = ἡμέτεραι.

ἀπειρήκαντι = ἀπειρήκασι. Doric -καντι for -κασι occurs only here in Callimachus.

105. χῆραι: the adjective means "widowed" and by extension, "bereft of."

μάνδραι: enclosed spaces for cattle.

αὔλιες: from αὖλις, a shelter, here for herd animals (cf. *HhHerm* 71, where the cattle of the Sun are stabled, and *hArt* 87).

106–110. Scholars debate whether Triopas' speech ends after 106 or 110. The list breaks into two parts: animals destined for slaughter (through 106) followed by those domesticated for other purposes (107–10), which could support ending Triopas' speech with μάγειροι (106). But since μάγειροι is also the subject of ὑπέλυσαν in 107, the direct speech probably continues. Together 104–10 chronicle the economic demise of the house—all of the stores, the service animals, the horse that marks status for competitors in games, the warhorse for fulfilling a civic obligation, and finally even the lowly "white tail," whose task is to keep vermin under control. Finally, the tight organization of 108–10 acts as a coda to the speech. The outer two lines have καί + noun followed by a relative, the inner line two nouns linked by καί.

106. μάγειροι "cooks," who also functioned as butchers; here they unhitch and serve up even the cart animals for Erysichthon.

108. Ἑστίᾳ: Hestia, the goddess of the hearth, to whom families routinely made sacrifices, though the cow (τὰν βῶν) is not known to have been a usual offering.

110. μάλουριν: a *hapax*, the reading of POxy 2226, where the medieval mss. have αἴλουρον ("cat"). According to Hesychius, μάλουριν means "with a white tail"; apparently a compound of the rare μαλός = "white" and οὐρά = an animal's "tail" (especially that of the lion in Homer). If μάλουριν is correct, then αἴλουρον would have crept into the archetype as a gloss. Gow 1967 argues that "white tail" must indicate generic features, and since not all Egyptian cats had white tails, he considers other known domesticated species, settling on the mongoose. One species was characteristically white-tailed (though they are no longer found in Egypt). He further suggests that the γαλέαι at Theoc. 15.28 are not ferrets, as he originally thought, but also mongooses.

ἔτρεμε "were accustomed to tremble," but no longer since the "white tail" is gone.

μικκά: Doric for μικρά.

111–15. As long as stores held out, only Erysichthon's family were aware of his all-consuming needs, but when they were exhausted, his only recourse is begging at a public crossroads.

111. μέστα μὲν ἐν: the papyrus reading for μεσφ᾽ ὅτε μέν of the medieval mss.

ἔτι: ἔνι, the reading of the medieval mss., had long troubled scholars since it was difficult to construe. Pfeiffer (and subsequent editors) have accepted the papyrus reading μέστα μὲν ἐν and Lobel's conjecture of ἔτι for ἔνι.

113. βαθύν: the house with its deep pockets of wealth.

ἀνεξήραναν: from ἀναξηραίνω; the scholiast glosses as ἔρημον ἐποίουν ("empty"). Previously once each in Hom. *Il.* 21.347 (ἀγξηράνῃ, a form disputed in antiquity) and Hdt. 7.109, which offers a parallel for excess: the pack animals in Xerxes' advancing army dry up (ἀνεξήρηνε) a whole lake when they drink from it.

114. ὁ τῶ βασιλῆος (*sc.* υἱός): Erysichthon.

ἐνὶ τριόδοισι: from τρίοδυς; the meeting of three roads was dedicated to Hecate; it was a place where refuse and purificatory offscourings were deposited as "meals for Hecate," hence a place where beggars would gather (Parker 1983: 30n65).

καθῆστο: the line end is parallel to 102 (ἐν ὀφθαλμοῖσι κάθηται); the first encapulates a private anguish, in the second Erysichthon is exposed to eyes of the world at large.

115. αἰτίζων: an imitation of *Od.* 17.228; see above 88n.

ἔκβολα: previously in Euripides, at *Phoen.* 804 (βρέφος ἔκβολον) and *Ion* 555, of a child who has been exposed at birth. The choice of adjective suggests the practice of exposing unwanted children in public places—an ironic comment on Erysichthon's fate.

λύματα: cf. *hZeus* 17 (of Rhea's afterbirth) and *hAp* 109 (of the detritus carried by large rivers).

116–17. These lines are either based on Aesch. *Ag.* 1003–4: νόσος γὰρ | γείτων ὁμότοιχος ἐρείδει ("For sickness, its [*sc.* health's] common-wall neighbor, presses in") or more probably on a proverb common to both. Callimachus expresses two thoughts: "may I not have a common wall with someone who is Demeter's enemy" and "bad neighbors are hateful to me." The second phrase is clearly a proverb (see Lelli 2011: 386). Triopas describes his son's plight as a "sickness" at 103.

117. ὁμότοιχος "sharing a common wall." Apart from Aeschylus and Antiphanes (*PCG* 2 fr. 287 K-A) the word occurs elsewhere only in prose.

κακογείτονες: the compound occurs previously only at Soph. *Phil.* 692.

118. The opening metron of this line was damaged in the medieval mss. and falls within a section omitted in the papyrus. What remains repeats ἐπιφθέγξασθε from the opening line and now divides γυναῖκες into παρθενικαί (virgins) and τεκοῖσαι (women who have borne a child). Schneider's εἰ δ᾽ ἄγε ("come") or Wilamowitz's ἄρχετε ("begin") will be close to the mark.

120–28. The hymn concludes with a series of correlations, introduced by ὡς, expressing a symbiotic relationship between ritual behaviors at the conclusion of the procession (124, 126) and the desired favor of the goddess (125, 127). For this motif in sympathetic magic, see Theoc. 2.26–57 (cf. *hDelos* 84–85n).

120. The extreme hyperbaton of this line (τὸν κάλαθον between the article-noun group, αἱ . . . ἵπποι) has the effect of locating the κάλαθον upon the chariot, with the four mares leading them both (ἄγοντι | τέσσαρες).

λευκότριχες: rituals often stipulated the color of garments (Connelly 2007: 90–92) or skin (on animals) and sex of the participants (both humans and animals). Proper execution of the ritual led, in principle, to a propitious outcome, as at 122, where white becomes a marker of divine favor and bounty. (Cf. Pi. *Ol.* 6.95–96 for "the festival of [Demeter's] daughter with the white horses.")

121. εὐρυάνασσα: for the epithet see Pi. *Ol.* 13.24: εὐρὺ ἀνάσσων, of Zeus. It is appropriate for Demeter, whose domain of agriculture affects the whole human order.

123. φθινόπωρον "autumn," previously in Ionic prose.

ἔτος δ᾽ εἰς ἄλλο φυλαξεῖ: for similar ritual requests for a propitious outcome for harvest or another year, see, e.g., *Homeric Hymn* 26.11–13 (Dionysus); Ar. *Thesm.* 950–52 and *Ran.* 382–83 (Demeter).

124. ἀπεδίλωτοι: a variant of ἀπέδιλος, "unshod"; only in Callimachus. For stipulations about footwear in ritual, see Connelly 2007: 92.

ἀνάμπυκες "without a headband," i.e., with unbound hair; first in Callimachus, then imitated by Nonnus.

πατεῦμες: the use of the first person plural indicates that Callimachus' narrator is female in this hymn. For πατέω with a direct object, cf. Soph. *Phil.* 1060, Theoc. 18.20.

125. παναπηρέας "completely unharmed"; only in Callimachus; the scholiast glosses as ἀβλαβεῖς (see Schmitt 122.65n).

126. λικνοφόροι: those who carry the λίκνον or winnowing fan in procession (see Connelly 2007: 66, 171–72). This was a type of shallow scoop or basket used for separating wheat from chaff. It seems also to have been used as a cradle (see *hZeus* 48). For λίκνα in worship of Demeter see Brumfield 1997. In Theoc. 7.156 Simichidas plants another type of winnowing fan (πτύον) in a heap of grain in celebration of a harvest festival of Demeter.

χρυσῷ πλέα λίκνα: various implements were carried in these baskets as well as dedicatory cakes. According to the scholiast, the λίκνα are "filled with gold," i.e., with implements made of gold, or the λίκνα themselves were "gilded." Alternatively "gold" refers to the color of either the harvested grains or the cakes. For golden implements McKay (1962a: 129–30) points to the description of the (Dionysiac) Grand Procession of Ptolemy Philadelphus (Ath. 5.197c –203b, especially 198C-D, where the implements accompanying the tableau of Dionysus are of gold). And see below.

127. πασεύμεσθα: the mss. read πασσαίμεσθα (aorist optative of πατέομαι, "may we eat"); the scholiast glossed the verb as κτησόμεθα ("we shall get"), which has led to the emendations of πασαίμεσθα (from πάομαι, "may we get") or πασεύμεσθα (Doric future of πάομαι), though neither form is independently attested (see Hopkinson ad loc. for further details). McKay (1962a: 131–35) links the fruitful Nile (described as "flowing with gold") to this passage, arguing that the equivalence of corn and gold would allow the ms. reading to stand as a pun: πασσαίμεσθα, "may we eat gold = corn," or πασαίμεσθα, "may we get gold." Given the evidence for cakes carried in winnowing fans as offerings for Demeter (see Brumfeld 1997), his observation has merit. Against it is the scholiast's gloss, which requires a future tense, not an optative, and the fact that other verbs in the section are futures.

128. τὰ ... πρυτανήια: the *prytaneion* was a civic structure in the agora that contained the city's hearth, or shrine to Hestia, and was used for the conduct of official business, including banquets. This Ionic plural for singular occurs elsewhere only in a Delphic oracle quoted at Hdt. 3.57.

129. †τὰς δὲ τελεσφορίας†: this reading of the medieval mss. has been questioned because (1) sense seems to require a noun to contrast with ἀτελέστως (the "uninitiated"); (2) at *hAp* 78 τελεσφορίην means festival (glossed as ἑορτήν, θυσίαν) and at A.R. 1.917, τελεσφορίῃσι refers specifically to the Samothracian Mysteries. Anon. Bernensis and Th. Bentley conjectured the unattested τελεσφορέας, taking it to be the equivalent of τελεσφόρας ("initiates"). This has been accepted by most editors, but (3) West 1986: 31 maintains that "-φορέας is anomalous; preferable would be -φερέας," and (4) POxy 2226 seems to have the dative article: τ]αῖς, based on which Pfeiffer conjectures τ]αῖς δὲ τελεσφορίαις, which requires an ellipse of the subject of ὁμαρτεῖν in this line. The sense would then be: "as far as the city's prytaneion let the uninitiated follow, but for the rites [*sc.* let those who are initiated follow] all the way to the shrine of the goddess." The picture is complicated by the fact that τελεσφορ- compounds used in Cyrenean inscriptions for cults of Apollo and Artemis do not seem to be connected to mysteries (see Dobias-Lalou 2000: 209–10).

ὁμαρτεῖν: use of an infinitive for the third person imperative is not common outside of legal contexts (see Smyth §2013b); its use here conveys the impression that the speaker is quoting regulatory laws for the rites.

130. κατώτεραι: comparative adjective from κάτω, "lower than," i.e., those under sixty years of age.

αἱ δὲ βαρεῖαι: the adjective βαρύς ("heavy") is in regular use for those burdened by age, or ill health, or pregnant, and is here qualified to make the condition clear. Repeated χἄτις (= καὶ ἥτις) then separates them into those who are pregnant and those "in pain," while the final qualification (ὥς ... ὥς) stipulates that if they are unable to walk the full distance they should go as far as their limbs allow.

131. Ἐλειθυίᾳ: the goddess whom women supplicate to help them in child-birth. For the spelling see *hDelos* 257n.

132. ἰθαρόν: the medieval mss. have ἱκανόν; POxy 2226 has ἰθαρόν, which occurs also at *Aet.* fr. 85.15 (on which see Harder ad loc.). The rare adjective oc-curred previously in Alcaeus (fr. 58.18 V, with the meaning "more cheerful") and Simmias, fr. 25.6 Powell. Hesychius glosses variously as "fair," "pure," "light," "swift." The sense must be as far as their knees permit, cf. Hopkinson's "as far as their knees bear up lightly."

132–33. ταῖσι δὲ Δηώ | … †ὡς ποτὶ ναὸν ἵκωνται: scholars have taken two lines in emending the offending ὡς (or ὡς ποτί): (1) Demeter will grant every-thing to those who cannot complete the route to the sanctuary so that one day they may do so (Meineke: ὥς ποκα or Diggle: ὥς ποκα… ἱκέσθαι) or (2) she will give them the same benefits as those who reach the sanctuary (Barber: καὶ αἷς or Danielsson: καὶ αἵ). The scholiast's paraphrase takes the lines as (2), and he must have had a slightly different text. For details see Hopkinson ad loc.

133. ἐπίμεστα: adverb, previously only as a conjecture at Pherecrates (*PCG* 7 fr. 203 K-A); if correct, a nice parallel: βριθομένης ἀγαθῶν ἐπίμεστα τραπέζης ("of a table laden with a full measure of good things").

134. χαῖρε, θεά, καὶ τάνδε σάω πόλιν (see p. 266).

σάω = σάου: second person middle imperative from σάω/σάωμι, "preserve." The etymology of the form is complex; see Chantraine 1.364–65.

135. εὐηπελίᾳ: only in Callimachus; Hesychius glosses as εὐθηνία ("pros-perity"), εὐεξία ("good health").

ἀγρόθι "in the country," only here.

νόστιμα: of plants, "yielding a high return," hence "abundant."

136. φέρβε "feed" or "nourish"; cf. *Homeric Hymn* 30.2 to Gaia: φέρβει ἐπὶ χθονὶ πάνθ' ὁπόσ' ἐστίν ("[Gaia] nourishes everything that is upon the land").

μᾶλα: either Doric for "apples" or, generically, "fruit," or a hyperdoricism for μῆλα = "sheep," possibly with an intentional ambiguity. *Malephoros* was an epithet of Demeter at Megara and at Selinus; in terracottas found in the latter sanctuary, she seems to be carrying a piece of fruit.

θερισμόν "reaping time," "harvest"; found in documentary papyri and prose.

137. εἰράναν: the relationship of peace to agricultural bounty is a familiar theme; see, e.g., Theoc. 16 and 17.

ἵν' ὃς ἄροσε τῆνος ἀμάσῃ: a proverbial expression, see Diogenianus 2.62.

138. ἵλαθι (= Homeric ἵληθι) "be gracious." The form and etymology have generated considerable discussion (see Chantraine *DE* s.v. ἱλάσκομαι). In general ἵληθι appears in Homer and the Homeric hymns, while ἵλαθι, dialect consider-ations aside, is found in Hellenistic and later Greek.

τρίλλιστε: a Homeric *hapax* (*Il.* 8.488). That passage describes the coming of night over gift-giving earth (ζείδωρον ἄρουραν) and concludes: ἀσπασίη τρίλλιστος ἐπήλυθε νὺξ ἐρεβεννή ("Thrice prayed for came black night"). *HDem* opened at the coming of evening and now concludes, via the borrowing, with full nightfall. Cf. the end of the procession in honor of Ptolemy I as described by Athenaeus (5.197D): "the last group [*sc.* in the procession] happened to be of Hesperus, since the season brought the time [*sc.* consumed in the procession] to that point [*sc.* evening]." If Callimachus ordered the hymns himself, the fall of night at their conclusion is a fitting closure.

μέγα κρείοισα θεάων: cf. *hArt* 268.

Lines 118–37 are omitted from POxy 2226, which in other respects presents a text that is as good as or superior to **Ψ**. Because the Erysichthon narrative ends at 117, and 118–137 return us to the events of the festival procession with which the hymn began, the omission of these lines is almost certainly deliberate. The papyrus then continues with what seems to be letters from the last line of the received hymn (138) immediately followed by another line that Lobel, the original editor, read as: .. […]ασιδ[, tentatively suggesting δω[μ]ασι, but with no mark to indicate that a new poem is beginning. Another very small fragment that does not coincide with lines from any extant text of Callimachus is in the same hand. This led Lobel and Pfeiffer, and Hopkinson following them (pp. 188-89), to conclude that this papyrus text may have recorded an alternative ending to the hymn. Unfortunately, without further evidence it is impossible to draw firm conclusions.

Works Cited

Acosta-Hughes, B. 2010. *Arion's Lyre*. Princeton.

Acosta-Hughes, B. and C. Cusset. 2012. "Callimaque face aux Hymnes homériques," in R. Bouchon, P. Brillet-Dubois, and N. Le Meur-Weissman (eds.), *Hymnes de la grèce antique. Approches littéraires et historiques*. Lyon: 85–93.

Acosta-Hughes, B., L. Lehnus, and S. A. Stephens, eds. 2011. *Brill's Companion to Callimachus*. Leiden.

Acosta-Hughes, B. and S. A. Stephens. 2012. *Callimachus in Context*. Cambridge.

Ambühl, A. 2005. *Kinder und junge Helden. Innovative Aspekte des Umgangs mit der literarischen Tradition bei Kallimachos*. Leiden.

Athanassaki, L. 2009. "Narratology, Deixis, and the Performance of Choral Lyric. On Pindar's *First Pythian Ode*," in J. Grethlein and A. Rengakos (eds.), *Narratology and Interpretation: The Content of Narrative Form in Ancient Literature*. Berlin and New York: 241–73.

Bagnall, R. S. 1976. *The Administration of Ptolemaic Possessions*. Leiden.

Barber, E. A. 1954. Review: "The Hymns and Epigrams of Callimachus," *CR* 4: 227–30.

Barnes, H. R. 1995. "The Structure of the Elegiac Hexameter: A Comparison of the Structure of Elegiac and Stichic Hexameter Verse," in M. Fantuzzi and R. Pretagostini (eds.), *Struttura e storia dell'esametro greco*. 2 vols. Studi di metrica classica 10. Rome: 1.135–62.

Bassi, K. 1989. "The Poetics of Exclusion in Callimachus' *Hymn to Apollo*," *TAPA* 119: 219–31.

Berman, D. W. 2007. "Dirce at Thebes," *G&R* 54.1: 18–39.

Bernabé, A. 1987. *Poetarum epicorum Graecorum testimonia et fragmenta*. Leipzig.

Betegh, G. 2004. *The Derveni Papyrus. Cosmology, Theology and Interpretation*. Cambridge.

Bieber, M. 1961. *The Sculpture of the Hellenistic Age*. Rev. edn. New York (orig. 1955).

Billot, M.-Fr. 1997–98. "Sanctuaires et cultes d' Athéna à Argos," *Opuscula Atheniensia* 22–23: 7–52.

Bing, P. 1986. "Two Conjectures in Callimachus' *Hymn to Delos* V.178 and 205," *Hermes* 114: 121–24.

———. 1988. *The Well-Read Muse. Present and Past in Callimachus and the Hellenistic Poets*. Hypomnemata 90. Göttingen (repr. Ann Arbor 2008).

———. 2009. *The Scroll and the Marble. Studies in Reading and Reception in Hellenistic Poetry*. Ann Arbor.

Bing, P. and V. Uhrmeister. 1994. "The Unity of Callimachus' *Hymn to Artemis*," *JHS* 114: 19–34.

Blum, R. 1991. *Kallimachos: The Alexandrian Library and the Origins of Bibliography*. Trans. H. H. Wellisch. Madison.

Bonacasa, N. and S. Ensoli. 2000. *Cirene*. Milan.

Bornmann, F. 1992. "Der Text der Phönissen des Euripides und der Demeterhymnus des Kallimachos," *ZPE* 91: 15–17.

Brumfield, A. 1997. "Cakes in the Liknon: Votives from the Sanctuary of Demeter and Kore on Acrocorinth," *Hesperia* 66.1: 147–72.

Bruneau, P. 1970. *Recherches sur les cultes de Délos à l'époque hellenistique et à l'époque impériale.* Paris.

Bulloch, A. S. 1970. "A Callimachean Refinement to the Greek Hexameter," *CQ* 20: 258–68.

———. 1977. "Callimachus' Erysichthon, Homer and Apollonius Rhodius," *AJP* 98: 97–123.

Burkert, W. 1985. *Greek Religion.* Trans. J. Raffan. Cambridge, MA.

Cahen, E. 1930. *Les Hymnes de Callimaque.* Bibliothèque des écoles françaises d' Athènes et de Rome 134. Paris.

Calame, C. 1993. "Legendary Narration and Poetic Procedure in Callimachus' *Hymn to Apollo*," *Hellenistica Groningana* 1: 37–56.

———. 1997. *Choruses of Young Women in Ancient Greece. Their Morphology, Religious Role, and Social Functions.* Trans. D. Collins and J. Orion. New York.

———. 2004. "Deictic Ambiguity and Auto-Referentiality: Some Examples from Greek Poetics," *Arethusa* 37: 415–43.

———. 2011. "The Homeric Hymns as Poetic Offerings: Musical and Ritual Relationships with the Gods," in Faulkner 2011a: 334–57.

Cameron, A. 1995. *Callimachus and his Critics.* Princeton.

———. 2004. *Greek Mythography in the Roman World.* American Philological Association Monographs 48. Oxford and New York.

Carney, E. 2013. *Arsinoë of Egypt and Macedon: A Royal Life.* New York and Oxford.

Carrière, J. 1969. "Philadelphe ou Sotêr? À propos d'un hymne de Callimaque," *Studii Clasice* 11: 85–93.

Ceccarelli, P. 1998. *La Pirrica nell' antichità greco romana. Studi sulla danza armata.* Rome and Pisa.

———. 2004. "Dancing the Pyrrhiche in Athens," in P. Murray and P. Wilson (eds.), *Music and the Muses: The Culture of Mousike in the Classical Athenian City.* Oxford: 91–117.

Chamoux, F. 1953. *Cyrène sous la monarchie des Battiades.* Paris.

Chaniotis, A. 2001. "Ein alexandrinischer Dichter und Kreta: Mythische Vergangenheit und gegenwärtige Kultpraxis bei Kallimachos," in S. Böhm and K.-V. von Eickstedt (eds.), *ITHAKE: Festschrift für Jörg Schäfer zum 75. Geburstag am 25. April 2001.* Würzburg: 213–17.

Cheshire, K. 2005. "Thematic Progression and Unity in Callimachus' 'Hymn' 2," *CJ* 100: 331–48.

———. 2008. "Kicking ΦΘΟΝΟΣ: Apollo and his Chorus in Callimachus' *Hymn 2*," *CP* 103: 354–73.

Clauss, J. J. 1986. "Lies and Allusions: The Addressee and Date of Callimachus' *Hymn to Zeus*," *ClAnt* 5: 155–70.

———. 1993. *The Best of the Argonauts.* Berkeley and Los Angeles.

Clay, J. S. 1989. *The Politics of Olympus.* Princeton.

Clayman, D. 2014. *Berenice II and the Golden Age of Ptolemaic Egypt.* New York and Oxford.

Colvin, S. 2011. "The Koine: A New Language for a New World," in A. Erskine and L. Llewellyn-Jones (eds.), *Creating a Hellenistic World.* Llandysul, Wales: 31–46.

Connelly, J. B. 2007. *Portrait of a Priestess. Woman and Ritual in Ancient Greece.* Princeton.

Cook, A. B. 1902. "The Gong at Dodona," *JHS* 22: 5–28.

Cuypers, M. 2004. "Prince and Principle: The Philosophy of Callimachus' *Hymn to Zeus*," *Hellenistica Groningana* 7: 95–116.

D'Alessio, G.-B. 2004. "Textual Fluctuations and Cosmic Streams: Ocean and Acheloios," *JHS* 124: 16–37.

———. 2009. "Reconstructing Pindar's *First Hymn*: The Theban 'Theogony' and the Birth of Apollo," in L. Athanassaki, R. P. Martin, and J. F. Miller (eds.), *Apolline Politics and Poetics*. Athens: 129–48.

Danielsson, O. 1901. "Callimachea," *Eranos* 4: 77–133.

De Stefani, C. and E. Magnelli. 2011. "Callimachus and Later Greek Poetry," in Acosta-Hughes, Lehnus, and Stephens 2011: 534–65.

Depew, M. 1993. "Mimesis and Aetiology in Callimachus' Hymns," *Hellenistica Groningana* 1: 57–78.

———. 1994. "*POxy* 2509 and Callimachus' *Lavacrum Palladis*: αἰγιόχοιο Διὸς κούρη μεγάλοιο," *CQ* 44: 410–26.

Deubner, L. 1932. *Attische Feste*. Berlin.

Dickey, E. 2006. *Ancient Greek Scholarship*. Oxford.

Dobias-Lalou, C. 2000. *Le Dialecte des inscriptions grecques de Cyrène*. Karthago 25. Paris.

Dover, K. J. 1968. *Aristophanes*, Clouds. *Edited with an Introduction and Commentary*. Oxford.

Eichgrün, E. 1961. "Kallimachos und Apollonios Rhodios." Diss. Berlin.

Falivene, M. R. 2011. "The *Diegeseis* Papyrus: Archaeological Context, Format, and Contents," in Acosta-Hughes, Lehnus, and Stephens 2011: 81–92.

Fantuzzi, M. 2011. "Speaking with Authority: Polyphony in Callimachus' *Hymns*," in Acosta-Hughes, Lehnus, and Stephens 2011: 429–53.

Fantuzzi, M. and R. Hunter. 2004. *Tradition and Innovation in Hellenistic Poetry*. Cambridge.

Faraone, C. 1993. "Molten Wax, Spilt Wine and Mutilated Animals: Sympathetic Magic in Near Eastern and Early Greek Oath Ceremonies," *JHS* 113: 60–80.

Faulkner, A. 2008. *The Homeric Hymn to Aphrodite*. Oxford.

———. (ed.) 2011a. *The Homeric Hymns: Interpretative Essays*. Oxford.

———. 2011b. "Introduction," in Faulkner 2011a: 1–25.

———. 2011c. "The Collection of Homeric Hymns: From the Seventh to the Third Centuries BC," in Faulkner 2011a: 175–205.

———. 2013. "*Et in Arcadia Diana*: An Encounter with Pan in Callimachus' *Hymn to Artemis*," *CP* 108: 223–34.

Fearn, D. 2007. *Bacchylides. Politics, Performance, Poetic Tradition*. Oxford.

Fraenkel, E. 1962. *Aeschylus*, Agamemnon, *Prolegomena, Text, Translation, and Commentary*. 3 vols. Oxford.

Fraser, P. 1972. *Ptolemaic Alexandria*. 3 vols. Oxford.

Frazer, J. G. 1921. *Apollodorus*: The Library. 2 vols. Cambridge, MA.

Furley, W. D. and J. M. Bremer, eds. 2001. *Greek Hymns*. 2 vols. Tübingen.

Gallavotti, C. 1963. "Una defixio dorica e altri nuovi epigrammi cirenaici," *Maia* 15: 449–63.

Gardner, P. 1882. *Samos and Samian Coins*. London.

Gasperini, L. 1995. "Nuove dediche vascolari all'Apollo di Cirene," *Quaderni di archeologia della Libia* 17: 5–12.

Gelzer, T. 1994. "Zur Codex Mosquensis und zur Sammlung der *Homerischen Hymnen*," *Hyperboreus* 1: 113–30.

Giangrande, G. 1967. "Hellenistische Konjekturen," *RhM* 110: 151–57.

Giuseppetti, M. 2007. "Callimaco, *Inno a Delo* 52–69, 80–97: Oxford, Bodleian Library Ms. Gr. class. F 109 (P)," *ZPE* 162: 51–56.

———. 2013. *L'isola esile. Studi sull' Inno a Delo di Callimaco*. Rome.

Goldhill, S. 1986. "Framing and Polyphony," *PCPhS* 212: 27–29.

Gow, A. S. F. 1967. "Mousers in Egypt," *CQ* 17: 195–97.

Graninger, D. 2011. *Cult and Koinon in Hellenistic Thessaly*. Leiden.

Griffiths, A. 1981. Review: Hymn to Zeus *by* Callimachus: G. R. McLennan; *Callimachus, Hymn to Apollo: A Commentary*: F. Williams, *JHS* 101: 159–61.

Griffiths, A. 1988. Review: *Callimachus*. Hymn to Delos. Ed. W. H. Mineur; *Callimachus*. The Fifth Hymn. Ed. A. W. Bulloch; *Callimachus*. Hymn to Demeter. Ed. N. Hopkinson, *JHS* 108: 230–34.

Griffiths, F. T. 1979. *Theocritus at Court*. Leiden.

Hadjittofi, F. 2008. "Callimachus' Sexy Athena: The *Hymn to Athena* and the *Homeric Hymn to Aphrodite*," *MD* 60: 9–37.

Hagel, S. 2004. "Tables beyond O'Neill," in F. Spaltenstein and O. Bianchi (eds.), *Autour de la césure*. Bern: 135–215.

Hall, J. 1997. *Ethnic Identity in Greek Antiquity*. Cambridge.

Harder, M. A. 1992. "Insubstantial Voices. Some Observations on the Hymns of Callimachus," *CQ* 42: 384–94.

Haslam, M. W. 1993. "Callimachus' Hymns," *Hellenistica Groningana* 1: 111–25.

Herda, A. 1998. "Der Kult des Gründerheroen Neileos und die Artemis Kithone in Milet," *ÖJh* 67: 1–48.

Heyworth, S. 2004. "Looking into the River: Literary History and Interpretation in Callimachus' Hymns 5 and 6," *Hellenistica Groningana* 7: 139–60.

Higbie, C. 1990. *Measure and Music. Enjambement and Sentence Structure in the* Iliad. Oxford.

Higgs, P. 1994. "The Cyrenean Apollo," *History Today* 44.11: 50–54.

Hölbl, G. A. 2001. *History of the Ptolemaic Empire*. London.

Hopkinson, N. 1984a. "Rhea in Callimachus' *Hymn to Zeus*," *JHS* 104: 176–77.

———. 1984b. "Callimachus' *Hymn to Zeus*," *CQ* 34: 139–48.

———. 1985. Review: W. H. Mineur (ed.), *The Hymn to Delos*, *CR* 35: 249–52.

———. 1989. *A Hellenistic Anthology. Selected and Edited*. Cambridge.

Hordern, J. H. 2002. *The Fragments of Timotheus of Miletus*. Oxford.

Hunter, R. 1992. "Writing the God: Form and Meaning in Callimachus, *Hymn to Athena*," *MD* 29: 9–34.

———. 1999. *Theocritus: A Selection*. Idylls *1, 3, 4, 7, 10, 11 and 13*. Cambridge.

Hunter, R. and T. Fuhrer. 2002. "Imaginary Gods? Poetic Theology in the Hymns of Callimachus," in F. Montanari and L. Lehnus (eds.), *Callimaque*. Entretiens Hardt 48. Geneva: 145–87.

Huss, W. 2008. "Die Tochter Berenike oder die Schwiegertochter Berenike? Bemerkungen zu einigen Epigrammen des Poseidippos von Pella," *ZPE* 165: 55–57.

Jan, F. von (= de Ian). 1893. "De Callimacho Homeri interprete." Diss. Strassburg.

Janko, R. 1992. *The Iliad: A Commentary. Books 13–16*. Cambridge.

Kaibel, G. 1877. "Observationes criticae in Anthologiam Graecam," in *Commentationes philologae in honorem Theodori Mommseni*. Berlin: 326–36.

Kane, S. 1998. "Cultic Implications of Sculpture in the Sanctuary of Demeter and Kore/Persephone at Cyrene, Libya," in E. Catani and S. M. Marengo (eds.), *La Cirenaica in età antica*. Macerata: 289–300.

Kirichenko, A. 2012. "Nothing to Do with Zeus? The Old and New in Callimachus' First Hymn," *Hellenistica Groningana* 16: 181–202.

Kirk, G. S. 1985. *The Iliad: A Commentary. Books 1–4*. Cambridge.

Kleinknecht, H. 1939. "ΛΟΥΤΡΑ ΤΗΣ ΠΑΛΛΑΔΟΣ," *Hermes* 74: 301–50.

Koenen, L. 1977. *Eine agonistische Inschrift aus Ägypten und frühptolemäische Königsfeste*. Beiträge zur klassischen Philologie 56. Meisenheim am Glan.

———. 1993. "The Ptolemaic King as a Religious Figure," in A. S. Bulloch, E. Gruen, A. A. Long, and A. Stewart (eds.), *Images and Ideologies. Self-Definition in the Hellenistic World*. Berkeley and Los Angeles: 25–115.

Köhnken, A. 2003. "Apoll-Aitien bei Apollonios und Kallimachos," in D. Accorinti and P. Chuvin (eds.), *Des géants à Dionysos: mélanges de mythologie et de poésie grecques offerts à Francis Vian*. Alessandria: 207–13.

Lacy, L. R. 1990. "Aktaion and a Lost 'Bath of Artemis,'" *JHS* 110: 24–42.

Lapp, F. 1965. "De Callimachi Cyrenaei tropis et figuris." Diss. Bonn.

Laronde, A. 1987. *Cyrène et la Libye hellénistique*. Paris.

Larsen, J. 2007. *Ancient Greek Cults. A Guide*. New York.

Legrand, Ph.-E. 1894. "Sur la date de quelques poèmes de Théocrite et Callimaque," *REG* 7: 276–85.

Lehnus, L. 2000. "P. Maas and the Crux in Callimachus, *Hymn to Delos* 41," *ZPE* 131: 25–26.

———. 2011. "Callimachus Rediscovered in Papyri," in Acosta-Hughes, Lehnus, and Stephens 2011: 23–38.

Lelli. E. 2011. "Proverbs and Popular Sayings in Callimachus," in Acosta-Hughes, Lehnus, and Stephens 2011: 384–403.

Lightfoot, J. L. 2014. *Dionysius Periegetes, Description of the Known World. With Introduction, Text, Translation, and Commentary*. Oxford.

Livrea, E. 1987. "Callimaco e la Beozia (*Suppl. Hell.* fr. 257, 1–8: Lav. Pall. 61)," *ZPE* 67: 31–36.

Lloyd-Jones, H. 1982. "Callimachus 4.246," *Hermes* 110: 119–20.

López, A. 1993. "Short Remarks on a Callimachean Fragment (*In Delum*, 138-149)," *ZPE* 98: 27–28.

Lüddecke, K. 1998. "Contextualizing the Voice in Callimachus' *Hymn to Zeus*," *MD* 41: 9–33.

Maas, P. 1956. "Hephthemimeres im Hexameter des Kallimachos," in *Festschrift für Bruno Snell*. Munich: 23–24 (=*Kleine Schriften*, Munich 1973: 92–93).

———. 1958. *Textual Criticism*. Trans. B. Flower. Oxford.

———. 1982. "Kallimachos, Hy. 4,1," *Hermes* 110: 118.

Maass, E. 1890. "Kallimachos und Kyrene," *Hermes* 25: 400–10.

Magnelli, E. 1995. "Le norme del secondo piede dell'esametro nei poeti ellenistici e il comportamento della 'parola metrica,'" *MD* 35: 135–64.

Manakidou, F. 2009. "Callimachus' Second and Fifth Hymn and Pindar: A Reconstruction of *Syggeneiai* between Old and New Greece," *RFIC* 137: 351–79.

———. 2013. ΚΑΛΛΙΜΑΧΟΣ, Εἰς λοῦτρα τῆς Παλλάδος. Athens.

———. Forthcoming. "Past and Present in the Fifth *Hymn* of Callimachus: Mimesis, Aetiology and Reality," *Hellenistica Groningana*.

Massimilla, G. 2002. "Artemis' Fourth Throw (Call. *Dian.* 121ff.)," *MH* 59: 51–54.

———. 2011. "The *Aetia* through Papyri," in Acosta-Hughes, Lehnus, and Stephens 2011: 39–62.

Mastronarde, D. 1994. *Euripides. Phoenissae*. Cambridge.

Matthews, V. J. 1996. *Antimachus of Colophon. Text and Commentary*. Leiden.

McKay, K. J. 1962a. *Erysichthon. A Callimachean Comedy*. Leiden.

———. 1962b. *The Poet at Play. Kallimachos, The Bath of Pallas*. Leiden.

———. 1963. "Mischief in Callimachus' *Hymn to Artemis*," *Mnemosyne* 16: 243–56.

McKenzie, J. 2007. *The Architecture of Alexandria and Egypt. 300 BC–AD 700*. New Haven.

Meadows, A. 2013. "The Ptolemaic League of Islanders," in K. Buraselis, M. Stefanou, and D. J. Thompson (eds.), *The Ptolemies, the Sea and the Nile*. Cambridge: 19–38.

Meillier, C. 1979. *Callimaque et son temps*. Lille.

Merker, I. L. 1970. "The Ptolemaic Officials and the League of the Islanders," *Historia* 19: 141–60.

Mitchell, S. 2003. "The Galatians: Representation and Reality," in A. Erskine (ed.), *A Companion to the Hellenistic World*. Oxford: 280–93.

Moorhouse, A. C. 1946. "AN with the Future," *CQ* 40: 7–8.

Morrison, A. D. 2005. "Sexual Ambiguity and the Identity of the Narrator in Callimachus' *Hymn to Athena*," *BICS* 48: 21–35.

———. 2007. *The Narrator in Archaic Greek and Hellenistic Poetry*. Cambridge.

Most, G. 1981. "Callimachus and Herophilus," *Hermes* 109: 191–96.

Moyer, I. 2011. "Court, Chora, and Culture in Late Ptolemaic Egypt," *AJP* 132: 15–44.

Mueller, K. 2005. "Geographical Information Systems in Papyrology," *BASP* 42: 63–92.

Müller, S. 2009. *Das hellenistische Königspaar in der medialen Repräsentation.* Berlin and New York.

Naber, S. A. 1906. "Ad Callimachum," *Mnemosyne* 34: 225–39.

Nagy, G. 1979. *The Best of the Achaeans.* Baltimore and London.

O'Neill, E. 1942. "The Localization of Metrical Word-Types in the Greek Hexameter," *YCS* 8: 105–78.

Oliver, G. J. 2002. "Callimachus the Poet and Benefactor of the Athenians," *ZPE* 140: 6–8.

Oppermann, H. 1925. "Herophilos bei Kallimachos," *Hermes* 60: 14-32.

Parke, H. W. 1967. *Greek Oracles.* London.

Parker, R. 1983. *Miasma: Pollution and Purification in Early Greek Religion.* Oxford.

Parsons, P. 2011. "Callimachus and His *Koinai*," in Acosta-Hughes, Lehnus, and Stephens 2011: 134–52.

Perpillou-Thomas, F. 1993. *Fêtes d'Égypte ptolémaïque et romaine d'après la documentation papyrologique grecque.* Studia Hellenistica 31. Louvain.

Petrovic, I. 2007. *Von den Toren des Hades zu den Hallen des Olymp: Artemiskult bei Theokrit und Kallimachos.* Mnemosyne Supplement 281. Leiden.

———. 2010. "Transforming Artemis: from the Goddess of the Outdoors to City Goddess," in J. Bremmer and A. Erskine (eds.), *The Gods of Ancient Greece. Identities and Transformations.* Edinburgh: 209–27.

———. 2011. "Callimachus and Contemporary Religion," in Acosta-Hughes, Lehnus, and Stephens 2011: 264–85.

Pettersson, M. 1992. *Cults of Apollo at Sparta. The Hyakinthia, the Gymnopaidiai, and the Karneia.* Stockholm.

Pfrommer, M. 2001. *Greek Gold from Hellenistic Egypt.* Malibu.

Plantinga, M. 2004. "A Parade of Learning: Callimachus' *Hymn to Artemis* (lines 170-268)," *Hellenistica Groningana* 7: 257–77.

Polignac, F. de. 2002. "Cultes de sommet en Argolide et Corinthie: éléments d'interprétation," in R Hägg (ed.), *Peloponnesian Sanctuaries and Cults.* Stockholm.

Pontani, F. 2011. "Callimachus Cited," in Acosta-Hughes, Lehnus, and Stephens 2011: 93–117.

Quack, J. F. 2008. "Innovations in Ancient Garb? Hieroglyphic Texts from the Time of Ptolemy Philadelphus," in P. McKechnie and P. Guillaume (eds.), *Ptolemy II and His World.* Leiden: 276–89.

Ragone, G. 2006. "Callimaco e le tradizioni locali della Ionia asiatica," in A. Martina and A.-T. Cozzoli (eds.), *Callimachea* I. Rome: 71–114.

Reed, J. D. 1997. *Bion of Smyrna: The Fragments and the Adonis.* Cambridge.

Reinsch-Werner, H. 1976. *Callimachus Hesiodicus. Die Rezeption der hesiodischen Dichtung durch Kallimachos von Kyrene.* Berlin.

Renehan, R. 1987. "Curae Callimacheae," *CP* 82: 240–54.

Rengakos, A. 1992. "Homerische Wörter bei Kallimachos," *ZPE* 94: 21–47.

———. 1993. *Der Homertext und die hellenistischen Dichter.* Stuttgart.

Richardson, N. 1974. *The Homeric Hymn to Demeter.* Cambridge.

———. 1993. *The Iliad: A Commentary. Books 21–24.* Cambridge.

———. 2010. *The Homeric Hymns to Apollo, Hermes, and Aphrodite.* Cambridge.

Robertson, N. 1984. "The Ritual Background of the Erysichthon Story," *AJP* 105: 369–408.

Rogers, G. M. 2012. *The Mysteries of Artemis of Ephesos.* New Haven and London.

Rosen. R. 2007. *Making Mockery: The Poetics of Ancient Satire.* Oxford.

Ruijgh, C. J. 1971. *Auteur de 'te epique.'* Amsterdam.

———. 1981. "L'emploi de HTOI chez Homère et Hésiode," *Mnemosyne* 34: 272–87.

————. 1984. "Le dorien de Théocrite: dialecte cyrénien d'Alexandrie et d'Égypte," *Mnemosyne* 37: 56–88.

Schachter, A. 1981. *Cults of Boiotia 1: Archeloos to Hera.* Bulletin of the Institute of Classical Studies Supplement 38.1. London.

————. 1994. *Cults of Boiotia 3: Potnia to Zeus.* Bulletin of the Institute of Classical Studies Supplement 38.3. London.

Schmiel, R. 1987. "Callimachus' *Hymn to Delos.* Structure and Theme," *Mnemosyne* 40: 45–55.

Selden, D. 1998. "Alibis," *ClAnt* 17: 289–412.

Sens, A. 1997. *Theocritus:* Dioscuri (Idyll 22). Hypomnemata 114. Göttingen.

————. 2004. "Doricisms in the New and Old Posidippus," in B. Acosta-Hughes, E. Kosmetatou, and M. Baumbach (eds.), *Labored in Papyrus Leaves. Perspectives on an Epigram Collection Attributed to Posidippus (P. Mil. Vogl. VIII 309).* Washington, DC: 65–83.

————. 2011. *Asclepiades of Samos. Epigrams and Fragments.* Oxford.

Sherwin-White, S. 1978. *Ancient Cos.* Hypomnemata 51. Göttingen.

Silva Sanchez, T. 2003. "La elisión en el hexámetro de Calímaco. Actualización," *Habis* 34: 73–85.

Smiley, M. T. 1911. "A Note on Callimachus Hymn I.23," *CQ* 5: 89–90.

————. 1920a. "The Manuscripts of Callimachus' Hymns," *CQ* 14: 1–15.

————. 1920b. "The Manuscripts of Callimachus' Hymns (Continued)," *CQ* 14: 57–77.

————. 1920c. "The Manuscripts of Callimachus' Hymns (Continued)," *CQ* 14: 105–122.

————. 1921a. "The Manuscripts of Callimachus' Hymns (Continued)," *CQ* 15: 57–74.

————. 1921b. "The Manuscripts of Callimachus' Hymns (Concluded)," *CQ* 15: 113–25.

Sokolowski, F. 1955. *Lois sacrées de l' asie mineure.* Paris.

Sourvinou-Inwood, C. and R. Parker. 2011. *Athenian Myths and Festivals: Aglauros, Erechtheus, Plynteria, Panathenaia, Dionysia.* Oxford.

Stephens, S. A. 2003. *Seeing Double: Intercultural Poetics in Ptolemaic Alexandria.* Berkeley and Los Angeles.

————. 2005. "Battle of the Books," in K. Gutzwiller (ed.), *The New Posidippus. A Hellenistic Poetry Book.* Oxford: 229–48.

————. 2008. "Ptolemaic Epic," in T. Papanghelis and A. Rengakos (eds.), *Brill's Companion to Apollonius Rhodius.* Leiden: 95–114.

Svarlien, D. A. 1991. "Callimachus and the Path of Song: οἶμον for οἶτον at *Lav. Pall.* 94," *Hermes* 119: 473–77.

Swift, L. 2010. *The Hidden Chorus: Echoes of Genre in Tragic Lyric.* Oxford.

Tarán, S. L. 1985. "Εἰσὶ τρίχες : An Erotic Motif in the *Greek Anthology,*" *JHS* 105: 90–107.

Thomas, O. 2011. "The Homeric Hymn to Pan," in Faulkner 2011a: 151-72.

Thompson, D. W. 1895. *A Glossary of Greek Birds.* Oxford.

Traill, D. 1998. "Callimachus' Singing Sea (*Hymn* 2.106)," *CP* 93: 215–22.

Ukleja, K. 2005. *Der Delos-Hymnos des Kallimachos innerhalb seines Hymnensextetts.* Münster.

Vamvouri Ruffy, M. 2004. *La Fabrique du divin. Les Hymnes de Callimaque à la lumière des Hymnes homériques et des Hymnes épigraphiques.* Liège.

Wackernagel, J. 1916. "Sprachliche Untersuchungen zu Homer," *Glotta* 7: 161–319.

Weinreich, O. 1929. "Türöffnung im Wunder-, Prodigien-, und Zauberglauben der Antike," in *Genethliakon Wilhelm Schmid zum siebzigsten Geburtstag.* Stuttgart: 200–452.

West, M. L. 1966. "Conjectures on 46 Greek Poets," *Philologus* 110: 147–68.

————. 1982. *Greek Metre.* Oxford.

————. 1986. Review: A.W. Bulloch (ed.), *Callimachus.* The Fifth Hymn *by Callimachus,* and N. Hopkinson (ed.), Hymn to Demeter *by Callimachus, CR* 36: 27–31.

————. 1992. *Ancient Greek Music.* Oxford.

West, M. L. 2001. "The Fragmentary Homeric Hymn to Dionysus," *ZPE* 134: 1–11.

———, ed. 2003. *Homeric Hymns, Homeric Apocrypha, Lives of Homer*. Cambridge, MA and London.

———. 2011. "The First *Homeric Hymn* to Dionysus," in Faulkner 2011a: 29–43.

White, D. 1984. *The Extramural Sanctuary of Demeter and Persephone at Cyrene, Libya*. Vol.1. Philadelphia.

Wilson, N. G. 1974. "A Puzzle in Stemmatic Theory Solved," *Revue d'Histoire des Textes* 4: 139–42.

Wilson, P., ed. 2007. *The Greek Theatre and Festivals. Documentary Studies*. Oxford.

Wimmel, W. 1960. *Kallimachos in Rom. Die Nachfolge seines apologetischen Dichtens in der Augusteerzeit*. Wiesbaden.

Index of Subjects

Index of Selected Greek Words Discussed

Numbers refer to hymns (1 = hZeus, 2 = hAp, 3 = hArt, 4 = hDelos, 5 = hAth, 6 = hDem), followed by line number of the commentary.

Index of Passages Discussed